NEUROCOMPUTING

Robert Hecht-Nielsen

HNC, Inc. and University of California, San Diego

Addison-Wesley Publishing Company

Reading, Massachusetts • Menlo Park, California • New York
Don Mills, Ontario • Wokingham, England • Amsterdam • Bonn
Sydney • Singapore • Tokyo • Madrid • San Juan

ANZA, ANZA Plus, AXON, User Interface Subroutine Library, and UISL are trademarks of HNC, Inc. All rights reserved. ©1987, 1988, 1989 by HNC, Inc. The distinctive list of UISL commands (including AL-LOCATE_NEUROCOMPUTER, LOAD_NETWORK, UNLOAD_NETWORK, ITERATE, PUT_STATES, PUT_WEIGHTS, PUT_CONSTANTS, GET_STATES, GET_WEIGHTS, GET_CONSTANTS, SAVE_NETWORK, and DEALLOCATE_NEUROCOMPUTER) are ©1987, 1988 by HNC, Inc.

Library of Congress Cataloging-in-Publication Data

Hecht-Nielsen, Robert.
    Neurocomputing / Robert Hecht-Nielsen.
        p.   cm.
    Includes bibliographical references.
    ISBN 0-201-09355-3
    1. Neural computers. I. Title.
QA76.5.H4442   1989
006.3--dc20   89-18261
                                                  CIP

Preface

Neurocomputing is a subject that has captivated the interest of thousands of technologists, scientists, and mathematicians. The idea of training a system to carry out an information processing function (instead of programming it) has intrinsic appeal, perhaps because of our personal familiarity with training as an easy and natural way to acquire new information processing capabilities. Neurocomputing systems are often endowed with a "look and feel" vaguely reminiscent of animals. Like a pet, this is a technology that is easy to fall in love with. I did, 22 years ago.

I hope you find this book useful and enjoyable.

About This Book

The author of this book is an industrialist, an adjunct academic, and a philanthropist without financial portfolio. Activities of these sorts heighten one's awareness of the need for technology textbooks to have industrially oriented material sprinkled in with the purely academic grist. This book is designed with this idea in mind. It contains auxiliary material on subjects as diverse as business plan development, venture capital, proposal writing, and development project planning and management. Discussions about the history of neurocomputing and historical vignettes summarizing the stories of pioneering neurocomputing companies are also presented. The observations that have led to the decision to include this material are sketched below.

Until about 1960, the primary focus of technology was the near-term betterment of the life of the average human being (with the development of weaponry running a close second). However, over the past 30 years some countries (such

as the United States and the Soviet Union — but not, for example, Japan) have
built up large technology research infrastructures (separate from the science and
mathematics infrastructures) that are, to a distressing extent, disconnected from
the practical civilian and military applications of technology (both short-term
and long-term). These infrastructures have diverted large numbers of highly
talented technologists from useful work. A concomitant of the rise of these infrastructures has been the emergence of a reprehensible snobbery that places all
technological efforts into one of two categories: high-tech or I'd-rather-die-than-
do-that. The social damage caused by these aberrations has been enormous.

It is now time for technology to regain its traditional primary focus. The
formula is the same one that has always worked. Namely: young technologists should work on design, project management, product development, and/or
manufacturing. Those of supreme talent and/or pedagogic ability who are appropriately motivated *and* who have proven themselves in practical work can,
later in their careers, carry out research and/or teach technology in universities.
By addressing some of the issues surrounding the practice of technology in industry, as part of the presentation of a popular and potentially important new
information processing technology, perhaps this book can, in some small way,
serve to help bring about this renaissance.

Use of this Book in a Course

This text is designed to provide technologists, scientists, and mathematicians
with an introduction to the field of neurocomputing. It is intended for use
at the graduate level, although seniors would typically have all of the required
background. The text is written to support a year-long course. It can also be
used for shorter courses if some of the material is skipped or skimmed.

A year-long course can go through the whole book, in order. This would
afford an opportunity to explore all three aspects of the subject (theory, implementation, and applications). Instructors can expand or contract the various
topics to fit their personal preferences.

A semester-long course can probably still cover the whole book. Chapters
1, 2, 3, 4, 5, and 9 can be covered in detail, and the rest of the book can be
skimmed. A quarter-long course can cover most of Chapters 1, 2, 3, 4, and
5, along with a small amount of material selected by the instructor from other
chapters.

Concurrent Laboratory Projects

One of the realities of neurocomputing is that hands-on practice is as important as classroom learning. Thus, students learning neurocomputing should,
if possible, be involved in laboratory projects concurrent with their classroom
instruction. This activity can be done on a group basis or, preferably, on an

individual basis. To help in the planning of a laboratory section to complement a course based on this book, the following suggestions for projects are offered:

- Develop a backpropagation image compression system based on the example in Section 9.2.2. Images of the members of the class can be used for training and testing, with images of automobiles used to demonstrate the problems caused by data that are not statistically consistent with those used during training.
- Simulate a broomstick-balancing system based upon visual feedback, as discussed in Section 9.3.1.
- Write a neurosoftware description (in AXON, for example) of a famous neural network architecture, such as the Boltzmann Machine or GMDH and build a demonstration program that illustrates the architecture's capabilities.
- Solve a "toy problem" using multiple neural networks. The group can first define a suitable toy problem, and then solve it.
- Carry out experimental validation of theoretically derived results from Chapters 3 through 6.
- Develop variants of some of the simpler neural networks described in Chapters 4, 5, and 6.
- Define and solve a simple application problem from start to finish.

It is suggested that projects be organized via the writing of a brief (one or two page) development plan in accordance with the planning approach presented in the Appendix. Projects can last from 1 week to 4 weeks and can be concluded with a detailed report describing the development plan, the work carried out, the results, the software and neurosoftware developed (with listings and permanent archival diskette provided), and recommendations for future work.

Acknowledgments

Writing a textbook involves a major commitment of time and energy and a commensurate loss of availability of that time and energy for other uses. Robert L. North and Gerald I. Farmer (President and Executive Vice President of HNC, Inc.) have been extremely generous in supporting the development of this book during the past 3 years. Thanks are also due to the 100+ students who have patiently sat through an entire year of ECE-270 A/B/C (*Neurocomputing*) in the Electrical and Computer Engineering Department of the University of California, San Diego in 1986/1987, 1987/1988, and 1988/1989. They have been both the guinea pigs for the material of the text and the most helpful assistants in making improvements. The class of 1989/1990 has been helpful in doing final proofreading. Special thanks are also due Lawrence Milstein and Manuel Rotenberg, the successive Chairs of the UCSD ECE Department over the past 4 years, for their unwavering support. Also, the lively interdisciplinary interaction in neural networks at UCSD (across 14 academic departments and the Salk Institute) has been of great value in this project.

The process of synthesizing and refining the material for this book was aided significantly by the following people, whose help is greatly appreciated: Karen Haines (teaching and laboratory assistant for ECE-270 during 1987/1988 and 1988/89), Barton Addis, Timur Ash, Dale Barbour, Steve Biafore, Groff Bittner, Richard Bocker, Dale Bryan, Bill Caid, Maureen Caudill, Subhasis Chaudhuri, Jen Chou, Brad Coté, David DeMers, Duane Desieno, Andrew Diamond, Michael Fennel, Alexander Glockner, Joel Gross, Takeo Hamada, Adam Harris, Hillary Heinmets, David Holden, Geoffrey Hueter, William Jasper, Richard Kasbo, Fouad Kiamilev, John Kim, Myung Soo Kim, Paul Klimowitch, Dennis Kocher, Hari Kuchibhotla, Markham Lasher, Yun-Parn Thomas Lee, Harry Luithardt, Stephen Luse, Tracy Mansfield, Harold McBeth, John McDonnell, John McInerney, Martin McNeill, Robert Means, Phillippe Mercier, Hoa Nguyen, David Olsen, Robert Osborne, Frank Overton, Mark Plutowski, Carl Rindfleisch, John Robinson, John Sabin, Robert Sasseen, Valery Secarea, Holly Shen, Vincent Stuart, Robert Tekolste, Max S. Tomlinson, Anthony Weathers, Eric Wolin, Barnes Woodhall, and Hedong Yang. Comments by Stephen Grossberg and David Casasent were of great value. The author's numerous conversations about the contents of this book with Duane Desieno, Robert Sasseen, and Geoffrey Hueter have been both enjoyable and helpful. Harley Hahn's assistance is also appreciated.

The greatest thanks are owed to Carol Bonomo. She did the majority of the typing, many of the corrections, the initial versions of the figures, and the initial proofreading. She also functioned as a critic, promoting a number of important improvements in the book. Without Carol's contributions this book would not exist. Anna Ewers' help with finishing the last draft of the book has also been invaluable.

The love, patience, understanding, and encouragement of my wife Judi Hecht-Nielsen and our son Andy Hecht-Nielsen are greatly appreciated. Also reflected in this book are the early influences of my mother, Elisabeth Kost; father, Robert Hecht-Nielsen; and grandmother, Jessie Laing Wilson; and the later influences of friends Roy McAlister, David Hestenes, and Alan Wang.

This is a perfect opportunity to thank all of those individuals and organizations that so generously supported my neurocomputing activities when the subject was not fashionable. These include (in chronological order, from 1968 through 1986) the following individuals and organizations: Rennie Molumby, Roy McAlister, Jim Torbert, Hap James, Sid Swanson, Russ Yost, Jerald Bauck, Don Spencer, Todd Gutschow, Robert L. North, Ira Skurnick, Charles Kellum, Robert Launer, Jagdish Chandra, Hugo Poza, Richard Booton, Terry Dolan, Paul Glenn, A. T. LaPrade, Mark Collins, and Gordon Davidson; Arizona State Hospital, Arizona State University, TransEnergy Corporation, Jet Propulsion Laboratory, Chandler Flyers, Ramada Laboratories, Advance Aviation, Talley Industries, TAD Tech, Motorola, and TRW. The encouragement and generous support of DARPA over the years 1982 through 1986 is especially appreciated.

Special thanks go to my friend and business partner Todd Gutshow. He has been a constant source of new insights and ideas, as well as a superb critic and evaluator. During our years at TRW, Todd and I accumulated neurocomputing applications skills and advanced the state of the art in implementation technology. These experiences became the launching pad for the development of a new generation of approaches at HNC. His help has been an essential ingredient for this book.

After the initial draft of the book was completed it was reviewed by Harold K. Brown, David Casasent, Hans Peter Graf, Stephen Grossberg, Karen Haines, David Hestenes, Stefan Shrier, and Carme Torras. Their many comments and criticisms were of enormous value. Many thanks to them for their generous help.

Finally, I want to thank Tom Robbins of Addison-Wesley for his encouragement, patience, and wise counsel. It was almost axiomatic that a publisher with a hyphenated name would turn out to be a good choice.

Contents

1

Introduction: What Is Neurocomputing?

Neurocomputing is the technological discipline concerned with information processing systems (for example, *neural networks*) that autonomously develop operational capabilities in adaptive response to an information environment. Neurocomputing is a fundamentally new and different approach to information processing. It is the first alternative to *programmed computing*, which has dominated information processing for the last 45 years. This book provides a graduate-level introduction to neurocomputing, including theory, implementation, and applications.

This chapter begins with an overview of neurocomputing. The structure of the field of neurocomputing is then discussed, followed by a discussion of the relationship between neurocomputing and neuroscience. The history of the subject is then surveyed, and finally, a brief overview of the structure of the rest of the book is presented.

1.1 Introduction

1.1.1 Overview of Neurocomputing

From the advent of the first useful electronic digital computer (ENIAC) in 1946 [23] until the late 1980s, essentially all information processing applications used a single basic approach: *programmed computing*. Solving a problem using programmed computing involves devising an algorithm and/or a set of rules for solving the problem and then correctly coding these in software (and making necessary revisions and improvements).

Clearly, programmed computing can be used in only those cases where the processing to be accomplished can be described in terms of a known procedure or a known set of rules. If the required algorithmic procedure and/or set of rules are not known, then they must be developed — an undertaking that, in general, has been found to be costly and time consuming. In fact, if the algorithm required is not simple (which is frequently the case with the most desirable capabilities), the development process may have to await a flash of insight (or several flashes of insight). Obviously, such an innovation process cannot be accurately planned or controlled. Even when the required algorithm or rule set can be devised, the problem of software development still must be faced.

Because current computers operate on a totally logical basis, software must be virtually perfect if it is to work. The exhaustive design, testing, and iterative improvement that software development demands makes it a lengthy and expensive process.

A new approach to information processing that does not require algorithm or rule development and that often significantly reduces the quantity of software that must be developed has recently become available. This approach, called *neurocomputing*, allows, for some types of problems (typically in areas such as sensor processing, pattern recognition, data analysis, and control), the development of information processing capabilities for which the algorithms or rules are not known (or where they might be known, but where the software to implement them would be too expensive, time consuming, or inconvenient to develop). For those information processing operations amenable to neurocomputing implementation, the software that must be developed is typically for relatively straightforward operations such as data file input and output, peripheral device interface, preprocessing, and postprocessing. The Computer Aided Software Engineering (CASE) tools often used with neurocomputing systems can frequently be utilized to build these routine software modules in a few hours. These properties make neurocomputing an interesting alternative to programmed computing, at least in those areas where it is applicable.

Formally, *neurocomputing* is the technological discipline concerned with parallel, distributed, adaptive information processing systems that develop information processing capabilities in response to exposure to an information environment. The primary information processing structures of interest in neurocomputing are *neural networks* (although other classes of adaptive information processing structures are sometimes also considered, such as learning automata, genetic learning systems, data-adaptive content addressable memories, simulated annealing systems, associative memories, and fuzzy learning systems). The formal definition of a neural network follows.

■ *DEFINITION 1.1.1 A* neural network *is a parallel, distributed information processing structure consisting of* processing elements *(which can possess a local memory and can carry out localized information processing operations)* interconnected via unidirectional signal channels called connections. *Each processing element has a single output connection that branches ("fans out") into as many collateral connections as desired; each carries the same signal*

— *the* processing element output signal. *The processing element output signal can be of any mathematical type desired. The information processing that goes on within each processing element can be defined arbitrarily with the restriction that it must be completely local; that is, it must depend only on the current values of the input signals arriving at the processing element via impinging connections and on values stored in the processing element's local memory.* ∎

One might wonder why this particular type of Multiple Instruction Multiple Data (*MIMD*) parallel processing architecture should be worthy of such concentrated attention (beyond the obvious fact that biological neuron networks seem to be neural networks in the above sense). In particular, why not simply study some of the more general MIMD architectures (such as dataflow architectures [57]) which contain neural networks as a subclass? Surprisingly, no completely satisfactory answer to this question is yet known. However, it seems very likely to me that the neural network definition will someday be shown to be a particularly good compromise that allows substantial information processing capability while at the same time providing sufficient structure to allow the development of efficient general-purpose implementations (methods for efficiently implementing arbitrary general MIMD architectures are not known and may not exist). All we can say for sure now is that the neural network definition does produce a class of powerful and potentially useful information processing structures that lend themselves to efficient implementation by general-purpose neurocomputers. It is these consequences of the definition that we will discuss in this book.

To illustrate the nature of neural networks we shall describe briefly a classical neural network architecture known as the *perceptron*. Because it has been largely superceded by more powerful neural networks (for example, some of those discussed in Chapters 3, 4, 5, and 6), the perceptron is primarily of historical interest, although it is still occasionally used.

The perceptron is a neural network that consists of one or more of the processing elements shown in Figure 1.1 (which are themselves also referred to individually as perceptrons). For simplicity, we shall concentrate on the operation of a single perceptron processing element.

The goal of the perceptron is illustrated in Figure 1.2. Here we see two classes of *patterns* (class 0 and class 1). A pattern is simply a point in *n*-dimensional space (the coordinates of the point represent *attributes* or *features* of the object to be classified, such as weight, height, density, or frequency). In the case illustrated in Figure 1.2 (which is the situation of interest relative to the perceptron), the two classes can be separated from each other by a simple linear hyperplane (in 2-dimensional space a hyperplane is a line, in 3-dimensional space it is an ordinary plane, and in *n*-dimensional space it is an $(n-1)$-dimensional flat surface). Classes that have this property are termed *linearly separable*. The goal is to find a set of *weights* or *adaptive coefficients* $w_0, w_1, \ldots, w_n$ (which, it turns out, determine a unique hyperplane — as will

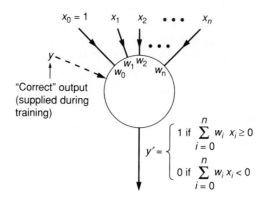

Fig. 1.1. • The perceptron. The perceptron has an input consisting of an $(n + 1)$-dimensional vector $\mathbf{x} = (x_0, x_1, x_2, \ldots, x_n)$, where x_0 is permanently set to 1 (this is called a *bias input*). The output of the perceptron is 1 if the weighted input sum $x_0 w_0 + x_1 w_1 + \cdots + x_n w_n$ is greater than or equal to zero; the output is 0 if this weighted input sum is less than zero.

be discussed in Chapter 3) such that the output of the perceptron is 1 if the input pattern vector $(x_1, x_2, \ldots, x_n)$ belongs to class 1, and 0 if the pattern vector belongs to class 0.

The weights are stored within the processing element and are automatically modified by the processing element itself in accordance with the *perceptron learning law*. This learning law operates during a training process where the perceptron is shown a sequence of randomly selected $\mathbf{x}$ pattern vectors (one at a time). Each time an $\mathbf{x}$ example is presented to the perceptron (as part of a *training trial*), the system is also told to which class (0 or 1) the example belongs. On each training trial, the learning law modifies the weight vector $\mathbf{w}$ in accordance with the equation

$$\mathbf{w}^{\text{new}} = \mathbf{w}^{\text{old}} + (y - y')\, \mathbf{x}, \tag{1.1}$$

where y is the correct class number of the input pattern $\mathbf{x}$ (which is supplied, along with $\mathbf{x}$, on each training trial), and y' is the output of the perceptron. The idea of this learning law is that, if the perceptron makes an error $(y - y')$ in its output, this error indicates a need to reorient the $\mathbf{w}$ hyperplane so that the perceptron will tend not make an error on this particular $\mathbf{x}$ vector (or any other vector near it) again. Note that the output error $(y - y')$ will be 0 if the output of the perceptron is correct. In this situation the weight will not change. If the output is wrong, then $(y - y')$ will be either $+1$ or -1, and $\mathbf{w}$ will be modified appropriately (so that the perceptron will do better in the future).

The perceptron was invented in 1957 by Frank Rosenblatt [199] (who also wrote *Principles of Neurodynamics*, one of the two early books on neurocomputing [198] — the other being *Automat und Mensch* by Karl Steinbuch [216]). Following his invention of the perceptron, Rosenblatt proved that, given linearly separable classes, a perceptron will, in a *finite number* of training trials, develop

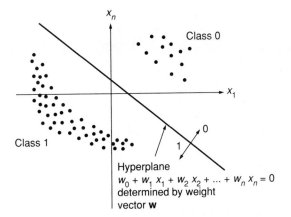

Fig. 1.2. • A pattern classification problem in *n*-dimensional space. Each of the points shown is a pattern in either class 0 or class 1. The goal is to find a set of weights for which the output of the perceptron will always match the class number of the point entered into the perceptron. The perceptron weight vector **w** determines a hyperplane in *n*-dimensional space. If a point $(x_1, x_2, \ldots, x_n)$ lies on one side of the hyperplane (marked with a "0"), then the output of the perceptron is 0. If the point lies on the hyperplane or on the "1" side of the hyperplane, then the perceptron output is 1. In the situation illustrated, the perceptron will perform correctly because its hyperplane has been oriented properly relative to the two (linearly separable) classes.

a weight vector that will separate the classes (that is, the perceptron would thereafter perform its pattern classification task perfectly, with $(y - y') = 0$). This proof holds independent of the starting values of the weights. This startling result caused great excitement in the late 1950s and early 1960s.

Beyond his discovery of the perceptron and his visionary view of the future of neurocomputing, Rosenblatt also designed and helped to build (along with Charles Wightman and others) the first successful neurocomputer, the *Mark I Perceptron*. Although the Perceptron was not the first neurocomputer, it was the first to carry out a useful function.

The Mark I Perceptron (which is shown in Figures 1.3 – 1.6) functioned as a character recognizer. As shown in Figure 1.3, a character was placed on a floodlight-illuminated board, and the image of this character was focused upon a 20 × 20 array of CdS photoconductors (shown in Figure 1.4) — which provided a 400 pixel image sensor input to the neural network. The Mark I Perceptron had 512 weights, implemented as an 8 × 8 × 8 array of electric motor driven potentiometers (one motor per potentiometer — see Figure 1.5), which could be allocated amongst multiple individual perceptron processing elements as desired. There were also several threshold units to determine the correct sign of a weighted sum for use in producing perceptron output signals. Finally, as shown in Figure 1.6, a patch panel was provided so that the functional

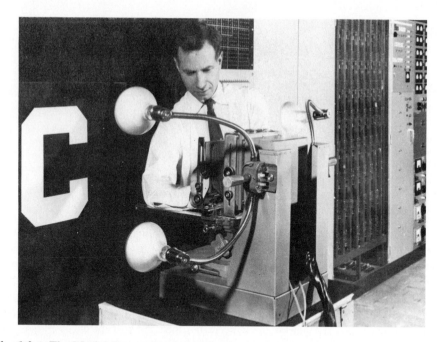

Fig. 1.3. • The Mark I Perceptron image input system being adjusted by Charles Wightman, Mark I Perceptron project engineer. A printed character was mounted on the board and illuminated with four floodlights. The image of the character was focused on a 20 × 20 array of CdS photoconductors — which then provided 400 pixel values for use as inputs to the neural network (which then attempted to classify the figure into one of M classes — "A", "B", etc.). Photo courtesy of Arvin Calspan Advanced Technology Center.

elements of the neurocomputer could be connected together to implement any desired perceptron neural network (up to the capacity of the machine).

The Mark I Perceptron was built and successfully demonstrated in 1957 and 1958 [199] — over 30 years ago. Thus, neurocomputing is by no means a new subject. What has made neurocomputing suddenly take off is the emergence of information processing hardware that is both powerful and affordable. Unlike programmed computing, where even extremely primitive hardware provided significant useful capability, neurocomputing demands minimum capabilities that could not be delivered until the sufficient maturation in the mid-1980s of silicon Very Large Scale Integration (VLSI) circuit technology. It was only then that the field could emerge from its former status as an esoteric research subject to become an important "new" practical technology.

Application of the neurocomputing information processing approach begins with the selection of an appropriate neural network architecture for solving the problem at hand (if such a network exists) and the exposure of that network to a statistically adequate set of training data. There are multiple neural network architectures that have been studied and characterized sufficiently to allow their

Fig. 1.4. • Frank Rosenblatt (the inventor of the perceptron and designer of the Mark I Perceptron neurocomputer) with the 400 pixel (20 × 20) Mark I Perceptron image sensor. Photo courtesy of Arvin Calspan Advanced Technology Center.

use in solving practical problems. Each of these architectures has its own unique mix of information processing capabilities, domains of applicability, techniques for use, required training data, training regimen, and so on. At present, however, the capabilities offered by these architectures are limited; usually, only certain problems in areas such as sensor processing, pattern recognition, data analysis, and control can be solved.

Because they typically require large numbers of mathematical computations to carry out their functions, neural networks are often implemented using specialized processors called *neurocomputers* that have the ability to implement neural networks efficiently and cost effectively. A surprisingly large variety of neurocomputers have been built (using both digital and analog designs executed in electronic, optical, electro-optical, and even electrochemical hardware). Most of these machines are experimental. However, some digital electronic neurocomputer designs are now offered for commercial sale.

In the example of the perceptron pattern classifier, the neural network was trained using *supervised training*. In other words, for each input **x** to the network, the correct output *y* also was supplied. Two other types of training also are commonly used: *graded* or *reinforcement* training and *self-organization*. In the case of graded training, the network is given data inputs, but is not supplied with the desired outputs. Instead, it is occasionally given a "grade" or "performance score" that tells it how well it has done overall since the last time it was graded. In self-organization training, the network is given only data inputs.

Fig. 1.5. • Charles Wightman holding a subrack of 8 motor/potentiometer pairs. Each motor/potentiometer pair functioned as a single adaptive weight value. The perceptron learning law was implemented in analog circuits that (when properly wired through the patchboard shown in Figure 1.6) would control the motor of each potentiometer (the resistance of which functioned to implement one weight). Photo courtesy of Arvin Calspan Advanced Technology Center.

From just these pieces of information, it is expected to organize itself into some useful configuration.

Because neurocomputing is a new technology and because currently only a relatively small set of well-characterized neural network architectures is available for use, most practitioners of neurocomputing solve problems by working "in reverse". Instead of taking an arbitrary problem and trying to solve it with neurocomputing (an approach that neurocomputing's currently limited technical armamentarium will typically not support), they take the available neural network architectures and seek out important problems within their domain of expertise that the capabilities of these networks can solve. This approach has been shown to be effective in a wide variety of application areas. Clearly, it places a premium on domain expertise — rather than on neurocomputing expertise. This emphasis accounts for the fact that the majority of real-world applications of neurocomputing (in areas such as defense, finance, insurance, and the automotive industry) have been accomplished by domain experts, not neurocomputing specialists (although technical support from neurocomputing specialists is sometimes employed).

Finally, lest you gain the wrong impression, it is important to point out that, even in those applications where neurocomputing is successful, it typically

Fig. 1.6. • The Mark I Perceptron patchboard. The connection patterns were typically "random", so as to illustrate the ability of the perceptron to learn the desired pattern without need for precise wiring (in contrast to, unlike the precise wiring required in a programmed computer). Photo courtesy of Arvin Calspan Advanced Technology Center.

solves only the "core problem". For example, in a medical diagnosis system, the neural network would typically carry out only the transformation from test results to diagnosis. Polling the medical instruments to obtain the test results, properly formatting these data for entry into the network, and using the network output to produce a screen display for use by the physician must all still be accomplished using programmed computing. Thus, neurocomputing is best thought of as an *adjunct* to programmed computing, rather than a replacement. In fact, neural networks are usually treated essentially as *software-callable procedures* or subroutines that can be embedded into software wherever their capabilities are needed (this is done using software routines that hide the fact that the neural network is typically running on a neurocomputer coprocessor). By this means, neurocomputing capabilities can be easily integrated with existing programmed computing systems (including both algorithmic systems and rule-based systems). All told, the reduction in algorithm development and software development afforded by neurocomputing often leads to a dramatic reduction in system development time and expense. The level of technical expertise required to solve a particular problem also is often reduced substantially. In the end, it may be these reduced cost, time, and skill characteristics of neurocomputing that will have the most profound impact on the technology's near-term acceptance as a practical information processing approach.

Neurocomputing and programmed computing are fundamentally different approaches to information processing. Neurocomputing is based on transformations, whereas programmed computing is based on algorithms and rules. Experience has shown that these two types of information processing are operationally complementary but conceptually incompatible. In other words, it may often be impossible to describe the operation of a transformation in terms of a high-level information processing "principle" (expressed as a canonical algorithm or as a set of high-level rules).[1] In essence, neurocomputing systems tend to operate on information in an entirely different way than the algorithmic and rule-based information processing systems that we are familiar with.

Although we can prove theorems that guarantee certain neural network capabilities and properties (such as failure tolerance, robustness, and the ability to implement a particular class of transformations), such results only give us assurance that neural networks can be usefully and safely employed. They do not answer the more academically interesting question of how (in higher conceptual terms) the network does its job. In fact, there is a growing suspicion that discovering the answers to questions of this type may require an intellectual revolution in information processing as profound as that in physics brought about by the Copenhagen interpretation of quantum mechanics.

1.2 Neurocomputing as a Subject

As a subject, neurocomputing is comprised of three main areas of activity:

- Architecture and Theory
- Implementation
- Applications

Each of these areas is now briefly described.

ARCHITECTURE AND THEORY   In neurocomputing, the word *architecture* is used to indicate the formal "machine independent" mathematical definition of a neurocomputing structure (for example, a neural network). The neurocomputing area of architecture and theory is concerned with the development and study of neurocomputing architectures (primarily neural network architectures) and the development of theories of operation for those architectures. Besides developing new architectures and theories, researchers in this area perform countless

---

[1] However, the operation of a neural network can sometimes be expressed as a functionally equivalent set of low-level rules [81].

experimental evaluations of neurocomputing systems — typically employing what are known as *toy problems* (problems that are simple to state and that require no significant application domain knowledge to understand and appreciate). It has been the study of architecture and theory that has given us the neural network architectures that we use today, along with an understanding of their theory of operation, capabilities, techniques for effective use, and limitations. This knowledge forms the basis for successful real-world applications.

IMPLEMENTATION   The implementation area of neurocomputing involves research into, and development of, ways to implement neurocomputing architectures in physical hardware. Implementation includes work in areas such as neurosoftware languages (languages for describing neural network architectures in a machine-independent way), design and development of neurocomputers, and design and development of interfaces between programmed computing systems and neurocomputing systems. It is the results of implementation research and development that today provide us with the capability to apply neurocomputing to practical problems quickly and easily.

APPLICATIONS   By far the largest area of activity in neurocomputing is that of applications. Thousands of technologists, business analysts, scientists, and mathematicians are now applying neurocomputing to a wide variety of problems. The primary ingredient in the success of these projects seems to be domain knowledge (as is true for almost all real-world applications of technology). Thus, most successful applicators of neurocomputing are not neurocomputing specialists, but rather are domain specialists. Neurocomputing is relatively easy to learn, compared with most domain knowledge. This contrasts sharply with information processing fields such as artificial intelligence, where typically only highly skilled and trained "knowledge engineers" can apply the technology successfully. Because neurocomputing became practical for real-world applications only in the very recent past, not enough time has elapsed yet for large numbers of applications to be developed. We have, however, gained enough experience to work out some methodologies for neurocomputing application. The most successful methodology seems to be the "answer in search of a question" approach (alluded to previously) in which application domain experts learn the capabilities and limitations of multiple neural network architectures, and then look in their area of expertise for an appropriate important problem to solve. This methodology is characteristic of many new technologies. As time passes and the set of neurocomputing capabilities expands, it may be possible to begin attacking problems directly. One area of potential future development in neurocomputing that may radically alter the approach to applications is automated tool sets that perform powerful general-purpose information processing functions, but require essentially no neurocomputing knowledge. Such tools, which might be as easy to use as a word processor or spreadsheet program, would serve to broaden the scope of the neurocomputing applications area to include hundreds of thousands of people, many of whom would be non-technical.

1.3 The Relationship Between Neurocomputing and Neuroscience

The very name neurocomputing begs the question of how this technological field is related to neuroscience. This section describes the nature of the reciprocal interactions between neurocomputing and neuroscience and the mutual benefit that may result from this interaction. The subject of "hype" in neurocomputing is also discussed.

1.3.1 Neurocomputing and Neuroscience

Neuroscience, broadly taken, can be defined as the scientific discipline concerned with understanding both the brain and the mind (which are usually presumed to be, respectively, the "hardware" and "software" aspects of the same object). Clearly, the brain is composed of networks of neurons. However, these neurons are much more complicated than are the processing elements used in neurocomputing, and their functions are not yet understood.

As with any science, progress in neuroscience is made by creating functional concepts and models based upon experimental results and then refining or refuting these concepts and models by carrying out more experiments. So far, essentially all of the models that have been put forward have been either refuted or shown to be excessively oversimplified. In fact, the current level of understanding of brain and mind function is so primitive that it would be fair to say that not even one area of brain or one type of mind function is yet understood at anything approaching a first-order level. A good way to think of the brain is as an exceedingly complex object built using an alien technology so advanced that we are only now, after more than a century of concentrated study, beginning to understand its simplest components.

The production of functional concepts and models in neuroscience is continuous and prodigious. These provide an excellent source of new concepts and principles for use in neurocomputing. The beauty is that this source of inspiration and ideas will probably keep increasing in both the quantity and quality of its output for the indefinite future. Naturally, since these neuroscience concepts and models are *not* (as of yet) accurate representations of brain function, neurocomputing systems based upon these ideas cannot be described as being "based upon the operation of the human brain" (a claim that is all too often heard). A more accurate statement would be that neurocomputing systems based upon these ideas "probably have no close relationship whatsoever to the operation of the human brain". Notwithstanding the general inadequacies of the functional concepts and models provided by neuroscience, the benefit to the neurocomputing community of this flow of ideas has been substantial, and this flow will probably continue to expand.

The flow of ideas from neuroscience to neurocomputing is only half of the story. There is also beginning to be a flow of ideas from neurocomputing to neuroscience. Members of the neurocomputing community are constantly developing new neural network architectures, as well as new concepts and theories to explain the operation of these architectures. Many of these developments can be used by neuroscientists as new paradigms for building functional concepts and models of elements of brain and mind. These can then lead to new predictions and new experiments. Thus, neurocomputing may have valuable new insights to offer neuroscience. Due to the deliberate actions of leaders of both the neuroscience and neurocomputing communities, there is a growing level of effective communication between these disparate groups. This communication will hopefully continue and expand.

1.3.2 Hype

Almost from the beginning, neurocomputing has been harmed by wild speculations that the subject will someday produce machines with human or near-human perceptual, reasoning, and movement capabilities. The press loves these statements, but many technical people are angered by them. Such pronouncements (along with milder statements concerning, for example, machines that could understand speech or unconstrained images) have become known in neurocomputing as *hype*.

Many members of the neurocomputing community decry hype as dangerous, since a widespread legend says that the subject was almost eradicated by hype in the mid-1960's (this is not really true — see Section 1.3.2 below). However, as is so often the case with righteous indignation, there are very few technical people (technologists, scientists, and mathematicians) who have not themselves engaged in egregious hype at one point or another (usually at many points). Nonetheless, hype is something to be assiduously avoided — particularly by technologists, since personal credibility is essential in technology.

In my view, the tendency for people in neurocomputing to produce hype has a rational basis; namely, a system of beliefs. Typical of these beliefs is the notion that human-like "android robots" based upon neurocomputing systems will someday be built in large quantities to serve humans as willing slaves. These beliefs are frequently quite strong. In many instances they have been fueled by the reading of science fiction stories during puberty (for example, Isaac Asimov's classic book *The Naked Sun*, Doubleday and Company, Inc., New York, 1956, which described "Three Laws of Robotics").

Such beliefs are often also fueled by idealism and altruism. For example, if such human-like machines do someday emerge they might operate their own highly efficient economy; obtaining raw materials, producing finished products, and replicating themselves — a class of producers who do not consume. A common vision is of a future Earth having perhaps a few billion humans served by a few tens of billions of these machines. They could be used to maintain the Earth itself in perfect condition and to provide all humans with essentially unlimited material wealth, security, and comfort. Such machines could grow food, build cities, patrol the streets, keep everything clean and in good repair, and take humans to the stars. It has even been postulated that the advent of such machines would launch the human species into a new anthropologic era (following the original era of Culture and the now-current era of Civilization) — namely, an era of Universal Nobility (Ubility) in which economics (the connection between individual effort and survival) would no longer play any role and where the creation of harmonious ecosocial systems would become the driving force. It has also been suggested that such highly competent machines, should they actually ever emerge, might also become the technologists. In this scenario, neurocomputing would turn out to be the *last* human technology – since all future technologies would be developed primarily by these machines.

Given the powerful idealism and soaring altruism of such speculations, it is easy to appreciate the strength of belief that accompanies them. Unlike religion, which promises a vague eventual spiritual salvation, these ideas promise a hard, palpable, technological salvation. Notwithstanding their attractiveness, it is essential that the connection between these ideas and here-and-now reality be objectively assessed.

The reality is that if human-like machines are ever developed — and it is by no means certain that they will be (for example, insurmountable technological and/or ethical problems could emerge) — their advent would almost certainly lie far in the future (probably centuries from now). Thus, it is a waste of time for technologists to think about them today. Further, it is clearly counterproductive for this issue (and other forms of hype) to continue hovering around neurocomputing, because their presence acts to alienate and repel people outside the field. As a community we need to rid ourselves of this problem. One way of doing this might be for neurocomputing technologists (regardless of their personal beliefs — which should be kept private) to develop a bemused reaction to the mention of "thinking machines" or other neurocomputing anthropomorphisms. Perhaps by dismissing such concepts as humorously preposterous we can make this bad odor go away.

1.4 History of Neurocomputing

As illustrated by the 30 year old example of the perceptron, neurocomputing has an interesting history. Although it is not possible to review this history in any depth in this book, this section presents a brief overview. Understanding the basic history of any subject enhances one's ability to appreciate results from the past and to assess future trends.

The book *Neurocomputing: Foundations of Research* by James Anderson and Edward Rosenfeld [11] is highly recommended as a resource for understanding neurocomputing's past. It contains most of the classic papers of neurocomputing through 1986. Many of the pre-1987 papers referenced in this and later chapters are reprinted in the Anderson and Rosenfeld book.

1.4.1 The Beginning

The beginning of neurocomputing is often taken to be the 1943 paper of Warren McCulloch and Walter Pitts [165] (even though these authors never mentioned practical uses of their work). This paper, which showed that even simple types of neural networks could, in principle, compute any arithmetic or logical function, was widely read and had great influence. Other researchers, principally Norbert Wiener and John von Neumann, wrote books and papers [225, 224] in which the suggestion was made that research into the design of brain-like or brain-inspired computers might be interesting. These suggestions were widely read and appreciated, but little of substance happened as a result of them for a long time.

In 1949 Donald Hebb wrote a book entitled *The Organization of Behavior* [115] which pursued the idea that classical psychological conditioning is ubiquitous in animals because it is a property of individual neurons. This idea was not itself new, but Hebb took it further than anyone before him had by proposing a specific learning law for the synapses of neurons. Hebb then used this learning law to build a qualitative explanation of some experimental results from psychology. This bold step served to inspire many other researchers to pursue this same theme — which further laid the groundwork for the advent of neurocomputing. Although there were many other people examining the issues surrounding neurocomputing in the 1940s and early 1950s, their work had more the effect of setting the stage for later developments than of actually causing those developments. Typical of this era was the construction of the first neuro-computer (the *Snark*) by Marvin Minsky in 1951 [172]. The Snark did operate successfully from a technical standpoint (it adjusted its weights automatically), but it never actually carried out any particularly interesting information processing function. Nonetheless, it provided design ideas that were used later by other investigators.

1.4.2 First Successes

As mentioned in Section 1.1, the first successful neurocomputer (the Mark I Perceptron) was developed during 1957 and 1958 by Frank Rosenblatt, Charles Wightman, and others [199]. Given his many deep insights, his technical contributions, and his modern way of thinking about neural networks, many people see Rosenblatt as the founder of neurocomputing as we know it today. His primary interest was pattern recognition. Besides inventing the perceptron, Rosenblatt also wrote an early book on neurocomputing, *Principles of Neurodynamics* [198] — a book that is still worth reading.

Slightly later than Rosenblatt, but cut from similar cloth, was Bernard Widrow. Widrow, working with his graduate students (most notably Marcian E. "Ted" Hoff, who later went on to invent the microprocessor) developed a different type of neural network processing element called the ADALINE (see Section 3.3 for details), which was equipped with a powerful new learning law which, unlike the perceptron learning law, is still in widespread use. Widrow and his students applied the ADALINE successfully to a large number of toy problems, and produced several films of their successes. Widrow also founded the first neurocomputer hardware company (the Memistor Corporation; see Section 8.2.2 for details), which actually produced neurocomputers and neurocomputer components for commercial sale during the early to mid 1960s.

Besides Rosenblatt and Widrow, there were a number of other people during the late 1950s and early 1960s who had substantial success in the development of neurocomputing architectures and implementation concepts. Examples of such people are Karl Steinbuch [217, 216] (who developed a binary associative network architecture called the *learnmatrix* and several concepts for implementing it in hardware; see Section 4.3 for details) and Roger Barron and Lewey Gilstrap [20] (who, in 1960, founded the first neurocomputing applications company, the Adaptronics Corporation — which, during the 1970s, also sold neurocomputers; the company remained in business continuously and profitably until 1982, when it was acquired by the Flow General Corporation). The 1965 book *Learning Machines* by Nils Nilsson [178] summarizes much of the work of this period.

Notwithstanding the considerable success of these early neurocomputing researchers, the field suffered from two glaringly obvious problems. First, the majority of researchers approached the subject from a qualitative and experimental point of view, rather than from an analytical point of view (although there were notable exceptions to this, such as Widrow). This experimental emphasis resulted in a significant lack of rigor and a looseness of thought (all too reminiscent of alchemy) that bothered many established scientists and engineers who observed the field.

Second, an unfortunately large fraction of neurocomputing researchers (and the press people with whom they spoke) were carried away by their enthusiasm in their statements and writings. For example, there were widely publicized predictions that artificial brains were just a few years away from development, and other incredible statements. This hype further discredited the field and angered technical people in other fields.

Besides the hype and the general lack of rigor, by the mid 1960s researchers had run out of good ideas. It became clear that if further progress was to be made, some radically new ideas had to be introduced — and it was not apparent that these would come along anytime soon. In fact, this latter assessment was correct. This intellectual exhaustion caused many of the best people to leave the field. Many of these people switched to related fields such as pattern recognition, image processing, and signal processing.

By the mid 1960s it was clear that neurocomputing's era of first successes was drawing to a close. The final episode of this era was a campaign led by Marvin Minsky and Seymour Papert to discredit neural network research and divert neural network research funding to the field of "artificial intelligence."[2] The campaign was a success, although the victory was largely illusory, since neurocomputing was already a moribund field. The campaign was waged by means of personal persuasion by Minsky and Papert and their allies, as well as by limited circulation of an unpublished technical manuscript (which was later

---

[2] Until recently, the term "artificial intelligence" seemed secure in its position at the zenith of the firmament of hype. Not anymore. There is now a field called "artificial life".

de-venomized and, after further refinement and expansion, published in 1969 by Minsky and Papert as the book *Perceptrons* [171]).

Minsky and Papert's book *Perceptrons* proved mathematically that a perceptron could not implement the EXCLUSIVE OR (*XOR*) logical function ($f(0,0) = f(1,1) = 0$, $f(0,1) = f(1,0) = 1$ — see Figure 1.7), nor many other such *predicate* functions (binary scalar functions of binary vector variables). As can be seen from Figure 1.7, the inability of the perceptron to implement the XOR function is a trivial fact. Minsky and Papert bulked up this trivial fact (which had been discovered several years earlier by one of Rosenblatt's friends) into the book *Perceptrons*, which was rife with innuendos denigrating neural networks. The following excerpts (pp. 4 and 242) serve to illustrate the book's viewpoint (see [184, 54] for a deeper analysis of *Perceptrons*).

Our discussions will include some rather sharp criticisms of earlier work in this area. Perceptrons have been widely publicized as "pattern recognition" or "learning" machines and as such have been discussed in a large number of books, journal articles, and voluminous "reports." Most of this writing (some exceptions are mentioned in our bibliography) is without scientific value and we will not usually refer by name to the works we criticize. ...

Our first formal presentation of the principal results in this book was at an American Mathematical Society symposium on Mathematical Aspects of Computer Science in April 1966. ...

We were pleased and encouraged by the enthusiastic reception by many colleagues at the A.M.S. meeting and no less so by the doleful reception of a similar presentation at a Bionics meeting [note: *bionics* was one of the names used for the field of neurocomputing during the 1960s]. However, we were now involved in establishing at M.I.T. an artificial intelligence laboratory largely devoted to real "seeing machines," and gave no attention whatsoever to perceptrons until we were jolted by attending an I.E.E.E. Workshop on Pattern Recognition in Puerto Rico early in 1967.

Appalled at the persistent influence of perceptrons (and similar ways of thinking) on *practical pattern recognition*, we determined to set out our work as a book. ....

The implicit thesis of *Perceptrons* was that essentially all neural networks suffer from the same "fatal flaw" as the perceptron; namely, the inability to usefully compute certain essential predicates such as XOR. To make this point the authors reviewed several proposed improvements to the perceptron and showed that these were also unable to perform well. They left the impression that neural network research had been *proven* to be a dead end.

Minsky and Papert's campaign achieved its purpose. The common wisdom that neural networks were a research dead-end became firmly established. Artificial intelligence researchers got all of the neural network research money and more. The world had been reordered. And neurocomputing had to go underground.

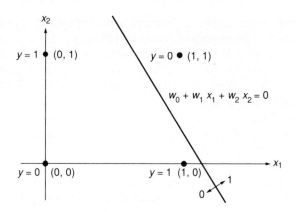

Fig. 1.7. • Impossibility of computing the EXCLUSIVE OR (XOR) function with a perceptron. In order for the perceptron to compute XOR, a line (the hyperplane corresponding to the weights w_0, w_1 and w_2) must be found that puts points $(0,0)$ and $(1,1)$ on one side of the line and $(0,1)$ and $(1,0)$ on the other side of the line. This is obviously impossible. This trivial proof was generalized and expanded by Minsky and Papert in the mid-1960's into a damnation of the entire field of neurocomputing.

1.4.3 The Quiet Years

During the period from 1967 to 1982 little explicit neurocomputing research was carried out in the United States (research in Japan, Europe, and the Soviet Union was somewhat less affected by the *Perceptrons* debacle). However, a great deal of neural network research went on under the headings of adaptive signal processing, pattern recognition, and biological modeling. In fact, a good percentage of the material presented in this book emerged during this period. An interesting aspect of this era of quiet research was the great influx of talented new researchers during the 4 years from 1966 to 1969. Examples include Shun-ichi Amari [9], James Anderson [16], Kunihiko Fukushima [77], Stephen Grossberg [99], Harry Klopf [137], Teuvo Kohonen [147], and David Willshaw [243]. These people, and those who came in over the next 13 years, were the people who put the field of neurocomputing on a firm footing and prepared the way for the renaissance of the field.

1.4.4 Neurocomputing Takes Off

By the early 1980s many neurocomputing researchers became bold enough to begin submitting proposals to explore the development of neurocomputers and of neural network applications. The first breakthrough was at the Defense Advanced Research Projects Agency (DARPA), where Ira Skurnick (a program manager in the Defense Sciences Office) refused to follow conventional wisdom blindly, and instead listened to the substantive arguments that neurocomputing researchers made in favor of their proposed projects. Boldly diverging from tradition, Skurnick began funding neurocomputing research in 1983. Given DARPA's status as one of the world's chief arbiters of technological fashion, this action opened the floodgates. Within months, program managers at other research funding organizations (many of whom had already become interested in the field, but lacked Skurnick's courage) had jumped on the bandwagon. Skurnick was at the right place at the right time to make a key decision that helped launch the renaissance of neurocomputing.

Another potent force in the years 1983 to 1986 was John Hopfield, an established physicist of worldwide reputation who had become interested in neural networks a few years earlier. Hopfield wrote two highly readable papers on neural networks in 1982 [124] and 1984 [123] and these, together with his many lectures all over the world, persuaded hundreds of highly qualified scientists, mathematicians, and technologists to join the emerging field of neural networks. In fact, by the beginning of 1986, approximately one-third of the people in the field had been brought in directly by Hopfield or by one of his earlier converts. Hopfield's work as a recruiter was perhaps the single most important contribution to the early growth of the revitalized field. In fact, in some circles, there developed a confusion that Hopfield had *invented* neurocomputing (or had at least supplied the key discoveries that led to the revitalization of the field). This belief engendered significant discomfort on the part of many of the actual pioneers of the field — particularly the ones who had struggled through the entire span of quiet years in obscurity and were now expecting their due adulation for cumulative services rendered (which did finally come, but not until 1987).

By 1986, with the publication of the "PDP books" (*Parallel Distributed Processing, Volumes I and II*, edited by David Rumelhart and James McClelland [203]), the field exploded. In 1987, the first open conference on neural networks in modern times, the IEEE International Conference on Neural Networks (1700 participants), was held in San Diego (previous neural network conferences were by invitation only or were severely limited in the number of attendees), and the International Neural Network Society (*INNS*) was formed. In 1988 the INNS journal *Neural Networks* was founded, followed by *Neural Computation* in 1989 and the *IEEE Transactions on Neural Networks* in 1990 (and subsequently, many others). Beginning in 1987, several leading universities announced the formation of research institutes and educational programs in neurocomputing.

Although neurocomputing has had an interesting history, the field is still at an early stage of development. As Winston Churchill might have put it: we are now at the end of the beginning.

1.5 Guide to This Book

This section presents a guide for reading this book. The layout of the remainder of the book and the contents of the individual chapters are reviewed briefly.

The book is divided into three major parts:

- Neural Network Architectures and
  Theory — Chapters 2 through 6
- Neural Network Description Languages and Neurocomputer
  Design — Chapters 7 and 8
- Applications of Neurocomputing and Neurocomputing Project Planning
  and Project Management — Chapter 9 and the Appendix

Part 1, Neural Network Architectures and Theory, begins in Chapter 2 with
a presentation of the basic concepts and definitions of neural networks. Chapter
3 then presents five of the learning laws used in neurocomputing. Chapter 4 discusses associative networks (the simplest and most thoroughly understood class
of neural networks); followed by a discussion of mapping networks in Chapter
5. Chapter 6 finishes up Part 1 with a discussion of three additional classes of
neural network architectures: spatiotemporal, stochastic, and hierarchical.

The goal of Part 1 of the book is to provide a synthesized exposition of the
theory of many of the basic neural networks widely used in neurocomputing
today (and of a few advanced networks not currently in use). In producing this
synthesis, ideas from historically disconnected schools of thought have been
freely mashed together. However, references to the original papers are provided.

Part 2, Neural Network Description Languages and Neurocomputer Design, discusses implementation of neural networks. Chapter 7 explains the
concept of neurosoftware languages. These are languages designed expressly
for the purpose of describing the structure of neural networks in a machine-
independent form (to allow automatic compilation of such networks into an ex-
ecutable form). As an example of a specific neurosoftware language, the AXON
language is presented. Chapter 8 discusses neurocomputer design principles
and performance measures, and provides descriptions of a variety of classic
neurocomputers.

Finally, Part 3, Applications of Neurocomputing and Neurocomputing
Project Planning and Project Management, discusses the applications of neurocomputing and some practical matters confronting technologists in industry.
Chapter 9 presents neural network applications engineering and then a number of examples of toy problem applications in the areas of sensor processing,
control, and data analysis. These examples illustrate some important neurocomputing techniques and principles that can be applied to real-world applications.
The Appendix explores the issues of project evaluation, proposal writing, project
planning, and project management.

Neural Network Concepts, Definitions, and Building Blocks

2

Neural networks are fundamentally simple structures. However, as with almost any class of structured objects (aircraft, governments, languages, etc.), it is helpful to have a detailed general or canonical model for the members of the class. Such a model typically provides a set of descriptive terms (for example, aileron, social democracy, and noun) and measurements (for example, wingspan, term of office, and number of noun cases) that can be used to characterize a particular member of the class. This chapter presents a general model and a set of descriptive terms and measurements for neural networks. In addition, some useful facts and definitions concerning *n*-dimensional geometry are presented.

2.1 Neural Networks

As pointed out in the neural network definition given in Chapter 1, neural networks are composed of processing elements and connections. This earlier definition is now restated in an equivalent, but more useful, form. This refined definition is then elaborated upon to form a general structural model of a neural network. Additional aspects of this model are explored in later sections of this chapter.

The general model presented here is known as the *AXON model*. It underlies the AXON neural network description language (which is discussed in Chapter 7). The AXON model not only provides a convenient way to specify the structure of a neural network. It also provides us with a set of descriptive terms for neural networks that will be useful in the remaining chapters of the book.

21

2.1.1 Definition of a Neural Network

A *directed graph* is a geometrical object consisting of a set of points (called *nodes*) along with a set of directed line segments (called *links*) between them. A *neural network* is a parallel distributed information processing structure in the form of a directed graph, with the following sub-definitions and restrictions:

1. The nodes of the graph are called *processing elements.*

2. The links of the graph are called *connections.* Each connection functions as an instantaneous unidirectional signal-conduction path.

3. Each processing element can receive any number of incoming connections (also called *input connections*).

4. Each processing element can have any number of outgoing connections, but the signals in all of these must be the same. In effect, each processing element has a single *output connection* that can branch or *fan out* into copies to form multiple output connections (sometimes called *collaterals*), each of which carries the same identical signal (the processing element's *output signal*).

5. Processing elements can have *local memory.*

6. Each processing element possesses a *transfer function* which can use (and alter) local memory, can use input signals, and which produces the processing element's output signal. In other words, the only inputs allowed to the transfer function are the values stored in the processing element's local memory and the current values of the input signals in the connections received by the processing element. The only outputs allowed from the transfer function are values to be stored in the processing element's local memory and the processing element's output signal. Transfer functions can operate *continuously* or *episodically.* If they operate episodically, there must be an input called *"activate"* that causes the processing element's transfer function to operate on the current input signals and local memory values and to produce an *updated* output signal (and possibly to modify local memory values). Continuous processing elements are always operating. The "activate" input arrives via a connection from a *scheduling* processing element that is part of the network.

7. Input signals to a neural network from outside the network arrive via connections that originate in the outside world. Outputs from the network to the outside world are connections that leave the network.

   Figure 2.1 shows a typical neural network architecture. In neurocomputing, the word *architecture* is reserved for the formal mathematical description of a neural network. Just as the definition of an algorithm in programmed computing has nothing to do with how that algorithm is run on a computer, so in neurocomputing the definition of a neural network architecture has nothing to do with that architecture's *implementation* (meaning the manner in which a neural network is implemented in software, neurosoftware, and/or hardware). Figure 2.1 illustrates some inputs (which can be thought of collectively as an input data array **x**) entering the network from the outside world and copies of selected processing element output signals (which can be thought of collectively as an output data array **y**) leaving the network and being supplied to the outside world. Processing elements within the network receive inputs from other processing elements (and from these external inputs) and send copies of their output signals to other processing elements (and to the outside world).

Referring again to Figure 2.1, notice that the general functional form of a neural network is similar to that of a software subroutine or procedure (input → processing → output). This simple observation is the basis for the mechanism used to embed neural networks into programmed computing systems. This mechanism is described in detail in Chapter 7.

Figure 2.2 shows internal details of a neural network processing element.[1] The processing element transfer function receives as input the signals arriving via the incoming connections which impinge upon the processing element (including the "activate" input from a scheduling processing element, if this processing element is episodically updated), as well as values from local memory (assuming that the processing element has a local memory). Given these inputs, the transfer function outputs values to be stored in specified locations in local memory, as well as supplying the processing element's output signal y. The output signal y fans out (branches into copies or collaterals) after leaving the processing element.

In addition to the structure presented above, all known neural networks have their processing elements divided into disjoint subsets, called *layers* or *slabs* (we will use both of these terms, which mean exactly the same thing), in which all of the processing elements possess essentially the same transfer function. In fact, this definition is universal for all neural networks because *any* neural network can be configured as a collection of layers; namely, by defining each layer to have a single processing element in it.

Figure 2.3 shows a neural network with six slabs. Each slab in the figure consists of a 2-dimensional array of processing elements. Slabs can have any geometrical form desired. As illustrated, processing elements can send connections to other processing elements on the same slab, as well as to processing elements on other slabs.

Many neural networks include a type of slab, called an *input slab*, in which each processing element receives exactly one input, which arrives from the outside world. Input slabs have their incoming signals defined by an array of data supplied by an external agent — such as a computer program running on a host computer. The processing elements of the input slab typically have no function

---

[1] Processing elements are sometimes referred to as *units*, *formal neurons*, or even just as *neurons*. However, use of the term neuron, which has a certain appeal, is viewed as pure hype by many people, so this term is eschewed here

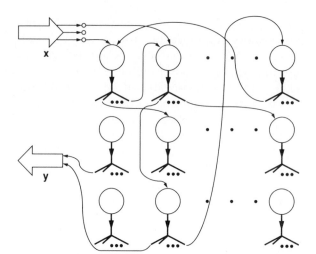

Fig. 2.1. • A typical neural network architecture. Each processing element can have multiple input connections (which can originate from other processing elements or from outside the network), but only one output signal. The single output branches into copies (in other words, multiple connections carrying the same signal) which are distributed to other processing elements, or which leave the network altogether. The input to the network can be viewed as a data array **x** and the output of the network is a data array **y**. When viewed in this way, the network can be thought of as a *function, subroutine,* or *procedure* **y(x)**. This observation is the basis for the mechanism used to embed neural networks into programmed computing systems.

other than to distribute the signals impinging upon them to other processing elements of the network. Such processing elements are called *input units* or *fanout units*. They have no local memory and their transfer function is simply a latch (which releases the input signal to the outgoing collateral connections of the unit whenever the "activate" signal is received).

Processing element transfer functions usually have a subfunction, called a *learning law*, that is responsible for adapting the input–output behavior of the processing element transfer function (over a period of time) in response to the input signals that impinge on the processing element. This adaptation is usually accomplished by modification of the values of variables stored in the processing element's local memory.

Not all neural network adaptation and learning take place via modification of values stored in local memory. Other possibilities exist. For example, connections between processing elements can be created or destroyed. In other schemes the transfer function of a processing element might be replaced by a new one. These sorts of ideas can typically be accommodated by the AXON neural network model presented here. If an idea can't be accommodated by the AXON model then it probably represents a process that is not compatible with

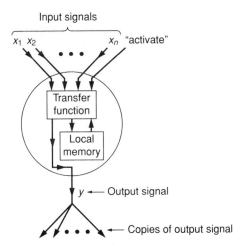

Fig. 2.2. • A generic processing element. The input signals $x_1, x_2, \ldots x_n$ arriving at the processing element are supplied to the transfer function, as is the "activate" input. The "activate" input causes the transfer function to be activated. Continuous-time processing elements do not have an "activate" input — their transfer functions are always active. The transfer function of an episodically updated processing element, when activated, uses the current values of the input signals, as well as values in local memory, to produce the processing element's new output signal value y. The transfer function can also modify values stored in local memory to effect learning.

neural networks. In this event, some other, more general, information processing architectural context (such as the class of general dataflow architectures or even the class of general MIMD architectures) should be considered.

In networks that have episodic transfer functions, each slab is equipped with a processing element that generates the "activate" signal for all of the processing elements of the slab (this processing element is actually located on a separate one-unit slab; but this detail will be suppressed for clarity). For convenience, from now on we shall consider only neural networks that are either composed entirely of episodically updated processing elements or entirely of continuously updated processing elements. Mixed cases will not be treated (obvious modifications of the structures presented here will handle these cases).

The processing element that generates the "activate" signal for a slab has a transfer function that is known as the *scheduling function* of the slab. Because of the large-scale action of this processing element, we often speak of the scheduling function for a particular slab as though it were disembodied. Note that this convention effectively narrows the definition of an episodically updated slab to a set of processing elements with the same transfer function *and* the same scheduling function. In other words, all of the processing elements of the slab get updated together.

In the next two sections we shall discuss more details of connections, processing elements, and scheduling functions.

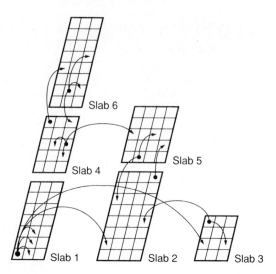

Fig. 2.3. • A neural network with six slabs. The term *layer* is used interchangeably with the term *slab*. The processing elements of each slab share the same transfer function, and are updated together. The slab definition does not comment on the configuration of connections into, on, and out of the slab. These can be defined in any way desired.

Exercises

2.1.1. A parallel image processing architecture, in the form of a regular rectangular grid with one processing element per pixel, has separate bidirectional communications links between each processing element and its North-South-East-West neighbors. Is this a neural network? Explain why or why not.

2.1.2. Write down sets of sensible English synonyms for the terms "processing element" and "connection" (also feel free to invent new ones). Then write a few sentences describing both the advantages and disadvantages of each element of each list.

2.1.3. A *dataflow* information processing architecture is a MIMD architecture without global or shared memory in which each processing element only operates when all of the necessary information that it needs to function has arrived. Show that neural networks are dataflow architectures.

2.1.4. Invent a concrete, detailed example of a dataflow architecture that is not a neural network.

2.2 Connections

This section discusses the details of connections. The data type of the signal carried by a connection and the input class of a connection are defined. The

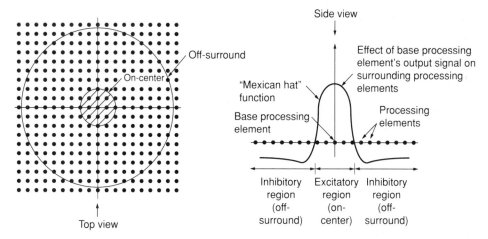

Fig. 2.4. • The on-center/off-surround structure. Each processing element receives excitatory inputs from its close neighbors and inhibitory inputs from more distant processing elements. The excitatory and inhibitory input connections belong to separate *input classes*.

those connections. In fact, the different output collaterals of a single processing element can belong to different input classes. For the purposes of this book, we shall assume that input classes for a particular slab are numbered sequentially by integers. For example, a slab might have input classes 1, 2, 3, and 4.

Figure 2.4 shows a commonly encountered architectural arrangement called an *on-center/off-surround* or *lateral-inhibition* structure. In this architecture, each processing element receives two different classes of input: "excitatory" class 1 inputs from nearby processing elements, and "inhibitory" class 2 inputs from more distant processing elements. The effect of a single processing element's output on surrounding processing elements is plotted in Figure 2.4. This plot takes the approximate form of a so-called "Mexican hat function" [141].

As shown in Figure 2.5, the inputs arriving at a processing element in the on-center/off-surround architecture need to be grouped so that their effects can be combined by the processing element's transfer function. Thus, the connections impinging on a processing element need to be identified as belonging a particular input class.

Since in some networks (particularly in those with random sparse connections) it can be inconvenient to have to predict in advance how many inputs of a given class will be arriving at a particular processing element in a slab, the transfer function must, in these cases, be formulated so that it can deal with a varying number of inputs of each class (including none). This requirement will be discussed in the next section.

2.2.3 Connection Geometries

Besides describing a connection's signal data type and input class, we must also be able to tell where the connection originates and terminates. We need

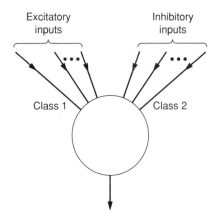

Fig. 2.5. • A typical processing element in the on-center/off-surround network. There are two input classes, one for excitatory inputs (Class 1) and one for inhibitory inputs (Class 2).

a wiring diagram. One way to construct this diagram is to simply number the processing elements of the network from 1 to N and then write down an *interconnection matrix* $M = [m_{ij}]$, in which $m_{ij} = 1$ if there is a connection going *to* processing element i *from* processing element j, and $m_{ij} = 0$ if there is no such connection. This is, of course, a universally applicable approach to defining connections. However, it is difficult to construct an interconnection matrix for large networks, since the number of entries in the connection matrix grows as N^2. Further, the interconnection matrix approach does not allow us to exploit geometrical intuition and visualization.

Rather than deal with connections at the primitive interconnection matrix level, we will use a higher–level geometric approach. The idea is based on the observation that, in almost every network, the connections are made up of disjoint bundles of fibers (analogous to the *fascicles* of neuroscience — a term we will adopt) going from one geometrical region of processing elements to another such region. Before formally defining fascicles, we will give the definitions of slab geometry, slab slice, and region.

■ *DEFINITION 2.2.1 A* geometry *for a neural network slab is defined to be a pair* (G, θ) *consisting of a set G containing N points (not necessarily in a regular or rectangular configuration), known as a* grid, *located in n-dimensional Euclidean space, along with a one-to-one and onto mapping θ of the processing elements of the slab onto the points of the grid. The processing elements of the slab are indexed by the integers from 1 to N (which induces an indexing of the grid via the mapping θ). A* geometry *for a neural network is a collection of geometries for all of its slabs.* ■

In neurocomputing, it is frequently useful to be able to specify a subset of a network constructively. In order to facilitate this, we introduce the concepts of *slice* and *region*.

■ **DEFINITION 2.2.2** *A* slice *of a slab with N processing elements (assumed to be indexed from 1 to N) is a set of processing elements of the slab with indices i between a starting index n_1 and an ending index n_2 (i.e., $1 \le n_1 \le i \le n_2 \le N$) with i of the form $i = n_1 + k\,r$, where r is some non-negative integer constant and where k ranges over all non-negative integers.* ■

■ **DEFINITION 2.2.3** *A* region *is a set of processing elements of a neural network derived from slab slices (of one or more slabs) by means of set unions, set intersections, and set differences.* ■

Notice that Definition 2.3 could just as well have been formulated recursively to also allow unions, intersections, and differences with other regions (because regions would still ultimately be made up of slices). This trivial modification (which we hereby adopt) is useful in practice because once a region has been defined in terms of slab slices, it can then be combined using set union, intersection, and difference operations with other regions or slices to build new regions. Slices and regions give us additional terminology for describing connection geometries. As we will see in Chapter 7, slices and regions are also useful in describing connection geometries in neurosoftware.

Most neurocomputing architectures involve connections that occur in large collections or bundles that we will call *fascicles*. To make the fascicle concept useful it is necessary to attach a number of attributes to each fascicle. These attributes are described in the following definition.

■ **DEFINITION 2.2.4** *A* fascicle *is a collection of connections that satisfies the following five conditions:*

1. *The connections that make up the fascicle must all originate within a single region of the network. This region is called the* source *region of the fascicle.*

2. *All of the signals carried by the connections of the fascicle must be of the same mathematical data type.*

3. *All of the connections of the fascicle must terminate within a region that is a subset of a single slab. This region is called the* target *region of the fascicle.*

4. *All of the connections of the fascicle must be of the same input class relative to the slab which contains the target region of the fascicle.*

5. *The fascicle must have a* selection function *σ defined for it. The selection function $\sigma : T \longrightarrow 2^S$ maps the fascicle's target region T into the power set (the set of all subsets) of the fascicle's source region S. In other words, for each processing element $i \in T$ in the target region T the selection function assigns a subset $\sigma(i)$ of the source region S. This subset defines the set of all*

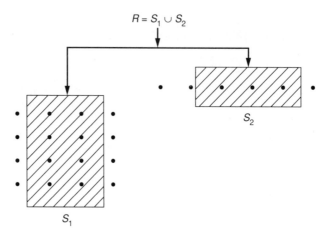

$R = S_1 \cup S_2$

S_2

S_1

Fig. 2.6. • A region R consisting of the union of a region S_1 and a slice S_2 of two rectangular slabs. Note that S_1 is a region but not a slice because it cannot be defined in terms of a single offset formula (assuming that the processing elements are numbered in left-to-right then top-to-bottom raster order).

processing elements in S which supply connections belonging to the fascicle to processing element i of T (note that, for example, in networks with "random" connections, it is possible that some of the sets $\sigma(i)$ could be empty).

■

Fascicles provide a convenient building block for constructing neural networks. Typically, all of the connections needed for a network (even an unusually complicated network) can be defined in terms of a small number of fascicles. Note that the connections of *any* neural network can be defined in terms of fascicles, because, in the worst case (where all of the connections have different characteristics), we can simply assign one fascicle to each connection. Thus, fascicles are universally applicable.

To make these definitions clearer, let us look at some example situations. Figures 2.6 and 2.7 present typical regions. Note that the region S_1 in Figure 2.6 is composed of two vertical slices (or four horizontal slices) of the two-dimensional rectangular slab. Region S_2 is a slice. In Figure 2.7, all four of the regions used to define R are the unions of multiple slices, except for S_3, which is a single slice.

Figure 2.8 shows two fascicles. Fascicle 1 originates in source region R_1 and goes to target region R_3. Fascicle 2 originates in source region R_2 and lands in target region R_4. Notice that source region R_2 consists of the union of two slab subsets — one on slab 1 and one on slab 2 — which indicates that the output signals of processing elements on both slab 1 and slab 2 have the same mathematical data type. As shown in Figure 2.8, a typical processing element in the intersection of regions R_3 and R_4 receives inputs from both fascicle 1

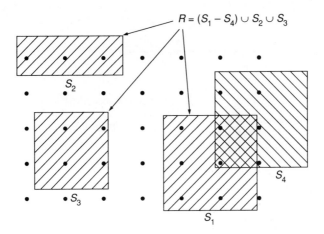

$$R = (S_1 - S_4) \cup S_2 \cup S_3$$

Fig. 2.7. • R is a region formed when the union of the difference $S_1 - S_4$ (of regions S_1 and S_4) is taken with the regions S_2 and S_3. Again, as in Figure 2.6, raster indexing of the slabs is assumed.

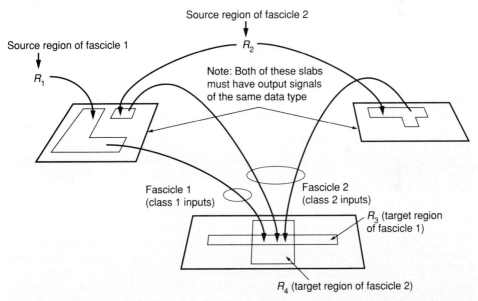

Fig. 2.8. • Two fascicles. The source region and target region of each fascicle are shown. Note that region R_2 is the union of two regions.

and fascicle 2. Note that the selection function geometry is not specified in this figure for either fascicle.

In Figure 2.9, connections for an on-center/off-surround network are defined. Here, there are two fascicles — one for excitation and the other for inhibition. In this example, the source and target regions for both fascicles are

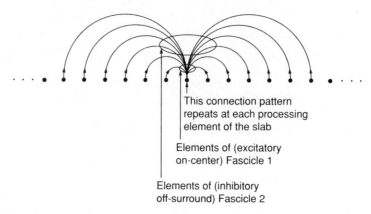

This connection pattern
repeats at each processing
element of the slab

Elements of (excitatory
on-center) Fascicle 1

Elements of (inhibitory
off-surround) Fascicle 2

Fig. 2.9. • Fascicle designs for an on-center/off-surround architecture on a slab with regular linear grid geometry in R^1. This architecture includes two fascicles (one consisting of "excitatory" connections and the other consisting of "inhibitory" connections) that both have this entire slab as both their source and target regions. This figure shows only those fascicle connections that impinge upon the processing element at the center of the figure. This defines the selection functions for both of the fascicles. Each processing element in the slab receives an excitatory connection from those other processing elements within 2 grid units distance from it (excluding itself). These excitatory connections are defined to be of input class 1. Each processing element also receives an inhibitory connection from each processing element lying between 3 and 6 grid units distance from it. These inhibitory connections are defined to be of input class 2. Note that the mathematical types of the signals in both of these fascicles *must* be the same.

the whole slab. In Figure 2.9, the selection functions of the two fascicles are illustrated for a typical processing element. These selection functions are defined by the rule that each processing element receives (excitatory) Class 1 inputs (elements of Fascicle 1) from the other processing elements that lie within 2 processing element grid spacing units (*distance units*) and (inhibitory) Class 2 inputs (elements of Fascicle 2) from those processing elements that lie between 3 and 6 distance units away (inclusive). Note that these selection function geometries are defined in a uniform manner across the target region. Also note that the preceding selection function definition can handle the processing elements at the ends of the slab. Finally, notice that in this scheme each processing element emits both excitatory (Class 1) and inhibitory (Class 2) connections. Since these must, in fact, be the exact same signal (because they are just collaterals of the same output connection) the mathematical data type of both fascicles must be the same. Thus, the excitatory and inhibitory effects of these signals are determined by how the Class 1 and Class 2 signals are processed as they are received by the processing elements.

Fascicle selection functions are *target based*. They define from where within the source region the connections impinging upon a particular processing element in the target region come. Thus, rather than the familiar "GOTO" type of operation (which would correspond to a *source based* approach), selection functions implement a "COMEFROM" type of operation. The reason for choosing target basing rather than source basing is that all we really care about when we are operating a particular processing element is where the inputs to that processing element come from. And since running a neural network consists of nothing more than the operation of its processing elements (either continuously or episodically) the source based picture is of no great value.

Another reason for target basing is that it typically makes design simpler and more foolproof. By concentrating on the input signal needs of the processing elements of each slab we can be sure that all of the connections required by those units are provided. If we were instead concentrating on where the connections of each unit were going we might not notice if some units were not receiving all of the inputs they require. Finally, target basing is also of value relative to the design of neurosoftware languages and their compilers. This point will be discussed in Chapter 7.

While selection functions can be defined in any manner desired, certain commonly encountered patterns of connection have had *standardized* selection functions defined for them. Some of these standardized selection functions are described below.

- FULL — each processing element in the target region receives one input connection from each processing element of the source region.
- UNIFORMLY_RANDOM(n) — supplies each processing element in the target region with n inputs from n different processing elements in the source region chosen uniformly at random. This selection function employs either a random or pseudorandom number generator.
- ONE_TO_ONE(f,g) — assuming that the target region T has M processing elements indexed from 1 to M by the function $f : \{1, 2, \ldots, M\} \longrightarrow T$ and assuming that the source region S has N processing elements indexed from 1 to N by the function $g : \{1, 2, \ldots, N\} \longrightarrow S$, this selection function supplies processing element $f(i)$ of the target region with an input connection from processing element $g(i)$ of the source region, for all i between 1 and $\min[M, N]$.

The standardized selection functions defined above will be used later in this book without further comment.

Exercises

2.2.1. Given any source region S (containing more than 10 processing elements) and target region T of a fascicle, explicitly define a selection function from T to S such that each processing element in T receives input from two different processing elements in S chosen uniformly at random (state the scheme by which you will generate these random numbers). For simplicity, assume that the processing elements of both

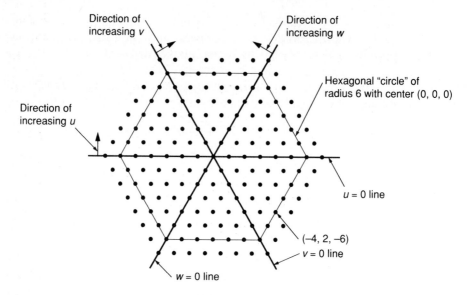

Fig. 2.10. • Two-dimensional hexagonal (u, v, w) coordinate system. The regular hexagonal grid of points has three natural axes, rather than the two axes customary for rectangular grids. Although one of the axes is redundant, it is useful to use all three coordinates because many formulas are both simplified and made hexagonally symmetric.

T and S are indexed by sequential integers from 1 to M and 1 to N, respectively.

2.2.2. Given the processing elements of a regular 2-dimensional hexagonal grid of points as shown in Figure 2.10, develop a mapping f from the integers 1 to $N(r)$ to the set of points within a hexagonal "circle" of radius r (centered on the origin) in some specified inside-to-outside spiral ordering, where $N(r)$ is the number of points within the circle. Derive a formula for $N(r)$ for arbitrary r. Derive formulas for both the Euclidean distance and "hexagonal circle radius"distance between any two grid points (u_1, v_1, w_1) and (u_2, v_2, w_2).

2.2.3. For any two two-dimensional hexagonal circles S and T (as in Exercise 2.2.2) with non-negative radii and arbitrary centers, define a mapping f from T to S such that, if $S=T$, then f is the identity mapping.

2.2.4. Let S and T be regular (in other words, with the same grid spacing in all dimensions) m-dimensional and n-dimensional rectangular point grids, respectively. Define a mapping f from T to S such that f is the identity mapping if $T=S$.

2.2.5. Define fascicles for implementing an on-center/off-surround structure for a general two-dimensional hexagonal circle slab.

2.2.6. Explicitly define a neural network having a fascicle with a selection function σ for which $\sigma(i) = \emptyset$ for some processing element i in the target region of the fascicle, where $\emptyset$ is the empty set.

2.2.7. Define an n-dimensional version of the two-dimensional hexagonal coordinate system of Exercise 2 and derive the corresponding formulas. (NOTE: this is a more difficult problem.)

2.2.8. Describe the 2's–complement number representation scheme and explain in detail how such numbers can be added and multiplied.

2.3 Processing Elements

This section discusses the details of the primary structures associated with processing elements; namely, transfer functions and slabs. After reading this section, you may find it profitable to reread Section 2.2.

2.3.1 Transfer Functions and Local Memories

Episodically updated processing elements are best thought of as having the basic form shown in Figure 2.11. As discussed in Section 2.2, processing elements can receive inputs belonging to multiple *input classes*. The inputs of each class enter the transfer function as a group.

Figure 2.11 shows that transfer functions receive values from incoming connections and from local memory. Transfer functions can produce two types of output values: those to local memory and the processing element's output signal. In processing elements that operate episodically, one of the inputs is an "activate" signal from a scheduling processing element. The arrival of this input connection signal (which can be of any mathematical data type desired) causes the processing element transfer function to be applied to the signal values currently being supplied by the connection inputs (including the "activate" input itself — which can be used to broadcast information, such as updating instructions, to all of the processing elements of the slab) and to the values stored in local memory. After the transfer function has completed its operation and has updated the desired values stored in local memory (which, like the connection signals, can be of any mathematical data type) and generated the processing element's output signal y, it ceases operation. The processing element then remains dormant until the next "activate" signal is sent. Naturally, in continuously running neural networks these updating ideas do not apply, since the transfer function is updating continuously in time.

Note that since all of the processing elements of an episodically updated slab are provided with their "activate" inputs from a common scheduling processing element, all of the processing elements of a slab are updated simultaneously. Thus, processing elements on the same slab cannot communicate during updating. This parallelism of updating provides opportunities for parallelization

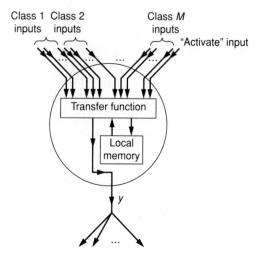

Fig. 2.11. • A general episodically updated processing element. Incoming connections belonging to M classes are shown, as is the "activate" input from the slab scheduling function processing element.

of neurocomputing hardware. This idea will be explored further in Chapters 7 and 8.

For any slab, the fascicles supplying the inputs of each class determine how many inputs of a particular class each particular processing element will receive. Note that the inputs of a particular class might be supplied by one fascicle or they might be supplied by more than one fascicle. This is so because the fascicle definition only specifies that all of the connections in the fascicle be of the same input class. It does *not* require the converse (namely, that all connections of one input class belong to one fascicle).

Given the fact that different processing elements on the same slab can have different numbers of inputs of a given class (varying from none to many), the question then arises as to how a transfer function can be defined to deal with this situation. A typical way in which this can be accomplished is to specify how the contribution of each input will be assessed along with how these contributions will be combined to yield the total effect of inputs from that class. By giving a general mathematical prescription for this process, we can accommodate any number of inputs.

A typical example of such a transfer function is a case where the input signals (assumed here to belong to the real numbers) of the connections belonging to a particular input class k are combined in a weighted sum of the form:

$$I_k = \sum_{j \in \text{Class } k} w_{kj}\, x_{kj} = \mathbf{w}_k \cdot \mathbf{x}_k, \qquad (2.1)$$

where w_{kj} is a multiplicative coefficient for x_{kj} — the jth input of Class k. The quantity w_{kj} is a local memory variable associated with each input of Class k. The vectors $\mathbf{w}_k$ and $\mathbf{x}_k$ have j^{th} components equal to w_{kj} and x_{kj}, respectively. If there are no inputs belonging to Class k impinging on a particular unit, then I_k is set to 0.

Note that since the number of inputs of Class k may vary from one unit to another that the size of the local memory required to store the w_{kj} values associated with the inputs of this class will vary also. This problem of variable local memory size is handled by defining a special type of local memory variable called a *weight*. A weight is a local memory variable of a specified mathematical data type that is assigned to each input connection or to specified mathematical combinations of input connections[4] of a particular input class. A vector which has weights as components is known as a *weight vector*. Processing element transfer functions use a weight to calculate the input contribution of the input connection(s) associated with the weight. Although the method of weight use illustrated in Equation 2.1 (a *weighted sum*) is commonly encountered, this is by no means the only possibility. For example, the transfer functions of the second layer of the counterpropagation neural network architecture introduced in Chapter 5 calculate the Euclidean distance between their weight vectors and their incoming signal vectors.

Not all input classes need to have weights assigned to them. Some input classes of a slab may have weights and others may not. Further, the mathematical data type of the weights associated with the connections of a particular input class can be defined in any way desired, and this data type can vary from one input class to another.

Besides weights, each processing element's local memory can have other values stored in it. These values are called *data variables*. The number of data variables and their mathematical types can be defined in any way that is desired. As with weights, the value of a data variable can vary from processing element to processing element. However, unlike weights, the number and types of data variables are the same for all of the processing elements of the slab. Thus, the local memory of a processing element contains two types of quantities: weights and data variables.

This subsection has described some of the inner workings of transfer functions and local memories. These comments also serve to explain the meaning of the phrase "all of the processing elements of a slab have the same transfer function" used earlier in this chapter. The next subsection discusses the requirements that we have accumulated concerning slabs.

---

[4] For simplicity, this multiple–input combination feature of the AXON model will be ignored in this book. It is primarily useful where multiple inputs are combined into more complicated expressions — such as a multinomial form.

2.3.2 Slabs

As indicated in Section 2.1, neural networks are composed of layers or slabs. In this subsection, we collect the structural features that have been explicitly and implicitly attached to slabs in this chapter.

The accumulated attributes of slabs in the AXON model are defined by the following list:

- Geometry — a grid of N points (not necessarily in a regular or rectangular configuration) located in n-dimensional Euclidean space, with a one-to-one and onto mapping from the processing elements of the slab to the points of the grid. The processing elements of the slab are indexed by integers 1 to N, which induces an indexing of the points of the grid.
- Transfer function — all processing elements of a slab must have the same transfer function.
- Input classes and connections — each processing element in the slab must have the same set of input classes, and all connections impinging on the processing elements of the slab must belong to one of these classes.
- Scheduling function — the transfer functions of the processing elements of an episodically updated slab are operated by an "activate" input signal from a single slab scheduling processing element that serves the entire slab.

Finally, an episodically updated neural network also has a *network scheduling processing element* (again resident on its own slab). This processing element has a transfer function (which, like the slab scheduling units' transfer functions, are often thought of as disembodied) called the *network scheduling function*. The network scheduling processing element provides the "activate" inputs to all of the slab scheduling units. The network scheduling unit receives its own "activate" input from outside the neural network. In other words, episodically updated networks are ultimately operated as an information processing unit that functions in response to some event outside the network. The network scheduling function is discussed further in Chapter 7 in connection with neurosoftware.

The final section of this chapter discusses some definitions and facts concerning n-dimensional geometry.

Exercises

2.3.1. Precisely define a transfer function, other than a weighted sum, that can accept a variable number (from none to many) of inputs of a single class.

2.3.2. Assume that each processing element of a slab receives exactly two input connections, each of which carries a Boolean (in other words, a 1-bit binary) signal (call these input signals A and B). Devise an explicit scheme of weights and an explicit transfer function such that by properly specifying the weights the processing element can produce any of the following two-input/one-output Boolean functions of A and B as the output signal of the processing element: XOR, AND, OR, NAND, NOR, A, B, NOTA, and NOTB.

2.3.3. Completely define a specific, continuously updated, neural network.

2.3.4. Provide an example of how the signal in an "activate" connection could be used to control or regulate the operation of a slab. Give all details.

2.4 *N*-Dimensional Geometry

This section discusses certain aspects of n-dimensional Euclidean geometry needed in this book that are sometimes not covered in mathematics courses.

2.4.1 Cubes

Many neural networks have processing elements with output signals in the ranges $[-1, +1]$ or $[0, 1]$, or in the discrete sets $\{-1, +1\}$ or $\{0, 1\}$. Given a set of n processing elements of one of these types (indexed from 1 to n), we can view the entire set of their n output signals as a single vector $\mathbf{x} = (x_1, x_2, \ldots, x_n)$, where x_i is the output signal of the processing element with index i. The domains of such vectors are the cubes:

$$[0, 1]^n \equiv \{\mathbf{x} = (x_1, x_2, \ldots, x_n) \in \mathbf{R}^n \mid 0 \leq x_i \leq 1, \text{for all } 1 \leq i \leq n\}, \quad (2.2)$$

$$[-1, 1]^n \equiv \{\mathbf{x} = (x_1, x_2, \ldots, x_n) \in \mathbf{R}^n \mid -1 \leq x_i \leq 1, \text{for all } 1 \leq i \leq n\}, \quad (2.3)$$

$$\{0, 1\}^n \equiv \{\mathbf{x} = (x_1, x_2, \ldots, x_n) \in \mathbf{R}^n \mid x_i \in \{0, 1\}, \text{for all } 1 \leq i \leq n\}, \quad (2.4)$$

and

$$\{-1, 1\}^n \equiv \{\mathbf{x} = (x_1, x_2, \ldots, x_n) \in \mathbf{R}^n \mid x_i \in \{-1, 1\}, \text{for all } 1 \leq i \leq n\}, \quad (2.5)$$

where the latter two cubes will be called the *discrete binary* cube and the *discrete bipolar* cube, respectively.

Vectors in $\{0, 1\}^n$ are termed *binary vectors* and vectors in $\{1, 1\}^n$ are termed *bipolar vectors*. Note that $\{0, 1\}^n$ and $\{-1, 1\}^n$ are the sets of corners or vertices of $[0, 1]^n$ and $[-1, 1]^n$ respectively. Also note that the points in $\{0, 1\}^n$ are located at varying distances from the origin (from 0 to $\sqrt{n}$), whereas the vectors in $\{-1, 1\}^n$ are all of length $\sqrt{n}$. $\{-1, 1\}^n$ is therefore a subset of the sphere of radius $\sqrt{n}$ in $\mathbf{R}^n$.

2.4.2 Spheres and Cubes

In 2-dimensional space and 3-dimensional space, we think of cubes and spheres as pretty much alike — spheres are just rounded cubes. In high–dimensional spaces, however, this model no longer holds true; the primary purpose of this subsection is to discuss this seeming inconsistency.

In n-dimensional Euclidean space, let the volume and area of a sphere of radius r be $V_s(n, r)$ and $A_s(n, r)$, respectively, and let the volume and area of a cube of side length l be $V_c(n, l)$ and $A_c(n, l)$, respectively. For reference, the formulas for these quantities are given below [141].

$$V_s(n, r) = \begin{cases} \frac{\pi^{n/2}}{(n/2)!} r^n & \text{if } n \text{ is even} \\ \frac{2^n \pi^{(n-1)/2} ([n-1]/2)!}{n!} r^n & \text{if } n \text{ is odd.} \end{cases}$$

(2.6)

$$A_s(n, r) = \begin{cases} \frac{n\pi^{n/2}}{(n/2)!} r^{n-1} & \text{if } n \text{ is even} \\ \frac{2^n \pi^{(n-1)/2} ([n-1]/2)!}{(n-1)!} r^{n-1} & \text{if } n \text{ is odd.} \end{cases}$$

(2.7)

$$V_c(n, l) = l^n.$$

(2.8)

$$A_c(n, l) = 2n \, l^{n-1}.$$

Naturally, the volume of a unit–side–length cube $V_c(n, 1)$ is equal to 1 (independent of n). However, the volume of the sphere inscribed in the unit cube, $V_s(n, 0.5)$ goes to 0 as $n \longrightarrow \infty$. Thus, contrary to our intuition, the sphere and the cube are very different indeed in high–dimensional spaces. The reason for this difference is that the distance from the center of the cube to the corners of the cube grows without bound as the dimension increases. Specifically, the distance from the center of a unit–volume cube to its vertices in n dimensions is $\sqrt{n/2}$, whereas the distance from the center of the sphere inscribed in the unit cube to any point on its surface is $1/2$.

Thus, cubes (and other rectangles) in n-dimensional space are *highly* anisotropic and should be thought of as illustrated in Figure 2.12. A sphere is always smooth and round and sensual, regardless of its dimensionality (except for $n = 1$, of course!). But cubes in high dimensions are best thought of as spherical porcupines. Their central portion is a tiny spherical region, which has zillions (2^n, to be exact) of very long spines attached to it. The surfaces of cubes are so horribly jagged that they might even be thought of as being almost fractal.

Finally, keep in mind that other strange things that defy intuition can happen in high-dimensional spaces. For example, unlike great circles on Earth, which must always intersect, most pairs of great circles of dimension less than $n - 1$ on the n-dimensional sphere do not intersect. For example, in 4 dimensions (x, y, z, w), the 1-dimensional great circles $x^2 + y^2 = 1$ and $z^2 + w^2 = 1$ do

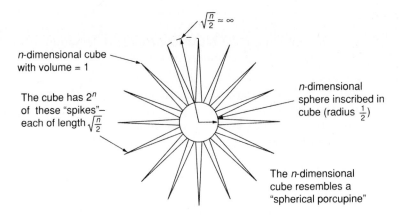

$\sqrt{\frac{n}{2}} \approx \infty$

n-dimensional cube
with volume = 1

The cube has 2^n
of these "spikes"–
each of length $\sqrt{\frac{n}{2}}$

n-dimensional
sphere inscribed in
cube (radius $\frac{1}{2}$)

The *n*-dimensional
cube resembles a
"spherical porcupine"

Fig. 2.12. • A unit volume cube and its inscribed sphere in *n*-dimensional Euclidean space. The cube's $2n$ faces (the flat $(n-1)$-dimensional outer sides of the cube) are all $1/2$ unit distance from the center of the cube at their point of closest approach (where they are tangent to the inscribed sphere), but the 2^n corners or vertices of the cube are at distance $\sqrt{n/2}$, which grows without bound as the dimension increases. Thus, a high-dimensional cube resembles a *porcupine*. It has a small central core (delineated by the inscribed sphere) with zillions of long spikes or spines sticking out of it.

not intersect on the sphere $x^2 + y^2 + z^2 + w^2 = 1$. Likewise, the two-dimensional planes $x = y = 0$ and $z = w = 0$ in 4-dimensional space have exactly one point (namely, $(0,0,0,0)$) in common!

In the next chapter, we shall examine five learning laws used in neural networks.

Exercises

2.4.1. How many points are in the sets $\{0,1\}^n$ and $\{-1,1\}^n$? What are the *n*-dimensional volumes of $[0,1]^n$ and $[-1,1]^n$?

2.4.2. The *Hamming distance h* between two points in $\{0,1\}^n$ or two points in $\{-1,1\}^n$ is defined to be the number of mismatched coordinates between the points. Derive a formula for the Euclidean distance $d(\mathbf{x},\mathbf{y})$ between two points $\mathbf{x}$ and $\mathbf{y}$ in $\{0,1\}^n$, as an explicit function of their Hamming distance $h(\mathbf{x},\mathbf{y})$. Do the same for two points in $\{-1,1\}^n$.

2.4.3. Calculate the ratio of surface area (actually, $(n-1)$-dimensional hyper-area) of a cube in *n* dimensions to that of its inscribed sphere. What is the limit of this ratio as *n* grows without bound?

2.4.4. What are the mean and standard deviation of the angle in degrees between the surface normal vector (the vector perpendicular to the surface) at a point on the surface of a cube of side length *l* in *n* dimensions and the vector from the center of the cube to that point (in other words, the mean and standard deviation of this angle calculated over all the points on the surface of the cube)? This value is a measure of the jaggedness of the surface. What are the mean and standard deviation of this angle for the surface of the sphere inscribed in the cube?

2.4.5. Show that the number density (that is, the average number of vertices per unit of surface hyperarea) of cube vertices on the sphere circumscribing the cube *decreases* with increasing dimension. Interpret this relationship in terms of how fast the spines grow in length versus how many new spines appear as the dimension is increased.

2.4.6. If we were to put sequential integer numbers $(1, 2, \ldots, 2n)$ on the $(n - 1)$-dimensional faces of both of two n-dimensional cubes in order to form n-dimensional dice, and were to throw the dice in a uniformly random fashion (so that after each throw each die would have only one $(n - 1)$-dimensional face "up"), what would be the probability of rolling a combined total of 40?

2.4.7. Invent a method for choosing points at random on the unit–radius sphere in n dimensions so that the probability density of the points is uniform on the sphere. Is your method computationally efficient? (An efficient method is presented in Chapter 2 of [229].)

2.4.8. Derive an asymptotic formula for the side length l of a cube inscribed in a unit volume sphere as $n \longrightarrow \infty$.

2.4.9. Calculate the maximum number of angels that can dance on the circular (1.8 millimeter diameter) head of a pin, given that each angel requires its own dedicated regular hexagonal dancing area of 220 square nanometers. If it is further required that each angel's dancing area be individually "lit" from below (as in the 1978 movie *Saturday Night Fever*) at a minimum illumination of 2.5 photons per second, what minimum frequency of light will be required for this purpose, and what will the minimum power consumption be? Propose a method for building an energy source for this lighting system into the shaft of the pin (which measures 0.3 millimeters in diameter and 15 millimeters in length) such that this power source will have energy storage sufficient to light a 90-minute disco session with all of the angels dancing at once.

Learning Laws: Self-Adaptation Equations

3

This chapter presents five of the classical neural network learning laws. These laws are expressed as equations that can be used in the transfer functions of processing elements in a variety of network architectures. The five laws presented here were chosen from a large set of candidates on the basis of their widespread applicability and their pedagogic value. Some additional learning laws, as well as variants of the laws discussed here, are presented in later chapters.

3.1 Definitions

Learning law equations are not very useful or interesting by themselves. The information milieu in which the equation operates is important. So is the training regimen. This section presents the basic definitions surrounding the use of learning laws, in preparation for the discussions of the laws themselves.

3.1.1 Information Environments

Each learning law operates in an *information environment*. The processing element that has the learning law as part of its transfer function is bombarded by incoming signals of one or more input classes. Since neural networks are distributed information processing structures, each processing element is a totally isolated island. All the processing element can do is respond, in accordance with its transfer function, to the incoming signals impinging on it (which constitute its *local information environment*).

Thus, if learning is to carry out some useful purpose, we must understand how each processing element will self-adjust in response to its local information environment. To do this, we must typically consider the global information environment in which the entire network operates; and from this derive the local picture for each individual processing element.

Finally, it is important to be just as precise in the specification of information environments as in the specification of processing element transfer functions, connections, and slab scheduling. Since information environments tend to be statistical, they are often described in terms of probability density functions. For each of the five learning laws discussed in this chapter, constraints are placed on the information environments used. These specific examples provide a good introduction to the range of situations that are encountered in practice. Later chapters provide further examples.

3.1.2 Weight Space

As pointed out in Chapter 2, in most (but not all) neural networks that have learning capabilities, the learning is accomplished through modification of processing element weights (see Section 2.3 for the definition of a weight). Because of the predominance of weight-modification learning, it is important to develop a good mental model of the weight modification process. That is the purpose of this subsection.

To keep the mathematical notation simple it will be assumed for the remainder of this subsection that all weights belong to the real numbers and that each processing element has exactly n weights. Expanding the discussion to arbitrary weights is trivial, but messy.

In a neural network possessing N processing elements (assumed to be indexed from 1 to N) with adaptive weights (that is, weights that are modified by a learning law), a key concept is the idea of a *network weight vector*. This is the vector formed by concatenating all of the weights of all of the individual processing elements of the network. The network weight vector can be written as

$$
\begin{aligned}
\mathbf{w} &= (w_{11}, w_{12}, \ldots, w_{1n}, w_{21}, w_{22}, \ldots, w_{2n}, \ldots, w_{N1}, w_{N2}, \ldots, w_{Nn})^{\mathrm{T}} \\
&= (\mathbf{w}_1^{\mathrm{T}}, \mathbf{w}_2^{\mathrm{T}}, \ldots, \mathbf{w}_N^{\mathrm{T}})^{\mathrm{T}}.
\end{aligned}
$$

where the vectors $\mathbf{w}_1, \mathbf{w}_2, \ldots, \mathbf{w}_N$ are the *processing element weight vectors* of the processing elements $1, 2, \ldots, N$, respectively. These processing element weight vectors are thus defined to be

$$
\mathbf{w}_1 = \begin{pmatrix} w_{11} \\ w_{12} \\ \vdots \\ w_{1n} \end{pmatrix} = (w_{11}, w_{12}, \ldots, w_{1n})^{\mathrm{T}},
$$

$$\mathbf{w}_2 \;=\; \begin{pmatrix} w_{21} \\ w_{22} \\ \vdots \\ w_{2n} \end{pmatrix} = (w_{21}, w_{22}, \ldots, w_{2n})^{\mathrm{T}},$$

$$\vdots$$

$$\mathbf{w}_N \;=\; \begin{pmatrix} w_{N1} \\ w_{N2} \\ \vdots \\ w_{Nn} \end{pmatrix} = (w_{N1}, w_{N2}, \ldots, w_{Nn})^{\mathrm{T}}. \tag{3.1}$$

Note that the network weight vector $\mathbf{w}$ lies in Nn-dimensional Euclidean space. We shall now discuss the meaning of $\mathbf{w}$ and of changes to it.

First, it may seem unnatural to discuss $\mathbf{w}$ when this weight vector is made up from weights that are elements of the local memories of separate and potentially disparate processing elements. The advantage of thinking about $\mathbf{w}$ is that the set of all possible $\mathbf{w}$ vectors determines the set of all possible information processing configurations for this network (again, assuming that the weights are the only adaptive elements of the network). In other words, *if the information processing performance we seek is to be realized by this network, it will be found at some value of the vector* $\mathbf{w}$.

For neural networks that use weight training, the challenge is to develop a learning law (or a set of learning laws) that will efficiently guide the weight vector $\mathbf{w}$ to a location that yields the desired network performance. As we shall see, there are many different approaches to this problem.

Most learning laws are formulated with a specific goal in mind. A commonly encountered type of goal is to move $\mathbf{w}$ to a position that yields a network that minimizes or maximizes some particular global neural network cost or performance function, such as mean squared error, net profit, fuel consumed, or average pattern classification error (such learning laws belong to the learning law category called *performance learning*). Learning laws that do not attempt to optimize specific cost functions typically have a goal that can be expressed in behavioral or mathematical terms; such as learning the average (or some other function) of an input signal over a period of time (which is the goal of laws that belong to the *filter learning* category).

This observation that learning involves modifying a system to better achieve a stated goal leads to the notion that learning can be studied somewhat independently from the systems that are being modified. For example, we could consider systems defined by an input/output function

$$\mathbf{y} = G(\mathbf{x}, \mathbf{w}), \tag{3.2}$$

where $\mathbf{x}$ is the vector of inputs to the system, $\mathbf{y}$ is the vector of outputs from the system, and $\mathbf{w}$ is the weight vector that determines the precise form of the input/output function. We might then be interested in finding a weight vector that minimizes the function

$$F(\mathbf{w}) = \int_A |f(\mathbf{x}) - G(\mathbf{x}, \mathbf{w})|^2 \, \rho(\mathbf{x}) \, dV(\mathbf{x}), \qquad (3.3)$$

(which represents the mean squared error of approximation between G and a fixed function f that G is attempting to approximate over a region A, with the $\mathbf{x}$ vectors chosen randomly in accordance with a probability density function ρ). Given such a formulation, we could then study general methods of modifying $\mathbf{w}$ to lower the error F (which is our goal) without knowing much about the function G. Studies of this type have been pursued for decades in several different fields (statistics, signal processing, information theory, estimation theory, and communications theory). In fact, there is even a field called *learning theory* that has concentrated on studies of this sort. This body of work can be thought of as a precursor or predecessor of neurocomputing. One of the premier reviews of learning theory is the 1973 book of Yakov Tsypkin [221] (and his earlier book on the applications of adaptation and learning methods [222]). The literature of learning theory is clearly relevant to neurocomputing and is well worth studying.

The next subsection discusses the three general categories of incremental training that are commonly used in neurocomputing to adjust a neural network's weight vector.

3.1.3 Varieties of Training
Neural network adaptation always takes place in accordance with a *training regimen*. That is, the network is subjected to particular information environments on a particular schedule to achieve the desired end result. As mentioned in Chapter 1, training regimens can, at the most fundamental level, be divided into three categories: *supervised training*, *graded* (or *reinforcement*) *training*, and *self-organization*. These are now described.

Supervised training implies a situation in which the network is functioning as an input/output system. In other words, the network receives an input vector (or other quantity) $\mathbf{x}$ and emits a vector (or other quantity) $\mathbf{y}$. Supervised training for such a system implies a regimen in which the network is supplied with a sequence of examples $(\mathbf{x}_1, \mathbf{y}_1), (\mathbf{x}_2, \mathbf{y}_2), \ldots, (\mathbf{x}_k, \mathbf{y}_k), \ldots$ of "desirable" or "correct" input/output pairs. As each input $\mathbf{x}_k$ is entered into the neural network, the "correct output" $\mathbf{y}_k$ also is supplied to the network. The network is thus told precisely what it should be emitting as its output. To distinguish the actual output of the neural network from the desired output of the network (as determined, for example, by the data used for supervised training) a special notation will be used. The actual output of the network will be labeled $\mathbf{y}'$; whereas, the correct or desired output will be denoted by $\mathbf{y}$. This notation is used because, in some sense, the actual output $\mathbf{y}'$ is an "estimate" of the correct output $\mathbf{y}$.

In many supervised training situations the $(\mathbf{x}_k, \mathbf{y}_k)$ pairs used during training are assumed to be examples of a fixed function f. In this instance $\mathbf{y}_k = f(\mathbf{x}_k)$. Another commonly encountered situation is where the relationship between $\mathbf{x}_k$

and $\mathbf{y}_k$ is stochastic. For example, we might have $\mathbf{y}_k = f(\mathbf{w}_k) + \mathbf{n}_k$, where $\mathbf{n}_k$ is a zero-mean random noise vector of small average magnitude.

Graded training (which is also known as reinforcement training) is similar to supervised training except that, instead of being given the correct $\mathbf{y}_k$ output on each individual training trial, the network receives only a score or grade that tells it how well it has done over a sequence of multiple training (i.e., input/output) trails. In other words, at time intervals (periodic or aperiodic) encompassing multiple input/output episodes, the network is given a numeric score or grade that represents the value of some network performance measurement (or "cost") function measured or evaluated over this time interval. Many different cost functions have been used in graded learning schemes. In one famous example (Barto, Sutton, and Anderson's 1983 Broomstick Balancer [22]), the cost function was a binary value that told the network that it had allowed the broomstick that it was supposed to be balancing either to fall down or to move too far from the center of the track (the broomstick was mounted on a 1-degree-of-freedom pivot mounted on a cart confined to a finite-length track). Another graded learning system uses the total time integral of sum of the broomstick's absolute angle deviation from vertical plus its absolute distance deviation from the center of the track since its last fall, as its cost function. The advantage of graded learning is that it is not necessary to know the correct answer for each input/output trial in order to train the network to perform a task. Unfortunately, graded training networks are typically less capable and less generally applicable than are supervised training networks, although this may not remain true indefinitely. Graded training networks are particularly applicable to control and process–optimization problems where there is no way to know what the desired outputs should be, and where the network required to solve the problem is typically small. Graded training will not be discussed in detail in this book because currently the only practically useful learning laws are commercially proprietary.

In self-organization, a network modifies itself in response to $\mathbf{x}$ inputs. There are no $\mathbf{y}$ inputs nor grade inputs. This category of training may seem rather pointless, but a surprising number of information processing capabilities can be obtained using it. Examples include estimation of probability density functions, development of pattern categories based on clustering, and development of continuous topological mappings from Euclidean space to curved manifolds. Examples of the use of self-organizing training include the competitive learning law presented in Section 3.4 and the self-organizing map neural network presented in Section 5.4.

Given these preliminaries, five specific learning laws are discussed in the following five sections. Each of the five laws is a member of a different general category of learning laws.[1] The section describing each learning law is named

---

[1] There are more than five categories of learning laws used in neurocomputing, but five are plenty for an introductory text.

for the category to which that law belongs. Some other members of some of these categories are introduced in later chapters.

Exercises

3.1.1. Consult a book on classical psychological conditioning and find a type of conditioning that is qualitatively different from supervised training, graded training, and self-organization in neurocomputing.[2] Describe that conditioning paradigm in detail. Comment on whether you feel that a neural network capable of learning in this manner would be useful. Explain your reasoning.

3.1.2. Show that if a weight vector $\mathbf{w} \in \{-1, 1\}^n$ can only have one component changed at each discrete time step that it will take a minimum of $h(\mathbf{w}, \mathbf{u})$ time steps for $\mathbf{w}$ to be changed into $\mathbf{u}$ (where $\mathbf{u} \in \{-1, 1\}^n$ and where $h(\mathbf{w}, \mathbf{u})$ is the Hamming distance from $\mathbf{w}$ to $\mathbf{u}$).

3.1.3. Give examples of training processes for household pets that resemble supervised training, reinforcement training, and self-organization.

3.1.4. If a weight vector $\mathbf{w} \in \mathbf{R}^n$ is to be moved continuously and smoothly from its current position $\mathbf{w}$ to a new position $-\mathbf{w}$ along a circular arc about the origin, write an equation that will accomplish this. [Hint: write down an explicit smooth function $\mathbf{v} : [0, 1] \longrightarrow \mathbf{R}^n$ such that $\mathbf{v}(0) = \mathbf{w}$, $\mathbf{v}(1) = -\mathbf{w}$, $|\mathbf{v}(t)| = |\mathbf{w}|$ for all $t \in [0, 1]$, and such that $\mathbf{v}(t)$ is always located in a fixed two-dimensional plane for all $t \in [0, 1]$.]

3.2 Coincidence Learning

In 1949, Canadian psychologist Donald Hebb published a book entitled *The Organization of Behavior* [115], in which he postulated a plausible mechanism for learning at the cellular level in brains. This section presents Hebb's learning law in its neurocomputing form.

3.2.1 Hebb's Biological Learning Law

The basic idea espoused by Hebb was that, when an axonal input to a neuron (arriving via a synapse) helps cause that neuron to immediately emit a pulse, then the efficacy of that axonal input — in terms of its ability to help the target cell produce pulses in the future — will somehow be increased. Hebb

---

[2] Note: neural networks that can exhibit all 16 types of classical psychological conditioning have been constructed. See [136] for details.

postulated that the increase in efficacy occurs within the synapse that transducts the incoming signal into the target neuron.[3]

Hebb's learning concept is most appealing because it allows behavioral reward concepts to be pushed all the way down to the cellular level. Later work in neurobiology has confirmed that Hebb's idea was at least approximately correct neurophysiologically. However, it is also known that there are other mechanisms of biological learning, including the growth and withering of axon collaterals, modifications to local chemical metabolism, and development of new cells. Nevertheless, in recognition of Hebb's pioneering contributions to neuroscience and neurocomputing, the particular learning law presented in this section has come to be known as *Hebb learning*. Hebb learning belongs to the *coincidence* category of learning laws. These laws cause weight changes in response to events within a processing element that happen simultaneously. The learning laws of this category are characterized by their completely local (both in time and space) character.

3.2.2 The Linear Associator

Figure 3.1 shows a neural network architecture (or architectural element) called the *linear associator*. This network will be used in the next subsection as a substrate for the discussion of Hebb learning.

The input to the linear associator network is a vector $\mathbf{x}$, assumed to be drawn from $\mathbf{R}^n$ in accordance with a fixed probability density function $\rho(\mathbf{x})$. The output vector $\mathbf{y}'$ is derived from the input vector $\mathbf{x}$ by means of the following formula:

$$\mathbf{y}' = W\mathbf{x}, \tag{3.4}$$

where $W = (w_{ij})$ is the $m \times n$ *weight matrix* having vectors $\mathbf{w}_1^\mathrm{T}, \mathbf{w}_2^\mathrm{T}, \ldots, \mathbf{w}_m^\mathrm{T}$ as its rows. In other words,

---

[3] Everyone in neurocomputing should have a basic knowledge of neuroscience, if for no other reason than to be properly humbled by the super-advanced alien technology used in the construction of brains. The following introductory books are highly recommended: *From Neuron to Brain, Second Edition* by Stephen Kuffler, John Nicholls, and A. Robert Martin [155], *Neurophilosophy* by Patricia Churchland [38], and *The Human Brain Coloring Book* by Marian Diamond, Arnold Scheibel, and Lawrence Elson [53]. The latter book is a superb tool for learning the intricacies of brain structure. As you make your way through the book you literally color in the various brain structures with crayons. This is a learning experience that can be shared with young children (although they enjoy it for different reasons, and are unlikely to remember the difference between the infundibulum and the interventricular foramen!).

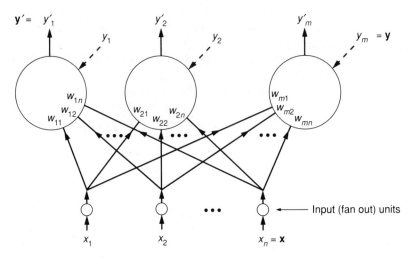

Fig. 3.1. • The linear associator neural network. The vector **x** is entered into the network at the bottom, and the vector **y**′ is emitted at the top. The components of **x** are provided to input units which simply fan out these values to the top layer of processing elements, which is known as the *output layer*. Each output layer processing element output signal y_i' is simply a linear combination of the x input signals. During each training trial, each output unit is supplied with the output signal y_j that it should have emitted. Since these y_j inputs are only provided during training, these inputs are indicated by dotted lines. This neural network uses Hebb learning.

$$W = (\mathbf{w}_1 \quad \mathbf{w}_2 \dots \mathbf{w}_m)^{\mathrm{T}} = \begin{pmatrix} \mathbf{w}_1^{\mathrm{T}} \\ \mathbf{w}_2^{\mathrm{T}} \\ \vdots \\ \mathbf{w}_m^{\mathrm{T}} \end{pmatrix}, \tag{3.5}$$

where $\mathbf{w}_i = (w_{i1}, w_{i2}, \dots, w_{in})$ is the weight vector of the ith processing element in Figure 3.1.

The basic idea of the linear associator neural network is that the network should learn L pairs of input/output vectors $(\mathbf{x}_1, \mathbf{y}_1), (\mathbf{x}_2, \mathbf{y}_2), \dots, (\mathbf{x}_L, \mathbf{y}_L)$. When one of these input vectors, say $\mathbf{x}_k$, is entered into the network, the output vector **y**′ should be $\mathbf{y}_k$. When a vector $\mathbf{x}_k + \epsilon$ (close to $\mathbf{x}_k$) is entered into the network, the output vector should be $\mathbf{y}_k + \delta$ (a vector close to $\mathbf{y}_k$). In the remainder of this section some ways of accomplishing this input/output behavior, at least approximately, are examined. The linear associator neural network, per se, is discussed in more detail in Chapter 4.

3.2.3 Hebb's Learning Law

The problem of getting the linear associator to associate $\mathbf{x}_k$ with $\mathbf{y}_k$ properly is, of course, a problem of finding the best possible weight matrix W for this purpose.

In this section the most common mathematical expression of the classic Hebb learning law is introduced.

Hebb's biological learning law conjecture, as already heuristically discussed, is the basis for neurocomputing's *Hebb learning law*:

$$w_{ij}^{\text{new}} = w_{ij}^{\text{old}} + y_{ki}x_{kj}, \tag{3.6}$$

(where x_{kj} and y_{ki} are the jth and i^{th} components of $\mathbf{x}_k$ and $\mathbf{y}_k$, respectively) or, rewritten as a weight matrix updating rule

$$\mathbf{W}^{\text{new}} = \mathbf{W}^{\text{old}} + \mathbf{y}_k\mathbf{x}_k^{\mathsf{T}}. \tag{3.7}$$

The idea is that to add another associated vector pair $(\mathbf{x}_k, \mathbf{y}_k)$ example to the network, all we need to do is enter components of the vector $\mathbf{x}_k$ into the usual input channels (as shown in the bottom of Figure 3.1) and enter the components of $\mathbf{y}_k$ into the channels shown as dotted lines in Figure 3.1. This learning law functions only when a $\mathbf{y}$ vector (i.e., a "correct output") is entered into the output layer processing elements of the network. In other words, when no $\mathbf{y}$ vector is entered, the Hebb learning law is not applied. The net result is that the w_{ij} vectors are changed only on learning trials (i.e., trials where both an $\mathbf{x}$ input and a desired $\mathbf{y}$ output are supplied). It is assumed that before any vector pairs $(\mathbf{x}_k, \mathbf{y}_k)$ are entered, the w_{ij} weight values are all initially set to 0.

Another way to look at Hebb learning is from the standpoint of what values the weights take on at the end of training (that is, after all L training examples $(\mathbf{x}_1, \mathbf{y}_1), (\mathbf{x}_2, \mathbf{y}_2), \ldots, (\mathbf{x}_L, \mathbf{y}_L)$ have been entered). To explore this idea we note that, if there are L vector pairs $(\mathbf{x}_1, \mathbf{y}_1), (\mathbf{x}_2, \mathbf{y}_2), \ldots, (\mathbf{x}_L, \mathbf{y}_L)$ to be stored in the network, then the training process changes the W weight matrix from its initial state as the zero matrix to its final state by simply adding together all of the incremental weight changes caused by the L applications of the Hebb learning law. Thus, the end state of the matrix W is given by

$$W = \mathbf{y}_1\mathbf{x}_1^{\mathsf{T}} + \mathbf{y}_2\mathbf{x}_2^{\mathsf{T}} + \ldots + \mathbf{y}_L\mathbf{x}_L^{\mathsf{T}}. \tag{3.8}$$

This equation, which helps explain what is going on in Hebb learning, is called the *outer product sum* formula for W. This name stems from the fact that each of the Hebb learning law incremental changes to W is of the form $\mathbf{y}_k\mathbf{x}_k^{\mathsf{T}}$, which is the *outer product* of the vectors $\mathbf{y}_k$ and $\mathbf{x}_k$.

The outer product sum reformulation of the Hebb learning law allows us to gain additional insight into the capabilities of Hebb learning to carry out our goal of associating the $(\mathbf{x}_k, \mathbf{y}_k)$ vector pairs. The first observation is that if the vectors $\{\mathbf{x}_1, \mathbf{x}_2, \ldots, \mathbf{x}_L\}$ are orthogonal and of unit length — that is, if they are *orthonormal* — then

$$\mathbf{y}_k = W\mathbf{x}_k \tag{3.9}$$

for $k = 1, 2, \ldots, L$. In other words, the linear associator network will then perform the desired input/output transformation. This will occur because orthonormal $\mathbf{x}_k$ vectors obey the relationship

$$\mathbf{x}_i \cdot \mathbf{x}_j = \mathbf{x}_i^T \mathbf{x}_j = \mathbf{x}_j^T \mathbf{x}_i = \delta_{ij}, \qquad (3.10)$$

where δ_{ij} is the *Kronecker delta* ($\delta_{ij} = 1$ if $i = j$ and $\delta_{ij} = 0$ if $i \neq j$). Thus,

$$
\begin{aligned}
W\mathbf{x}_k &= (\mathbf{y}_1\mathbf{x}_1^T + \mathbf{y}_2\mathbf{x}_2^T + \ldots + \mathbf{y}_L\mathbf{x}_L^T)\mathbf{x}_k \\
&= \mathbf{y}_1(\mathbf{x}_1^T\mathbf{x}_k) + \mathbf{y}_2(\mathbf{x}_2^T\mathbf{x}_k) + \ldots + \mathbf{y}_k(\mathbf{x}_k^T\mathbf{x}_k) \ldots + \mathbf{y}_L(\mathbf{x}_L^T\mathbf{x}_k) \\
&= \mathbf{y}_k(\mathbf{x}_k^T\mathbf{x}_k) \\
&= \mathbf{y}_k.
\end{aligned}
\qquad (3.11)
$$

Therefore, if the $\mathbf{x}_k$ vectors are orthonormal, the linear associator works as desired. The problem is that this condition is very strict. For one thing, L must be less than or equal to n, the dimensionality of the $\mathbf{x}_k$ vectors. This restriction occurs because the maximum possible number of orthogonal vectors in an n-dimensional space is n. Thus, the number of vector pairs that we can associate is limited to $L = n$. Further, we are restricted to the condition that the $\mathbf{x}_k$ vectors be of unit length. It would be better if we could choose the $\mathbf{x}_k$ vectors and $\mathbf{y}_k$ vectors as we pleased, without restriction,[4] and could have as many of them as we wish. As we shall see in Chapter 4 and Chapter 5, this freedom can be achieved, but not with the linear associator.

If the $\mathbf{x}_k$ vectors are not orthogonal, then we get an error when attempting to reconstruct $\mathbf{y}_k$ using the product $W\mathbf{x}_k$. We can estimate this error (assuming that the $\mathbf{x}_k$ vectors are still of unit length) by using the *signal to noise expansion*:

$$
\begin{aligned}
W\mathbf{x}_k &= \mathbf{y}_1(\mathbf{x}_1^T\mathbf{x}_k) + \mathbf{y}_2(\mathbf{x}_2^T\mathbf{x}_k) + \ldots + \mathbf{y}_k(\mathbf{x}_k^T\mathbf{x}_k) \ldots + \mathbf{y}_L(\mathbf{x}_L^T\mathbf{x}_k) \\
&= \mathbf{y}_k(\mathbf{x}_k^T\mathbf{x}_k) + \sum_{j \neq k}\mathbf{y}_j(\mathbf{x}_j^T\mathbf{x}_k) \\
&= \mathbf{y}_k + \eta.
\end{aligned}
\qquad (3.12)
$$

Under certain circumstances the weight matrix W can be chosen so that the error vector η can be made to be small. In the next subsection an approach to making the error of the linear associator small is discussed. Although this *pseudoinverse* approach cannot be implemented with Hebb learning (it requires Widrow learning), it is presented here because it will be needed as background for the further discussion of the linear associator in Chapter 4.

3.2.4 The Pseudoinverse Formula

The problem of how best to choose the weights for the linear associator when the $\mathbf{x}_k$ vectors are not orthonormal can be answered using results from linear algebra. First, it is important to define what we mean by "best."

---

[4] Naturally, we must have the restriction that there not be two pairs of the form $(\mathbf{x}, \mathbf{y}_1)$ and $(\mathbf{x}, \mathbf{y}_2)$, where $\mathbf{y}_1 \neq \mathbf{y}_2$, since such a situation would violate causality and would not represent a valid functional relationship.

Given L pairs $(\mathbf{x}_1, \mathbf{y}_1), (\mathbf{x}_2, \mathbf{y}_2), \ldots, (\mathbf{x}_L, \mathbf{y}_L)$ of associated vectors that are to be used both for training the linear associator network and then evaluating its performance, the *mean squared error* F of the linear associator is defined to be

$$F(W) \equiv \left(\frac{1}{L}\right) \sum_{k=1}^{L} |\mathbf{y}_k - W\mathbf{x}_k|^2, \qquad (3.13)$$

where W is the weight matrix of the network. In the case where the $\mathbf{x}_k$ vectors are orthonormal, Hebb learning gives us a W matrix that yields zero mean squared error. To develop the general pseudoinverse formula, we need to show (see Exercise 3.2.3) that we can write the mean squared error formula shown in Equation 3.11 in the following form:

$$F(W) = \left(\frac{1}{L}\right) \|Y - WX\|^2, \qquad (3.14)$$

where X is the $n \times L$ matrix $X = (\mathbf{x}_1 \quad \mathbf{x}_2 \ldots \mathbf{x}_L)$ whose columns are the $\mathbf{x}_k$ vectors, and where Y is the $m \times L$ matrix $Y = (\mathbf{y}_1 \quad \mathbf{y}_2 \ldots \mathbf{y}_L)$ whose columns are the $\mathbf{y}_k$ vectors. In Equation 3.12, the square of the norm $\|(m_{ij})\|^2$ of a $p \times q$ matrix $M = (m_{ij})$ is defined to be

$$\|M\|^2 = \|(m_{ij})\|^2 = \sum_{i=1}^{p} \sum_{j=1}^{q} m_{ij}^2. \qquad (3.15)$$

Notice (see Exercise 3.2.1) that, in terms of the matrices X and Y, the Hebb outer product formula (Equation 3.6) can be rewritten as

$$W = YX^{\mathrm{T}}.$$

The *pseudoinverse formula* is simply

$$W = YX^+, \qquad (3.16)$$

where X^+ is the pseudoinverse of the matrix X (*every* matrix has a pseudoinverse). As shown in Exercises 3.2.3, 3.2.4, and 3.2.5, this choice of W minimizes the mean squared error F. The pseudoinverse is now discussed.

The *pseudoinverse* A^+ of an arbitrary $(p \times q)$ real matrix A is defined to be the (unique, it turns out — see [4, 215] for details) real matrix that has the following properties:

$$
\begin{aligned}
AA^+A &= A, \\
A^+AA^+ &= A^+, \\
AA^+ &= (AA^+)^{\mathrm{T}}, \\
A^+A &= (A^+A)^{\mathrm{T}}.
\end{aligned}
\qquad (3.17)
$$

While the pseudoinverse formula may seem radically different from Hebb learning, it can be shown that the Hebb weight matrix YX^{T} is the first term in a series expansion of the pseudoinverse formula weight matrix YX^{+}. Thus, they are actually closely related. The manner in which X^{+} can be computed in a neural network is discussed in Section 4.2.

In summary, Hebb learning is limited in its capabilities. However, it is simple to implement and, as we shall see, can be of use in some situations.

Exercises

3.2.1. Show that, if $W = (w_{ij})$ and $w_{ij} = y_i x_j$ for all i and j, then $W = \mathbf{y}\mathbf{x}^{\mathrm{T}}$. Also show that Equation 3.6 can be rewritten as $W = YX^{T}$.

3.2.2. Given vectors $\mathbf{x}_1 = (\frac{1}{\sqrt{30}})(1, 2, 3, 4)^{\mathrm{T}}$, $\mathbf{y}_1 = (3, 2, 1, 0, -1)^{\mathrm{T}}$, $\mathbf{x}_2 = (\frac{1}{\sqrt{81}})(8, -3, 2, -2)^{\mathrm{T}}$, and $\mathbf{y}_2 = (3, 5, -2, 9, -1)^{\mathrm{T}}$, construct the Hebb learning matrix W for these pairs using the outer product formula (Equation 3.6). Verify numerically that $\mathbf{y}_k = W\mathbf{x}_k$ for $k = 1, 2$.

3.2.3. Show that $F(W) = (1/L)\|Y - WX\|^2$, and then show that $F(W) = (\frac{1}{L})\, tr(S)$, where $S = (WX - Y)(WX - Y)^{\mathrm{T}}$ and where $tr(S)$ is the trace of the square matrix S (the sum of the m main diagonal entries of S).

3.2.4. Using the identities $A^{+}AA^{\mathrm{T}} = A^{\mathrm{T}}$ and $AA^{\mathrm{T}}(A^{+})^{\mathrm{T}} = A$ (which hold for any matrix A), show that the matrix S of Exercise 3.2.3 can be written as $S = (YX^{+} - W)XX^{\mathrm{T}}(YX^{+} - W)^{\mathrm{T}} + Y(I - X^{+}X)Y^{\mathrm{T}}$.

3.2.5. Using the result of Exercise 3.2.4, show that $F(W)$ is minimized for $W = YX^{+}$. [Hints: Show that the first term of the expanded expression for S is always non-negative and goes to zero for this choice of W, and show that the second term is constant. Note that the trace of a sum of matrices is the sum of their individual traces.]

3.3 Performance Learning

This section discusses the Widrow learning law, which is a member of the *performance learning* category of learning laws. Learning laws in this category attempt to find a set of weights that minimize or maximize a specified performance measurement function (sometimes called a *cost function*). In Widrow learning, the goal is to find the best possible weight vector (for a very simple type of processing element) in terms of a least mean squared error performance function criterion. The Widrow learning law is one of the most powerful in neurocomputing because it converges to this optimum weight vector from any starting point. The section begins with a description of the simple ADALINE affine combiner processing element. This discussion is followed by the careful definition of the performance measurement function to be used. Finally, the Widrow learning equation is defined.

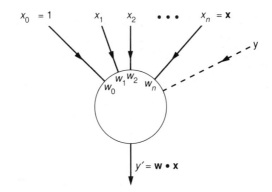

Fig. 3.2. • The ADALINE (ADAptive LINear Element), or *affine combiner*. The vector $\mathbf{x} = (x_0, x_1, \ldots, x_n)$ is entered into the processing element, and the number $y' = \mathbf{w} \cdot \mathbf{x} = w_0 x_0 + w_1 x_1 + \cdots + w_n x_n = w_0 + w_1 x_1 + \cdots + w_n x_n$ is emitted, where $\mathbf{w} = (w_0, w_1, \ldots, w_n)$ is the weight vector of the ADALINE processing element. Note that the zero[th] component of $\mathbf{x}$ (namely, x_0) is always equal to 1. This is called a *bias* input. The ADALINE uses Widrow learning.

3.3.1 The ADALINE

The ADALINE (ADAptive LINear Element) (see Figure 3.2) is a simple type of processing element that has a real vector $\mathbf{x}$ as its input and a real number y' as its output (complex values can also be accommodated, but this is not of interest for the purposes of this book) and uses Widrow learning.

The input to the ADALINE is $\mathbf{x} = (x_0, x_1, x_2, \ldots, x_n)^T$, where x_0, called a *bias term* or *bias input*, is permanently set to 1. The ADALINE has a weight vector $\mathbf{w} = (w_0, w_1, w_2, \ldots, w_n)^T$, and the output of the ADALINE processing element is simply $y' = \mathbf{w} \cdot \mathbf{x} = \mathbf{w}^T \mathbf{x} = w_0 + w_1 x_1 + w_2 x_2 + \cdots + w_n x_n$. Before we proceed with the discussion of the ADALINE and Widrow learning, it is important to understand the geometrical significance of the ADALINE's input/output relationship.

Figure 3.3 shows the geometry of the ADALINE. The basic idea is that the $\mathbf{w}$ vector defines a hyperplane in the n-dimensional space of the vectors $\underline{\mathbf{x}} = (x_1, x_2, \ldots, x_n)^T$. Since the input vector $\mathbf{x}$ is determined by $\underline{\mathbf{x}}$, the output y of the ADALINE is determined by this geometry. In short, the ADALINE's output is determined by which hyperplane (perpendicular to $\underline{\mathbf{w}}$) a particular $\underline{\mathbf{x}}$ lies on. Each such hyperplane is a $y' = constant$ surface. Notice that, if we did not have a bias term, the $y' = 0$ hyperplane would be forced to go through the origin.

A weighted sum of inputs $w_1 x_1 + w_2 x_2 + \ldots + w_n x_n$ is known as a *linear combination*. If we add a bias term w_0 to such a linear combination, we get what is called an *affine combination*. This is why the ADALINE is sometimes called an *affine combiner* (particularly when the connection with Widrow learning is not being emphasized).

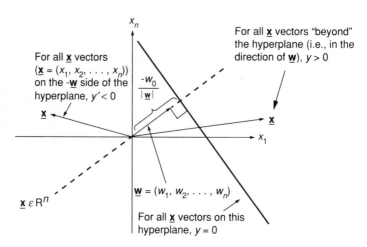

Fig. 3.3. • The geometry of the ADALINE input/output relationship. If the vector $\underline{x} = (x_1, x_2, \ldots, x_n)^T$ lies on the hyperplane perpendicular to $\underline{w} = (w_1, w_2, \ldots, w_n)^T$ at directed distance $(-w_0/|\underline{w}|)$ from the origin, then the output of the ADALINE will be 0. The $\underline{x}$ vectors lying on the "far side" of this hyperplane have positive y' output; $\underline{x}$ vectors lying on the $-\underline{w}$ side of the hyperplane have negative y' output. The output of the ADALINE depends linearly on the distance of $\mathbf{x}$ from the $\mathbf{w}$ hyperplane.

3.3.2 The Least Mean Squared Error Goal

Widrow learning is based on the idea that there is some sort of unknown "process" or "physical system" that we want to model as best we can with an ADALINE (based strictly on input/output examples from the process or system). This process involves the same $\mathbf{x} \to y$ input/output scheme as that of the ADALINE. The process chooses vectors $\underline{x}$ from $\mathbf{R}^n$ in accordance with a fixed probability density function ρ. The process augments each $\underline{x}$ with $x_0 = 1$ to form $\mathbf{x}$. This vector is then entered into the process. The output of the process is a number y (the *desired output*). What we want is to select a $\mathbf{w}$ vector such that the mean squared error of y', when compared with y, is minimized. In other words, if we consider a sequence of $\underline{x}$ vectors $\underline{x}_1, \underline{x}_2, \underline{x}_3, \ldots$, drawn in accordance with ρ (which are then augmented to yield a sequence of $\mathbf{x}$ vectors $\mathbf{x}_1, \mathbf{x}_2, \mathbf{x}_3, \ldots$), the goal is to find a $\mathbf{w}$ that minimizes the *mean squared error*

$$F(\mathbf{w}) \equiv \lim_{N \to \infty} (\frac{1}{N}) \sum_{k=1}^{N} (y_k - y_k')^2, \tag{3.18}$$

where y_k is the output of the process for input vector $\mathbf{x}_k$, and $y_k' = \mathbf{w} \cdot \mathbf{x}_k$ is the output of the ADALINE for that vector. Notice that this equation could also be written $F(\mathbf{w}) = \mathrm{E}[(y_k - y_k')^2]$, where E is the *expectation operator* from statistics. The expectation operator calculates the mean or average of the quantity within its bracket, based upon the assumption that this quantity is a random variable with some fixed probability density function. Since there is no information given about the process or plant being modeled, it may well turn out that the ADALINE affine combination approximation is very bad. That is not the issue we are concerned with here. What we care about is, no matter how good or bad an approximation it turns out to be, we want to find the **w** vector that does the *best possible job* of minimizing $F(\mathbf{w})$. As we shall see in later chapters, solving this problem for the ADALINE gives us an approach that, when generalized, allows us to solve much more difficult and highly nonlinear problems using more capable neural networks.

3.3.3 The Widrow Learning Law

To derive the Widrow learning law, we expand the expression for $F(\mathbf{w})$:

$$
\begin{aligned}
F(\mathbf{w}) &= \mathrm{E}[(y_k - y_k')^2] \\
&= \mathrm{E}[(y_k - \mathbf{w}^T\mathbf{x}_k)^2] \\
&= \mathrm{E}[y_k^2 - 2y_k\mathbf{w}^T\mathbf{x}_k + \mathbf{w}^T\mathbf{x}_k\mathbf{x}_k^T\mathbf{w}] \\
&= \mathrm{E}[y_k^2] - 2\mathbf{w}^T E[y_k\mathbf{x}_k] + \mathbf{w}^T E[\mathbf{x}_k\mathbf{x}_k^T]\mathbf{w} \\
&= p - 2\mathbf{w}^T\mathbf{q} + \mathbf{w}^T R\mathbf{w}.
\end{aligned}
\tag{3.19}
$$

This expansion depends on the facts that the expectation of a sum is the sum of the expectations of the terms, and that constants can be brought out of an expectation. Notice that we are treating **w** as a constant. In other words, once we have chosen a **w** vector, we let it remain fixed as we evaluate $F(\mathbf{w})$.

The equation $F(\mathbf{w}) = p - 2\mathbf{w}^T\mathbf{q} + \mathbf{w}^T R\mathbf{w}$ shows that the dependence of F on **w** is quadratic. By its nature, the square $(n + 1) \times (n + 1)$ matrix R is symmetric and positive semidefinite (see Exercise 3.3.3 for the definition of *positive semidefinite*). Thus, this quadratic form determines a paraboloidal surface (with height equal to $F(\mathbf{w})$ at each weight value **w**). As with an ordinary parabola, a paraboloid usually has a unique "bottom" point that lies at the minimum value of $F(\mathbf{w})$. Occasionally, however, the paraboloid may be degenerate and have one or more "troughs" (see Exercise 3.3.5), but the points along the bottoms of these troughs will all be at the same minimum F height. In either case, the function $F(\mathbf{w})$ is minimized at this particular point or set of points. Any **w** value that minimizes F will be denoted by the symbol $\mathbf{w}^*$.

The problem is to find a $\mathbf{w}^*$. One way to do this is to start at any initial weight and simply slide downhill on the mean squared error parabola. From basic vector calculus, we know that the gradient $\nabla_\mathbf{w}F(\mathbf{w})$ of the performance surface function $F(\mathbf{w})$ with respect to the vector **w** will always point in the direction that we should move **w** to *increase* $F(\mathbf{w})$ at the fastest possible rate (that is, in the direction that will move us uphill the fastest), except at $\mathbf{w}^*$, where it will be 0. Since we have a closed-form expression for $F(\mathbf{w})$, we can actually calculate the gradient and set it to zero. This gives us (see Exercise 3.3.6)

$$
\nabla F(\mathbf{w}) = \nabla(p - 2\mathbf{w}^T\mathbf{q} + \mathbf{w}^T R\mathbf{w})
$$

$$= -2\mathbf{q} + 2R\mathbf{w}^*$$
$$= \mathbf{0}, \tag{3.20}$$

or

$$\mathbf{w}^* = R^+\mathbf{q}. \tag{3.21}$$

In the case of a unique $\mathbf{w}^*$ (that is, a nondegenerate performance surface), this formula will converge to that unique weight vector (R will turn out to be invertible in this case, and R^+ will be equal to R^{-1}). In the case of a degenerate performance surface, this formula will give us the $\mathbf{w}^*$ with the shortest possible length (that is, the one closest to the origin).

In general, it is not desirable or convenient to attempt to calculate the statistical quantities $\mathbf{q}$ and R (although this approach can sometimes be useful). As a remedy to this numerical problem, in 1959 Bernard Widrow, along with his first graduate student Marcian E. Hoff, developed the idea of finding $\mathbf{w}^*$ by starting at any initial value of $\mathbf{w}$, call it $\mathbf{w}_0$, and simply sliding down the ADALINE performance surface until the bottom is reached [238]. Since the performance surface is a simple paraboloid, there are no obstructions or local minima to impede a direct slide from any starting point to the bottom (which will yield the smallest possible mean squared error). The value of $\mathbf{w}$ at the bottom will then be (a) $\mathbf{w}^*$. The amazing thing about this approach is that the calculations needed to carry it out are very simple.

We can understand the Widrow learning rule more easily if we note that, at any point on the performance paraboloid, the vector $-\nabla F$ points in the direction in which $F(\mathbf{w})$ will *decrease* at the fastest possible rate (that is, the opposite direction to ∇F, the direction of maximum *increase*; see Exercise 3.3.7). Widrow and Hoff reasoned that, if they could calculate or estimate $-\nabla F$, then they could simply move the weight vector in this direction by a small amount, which would then take them "downhill" toward (a) $\mathbf{w}^*$. The problem is estimating ∇F. Following the logic used by Widrow and Hoff, we once again derive ∇F, but this time from a different starting point. This time the limit form of F will be used:

$$
\begin{aligned}
\nabla_{\mathbf{w}} F(\mathbf{w}) &= \nabla[\lim_{N\to\infty} (\frac{1}{N}) \sum_{k=1}^{N} (y_k - y_k')^2] \\
&= \lim_{N\to\infty} (\frac{1}{N}) \nabla (\sum_{k=1}^{N} (y_k - y_k')^2) \\
&= \lim_{N\to\infty} (\frac{1}{N}) \sum_{k=1}^{N} \nabla (y_k - y_k')^2) \\
&= \lim_{N\to\infty} (\frac{1}{N}) \sum_{k=1}^{N} 2(y_k - y_k') \nabla(-y_k')
\end{aligned}
$$

$$= \lim_{N \to \infty} (\frac{1}{N}) \sum_{k=1}^{N} 2(y_k - y'_k)(-\mathbf{x}_k). \tag{3.22}$$

It is easy to prove that this interchanging of limit and derivatives is mathematically legal, but these details will be skipped here. Note that $\nabla_\mathbf{w}(-y'_k) = -\mathbf{x}_k$ because $y'_k = \mathbf{w}^\mathsf{T}\mathbf{x}_k$. If the error $(y_k - y'_k)$ made by the ADALINE on the kth input $\mathbf{x}_k$ is denoted by δ_k, then we get

$$
\begin{aligned}
\nabla_\mathbf{w} F(\mathbf{w}) &= \lim_{N \to \infty} (\frac{1}{N}) \sum_{k=1}^{N} 2(y_k - y'_k)(-\mathbf{x}_k) \\
&= -\lim_{N \to \infty} (\frac{1}{N}) \sum_{k=1}^{N} 2\delta_k \mathbf{x}_k \\
&= -2E[\delta_k \mathbf{x}_k].
\end{aligned}
\tag{3.23}
$$

Therefore, to estimate ∇F, all we have to do is average a large number of $\delta_k \mathbf{x}_k$ vectors and multiply by -2. Widrow and Hoff took this process one step further. In an intellectual leap, they, in effect, asked: Why not just use *each* $\delta_k \mathbf{x}_k$ vector as a correction to $\mathbf{w}$? In fact, they were able to show that the following weight update law (the *Widrow learning law* — also known as the *Widrow/Hoff learning law*, the *LMS learning law*, and the *delta rule*) will always converge to (a) $\mathbf{w}^*$ from any starting $\mathbf{w}_0$ value:

$$\mathbf{w}_{k+1} = \mathbf{w}_k + \alpha \, \delta_k \mathbf{x}_k, \tag{3.24}$$

where α is a positive constant smaller than 2 divided by the largest eigenvalue of the matrix R. Since there is no longer any need to calculate R, the upper bound for α is not easy to calculate. Thus, α is typically selected by trial and error. In general, if α is too large, the weight vector will not converge; if α is too small, convergence will take too long. Typically, $0.01 \le \alpha \le 10.0$; with a value of 0.1 often used as a starting value. Choosing and adjusting α is an art that neurocomputing practitioners need to learn.

There are two common variants of the Widrow learning law: the *batching* and *momentum* versions. In the batching variant, the weight vector is updated only after a long run of $\mathbf{x}_k$ inputs with a fixed weight vector. During this run, the $\delta_k \mathbf{x}_k$ vectors are averaged (per Equation 3.23), and this average is used in the Widrow learning law to replace the single-input-episode $\delta_k \mathbf{x}_k$ used in the usual form of the equation. This averaging has the effect of changing the weight only after a reasonable estimate of the gradient of F has been found, as in the previous argument (that is, using Equation 3.21).

The momentum variant of Widrow learning is given by the following equation:

$$\mathbf{w}_{k+1} = \mathbf{w}_k + \alpha(1 - \mu)\delta_k \mathbf{x}_k + \mu(\mathbf{w}_k - \mathbf{w}_{k-1}). \tag{3.25}$$

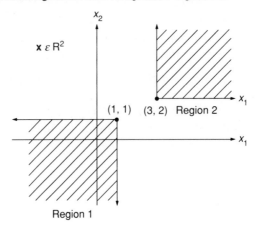

Fig. 3.4. • Geometry of regions 1 and 2.

By using a μ value that is considerably larger than α, we ensure that the weight vector corrections will tend to average over time (a μ value of about 0.9 is commonly chosen). This capability is particularly important when there is a need to ignore large fluctuations in one direction and to move the weight in an orthogonal direction (such as when trying to move downhill in a shallow trough). The emergence of such situations will be discussed in later chapters.

Deciding whether to use the Widrow learning law or its batching or momentum variants on a particular problem is not easy. Each of these approaches works better (i.e., converges to (a) $\mathbf{w}^*$ faster) than the others on some problems. However, in general, the differences between these approaches are not great. As of yet, no method exists for predicting which approach will work best on a particular problem.

Exercises

3.3.1. Given an ADALINE weight vector $\mathbf{w}$, show that the set of $\underline{x}$ vectors for which the ADALINE's output will be 0 all lie on a hyperplane located at directed distance $(-w_0/|\underline{\mathbf{w}}|)$ from the origin.

3.3.2. Find an ADALINE weight vector $\mathbf{w} = (w_0, w_1, \ldots, w_n)^{\mathrm{T}}$ such that, if $\underline{x}$ is in region 1 (see Figure 3.4), y' will be greater than 7; and if $\underline{x}$ is in region 2, y' will be less than or equal to 3.

3.3.3. Show that the matrix R is *positive semidefinite* (in other words, that $\mathbf{u}^{\mathrm{T}} R \mathbf{u} \geq 0$ for all vectors $\mathbf{u} \in R^{n+1}$).

3.3.4. Demonstrate that the geometric form of the ADALINE performance surface $z = F(\mathbf{w})$ is that of a paraboloid. Hint: Set $\mathbf{w} = \mathbf{w}^* + \mathbf{u}$ to move the origin of the $\mathbf{u}$ coordinate system to the bottom of the paraboloid of Equation 3.19, and then show that, for any direction (defined by a unit vector $\mathbf{v}$), the form of the 2-dimensional graph of z as a function of α, where $\mathbf{u} = \alpha\mathbf{v}$, is an ordinary parabola.

3.3.5. Explain in detail how the paraboloidal ADALINE performance surface can have "troughs." Under what conditions on p, $\mathbf{q}$, and R will they appear?

3.3.6. Prove that $\nabla_{\mathbf{w}} F(\mathbf{w}) = -2\mathbf{q} + R\mathbf{w}$.

3.3.7. Show that $-\nabla F$ points in the direction of maximum decrease of F and approximately in the direction of (a) $\mathbf{w}^*$ from any point on the ADALINE performance surface.

3.4 Competitive Learning

Learning laws belonging to the competitive learning category all have the property that a competition process, involving some or all of the processing elements of the neural network, always takes place before each episode of learning. The processing elements that emerge as the winners of the competition are then allowed to modify their weights (or modify their weights in a different way from those of the non-winning units). This section discusses a specific type of competition learning known as *Kohonen* learning.

Kohonen learning differs significantly from Hebb learning and Widrow learning in that it is a self-organization training principle (as opposed to a supervised training principle). The basic idea is to have a layer of processing elements arrange their weight vectors such that these weight vectors are distributed in $\mathbf{R}^n$ with a number density approximately proportional to the probability density function p according to which the $\mathbf{x}$ input vectors used to train the layer are selected.

The Kohonen learning law has a complicated history. The learning law itself originated in neurocomputing in 1962 or earlier. For example, it appears in the 1965 neurocomputing book *Learning Machines* by Nils Nilsson [178].[5] In this book, Nilsson states that this learning law was invented by L. M. Stark, M. Okajima, and G. H. Whipple in 1962 [214]. However, the idea may have had an even earlier origin in the related subject of "unsupervised clustering." The earliest origin of this learning law has not yet been established.

During the late 1960s and throughout the 1970s Stephen Grossberg introduced a variety of competitive neural network learning schemes [92]. The learning law we will study in this section was among those he discussed in considerable detail. Another competitive learning researcher during this period was Christoph von Malsburg, who wrote a highly influential 1973 paper [223]. This paper introduced a self-organization learning law (which was influenced by

---

[5] *Learning Machines* has recently been reprinted [179]. This book is still worth careful study by neurocomputing technologists. A related 1973 book, *Pattern Classification and Scene Analysis* by Richard Duda and Peter Hart [56] (which contains the majority of the material in Nilsson's book, and much more) is worth even more careful study. It is a gold mine of insights and clever methods.

Grossberg's earlier work) that attempted to provide (via computer experiments reported in the paper) an explanation for the (experimentally observed) continuous variation of local image edge feature detector orientation as a function of position across the mammalian primary visual cortex. The learning law used by von der Malsburg was based on the concept that the sum of the weights associated with the inputs at different units from a single source unit had to be constant. Thus, as one of these weights increased, the others had to decrease. This is a nonlocal learning law. Von der Malsburg postulated that learning depended on a chemical compound, supplied by the source unit, which would be in limited supply and would have to be shared by all of the axon collaterals.

Stephen Grossberg was significantly influenced by von der Malsburg's ideas, but he rejected von der Malsburg's nonlocal learning law. In working to eliminate the non-local character of the von der Malsburg law, Grossberg rediscovered the learning law equation discussed in this section, which he then presented in an influential 1976 paper [94]. At about the same time von der Malsburg and David Willshaw also presented a version of this learning law [242]. After considerable research effort during the mid and late 1970's Teuvo Kohonen (who was familiar with the work of von der Malsburg, Grossberg, Willshaw, and the earlier learning theory work of Yakov Tsypkin [221]) reached the important conclusion that the proper goal of this learning law should be the construction of a collection of vectors that form a set of equiprobable representatives of a fixed probability density function. Earlier work in other fields had emphasized equiprobability, but this was new to neurocomputing.

Although the learning law of this section was independently introduced by many people, Kohonen was the one who first clearly focused on the issue of equiprobability. The other contributors mentioned above had other goals in mind. For example, the goal stated in Nilsson's 1965 book was to find weight vectors to represent the modes of a probability density function (i.e., the places where the function has a local maximum). Tsypkin's 1970 goal was to minimize a mean squared distance performance function. Grossberg's 1976 goal was to demonstrate a stable learning scheme that would not destroy previously learned information in the process of storing new information. Willshaw and von der Malsburg sought a continuous topological mapping of one two-dimensional surface onto another two-dimensional surface by means of self-organizing simulated axons (Kohonen was also interested in the establishment of self-organizing mappings, but he explicitly sought equiprobable weight vector representations of probability density functions).

Oddly, although Kohonen's goal was to achieve equiprobability, his version of the learning law lacks an essential correction factor that would make this possible. It was not until Duane Desieno's 1987 discovery [51] of the *conscience mechanism* (which fixes this deficiency of the Kohonen learning law) that this problem was rectified. Without this correction the learning law does not perform well except in the case of uniform probability density.

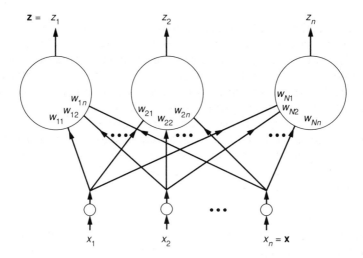

Fig. 3.5. • The Kohonen layer. The N Kohonen processing elements of this layer each receive n inputs $x_1, x_2, \ldots, x_n$. Each input has a weight w_{ij} assigned to it. When each $\mathbf{x}$ vector is entered into the Kohonen layer, the processing elements compete on the basis of which of them has its weight vector $\mathbf{w}_i$ ($\mathbf{w}_i = (w_{i1}, w_{i2}, \ldots, w_{in})$) closest to $\mathbf{x}$ (as measured by a distance function D). The winner emits signal $z_i = 1$; the others emit $z_i = 0$.

Due to his championship of the importance of equiprobability and his worldwide promulgation of this learning law in his classic book *Self-Organization and Associative Memory* [141], Kohonen's name has become almost universally associated with this style of learning.

The Kohonen learning law is now explained in terms of the operation of the neural network substrate in which it operates — the Kohonen layer.

3.4.1 Kohonen's Layer

Figure 3.5 shows the basic structure of the *Kohonen layer*. The layer consists of N processing elements, each receiving n input signals $x_1, x_2, \ldots, x_n$ from a layer of fan–out units below. The x_j input to Kohonen processing element i has real weight w_{ij} assigned to it.

Each Kohonen processing element calculates its *input intensity* I_i in accordance with the following formula:

$$I_i = D(\mathbf{w}_i, \mathbf{x}), \tag{3.26}$$

where $\mathbf{w}_i = (w_{i1}, w_{i2}, \ldots, w_{in})^{\mathrm{T}}$ and $\mathbf{x} = (x_1, x_2, \ldots, x_n)^{\mathrm{T}}$, and where $D(\mathbf{u}, \mathbf{v})$ is a distance measurement function (which need not be a distance metric in the mathematical sense — see Section 6.1). Two common choices for $D(\mathbf{u}, \mathbf{v})$ are Euclidean distance ($d(\mathbf{u}, \mathbf{v}) = |\mathbf{u} - \mathbf{v}|$) and spherical arc distance ($s(\mathbf{u}, \mathbf{v}) = 1 - \mathbf{u} \cdot \mathbf{v} = 1 - \cos \theta$, where $\mathbf{u}$ and $\mathbf{v}$ are assumed to both be unit–length vectors and where θ is the angle between $\mathbf{u}$ and $\mathbf{v}$). For the purposes of this book, Euclidean distance $d(\mathbf{u}, \mathbf{v})$ will always be used with Kohonen learning unless otherwise noted.

Once each Kohonen unit has calculated its input intensity I_i, a competition takes place to see which unit has the smallest input intensity (in other words, to find out which unit has its weight vector $\mathbf{w}_i$ closest to $\mathbf{x}$). Ties are broken on the basis of lowest processing element index number. This competition can be implemented in several ways. For example, the scheduling unit of the Kohonen layer can simply get I_i inputs from each of the Kohonen processing elements, sort these by size, and output the number of the winning unit (which is broadcast back to all of the Kohonen units). Another approach is to use lateral inhibition (on-center/off-surround type connections) so that only the Kohonen unit with the smallest distance ends up active. Finally, each processing element can compare its I_i value to those received from the other processing elements to see which value is smaller. Yet another approach is to have the scheduling unit transmit a threshold value Γ, starting at 0 and rising slowly. The first processing element to have a distance less than Γ wins the competition. Methods exist for computing the winner of such a competition in $O[1]$ time (i.e., in one unit of time, regardless of how many processing elements there are in the Kohonen layer) — see Exercise 3.4.1.

Regardless of how the competition is mediated, once the winning Kohonen unit is determined, its output z_i set to 1. All of the other Kohonen unit output signals are set to 0. At this point, Kohonen learning, which is discussed in the next section, takes place.

3.4.2 The Kohonen Learning Law

The training data for the Kohonen layer is assumed to consist of a sequence of input vectors $\mathbf{x}$, drawn at random in accordance with a fixed probability density function p. As each of these vectors is entered into the network, the Kohonen processing elements compete with one another to determine the winner on the basis of minimum distance. The winning Kohonen processing element then has its z_i set to 1, and all of the other Kohonen unit output signals are set to 0. At this point, weight modification takes place in accordance with the following equation, called the *Kohonen learning law*:

$$\mathbf{w}_i^{\text{new}} = \mathbf{w}_i^{\text{old}} + \alpha(\mathbf{x} - \mathbf{w}_i^{\text{old}})z_i, \qquad (3.27)$$

where α is a constant, $0 < \alpha \leq 1$. Because the second term of the right-hand side of this equation is multiplied by z_i, only the winning Kohonen processing element actually gets to modify its weight. Note that this learning law can be rewritten as

$$\mathbf{w}_i^{\text{new}} = (1 - \alpha)\mathbf{w}_i^{\text{old}} + \alpha\mathbf{x}$$

for the winning processing element, and as

$$\mathbf{w}_i^{\text{new}} = \mathbf{w}_i^{\text{old}}$$

for the losing processing elements. Thus, the new value of the winning unit's weight vector is merely the convex combination of the old weight vector and $\mathbf{x}$.

In other words, the Kohonen learning law moves the weight vector a fraction α of the way along the straight line from the old weight vector to the **x** vector. The winning weight can be thought of as being drawn toward the **x** vector, as though **x** were able to exert an attractive force only on this nearest weight vector. Thus, as new **x** vectors are entered into the network, the Kohonen unit weight vectors are drawn to them and form a cloud near where the **x** vectors actually appear, as determined by ρ.

At the beginning of training, α is often set to a value of approximately 0.8. As the $\mathbf{w}_i$ vectors move into the area of the data, α is then lowered to 0.1 or less for final equilibration.

In fact, as training progresses, the Kohonen weight vectors become densest where the **x**s are most common, and become least dense (or absent) where the **x** vectors hardly ever or never appear. In this way, the Kohonen layer adapts itself to conform approximately to ρ in a volume number density sense. This concept is discussed further in the next section.

Finally, it is worth noting the similarity of Kohonen learning to the statistical process of finding *k-means*. The k-means for a set of data vectors $\{\mathbf{x}_1, \mathbf{x}_2, \ldots, \mathbf{x}_L\}$, chosen at random with respect to a fixed probability density function ρ, comprise a set of k vectors $\{\mathbf{w}_1, \mathbf{w}_2, \ldots, \mathbf{w}_k\}$ that minimize the sum

$$\sum_{i=1}^{L} D^2\left(\mathbf{x}_i, \mathbf{w}(\mathbf{x}_i)\right),$$

where $\mathbf{w}(\mathbf{x}_i)$ is the closest **w** vector to $\mathbf{x}_i$, as measured using the distance measure D. In fact, as demonstrated by Tsypkin in his 1970 book [221], the Kohonen learning law can be used for finding k-means, as long as the α value used on each weight update is the reciprocal of the fraction of **x** vectors which lie closer to the current winning weight vector than to any other weight vector. Thus, much like Kohonen weight vectors, k-means are distributed in the same area as the **x** data vectors. However, the k-means are not equiprobable. Thus, the basic Kohonen learning law is essentially the k-means incremental adjustment law. For further information on k-means and other related statistical concepts, see [134, 221].

In conclusion, the Kohonen learning law does not, in general, produce a set of equiprobable weight vectors (i.e., a set of vectors such that an **x** vector chosen randomly in accordance with the probability density function ρ will have an equal probability of being closest to each of the weight vectors). In the next subsection some methods for fixing this problem are discussed.

3.4.3 Estimation of the Probability Density Function

As discussed above, what we would like is to have the $\mathbf{w}_i$ vectors arrange themselves in $\mathbf{R}^n$ such that they are approximately equiprobable, in a nearest neighbor sense, with respect to **x** vectors drawn from $\mathbf{R}^n$ in accordance with the probability density function ρ. In other words, given an **x** vector drawn from $\mathbf{R}^n$ in accordance with ρ, the probability that $\mathbf{x}$ is closest to $\mathbf{w}_i$ is approximately $1/N$, for all i, $i = 1, 2, \ldots, N$.

With the learning law as previously given in Equation 3.27, the actual probabilities of the $\mathbf{w}_i$ turn out to be only approximately $1/N$ in certain benign cases, such as where ρ is approximately constant on one and only one simply connected region of fairly simple geometry (*simply connected* means a region in which any two points in the region can be joined by a path contained entirely in the region; that is, the region is not composed of disconnected, separated, sub-regions). Even on a simply connected region, if the probability density function is far from being constant, then the Kohonen learning law produces a set of $\mathbf{w}_i$ vectors that are far from being equiprobable. To illustrate what can go wrong, we now consider a specific example.

If the region of sensible support of ρ (the region on which ρ is significantly greater than 0) is multiply connected, then weight vectors can get "stuck" in isolated regions and may not be able to move to where they are needed. For example, let us imagine that all of our $\mathbf{x}$ vectors are chosen to be on the surface of Earth. Assume that there are $1,000,000$ $\mathbf{w}_i$ vectors and that they all just happen to start out initially located at various of my friends' homes in San Diego, Phoenix, New York, Boston, Pensacola, and Denver. Training now begins. The first $\mathbf{x}$ vector comes in from Timbuktu, Mali. Since one of the Pensacola, Florida weight vectors will be closest, it will move over toward Africa. The second $\mathbf{x}$ vector comes in from Tel Aviv, Israel. The *same* former Pensacola weight vector (now located deep within the Earth under the Canary Islands) will win the competition and will move to a new location, say under Algeria. If ρ is positive only in North America and in Africa, we have a problem. The $999,999$ weight vectors back in North America will spread out and follow the $\mathbf{x}$ vectors that appear there. But no more of them will ever migrate to Africa. Why? Because the one $\mathbf{w}$ vector already over in Africa will *always* be closer to any African $\mathbf{x}$ vector than any of the North American weight vectors will be. Thus, it will always win; all of Africa gets represented by a single weight vector (which keeps bouncing around from Togo to Madagascar and from Zimbabwe to Egypt), while North America gets $999,999$ weight vectors that pepper every county in the contiguous United States, as well as Canada, and Mexico. This result holds true even if ρ chooses $\mathbf{x}$ vectors in Africa much more frequently than in North America.

A number of solutions have been developed for the problems of the basic Kohonen learning law. In one approach, called *radial sprouting* (which works best for Euclidean and similar distance measurement functions), all of the weight vectors start off equal to the zero vector $\mathbf{0} \equiv (0, 0, \ldots, 0)$. The $\mathbf{x}$ vector inputs are all multiplied by small positive number β. The learning process starts off with a very low value of β (near 0). This forces all of the data vectors to be close to the weight vectors. As time goes on, the value of β is raised slowly to 1. As this happens, the weight vectors are "peeled off" from the origin and follow the input data vectors as they move outward from $\mathbf{0}$.

This scheme works fairly well (a few weight vectors are usually left behind, and therefore are wasted), but it slows learning considerably.

Another approach is to add uniformly distributed noise vectors to the data vectors, which has the effect of making ρ positive everywhere. The noise power is started off at a high enough level that the noise vectors are much larger than the data vectors. As training proceeds, the noise power is lowered slowly. This approach works all right too, but it is typically even slower than radial sprouting. The radial sprouting and noise addition approaches solve the problem of underrepresented regions. However, they do not solve the problem of creating an equiprobable positioning of the $\mathbf{w}_i$ vectors (the vector density achieved by the basic Kohonen learning law tends to be too low where ρ is small and too high where ρ is large; in other words, the $\mathbf{w}_i$ vectors oversample regions from which $\mathbf{x}$ vectors are more likely to come, and undersample regions from which $\mathbf{x}$ vectors are less likely to come). Fortunately, there is also a fix for this problem.

The idea (which was discovered by Duane Desieno [51]) is to build a "conscience" into each Kohonen processing element's transfer function (or into the competition mediating scheduling unit) to monitor the processing element's history of success in the Kohonen layer competition. If a Kohonen processing element wins the competition substantially more often than $1/N$ of the time, then its conscience takes that unit out of the competition for a while, allowing units in oversampled areas to spread out into nearby undersampled areas. This approach often works very well and is able to yield a surprisingly good set of equiprobable weight vectors. The basic concept of the conscience mechanism is to keep track of the fraction of the time f_i that processing element i wins the competition. This value can be calculated locally by each processing element using the formula

$$f_i^{new} = f_i^{old} + \beta(z_i - f_i^{old}) \tag{3.28}$$

immediately after the z_i competition has been finished and the current z_i value (0 or 1) has been assigned (in the same manner as before). The constant β is chosen to be a small positive number (0.0001 is a typical value). Once the fraction f_i^{new} has been calculated, the current *bias value* b_i is calculated using

$$b_i = \gamma(1/N - f_i), \tag{3.29}$$

where γ is a positive constant (a typical value is $\gamma = 10$). The weight updating then takes place. However, unlike the usual situation (in which the weight is updated in the one processing element with $z_i = 1$), here a *separate* competition, solely for determining which processing element will undergo weight adjustment, is held. The competition is held on the basis of which processing element has the smallest value of

$$D(\mathbf{w}_i, \mathbf{x}) - b_i. \tag{3.30}$$

Ties are again broken on the basis of smallest index. The processing element that wins this competition then updates its weight in accordance with the usual Kohonen learning law (Equation 3.27).

The bias terms represent the amount by which each processing element's frequency of winning the pure distance competition is below or above the desired equiprobable level ($1/N$). Processing elements that win far too often have large negative bias values. Processing elements that hardly ever win have large positive bias values. These latter processing elements are thus favored by Equation 3.28 to win the weight modification competition. The net result is that, in almost every case, the weight vectors distribute themselves in an almost perfectly equiprobable configuration.

Finally, a few comments are in order as to why being able to build a highly accurate representation for a probability density function is so interesting. The reason (which is elaborated greatly in following chapters) is that, for many types of data where the time sequence of presentation is unimportant, essentially everything that can be known about the data is contained in its probability density function ρ (as many results in information theory, statistics, and pattern recognition theory demonstrate [52, 129, 167]). This principle applies to many problems in pattern recognition, statistical data analysis, control, and knowledge processing. As we shall see, the ability of a Kohonen layer to form an accurate, yet compact, representational model for probability density function of the training data can be of great value.

Exercises

3.4.1. Develop a method for conducting the Kohonen layer competition in a single unit of time, independent of N.

3.4.2. What could go wrong if the value α in the Kohonen learning law were chosen to be larger than 1?

3.4.3. If the **x** vectors are chosen uniformly at random from inside the unit-radius sphere in $\mathbf{R}^{10,000}$, approximately how many Kohonen processing elements will be required to ensure that there is a weight vector within 0.1 units of Euclidean distance from any vector within the sphere? Hint: First figure out the volume density of points that will be required to meet the maximum distance criterion using, say, a rectangular array assumption. Then multiply this volume density by the volume of the sphere.

3.4.4. A solid cylinder of unit radius and length 12 is located in $\mathbf{R}^{943}$ with one end of the cylinder touching the origin. The vector $\mathbf{v} = (\frac{12}{\sqrt{943}}, \frac{12}{\sqrt{943}}, \ldots, \frac{12}{\sqrt{943}})^{\mathsf{T}}$ defines both the axis of the cylinder and the position of the other end. How many Kohonen units will be required if every point within the cylinder is to have a distance to the nearest Kohonen weight vector of less than 0.1?

3.5 Filter Learning

The learning laws belonging to the *filter learning* category have the common feature that the weights are determined by a filtering process in which one of the inputs to the processing element is treated as a time series signal and the designated weight (not necessarily associated with this particular input) takes on a value given by the output of a filter applied to this time series. Grossberg learning was invented and developed by Stephen Grossberg as part of his early studies of *embedding fields* during the mid-1960s [97]. It provides a mechanism for the weight associated with a particular input connection to a processing element to learn the average activity in a second input connection, multiplicatively weighted by the signal activity in the first connection. After learning, the processing element can then 'recall' this average every time it is stimulated by a high input signal from the weighted connection.

3.5.1 The Flywheel Equation

The central mathematical result required for Grossberg learning is an understanding of the behavior of the following scalar difference equation (where time is treated as an integer variable)

$$z(t+1) = z(t) + a\,[I(t) - z(t)], \tag{3.31}$$

or

$$z(t+1) - bz(t) = aI(t), \tag{3.32}$$

where $0 < a < 1$, $b = 1 - a$ and $I(t)$ is the external input to the equation at time t. This equation is known as the *flywheel equation* because it can be used to model the time–varying behavior of the angular velocity z of a flywheel with angular-velocity-proportional braking torque increment $-az$ per unit time and external driving torque increment aI per unit time. To solve this equation, we exploit a trick from the mathematical subject of difference equations [87]. Namely, we let $z(t) = u(t)v(t)$. Then,

$$
\begin{aligned}
z(t+1) - bz(t) \quad &= u(t+1)v(t+1) - bu(t)v(t) \\
&= u(t+1)\,(v(t) + [v(t+1) - v(t)]) \\
-bu(t)v(t) \\
&= v(t)[u(t+1) - bu(t)] \\
+u(t+1)[v(t+1) - v(t)] \tag{3.33}
\end{aligned}
$$

Now, without loss of generality, we can choose $u(t)$ such that

$$u(t+1) - bu(t) = 0$$

for all t, $t = 1, 2, \ldots$ (see Exercise 3.5.2). Solving this equation for $u(t+1)$ gives us $u(t+1) = b^t u(1)$. Given this choice of $u(t)$, we get

$$u(t+1)[v(t+1) - v(t)] = aI(t), \tag{3.34}$$

or

$$v(t+1) - v(t) = \frac{a}{b^t u(1)} I(t). \tag{3.35}$$

Using the fact that

$$v(t+1) - v(1) = v(t+1) - v(t) + v(t) - v(t-1) + \ldots + v(2) - v(1),$$

we get

$$v(t+1) - v(1) = \sum_{s=1}^{t} \frac{aI(s)}{b^s u(1)} = \frac{a}{u(1)} \sum_{s=1}^{t} \frac{I(s)}{b^s}. \tag{3.36}$$

To allow comparison of this discrete case with that of the continuous case previously described, assume that

$$I(t) = \bar{I} + \Delta(t),$$

where $\bar{I}$ is the average value of $I(t)$, and $\Delta(t)$ is the deviation of $I(t)$ from this average (a variable with zero mean). Then, we get

$$v(t+1) - v(1) = \frac{a}{u(1)} \left[\bar{I} \sum_{s=1}^{t} \left(\frac{1}{b} \right)^s + \sum_{s=1}^{t} \frac{\Delta(s)}{b^s} \right]. \tag{3.37}$$

Reexpressing $z(t)$ in these terms gives

$$z(t) = u(t)v(t)$$

$$= [b^{t-1} u(1)] \left(\left[\frac{a}{u(1)} \right] \left[\bar{I} + \sum_{s=1}^{t-1} b^{-s} + \sum_{s=1}^{t-1} b^{-s} \Delta(s) \right] + v(1) \right) \tag{3.38}$$

$$= a\bar{I} \sum_{s=1}^{t-1} b^{t-1-s} + \sum_{s=1}^{t-1} b^{t-1-s} \Delta(s) + b^{t-1} u(1) v(1).$$

Note that this last term goes to zero as t gets large (since $0 < b < 1$). Also note that

$$\sum_{s=1}^{t-1} b^{t-1-s} = b^{t-2} + b^{t-3} + \ldots + b + 1 = \frac{1 - b^{t-1}}{1 - b},$$

which approaches $\frac{1}{1-b} = \frac{1}{a}$ as t gets large. Thus, we get

$$z(t) \doteq \bar{I} + \sum_{s=1}^{t-1} b^{t-1-s} \Delta(t). \tag{3.39}$$

If we assume that $I(t)$ has the property that its average value over intervals of time greater than some fraction of $1/a$ is always close to $\bar{I}$ (where $1/a$ is assumed to be a large number), then the second term of this equation turns out to be approximately zero (since it is the fading average of a zero-mean quantity).

Thus, in this case

$$z(t) \doteq \bar{I}.$$

We shall use this result to discuss Grossberg learning. First, however, we shall define the training regime within which Grossberg learning occurs.

3.5.2 The Instar

Figure 3.6 shows the basic setting for Grossberg learning. A processing element of unspecified transfer function receives multiple input signals, including x_i and y. The x_i input (which is assumed to be a non–negative real value) has a weight w_i associated with it. Typically there would be several x_i inputs with weights, but only one y input. In Grossberg's original neurobiological model [99], the x_i were thought of as "conditioned stimuli" (signals from specific internal brain areas), and the y signal was the "unconditioned stimulus" (a sensor input, or a signal from a distant internal brain area). Grossberg assumed that x_i was 0 most of the time and took on a large, fixed positive value when it became active. The idea is that, whenever the x_i input is *active* (that is, not 0), that connection's weight w_i will learn the average value of the concurrent y input multiplicatively weighted by x_i. Under some circumstances, it is desirable to let $y = y'$ (the output of the unit), but this case will not be discussed here (see [92] for more details).

3.5.3 Grossberg's Learning Law

Grossberg's learning law is expressed by the equation

$$w_i^{\text{new}} = w_i^{\text{old}} + a[x_i y - w_i^{\text{old}}] U(x_i), \tag{3.40}$$

where $0 < a < 1$, and where

$$U(s) = \begin{cases} 1 & \text{if } s > 0 \\ 0 & \text{otherwise} \end{cases}$$

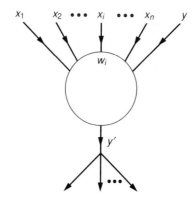

Fig. 3.6. • An instar is a single processing element that typically receives multiple input signals $x_1, x_2, \ldots, x_n$, as well as other inputs, including input signal y. The weights on the x_i inputs learn the average value of the y input that occurs when each of them is active.

is a *unit step function.* The basic idea is that the weight will not change unless $x_i > 0$. This learning law is equivalent to the flywheel equation, except that we must ignore those time intervals during which $x_i = 0$. One way to think of this occasional activation characteristic is simply to imagine that these time intervals were snipped out of the t time axis to form an s time axis. In this, case we would have

$$w_i^{\text{new}} = w_i^{\text{old}} + a[x_i y - w_i^{\text{old}}], \tag{3.41}$$

which now fits in with the flywheel equation form. As shown by Equation 3.39, after a long period of training, this weight will take on the value

$$w_i \doteq \overline{x_i y},$$

where $\overline{x_i y}$ is the time average of the product $x_i y$ (which is assumed to meet the averagability conditions of the previous subsection) during those times when $x_i > 0$.

Exercises

3.5.1. Show by numerical experiment that, for an averagable driving function $I(t)$, the solution to the difference equation $z(t+1) = z(t) - a[I(t) - z(t)]$ is approximately the same as that of the flywheel equation, assuming that the discrete time increments of the difference equation are significantly shorter than the Nyquist sample interval for the signal $I(t)$, and assuming that $0 < a < 1$.

3.5.2. Show that we can choose $u(t)$ such that $u(t+1) - bu(t) = 0$ for all t, without restricting the generality of the solution to the difference equation $z(t+1) = bz(t) + aI(t)$. Show that the general solution to this equation for u is $u(t+1) = b^t u(1)$.

3.5.3. Demonstrate that if the continuous time function $I(t)$ has the property that

$$\left(\frac{1}{\Delta}\right) \int_t^{t+\Delta} I(t)\,dt \doteq \bar{I},$$

for all $t > 0$, as long as $\Delta \gg 1/a$ (this is the definition of continuous time averagability), then the solution of the differential equation

$$\frac{dz(t)}{dt} = a[I(t) - z(t)],$$

where $t > 0$ and $0 < a < 1$, is approximately $z(t) = \bar{I}$ for $t \gg (1/a)$, regardless of the value of $z(0)$.

3.6 Spatiotemporal Learning

Learning laws belonging to the *spatiotemporal learning* category modify weight values in response to the derivatives of selected processing element input signals, as well as in response to the input signal values themselves. This allows the weights to represent temporal aspects of the network's dynamics.

The idea of using input signal derivative values in learning laws was independently invented during the mid-1980s by both Bart Kosko [151] and Harry Klopf [136]. This section presents the *Kosko/Klopf learning law*, which is somewhat different from either of the learning laws developed by Kosko and Klopf, but which incorporates their basic idea that the time derivatives of signals should be used in learning. Thus, the Kosko/Klopf learning law is a member of the spatiotemporal learning category.

3.6.1 Temporal Sequences

Figure 3.7 depicts two reciprocally connected processing elements of a slab. The processing element on the left (with output signal x_i) sends its output signal to the processing element on the right (which has output signal x_j), and vice versa. The x_i input to the processing element on the right has weight w_{ji} assigned to it, and the input of x_j to the processing element on the left has weight w_{ij} assigned to it.

Figure 3.8 shows a typical sequence of activations of the two processing elements of Figure 3.7. The reason why activation sequences of this form are used will be indicated in Chapter 6. For now, it is sufficient to note that both processing elements have non–negative output signal values and that the x_i activation precedes the x_j activation in time.

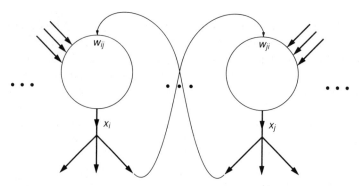

Fig. 3.7. • Reciprocally connected processing elements. The connections between processing elements are used in some neural networks to transmit data concerning the anticipated activation of one processing element following another (in this case, the activation of x_i followed by the activation of x_j — an event that is assumed to commonly occur during training). For this effect to occur, the weight w_{ij} should be small and the weight w_{ji} should be large. Kosko/Klopf learning can be used to achieve such temporal pattern learning.

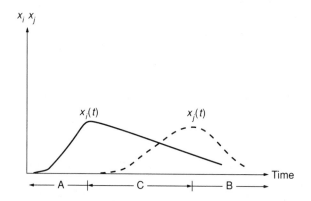

Fig. 3.8. • A temporal sequence of processing element activations. The processing element with output signal x_i becomes active first, and that with output signal x_j becomes active shortly thereafter. Kosko/Klopf learning is based on the concept that a temporal connection weight should be increased only when the target unit's output signal is increasing (which indicates that the unit is just now being activated) and the supplying unit's output signal is decreasing (which indicates that the unit has been activated *previously*, but is now spinning down). In this case, w_{ij} will not increase, but w_{ji} will. The learning activity that leads to this increase will occur during the time epoch labeled C.

3.6.2 The Kosko/Klopf Learning Law

The basic idea of Kosko/Klopf learning is that we want to form strong *temporal connections* between processing elements that are frequently activated in close succession in a particular order during training. In the case of the processing elements in Figure 3.7, we want to increase weight w_{ji}, and decrease weight w_{ij} when this happens (all weights are assumed to be non-negative real numbers and a large value weight allows the input with which it is associated to have a larger effect on the target unit). Thus, if this sequence of activations is repeated many times during training weight w_{ji} will become large and weight w_{ij} will become small.

Assuming that the weights w_{ji} and w_{ij} have been modified as indicated, every time the left-hand processing element becomes active in the future, it will help the right–hand unit of Figure 3.7 to start to become active by means of the large w_{ji} weight on its x_i signal (assuming that the transfer function used responds positively to large inputs). The reverse will not occur (assuming that the sequence $x_j \rightarrow x_i$ does not frequently occur at some other point in training), because the weight w_{ij} is small. Nonsymmetrical connections of this type, called *temporal connections*, serve to introduce time-varying dynamics into neural networks. By building connections that represent commonly encountered sequences of historical activations, networks can learn spatiotemporal information. By forming connections that are sensitive to the temporal *order of activation* of processing elements, we introduce an *arrow of time* into the network. Before Kosko and Klopf, neural network learning laws used for learning temporal relationships simply strengthened connections between simultaneously active processing elements. In other words, they strengthened *both* w_{ji} and w_{ij}, reciprocally. This yielded a situation where the network would respond equally well to a pattern played forward or backward, which is often an undesirable behavior.

The Kosko/Klopf learning law is expressed by the formula

$$w_{kl}^{new} = w_{kl}^{old} - aw_{kl}^{old} + [-bw_{kl}^{old} + cx_k x_l]U(\dot{x}_k)U(-\dot{x}_l), \qquad (3.42)$$

where U is the unit step function defined in the previous section; a, b, and c are positive constants, with a typically much smaller than b; and $\dot{x}_k$ and $\dot{x}_l$ are the time rates of change of x_k and x_l. The purpose of a is to cause weights that are never or almost never increased (by the third term on the right-hand side of the equation) to eventually go to zero. This term causes a slow decay of never or infrequently increased weights, but does not interfere with the learning of weights that are frequently reinforced. This term can sometimes be left out if all the weights are started at 0. The portion of the third term in brackets ($[-bw_{mn}^{old} + cx_m x_n]$) is essentially just like the similar term in the flywheel equation of Grossberg learning. The main difference is that here it is "gated" by the product of unit step functions, instead of a single unit step function.

We can best illustrate the purpose of the unit step function product in the Kosko/Klopf learning law by following the output signal activation sequence in Figure 3.8. During time interval A, $U(\dot{x}_i)U(-\dot{x}_j) = 0$ and $U(\dot{x}_j)U(-\dot{x}_i) = 0$, since $\dot{x}_i \geq 0$ and $\dot{x}_j \leq 0$. During time interval B, $U(\dot{x}_i)U(-\dot{x}_j) = 0$ and $U(\dot{x}_j)U(-\dot{x}_i) = 0$, since $\dot{x}_i \leq 0$ and $\dot{x}_j \leq 0$. However, during time interval

C, $U(\dot{x}_i)U(-\dot{x}_j) = 0$ and $U(\dot{x}_j)U(-\dot{x}_i) = 1$, since $\dot{x}_i < 0$ and $\dot{x}_j > 0$. Thus, these gating factors ensure that weight increase takes place only during the period when the target processing element is increasing its output signal (spinning up) and the source processing element of the connection is decreasing its output signal (spinning down). Assuming that the form of the processing element output signal responses always follows the pattern shown in Figure 3.8, the Kosko/Klopf learning law does indeed ensure the formation of temporal connections that reflect the historical sequences of activation of the processing elements. The value of this capability will be indicated in Chapter 6.

Exercises

3.6.1. Show, under a positive transient $I(t)$ input, say

$$I(t) = \begin{cases} 0 & \text{if } t \le 0 \\ 1 & \text{if } 0 < t \le 1 \\ 0 & t > 1 \end{cases}$$

(with $z = 0$ before the onset of the transient), that the continuous-time flywheel equation

$$\frac{dz(t)}{dt} = a[I(t) - z(t)],$$

and the discrete-time flywheel equation

$$z(t+1) = z(t) + a[I(t) - z(t)],$$

(where $0 < a < 1$ for both equations), will both behave in a manner qualitatively similar to, but not exactly the same as, the x_i and x_j responses shown in Figure 3.8 (the x_i and x_j responses in Figure 3.8 decrease much more slowly than the solutions of the flywheel equations do). This problem can be solved either analytically or by means of a set of computer experiments.

3.6.2. Why might it be useful to have the processing element output signals tail off at a slower rate than that at which they ramp up? Interpret the value of this characteristic in terms of its value for creating weights capable of representing commonly encountered temporal sequences of processing element activation.

3.6.3. Provide an example of a situation where it would be useful to be able to predict which processing elements in a network are about to be activated by an external spatiotemporal input.

In the next chapter we discuss the simplest category of neural network architectures — associative networks.

4

Associative Networks: Data Transformation Structures

One of the early goals of neurocomputing researchers was to get the maximum possible performance out of the simplest possible architectures. Although later developments have brought into question the need for these efforts, this early work remains interesting because of its potential for implementation in simple hardware. This chapter discusses the primary class of these simple architectures — *associative networks*. In Chapter 5, we introduce less simple networks that are capable of solving the problems that are incompletely addressed by the associative networks.

4.1 Basic Definitions

In this section, the basic definitions for associative networks are introduced. Some of these definitions are also applicable to other types of networks

An *associative network* is a neural network with essentially a single functional layer or slab (which is sometimes divided into multiple slabs to allow desynchronized updating) that associates one set of vectors with another set of vectors. More precisely, an associative network is a network with essentially a single functional layer (i.e., ignoring fan–out units and any division into multiple slabs for the purpose of desynchronized updating) designed to map user–selected vectors $\mathbf{x}_1, \mathbf{x}_2, \ldots, \mathbf{x}_L$ into user-selected vectors $\mathbf{y}_1, \mathbf{y}_2, \ldots, \mathbf{y}_L$, respectively. For the purposes of this chapter, the vectors $\mathbf{x}_i$, $i = 1, 2, \ldots, L$ will be assumed to belong to $\mathbf{R}^n$ and the vectors $\mathbf{y}_i$, $i = 1, 2, \ldots, L$ will be assumed to belong to $\mathbf{R}^m$. If we think of the input–output action of the network as being described by a function ψ, then our goal is to have $\psi(\mathbf{x}_i) = \mathbf{y}_i$ for $i = 1, 2, \ldots, L$. Naturally, this vector association must be logically consistent.

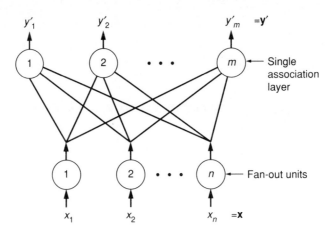

Fig. 4.1. • A typical feedforward associative network. The input vector **x** leads to the output vector **y**′ in a single feed-forward pass.

In other words, there can never be two different **y** values assigned to the same **x** value. Consistency of the intended association will be assumed throughout this chapter.

The typical goal in the study of associative networks is to understand how large L (the number of associated vectors) can be, given correct and robust operation, for an associative network with a given number of processing elements.

Associative networks come in a variety of forms. To help sort these out, a taxonomy of associative networks is presented next.

The primary classification of associative networks is into *feedforward* and *recurrent* classes. In a feedforward associative network (see Figure 9.1) the **x**-vector input to the single functional layer of processing elements (this input typically occurs via a layer of input units) leads to the **y**′-vector output in a single feedforward pass. For example, the linear associator network introduced in Section 3.2 is a feedforward associative network.

In a recurrent associative network (see Figure 4.2), the output signals of the processing elements of the layer are connected to those same processing elements as input signals. In these networks, the components of the **x** vector input are entered through separate input connections to the processing elements. The insertion of the **x** vector causes the feedback loop of the network to become active. The basic idea is that the network must converge (at least asymptotically as $t \to \infty$) to a "stable state" that is then read out as the final **y**′ output of the network.

Another categorization of associative networks is into *autoassociative* and *heteroassociative* classes. In an autoassociative network, the **y** vectors $\{y_1, y_2, \ldots, y_L\}$ are assumed to be equal to the corresponding **x** vectors $\{x_1, x_2, \ldots, x_L\}$. In other words, $m = n$ and $y_i = x_i$. In a heteroassociative network $y_i \neq x_i$.

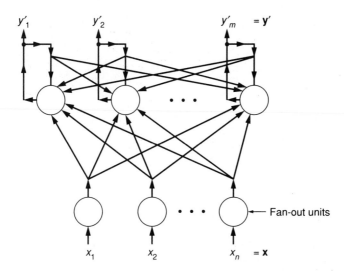

Fig. 4.2. • A typical recurrent associative network. The arrival of the input vector **x** initiates a dynamic evolution of the processing element output states of the functional layer. For example, this dynamical evolution can be used to allow the network to exhibit accretive behavior. The output vector **y'** is typically ignored until the system *converges* (that is, stabilizes and ceases to change significantly).

Finally, there are two ways in which associative networks handle errors in the **x** input. In an *accretive* network, $\psi(\mathbf{x}_i + \epsilon) = \mathbf{y}_i$, where ϵ is a sufficiently small error vector. In an *interpolative* network, $\psi(\mathbf{x}_i + \epsilon) = \mathbf{y}_i + \delta$, where $|\delta| \to \mathbf{0}$ as $|\epsilon| \to \mathbf{0}$.

4.2 Linear Associator Network

The architecture of the linear associator network was introduced in Section 3.2 in connection with Hebb learning. Figure 4.3 shows this architecture. The linear associator was invented by multiple people during the period from 1968 through 1972. The 1972 papers by James Anderson [15] and Teuvo Kohonen [146] are considered the classic references on the subject.

This section provides a detailed analysis of the linear associator neural network. It extends the analysis presented in Section 3.2. The results obtained are not particularly impressive, but the methods employed are useful for analyzing many different neural networks.

In Section 3.2 we showed that, if the set of **x** vectors $\{\mathbf{x}_1, \mathbf{x}_2, \ldots, \mathbf{x}_L\}$ (derived from the set of vector pairs $\{(\mathbf{x}_1, \mathbf{y}_1), (\mathbf{x}_2, \mathbf{y}_2), \ldots, (\mathbf{x}_L, \mathbf{y}_L)\}$ to be associated) is orthonormal, then Hebb learning gives weight values that yield the desired $\psi(\mathbf{x}_i) = \mathbf{y}_i$ associations. Note again that this is an interpolative network. It turns out that, if the pseudoinverse weight matrix $W = YX^+$ is used, then this result

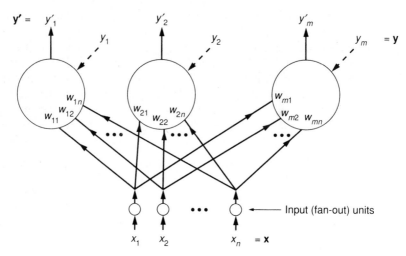

Fig. 4.3. • The linear associator neural network. The vector **x** is entered into the system at the bottom and the vector **y′** is emitted at the top. Each output processing element signal y_i' is simply a linear combination of the x input signals. During training, each output unit is supplied with its "correct" output signal y_j. This network uses Hebb learning.

extends to the case where the set $\{x_1, x_2, \ldots, x_L\}$ is merely linearly independent. This extension holds because, if these **x** vectors are linearly independent, then it can be shown that $X^+X = I$ (see Exercise 4.2.2), and so (taking $W = YX^+$, as in Section 3.2) $F(W) = \|Y - WX\|^2 = \|Y - YX^+X\|^2 = \|Y - Y\|^2 = 0$. Thus, $\psi(x_i) = y_i$ for $i = 1, 2, \ldots, L$ in this case also. If the set $\{x_1, x_2, \ldots, x_L\}$ is linearly dependent, then we can write $x_j = \sum_{i \neq j} \alpha_i x_i$, and so

$$
\begin{aligned}
W x_j &= \sum_{i \neq j} \alpha_i W x_i \\
&= \sum_{i \neq j} \alpha_i y_i \\
&= y_j.
\end{aligned}
\tag{4.1}
$$

Thus, y_j *must* have this specific value if we are to have $F(W) = 0$. Otherwise, $F(W)$ will be larger than 0. In this case, the network will fail to exactly map one or more x_j into the corresponding y_j.

In summary, the linear associator can have at most n pairs of vectors (x_i, y_i) stored in it, if it is to map x_i into y_i exactly. Again, as shown in Section 3.2, even this limited capability is available if and only if the x_i vectors form a linearly independent set.

Now let us explore the case where we do not require exact mapping of each x_k into the associated y_k but merely seek the best possible approximate mapping (using, say, mean squared error as the measure of goodness of approximation). In this case, as shown in Section 3.2, the mean squared error $F(W)$ of this mapping will be minimized if $W = YX^+$ is used. $F(W)$ will then take on the value $F(W) = \|YX^+X - Y\|^2 = \|Y(X^+X - I)\|^2$. This mathematical form clearly shows the dependence of F on the rank of X.

Next, it is interesting to consider the performance of the linear associator when the input vectors have noise added to them. For this discussion it will be convenient to restrict the number of vector pairs to be associated (L) to be less than the dimensionality of the space of **x** vectors (namely, n). The first step is to introduce the *singular value decomposition* (SVD) of a matrix. Given *any* $n \times L$ matrix X with $n \geq L$, we can express X as follows:

$$X = \sum_{i=1}^{L} \lambda_i^{1/2} \, \mathbf{p}_i \, \mathbf{q}_i^{\mathrm{T}}, \tag{4.2}$$

where

$$X X^{\mathrm{T}} \mathbf{p}_i = \lambda_i \, \mathbf{p}_i \tag{4.3}$$

and

$$X^{\mathrm{T}} X \mathbf{q}_i = \lambda_i \, \mathbf{q}_i, \tag{4.4}$$

and the sets

$$\{\mathbf{p}_1, \mathbf{p}_2, \ldots, \mathbf{p}_L\} \tag{4.5}$$

and

$$\{\mathbf{q}_1, \mathbf{q}_2, \ldots, \mathbf{q}_L\} \tag{4.6}$$

are each orthonormal (see [215] for more discussion on the SVD representation). The eigenvalues λ_i (which are all non–negative real numbers — see Exercise 4.2.4) are ordered in terms of their sizes, with the largest being listed first. Eigenvalues with equal values are repeated according to their multiplicity. Thus, $\lambda_i \geq \lambda_{i+1}$. Naturally, the $\mathbf{p}_i$ vectors are n-dimensional, and the vectors $\mathbf{q}_i$ are L-dimensional. Given this decomposition, it turns out (see [215] for details) that the pseudoinverse of X can easily be written as

$$X^+ = \sum_{i=1}^{r} \lambda_i^{-1/2} \mathbf{q}_i \, \mathbf{p}_i^{\mathrm{T}}, \tag{4.7}$$

where the number r is the *rank* of the matrix X (that is, the number of linearly independent rows of X — which, it turns out, is also the number of linearly independent columns of X). Also, r turns out to be the number of non–zero eigenvalues λ_i (see Exercise 4.2.1). Finally, note that the SVD is not unique, since, for example, any pair of the $\mathbf{p}_i$ or $\mathbf{q}_i$ eigenvectors could each be multiplied by -1 without anything being changed. If $n < L$, then one simply does the SVD on X^{T}.

The problem of interest here is how to achieve maximum accuracy retrieval from the linear associator network under the condition that noise is added to the x input vectors. In other words, we want the network to map a vector

$$\mathbf{z}_i = \mathbf{x}_i + \mathbf{n}, \tag{4.8}$$

into a vector as close to $\mathbf{y}_i$ as possible in the least mean squared error sense, where the noise vector $\mathbf{n}$ (which is selected in accordance with a fixed probability density function) has zero mean, uncorrelated components, and the same standard deviation σ in each coordinate. In other words, we want to minimize the expected mean squared error

$$F(W) = E\left[|\mathbf{y}_i - W\mathbf{z}_i|^2\right]. \tag{4.9}$$

Murakami has shown [174] that, if $W = YX^+$, then $F(W)$ can be written as

$$F(W) = \sum_{i=r+1}^{L} |Y\mathbf{q}_i|^2 + L\sigma^2 \sum_{i=1}^{r} \lambda_i^{-1} |Y\mathbf{q}_i|^2. \tag{4.10}$$

The first term of this sum is attributable to the linear dependency of the $\mathbf{x}_i$ vectors. If they are linearly independent, the rank r of X will be L, and this sum would have no terms in it and would thus be 0. The second sum is due to the noise vectors. Note that, if the noise drops to 0 (that is, if $\sigma = 0$), then this term is 0. Further, note that each term of the second sum depends linearly on the value of the associated λ_i^{-1}.

An effective way to minimize $F(W)$ for this case of additive noise is to change W by suppressing small eigenvalue terms in the SVD expansion of X. In other words, we take $W = Y\bar{X}^+$, where

$$\bar{X}^+ = \sum_{i=1}^{s} \lambda_i^{-1/2} \, \mathbf{q}_i \, \mathbf{p}_i^{\mathrm{T}}. \tag{4.11}$$

The number s ($s \le r$) is chosen such that

$$\frac{L\sigma^2}{\lambda_s} \le 1 \le \frac{L\sigma^2}{\lambda_{s+1}}. \tag{4.12}$$

This condition will ensure that, in the new version of Equation 4.10 that can be derived for this new W, the terms that are moved from the second sum of

Equation 4.10 to the first sum of Equation 4.10 (this movement must occur since the sums together always have L terms) will decrease $F(W)$, since $|Y\mathbf{q}_i|^2$ will be less than $L\sigma^2|Y\mathbf{q}_i|^2/\lambda_i$ for each of the terms that are moved. Thus, by removing terms from the SVD expansion we can often improve the performance of the linear associator in additive noise. This is an idea that has also been exploited in related fields such as computed tomography and synthetic aperture radar.

Finally, note that in the case of the autoassociative linear associator network (in which $Y = X$), for $W = XX^+$,

$$F(W) = L\sigma^2 r, \qquad (4.13)$$

and for $W = X\bar{X}^+$,

$$F(W) = L\sigma^2 s + \sum_{i=s+1}^{r} \lambda_i. \qquad (4.14)$$

Thus, if $\sum_{i=s+1}^{r} \lambda_i < L\sigma^2(r-s)$, then we have lowered the expected mean squared error of the network. Note that, in the autoassociative case with $W = XX^+$ and no noise ($\sigma = 0$), perfect recall can be obtained no matter how large L ($L \le n$, of course) is! We can be understand this surprising fact by noting that W becomes approximately equal to the identity matrix I in this situation. Thus, essentially every vector is autoassociated with itself, completely eliminating any accretive behavior — once again proving that there is no free lunch.

Another interesting fact is that a form of Widrow learning can often be used to compute $W = YX^+$ recursively. This fact is based on *Greville's theorem* [4] which, when used for this purpose, states that if W^{old} is the weight matrix based on $W^{\text{old}} = Y^{\text{old}}(X^{\text{old}})^+$, where Y^{old} and X^{old} are the $m \times (k-1)$ and $n \times (k-1)$ matrices, respectively composed of the first $(k-1)$ $\mathbf{y}_i$ vectors and $(k-1)$ $\mathbf{x}_i$ vectors, then when $\mathbf{y}_k$ and $\mathbf{x}_k$ are added to the list, the new W is given by

$$W^{\text{new}} = W^{\text{old}} + (\mathbf{y}_k - W^{\text{old}}\mathbf{x}_k)\mathbf{p}_k^{\mathsf{T}}, \qquad (4.15)$$

where

$$\mathbf{p}_k = \begin{cases} \dfrac{[I - X^{\text{old}}(X^{\text{old}})^+]\mathbf{x}_k}{|[I - X^{\text{old}}(X^{\text{old}})^+]\mathbf{x}_k|^2} & \text{if the denominator is} \ne 0, \\[4mm] \dfrac{(X^{\text{old}})^{\mathsf{T}}(X^{\text{old}})^+\mathbf{x}_k}{1 + |(X^{\text{old}})^+\mathbf{x}_k|^2} & \text{otherwise.} \end{cases} \qquad (4.16)$$

By starting with $W^{\text{old}} = 0$ and successively adding the pairs $(\mathbf{x}_1, \mathbf{y}_1), (\mathbf{x}_2, \mathbf{y}_2), \ldots, (\mathbf{x}_L, \mathbf{y}_L)$, we can construct the final pseudoinverse-based W matrix. The problem with this approach is that this recursive rule cannot be implemented locally because of the $\mathbf{p}_k$ calculations. However, experimental experience has shown that many times the same eventual effect can be approximately obtained by use of the following variation of the result of Equation 4.15:

$$W^{\text{new}} = W^{\text{old}} + \alpha \, (\mathbf{y}_k - W^{\text{old}}\mathbf{x}_k) \, \mathbf{x}_k^{\text{T}}, \qquad (4.17)$$

where α is a small positive constant (the *learning rate*). This learning law is clearly Widrow learning, which can be implemented locally in each processing element by means of the following equation:

$$\mathbf{w}_i^{\text{new}} = \mathbf{w}_i^{\text{old}} + \alpha \, (y_{ki} - (\mathbf{w}_i^{\text{old}})^{\text{T}}\mathbf{x}_k) \, \mathbf{x}_k, \qquad (4.18)$$

where $\mathbf{w}_i$ is the weight vector of the ith processing element of the linear associator. With this scheme, it is often necessary to enter the pairs $(\mathbf{x}_1, \mathbf{y}_1), (\mathbf{x}_2, \mathbf{y}_2), \ldots,$ $(\mathbf{x}_L, \mathbf{y}_L)$ many times (with each training example chosen uniformly at random).

In many cases, this procedure for calculating W works quite well. By means of the addition of this learning law, a linear associator network can adaptively form an approximation to the weight matrix $W = YX^+$. No method for adaptively learning $W = YX^+$ is known.

Before we leave the linear associator, we should note that it is often useful to allow the processing elements of the network to have a bias input, as with the ADALINE (see Section 3.3). We can easily arrange for a bias input by simply adding to the $\mathbf{x}_i$ vectors a new coordinate that is always equal to 1. For the purpose of standardization, this coordinate, if used, is traditionally given index 0 (again, as with the ADALINE). Thus, in this instance, we would use an $\mathbf{x}$ vector of the form $\mathbf{x} = (x_0, x_1, x_2, \ldots, x_n) = (1, x_1, x_2, \ldots, x_n)$. This alteration is essential if, for example, Equation 4.18 is to be exploited fully.

In mathematical terms, when we add bias terms to $\underline{\mathbf{x}}$ vectors and then subject these augmented vectors to a linear transformation (such as $W\mathbf{x}$), we are actually performing an *affine transformation*, as with the ADALINE. The difference is that, geometrically speaking, linear transformations can carry out only arbitrary rotation and scaling operations, whereas affine transformations can carry out arbitrary rotation, scaling, *and* translation operations. Thus, affine transformations are much more powerful than linear transformations.

In conclusion, the linear associator network can, in its general heteroassociative form, store at most n vector pairs and still provide exact recall, where n is the dimensionality of the $\mathbf{x}$ vectors. If more patterns are stored, error is introduced. For many practical problems, this linkage between the dimensionality of the data and the number of data items that can be stored is an unacceptable restriction. For example, this means that if we are trying to store associations between 10 attributes of people (the $\mathbf{x}_i$ vectors) and 7 attributes of people's cars (the $\mathbf{y}_i$ vectors), then we can store data on only at most 10 people without errors. This capacity is practically useless, since we might need to store such associations for 10 million people.

As will be shown in Chapter 5, there are neural networks that can solve this problem completely. The remaining sections of this chapter consider other associative networks. As we shall see, essentially the same capacity restrictions that apply to the linear associator also apply to these networks. By means of *coding* schemes, however, the dimensionality of the data to be stored can sometimes be increased artificially, thus allowing more pairs of items to be stored.

Exercises

4.2.1. Show that the number of linearly independent rows of any matrix equals both the number of linearly independent columns and the number of non-zero eigenvalues of the matrices $X X^T$ and $X^T X$.

4.2.2. For any $n \times L$ matrix X (with $n \geq L$) that has L linearly independent columns (and therefore L linearly independent rows), show that $X^+ X = I_{L \times L}$ (and thus $Y - (Y X^+) X = 0$). [Hint: Use the SVD expansions for X and X^+.]

4.2.3. Show that the matrix $X X^+$ is the projection operator for the subspace defined by the set of orthonormal vectors $\{\mathbf{p}_1, \mathbf{p}_2, \ldots, \mathbf{p}_L\}$ (Equation 4.5). In other words show that, for every vector $\mathbf{x}$ in this subspace, $X X^+ \mathbf{x} = \mathbf{x}$, and that for every vector $\mathbf{x}$ in $\mathbf{R}^n$, $X X^+ \mathbf{x}$ is the subspace and $(X X^+)(X X^+)\mathbf{x} = X X^+ \mathbf{x}$.

4.2.4. Given any $n \times L$ real-valued matrix X, show that the eigenvalues of the matrix $X X^T$ will all be real and non–negative. [Hint: Show that the matrix is symmetric, and then show that $\mathbf{p}^T X X^T \mathbf{p}$ must be a non–negative real number for any vector $\mathbf{p}$ in $\mathbf{R}^n$. Then apply this result to the eigenequation $X X^T \mathbf{p} = \lambda \mathbf{p}$ by premultiplying both sides by $\mathbf{p}$.]

4.3 The Learnmatrix Network

The learnmatrix network was invented in 1958 by Karl Steinbuch [216], whose goal was to produce a network that could use a binary version of Hebb learning to form associations between pairs of binary patterns. This goal arose from Steinbuch's desire to build such networks out of simple physical elements, such as wires and resistors. Steinbuch's 1961 book, *Automat und Mensche* [216], was one of the first books on neurocomputing, and is a classic. The storage capacity of the learnmatrix was later studied by David Willshaw and his colleagues in 1969 [243]. The learnmatrix is important because of this extremely clever capacity analysis, which provides us with an approach for using associative networks in a way that yields very efficient utilization of their available information storage capacity. This approach requires the use of *sparse codes*, which are best

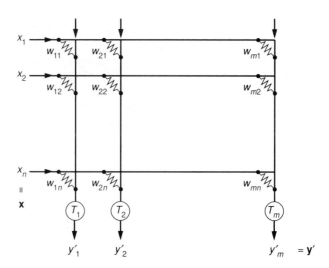

Fig. 4.4. • Binary learnmatrix network. This network accepts a binary input vector **x** as input and produces a binary vector **y** as output. The weighted sums $\sum_{j=1}^{n} w_{ij}x_j$ are thresholded at threshold values T_i to yield the binary output signals y_i'. Learning takes place via a Boolean form of Hebb learning that utilizes **y** vectors input through the input ports shown at the top of each vertical line. All of the weight values w_{ij} are binary.

introduced via a discussion of the learnmatrix network. The purpose of this section is to provide that discussion.

4.3.1 Definition of the Learnmatrix Network

Figure 4.4 shows the learnmatrix network as originally envisioned by Steinbuch. The binary input vector **x** is introduced as a set of n voltages. The components of the **y'** vector output are expressed as threshold functions of the currents, which are the sums of the currents through the resistors connecting the horizontal input lines with the vertical output lines (which are maintained at a constant zero voltage). The resistor values are actually the inverses of the w_{ij} values shown. This fact is easy to understand, since we want the current flow through each resistor to be proportional to $w_{ij}x_j$. We can obtain this form if we rearrange Ohm's law as $I = (1/R)V$. Thus, we must set the resistances to $R_{ij} = 1/w_{ij}$. See Chapter 8 for a more detailed discussion of this issue. The **y'** vector's binary components are simply thresholded versions of the currents summed by the vertical lines. Specifically,

$$y_i = \begin{cases} 1, & \text{if } \sum_{j=1}^{n} w_{ij}x_j \geq T_i, \\ 0, & \text{otherwise.} \end{cases} \tag{4.19}$$

Although, from this formula, the learnmatrix is clearly nothing but a simple threshold logic device (see [50]), the network is distinguished by its use of binary weights (the w_{ij}) and its use of a sort of Boolean Hebb learning. In this learning law, each pair of binary vectors (**x**, **y**) to be stored (the **y** vector's components are entered via the vertical line extensions shown at the top of Figure 4.4) causes a weight change as follows:

$$w_{ij}^{\text{new}} = \begin{cases} 1 & \text{if } w_{ij}^{\text{old}} = 1, \\ 1 & \text{if } y_i x_j = 1, \\ 0 & \text{otherwise.} \end{cases} \qquad (4.20)$$

This learning law is equivalent to simply adding together all of the products $y_i x_j$ (for all of the L pairs of vectors to be stored in the network), as in Hebb learning, but using Boolean arithmetic in which $0 + 0 = 0$, $0 + 1 = 1$, $1 + 0 = 1$, $1 + 1 = 1$.

4.3.2 Learnmatrix Optical Analysis

To facilitate analysis of the learnmatrix, we now present a clever "optical" equivalent of the network (developed by Willshaw and his colleagues [243]). This optical scheme will be used in the next section to derive the capacity of the learnmatrix.

For the purposes of the rest of this chapter, we shall restrict the learnmatrix as follows. First, the thresholds T_i shall all be set equal to a fixed positive integer M, $M \leq n$. Second, to make the analysis easier, we shall assume that $m = n$ (this restriction can be easily removed, but saves some bookkeeping). Notice that this is still a heteroassociative situation. Only the dimensions of the associated $\mathbf{x}$ and $\mathbf{y}$ vectors are being set equal; their entries need not be equal. Finally, we shall assume that each of the L binary vector pairs $(\mathbf{x}_k, \mathbf{y}_k)$ to be associated by the network are such that each $\mathbf{x}_k$ vector and each $\mathbf{y}_k$ vector have *exactly* M entries that are 1s and $n - M$ entries that are 0s. This is the same M used as the threshold value. As we shall see, this assumption makes it possible to analyze the behavior of the network in considerable detail.

Figure 4.5 shows an optical analog of the learnmatrix network consisting of three opaque planes (A, B, and C) and a diffuse light source. Plane A has had m holes drilled in it and plane B has had n holes drilled in it (again, for simplicity, we shall assume that $m = n$). Each of these holes is equipped with a cover that can be opened or closed — allowing light to pass freely or blocking it completely. These holes are drilled such that, if they are all opened up, mn ($= n^2$) distinct spots of light will fall on plane C. In other words, no two pairs of holes on planes A and B are aligned such that rays of light passing through them will intersect on plane C. This situation can easily be accomplished (see Exercise 4.3.1).

To program the optical learnmatrix, assume that the n holes in planes A and B have been numbered from 1 to n. Beginning with the pair $(\mathbf{x}_1, \mathbf{y}_1)$, we program the M entries in $\mathbf{y}_1$ that are equal to 1 into plane A by opening the holes with numbers corresponding to the coordinate numbers of those entries. The other holes in plane A are left covered. Then, we program the vector $\mathbf{x}_1$ into plane B in the same manner. The result is a total of M^2 spots of light on plane C. Figure 4.5 shows three of the open holes of plane A (labeled 7, 8, and 9), two of the open holes of plane B (labeled 10 and 11), and the six spots of

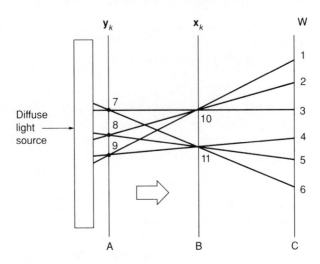

Fig. 4.5. • Optical learnmatrix analog system during training. Light from the diffuse light source shines through M holes in plane A (the holes that are opened are those representing the entries in vector $\mathbf{y}_k$ that are equal to 1). Light passing through these holes also passes through the M open holes of plane B (representing the components of vector $\mathbf{x}_k$ that are equal to 1), forming M^2 distinct spots of light on plane C. Holes are then drilled in plane C at the positions of these spots.

light on plane C (labeled 1, 2, 3, 4, 5, 6) that result. To store the associated vector pair $(\mathbf{x}_1, \mathbf{y}_1)$ in this system, we simply drill holes in plane C (which starts out completely opaque) at the positions of these six spots (these holes are not equipped with covers). The pair $(\mathbf{x}_2, \mathbf{y}_2)$ is then brought in, and the process is repeated. Whenever a hole is to be drilled in plane C we drill it, even if it has been drilled before (this redrilling simply results in the same size of hole as before). This process continues until all L vector pairs to be stored have been entered. It is easy to show that this "learning law" is the same as the Boolean Hebb learning law of the learnmatrix — if we interpret the value of w_{ij} to be 1 or 0 in accordance with the presence or absence of a hole at the corresponding spot position on plane C (see Exercise 4.3.2).

Figure 4.6 shows how an $\mathbf{x}_k$ vector is entered into the (already trained) optical learnmatrix system and how (we hope) the associated $\mathbf{y}_k$ vector is reconstructed. The method works as follows: Light from the diffuse light source (which has now been moved to the right of plane C) shines through the holes that were drilled in plane C during training. The M holes in plane B corresponding to the coordinates of $\mathbf{x}_k$ that are equal to 1 have been opened (the other holes in plane B are covered). The light shining through the drilled holes in plane C and the opened holes in plane B falls onto plane A. It is evident (see Exercise 4.3.3) that each spot on plane A that corresponds to a coordinate of $\mathbf{y}_k$ that is equal to 1 has exactly M beams shining onto it. In fact, it is easy to show that no spot

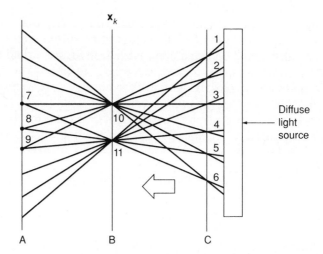

Fig. 4.6. • Optical learnmatrix analog system during recall. Light from the diffuse light source shines through the holes in plane C (the ones that were drilled to store the L vector pairs). The holes in plane B corresponding to the components of vector x_k that are equal to 1 have been opened. The light from the drilled holes in plane C shines through these holes in plane B and hits plane A. Wherever exactly M beams hit one of the n spots on plane A, there is assumed to be a 1 in that coordinate of the reconstructed y_k vector. All other coordinates of y_k are assumed to be equal to 0.

can have more than M beams shining onto it (see Exercise 4.3.4). We construct the y (that is, y') vector output of the system by thresholding the number of beams impinging on each of the n holes of plane A at threshold value M. It is easy to show (see Exercise 4.3.5) that this optical system functions identically to the learnmatrix network.

Clearly, the only thing that can go wrong with the reconstruction of y_k from x_k is that some of the holes on plane A may accidently receive M spots when they should not receive them. This will cause the y' vector output to have some spurious 1s in it that are not in y_k. The next section analyzes the likelihood of this occurrence.

4.3.3 Learnmatrix Capacity
Given the learnmatrix neural network and its optical equivalent, some questions naturally arise. For example, how many pairs of (x, y) vectors can we store before the network will begin to make mistakes on recall? Further, what is the optimal value of M to achieve maximum storage capacity? These questions are now examined. This discussion uses the 1969 approach of Willshaw and his colleagues [243]. In 1980 Günther Palm [183] provided an amplification of this earlier work.

First, to make the analysis tractable, we shall assume that the associated x_k and y_k, $k = 1, 2, \ldots, L$ vectors are chosen randomly such that the M 1s are as likely to be in any coordinate as in any other. In other words, if we were to generate a large number of such vectors to be stored, and were to add them all together (including all $\mathbf{x}_k$ and all $\mathbf{y}_k$), the sum vector would be expected to have all of its components approximately equal to $(2LM)/n$ (see Exercise 4.3.6). Let us assume that these L pairs of vectors have been entered into the optical version of the network, as in Figure 4.5.

Notice that, since plane C has n^2 spots, its total information capacity is n^2 bits of information (since each spot can store 1 bit of information — either it is drilled or it is not). One of our goals is to maximize the total amount of information stored in the network in the $(\mathbf{x}_k, \mathbf{y}_k)$ pairs. To calculate this *information storage capacity*, we recall from elementary information theory that the information content of a quantity is equal to the logarithm to the base 2 of the number of ways of choosing that quantity (assuming the quantities are equally likely to be chosen). Since in the learnmatrix we are actually storing L $\mathbf{y}_k$ vectors (the $\mathbf{x}_k$ vectors are not stored — they are merely entered as keys), the amount of information stored in the learnmatrix is L times the amount of information stored in each $\mathbf{y}_k$ vector.

To help calculate the number of bits of information stored in each $\mathbf{y}_k$ vector, we note that there are exactly $C(n, M)$ ways of choosing such a vector (where $C(n, M) = n!/[(n - M)!M!]$ is the number of combinations of n things (the components of the vector) taken M at a time — the number of those components set equal to 1). Thus, the total amount of information I stored in the network is

$$I = L \, \log_2 C(n, M). \tag{4.21}$$

Next, turning to Figure 4.6, we determine the probability p of a spot on plane C having a hole drilled in it. To do this, we consider the probability $1 - p$ of a spot *not* having a hole drilled in it. Referring to Figure 4.6, let us think about a particular spot with associated weight w_{ij}. This spot will not be drilled only if *all* of the L pairs of vectors have a $y_i x_j$ value of 0. For each of these L independent events, the probability of this happening is $(n^2 - M^2)/(n^2)$. Thus,

$$(1 - p) = \left[\frac{(n^2 - M^2)}{(n^2)} \right]^L, \tag{4.22}$$

or

$$p = 1 - \left[1 - \frac{M^2}{n^2} \right]^L, \tag{4.23}$$

since the probability of an independent sequence of events occurring is the product of the events' individual probabilities.

Given the preceding derivations, it is now possible to determine the probability of obtaining extra 1s during the recall of $\mathbf{y}_k$. To do this, let us focus our attention on a hole in plane A that is *not* supposed to get M beams of light. Let us determine the probability of this spot erroneously getting M beams. First, we know that there are exactly M holes open in plane B (because the $\mathbf{x}_k$ vector has been entered there), and that the probability of a spot on plane C being drilled is p. If we look back toward plane C from the hole that we are considering on plane A, we can see exactly M spots on plane C (because there are exactly M open holes in plane B to look through). For there to be a spurious output at our hole on plane A, *every one* of the spots that we can see on plane C must be drilled. However, the probability of this happening is p^M. Thus, the probability of getting a spurious output at this hole on plane A is p^M. To fix the numbers, let us demand that the expected number of spurious 1s on each $\mathbf{y}_k$ vector recall be 1. Thus, the product of $(n - M)$ (the number of 0s in $\mathbf{y}_k$) and p^M (the probability of each 0 being inadvertently set to 1) will be assumed to be equal to 1. In other words, when we enter $\mathbf{x}_k$ into the system we will normally get back a $\mathbf{y}'$ vector that is the same as $\mathbf{y}_k$ except that it will have, on average, one extra 1 in it. For this to be true, we must have

$$(n - M)p^M = 1. \tag{4.24}$$

Combining Equations 4.21, 4.23, and 4.24 (see Exercise 4.3.7) yields

$$I = \frac{1}{\ln(2)} \left(\frac{\ln(1 - [n - M]^{-\frac{1}{M}})}{\ln(1 - M^2/n^2)} \right) [(n + 1/2)\,[\ln n - \ln(n - M)]$$
$$+ M \ln(n - M) - (M + 1/2)\ln M - 0.92]. \tag{4.25}$$

If we use a computer, it is trivial to find the value of M that maximizes I/n^2 (the fraction of realized information storage capacity to available information storage capacity) for each value of n. The results of this computation for several values of n are shown in Table 4.1.

Several conclusions can be drawn from Table 4.1. First, the optimum value of M is approximately

$$M = \log_2 n - 2 = \log_2 \left(\frac{n}{4} \right). \tag{4.26}$$

Second, by substituting Equation 4.26 into Equation 4.24, we can prove that, for large n, $p \doteq 1/2$. Thus, half of the n^2 spots on plane C are drilled. Third, the number of vector pairs that can be stored in the network is approximately

$$L = (\ln 2)(n^2/M^2).$$

This is obtained by dividing the information stored in the entire network by the information required to represent a single $\mathbf{y}_k$ vector. Note that this value is *much* greater than n, which is quite different from the result obtained for the linear associator. Finally, the information storage efficiency ($I_{\max}/n^2$) clearly approaches some upper bound asymptotically as $n \to \infty$. To determine the value of this bound, we can substitute Equation 4.26 into Equation 4.25, thus yielding (see Exercise 4.3.8)

n	M	I_{max}/n^2
10^2	5	0.54
10^3	8	0.55
10^4	11	0.57
10^5	14	0.58
10^6	18	0.59
10^7	21	0.60
10^8	24	0.61
10^9	28	0.62
10^{20}	64	0.63
10^{80}	263	0.67
10^{100}	330	0.68

Table 4.1• Learnmatrix storage capacity. The information storage capacity is maximized when number of 1s in each vector is equal to M. All of the other entries in the vectors are 0. Thus, a vector with a million components will have only *18* of those components equal to 1. The rest will be 0. This approach to information storage is called *sparse coding*.

$$I = n^2 \ln 2. \tag{4.27}$$

Therefore, the asymptotic percentage information capacity of the learnmatrix network is 100 ln 2 percent, or 69.31 percent. As it turns out, this capacity is far better than those of most other associative memory schemes.

The use of x_k and y_k vectors with enormous numbers of 0s and a very small number (M) of 1s is extremely inconvenient (albeit efficient). Transforming ordinary sorts of information (such as binary number representations, ASCII-coded character strings, or EBCDIC numerals) into this form requires a scheme for mapping *dense codes* into these uniformly randomly selected *sparse* x_k and y_k vectors. A procedure that does this mapping is called a *sparse coding scheme*, and the resulting code is a *sparse code*. No sparse coding schemes have yet been discovered, although some preliminary ideas have emerged (see Section 6.3 for discussions of competitive slabs and combinatorial hypercompression). To appreciate just how "sparse" these vectors are, note that if $n = 1,000,000$, then $M = 18$. Each of these 1-million-bit vectors can represent only about 324 bits of information. That's sparse!

Finally, it is interesting to redo the above derivations for the case of a smaller allowed error rate. For example, if the error condition of one expected error (additional 1) per y_k associative recall were reduced to one expected error per 100 recalls, the asymptotic percentage information capacity would drop to approximately 68 percent, and the optimum M would increase to about $\log_2(n)+4$. Thus, the error rate can be decreased considerably without a significant decrease in storage capacity.

In conclusion, the learnmatrix is instructive because it suggests a scheme for utilizing up to 69 percent of the available storage capacity in a particular associative network, while still achieving heteroassociative access to desired data with only small errors.

Exercises

4.3.1. Define a pattern of n holes on planes A and B in Figure 4.5 such that the number of distinct spots of light falling on plane C is n^2, and the minimum distance between any of these spots on plane C is equal to 1 distance unit. Assume that the planes A, B, and C are parallel and lie 10 distance units apart. Further assume that the planes and the diffuse light source are infinite in extent.

4.3.2. Given the scheme for drilling holes in plane C described in the Figure 4.5, show that this procedure is exactly equivalent to the learnmatrix learning law (Equation 4.20).

4.3.3. Given the $\mathbf{y}$ vector retrieval scheme outlined in the text for the optical system of Figures 4.5 and 4.6, show that each of the holes of plane A corresponding to a coordinate of $\mathbf{y}_k$ that is equal to 1 will have exactly M beams of light shining on it.

4.3.4. Show that each of the n holes of plane A can have no more than M beams of light shining on it during recall of a $\mathbf{y}_k$ vector (see Figure 4.6).

4.3.5. Show that the optical system of Figures 4.5 and 4.6 is functionally identical to the learnmatrix network.

4.3.6. Show that $(2LM)/n$ is the expected value of each component of a vector that is the sum of $2L$ uniformly randomly chosen n-dimensional binary vectors that have M 1s each.

4.3.7. Combine Equations 4.21, 4.23, and 4.24 to get Equation 4.25. (Hint: Use the logarithmic version of Sterling's formula, $\ln(n!) \doteq (n+1/2)\ln n -n + (1/2)\ln(2\pi)$, to reexpress $C(n, M)$. Then, write a computer program to find the value of M that maximizes I for $n = 10^2,\ 10^3, \ldots, 10^{100}$ (that is, verify the entries in Table 4.1).

4.3.8. Derive Equation 4.27 from Equations 4.25 and 4.26.

4.4 Recurrent Associative Networks

This section considers five different recurrent associative networks. Recurrent associative networks offer one capability that feedforward associative networks exhibit only weakly: accretive behavior. Typically, recurrent associative networks are started at some initial state (or have a constant input of an "initial state"), and then converge to one of a finite number of stable states.

There are three basic goals in the design of recurrent associative networks. First, given any initial state, the network should always converge to some stable state. Second, the stable state to which the network converges should be the one closest to the initial state, as measured by some metric. Third, it should be possible to have as many stable states as desired. In other words, these networks should behave like a sort of restricted gravitational system in which any desired number of equal-mass glue balls (the stable states) are located at any desired positions in an n-dimensional space. The gravitational force of each glue ball extends only to points that are closer to that ball than to any other ball. The initial state is then entered when a test mass is placed at the desired location and then released with an infinitesimal push. It will then always fall into the nearest stable state, and will "stick." As we shall see, only the first of these three goals can be achieved with associative networks. However, all of them can be achieved using the mapping networks discussed in the next chapter.

4.4.1 The Hopfield Network

As discussed in Chapter 1, many people contributed to neurocomputing's renaissance. However, the efforts of John Hopfield in the years 1983 to 1986 were unique in their effectiveness. In this subsection we study a neural network that has come to be known as the Hopfield network. This network is similar to the one Hopfield described in his 1982 paper [124].

The Hopfield network is shown in Figure 4.7. This structure is similar to the learnmatrix, except that the processing element outputs are wrapped around to become the inputs to the system and the weights can be given any desired (real number) values (with the restrictions that $w_{ij} = w_{ji}$ and $w_{ii} = 0$). The Hopfield network processing element transfer function is given by

$$x_i^{\text{new}} = \begin{cases} 1 & \text{if } \sum_{j=1}^{n} w_{ij} \, x_j^{\text{old}} > T_i, \\ x_i^{\text{old}} & \text{if } \sum_{j=1}^{n} w_{ij} \, x_j^{\text{old}} = T_i, \\ -1 & \text{if } \sum_{j=1}^{n} w_{ij} \, x_j^{\text{old}} < T_i, \end{cases} \tag{4.28}$$

for $i = 1, 2, \ldots, n$. The processing elements of the network are updated one at a time. The only constraint on the scheduling of these updates is that all of the processing elements must be updated at the same average rate. A uniformly random updating schedule is often specified. The time evolution of the state of the network clearly depends on the updating schedule. The subsequent movement of the network's state vector $\mathbf{x} = (x_1, x_2, \ldots, x_n)^{\mathrm{T}}$ on cube $\{-1, 1\}^n$ (see Section 2.4 for the definition of $\{-1, 1\}^n$) is therefore not uniquely defined by the initial state.

The Hopfield network does not have a learning law associated with its transfer function. The $n \times n$ weight matrix $W = (w_{ij})$ (which is therefore fixed) is assumed to be specified in advance. No restrictions on the real number values w_{ij} are made, except that (as mentioned above) the matrix W must be symmetric and have a 0 diagonal. In other words,

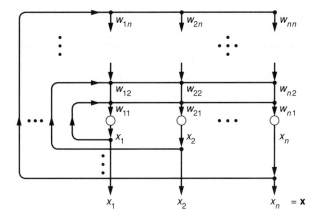

Fig. 4.7. • The Hopfield neural network. This recurrent associative network has n processing elements, each of which receives inputs from all the others. The input that a processing element receives from itself is ignored. All of the processing element output signals are bipolar. The network has an *energy function* associated with it; whenever a processing element changes state, this energy function always decreases. Starting at some initial position, the system's state vector simply moves downhill on the network's *energy surface* until it reaches a local minimum of the energy function. This convergence process is guaranteed to be completed in a fixed number of steps.

$$w_{ij} = w_{ji} \text{ for all } i, j \in \{1, 2, \dots, n\}, \tag{4.29}$$

and

$$w_{ii} = 0 \text{ for all } i \in \{1, 2, \dots, n\}. \tag{4.30}$$

The diagonal of W must be 0 in order for the energy function scheme presented later to work (see Exercise 4.4.5).

The values $T_1, T_2, \dots, T_n$ are called *thresholds*. They play the same role as do the bias terms in the ADALINE (see Section 3.3). The hyperplane determined by the vector $\mathbf{w}_i$ (where, as usual, $\mathbf{w}_i = (w_{i1}, w_{i2}, \dots, w_{in})^{\mathrm{T}}$) and the threshold T_i is perpendicular to $\mathbf{w}_i$, and is located at a directed distance (measured from the origin along $\mathbf{w}_i$, with positive distance measured in the direction of $\mathbf{w}_i$) $T_i/|\mathbf{w}_i|$, just as with the ADALINE. Each processing element has such a plane. When the state of a processing element is being updated, if the current state $\mathbf{x}$ of the network (in other words, the vertex of the cube that the network is currently located at) lies on the "plus" side of this plane, then the new output of the processing element will be $+1$; if $\mathbf{x}$ lies on the "minus" side of the hyperplane, then the new output will be -1; finally, if the state happens to lie on this plane, then the processing element's state remains unchanged. Notice that, since points have zero size, if any of the n planes go through one or more of the vertices of the $\{-1, 1\}^n$ cube, then we can tilt or move these planes (by infinitesimally modifying W or the T_is) so as to avoid these vertices. Thus, if we were to adopt the convention that none of the n hyperplanes would be allowed to contain any of the 2^n vertices of the cube $\{-1, 1\}^n$ (which, as noted, is a harmless restriction), then we could re–express the updating law for the Hopfield network as

$$x_i^{\text{new}} = \text{sgn}\left(\sum_{j=1}^{n} w_{ij}\, x_j^{\text{old}} - T_i\right), \tag{4.31}$$

where

$$\text{sgn}(u) = \begin{cases} +1 & \text{if } u \geq 0, \\ -1 & \text{if } u < 0. \end{cases} \tag{4.32}$$

This form of the network will not be used in this section, but is often encountered in literature. It is essentially identical to the perceptron input/output relationship. Note that we might just as well have used a bias input weight in each processing element, and have thresholded at 0 instead of using an explicit threshold. However, as we shall see, the threshold values (or the bias weights) must be treated specially, which makes it sensible to distinguish them from the other weights.

The initial bipolar values $I_1, I_2, \ldots, I_n$ of the processing element states (that is, the initial values of $x_1^{\text{old}}, x_2^{\text{old}}, \ldots, x_n^{\text{old}}$) are brought in on the vertical input lines, as shown in Figure 4.7. As with the learnmatrix network, these inputs and their associated weight application mechanisms are actually part of the internal structure of the Hopfield network processing elements. The representation of these values as extended external entities, as exhibited in Figures 4.4 and 4.7, is intended to acquaint you with a graphical notation that is commonly encountered in neurocomputing literature.

We can characterize the behavior of the Hopfield network by means of an *energy function* analysis. The idea is that the function

$$H(\mathbf{x}) = -\sum_{i=1}^{n}\sum_{j=1}^{n} w_{ij}\, x_i\, x_j + 2\sum_{i=1}^{n} T_i\, x_i \tag{4.33}$$

always decreases whenever the state of any processing element changes. This fact is easy to demonstrate. Let us assume that processing element k ($k \in \{1, 2, \ldots, n\}$) just changed state. In other words, its state changed from $+1$ to -1, or vice versa. The change in energy ΔH is then

$$\begin{aligned} \Delta H &= H(\mathbf{x}^{\text{new}}) - H(\mathbf{x}^{\text{old}}) \\ &= -\sum_{i=1}^{n}\sum_{j=1}^{n} w_{ij} x_i^{\text{new}} x_j^{\text{new}} + 2\sum_{i=1}^{n} T_i\, x_i^{\text{new}} \\ &\quad + \sum_{i=1}^{n}\sum_{j=1}^{n} w_{ij} x_i^{\text{old}} x_j^{\text{old}} - 2\sum_{i=1}^{n} T_i\, x_i^{\text{old}} \end{aligned} \tag{4.34}$$

$$= -2x_k^{\text{new}} \sum_{j=1}^{n} w_{kj} x_j^{\text{new}} + 2T_k \, x_k^{\text{new}} + 2x_k^{\text{old}} \sum_{j=1}^{n} w_{kj} x_j^{\text{old}} - 2T_k \, x_k^{\text{old}}. \tag{4.35}$$

This last result follows (see Exercise 4.4.1) because, except for the kth processing element state x_k, none of the other states have changed. Thus, $x_i^{\text{new}} = x_i^{\text{old}}$ for $i \neq k$, and so the terms of the sums that do not contain x_k cancel each other out. Equation 4.34 also exploits the facts that $w_{ij} = w_{ji}$ and $w_{ii} = 0$. By factoring out the term $(x_k^{\text{old}} - x_k^{\text{new}})$, we can reduce the final expression in Equation 4.34 to

$$\Delta H = 2(x_k^{\text{old}} - x_k^{\text{new}}) \left[\sum_{j=1}^{n} w_{kj} x_j^{\text{old}} - T_k \right]. \tag{4.36}$$

However, from Equation 4.28, if x_k has changed from $x_k^{\text{old}} = -1$ to $x_k^{\text{new}} = +1$, then $\sum_{j=1}^{n} w_{kj} x_j^{\text{old}} - T_k$ must have been positive — and, since $x_k^{\text{old}} - x_k^{\text{new}} = -2$ in this case, ΔH will be negative. Similarly, if x_k has changed from $+1$ to -1, then $\sum_{j=1}^{n} w_{kj} x_j^{\text{old}} - T_k$ must have been negative — and, since $x_k^{\text{old}} - x_k^{\text{new}} = +2$ in this case, ΔH will again be negative. If x_k has not changed, then $(x_k^{\text{old}} - x_k^{\text{new}}) = 0$, in which case ΔH will be 0. Thus,

$$\Delta H \leq 0. \tag{4.37}$$

In short, ΔH is negative whenever a processing element changes state, and ΔH is 0 whenever no change in state occurs.

It is easy to show (see Exercise 4.4.2) that H must have an absolute minimum value and that, each time H changes, it must decrease by at least some fixed minimum amount. Given these facts, it is inescapable that H must reach some minimum value in a finite number of steps (state changes). If all of the processing elements of the network are updated without any of them changing state, then none of them will ever again change state — the network has then reached a stable state. Further, every stable state must lie at a local minimum of the energy function H, since the preceding argument regarding ΔH always being negative can be used (see Exercise 4.4.3) to show that, if H has a lower value at one or more neighboring state values, then the network will move to one of these on an upcoming processing element update. Combining these facts demonstrates that the network must converge to a stable state in a finite number of updates. Thus, no matter what its initial state is, the Hopfield network always converges to a stable state in a finite number of processing element update steps.

It turns out, however, that the Hopfield network does not always go from an initial state to the nearest stable state (with distance measured using Hamming distance). Sometimes, it goes to a stable state that is farther away than the nearest stable state. No way to fix this is known (this problem probably cannot, in general, be fixed). The next subsection considers a network with states in the range $[-1, 1]$ that is closely related to the Hopfield network.

4.4.2 The Brain State in a Box Network

James Anderson introduced the *brain state in a box* (BSB) network in 1977 [14]. The idea is that the state **x** of the network, instead of being confined to the vertices of the discrete cube $\{-1, 1\}^n$, can lie anywhere within the closed solid cube $[-1, 1]^n$ that contains the cube $\{-1, 1\}^n$ (see Section 2.4 for the definitions of $[-1, 1]^n$ and $\{-1, 1\}^n$). The state of the network can start out at any point within $[-1, 1]^n$. As time passes, it migrates out to one of the vertices, where it stays. As in the Hopfield network, those vertices that form the "attractors" of the network are referred to as the *stable states* of the network.

The BSB network consists of n processing elements that are all updated simultaneously. The state vector of the network $\mathbf{x} = (x_1, x_2, \ldots, x_n)$ evolves in accordance with the following equation:

$$\mathbf{x}^{\text{new}} = C\left(\mathbf{x}^{\text{old}} + \alpha W \mathbf{x}^{\text{old}},\right) \tag{4.38}$$

where $\alpha > 0$ is a constant, where

$$C(\mathbf{u}) = C((u_1, u_2, \ldots, u_n)^{\text{T}}) = (\kappa(u_1), \kappa(u_2), \ldots, \kappa(u_n))^{\text{T}}, \tag{4.39}$$

and where

$$\kappa(s) = \begin{cases} +1 & \text{if } s > 1 \\ s & \text{if } -1 \leq s \leq +1 \\ -1 & \text{if } s < -1. \end{cases} \tag{4.40}$$

The behavior of the BSB network is quite simple. The state **x** starts out somewhere inside the cube at point **x** (the input vector to the network). It then migrates outward (via updating by Equation 4.37) until it reaches a particular vertex. At that point, the state vector stops — and it never moves again.

Once the system state has stopped changing (that is, it has reached a vertex), the processing element weight vectors $\mathbf{w}_i = (w_{i1}, w_{i2}, \ldots, w_{in})^{\text{T}}$ are updated in accordance with the learning law

$$w_{ij}^{\text{new}} = w_{ij}^{\text{old}} + \eta \left(x_i^{\text{actual}} x_j^{\text{actual}}\right), \tag{4.41}$$

where $\mathbf{x}^{\text{actual}}$ is the bipolar vector state in which the network ended up. The BSB network's weights all start out initially at very small ($|w_{ij}| \ll 1$) random values.

This learning law has the effect of causing the network to learn the bipolar vectors that are visited during the course of its experience. If the number of vertices actually visited during a significant period of training is relatively small, then these vertices will represent *categories* of inputs. In other words, each of the learned vertices becomes a stable state of the network, and some portion of the cube becomes its attractive basin. It is easy to show (see Exercise 4.4.5) that each stable state $\mathbf{x}^{\text{stable}}$ has a paired stable state $-\mathbf{x}^{\text{stable}}$ (its "twin"). Thus, the cube is partitioned into K regions, where $2K$ is the number of stable states of the network. As with the linear associator, we can introduce a bias term into the BSB processing elements by simply adding a 0th x_0 coordinate and permanently setting it to 1. This modification will usually eliminate the twins of the stable states. Finally, if desired, η in Equation 4.40 can be set to 0, and a fixed weight matrix W can be used. Widrow learning can also be used with the BSB network. In this case, the learning law of Equation 4.40 becomes $W^{new} = W^{old} + \eta(\mathbf{x}^{desired} - \mathbf{x}^{actual})(\mathbf{x}^{input})^T$, where $\mathbf{x}^{desired}$ is the desired final state of the network ($\mathbf{x}^{desired} \in \{-1, 1\}^n$). In this case, all of the $\mathbf{x}$ vectors have been augmented with bias terms set to 1, and W has been augmented with bias weights.

4.4.3 Associative Network Theorems

In 1983, Michael Cohen and Stephen Grossberg introduced an important new theorem concerning the behavior of a broad class of continuous-time associative networks [39]. This theorem built on Grossberg's work during the previous decade on the use of energy — or *Liapunov* — function methods (named after mathematician Alexander Liapunov, who discovered this approach to proving the stability of differential equations in the early 1900s — see [19] for a modern perspective on this approach). The idea of using energy functions for discerning the behavior of neural networks was introduced during the first half of the 1970s independently by Shun-ichi Amari [8], Stephen Grossberg [96], and W. A. Little [161]. The Cohen/Grossberg theorem follows.

■ *THEOREM 4.4.1* **The Cohen/Grossberg Theorem** *Given an associative neural network with n processing elements having output signals x_i and transfer functions of the form*

$$\dot{x}_i = a_i(x_i) \left[b_i(x_i) - \sum_{j=1}^{n} w_{ij} \, f_j(x_j) \right] \qquad (4.42)$$

such that

1. *matrix $[w_{ij}]$ is symmetric (that is, $w_{ij} = w_{ji}$) and all $w_{ij} \geq 0$*
2. *function $a_i(u)$ is continuous for $u \geq 0$ and $a_i(u) > 0$ for $u > 0$*
3. *function $b_i(u)$ is continuous and never "levels out" over any open interval for $u > 0$*
4. *function $f_j(u)$ is differentiable and $f'_j(u) > 0$ for $u \geq 0$*
5. *$[b_i(u) - w_{ii} f_i(u)] < 0$ as $u \to \infty$*
6. *either $\lim_{u \to 0+} b_i(u) = \infty$ or $\lim_{u \to 0+} b_i(u) < \infty$ and $\int_0^u [1/a_i(s)] \, ds = \infty$ for some $u > 0$,*

if the network's state $\mathbf{x}(0)$ at time 0 is in the positive orthant of $\mathbf{R}^n$ (that is, $x_i(0) > 0$ for $i = 1, 2, \ldots, n$), then the network will almost certainly converge to some stable point (that is, a point $\mathbf{p}$ such that $\dot{\mathbf{x}}(\mathbf{p}) = 0$) also in the positive orthant. Further, there will be at most a countable number of such stable points. ■

Notice that the function f_j is applied to only the corresponding processing element output signal x_j, no matter which processing element output signal x_i is being updated. This means that f_j is actually being applied to x_j before this composite signal is transmitted to the other processing elements. Thus, in actuality, $f_j(x_j)$ is the output signal of each processing element. The statement that b_i does not "level out" in condition 3 of the theorem means that none of the sets

$$S(c) = \{u > 0 \mid b_i(u) = c\} \tag{4.43}$$

contains an open interval $\{u | \alpha < u < \beta\}$. The statement that the network will "almost certainly" converge to a stable point means that this will happen except for certain rare choices of the W weight matrix. The set of such choices for W within the n^2-dimensional space of all possible W choices is of "measure zero" — meaning that, if W weight matrices are chosen uniformly at random, then it is virtually certain that a bad one never will be chosen.

The proof of this theorem uses an energy or Liapunov function approach. The key idea is to show that, under the conditions described, the Liapunov function

$$H(\mathbf{x}) = -\sum_{i=1}^{n}\sum_{j=1}^{n} w_{ij} f_i(x_i) f_j(x_j) - 2 \sum_{i=1}^{n} \int_{0}^{x_i} b_i(u_i)\, f_i'(u_i)\, du_i \tag{4.44}$$

is such that $\dot{H}(\mathbf{x}(t)) < 0$ on every possible trajectory that the network's state can follow. This seems fairly easy to show because (see Exercise 4.4.6)

$$\dot{H}(\mathbf{x}(t)) = -\sum_{i=1}^{n} a_i(x_i)\, f_i'(x_i) \left[b_i(x_i) - \sum_{j=1}^{n} w_{ij}\, f_j(x_j) \right]^2, \tag{4.45}$$

so every term of this sum is positive if $\mathbf{x}$ is in the positive orthant and is changing (that is, if $\dot{\mathbf{x}} \neq \mathbf{0}$). The difficulty arises in showing that the solution always stays in the positive orthant and in satisfying some other detailed mathematical requirements. Verifying these details requires the assumptions listed in the theorem and some sophisticated mathematics.

The Cohen/Grossberg theorem is deceptively simple. In fact, the functional form of the processing element transfer function assumed by the theorem (Equation 4.41) is extremely general. To illustrate this generality, we can show (see Exercise 4.4.7) that the following two transfer functions (with suitable restrictions on the constants and functions used) can be put into the form of Equation 4.41:

$$\dot{x}_i = -A_i x_i + (B_i - C_i x_i)[I_i + f_i(x_i)]$$

$$-(D_i x_i + E_i) \left[J_i + \sum_{j=1}^{n} w_{ij} g_j(x_j) \right] , \qquad (4.46)$$

$$\dot{x}_i = G_i x_i \left(1 - \sum_{j=1}^{n} H_{ij} x_k \right) . \qquad (4.47)$$

Equation 4.46 is known as the *Volterra–Lotka equations* and has been studied extensively in the field of population biology. In fact, the network equations of the Cohen/Grossberg theorem include many famous and well studied sets of equations as subcases [39]. There are equations for describing the evolutionary fitness selection of macromolecular species, models of voting behavior, and a mathematical morphogenic model of how zebras and cats get their stripes!

Finally, it is important to point out that the convergence result of the Cohen/Grossberg theorem depends critically on the symmetry of W. In fact, it is possible to construct cases in which even infinitesimal deviations from symmetry can cause endless oscillation of the network's state. For example, a network with three processing elements with initially (that is, at $t = 0$) positive and different output signals x_1, x_2, and x_3 with the following Cohen/Grossberg transfer functions

$$\begin{aligned}
\dot{x}_1 &= x_1 \left(1 - x_1 - \alpha x_2 - \beta x_3 \right), \\
\dot{x}_2 &= x_2 \left(1 - \beta x_1 - x_2 - \alpha x_3 \right), \\
\dot{x}_3 &= x_3 \left(1 - \alpha x_1 - \beta x_2 - x_3 \right),
\end{aligned} \qquad (4.48)$$

where $\beta > 1 > \alpha$ and $\alpha + \beta > 2$, will oscillate forever, even if α and β are made infinitesimally close to 1 (making the matrix W almost perfectly symmetric [39]).

We now examine another associative network theorem — Kosko's theorem. This theorem, which follows from the Cohen/Grossberg theorem, presents a different type of associative neural network — a continuous time network with continuous real states that has its functional layer split into two parts. The state of one part of the network is called **x** and the state of the other part is called **y**. So, in a sense, the network is both autoassociative and heteroassociative (formally, it is strictly an autoassociative network).

Bart Kosko introduced the *Bidirectional Associative Memory* (BAM) network in 1987 (see [151] for a detailed discussion). This associative network is related to the Hopfield network and to the networks of the Cohen/Grossberg theorem. As we shall see, there are multiple types of BAM network. In this section, we will examine two of them: the *continuous* BAM network and the *discrete* BAM network. The description and behavior of the continuous BAM network is encapsulated in the following theorem:

■ **THEOREM 4.4.2 Kosko's Theorem** *Given a network consisting of two sets of processing elements, with one set of n processing elements having output signals*

$x_1, x_2, \ldots, x_n$ and the other set of m processing elements having output signals $y_1, y_2, \ldots, y_m$, let these processing elements have transfer functions given by

$$
\begin{aligned}
\dot{x}_i &= -a_i\, x_i + \textstyle\sum_{j=1}^{m} w_{ij}\, f(y_j) + S_i, \\
\dot{y}_j &= -c_j\, y_j + \textstyle\sum_{i=1}^{n} w_{ij}\, f(x_i) + T_j,
\end{aligned}
\tag{4.49}
$$

where a_i, c_j, S_i, and T_j are positive constants for all $i \in \{1, 2, \ldots, n\}$ and all $j \in \{1, 2, \ldots, m\}$, f is a sigmoid function (see Figure 4.8), and $W = [w_{ij}]$ is any $n \times m$ real matrix. Then, given any starting state $(\mathbf{x}(0), \mathbf{y}(0))$, this network will converge to a stable point $(\mathbf{x}(\infty), \mathbf{y}(\infty))$. ∎

The Kosko theorem is easy to prove using the Cohen/Grossberg theorem (see Exercise 4.4.8). As with all of the networks encompassed by the Cohen/Grossberg theorem, the continuous BAM network has a Liapunov energy function, which is given by

$$
\begin{aligned}
H(\mathbf{x}, \mathbf{y}) = {}& -\sum_{i=1}^{n}\sum_{j=1}^{m} w_{ij}\, f(x_i)\, f(y_j) \\
& + \sum_{i=1}^{n} a_i \int_{0}^{x_i} f'(u_i)\, u_i\, du_i \\
& + \sum_{j=1}^{m} c_j \int_{0}^{y_j} f'(v_j)\, v_j\, dv_i \\
& - \sum_{i=1}^{n} f(x_i)\, S_i - \sum_{j=1}^{m} f(y_j)\, T_j.
\end{aligned}
\tag{4.50}
$$

Taking the time derivative of this energy function yields

$$
\begin{aligned}
\dot{H}(\mathbf{x}, \mathbf{y}) = {}& -\sum_{i=1}^{n}\sum_{j=1}^{m} w_{ij}\, f'(x_i)\, \dot{x}_i\, f(y_j) \\
& - \sum_{i=1}^{n}\sum_{j=1}^{m} w_{ij}\, f(x_i)\, f'(y_j)\, \dot{y}_j \\
& + \sum_{i=1}^{n} a_i\, f'(x_i)\, x_i\, \dot{x}_i + \sum_{j=1}^{m} c_j\, f'(y_j)\, y_j\, \dot{y}_j \\
& - \sum_{i=1}^{n} f'(x_i)\, \dot{x}_i\, S_i - \sum_{j=1}^{m} f'(y_j)\, \dot{y}_j\, T_j,
\end{aligned}
\tag{4.51}
$$

which can be simplified to

$$\dot{H}(\mathbf{x},\mathbf{y}) = -\sum_{i=1}^{n} f'(x_i)\,\dot{x}_i \left[-a_i\,x_i + \sum_{j=1}^{m} w_{ij}\,f(y_j) + S_i \right]$$
$$-\sum_{j=1}^{m} f'(y_j)\,\dot{y}_j \left[-c_j\,y_j + \sum_{i=1}^{n} w_{ij}\,f(x_i) + T_j \right]. \qquad (4.52)$$

However, the terms in brackets are just $\dot{x}_i$ and $\dot{y}_j$, by Equations 4.48, and so

$$\dot{H}(\mathbf{x},\mathbf{y}) = -\sum_{i=1}^{n} f'(x_i)\,(\dot{x}_i)^2 - \sum_{j=1}^{m} f'(y_j)\,(\dot{y}_j)^2. \qquad (4.53)$$

Since the derivative of f is always positive, and since the squared quantities are always positive (unless $\dot{x}_i = 0$ or $\dot{y}_j = 0$), this quantity will always be negative unless *all* of the $\dot{x}_i$ and $\dot{y}_j$ are equal to 0 — in which case a stable state has been reached. Thus, $\dot{H}$ will always be decreasing along any trajectory followed by the state of the network. The absolute maximum value that $\dot{H}$ can reach is 0 — which is attained only at the stable states of the network.

Some questions immediately arise from the preceding analysis. First, why must the network converge to a stable state? The answer flows from the Cohen/Grossberg theorem (see Exercise 4.4.7). Second, what can we say about these stable states? The answer is: Not much, without further constraining the function f and the constants associated with the network. However, if we assume that f is a sigmoid function with sufficiently high gain (see Figure 9.8 for the definition of the gain of a sigmoid function) and with upper limit $+1$ and lower limit -1, and that $a_i = 1$ for all i and $c_j = 1$ for all j, then experiment has shown that the continuous BAM will converge to a state such that the vectors $f(\mathbf{x}) \equiv (f(x_1), f(x_2), \ldots, f(x_n))^{\mathrm{T}}$ and $f(\mathbf{y}) \equiv (f(y_1), f(y_2), \ldots, f(y_m))^{\mathrm{T}}$ approach vertices of the cubes $\{-1, 1\}^n$ and $\{-1, 1\}^m$, respectively.

The discrete BAM is defined in a manner similar to the Hopfield network. In fact, except for a few small details, it can be viewed as a Hopfield network in which the processing elements have been divided into two subsets and all of the connections from each subset to itself have been eliminated. The discrete BAM is defined by the transfer function equations

$$x_i^{\mathrm{new}} = \begin{cases} 1 & \text{if } \sum_{j=1}^{m} w_{ij}\,y_j^{\mathrm{old}} > S_i \\ x_i^{\mathrm{old}} & \text{if } \sum_{j=1}^{m} w_{ij}\,y_j^{\mathrm{old}} = S_i \\ -1 & \text{if } \sum_{j=1}^{m} w_{ij}\,y_j^{\mathrm{old}} < S_i \end{cases} \qquad (4.54)$$

$$y_j^{\mathrm{new}} = \begin{cases} 1 & \text{if } \sum_{i=1}^{n} w_{ij}\,x_i^{\mathrm{old}} > T_j \\ y_j^{\mathrm{old}} & \text{if } \sum_{i=1}^{n} w_{ij}\,x_i^{\mathrm{old}} = T_j \\ -1 & \text{if } \sum_{i=1}^{n} w_{ij}\,x_i^{\mathrm{old}} < T_j, \end{cases} \qquad (4.55)$$

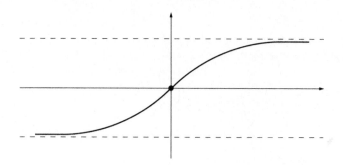

Fig. 4.8. • A sigmoid function. A *sigmoid function* is a bounded differentiable real function that is defined for all real input values and that has a positive derivative everywhere. Further, a sigmoid function is assumed to rapidly approach a fixed finite upper limit asymptotically as its argument gets large, and to rapidly approach a fixed finite lower limit asymptotically as its argument gets small. The central portion of the sigmoid (whether it is near 0 or displaced) is assumed to be roughly linear. The average slope of this central portion is called the *gain* of the sigmoid. A typical sigmoid function is $f(u) = 1/1 + e^{-u}$.

where the **x** and **y** state vectors start out at selected vertices of the cubes $\{-1, 1\}^n$ and $\{-1, 1\}^m$, respectively. The x processing elements are all updated together during one time step, and the y processing elements are all updated together during the next time step, and so on (thus, these make up two separate slabs — although they are each made up of the same type of processing elements).

The discrete BAM network functions exactly like the Hopfield network does (see Exercises 4.4.9 and 4.4.10). It starts at some particular pair of states, and then runs downhill on its energy surface until it reaches a local minimum (although not necessarily the closest one to the starting point). Note that this is not like the continuous BAM, for which we have *not* shown that the state of the network necessarily ends up in a local minimum of its Liapunov energy function. The BAM can be made adaptive [150].

Exercises

4.4.1. Establish the correctness of Equations 4.34 and 4.35.

4.4.2. Show that H (Equation 4.33) must have a finite minimum value, and that each time H changes it must decrease by at least some minimum amount.

4.4.3. Show that, if the state of the Hopfield network lies one Hamming distance unit away from one or more states with lower energies, then the network will transition to one of these lower energy states during the next updating of one of the relevant processing elements. Show that this fact implies that the network's state must end up at a local minimum of the energy function. Hint: Use Equations 4.35 and 4.36.

4.4.4. Explain why the diagonal entries w_{ii} of the Hopfield network weight matrix must be 0. Hint: Carry through the energy function decrease argument with these diagonal weight matrix entries set to non-zero values, and argue why it would not be possible to add compensatory terms to the energy function to get rid of the new terms that appear.

4.4.5. Show that, if the BSB network (without biases) converges to the bipolar vector $\mathbf{x}^{\text{stable}}$ from initial state $\mathbf{x}^{\text{initial}} \in [0, 1]^n$, then the BSB network will converge to $-\mathbf{x}^{\text{stable}}$ if its initial state is $-\mathbf{x}^{\text{initial}}$.

4.4.6. Derive Equation 4.44 from Equation 4.43 and show that, given the assumptions of the Cohen/Grossberg theorem, $\dot{H}(\mathbf{x}(t)) < 0$ whenever $\mathbf{x}(t)$ is in the positive orthant and $b\dot{f}x \neq \mathbf{0}$.

4.4.7. Show that Equations 4.45 and 4.46 can be put into the form of Equation 4.41.

4.4.8. Prove the Kosko theorem using the Cohen/Grossberg theorem.

4.4.9. Derive an energy function $H(\mathbf{x}, \mathbf{y})$ for the discrete BAM. Prove that the value of this function decreases every time the state of the network changes. Hint: Use the Hopfield network and continuous BAM network energy functions as guides.

4.4.10. Show that the discrete BAM, just like the Hopfield network, ends up in a local minimum of its energy function. Hint: Use the same argument as in Exercise 3.

4.4.11. Numerically calculate all of the stable states of the Hopfield network with weight matrix

$$
W = \begin{pmatrix}
0 & 1 & -3 & 2 & -0.3 & -2.1 & 1 \\
1 & 0 & 1 & 1 & 3 & -4 & 0 \\
-3 & 1 & 0 & 0 & 1 & -1 & -1 \\
2 & 1 & 0 & 0 & 0 & -2.4 & 3.3 \\
-0.3 & 3 & 1 & 0 & 0 & 1 & 1 \\
-2.1 & -4 & -1 & -2.4 & 1 & 0 & -1 \\
1 & 0 & -1 & 3.3 & 1 & -1 & 0
\end{pmatrix},
$$

with even numbered thresholds all equal to -0.12 (i.e., $T_2 = T_4 = T_6 = -0.12$) and all odd numbered thresholds equal to 0.003 (i.e., $T_1 = T_3 = T - 5 = T_7 = 0.003$). Also calculate the energy function value at each of these stable states.

4.5 Association Fascicles

As we have seen above, associative networks are fundamentally unable to carry out the desired function of robustly mapping one set of vectors onto an associated set of vectors, unless sparse coding is used. Further, the information storage efficiency of associative networks (a topic that we only pursued for the

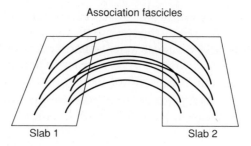

Fig. 4.9. • An association fascicle provides a means for two otherwise independent slabs to activate each other associatively, when desired. The processing elements of slab 1 send their output signals to the processing elements of slab 2, and vice versa. Whenever it is desired, the processing elements of either slab can allow themselves to be associatively activated or presensitized by the processing elements of the other slab. Such interactions work to reestablish mutual constellations of activation (or, at least, presensitization) that correspond to paired activations that have previously occurred.

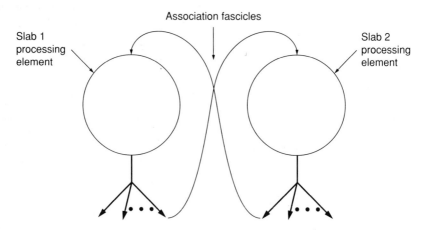

Fig. 4.10. • Details of an association fascicle. Processing elements of slab 1 send copies of their output signals to processing elements of slab 2, and vice versa, forming an association fascicle. In most situations, these associative fascicles provide only a fraction of the inputs to the processing elements of slabs 1 and 2. These associative connections allow the processing elements of one or both of these slabs to be activated (either partially or totally) by means of associative inputs from the other. This might be used for associative recall of constellations (as in the learnmatrix network) or for consensus formation (as in the BAM networks).

learnmatrix, but which has been investigated for many other associative networks — see [167, 101]) is usually abysmally low, unless sparse coding is used (in which case efficiencies as high as 68% can be attained). Clearly, if there is one lesson in the study of associative networks it is that the use of sparse codes is important.

Because of the simplicity of associative networks, it is conceivable that they might someday be implementable in extremely large sizes in inexpensive hardware. Given such a capability, and given a scheme for ensuring that the activity patterns of slabs are always sparse (for example, using competition — see the discussion of combinatorial hypercompression in Section 6.3), then associative networks might be usable as a means for forming associations between the states of different slabs. Under these circumstances, associative networks might be thought of as a neural network building block. In other words, as an element that can be added to a neural network design, where needed, to achieve a specific information processing goal. Such a neural network building block might be called an *association fascicle*. This idea is illustrated in Figures 4.9 and 4.10.

Association fascicles used to link slabs with sparse activity patterns can often learn to associate those patterns. In other words, on future occasions where one slab exhibits a known pattern of activity[1] the association fascicle can cause a previously frequently associated pattern of activity to be (approximately) reproduced on the other slab. Alternatively, the association fascicle inputs can simply be used to *presensitize* the processing elements of the target slab. In other words, these inputs can be used to prepare these processing elements for possible inputs that may arrive in the near future. Such schemes can be used to implement *expectation mechanisms* for use with time-varying inputs.

In summary, associative networks hold the potential (given further development — see [160] for an example of research in this direction) of providing us with a robust and reliable neural network building block — the association fascicle. It is in this way that we will probably best be able to exploit the capabilities of associative networks. The original goal of associating arbitrary sets of vectors can probably never be met by these simple structures. However, this goal (and much more ambitious goals) can be completely realized by the *mapping networks*, which are discussed in the next chapter.

---

[1] A pattern of sparse slab activity (i.e., where only a few processing elements have "large" output signals at any time and all of the other processing elements have "small" output signals) is often termed a *constellation*. If a constellation of activity on one slab frequently appears simultaneously with a constellation of activity on another slab (say, due to both slabs responding to a set of causally related external inputs), then these constellations can often be associated with each other by means of an association fascicle using Hebb or Grossberg learning.

Mapping Networks: Multi-Layer Data Transformation Structures

The approximation of a mathematical function or mapping (using examples of the mapping's action) is a central issue in subjects as diverse as pattern recognition, control theory, and statistics. In the past, each of these subjects has developed an armamentarium of approaches for solving problems of this type. However, essentially all of these approaches revolve around the least-sum-of-squared-errors method of Carl Gauss [4]. In other words, these approaches can be viewed as variants of the methods of statistical regression analysis.

In this chapter, some neural networks capable of solving this mapping implementation problem are presented. In every case, the capabilities offered by these networks are substantially different from those offered by regression approaches. In fact, some of the methods presented could even be viewed as a type of "superregression" that in some ways generalizes traditional regression approaches.

The networks presented in this chapter by no means represent the final word on mapping neural networks. However, these architectures are fairly well understood, and procedures for applying them successfully in a number of application domains have been worked out. Thus, they provide a good a starting point for the study of the rapidly growing subject of mapping networks.

5.1 The Mapping Implementation Problem

This section describes the general mapping implementation problem, as well as the underlying issues and assumptions that accompany such problems.

5.1.1 Mapping Neural Networks

The problem addressed by mapping neural networks is the approximate implementation of a bounded mapping or function $f : A \subset \mathbf{R}^n \longrightarrow \mathbf{R}^m$, from a bounded subset A of n-dimensional Euclidean space to a bounded subset $f[A]$ of m-dimensional Euclidean space, by means of training on examples $(\mathbf{x}_1, \mathbf{y}_1)$, $(\mathbf{x}_2, \mathbf{y}_2), \ldots, (\mathbf{x}_k, \mathbf{y}_k), \ldots$ of the mapping's action, where $\mathbf{y}_k = f(\mathbf{x}_k)$. For the purposes of this chapter, we will always assume that we can generate such examples of a mapping f by selecting $\mathbf{x}_k$ vectors randomly from A in accordance with a fixed probability density function $\rho(\mathbf{x})$ (ρ is assumed to be 0 outside A). We will also assume that, after training, the network will be used to select random input vectors $\mathbf{x}$ in accordance with $\rho(\mathbf{x})$. Mapping networks can also handle the case where noise is added to the examples of the function being approximated, but this capability will be ignored here.

There are basically two types of mapping networks: *feature-based* (or simply *feature*) networks and *prototype-based* (or simply *prototype*) networks. Examples of both of these network types are discussed in this chapter. A feature network implements a functional input/output relationship that is expressed in terms of a general, modifiable functional form; this functional form is modified (typically via the adaptive setting of weights by means of the application of one or more learning laws within the processing elements of the network) to fit the specific mapping that is to be approximated. Backpropagation and GMDH (the Group Method of Data Handling) are examples of feature networks.

Prototype-based networks operate by creating (by the use of one or more learning laws) a set of specific input/output examples $(\mathbf{w}_1, \mathbf{v}_1)$, $(\mathbf{w}_2, \mathbf{v}_2), \ldots,$ $(\mathbf{w}_L, \mathbf{v}_L)$ that statistically represent the action of the mapping. The network then determines the action of the mapping on some new unknown vector $\mathbf{x}$ by comparing $\mathbf{x}$ with the set of $\mathbf{w}_i$ vectors stored in the network, and then using the results of these comparisons (for example, the distances from $\mathbf{x}$ to each of the $\mathbf{w}_i$ vectors) to combine the $\mathbf{u}_i$ vectors appropriately to produce an estimate of $f(\mathbf{x})$ (for example, by proportional interpolation between the $\mathbf{u}_i$ vectors based on the coefficients used to express $\mathbf{x}$ as some linear combination of the $\mathbf{w}_i$ vectors). The counterpropagation and self-organizing map neural networks are examples of prototype networks.

To understand mapping networks, we must understand the basic function approximation issues of measuring approximation accuracy and determining when we are "overfitting" or "underfitting" the training data. These issues will be covered in the next two subsections.

5.1.2 Measuring Function Approximation Accuracy

For the purposes of this chapter, let us assume that every mapping network in which we will be interested adapts itself to the example data by modifying adaptive coefficients (i.e., weights), as opposed to modifying its connectivity.

When the vector $\mathbf{x}$ (as always, assumed to be chosen at random in accordance with a fixed probability density function $\rho(\mathbf{x})$) is entered into the neural network, we refer to the output vector of the mapping network as $Y(x, w)$, where w is the weight vector of the network. To measure the approximation accuracy of the network, all we then need to do is to somehow compare the actual output $Y(x, w)$ of the network to the "correct" output $f(x)$ over a large number of testing trials. This is the concept that is explored in this subsection.

To test the approximation accuracy of a mapping network, we shall require additional randomly selected examples $(x_1, y_1), (x_2, y_2), \ldots, (x_k, y_k), \ldots$ of the mapping's action, beyond those used for training the network. We will call this set of examples, which shall be used only for testing, the *test set*. These examples must be "fresh" because, if we use the same examples for training as are used for testing, all we are determining is how well the network learned the training examples. What we are really interested in determining is how well the network has learned to approximate the function for *arbitrary* values of x. For now, we will assume that the test set is infinite in size. Techniques have been developed for dealing with situations where an unlimited supply of data for training and testing is not available. These will be described briefly in the next subsection.

Given a mapping network and a test set, we now test the network by comparing its output with the correct functional value provided by the mapping. This testing takes place one example at a time. Each individual evaluation of the network with a single test example is called a *testing trial*. Let (x_k, y_k) be the example used on the kth testing trial (i.e., $y_k = f(x_k)$). As before, it is assumed that x_k has been drawn at random from the domain set A in accordance with a fixed probability density function p. Next, we let

$$F_k(x_k, w) = |f(x_k) - Y(x_k, w)|^2.$$

F_k is the square of the approximation error made by the mapping network on the kth testing trial. For the purposes of this discussion we shall assume that w is fixed during testing. Thus, whatever training process we have carried out has been terminated and the neural network is no longer allowed to adapt (it is important that the network not be trained while it is being tested — erroneous results may be obtained). Given all of this, the *mean squared error* $F(w)$ of the network is defined to be

$$F(w) \equiv \lim_{N \to \infty} \frac{1}{N} \sum_{k=1}^{N} F_k(x_k, w), \tag{5.1}$$

assuming this limit exists for almost any set of randomly chosen x_k. Note that $F(w) \geq 0$ because F is the average of non-negative quantities. Alternatively (see Exercise 5.1.1), we can define $F(w)$ by means of the probability integral

$$F(w) \equiv \int_A |f(x) - Y(x, w)|^2 \, p(x) \, dx. \tag{5.2}$$

The mean squared error $F(\mathbf{w})$ is well defined for most neural networks (such as backpropagation, counterpropagation, GMDH, etc.). However, it is possible to define a neural network for which the mean squared error is not well defined (see Exercise 5.1.2). By "well defined," it is meant that the limit in Equation 5.1 converges "almost surely" (i.e., with probability 1) and/or that the function $|f(\mathbf{x}) - \mathbf{Y}(\mathbf{x}, \mathbf{w})|^2$ $\rho(\mathbf{x})$ is integrable over the region A. Since these conditions are met for all of the neural networks with which we will be concerned, $F(\mathbf{w})$ will hereafter be assumed to exist. Further, $F(\mathbf{w})$ is almost always a continuous and differentiable function of $\mathbf{w}$.

The remarkable thing about $F(\mathbf{w})$ is that as long as we select the testing examples randomly in accordance with ρ it makes no difference which examples we use (this will not be proved here, but it is easy to demonstrate). The limit in Equation 5.1 will almost always converge to the same value as the number (N) of testing examples gets large. The probability of choosing a set of examples for which this series will not converge is zero (although such example sets *do* exist – see Exercise 5.1.3). One of the ways of deciding how large a test set must be used is to (if possible) try out progressively larger test sets until the value of the mean squared error starts to converge to a fixed value. This procedure (if it is feasible) will indicate how large a test set must be used for that particular mapping and that particular neural network.

Mean squared error is not the only measure of error that might be of interest. However, it is by far the most popular. The advantage of mean squared error is that it uniformly weights each training trial error in accordance with the square of magnitude of the error vector

$$f(\mathbf{x}_k) - \mathbf{Y}(\mathbf{x}_k, \mathbf{w}).$$

This error measurement scheme ensures that large errors receive much greater attention than small errors, which is usually what is desired (in most situations large errors hurt much more than small errors). Also, the mean squared error takes into account the frequency of occurrence of particular inputs. It is much more sensitive to errors made on commonly encountered inputs than it is to errors on rare inputs. Again, this is exactly what we want for many applications.

Notwithstanding its general utility, the mean squared error measure of network performance is not universally desirable. For example, if the outputs of the mapping and the network are images, the mean squared error will not do a good job of measuring errors that would be significant to a human observer. A specific instance of this would be if the image output of the mapping and the image output of the network are the same image except for a constant offset of 30 grey scale levels (out of 256), then the mean squared error will be 900; and yet, a human observer would probably not be able to perceive any significant difference between the images. However, if the mapping output image and the network output image are the same except that the network has an average of one pixel out of a hundred set to a random value (between 0 and 255) then the mean squared error will be small but the images will look *very* different to a human observer. Thus, in the case of images, the mean squared error criterion does not do an adequate job of measuring the important errors (in fact, there are no really good numerical measures of image similarity known).

Examples of alternative error measures are maximum absolute error, mean absolute error, and median squared error. Mean absolute error measures the average length of the error vector, weighted by the probability density function. This error measure weights all errors in proportion to their magnitude (unlike the mean squared error, which emphasizes larger error values by squaring). For applications such as control problems (where trying very hard to avoid larger position errors — as with the mean squared error — can lead to unacceptably large accelerations and jerks) mean absolute error is sometimes preferable.

Other error measures (such as maximum absolute error and median squared error) have even greater advantages in many situations. For example, maximum absolute error is useful for numerical analysis because it quantifies the absolute maximum error that can ever occur. Median squared error is useful because (unlike the mean) the median is a *robust statistic* (its value is insensitive to occasional gross errors in the training data — such as an additive error of 10^{41} on the data used on every tenth testing trial, which would completely destroy a mean squared error approach).

Unfortunately, practical techniques for implementing these more desirable error measures do not yet exist. Thus, most neural networks today are inexorably tied to mean squared error measurement. The few that are not (such as the self-organizing map, which uses a probability density function matching criterion — see Section 5.4) are not capable of solving many of the problems that the others (such as backpropagation and counterpropagation) can solve. So, for the remainder of this chapter the emphasis will be on mean squared error measurement.

As discussed above, the mean squared error $F(\mathbf{w})$ is a function of the weight vector $\mathbf{w}$ of the neural network being evaluated. For each selection of weights a different mean squared error arises. Thus, we can think of $F(\mathbf{w})$ as a surface sitting "above" the weight space of the network, where F is the height of the surface at weight value $\mathbf{w}$. This surface is known as the *error surface* of the neural network.

Clearly, because F is a non-negative function, the error surface always lies at a non-negative altitude above the weight space. Figure 5.1 illustrates a typical error surface. Obviously, the idea is to find those weights that minimize F. Typically, the minimum value of F will not be zero; because the neural network is unable to *exactly* implement the desired mapping. Thus, the minimum value of F will typically be $F_{min} > 0$. If we could find a weight vector $\mathbf{w}^*$ for which $F(\mathbf{w}^*) = F_{min}$, then the neural network would do the best possible job of approximating the mapping (as measured using mean squared error). As we shall see, the structure of error surfaces is a crucial issue for the backpropagation

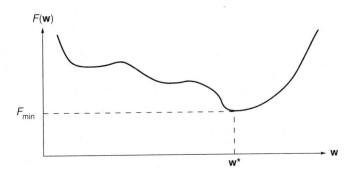

Fig. 5.1. • A typical error surface. A goal of neural network training is to find a network weight vector $\mathbf{w}^*$ that minimize the error F.

neural network. For other networks it merely gives us a way of understanding network performance in absolute terms.

5.1.3 Training and Overtraining

One of the perennial problems in function approximation is that in most situations infinite supplies of training and testing examples are not available. If they are, then we train the network using the largest possible set of data and then test its performance on the largest possible set of data. One way to be sure that these sets are large enough is to show that substantially increasing their size does not affect performance. Another way is to test the performance of the network on both the training and testing sets and show that the results are the same. However, given that this ideal case is rarely applicable (even when the data is available practical considerations may keep us from using it), this subsection concentrates on the case where only a modest amount of data is available.

First of all, it is important to remember that if the amount of available data is too small then neurocomputing techniques simply won't work. In this event it may be more profitable to attempt to develop a set of rules for solving the problem or to devise an appropriate algorithm, or to simply forget the whole thing (often a prudent course of action in the face of the impossible). If a reasonable amount of data is available (the definition of "reasonable" is discussed below), then we can proceed.

In general, the best procedure is to begin by constructing the test set. The ideal criterion is that the test set be sufficiently comprehensive so that if the network performs well on it then the ultimate problem will be considered solved. In other words, the test set is constructed so that it contains essentially every possible case that will be encountered in the real world. If such a test set is available then make performance on it (by a neural network that was *not* trained on it) the "buy-off" condition for the project. In other words, if the network does well on this test set then the project is a success. If it doesn't, then it is not a success. To keep things honest this *acceptance test set* is often retained by the "customer" or sponsor of the project and is never given to the engineers performing the work on the project. The engineers working on the project get similar but different data for use in constructing their *validation test set, training set* and *training test set*. The developers use the training set to train the network and they use the training test set to evaluate its performance (see below). After the network has been developed, the engineers use their validation test set to validate the network's performance before submitting it to the customer for acceptance testing. If the network fails the validation testing it is reworked using the training set and training test set.

It is crucial that the validation and acceptance test sets only be used for final "safety" checks of the network's performance at the end of the development cycle. They must not be directly used during the network's development. This segregation is necessary because some neural networks (notably, the backpropagation network, as it is normally used) have the capability to learn a specific data set much better than they can learn a general problem. Since the goal of most mapping network systems (and, actually, most neural network based systems in general — many of the comments in this section apply to almost all neural networks) is to perform well in an operational setting in which the environmental inputs have more variability than is evidenced in a training set, learning the specific examples of a training set too well is not desirable. What we want is for the neural network to *generalize* from the training set examples to the entire problem environment.

In this context, the term generalize could almost be replaced with the word "interpolate." In other words, if a real-world input vector lies *between* or *close to* training set examples, then we want the output of the network to be reasonably related to the outputs it would give for the training set examples. If the input is far away from any training examples then the output of the network cannot be expected to be meaningful.

An unexpected and peculiar phenomenon found in some feature-base mapping networks (notably, backpropagation) is the problem of *overtraining*. While the exact origin of this problem has still not been fully elucidated, it seems to be related to the manner in which the afflicted networks form their mapping approximations. The source of this problem seems to be a tendency of some networks to start out by implementing a very "flat" approximating function. In other words, the prescription for choosing their initial weight values causes the network to start in a configuration in which the derivatives of the output variables with respect to the input variables all have small values at every point in the input space. Thus, the "surface" defined by the functional form of the network is very "flat" and "unwrinkled." Such a surface does a good job of interpolating between points on its surface.

As training of one of these peculiar mapping networks progresses, it seems to be the case that the initially flat surface defined by the functional form of the network begins to "crinkle" and develop undulations — as it must if it is to better fit the training set examples. However, as this process continues, if the same set of training examples are shown repeatedly to the network many, many times, then the surface becomes even more crinkled and convoluted in its

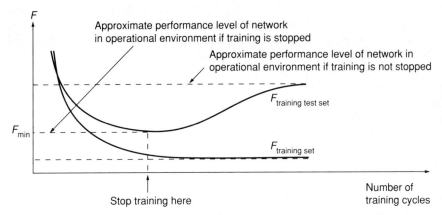

Fig. 5.2. • Training set error vs. training test set error as a function of the number of training cycles. This illustrates the phenomenon of *overtraining* seen in some feature-based mapping networks.

attempt to fit this fixed set of points. In behavioral terms, all it "cares about" is fitting these points. The ability to interpolate well between them is unimportant.

In fact, as the surface progresses from flat to convoluted there is almost always an intermediate stage at which the surface reaches a good balance between accurately fitting the training set examples and yet still exhibiting a reasonably good interpolation capability between these examples. It is typically at this intermediate point that training of such networks should be stopped.

The problem then becomes: how do we know when this stopping point has been reached? Unfortunately, research has not yet given us a clear answer to this problem (in fact, the whole problem of overtraining can possibly be eliminated by means of a slightly modified weight initialization and training methodology). However, experimental experience suggests that the behavior exhibited in Figure 5.2 is typical. In this situation, the horizontal axis is measuring the number of presentations of the training set to the network. At periodic intervals in this process the network training is stopped, the weights are temporarily frozen, and the network's error performance is tested using, let us say, mean squared error. The levels of performance are measured along the vertical axis.

The network's performance is measured using two different data sets: the training set and the *training test set* (which is only typically used with networks that suffer from this problem). The training test set is a separate body of data, drawn, like the training set, in accordance with the fixed probability density function that governs the real-world problem being solved. While the training set is used directly for training of the network the training test set is used only for this evaluation process (which applies it indirectly to the training process).

Notice in Figure 5.2 that the error of the network as measured using the training set constantly decreases. This is what would be seen for just about any mapping network.   However, the odd thing is that the training test set error typically decreases for a while, but then begins to *increase* again (often it eventually seems to level out, but not always). If we were somehow able to increase the size of the training test set to the point where further increases in size would not change the error values measured with it (it can be proven that this will always happen), there is good experimental evidence that this same behavior would obtain. In other words, overtraining is a real phenomenon that must be dealt with.

If we assume that the error curve of the network tested against the entire infinite set of possible examples would be approximately the same as that of the training test set curve (which is often only a crudely correct assumption) then, clearly, we want to stop training when this curve reaches its minimum. At this point, the network can be tested against the validation test set to verify adequate performance. If it demonstrates satisfactory performance than it is shipped to the "customer," who then tests the network again, using the acceptance test set.

The training test set typically consists of half of the available training data (with the other half used for the training set). However, this is not a hard and fast rule. In fact, if data is scarce, then it is often wise to simply use all of the data for training and to simply stop training when both an adequate level of performance is reached and when the training set error curve first begins to level out. Many other ideas and prescriptions for handling overtraining problems have been devised (some of these have a rational basis, while others are simply superstitious behaviors passed from one neural alchemist[1] to another). However, such material is too tentative for an introductory textbook.

For networks that do not suffer from overtraining (e.g., counterpropagation, self-organizing map, and, typically, other prototype networks) the performance of the network typically continues to improve monotonically as training progresses. For these networks there is little utility in having a training test set, since the error curve measured using it is also monotonically decreasing. Thus, for these networks the best strategy is usually to simply use all of the available training data for training (and for testing). As the error curve of the network, as measured using the training set, flattens out at an acceptable error level, training is halted. The network can then be tested with the validation test set and, if it passes this test, delivered to the "customer" for final acceptance testing.

In training any network the worst possible situation (which, unfortunately, arises all too often) is that there is enough data to probably adequately train the neural network, but not enough to hold out for validation and acceptance test

---

[1] Neurocomputing has attracted its share of alchemistic tinkerers, whose experimental efforts rely more on hope, intuition, and luck than on detailed understanding. However, on surprisingly frequent occasions the efforts of such individuals yield interesting results. This serves to illustrate the fact that in the application of neurocomputing to real-world problems, behavioral intuition can often be just as important as deep technical understanding. The ideal situation is to have both.

sets (and a training test set, should that be required). In this instance there are a few options that can help. One option is if there are L examples available, then train the network L different times using $L - 1$ of the examples, each time holding out a single different example as a singleton test set. On each of these L trials, the training set is used for testing the network during training and training is ended when the error curve levels out. Then the error of the network on the held-out test example is measured. After doing this L times the mean of the squared errors made on the held-out examples is calculated. This is the estimate of the overall network performance that would be achieved if more data from the final environment were available. The network can be retrained using all L examples, if desired, or the last already trained version of the network (trained on the last set of $L - 1$ examples) can be used.

Another approach to dealing with meager data is to use it to build additional "fake" training and testing data; e.g., using the provided training set as a starting point. The idea is to discover what kinds of differences occur between real data examples and then create new examples by appropriately perturbing or combining the existing examples. For example, if the problem is character recognition using pixel images, many new examples can be produced by simply translating and geometrically distorting the given character images. Another example is in speech recognition; where the example speech stream can be changed in pitch and time-warped to create many new realistic examples. Additional training examples can also be created by appropriately adding noise to the initial examples.

In the worst case, where barely sufficient training data exists, but where (for whatever reason) none of the above training set extension or performance testing approaches can be used, the only option is to simply train the network until the "learning curve" (the error measured using the training set itself) begins to level off, and leave it at that. This approach offers no assurance that anything of value has been produced, but at least the performance on the training set can be quantified.

No matter how it is trained, ultimately each particular neural network can only do so well on a particular problem. The final challenge is to produce a network that can do well enough to meet the requirements of the particular application being attempted. This often requires that a sequence of neural networks of different sizes and configurations (and possibly different architectures) be tried. One then picks the best performing network as the final choice. Again, for the same reasons as before, it is crucial that only the training set data be used for deciding between these alternative networks. Using the validation and/or acceptance test sets for this purpose effectively makes them part of the training/selection process and ruins them for use as final testing means. This issue of leaving the testing sets completely out of the network development process and using them only as a final, ultimate safety check is a common point of confusion. When evaluating other people's work it is essential to determine if their performance numbers were derived by use of a comprehensive and pristine test set. If not, the validity of the results should be seriously questioned.

5.1.4 Relationship to Statistical Regression

The manner in which mapping networks approximate functions can be thought of as a generalization of statistical regression analysis. In regression, the specific form of a function to be fitted to data is first chosen and then fitting according to some error criterion (such as mean squared error) is carried out. This procedure is, at its core, based upon the *least mean of squared errors* (or simply *least squares*) technique for fitting a straight line to irregular data invented almost 200 years ago by Carl Gauss. The least squares method has been essentially the only available approach to the approximation of mappings from data. Examples of this approach include such well-known techniques as polynomial curve fitting, Fourier analysis, and Kalman filtering. Mapping networks can be thought of as going "Beyond Regression" (which was the title of the 1974 Ph.D. dissertation of Paul Werbos [233] in which the backpropagation network was first introduced in essentially its current form).

A primary advantage of mapping networks over classical statistical regression analysis is that the neural networks have more general functional forms than the well developed statistical methods can effectively deal with. For example, in Fourier analysis the "training" examples are used to compute the amplitudes and phases of sine waves (which are then simply added together in a *linear superposition* to give the approximation). However, Joseph Fourier has already selected the frequencies for us (integer multiples of some user-selected base frequency). In neurocomputing (for example, in a backpropagation network) the neural network uses the training examples to effectively adjust the amplitudes, phases, *and* the "frequencies" — thus providing a significantly increased ability to accurately approximate the function. Neural networks are free from dependency on linear superposition and orthogonal functions — which linear statistical regression approaches must use because without them the known mathematics upon which linear regression is based does not go through.[2]

---

[2] In linear statistical regression analysis the fitting functions can be nonlinear functions of the input data, but only linear functions of the parameters (this is why linear superposition is required). In nonlinear statistical regression the fitting function can be a nonlinear function of both the input data and the parameters. Thus, the methods of nonlinear statistical regression analysis resemble those of neurocomputing. However, few, if any, individual statistical regression function methods (i.e., a method connected to a specific broad class of fitting functions) have been developed as thoroughly as the neurocomputing architectures presented in this chapter. The main advantage of neurocomputing over statistics (in the area of function approximation) seems to be neurocomputing's ability to draw from many more sources of inspiration (pattern recognition theory, signal processing theory, image analysis theory, cognitive science, control theory, and, potentially, neuroscience) for its methods than are typically exploited by workers in statistics.

In essence, in terms of its everyday practice, there has been only modest progress in regression analysis since the days of Gauss.[3] Neurocomputing is now providing a breath of fresh new air to this 200 year old subject.

In summary, enough experimental evidence has now been gathered to state with some confidence that mapping networks are, in general, different than statistical regression approaches. The function approximations that arise from properly applied mapping networks (at least in instances where sufficient training data is available) are usually better than those provided by regression techniques (which often exhibit artifacts such as excessive polynomial-type "humps" or Fourier series-type overshoots and ringing). This difference is particularly important in high-dimensional spaces (input dimensions greater than 3 to 10), where many of the more "automated" regression techniques often fail to produce an appropriate approximation.

Exercises

5.1.1. Demonstrate, using elementary probability theory, that Equations 5.1 and 5.2 are equivalent, given certain conditions. Produce a sufficient set of conditions that would guarantee this equivalence.

5.1.2. Construct a neural network (as well as a function f, a set A, and a probability density function ρ) for which the mean squared error function $F(\mathbf{w})$ is not well defined for some, but not all, values of $\mathbf{w}$. Define a network for which $F(\mathbf{w})$ is not well defined for any value of $\mathbf{w}$. [HINT: The first network will have to have a really serious pathology. The second network will have to be a mathematical monstrosity.]

5.1.3. Given a neural network consisting of a single ADALINE processing element with four non-bias inputs (see Section 3.3), with an arbitrary fixed weight vector $\mathbf{w}$, where the unaugmented input vectors $\underline{\mathbf{x}}$ are chosen uniformly randomly from the unit cube $[0, 1]^4 \subset \mathbf{R}^4$, find an infinite sequence of example vectors $\mathbf{x}_1, \mathbf{x}_2, \ldots, \mathbf{x}_k, \ldots$ for which the sum of Equation 5.1 will not converge. [Hint: make the average oscillate forever.]

---

[3] Gauss invented regression to predict the orbit of the asteroid Ceres from an incomplete set of observations (it had been discovered by astronomers only a few days before it entered daylight). Gauss' fame was launched when Ceres was found again several months later (when it could again be seen at night), exactly where he had predicted it would reappear.

5.2 Kolmogorov's Theorem

In 1957 mathematician Andrei Kolmogorov published an astounding theorem concerning the representation of arbitrary continuous functions from the n-dimensional cube $[0, 1]^n$ to the real numbers R in terms of functions of only one variable [148]. This theorem intrigued a number of mathematicians and over the next twenty years several improvements to it were discovered, notably those of G. G. Lorentz [163, 213].

The Kolmogorov theorem was discovered during a friendly mathematical duel between Kolmogorov and his colleague mathematician V. I. Arnol'd in which they each tried to be the first to put to rest the remaining questions surrounding the 13th problem of Hilbert (a prominent mathematician who, in 1900, announced a list of difficult problems for 20th century mathematicians to solve). In a series of papers in the mid to late 1950's Kolmogorov and Arnol'd fought their battle, each one-upping the other in successive papers. In the end, Kolmogorov won. His result was a mathematical supernova.

Although Kolmogorov's theorem is both powerful and shocking (many mathematicians do not believe it can be true when they first see it), it has not been found to be of much value in mathematics in terms of its utility for proving other important theorems. However, as we shall see in this section, this is *not* the case in neurocomputing!

Kolmogorov's mapping neural network existence theorem is stated below.

■ *THEOREM 1* **Kolmogorov's Mapping Neural Network Existence Theorem** *Given any continuous function $f : [0, 1]^n \longrightarrow \mathbf{R}^m$, $f(\mathbf{x}) = \mathbf{y}$, f can be implemented exactly by a three-layer feedforward neural network having n fanout processing elements in the first (**x** - input) layer, (2n+1) processing elements in the middle layer, and m processing elements in the top (**y** - output) layer (see Figure 5.3).* ■

The proof of this theorem relies directly upon the result of David Sprecher [213], which was an improvement on Kolmogorov's original result. The proof (which can be found in [109]) will not be presented here, because it does not provide any technologically useful insights.

As stated in the theorem, the *Kolmogorov mapping network* consists of three layers of processing elements (see Figure 5.3). The processing elements on the bottom layer are fanout units that simply distribute the input **x** vector components to the processing elements of the second layer. The processing elements of the middle or *hidden* layer (the term hidden means that this layer does not directly receive inputs from the outside world, nor does it provide outputs directly to the outside world — thus it is hidden from external view) implement the following transfer function:

$$z_k = \sum_{j=1}^{n} \lambda^k \, \psi(x_j + k\epsilon) + k$$

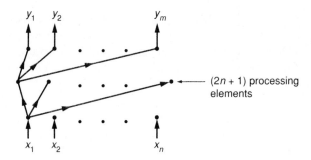

Fig. 5.3. • Topology of the Kolmogorov network. This network can *exactly* implement any continuous mapping. The network has three layers. The first layer consists of n input fanout units. The second layer consists of $2n+1$ semilinear units (i.e., the transfer function of these units is similar to a linear weighted sum). Finally, the third (output) layer has m processing elements with highly nonlinear transfer functions.

where the real constant λ and the continuous real monotonically increasing function ψ are independent of f (although they do depend on n). The constant ϵ is a rational number $0 < \epsilon \leq \delta$, where δ is an arbitrarily chosen positive constant.

The m top layer processing elements (*output units*) have the following transfer functions:

$$y_i = \sum_{k=1}^{2n+1} g_i(z_k)$$

where the functions g_i $i = 1, 2, \ldots, m$ are real and continuous (and depend on f and ϵ).

This is all that is known. No specific example of a function ψ and constant ϵ are known. No example of a g function is known. The proof of the theorem is not constructive, so it does not tell us how to determine these quantities. It is strictly an existence theorem. It tells us that such a three-layer mapping network must exist, but it doesn't tell us how to find it. Unfortunately, there does not appear to be too much hope that a method for finding the Kolmogorov network will be developed soon. Thus, the value of this result is its intellectual assurance that continuous vector mappings of a vector variable on the unit cube (actually, the theorem can be extended to apply to any *compact*, i.e., closed and bounded, set) can all be implemented *exactly* with a three-layer neural network.

5.2.1 Implications for Neurocomputing

Kolmogorov's Mapping Neural Network Existence Theorem is a statement that our quest for approximations of functions by neural networks is, at least in theory, sound. However, the direct usefulness of this result is doubtful, because no constructive method for developing the g_i functions is known.

I derived this theorem from Kolmogorov's original work (and improvements by others) in 1986 [111]. At the time it was interesting, because no other similar neural network performance guarantee had been found. Now there are even more powerful results, such as the backpropagation theorem presented in Section 5.3 below.

Exercises

5.2.1. How might Kolmogorov's theorem be thought of in terms of mathematical transformations? How can we visualize the action of the middle layer of the network, given its simple mathematical form and given that it depends only upon n and not on the choice of f? What about the top (output) layer? Try to construct a geometric picture of the action of the network.

5.2.2. Construct a Kolmogorov neural network (i.e., a network with transfer functions of the proper mathematical form) with two inputs and one output by specifying all of the transfer functions. Using a computer, plot the two-dimensional graph of the output (expressed as the height y) as a function of the two inputs (x_1 and x_2). Experiment to see how the shape of this surface changes as the g function is changed.

5.2.3. Try to guess why $2n + 1$ hidden layer processing elements are required (it is known that there are functions for which $2n$ will not suffice). State why this fact doesn't seem to have anything to do with linear algebra.

5.2.4. Could the function ψ possibly be the identity function? What implications would this have for the utility of the theorem?

5.2.5. Do you believe that a learning law for adaptively adjusting the g_i functions can ever be found? Give concrete reasons.

5.3 The Backpropagation Neural Network

The backpropagation neural network is one of the most important historical developments in neurocomputing. It is a powerful mapping network that has been successfully applied to a wide variety of problems ranging from credit application scoring to image compression.

Backpropagation has a colorful history. Apparently, it was originally introduced by Paul Werbos in 1974 [233], by David Parker in 1984/85 [186, 187, 188] and by David Rumelhart, Ronald Williams and other members of the "PDP group" in 1985 [11, 203, 204]. A mathematically similar recursive control algorithm was presented by Arthur Bryson and Yu-Chi Ho [29] in 1969. The primary learning law used can be shown to follow from the

Robbins/Monro technique introduced in 1951 [234, 197]. As with Kohonen learning, the earliest incarnation of backpropagation has probably not yet been found.

Notwithstanding its checkered history, there is no question that credit for developing backpropagation into a usable technique, as well as promulgation of the architecture to a large audience, rests entirely with Rumelhart and the other members of the PDP group [203]. Before their work, backpropagation was unappreciated and obscure. Today, it is a mainstay of neurocomputing.

5.3.1 Architecture of the Backpropagation Network

The backpropagation neural network architecture is a hierarchical design consisting of fully interconnected layers or *rows* of processing *units* (with each unit itself comprised of several individual processing elements, as will be explained below). The information processing operation that backpropagation networks are intended to carry out is the approximation of a bounded mapping or function $f : A \subset \mathbf{R}^n \longrightarrow \mathbf{R}^m$, from a compact subset A of n-dimensional Euclidean space to a bounded subset $f[A]$ of m-dimensional Euclidean space, by means of training on examples $(\mathbf{x}_1, \mathbf{y}_1), (\mathbf{x}_2, \mathbf{y}_2), \ldots, (\mathbf{x}_k, \mathbf{y}_k), \ldots$ of the mapping, where $\mathbf{y}_k = f(\mathbf{x}_k)$. As always, it will be assumed that such examples of a mapping f are generated by selecting $\mathbf{x}_k$ vectors randomly from A in accordance with a fixed probability density function $\rho(\mathbf{x})$. The operational use to which the network is to be put after training is also assumed to involve random selections of input vectors $\mathbf{x}$ in accordance with $\rho(\mathbf{x})$. The backpropagation architecture described in this section is the basic, classical version. Many variants of this basic form exist (see discussion below).

The macroscopic-scale detail of the backpropagation neural network architecture is shown in Figure 5.4. In general, the architecture consists of K rows of processing units, numbered from the bottom up beginning with 1. For simplicity, the terms *row* and *layer* will be used interchangeably in this section, even though each row will actually turn out to consist of two heterogeneous layers or slabs. The first layer consists of n fanout processing elements that simply accept the individual components x_i of the input vector $\mathbf{x}$ and distribute them, without modification, to all of the units of the second row. Each unit on each row receives the output signal of each of the units of the row below. This continues through all of the rows of the network until the final row. The final (K^{th}) row of the network consists of m units and produces the network's estimate $\mathbf{y}'$ of the correct output vector $\mathbf{y}$. For the purposes of this section it will always be assumed that $K \geq 3$. Rows 2 through $K - 1$ are called *hidden* rows (because they are not directly connected to the outside world).

Besides the feedforward connections mentioned above, each unit of each hidden row receives an "error feedback" connection from each of the units above it. However, as will be seen below, these are not merely fanned out copies of a broadcast output (as the forward connections are), but are each separate connections, each carrying a different signal. The details of the individual "units" (shown as rectangles in Figure 5.4) are revealed in Figure 5.5

(which depicts two units on adjacent rows and shows all of their connections — except those from the scheduling element, see below). Note that each unit is composed of a single *sun* processing element and several *planet* processing elements. Each planet produces an output signal that is distributed to both its sun and to the sun of the previous layer that supplied input to it. Each planet receives input from one of the suns of the previous layer as well as its own sun. The hidden row suns receive input from one of the planets of each of the suns on the next higher row. The planet that sends a connection back to a sun is the same one that receives an input from that sun. The output row suns receive the "correct answer" y_i for their component of the output vector on each training trial. As discussed in detail below, the network functions in two stages: a forward pass and a backward pass. A network scheduling processing element (not shown) sends signals to each of the slab scheduling processing elements. These slab scheduling processing elements tell each of their slab's processing elements when to apply its processing element transfer function, and whether to apply the forward pass part of it or the backward pass part of it. After the transfer function is applied, the output signal is latched to the value determined during the update. This value is therefore constant until the next update. The exact equations of the processing elements of the network are given in Table 5.1.

The scheduling of the network's operation during training consists of two "sweeps" through the network. The first sweep (the *forward pass*) starts by inserting the vector x_k into the network's first row, the *input* (or *fanout*) layer. The processing elements of the first layer transmit all of the components of x_k to all of the units of the second row of the network. The outputs of the units of row two are then transmitted to all of the units of row three, and so on, until finally the *m output units* (the units of the top, K^{th}, row) emit the components of the vector y'_k (the network's estimate of the desired output y_k). After the estimate y'_k is emitted, each of the output units is supplied with its component of the correct output vector y_k, starting the second, backward, sweep through the network (the *backward pass*). The output suns compute their δ_{Ki}'s and transmit these to their planets. The planets then update their Δ_{Kij} values (and update their weights, if Batch_size training trials have elapsed since the last update) and then transmit the values $w^{\text{old}}_{Kij}\delta_{Ki}$ to the suns of the previous row. This weight modification law is similar to Widrow learning. The superscript "old" indicates that the (non-updated) weight value used on the forward pass is used in this calculation. This process continues until the planets of row 2 (the first hidden layer) have been updated. The cycle can then be repeated. In short, each cycle consists of the inputs to the network "bubbling up" from the bottom to the top and then the errors "percolating down" from the top to the bottom. This process is continued until the network reaches a satisfactory level of performance, as measured per Section 5.1; or until the user gives up and decides to try a new starting weight set or a new network configuration (see below for a discussion of backpropagation network training). After successfully training the network to a suitably low level of error the network can then be

Forward Pass

Backward Pass

Planet j of sun i
  of row l (l = 2, 3, ..., K):

Input Used: $z_{(l-1)j}$ (where $z_{(l-1)0} \equiv 1.0$)

Input Used: z_{li} $(= \delta_{li})$

Weight Value Used: w_{lij}

Weight Value Used: w_{lij}

Local Memory Value Used: None

Local Memory Values Used: count,

Output: $w_{lij} z_{(l-1)j}$

Δ_{lij}

Weight and Local Memory Value Update
and Storage: None

Output: $w_{lij}^{old} \delta_{li}$

Weight and Local Memory Value
Update and Storage:

IF (count = batch_size)

THEN {
$$w_{lij}^{new} = w_{lij}^{old} + \alpha\Delta_{lij}/\text{batch\_size}$$
$$\Delta_{lij}^{new} = \delta_{li}z_{(l-1)j}$$
$$\text{count} = 1 \}$$

ELSE {
$$w_{lij}^{new} = w_{lij}^{old}$$
$$\Delta_{lij}^{new} = \Delta_{lij}^{old} + \delta_{li}z_{(l-1)j}$$
$$\text{count} = \text{count} + 1 \}$$

Hidden Sun i of row l (l = 2, 3, ..., K − 1):

Inputs Used: $w_{li0}z_{(l-1)0}, w_{li1}z_{(l-1)1}, \ldots,$
$$w_{liM_{(l-1)}}z_{(l-1)M_{(l-1)}}$$

Inputs Used: $w_{(l+1)1i}\delta_{(l+1)1},$
$$w_{(l+1)2i}\delta_{(l+1)2}, \ldots,$$
$$w_{(l+1)M_{(l+1)}i}\delta_{(l+1)M_{(l+1)}}$$

Local Memory Value Used: None

Local Memory Value Used: I_{li}

Output: $z_{li} = s(\sum_j w_{lij}z_{(l-1)j})$

Output: $z_{li} = \delta_{li}$

Local Memory Value Stored:

$$I_{li} \equiv \sum_j w_{lij}z_{(l-1)j}$$

$$\equiv s'(I_{li}) \sum_k w_{(l+1)ki}\delta_{(l+1)k}$$

Local Memory Value Stored:
None

Output Sun i of row l = K:

Inputs Used: $w_{Ki0}z_{(K-1)0}, w_{Ki1}z_{(K-1)1}, \ldots,$
$$w_{KiM_{(K-1)}}z_{(K-1)M_{(K-1)}}$$

Input Used: y_i

Local Memory Value Used: None

Local Memory Value Used: None

Output: $y_i' = z_{Ki} = \sum_j w_{Kij}z_{(K-1)j}$

Output: $z_{Ki} = \delta_{Ki}$

$$\equiv (y_i - y_i')$$

Local Memory Value Stored:
None

Local Memory Value Stored:
None

where $s(I) = 1/(1 + e^{-I})$ is the *sigmoid function* of the network, $s' = ds/dI$ is the first derivative of the sigmoid function, M_l is the number of units on row l, w_{lij} is the weight of planet j of unit i of row l, $z_{1i} = x_i$ (where x_i is the ith component of the input vector **x**), and the network's output signals z_{Ki} are equal to the components y_i' of the network's output vector **y**' — the network's estimate of the "correct" or "desired" output **y** (the components y_i of which are supplied to the network during each training trial).

Table 5.1• Processing element transfer functions for the backpropagation neural network architecture. Three types of processing element are used (planets, hidden suns, and output suns). For each processing element type the transfer function used on the forward pass of the network and the backward pass of the network is given. The backward pass only occurs on training trials.

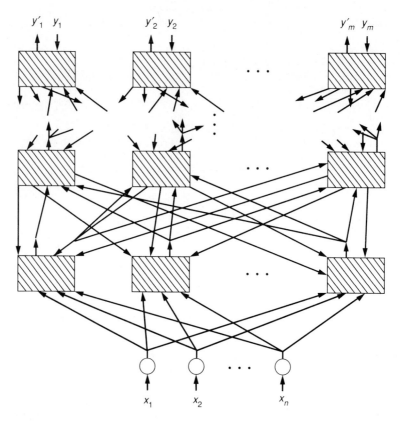

Fig. 5.4. • Macroscopic architecture of the backpropagation neural network. The boxes are called *units*. The detailed architecture of the units is elaborated in Figure 5.5. Each row can have any number of units desired, except the input row and the output row, which must have exactly n units and m units, respectively (because the input vector **x** is n-dimensional and the output vector **y**$'$ must be m-dimensional).

put through further operational testing to qualify it for deployment. If on-line training is not needed in the deployed version, the backward pass can be eliminated — allowing a considerable computational savings to be realized.

As pointed out by Gail Carpenter and Stephen Grossberg [33], the early forms of the backpropagation architecture were, in fact, not neural networks. They violated the restriction that all of the processing that occurs within a processing element must be localized. The backpropagation neural network architecture presented above (which I developed in 1986 — see [105]) eliminates this objection, while retaining the traditional mathematical form of the architecture.

5.3.2 Backpropagation Error Surfaces

This subsection discusses the backpropagation neural network mean squared error surface. First it is shown that the error function actually exists. Then some of its known properties are explored.

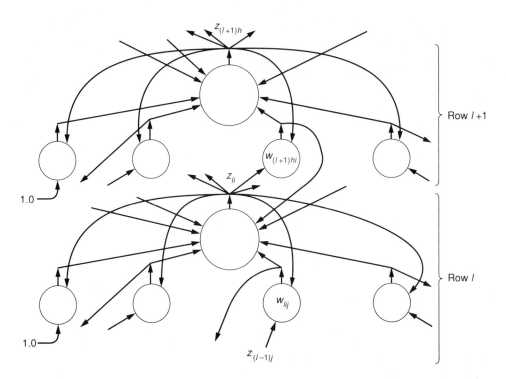

Fig. 5.5. • Architectural detail and interaction of two backpropagation network units on two adjacent rows (row l below and row $l + 1$ above). Each unit consists of a *sun* and several *planets*. Each hidden row sun sends its output to one planet of each unit of the next row. Each planet receives an input from the previous row (the *bias* planets all receive the constant input $z_{(l-1)0} \equiv 1.0$ from a single processing element which is not shown) sends a connection back to the sun that supplied that input. It is through these downward connections that the products of the errors times the weights ($w_{lij}\delta_{li}$) are "back-propagated."

First, let **w** be the network weight vector, with components consisting of the weights of all of the planets of the network, starting with the weight of the first planet of the first processing element of layer 2 (the first hidden layer) and ending with the weight of the last planet of the last unit of output layer K. To make things simple we will usually refer to the components of **w** as $w_1, w_2, \ldots$, rather than $w_{210}, w_{211}, \ldots$, although both indexing schemes will be used. To make our notation simple the vector $(z_{K1}, z_{K2}, \ldots, z_{Km})$ (the network's estimate **y**' of the correct output **y**) shall be called **B**. (This is the same as **Y** of Section 5.1). Note that **B** is a function of the input vector **x** and the network weight vector **w**. Thus, we will write **B(x, w)**. Let $(\mathbf{x}_k, \mathbf{y}_k)$ be the example used on the kth testing trial (i.e., $\mathbf{y}_k = f(\mathbf{x}_k)$). As before, the $\mathbf{x}_k$'s are drawn from A in accordance with the same fixed probability density function ρ used in the selection of the training examples.

Given the above situation, let $F_k = |f(\mathbf{x}_k) - \mathbf{B}(\mathbf{x}_k, \mathbf{w})|^2$. F_k is the square of the approximation error made by the network on the kth testing trial. For the purposes of the discussion below we shall assume that $\mathbf{w}$ is fixed. Then, as with Widrow learning, we define $F(\mathbf{w})$ to be

$$F(\mathbf{w}) \equiv \lim_{N \to \infty} \frac{1}{N} \sum_{k=1}^{N} F_k. \tag{5.3}$$

It is fairly easy to show (see Exercise 5.3.1) that this sum must almost surely converge to the expected value $F(\mathbf{w})$ of F_k. We call $F(\mathbf{w})$ the *mean squared error* function of the network; which is often just shortened to *error function*. Note that $F(\mathbf{w}) \geq 0$ because F is the average of non-negative quantities.

As discussed in Section 5.1, the *error surface* of a backpropagation network is the surface defined by the equation $F = F(\mathbf{w})$ in the $Q + 1$-dimensional space of vectors $(\mathbf{w}, F)$, where Q is the number of dimensions in the vector $\mathbf{w}$ (i.e., the number of planets in the network). The variable $\mathbf{w}$ ranges over the Q-dimensional space $\mathbf{R}^Q$ and for each $\mathbf{w}$ a non-negative surface height F is defined by $F(\mathbf{w})$. In other words, given any selection of weights $\mathbf{w}$, the network will make an average squared error $F(\mathbf{w})$ in its approximation of the function f. We now consider the shape of this error surface.

As will be shown below, the *generalized delta rule* learning law used with the backpropagation neural network has the property that, given any starting point $\mathbf{w}_0$ on the error surface that is not a minimum, the learning law will modify the weight vector $\mathbf{w}$ so that $F(\mathbf{w})$ will decrease. In other words, the learning law uses examples provided during training to decide how to modify the weight vector so that the network will do a better job of approximating the function f. In essence, it goes "downhill" from the starting point. The question then becomes: will this process eventually lead to a global minimum? Or will it lead to a local minimum or other difficulties? The answers to these questions all depend upon the shape of the error surface, which is discussed next.

Until recently, the shape of backpropagation error surfaces was largely a mystery. Three basic facts have emerged so far. First, experience has shown that many backpropagation error surfaces have extensive flat areas and troughs that have very little slope. In these areas it is necessary to move the weight value a considerable distance before a significant drop in error occurs. Since the slope is shallow it turns out that the generalized delta rule has a hard time determining which way to move the weight to reduce the error. Often, great numerical precision (e.g., 32-bit floating point) and patience (or a better learning law — see below) must be employed to make significant progress.

A second fact about backpropagation error surfaces is that they have many global minima. This is due to the fact that for each set of weights, there are many weight permutations that yield exactly the same overall network input/output function (see Exercise 5.3.2). In fact, each network weight vector $\mathbf{w}$ is equivalent to so many other weight vectors that the weights of the network collectively contain only a small amount of information (see Exercise 5.3.3).

Another basic fact about error surfaces that has emerged concerns the existence of local minima. Until recently, it was not known for certain whether backpropagation error surfaces have local minima at error levels above the levels of the global minima of the surfaces (due to weight permutations there are always many global minima). Experience suggested that such minima might not exist because usually when training failed to make downhill progress and the error level was high it was discovered that further patience (or the use of one of the training augmentations described below) would eventually lead to the weight moving away from what was clearly a shallow spot on the surface and onto a steeper part. Thus, it was somewhat surprising when John McInerney, Karen Haines, Steven Biafore, and I [168] discovered a local minimum (at a very high error level) in a backpropagation error surface in 1988. Finding this local minimum required a 12-hour run on a Cray-2 supercomputer.

In summary, three basic facts are known about backpropagation error surfaces. First, because of combinatoric permutations of the weights that leave the network input-output function unchanged, these functions typically have large numbers of global minima (which may lie at infinity for some problems). This causes the error surfaces to be highly degenerate and to have numerous "troughs." Secondly, error surfaces have a multitude of areas with shallow slopes in multiple dimensions simultaneously. These typically occur because particular combinations of weights cause the weighted sums of one or more hidden layer suns (with sigmoided outputs) to be large in magnitude. When this occurs the output of that sun (and therefore the value of F) is insensitive to small weight changes, since these simply move the weighted sum value back and forth along one of the shallow tails of the sigmoid function. Thirdly, it is now established that local minima do actually exist. Beyond these three facts, little is known. How many non-global local minima are there, compared to the number of global minima? Are such local minima excluded from regions near global minima? How large are the attractive basins of each of the different types of minima (the *attractive basin* of a minimum is the set of points from which the minimum will be reached by gradient descent)? What forms do the boundaries between attractive basins take? As the answers to these questions become available, our ability to use the backpropagation neural network will be increased even further.

5.3.3 Function Approximation with Backpropagation

The question of what functional forms can be approximated by neural networks has had pivotal importance in the history of neurocomputing, as discussed in Chapter 1.

The first clear insight into the versatility of neural networks for use in function approximation came with the discovery [109] of Kolmogorov's theorem (see Section 5.2). This result gave hope that neural networks would turn out to be able to approximate any function that arises in the real world.

Kolmogorov's theorem was a first step. The following result shows that the backpropagation network is itself able to implement any function of practical interest to any desired degree of accuracy. This result, and similar results, were discovered independently in 1987/1988 by myself [105] (stimulated by earlier work by Halbert White and A. Ronald Gallant [80]) and several other people, including Alan Lapedes and Robert Farber [156], Yann le Cun [159], Halbert White, Kurt Hornik and Maxwell Stinchcombe [125], B. Moore and Tomaso Poggio [173], and Bunpei Irie and Sei Miyake [128]. To provide definitions required in the statement of the theorem, we start with some background information.

Given any square-integrable function $g : [0, 1]^n \longrightarrow \mathbf{R}$ (i.e., any function for which $\int_{[0,1]^n} |g(\mathbf{x})|^2 d\mathbf{x}$ exists), it can be shown by the theory of Fourier series [58] that the series

$$\hat{g}(\mathbf{x}, N) = \sum_{\mathbf{k}} c_{\mathbf{k}} \exp(2\pi i \, \mathbf{k} \cdot \mathbf{x})$$

$$\equiv \sum_{k_1=-N}^{N} \sum_{k_2=-N}^{N} \cdots \sum_{k_n=-N}^{N} c_{k_1 k_2 \ldots k_n} \exp\left(2\pi i \sum_{q=1}^{n} k_q x_q\right) \quad (5.4)$$

where

$$c_{\mathbf{k}} \equiv c_{k_1 k_2 \ldots k_n} = \int_{[0,1]^n} g(\mathbf{x}) \, \exp(-2\pi i \, \mathbf{k} \cdot \mathbf{x}) \, d\mathbf{x} \quad (5.5)$$

converges to g in the sense that

$$\lim_{N \to \infty} \int_{[0,1]^n} |g(\mathbf{x}) - \hat{g}(\mathbf{x}, N)|^2 \, d\mathbf{x} = 0. \quad (5.6)$$

This is an example of the property of having the integral of the square of the error of approximation of one function by another go to zero. This property is described by the statement that the approximation can be achieved to within any desired degree of accuracy in the *mean squared error sense*. The following definition clarifies this terminology.

Given a function $f : [0, 1]^n \longrightarrow \mathbf{R}^m$, we say that f *belongs to* L_2 (or "*is* L_2") if each of f's coordinate functions is square-integrable on the unit cube. For functions of this class it is assumed that the $\mathbf{x}$ vectors are chosen uniformly in $[0, 1]^n$ (relaxing this condition is easy). Clearly if a vector function of a vector variable is in L_2 then each of its components can be approximated by its Fourier series to any desired degree of accuracy in the mean squared error sense. With this background as preamble, the backpropagation approximation theorem [105] is now presented.

■ **THEOREM 2** *Given any $\epsilon > 0$ and any L_2 function $f : [0, 1]^n \longrightarrow \mathbf{R}^m$, there exists a three-layer backpropagation neural network that can approximate f to within ϵ mean squared error accuracy.* ■

The proof of this theorem is carried out by showing that each of the sine waves in the Fourier series approximation of each component function of f can be approximated arbitrarily closely using some hidden layer units and a portion of the appropriate output unit's weighted sum. There are many subtle details that must be accounted for, but the proof is basically simple. The proof is omitted here, because it does not provide any significant enlightenment.

The space L_2 includes every function that could ever arise in a practical problem. For example, it includes the continuous functions and it includes all discontinuous functions that are piecewise continuous on a finite number of subsets of $[0, 1]^n$. L_2 also contains much nastier functions than these, but they are only of mathematical interest.

It is important to realize that although this theorem proves that "three layers are always enough," in solving real-world problems it is often essential to have four, five, or even more layers. This is because for many problems an approximation with three layers would require an impractically large number of hidden units, whereas an adequate solution can be obtained with a tractable network size by using more than three layers. Thus, the above result should not influence the process of selecting an appropriate backpropagation architecture for a real-world problem — except to provide the confidence that comes from knowing that an appropriate backpropagation architecture *must* exist.

Finally, although the above theorem guarantees the ability of a multilayer network *with the correct weights* to accurately implement an arbitrary L_2 function, it does not comment on whether or not these weights can be *learned* using any existing learning law. That is an open question.

5.3.4 Backpropagation Learning Laws

This subsection provides a derivation of the generalized delta rule.

The first step in the derivation is to recall that our goal is to move the $\mathbf{w}$ vector in a direction so that the value of F will be smaller at the new value. Obviously, the best approach would be to move in the $\mathbf{w}$ direction in which F is decreasing most rapidly. Assuming that F is differentiable, this direction of maximum decrease is given by $-\nabla_\mathbf{w} F(\mathbf{w}) = -\left(\frac{\partial F}{\partial w_1}, \frac{\partial F}{\partial w_2}, \dots, \frac{\partial F}{\partial w_Q}\right)$, where, again, there are Q weights in the network (i.e., the vector $\mathbf{w}$ has Q components). However, before proceeding with this line of thought it is essential to show that F is in fact differentiable. The proof of this is presented below, for those readers who would like to see the details.

First, note that because backpropagation networks are made up entirely of affine transformations and smooth sigmoid functions, $B(\mathbf{x}, \mathbf{w})$ is a C^∞ function of both $\mathbf{x}$ and $\mathbf{w}$ (i.e., its partial derivatives of all orders with respect to the components of $\mathbf{x}$ and $\mathbf{w}$ exist and are continuous) and the limits defining its derivatives all converge uniformly on compact sets. Thus, F_k, as a function of $\mathbf{w}$, inherits these same properties, since $F_k = |f(\mathbf{x}_k) - B(\mathbf{x}_k, \mathbf{w})|^2$, and since $f(\mathbf{x}_k)$ is a constant vector. What we will need later on are two facts: first, that F is a differentiable function, and second, that $\nabla_\mathbf{w} F(\mathbf{w}) = \lim_{N \to \infty} \frac{1}{N} \sum_{k=1}^{N} \nabla_\mathbf{w} F_k(\mathbf{w})$

almost surely. These two facts can be simultaneously established. First, fix $\mathbf{w}$ and, given an arbitrary test set example sequence $\{\mathbf{x}_1, \mathbf{x}_2, \ldots \mathbf{x}_k, \ldots\}$ (as defined above), let

$$G_i(\Gamma, \Delta) = \frac{1}{\lfloor 1/|\Gamma| \rfloor} \sum_{k=1}^{\lfloor 1/|\Gamma| \rfloor} \left(\frac{F_k(\mathbf{w} + \Delta \sigma_i) - F_k(\mathbf{w})}{\Delta} \right), \tag{5.7}$$

where σ_i is the unit basis vector along the ith coordinate axis in weight space, where the real variables Γ and Δ both range over a compact neighborhood U of zero (with zero removed) and where $\lfloor u \rfloor$ (the *floor* function) is the largest integer less than or equal to u. Because the limits that define the partial derivatives of F_k all converge uniformly on compact sets in weight space the limit

$$\lim_{\Delta \to 0} G_i(\Gamma, \Delta) = \lfloor 1/|\Gamma| \rfloor \sum_{k=1}^{\lfloor 1/|\Gamma| \rfloor} \frac{\partial F_k}{\partial w_i} \tag{5.8}$$

converges uniformly on U. Further, using the result of Exercise 5.3.1, for each Δ in U the limit

$$\lim_{\Gamma \to 0} G_i(\Gamma, \Delta) = \left(\frac{F(\mathbf{w} + \Delta \sigma_i) - F(\mathbf{w})}{\Delta} \right), \tag{5.9}$$

converges almost surely. Thus, by the elementary theory of iterated limits [149] the double limits

$$\lim_{\Gamma \to 0} \lim_{\Delta \to 0} G_i(\Gamma, \Delta) \tag{5.10}$$

and

$$\lim_{\Delta \to 0} \lim_{\Gamma \to 0} G_i(\Gamma, \Delta) \tag{5.11}$$

both exist and are equal, almost surely. Thus, we have shown that, almost surely, F is a differentiable function and that

$$\nabla_{\mathbf{w}} F(\mathbf{w}) = \lim_{N \to \infty} \frac{1}{N} \sum_{k=1}^{N} \nabla_{\mathbf{w}} F_k(\mathbf{w}).$$

Given these preliminaries, the generalized delta rule is now derived. The basic idea is to derive a formula for calculating

$$-\nabla_{\mathbf{w}} F(\mathbf{w}) = - \left(\frac{\partial F}{\partial w_1}, \frac{\partial F}{\partial w_2}, \ldots, \frac{\partial F}{\partial w_Q} \right)$$

by using training examples. To do this, we focus on the calculation of $\frac{\partial F}{\partial w_p}$. We first note that, using the above results,

$$\frac{\partial F(\mathbf{w})}{\partial w_p} = \lim_{N \to \infty} \frac{1}{N} \sum_{k=1}^{N} \frac{\partial F_k(\mathbf{w})}{\partial w_p} \tag{5.12}$$

but, reverting to full weight indices (where the pth weight has full index lij), and using the chain rule

$$\frac{\partial F_k(\mathbf{w})}{\partial w_p} \equiv \frac{\partial F_k(\mathbf{w})}{\partial w_{lij}} = \frac{\partial F_k}{\partial I_{li}} \frac{\partial I_{li}}{\partial w_{lij}}, \tag{5.13}$$

because any functional dependence of F_k on w_{lij} must be through I_{li}. If we now define δ_{li}^k to be $\frac{\partial F_k}{\partial I_{li}}$ and evaluate $\frac{\partial I_{li}}{\partial w_{lij}}$ in terms of the formula for I_{li}, we get

$$\frac{\partial F_k(\mathbf{w})}{\partial w_p} = \delta_{li}^k \frac{\partial}{\partial w_{lij}} \left(\sum_q w_{liq} z_{(l-1)q}^k \right) = \delta_{li}^k z_{(l-1)j}^k, \tag{5.14}$$

where z_{lj}^k is the output signal of the jth sun of the lth row on the forward pass of the kth training trial. If the lth row is not the output layer, then

$$\delta_{li}^k \equiv \frac{\partial F_k}{\partial I_{li}} = \frac{\partial F_k}{\partial z_{li}} \frac{\partial z_{li}}{\partial I_{li}} = \frac{\partial F_k}{\partial z_{li}} s'(I_{li}) \tag{5.15}$$

where $s'()$ is the ordinary derivative of the sigmoid function s with respect to its argument. If it is the output layer, then

$$\delta_{li}^k = \frac{\partial F_k}{\partial z_{li}}, \tag{5.16}$$

since $z_{li} = I_{li}$. Thus, if row l is the output layer, then

$$\frac{\partial F_k}{\partial z_{li}} = \frac{\partial}{\partial z_{li}} \sum_{p=1}^{m} \left(y_p^k - z_{lp}^k \right)^2 = -2 \left(y_i^k - z_{li}^k \right), \tag{5.17}$$

where y_p^k is the pth component of $\mathbf{y}_k$. Thus, for the output layer units

$$\delta_{li}^k = -2 \left(y_i^k - z_{li}^k \right). \tag{5.18}$$

If row l is a hidden layer, then by using the multi-dimensional chain rule, we get

$$\frac{\partial F_k}{\partial z_{li}} = \sum_{p=1}^{M_{(l+1)}} \frac{\partial F_k}{\partial I_{(l+1)p}} \frac{\partial I_{(l+1)p}}{\partial z_{li}}. \tag{5.19}$$

Thus, if we combine Equations 5.15 and 5.19 for the hidden layer units

$$\delta_{li}^k = s'(I_{li}) \sum_p \delta_{(l+1)p}^k w_{(l+1)pi}. \tag{5.20}$$

So, substituting these results back into the formula for $\frac{\partial F}{\partial w_{lij}}$ gives

$$\frac{\partial F}{\partial w_p} = \lim_{N \to \infty} \frac{1}{N} \sum_{k=1}^{N} \frac{\partial F_k}{\partial w_{lij}} = \lim_{N \to \infty} \frac{1}{N} \sum_{k=1}^{N} \delta_{li}^k \, z_{(l-1)j}^k. \qquad (5.21)$$

Thus, to move $\mathbf{w}$ in a direction that will decrease F (and thus improve the accuracy by which the network approximates the function f), all we need do is move in the direction $-\nabla_{\mathbf{w}} F(\mathbf{w})$. The amount to be moved must be small, to avoid the problem of overshooting the bottom of the hill. Thus, a reasonable learning law is

$$\mathbf{w}^{\text{new}} = \mathbf{w}^{\text{old}} - \alpha \nabla_{\mathbf{w}} F(\mathbf{w}), \qquad (5.22)$$

or

$$w_{lij}^{\text{new}} = w_{lij}^{\text{old}} - \alpha \lim_{N \to \infty} \frac{1}{N} \sum_{k=1}^{N} \delta_{li}^k \, z_{(l-1)j}^k \qquad (5.23)$$

where $\alpha > 0$ is a small constant called the *learning rate*. This is the *generalized delta rule* learning law.

The rigorous generalized delta rule is approximated by the learning law used in the backpropagation architecture presented above, which substitutes a finite averaging sum of *batch_size* terms for the infinite-size average of the formula. Since we know that the limit converges this *batching* version of the learning law will clearly be acceptable, assuming *batch_size* is chosen large enough.

A number of variants of this learning law (and of other parts of the backpropagation neural network architecture) have been presented [35, 127]. One learning law variant in common use is

$$w_{lij}^{\text{new}} = w_{lij}^{\text{old}} - \alpha \, \delta_{li}^k \, z_{(l-1)j}^k. \qquad (5.24)$$

This *jump every time* variant of the generalized delta rule is the backpropagation analog of Widrow learning. The proof that this law also carries out gradient descent on the backpropagation error surface was provided by Morris Hirsch [121] (see [234] for further details). Another common variant is the *momentum* version of the above law, in exact analogy with the momentum version of Widrow learning (i.e., replacing Equation 5.24 with Equation 3.25 — see [203] for details).

The above learning laws suffer from the same basic problem: they move downhill in short jumps. Thus, even if the network's initial weight vector lies within the attractive basin of a global minimum of the error surface, getting to the bottom can take many jumps. Further, the magnitude of the gradient vector gets small when a shallow area is reached — thus *shortening* the jumps that are taken — which is exactly the reverse of what is needed.

Many other backpropagation network learning laws have been developed. The general goal is to provide a faster descent to the bottom of the error surface. One line of investigation [228, 196, 24] is exploring the use of approximations to the pseudoinverse of the Hessian matrix $H = [(\partial^2 F / \partial w_i \partial w_j)]$ to calculate individually variable learning rates (α values in Equation (34)) for each weight w_{lij}. The underlying concept is to use Newton's method for finding a place where $\nabla_{\mathbf{w}} F(\mathbf{w}) = 0$. This method expands the error function $F(\mathbf{w})$ in a Taylor series and then truncates this series after the third term to yield $F(\mathbf{w}) \equiv F(\mathbf{w}_0) + [\nabla_{\mathbf{w}} F(\mathbf{w})]|_{\mathbf{w}_0} (\mathbf{w} - \mathbf{w}_0) + (\mathbf{w} - \mathbf{w}_0)^{\mathrm{T}} H|_{\mathbf{w}_0} (\mathbf{w} - \mathbf{w}_0)$, where, again, H is the Hessian. Setting the gradient of this quantity to zero and solving for $\mathbf{w}^{\text{new}}$ yields $\mathbf{w}^{\text{new}} = \mathbf{w}_o - H^+ \nabla F$. Under some circumstances, the new value of $\mathbf{w}$ will be a very intelligent jump in the right direction, leading to a large decrease in F. In other situations, it does not work so well. Calculating H^+ is difficult. So far, this work shows promise, but a major advance in convergence speed has yet to be realized for arbitrary problems. Another approach that shows promise in early tests is the incremental network growing technique of Timur Ash [17]. This method starts with a small number of units in each hidden layer and adds additional units in response to changes in the error level (as measured using test data). Many other methods have been proposed, many of which provide a significant increase in descent speed over the laws discussed here (see [211] for a discussion of a set of these improved laws).

Finally, it is important to note that this section has examined only one (albeit perhaps the most important) variant of the backpropagation neural network architecture. Other important variants exist. Examples of these include architectures in which connections skip layers [203], recurrent architectures [203, 189, 239] (also see Section 6.1), and the "sigma-pi" higher order architectures [203].

Exercises

5.3.1. Show that the random variable $F_k = |f(\mathbf{x}_k) - \mathbf{B}(\mathbf{x}_k, \mathbf{w})|^2$ is bounded. Show that it must therefore almost surely have a well defined mean or expectation value given by Equation 5.3

5.3.2. Given a backpropagation neural network with two or more inputs and outputs and two or more hidden units, demonstrate that there exist weight permutations that yield an unchanged input/output function. Show that this fact implies that backpropagation error surfaces will have numerous global minima.

5.3.3. Given a backpropagation neural network in which there are Q weights each quantized to n bits (fixed point or floating point), with K distinct weight vector permutations that leave the overall input/output function of the network unchanged, calculate the effective average number of bits of information storage per weight vector.

5.3.4. Establish Equation 5.14.

5.3.5. Demonstrate that Equation 5.18 is correct.

5.3.6. If we add connections from all of the input units to all of the units of some layer beyond layer 2, what learning law must be used for the new planets that are added?

5.3.7. If we add connections from all of the suns of some hidden layer to all of the units of a layer 2 or more layers above, how must the learning law of the planets of the suns supplying these new connections be changed? [Hint: generalize Equation 5.20.]

5.4 Self-Organizing Map

The self-organizing map neural network was developed by Teuvo Kohonen during the period 1979 – 1982 [144, 145]. Kohonen's work in self-organizing maps and the strongly related earlier work of David Willshaw and Christoph von der Malsburg [242] and Stephen Grossberg [94] were both inspired by the pioneering self-organizing map studies of von der Malsburg [223]. Historically, the self-organizing map was one of the most important neural networks discovered before the major expansion of neurocomputing in the mid-1980s.

5.4.1 Architecture of the Self-Organizing Map Neural Network

The self-organizing map is an unusual mapping network in that the mapping it approximates is defined implicitly, not explicitly. Instead of learning a mapping $f : A \subset \mathbf{R}^n \longrightarrow \mathbf{R}^m$, from some arbitrary bounded subset A of n-dimensional Euclidean space to m-dimensional Euclidean space by means of supervised training on examples of the mapping, the self-organizing map essentially learns a continuous topological mapping $f : B \subset \mathbf{R}^n \longrightarrow C \subset \mathbf{R}^m$ by means of self-organization driven by $\mathbf{y}$ examples in C, where B is a rectangular subset of n-dimensional Euclidean space and C is a bounded subset of m-dimensional Euclidean space, upon which a probability density function $\rho(\mathbf{y})$ is defined. The amazing thing about the self-organizing map neural network is that it develops this continuous topological mapping by self-organization on $\mathbf{y}$ examples chosen from C at random with respect to the probability density function ρ.

Although there are several embodiments of the self-organizing map neural network, the one shown in Figure 5.6, is perhaps the most commonly encountered. We shall work up to the definition of a more general self-organizing map in stages. The first stage is the situation illustrated in Figure 5.6. On the left side of Figure 5.6 is the "feeler" mechanism. This mechanism consists of a two-jointed arm with a pointer at the end. This arm, which operates in a two-dimensional plane, has a shoulder joint and elbow joint, with the shoulder joint

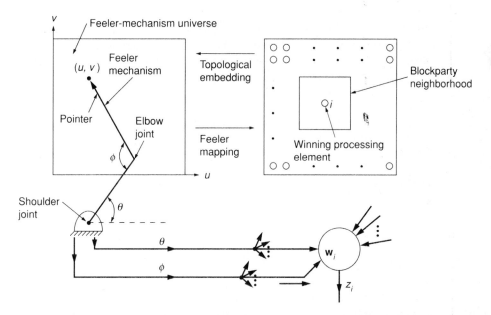

Fig. 5.6. • Self-organizing map training process. A point (u, v) is chosen at random in the feeler mechanism universe. The pointer is then moved to this point — sending signals θ and ϕ to the network (which then adapts to these values). This process continues through many thousands of trials.

pinned at a fixed location. Both of these joints are equipped with angle sensors and the angles θ and ϕ shown in Figure 5.6 can be read out at any time.

The pointer of the feeler mechanism can move to any position (u, v) within the rectangular "universe" of the feeler mechanism, as shown in Figure 5.6. At each position in the universe, the angles θ and ϕ are uniquely defined by the coordinates (u, v) of the pointer, and vice versa (the pointer elbow joint angle cannot exceed 180°, much like a human elbow joint). Further, notice that two nearby points in the universe generate angles that are close to one another, and vice versa (i.e., the mapping is continuous). Of course, the mapping from the angles (θ, ϕ) to the pointer coordinates (u, v) is highly nonlinear.

The self-organizing map neural network is shown on the right side of Figure 5.6. It consists of a rectangular array of N processing elements. For the moment, we will assume that both the feeler mechanism universe and the rectangular array of processing elements are squares.

The square processing element array at the right of Figure 5.6 consists of N processing elements, each of which receives the angle outputs of the feeler mechanism. In other words, each processing element receives the same input vector (θ, ϕ) from the feeler mechanism. Each processing element of the network has the form shown at the bottom right of Figure 5.6. A weight vector $\mathbf{w}_i$ (with two real-number components) is assigned to the input vector from the feeler mechanism. Each processing element also receives an input from each other processing element. These are used to implement a competition mechanism that will be described below. To keep the exposition concise, the mathematical details specifying how the processing element transfer function carries out the competition processing will not be described here. Exercises 5.4.1, 5.4.2, and 5.4.3 flesh out some of these details.

The output of each processing element is z_i (only the use of this output signal for non-competition processing will be described here).

The end goal of this particular embodiment of the self-organizing map is to have the neural network operate as a position indicator for the pointer of the feeler mechanism. Specifically, if the pointer is moved to the upper left hand corner of the universe, then the response of the (properly trained) network will be to have the processing element in the upper left hand corner of the rectangular network array have an output signal of 1 and all other processing elements have output signals of 0. Similarly, if the pointer is moved to the lower right hand corner, then the lower right processing element will have an output of 1 and all other processing elements will have an output of 0. In other words, no matter where we move the pointer within the universe, the appropriately placed processing element in the neural network will have its output signal near 1 and all of the other processing elements will have output signals of 0. If this can be arranged, the neural network will then have formed a Euclidean map of the feeler mechanism universe, even though the only inputs to the network are the non-Euclidean feeler mechanism joint angles. In fact, the self-organizing map can learn to carry out this function quite effectively. Our first job will be to understand how the training process leads to this desirable result. Following this, generalizations of this result and a discussion of its significance will be presented in the next subsection.

Training of the self-organizing map neural network begins by scrambling the weight values. Typically, the components of the two-dimensional weights $\mathbf{w}_i$ are selected uniformly randomly from a small neighborhood surrounding a fixed pair of angles representing a point near the center of the feeler mechanism universe. Training of the network then proceeds in a sequence of discrete self-organization training trials. At the beginning of each trial, a point (u, v) within the universe is selected uniformly at random. The feeler mechanism is then moved to position the pointer at this uniformly randomly chosen point. The joint angles θ and ϕ are then read out and supplied to all of the processing elements of the network. The Euclidean distance between the stored weight vector $\mathbf{w}_i$ of each processing element, and the input angle vector (θ, ϕ) is then measured. The processing elements of the network then compete with one another (as discussed above and in Exercises 5.4.1, 5.4.2, and 5.4.3) to determine which processing element's $\mathbf{w}_i$ is closest to (θ, ϕ). The processing element with the closest matching $\mathbf{w}_i$ is then declared the *winner*. The winning processing element has its output signal z_i set equal to 1. All other processing element output signals are set to 0.

Once the winning processing element is chosen, this processing element then holds a weight adjustment "block party." In other words, all of the processing elements that lie within a rectangular neighborhood surrounding the winning processing element are allowed to adjust their weights. Processing elements that are outside the block party do not adjust their weights. The weight adjustment law used by the processing elements within the block party is simply Kohonen learning:

$$\mathbf{w}_i^{\text{new}} = \alpha_i(\mathbf{z}, t)(\theta, \phi) + [1 - \alpha_i(\mathbf{z}, t)]\mathbf{w}_i^{\text{old}}. \tag{5.25}$$

The learning rate $\alpha_i(\mathbf{z}, t)$ is dependent on how far from the center of the block party neighborhood processing element i lies and also on time. The α value for the winning processing elements starts out near 1.0 at the beginning of training. The α values for other processing elements within the block party neighborhood fall off as a function of distance from the center (i.e., with distance from the winning processing element). In fact, the block party neighborhood can be defined by simply setting the $\alpha_i(z, t)$ values for processing elements outside the neighborhood to 0.

As time progresses, the block party neighborhood size shrinks (its initial size is a good fraction of the size of the entire slab) and the α values within the neighborhood also decrease towards zero. Both the shrinkage of the neighborhood and the decrease in the α values occur very slowly. Linear decrease of these values with time seems to work well.

Following the adjustment of the weights of the processing elements within the block party neighborhood, a new point in the feeler mechanism universe is selected uniformly at random, and the whole process begins again. This sequence of self-organizing training trials continues until the weight adjustments become negligibly small. At that point, the network is considered trained and can then be evaluated.

In practice, the self-organizing map is subject to the same problem as all other Kohonen learning systems: namely, the lack of conformity to the desired probability density function. Again, as in the discussion presented in Section 3.4, the conscience mechanism can be used to fix this problem.

The mathematical theory of the self-organizing map has not yet been worked out in general (although Kohonen has presented a theory of the one-dimensional case [141, 145]). As we will see in the next subsection, any such theory will have to take into account the fact that by changing the learning constants as a function of time, the response of the network to the training data alters correspondingly as a function of time. This feature of the self-organizing map neural network complicates attempts to build a mathematical explanation of its operation.

The next subsection reviews some examples of network configurations that can result from this training process. The intermediate states that the network goes through during training are also discussed.

5.4.2 Examples of the Operation of the Self-Organizing Map
This subsection presents examples of the operation of the self-organizing map. To make these examples clear, a specialized graphic representation developed by

Kohonen [141] will be used. This representation depends upon the fact that the weight vector in each of the processing elements of the network corresponds to a specific feeler mechanism position in the feeler mechanism universe — namely, the position at which the Euclidean distance between the angle vector (θ, ϕ) and the weight vector w_i is minimized. For weight vectors corresponding to feeler mechanism positions inside the feeler mechanism universe, this distance can be brought to zero. For weight vectors corresponding to feeler mechanism positions that would place the pointer outside the universe, the nearest point inside the universe would be selected. Thus, each processing element has associated with it a unique point in the universe that represents the current value of its weight vector.

To represent the points associated with the processing element weight vectors of the network, we will use an extra copy of the feeler mechanism universe; with the feeler mechanism itself removed. We will place a dot at the position of each of the weight vector points. Further, we will connect certain of these dots together with straight line segments. The dot corresponding to a particular processing element will be connected to the dots corresponding to the processing elements in the network that lie directly above, directly below, directly to the right, and directly to the left of the processing element. Thus, the dot of each processing element in the interior of the network will have four line segments connected to it. Dots associated with processing elements on the sides of the rectangular network array will have only three lines connected to them. Finally, the four dots corresponding to processing elements in the corners of the neural network processing element array will have only two lines connected to them. By using this graphic representation, we can visually represent the learning process of the self-organizing map neural network. Kohonen has used this graphic representation very effectively by making movies that show the movement of the dots as training progresses. In a typical movie, there will be approximately 100 training cycles between frames.

Figure 5.7 illustrates four frames from a "Kohonen movie." The starting configuration of the self-organizing map neural network is shown in the upper left hand corner of Figure 5.7. To dramatize the capability of the network, the weights are initially chosen so that they congregate in a cluster at the center of the feeler mechanism universe. After 20 feeler coordinate pairs have been presented to the network, the situation has evolved as shown in the upper right hand corner of Figure 5.7. Clearly the weight vectors have been "moved out" from the center of the universe in a manner that illustrates the topological continuity of the process. Following 100 training cycles, the weights have evolved to the positions shown in the lower left hand corner of Figure 5.7. While this is certainly not the desired final configuration, it is obviously well on its way. Finally, after 100,000 training cycles, the network achieves the configuration in the lower right hand corner of Figure 5.7. This configuration is clearly very close to that which was desired at the outset; namely, regardless of where the pointer moves within the feeler mechanism universe, the network's response will be appropriate. In other words, a Euclidean topological map of the feeler mechanism universe has been

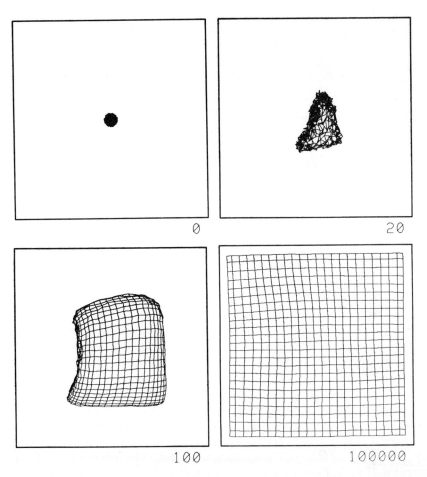

Fig. 5.7. • Four frames from a Kohonen self-organizing map neural network movie.

created by the self-organizing map neural network. The amazing thing about this map is the fact that it is derived by self-organization without the use of any explicit knowledge of the non-linear relationship between the angle coordinates (θ, ϕ) and the Euclidean feeler mechanism universe coordinates (u, v).

In order to obtain the results shown in Figure 5.7, the initial positions of the weights must be such that the "majority" of them are in the proper orientation relative to the final desired map. In other words, the weights that should eventually show up in the upper left hand corner of the universe should generally start in the upper left hand corner of the cluster, and so on. If one begins with a truly randomized weight vectors, then the outcome will very likely not correspond to that shown in Figure 5.7. One possibility is that a regular mesh will develop, but that it will be turned 90°, 180°, or 270° to the desired orientation. Another possibility is that the mesh will get twisted during the development as

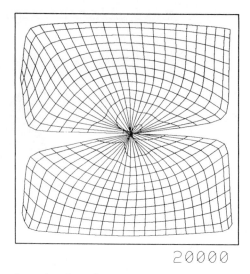

20000

Fig. 5.8. • Example of a twisted mesh.

shown in Figure 5.8. This was illustrated by one segment of Kohonen's original movie (shown, for example, at the 1985 annual meeting of the Optical
Society of America in Washington, D. C.). In this segment of the movie, one
witnesses the network becoming twisted during the training process and then
futilely struggling to untwist itself as it expands. Kohonen makes the point that
if the self-organizing map has any relevance to biology, it illustrates why it is so
important for genetics to provide a basically correct topological lay-out for the
nerve axon fascicles which later self-organize into precise topological mappings
(such as the somatosensory map connected with the sense of touch and the
movement of muscles, the tonotopic mapping of sounds onto the primary auditory cortex, and the log-polar mapping of the retina onto primary visual cortex).
In the end, whether it has biological relevance or not, the self-organizing map
provides us with a powerful tool for dealing with point sets with complicated
geometry.

Notice that when we utilize Kohonen's scheme for representing the weight
vectors in the feeler mechanism universe, this could be thought of as an embedding of the neural network array (and, by extension, the rectangular Euclidean
region in which it is contained) into the topological space of the feeler mechanism universe. In other words, after it is trained, the self-organizing map neural
network implicitly defines a continuous topological embedding map of the rectangular neural network array into the topological space of the feeler mechanism
universe. Naturally, this map operates in the opposite direction from the feeler
mapping that translates the position of the pointer into a corresponding neural
network activation (see Figure 5.6). This concept of an induced topological
embedding map will now be explored further by means of some additional examples.

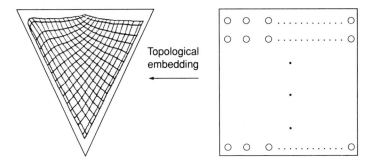

Fig. *5.9.* • Kohonen movie frame showing the induced mapping from a rectangular neural network array to a triangular region of $\mathbf{R}^2$.

Figures 5.9 and 5.10 show two additional examples of topological embedding maps induced by trained self-organizing map neural networks. In Figure 5.9, the same neural network shown in Figure 5.6 has been trained by using a slightly different set of training examples. In this instance, the examples were chosen uniformly at random from a triangular region inside the feeler mechanism universe. Thus, the only examples ever seen by the network came from the inside of this triangle. When we examine the weight vector mesh that results, we see that the network has been forced to find a way to embed the originally rectangular mesh inside the triangular region while still preserving topological continuity. Notice that three of the vertices of the rectangular mesh are located at the vertices of the triangle, while the fourth vertex is located along the upper left side of the triangle. Further notice that the rectangular mesh has been embedded in such a way that the area of each mesh rectangle is approximately equal. This is not an accident. In fact, for any set of points upon which a uniform probability density function is used to select examples, the self-organizing map will yield a topological embedding which (at least approximately) has this property. As indicated above, feeler mechanism universe subsets for which a non-uniform probability density function is used can also be accommodated if the conscience learning version of the Kohonen learning law is used instead of Equation 5.25 (see Section 3.4).

In Figure 5.10, a further variation of the self-organizing map is illustrated. In this situation, the self-organizing map neural network that is used is no longer a 2-dimensional rectangular array of processing elements. Instead, it is simply a long linear array. Thus, a topological embedding of this array would take the form of a line. This is indeed the case, as can be seen in the left side of Figure 5.10 (the training examples were again chosen uniformly randomly from the same triangle as in the example of Figure 5.9). Notice that the result is a topological embedding of the linear array of processing elements into the triangle as a continuous area-filling curve. Again, the numerical density of weight vectors per unit area is approximately constant.

Figures 5.9 and 5.10 illustrate the point that the feeler mechanism is not in itself a crucial element of the self-organizing map. In fact, virtually any system

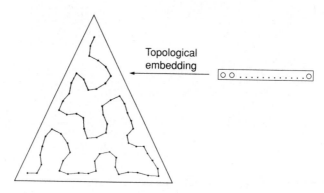

Fig. 5.10. • Kohonen movie frame showing the induced mapping from a long linear neural network array to a triangular region of $\mathbf{R}^2$. The result is an area filling curve.

of coordinates for expressing the example points can be used as long as they are continuous and free of singularities. The action of the self-organizing map is to spread out the weight vectors in the example topological space in such a way that two conditions are met: first, the number density of the weights in the target space is approximately proportional to the probability density used for selecting the examples. Secondly, the mapping from the rectangular grid of processing elements (actually, this grid does not even have to be rectangular) into the target space, must be topologically continuous. It is these two attributes that characterize the self-organizing map.

Exercises

5.4.1. Devise a processing element transfer function component to implement the competition between the self-organizing map processing elements to discover the one with the $\mathbf{w}_i$ vector that most closely matches the input from the feeler mechanism. During this competition, you can utilize the processing element output signal z_i any way you would like, and you may assume that the network is fully interconnected. However, at the end of the competition process, the winning processing element output signals z_i must be equal to 1 and all of the others must be 0. Both discrete time and continuous time approaches are allowed.

5.4.2. At the end of the competition process, the winning processing element has its output signal set to 1 and all others set to 0. Devise a method for each processing element in the network to decide what its learning rate $\alpha_i(\mathbf{z}, t)$ should be for participation in the block party. Note that time varying weights will be required to allow the block party neighborhood shrink as learning progresses. Note also that this neighborhood can be defined by simply setting the learning rates of processing elements outside the neighborhood to 0.

5.4.3. Define a specific self-organizing map learning rate/neighborhood function $\alpha_i(\mathbf{z}, t)$, as described in Exercise 5.4.2.

5.4.4. What geometrical form could we expect a 2-dimensional rectangular array of processing elements to take if we used a self-organizing map to embed the array in a 3-dimensional cube using a uniform probability density function on the cube for selecting the training examples?

5.5 Counterpropagation Network

By combining a Kohonen layer with another layer employing Grossberg learning a new type of mapping neural network is obtained. This *counterpropagation* network functions as a statistically optimal self-programming lookup table. The section begins with the definition of the counterpropagation network. Then discussions of counterpropagation network variants and counterpropagation network convergence and performance are presented. It is shown that (under nonpathological conditions) this network will learn a near-optimal lookup table approximation to the mapping being approximated. By using a sufficiently large network the mapping approximation can be made essentially as accurate as desired for continuous mappings.

5.5.1 Architecture of the Counterpropagation Neural Network

In this subsection the architecture of the counterpropagation neural network is defined.

The counterpropagation network architecture is a combination of a portion of the self-organizing map (see Section 5.4 above) and the instar/outstar structure of Stephen Grossberg [92, 97, 99] (i.e., a layer of the instar processing elements discussed in Section 3.). I invented counterpropagation in 1986 [112] while seeking a way to use the self-organizing map to learn explicit functions.

Figure 5.11 presents the topology of the full counterpropagation network. The network is designed to approximate a continuous function $f : A \subset \mathbf{R}^n \longrightarrow B \subset \mathbf{R}^m$, defined on a compact set A. The full network works best if f^{-1} exists and is continuous (i.e., if f is one-to-one and onto and if the inverse mapping $f^{-1} : B \subset \mathbf{R}^m \longrightarrow A \subset \mathbf{R}^n$ is continuous). The forward-only version of the network that will be presented in this section only requires continuity in the forward direction. As always, it is assumed that the $\mathbf{x}$ vectors are drawn (both during training and after training) from A in accordance with a fixed probability density function $p(\mathbf{x})$.

During training, examples $(\mathbf{x}_k, \mathbf{y}_k)$ of f (where $\mathbf{y}_k = f(\mathbf{x}_k)$) are presented to the network at layers 1 and 5, respectively (see Figure 5.11). These $\mathbf{x}$ and $\mathbf{y}$ vectors then *propagate* through the network in a *counterflow* manner to yield output vectors $\mathbf{x}'$ and $\mathbf{y}'$ that are intended to be approximations of $\mathbf{x}$ and $\mathbf{y}$. Thus the name *counterpropagation*. For further details and discussions of related issues, see [108, 110, 112].

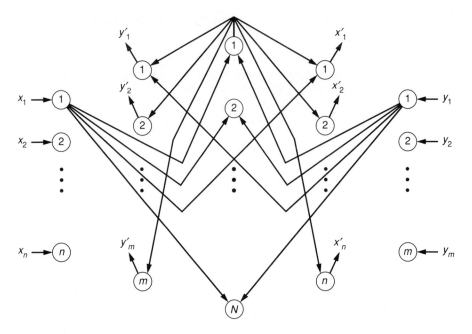

Fig. 5.11. • Topology of the full counterpropagation neural network. The vectors **x** and **y** are entered at opposite ends of the network. They then *propagate* through the network in opposite directions in a *counterflow* arrangement — thus the name *counterpropagation*.

For the purposes of this section the *forward-only* variant of the counter-propagation network (shown in Figure 5.12) shall be used. A description of this network's architecture, operation and capabilities is given below.

The forward-only counterpropagation network architecture consists of three slabs: an input layer (layer 1) containing n fanout units that multiplex the input signals $x_1, x_2, \ldots, x_n$ (and m units that supply the "correct" output signal values $y_1, y_2, \ldots, y_m$ to the output layer), a middle layer (layer 2) with N processing elements that have output signals $z_1, z_2, \ldots, z_N$, and a final layer (layer 3) with m processing elements having output signals $y'_1, y'_2, \ldots, y'_m$. The outputs of layer 3 represent approximations to the components $y_1, y_2, \ldots, y_m$ of $\mathbf{y} = f(\mathbf{x})$. During training these "correct" values are supplied to the units of the final layer from the **y** input units of layer 1 (see Figure 5.13).

During training the network is exposed to examples of the mapping f. After each $\mathbf{x}_k$ is selected, $\mathbf{y}_k = f(\mathbf{x}_k)$ is determined and both $\mathbf{x}_k$ and $\mathbf{y}_k$ are input to the network. During training, the transfer function equations for layer 2 are:

$$z_i = \begin{cases} 1 & \text{if } i \text{ is the smallest integer for which} \\ & \quad D(\mathbf{w}_i^{\text{old}}, \mathbf{x}) \leq D(\mathbf{w}_j^{\text{old}}, \mathbf{x}) \text{ for all } j \\ 0 & \text{otherwise,} \end{cases} \qquad (5.26)$$

where D is the distance metric being used to measure distance in the set A (this must be a metric that is equivalent to the Euclidean metric in the sense

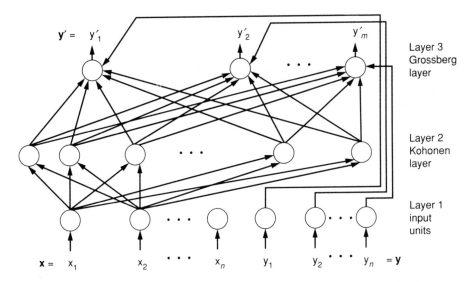

Fig. 5.12. • The forward-only counterpropagation network. This network implements a mapping from **x** to **y**.

that there exists a real constant $c > 1$ such that $(1/c)|\mathbf{a} - \mathbf{b}| \leq D(\mathbf{a}, \mathbf{b}) \leq c|\mathbf{a} - \mathbf{b}|)$. Following the completion of the competition process implicit in the above equation (see Exercises 3.4.1, 3.4.2, and 3.4.3 for methods of implementing this sort of competition process as part of a processing element transfer function), the next step is weight adjustment using the conscience mechanism (see Section 3.4). This occurs by means of Kohonen learning. In other words, the processing element that wins the weight adjustment competition adjusts its weight vector in accordance with the equation

$$\mathbf{w}_i^{\text{new}} = (1 - \alpha(t))\mathbf{w}_i^{\text{old}} + \alpha(t)\mathbf{x}.$$

The other processing elements do not adjust their weights. Notice that, just as with the self-organizing map, the learning constant $\alpha(t)$ is a function of time. Alpha starts out at a high value (such as 0.8) and gradually decreases towards zero. As always, a scheduling processing element (not shown in Figure 5.12) is used to coordinate all of these network activities (see Section 7.4 for a description of the scheduling function of the counterpropagation neural network — as expressed in the AXON neurosoftware language).

The usual final result of training is that the weight vectors distribute themselves in an almost equiprobable configuration. After training has ended the weight vectors are frozen and only Equation 5.26 is used.

To summarize the process of Kohonen learning with conscience, each time an **x** vector is submitted to the the network, layer 1 distributes all of the components of **x** to each of the processing elements of layer 2. A competition is then held among the units of layer 2 to determine which unit's weight vector lies closest to **x**. The winning processing element has its output signal set to

1 and all of the other processing elements have their output signals set to 0 (these values are stored so that the output signals can be used for the weight competition). Following this first competition, another competition is held to determine which processing element will be updated using Kohonen learning. The winning processing element of the original distance competition has its output signal again set to 1 and all other processing element output signals are set to zero. This completes the activity of layer 2 during training. Following the completion of layer 2 processing, layer 3 carries out its function.

Layer 3 of the counterpropagation network (see Figure 5.13) receives the $\mathbf{z}$ signals from layer 2 (one of which is 1 and all the others of which are 0). Each processing element of layer 3 receives all of the components of $\mathbf{z}$. The processing elements of layer 3 are governed by the following equations (which include Grossberg learning — see Section 3.5):

$$y'_j = \sum_{i=1}^{N} u_{ji}^{old} z_i$$

$$u_{ji}^{new} = u_{ji}^{old} + a(-u_{ji}^{old} + y_j)z_i,$$

where $\mathbf{u}_j = (u_{j1}, u_{j2}, \ldots, u_{jN})$ is the weight vector associated with the jth processing element of layer 3 and a is the learning rate ($0 < a < 1$) of the Grossberg learning law. The first transfer function equation serves to simply select the weight associated with the input to processing element j from the winning processing element of layer 2 (the one for which $z_i = 1$) and emit this weight value as the processing element output signal y'_j. The second equation is the Grossberg learning law from Section 3.5. This learning law modifies only the weight associated with input from the winning processing element of layer 2 (the one with $z_i = 1$). This weight is modified to, over time, learn the average of the "correct" y_j values associated with the $\mathbf{x}$ vector values that cause processing element i of layer 2 to win the final competition. As the weights of layer 2 equilibrate the layer 3 weights learn the averages of the y_j values associated with the $\mathbf{x}$ inputs within the equiprobable "win regions" of the processing elements of layer 2.

In other words, the layer 3 processing elements *sample* the "correct" y values associated with each particular layer 2 processing element that wins the final competition. It is easy to show (see Exercise 5.5.1) that, following equilibration of the layer 2 weights that the layer 3 weights learn the averages of these y values. In particular, after sufficient training, the network will output a vector $\mathbf{v}_i = (u_{1i}, u_{2i}, \ldots, u_{mi})$ whenever processing element i wins the final layer 2 competition (see Exercise 5.5.2). The $\mathbf{v}_i$ vector is very close to the vector average of the correct $\mathbf{y}$ vectors associated with $\mathbf{x}$ input vectors that cause processing element i of layer 2 to win.

In summary, after a large number of training inputs, the $\mathbf{w}_i$ vectors arrange themselves in $\mathbf{R}^n$ in such a way that they are approximately equiprobable in a nearest neighbor sense with respect to $\mathbf{x}$ vectors drawn from A in accordance with the probability density function p. In other words, given any i, $1 \leq i \leq N$,

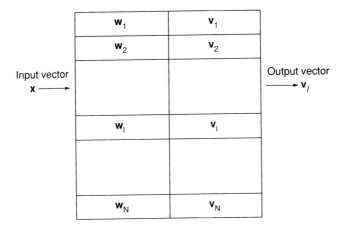

Fig. 5.13. • The counterpropagation neural network functions as an adaptive lookup table. The input vector $\mathbf{x}$ is compared with all of the $\mathbf{w}$ vectors to find the closest matching $\mathbf{w}_l$ vector using some distance measure D. The table then emits the associated $\mathbf{v}_l$ vector as its output.

and given an $\mathbf{x}$ vector drawn from A at random in accordance with ρ, the probability that $\mathbf{x}$ is closest to $\mathbf{w}_i$ (as measured by the distance metric D) is approximately $1/N$. As the Kohonen learning constant $\alpha(t)$ goes to zero these weight values stabilize and equilibrate. The weight vectors can then typically be frozen (although in some applications it may be necessary for training to continue indefinitely — e.g., in order to constantly update the network if probability density function ρ and/or the input/output function f slowly changes).

Once the Kohonen layer has equilibrated with equiprobable weights, the processing elements of layer 3 begin to learn the averages $\mathbf{v}_i$ of the correct $\mathbf{y}$ vectors associated with each processing element weight vector $\mathbf{w}_i$ of layer 2. Eventually the $\mathbf{v}_i$ vectors also equilibrate — assuming that the constant a is small enough (see Exercise 5.5.3). At this point training can be terminated and all of the weights of the network can be frozen (unless, as mentioned above, the functions ρ and f are expected to drift over time).

Following the completion of training (and the freezing of the weights) the network functions exactly as the lookup table shown in Figure 5.13. The input vector to the network ($\mathbf{x}$) is compared with the layer 2 weight vectors to find the closest match $\mathbf{w}_l$ (using the distance metric D). The layer 3 output vector $\mathbf{v}_l$ associated with $\mathbf{w}_l$ is then emitted by the network. This is exactly the function of a nearest-match lookup table. As shown in Figure 5.13, the number of entries in the lookup table is exactly equal to N, the number of processing elements in layer 2.

The counterpropagation network is statistically optimal in two ways: First, the $\mathbf{w}_i$ vectors are equiprobable. Secondly, the $\mathbf{v}_i$ network output vectors are the statistical averages of the $\mathbf{y}$ vectors associated with the $\mathbf{x}$ vectors that activate the associated layer 2 processing elements – thus taking on values that are, on average, best representative of the f function's value in each case. Therefore, in these ways, the counterpropagation neural network does as well as a lookup table can do to approximate the function f.

Since f is assumed to be a continuous function on the compact set A, it is easy to show that as the number of layer 2 processing elements N increases that the approximation accuracy of the network will increase. In fact, the mean squared error (and even the maximum absolute error!) of the network can be made as small as desired by choosing a sufficiently large N (see Exercises 5.5.4 and 5.5.5 for a simple example of this). Thus, for continuous functions the counterpropagation network is, in principle, just as effective as the backpropagation network — it is a universal continuous function approximator. Unfortunately, in practice this property is rarely useful, since the number of layer 2 processing elements needed to achieve a particular level of accuracy is often much greater than the number of units required by backpropagation. Nonetheless, there are situations where the counterpropagation network is superior to any other mapping network. Typical examples of situations where this is true are where it is crucial to be able to sense when training has ended (by testing for layer 2 weight vector equiprobability and output layer weight equilibration), when the **x** vectors lie in a small-dimensional subspace of the entire **x**-space, or in a situation where the absolute, fail-safe predictability of operation of the network is important (no weird or unexpected events can occur), or where the problem itself calls for a lookup table structure to be formed. Counterpropagation networks can also be used during rapid prototyping to build and test a complex system involving embedded mapping networks. Because, compared to other mapping networks, counterpropagation networks typically require orders of magnitude fewer training trails to achieve their best performance, this technique can speed up preliminary system development and checkout considerably. Following checkout a different, but "plug compatible" mapping network (such as backpropagation) can be substituted and trained once.

The next subsection describes some variants of the counterpropagation neural network.

5.5.2 Variants of the Counterpropagation Network

One important variant of the counterpropagation network is to operate it in an *interpolation* mode after training has been completed. In this mode more than one layer 2 processing element is allowed to win the competition. Not only is the processing element with the weight that most closely matches **x** allowed to win, but so are the processing elements with (say) the second closest and third closest matching weight vectors. The winning processing elements split the unit (1.0) output signal that formerly was concentrated in the single winning processing element's output signal. The split is ordinarily accomplished by letting the output of each unit be the ratio of the inverse of the distance between its weight vector and **x** to the sum of the inverses of the distances of the winning processing elements to **x**. The other processing elements have their outputs set to zero. Notice that because of the form of the layer 3 transfer function the network output vector $\mathbf{y}'$ will be a simple weighted blend of the $\mathbf{v}_i$ vectors associated with the winning layer 2 processing elements (see Exercise 5.5.6).

The number of winning processing elements and the way in which the output signals are set can be arranged in many ways. Unfortunately, the simple scheme presented above (a fixed number of winners on layer 2 and a distance-proportional blending) does not really work much better than the standard counterpropagation network (see Exercise 5.5.7 for an example of why this is so). A better way would be to use the *barycentric calculus* (invented by the mathematician August Möbius in 1827 [40]). In this scheme, the N $\mathbf{w}_k$ weight vector positions are treated as the positions of point masses having masses $p_1, p_2, \ldots, p_N$. The goal is to chose these masses so that their center of gravity (*barycenter*) is $\mathbf{x}$. It can be shown that this is always possible, assuming that $\mathbf{x}$ lies in the subspace of $\mathbf{R}^n$ determined by the weight vectors of layer 2. However, unless the point $\mathbf{x}$ lies inside the n-dimensional tetrahedron defined by the N weight vector positions, some of the masses will have to be negative. The sum of the masses can always be taken to be 1. Mathematically, these relationships can be expressed as

$$\mathbf{x} = \sum_{k=1}^{N} p_k \mathbf{w}_k$$

and

$$\sum_{k=1}^{N} p_k = 1.$$

Any set of masses $p_1, p_2, \ldots, p_N$ that meet these conditions are said to be *barycentric coordinates* for the point $\mathbf{x}$. Unfortunately, in general, barycentric coordinates are not unique. The ideal situation would be to have masses p_k that increase to 1 as $\mathbf{x}$ approaches weight vector $\mathbf{w}_k$ and gradually get small as $\mathbf{x}$ moves "far away" from $\mathbf{w}_k$. The output signal of each layer 2 processing element would then be set equal to the mass of its point mass (i.e., p_k). No usable method for accomplishing this is known. Presumably, such a scheme would yield a counterpropagation network that could smoothly interpolate between all of its $\mathbf{v}_k$ values as $\mathbf{x}$ moved between its $\mathbf{w}_k$ values. This is one of the major open research issues in connection with counterpropagation networks. For the moment we are stuck with distance-based blending schemes (although some of these do much better than the simple distance ratio blending described above).

The modular construction of the counterpropagation network illustrates the point that existing neural networks can be viewed as building block components that can be assembled into new configurations offering new and different information processing capabilities.

Exercises

5.5.1. Show that the jth processing element of layer 3 of the basic forward-only counterpropagation network will learn the averages of the y_j values associated with the training examples that cause each particular layer 2 processing element to win the layer 2 competition (once the layer 2 processing element weight vectors have stopped changing). Show that these averages are the weights u_{ji}.

5.5.2. Using the result of Exercise 5.5.1, show that after the layer 2 processing element weight vectors have equilibrated that the average of the **y** vectors associated with **x** vectors that cause layer 2 processing element k to win the activation competition is approximately given by the vector $\mathbf{v}_k = (u_{1k}, u_{2k}, \ldots, u_{mk})$. Demonstrate that $\mathbf{v}_k$ will be the output of the network whenever processing element k wins the final layer 2 competition.

5.5.3. Explain why the weights of the processing element of layer 3 will eventually equilibrate to fixed values (assuming a is small).

5.5.4. Given a function f from the set $A = [0, 1] \subset \mathbf{R}^1$ to $\mathbf{R}^1$ having continuous derivatives of all orders (i.e., an analytic function), show that if a set of N w_i weights are selected so that they are equiprobable in A in accordance with the uniform probability density function on A that the maximum euclidean distance between adjacent weights can be made as small as desired simply by increasing N. [Hint: consider what equiprobable means for uniform density.]

5.5.5. If the function of Exercise 5.5.4 is to be approximated by a counterpropagation neural network within a mean squared error accuracy of ϵ ($\epsilon > 0$), show that this can be accomplished by simply choosing N large enough. You should use the fact that the derivatives of such a function must be bounded (they are continuous functions on a compact set). In other words, given a point x in A as one moves from this point by a small amount Δ the value of f can change at a rate no greater than some maximum c. So, for sufficiently small Δ, $\|f(x+\Delta) - f(x)\| < c\Delta$ for all $x \in A$. [Hint: show, using the result of Exercise 5.5.4, that by selecting N large enough that the distances between weights can all be made less than the value for which the above inequality holds. Then show that the v_i vectors can be brought sufficiently close together (by increasing N further) such that no value $f(x)$ of the function for x within the equiprobable win region associated with w_i can be more than a distance ϵ from the associated v_i value produced by the network.]

5.5.6. Show that if interpolation is used that the network output vector **y** will be a weighted blend of the $\mathbf{v}_i$ vectors associated with the winning processing elements of layer 2. Also show that the weighting factors will be the output signal values of the winning layer 2 processing elements.

5.5.7.   Given a function f that maps a subset of $\mathbf{R}^2$ to $\mathbf{R}^1$ and given four
layer 2 weight vectors that form a square (with no other weight vectors
within the square) let the output values v_i associated with these weight
vectors be 1, 1, 1, and 100. Show that if $\mathbf{x}$ values are taken along a
diagonal of the square connecting the weight vector associated with an
output of 100 with one of the weight vectors with an output of 1 then
if interpolation with three winners is used the network output will be
discontinuous at the midpoint of the diagonal not including the point
with $v_i = 100$. State the values of the output on each side of the center
of this diagonal.

5.6 Group Method of Data Handling

The Group Method of Data Handling (GMDH) was introduced by A. G.
Ivakhnenko in 1968 [130, 131, 64]. GMDH is a feature-based mapping network. It is also an example of a *polynomial* neural network. Ivakhnenko developed GMDH for the purpose of building more accurate predictive models
of fish populations in rivers and oceans. GMDH worked well for modelling
fisheries and for many other modelling applications. In fact, what Ivakhnenko
developed was the first rational means for building mapping networks with hidden layers. In 1961, Frank Rosenblatt [198] had identified the lack of a means
for effectively selecting hidden layer processing element transfer functions as
the key weakness of neurocomputing at that epoch. Although other methods
were offered (including Shun-ichi Amari's 1966 paper in which he came very
close to discovering backpropagation [10] and the Adaptive Learning Network
method of Roger Barron and Lewey Gilstrap [20]), no really effective method
was developed until GMDH. Unfortunately, GMDH did not become widely
known until Ivakhnenko's 1971 paper [130].

A type of polynomial network related to GMDH formed the technological
basis for a company called Adaptronics, Inc. Adaptronics was probably the first
neurocomputing company [20]. Like Bernard Widrow's Memistor Corporation
(see Section 8.2), Adaptronics began its operations in the early 1960s. The company was focused on applications of polynomial networks to problems in pattern
recognition and control. Although the company remained small, Adaptronics
prospered for over 20 years. In 1982, Adaptronics became part of the Flow
General Corporation. The fact that a prosperous neurocomputing company existed throughout the 60s and the 70s is itself astonishing. However, the success
of Adaptronics, Inc. goes beyond its mere survival in an era when neurocomputing was a subject clearly ahead of it time. What makes the Adaptronics story
so much more interesting is the fact that the company successfully carried out
a number of application demonstrations (including the in-flight demonstration
of a flight control system component for a supersonic jet fighter aircraft in 1969
[210]). During the 1970s, Adaptronics sold a line of neurocomputers and associated ultrasonic non-destructive testing machines. This equipment was used

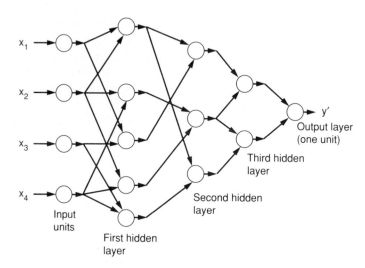

Fig. 5.14. • A typical GMDH neural network. The network maps a vector input **x** to a scalar output y'. Each processing element has two inputs, which it combines in a general quadratic form (with six weights) to yield the output signal. Layers of these units are combined to implement the mapping.

to test metallic aerospace parts for the presence of internal voids and cracks. In the early 1970s, Adaptronics added some of Ivakhnenko's GMDH concepts to their technology base. During the last half of the 1970s, Adaptronics personnel amply demonstrated the power of their version of GMDH.

5.6.1 The GMDH Neural Network

A typical GMDH neural network is shown in Figure 5.14. GMDH neural networks are typically used to approximate a continuous function $f : A \subset \mathbf{R}^n \longrightarrow \mathbf{R}$ that maps a subset of n-dimensional Euclidean space into the real numbers. Vector functions can be handled by creating one network per output coordinate (thus, this case will be ignored here).

The GMDH network shown in Figure 5.14 has four inputs (the components of the vector **x**) and one output (the estimate y' of the correct function value $y = f(\mathbf{x})$).

Following the layer of fanout units, note that each processing element has exactly two inputs. Thus, the output layer (which, of necessity, consists of a single processing element) is preceded by a final hidden layer having two units.

The scheduling of the GMDH network is a simple feed-forward sequence. The components of the input vector **x** are first supplied to the input units. These then distribute these components to the appropriate first hidden layer processing elements (the network is *not* fully interconnected between layers). The outputs of these hidden layer processing elements are then supplied to the next layer, and so on. The final output of the network is a single real number y'. The details of the GMDH network and the method for constructing it are now described.

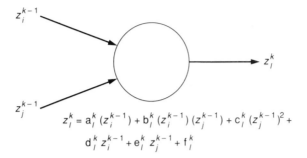

Fig. 5.15. • GMDH processing element of l layer k. The output signal z_l^k of the processing element is a general quadratic multinomial combination of the two inputs.

The processing elements of the input layer of the network are simply fanout units that distribute their component of the input vector **x** to the appropriate processing elements of the first hidden layer. After the input layer, all of the processing elements in the network have the form shown in Figure 5.15. Figure 5.15 illustrates a general processing element belonging to layer k of the network. In general, this element has two inputs, z_i^{k-1} and z_j^{k-1} (note that superscripts are used both to indicate the layer number and for exponentiation; parentheses are used for exponents to help avoid confusion). These are output signals from different processing elements of the previous layer $(k-1)$. The x_l inputs to the network are treated as z_l^0 values from a "zeroth layer." The output signal of this layer k processing element is given by the quadratic form transfer function

$$z_l^k = a_l^k \left(z_i^{k-1} \right)^2 + b_l^k \left(z_i^{k-1} \right) \left(z_j^{k-1} \right)$$
$$+ c_l^k \left(z_j^{k-1} \right)^2 + d_l^k z_i^{k-1} + e_l^k z_j^{k-1} + f_l^k.$$

(5.27)

In other words, the output of each of these GMDH processing elements is simply a quadratic combination of its two inputs. Thus, the GMDH network builds up a polynomial (actually, a *multinomial*) combination of the input components. Each layer of the network increases the degree of this polynomial expression by two. The output y' of the network can thus be expressed as a polynomial of degree $2K$, where K is the number of layers in the network following the input layer. This polynomial is called the *Ivakhnenko polynomial*.

As is clear from Figure 5.14, not all possible pairs of output signals from the previous layer are used at each subsequent layer. The selection of the signals to be used is made in accordance with an overall network development process that is now described.

The GMDH network is developed by starting at the input layer and growing the network progressively towards the output layer, one layer at a time. The process will be described in terms of the situation shown in Figure 5.16. Figure 5.16 illustrates the configuration of layer k of the network. Naturally, we begin

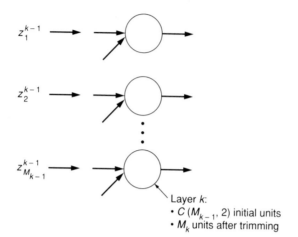

Layer k:
- $C(M_{k-1}, 2)$ initial units
- M_k units after trimming

Fig. 5.16. • Generic GMDH layer. The layer starts out with many processing elements and is later trimmed to a much smaller number.

with $k = 1$ and then proceed to $k = 2$, etc., until the entire network has been configured. Regardless of the value of k, the process used is the same.

The first step is to configure layer k with one processing element for each different pair of outputs from the previous layer. To make the notation precise, we shall assume that the number of processing elements in the previous layer (either the input layer or the previous hidden layer) is M_{k-1}. We start with a number of processing elements in layer k equal to $C(M_{k-1}, 2)$ (the number of combinations of M_{k-1} things taken two at a time). The M_{k-1} outputs of the previous layer are combined in all possible pairs to form the inputs to the processing elements of layer k. Each of these processing elements has the transfer function shown above in Equation 5.29. Thus, layer k has exactly $C(M_{k-1}, 2)$ of these equations.

As each new layer is added to the network, it is individually adapted and then frozen. Notice that this differs from backpropagation and counterpropagation in which all of the layers can participate simultaneously in the training process. The basic idea of GMDH is that each processing element on layer k wants to produce an output equal to y (the overall desired output of the network). In other words, each processing element would like to have its output match $f(\mathbf{x})$ as closely as possible for each network input vector $\mathbf{x}$. The manner in which this approximation is accomplished is through the use of linear regression.

The process of adjusting the six coefficients of each processing element is carried out using a large set of input/output examples $(\mathbf{x}_1, y_1), (\mathbf{x}_2, y_2), \ldots, (\mathbf{x}_p, y_p), \ldots$. Each example input vector $\mathbf{x}_p$ that is entered into the network during training (as always, these are chosen randomly in accordance with a fixed probability density function $p(\mathbf{x})$) eventually causes a $\mathbf{z}^{k-1}$ output vector to be emitted from layer $k - 1$. When these numerical values are entered into the transfer function of the lth processing element of layer k, the result is the quantity (processing element output signal) z_l^k expressed as a linear combination of the a_l^k, b_l^k, c_l^k, d_l^k, e_l^k, f_l^k coefficients for that processing element. Since all such GMDH processing elements want to have y_p as their output, we will substitute y_p (a given definitive numerical value — the correct output value for input vector x_p) for z_l^k. For example, if $z_i^{k-1} = 3$, $z_j^{k-1} = -2$, and $y_p = 19$ on a particular training trial, then the linear equation that will result for processing element l of layer k will be

$$9a_l^k - 6b_l^k + 4c_l^k + 3d_l^k - 2e_l^k + f_l^k = 19. \tag{5.28}$$

Each processing element of layer k accumulates one such equation for each training example. In order for GMDH to work properly, it is necessary to have a large amount of training data. It is assumed that each layer is trained on a statistically adequate set of training data that was not used for the training of previous layers.

After a sufficient number of training examples have been presented to the processing elements of layer k, the resulting linear equations for processing element l can be represented by the single linear equation (see Exercise 5.6.1)

$$\mathbf{Z}_l \begin{bmatrix} a_l^k \\ b_l^k \\ c_l^k \\ d_l^k \\ e_l^k \\ f_l^k \end{bmatrix} = \mathbf{Y}, \tag{5.29}$$

where $\mathbf{Z}_l$ is the matrix of numbers in which each row corresponds to the values in Equation 5.30 (above) of $(x_i^{k-1})^2$, $(z_i^{k-1})(z_j^{k-1})$, $(z_j^{k-1})^2$, z_i^{k-1}, z_j^{k-1}, and 1 for each of the examples used in training. The column vector $\mathbf{Y}$ has components equal to y_1, y_2, etc. (i.e., the set of corresponding y output values for the training trials). Since it is ordinarily impossible for any processing element of layer k (or any other layer, for that matter) to be able to give the exact correct output on each training trial, the set of linear equations expressed by Equation 5.25 will almost never have an exact solution, only an approximate solution. However, as discussed in Section 4.2, the solution to Equation 5.31 that minimizes the mean squared error of this approximation is given by

$$\begin{bmatrix} a_l^k \\ b_l^k \\ c_l^k \\ d_l^k \\ e_l^k \\ f_l^k \end{bmatrix} = \mathbf{Z}_l^+ \mathbf{Y}, \tag{5.30}$$

where $\mathbf{Z}_l^+$ is the pseudoinverse of the matrix $\mathbf{Z}_l$. Naturally, there will be one such solution for each of the $C(M_{k-1}, 2)$ processing elements of layer k. Each of the resulting sets of six polynomial coefficients a_l^k, b_l^k, c_l^k, d_l^k, e_l^k, f_l^k, represents the best possible selection of coefficients in terms of minimizing the mean squared error between the output of each processing element and the desired output. Notice that one way to assess the statistical sufficiency of the training data used for layer k is to double the number of examples used during training and then (by again solving the resulting system of equation using formula 5.32), seeing if the values of the six coefficients change much. If they don't change much, then the original training data was probably statistically representative of the overall data environment. If they change a lot, then still more training examples should be used.

Once all of the coefficient sets for each of the processing elements of layer k have been derived and statistically validated, the next step is to evaluate the overall performance of each processing element in terms of its goal. One convenient way to do this is to simply measure the mean squared error that each processing element makes on a set of new testing examples. To do this, all we need do is use these new testing examples to evaluate the mean squared error of each processing element by use of the formula (see Exercise 5.6.2):

$$\frac{1}{r} \left\| \mathbf{Z}_l' \begin{bmatrix} a_l^k \\ b_l^k \\ \vdots \\ f_l^k \end{bmatrix} - \mathbf{Y}' \right\|^2 \qquad (5.31)$$

where r is the number of testing examples used.

The mean squared error will usually differ enormously from one processing element to another. The next step in the GMDH process is to eliminate those processing elements on layer k that have a "large" mean squared error. The definition of "large" is up to the user. However, a typical approach is to set a threshold on the ratio of the mean squared error of one processing element versus the mean squared error of the best performing processing element and to simply eliminate processing elements whose error ratios lie above this threshold value. The end result of this step in the process is to eliminate all but the fittest polynomial units from layer k, thus overcoming the combinatorial explosion caused by initially taking all possible combinations of M_{k-1} things taken two at a time. The final set of remaining processing elements then supplies the $\mathbf{z}^k$ output vector that feeds layer $k + 1$. The number M_k is defined to be the final number of processing elements on layer k, after trimming.

This process of building the network layer by layer continues until a stopping criterion is satisfied. This criterion is illustrated in Figure 5.17, which

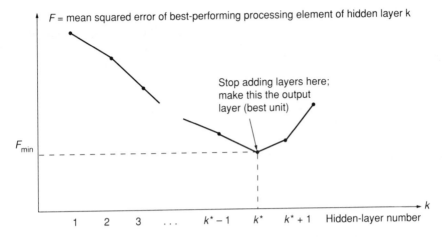

Fig. 5.17. • The GMDH layer addition stopping criterion. The best performing unit of layer k^* becomes the output unit of the network. Units on previous layers that do not connect to this output unit are eliminated.

shows a graph of the mean squared error of the best performing processing element of hidden layer k for $k = 1, 2, 3, \ldots$. Typically, the mean squared error of the best performing processing element is lower on each subsequent layer than on the previous layer. However, eventually an absolute minimum is usually reached (at layer k^*). If further layers are added, the mean squared error of the best performing processing element will actually rise. When this occurs, the layer addition process is stopped and the network is truncated at layer k^* (which then becomes the output layer). The best performing processing element on layer k^* is selected as the output unit for the entire network. Each of the preceding layers is then trimmed to eliminate those units whose outputs do not contribute to the final output of the network (i.e., units that do not connect to the final output unit). This trimming process often reduces the size of the network dramatically. Once all of this trimming has been accomplished, the network generation process is complete and the result is the final GMDH neural network for the function f. Notice that the output signal of the network y' can be expressed as a $2k^*$ degree polynomial (the *Ivakhnenko polynomial*) in the components of the input vector $\mathbf{x}$. An additional technique (developed at the Adaptronics Corporation) is to carry out a final regression of this polynomial against another large block of training data. Each input vector $\mathbf{x}$ of the training set is first entered into the polynomial to produce a linear expression in the polynomial coefficients. This expression is then set equal to the desired output value of the training example, forming a single linear equation. One such equation can then be accumulated for each training example. By assembling a large collection of such equations, the values of the coefficients in the processing element transfer functions can be further refined. Barron [21] reports that this global "post-fitting" typically increases the performance of the network.

5.6.2 GMDH Lessons

GMDH is one answer to the age-old question of how to fit a polynomial functional form to a set of data without overfitting or underfitting the data. Although a definitive statistical theory of GMDH has not yet been worked out, statisticians familiar with the technique tend to agree that it provides a novel approach to the solution of this centuries-old dilemma. Unfortunately, the price for using GMDH is that an enormous number of large matrix calculations must be carried out.

GMDH provides an example of a neural network that has adaptive coefficients which are not weights in the traditional sense of one weight per input. However, recall that in the AXON model, we *do* accept them as weights (see Chapter 2).

Finally, GMDH is a network that uses a localized mean squared error minimization procedure in each processing element. As pointed out in Section 3.3, the process of mean squared error minimization for a linear transfer function (which is what each processing element actually uses once the inputs are properly combined into the various numerical quantities of the quadratic form) can be optimized by means of Widrow learning. Thus, another approach to building a GMDH neural network would be to have each processing element utilize Widrow learning during training. Effectively, the "input vector" to each processing element would then be thought of as $((z_i^{k-1})^2, (z_i^{k-1})(z_j^{k-1}), (z_j^{k-1})^2, z_i^{k-1}, z_j^{k-1}, 1)^T$ and the processing element's weight vector would then be $(a_l^k, b_l^k, c_l^k, d_l^k, e_l^k, f_l^k)^T$.

Notice that GMDH is in some sense a "search for excellence." Each hidden layer of the network produces a set of output signals which are closer to the final goal of being equal to the desired y output than those units of the previous hidden layer. In other words, at the beginning, the **x** inputs are typically totally different from the desired y output. At the output of the first hidden layer, the processing element output numbers are closer to the final goal, but way off. As each subsequent layer is added, the dream of goal fulfillment gets closer, until the best possible fit is achieved.

The next chapter briefly considers three more classes of neural network architectures (beyond associative networks and mapping networks): spatiotemporal networks, stochastic networks, and hierarchical networks.

Exercises

5.6.1. Show that once a set of training examples for layer k have been used that the resulting set of linear equations for processing element l can be expressed in the form of Equation 5.31.

5.6.2. Show (using the result of Exercise 3.2.3) that the mean squared error of processing element l of layer k can be expressed as shown in Equation 5.33.

5.6.3. Describe another method for fitting an n-dimensional multinomial form to training examples, when the number of examples is very large. [Hint: reexpress the fitting problem as a linear matrix equation and comment on how this system might be solved.]

5.6.4. Characterize the similarities and differences between the Fourier series representation and the Taylor series representation of a smooth function.

5.6.5. A *Chebyshev polynomial* expansion provides a representation for a function that (for a given polynomial degree n) minimizes the absolute maximum error of approximation of a smooth real function of a single real variable. What is the corresponding goal of a Taylor polynomial expansion? What are the advantages and disadvantages of a Chebyshev polynomial representation in comparison to a Taylor polynomial representation? Finally, give an example of where a Chebyshev polynomial would be more useful than a Taylor polynomial. [Hint: consult a numerical analysis textbook.]

6

Spatiotemporal, Stochastic, and Hierarchical Networks: Frontiers of Neurocomputing

This chapter completes our discussion of neural network architectures and theory, which began in Chapter 2. In this chapter we discuss three additional classes of neural network architectures: spatiotemporal, stochastic, and hierarchical.

The networks discussed in this chapter lie at the outer edges of neurocomputing knowledge. In fact, two of the topics presented (the spatiotemporal pattern recognizer network and combinatorial hypercompression) have not yet been explored in detail.

6.1 Spatiotemporal Networks

In this section we will consider neural networks that can deal with inputs and outputs that are explicit functions of time. Essentially all such *spatiotemporal* neural networks share the characteristic that one or more of their layers or slabs have asymmetric intra-slab connections (or at least asymmetric weights for intra-slab connections). Notice that, with the exception of the brain state in a box network, the neural networks discussed in earlier chapters either had no intra-slab connections (as with backpropagation and counterpropagation) or had symmetrical intra-slab connections (as in the Hopfield network and the Cohen/Grossberg theorem networks). The brain state in a box network avoids being spatiotemporal by means the hard-limiting transfer function used, which captures the network state at a vertex of the cube (see Section 4.4). Asymmetrical intra-slab connections will (in the absence of such restrictions), in general, lead to spatiotemporal behavior.

164

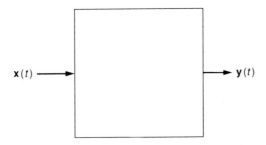

Fig. 6.1. • A spatiotemporal network. The input $\mathbf{x}(t)$ and the output $\mathbf{y}(t)$ are vector functions of time. Spatiotemporal pattern classification networks carry out the function of transforming the input pattern $\mathbf{x}(t)$ into a time-varying class number output code $\mathbf{y}(t)$. Controller networks carry out the function of transforming sensor readings $\mathbf{x}(t)$ from a system being controlled into control signals $\mathbf{y}(t)$ that are fed back to run the system. However, in each case, the network output at time t depends not just upon the input at that time; it also depends on inputs that arrived in the past. In fact, in some cases (none of which will be discussed here), the output of the network occurs at a retarded time $t - \delta$ and this output depends on inputs that occur both in the past and present, as well as in the future. Such *noncausal systems* are often used for retrospective off-line analysis and processing of data sets.

Spatiotemporal neural networks typically are generalizations of mapping networks, as illustrated in Figure 6.1. The input to the network is a vector function of time $\mathbf{x}(t)$, and the output of the network is a vector function of time $\mathbf{y}(t)$. Time t is assumed to move forward on an essentially continuous basis, although, in actual implementations, time usually moves forward in small discrete integer steps. This situation differs from that found in mapping networks, in that, in a mapping network, the input $\mathbf{x}$ is a static non-time-varying vector, as is the final output $\mathbf{y}$.

Most, but not all, spatiotemporal neural networks belong to one of two subclasses: networks primarily used for the classification of spatiotemporal patterns and networks primarily used for control. In this section we shall examine one example from each of these subclasses: the *spatiotemporal pattern recognizer* network and the *recurrent backpropagation* network. These networks serve to illustrate the substantially different considerations that apply in spatiotemporal pattern recognition and control.

In pattern classification networks, the input $\mathbf{x}(t)$ is a spatiotemporal pattern (such as speech), and the output is typically the class to which the most recently recognized object (such as a word) in the input stream belongs. In control networks, the components of the input vector $\mathbf{x}(t)$ are the system state variables (in other words, the plant sensor outputs) and the components of the output vector $\mathbf{y}(t)$ are the plant control signals.[1]

---

[1] In control the term *plant* is used to denote the system being controlled.

In spatiotemporal pattern classification, the emphasis is on developing networks that will be insensitive to certain transformations of the input pattern. For example, in speaker-independent speech recognition the word classifications should not change if the tempo of the speech is increased by 20%.

In control, the emphasis is on achieving the highest possible plant performance, as measured using one or more *cost functions* (functions that are minimized only by correct system performance) that are to be minimized. For example, for a personal tooth flossing machine the cost functions might be optimized if the entire non-toothbrush-reachable area of each tooth is well scrubbed (to just below the gum line) without having the flossing arm injure any mouth structures and without causing the user to gag.

Clearly, the design considerations pertinent to spatiotemporal pattern classifiers are quite different from those connected with control systems. Thus, it is not surprising that the neural networks used for each of these areas are typically different.

Another class of spatiotemporal networks (besides spatiotemporal pattern classifiers and controllers) are those designed to act as *command sequence memories*. Such networks (such as the Cerebellum Model Articulation Controller (*CMAC*) network developed by James Albus [5]) are designed to store, and (when properly cued) replay, individual command sequences. Most present-day control systems (which could be classified as *simple[2]*) do not utilize command sequence memories. Instead, they generate their output commands in real-time by applying a fixed spatiotemporal function to the current and recent past plant state sensor outputs and recent past control commands. Because of their primitive state of development, command sequence memory neural networks will not be discussed further in this book.

6.1.1 Spatiotemporal Pattern Recognizer Neural Network

This subsection presents the spatiotemporal pattern recognizer neural network. The discussion begins with an overview of some issues surrounding spatiotemporal patterns. We then examine ways to measure the distance between two patterns such that the distance measurement will be insensitive to the action of transformations that leave the classification of the pattern unchanged. Following this discussion, the spatiotemporal pattern recognizer network is defined.

SPATIOTEMPORAL PATTERNS   In traditional pattern recognition theory [52, 56], a *pattern* is simply an n-dimensional *feature vector* $\mathbf{x}$. A *spatiotemporal pattern* is a function $\mathbf{x} : [t_0, t_1] \longrightarrow R^n$ from a closed interval of time $[t_0, t_1]$ to n-dimensional Euclidean space. In other words, a spatiotemporal pattern is simply a trajectory or path in n-dimensional space, parameterized by time.

---

[2] The recurrent backpropagation network presented in this section is an example of a simple controller. In fact, there is strong evidence, but no proof yet, that this neural network is a *universal simple controller* that can implement any smooth simple controller.

Because the real world actually has no discontinuities, we shall assume that all spatiotemporal patterns are smooth functions (that is, they are continuous and have continuous derivatives of all orders). Further, because the rates of change of quantities in the real world are limited by factors such as inertia and capacitance, we shall feel free to make assumptions that put reasonable limits on the magnitudes of the derivatives of $\mathbf{x}$. Finally, to avoid some messy mathematical bookkeeping, we will often simply assume that spatiotemporal patterns are defined for all real values of t.

In spatiotemporal pattern recognition, the typical goal is to provide a classification for a relatively brief spatiotemporal pattern. The classification operation is typically carried out only after the entire pattern has been entered into the system. For simplicity, we will assume that each spatiotemporal pattern belongs to one of M classes. For example, in the problem of recognizing isolated words in speech classification, the input to the system might be a space–time pattern consisting of the time-varying "power spectrum" (an n-dimensional spatiotemporal pattern, with one non–negative power signal for each of n frequency channels) of the voltage output of a microphone monitoring an individual word utterance.[3] The classes in this instance are the words in the vocabulary. When each word utterance is entered into the system, the system is expected to emit a number between 1 and M, corresponding to the vocabulary number of the word that was spoken.

A basic difficulty with spatiotemporal pattern recognition is the issue of *cueing*. To explain this problem, and to provide a set of examples that are representative of the issues in general spatiotemporal pattern recognition, we shall use specific problems from speech classification. In the *isolated word recognition* problem, each word is entered into the system on cue, starting from the exact beginning of the word and progressing through until the end — at which point the system is told that the input has ended. A spatiotemporal pattern classifier of this type is called a *cued classifier*. A cued classifier is told when the input pattern begins, and when it ends. This cueing function is easy to arrange for in an isolated word recognition system, because the speaker must pause between words, and the beginning and end of each of these pauses can easily be detected using a power envelope threshold. An *uncued* spatiotemporal classifier is essentially provided with a continuous stream of spatiotemporal pattern input.

---

[3] Experience has shown that power spectra alone are not adequate as features for speech recognition. Recognition seems to work better if other features are used in addition to the power spectrum. Such features include measurements of the instantaneous responses of short-time signal amplitude detectors, harmonic energy detectors, extremely narrowband frequency filters, and vocal cord slap detectors. For the remainder of this section the term *power spectrum* will be taken to mean a power spectrum augmented with appropriate additional features.

The classifier system itself must figure out when a pattern of interest begins and ends, and must then carry out the classification operation. An uncued classifier is usually considerably more complicated than a cued classifier.

Notice that an uncued spatiotemporal classifier has much in common with a pattern recognition system for finding objects of interest in images. In both cases, the object must be effectively located and isolated ("clipped out") before the actual classification operation can begin. The process of locating and extracting the patterns of interest from a larger pattern is called *segmentation*. In both the image case and the sound–stream case, segmentation can be complicated if individual patterns of interest are partially *obscured* by other elements of the overall pattern (in other words, elements that are not objects of interest) or, worse yet, if *interference* occurs between different objects of interest. In images, obscuration and interference typically involve a situation where the particular object of interest lies partly behind or next to other objects that either are not of interest (obscuration) or are of interest (interference). In sound streams, obscuration and interference simply involve a mixing together of sounds from different sources. Unless some simple stratagem (such as bandpass filtering) can be used to separate these sounds, the problem of separating an object of interest from obscuring and interfering signals is currently considered intractable.

In this section, we will consider only patterns in which the objects of interest are not subject to obscuration or interference. Some neurocomputing approaches to the solution of obscuration and interference (for both spatial image patterns and spatiotemporal sound–stream patterns) have been discussed [103, 104], but these ideas are too speculative for an introductory text.

Spatiotemporal pattern classification has an issue associated with it that does not pertain to spatial pattern classification — namely, *spatiotemporal warping*. The term spatiotemporal warping refers to the action of a transformation $T : \mathscr{S} \subset \mathscr{A} \longrightarrow \mathscr{A}$ that maps each spatiotemporal pattern in a subset $\mathscr{S}$ of the set of all possible spatiotemporal patterns $\mathscr{A}$ (in other words, all smooth mappings from $(-\infty, +\infty)$ to R^n) to another spatiotemporal pattern in $\mathscr{A}$. Such spatiotemporal warping transformations can take many forms. One common example is the *time warp*. A time warp takes a pattern $\mathbf{x}(t)$ and transforms it into a pattern $\mathbf{x}(\theta(t))$, where θ is a strictly monotonically increasing smooth scalar function of time. Time warping has the effect of speeding up or slowing down the movement of the pattern $\mathbf{x}$ along its trajectory in R^n and of translating it forward or backward in time.

Figure 6.2 illustrates a typical spatiotemporal pattern in n-dimensional space. If a time warp transformation is applied to this pattern, it will still traverse the same trajectory, but will do so at a speed that differs from that of the original pattern. In fact (see Exercise 6.1.1), the ratio of the speeds at which the pattern will move after and before warping (at equivalent times) is given by $\frac{d\theta}{dt}$.

Another example of a spatiotemporal warp is the change that occurs to the sound power spectrum of a phonograph record when the same record is played at different speeds. In this instance, the spatiotemporal warp transformation

polynomial ratios) with which we are familiar only approach 0 asymptotically. Exercise 6.1.4 answers this question (see [119] for further details).

A space of objects on which a metric is defined is known as a *metric space*. Thus, $\mathscr{A}$ is a metric space with the metric D. Although this is mathematically neat and tidy, from a technological perspective the metric D leaves a lot to be desired. For example, let us imagine that the spatiotemporal output **u** of a neural network is exactly the same as the desired output **v**, except that it is slightly displaced in time (that is, $\mathbf{u}(t) = \mathbf{v}(t - 5)$). For most practical applications, we would want the distance between these two spatiotemporal patterns to be considered 0. Unfortunately, the metric D will assign a distance that could be quite large. In another situation a spatiotemporal neural network might be used to extract a human speech signal from a sound stream containing other obscuring and interfering signals. Because of the nature of the network, the output speech sound stream may be slightly time–warped from the sound stream of the original speaker (that is, the output speech might speed up and then slow down sporadically as the speech stream evolves). Again, in such an instance, the metric D might well produce a distance that is quite large between the original isolated speech stream of the speaker and the extracted, slightly time–warped version of that speech stream, even if the two are initially perfectly synchronized in time. In summary, there are many situations in which the metric D itself is not satisfactory. However, if we were to apply an appropriate *corrective* spatiotemporal warping transformation to one of the two patterns being compared, then D might serve quite adequately as a distance measurement. This is the theme that we will now pursue.

The basic concept is that, as in the previous examples, we want to create a distance measurement that is invariant, or at least insensitive, to the distortion of patterns by some preselected class $\mathscr{C}$ of spatiotemporal warping transformations. For example, if we wished to be insensitive to small time warps, we might define the class $\mathscr{C}$ to consist of transformations of the form $\mathbf{u}(t) \longrightarrow \mathbf{u}(\theta(t))$, where $0.5 \leq d\theta/dt \leq 2.0$. Of course, $\mathscr{C}$ might consist of even more complicated transformations, such as those connected with pitch changes or bandpass filtering.

Given the desire to have a distance measurement that is invariant with respect to a class $\mathscr{C}$ of spatiotemporal warping transformations, a natural choice would be

$$G(\mathbf{u}, \mathbf{v}) \equiv \inf_{T \in \mathscr{C}} D(\mathbf{u}, T\mathbf{v}). \tag{6.3}$$

Equation 6.3 says that we will now measure distance with a measurement G, which we obtain by measuring the D distance between **u** and every possible transformed version of **v** (that is, using every transformation T in the preselected set of transformations $\mathscr{C}$), and then taking the minimum of all of these D distances. Instead of using the minimum function, min, which is suitable only for finding the smallest of a finite set of real numbers, Equation 6.3 uses the function inf (standing for *infimum*), which is a generalization of min that will work for real number subsets with infinitely many members. The reason that inf must be used is an interesting mathematical detail. For example, the infinite set $(0, 1)$ of all real numbers between 0 and 1 does not have a minimum (there is no smallest positive real number), but it does have an infimum — namely, 0.

The distance measurement G has the advantage that it is no longer sensitive to spatiotemporal warping transformations of class $\mathscr{C}$ (the effects of which we have decided to ignore). Unfortunately, this means that $G(T\mathbf{u}, \mathbf{u}) = 0$ for any transformation $T \in \mathscr{C}$. Thus, G cannot be a metric, because $G(T\mathbf{u}, \mathbf{u}) = 0$ does not imply that $T\mathbf{u} = \mathbf{u}$. Nonetheless, the distance measurement G carries out exactly the operation we usually need for measuring the distance between spatiotemporal patterns.

In the next subsubsection, we consider a particular G distance measurement that has been used in engineering for decades.

MATCHED FILTERING   In the history of electrical engineering, there have been five technological epochs: the era of fundamental discoveries (1,000,000 B.C. to 1865 A.D.), the golden age of electricity (1866 to 1915), the radio years (1916 to 1935), the golden age of non–radio electronics (1936 to 1955), and the information processing age (1956 to present). It was in the fourth of these epochs that radar, sonar, and digital communications were developed. One of the key elements involved in all three of these fields has been the *matched filter* concept, invented by D. O. North in 1943 [180]. A matched filter is a device for detecting a particular signal. In traditional signal processing texts (see [185] for example), the matched filter for input (complex) scalar signal u, tuned to (complex) scalar signal v, is defined by the formula

$$H_v(u, t) = \int_{-\infty}^{\infty} u(\tau - t)v(\tau)\, d\tau.$$

The output of this filter is maximal only when the input waveform u matches the reference waveform v. It can be shown that the matched filter is the ideal detector for the waveform v in additive *white noise* (noise that has the same power level at all frequencies and is uncorrelated with itself at different times). This classical definition of a matched filter is suitable for only single–dimensional signals; the filter has the disadvantage that its output is based on an assumption that the unknown signal has a known power level. These restrictions are fine for radar, sonar, and communications, but are not appropriate for pattern recognition. Thus, we must generalize this definition.

For the purposes of this book, we define the *generalized multidimensional matched filter* (or simply *matched filter*, since we shall not use the traditional version in this book) for input spatiotemporal pattern $\mathbf{u}$, tuned to spatiotemporal pattern $\mathbf{v}$, over spatiotemporal warp class $\mathscr{C}$, to be

$$H_\mathbf{v}(\mathbf{u}, t) \equiv \inf_{T \in \mathscr{C}} \int_{-\infty}^{\infty} \mu(\tau - t) \mid \mathbf{u}(\tau) - T\mathbf{v}(\tau) \mid d\tau = G(\mu_t\, \mathbf{u}, \mu_t\, \mathbf{v}), \qquad (6.4)$$

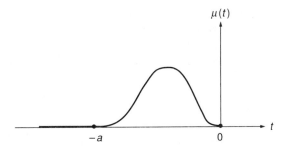

$\mu(t)$

$-a$ 0 t

Fig. 6.3. • A typical time windowing function μ. The function is zero everywhere except in the interval $[-a, 0]$, where it is non–negative.

where μ is a non–negative smooth function with $\mu(\tau) \geq 0$ for $\tau \in (-a, 0)$ (where a is a non–negative constant) and $\mu(\tau) = 0$ otherwise, and where $\mathscr{C}$ is a defined set of spatiotemporal warping transformations. The function μ is called a *time windowing function* (see Figure 6.3). It serves the purpose of focusing the attention of the distance measurement on the time interval $[t - a, t]$. H can be interpreted as the distance between the spatiotemporal pattern $\mathbf{u}$ over the time interval $[t - a, t]$, and the best matching warped portion (of duration $[t - a, t]$) of $\mathbf{v}$. It is also easy to show (see Exercise 6.1.5) that H can be written as $H_{\mathbf{v}}(\mathbf{u}, t) = G(\mu_t \mathbf{u}, \mu_t \mathbf{v})$, where $\mu_t(\tau) = \mu(\tau - t)$.

This matched filter generalizes the usual matched filter to the case of n-dimensional signals. It dispenses with the use of complex numbers (which are of little value for nonlinear systems such as neural networks anyway, since the required z-transforms are valid only for linear systems — see [185]), and it implements a matching process that can be made insensitive to a variety of signal distortions that are unimportant for a particular problem (by choosing the set $\mathscr{C}$ of spatiotemporal warping transformations correctly). Naturally, not all of the properties of the traditional linear matched filter are preserved (linearity, for example!). However, the property of being a good detector for the pattern in noise often *is* preserved (depending on the set $\mathscr{C}$). To see why, notice that, if we insert a noisy signal $\mathbf{u} + \mathbf{n}$ in place of $\mathbf{u}$ (where $\mathbf{n}$ is a general noise signal), then since $|\mathbf{u} + \mathbf{n} - T\mathbf{v}| \leq |\mathbf{u} - T\mathbf{v}| + |\mathbf{n}|$, we get

$$
\begin{aligned}
H_{\mathbf{v}}(\mathbf{u} + \mathbf{n}, t) &\leq H_{\mathbf{v}}(\mathbf{u}, t) + \inf_{T \in \mathscr{C}} \int_{-\infty}^{\infty} \mu^2(\tau - t) \, |\mathbf{n}(\tau)| \, d\tau \\
&= H_{\mathbf{v}}(\mathbf{u}, t) + \int_{-\infty}^{\infty} \mu^2(\tau - t) \, |\mathbf{n}(\tau)| \, d\tau \\
&= H_{\mathbf{v}}(\mathbf{u}, t) + \mathcal{N},
\end{aligned}
\tag{6.5}
$$

where $\mathcal{N}$ is the integrated "power" of the noise process $\mathbf{n}$ weighted by the window function μ over the time interval $[t - a, t]$. Thus, as with many situations involving euclidean distance, the triangle inequality gives us the ability to separate the noise from the non–noisy portion of the matched filtering process. Note that we could dispense with the inf because the noise integral does not depend on T.

As a result of Equation 6.5, it is clear that additive noise power, combined with the input signal to the filter, will contaminate the matched filtering process in a directly additive and average-power-linear way, which is essentially as well as we can, in general, hope to do. In fact, the generalized matched filter has the advantage that the effect of noise is felt only in terms of the noise's weighted average power level. In a sense, the noise is not put through the filter, as with the classical matched filter.

If a noise-free version u of the reference signal v is entered into the matched filter (where $u = Tv$ for some admissible transformation T), then the output of the filter will be zero. Thus, this matched filter has an output that is *smallest* when the correct signal is entered (this is the opposite of the traditional matched filter). When noise is added to such an input signal, the output signal is merely equal to the weighted average noise power over the time interval $[t - a, t]$. The output for signals that are not transformed versions of the reference signal, with the same noise added, will be higher than that for the signals that are equivalent. As with the usual matched filter, this property can be used to formulate pattern detection criteria.

Next, we use the generalized multidimensional matched filter to define a general type of spatiotemporal pattern classifier called the *nearest matched filter classifier*. Then, a neural network implementation of one such classifier, the *spatiotemporal pattern recognizer* network, is presented.

THE NEAREST MATCHED FILTER CLASSIFIER   Building a pattern classifier for spatiotemporal patterns usually requires the gathering of many examples of patterns belonging to each of the M classes into which each unknown input pattern is to be placed. To make the notation concrete, let us define such a *training set* of patterns to be the set $P = \{(v_1, \beta_1), (v_2, \beta_2), ..., (v_N, \beta_N)\}$, where $\beta_k \in \{1, 2, ..., M\}$ is the number of the class to which example pattern v_k belongs. The idea of the *nearest matched filter classifier* is simply to use the training set patterns as the reference patterns for N matched filters. The input signal, to the classifier u, is fed to all of these matched filters in parallel (all of the matched filters use the same weighting functions, or at least weighting functions with the same integral over time). The output of the classifier at time t is the class number β_i associated with the reference pattern having the smallest matched filter output $H_{v_i}(u, t)$, along with the actual value of that filter output. Clearly, the pattern class output typically will not be smooth (it will jump abruptly from one class number to another as the winning classifier of the competition process changes). The minimum filter output is supplied to give an estimate of the "value" or "believability" of the class output. I developed the nearest matched filter classifier during the period 1979 to 1982, while working on problems in time-series signal classification at Motorola, Inc.

In 1982, I introduced the nearest matched filter classifier along with a neural network implementation of the spatiotemporal pattern recognizer network [114] and, in a 1987 paper [112], I presented a detailed theory of this classifier and further described the related neural network. However, the spatiotemporal pattern classifier network described in both of these early papers was considerably simpler than the improved version presented here.

The nearest matched filter classifier can be defined for a variety of spatiotemporal warping transformations. However, common choices might be time warping or pitch change transformations. Time warping would be useful, for example, for speech recognition, where the changes in how words are pronounced are typically of a time–warp nature. Pitch change transformations (such as those that occur when we speed up or slow down a phonograph record) would be useful for recognizing vehicles by their sounds, since much of the sound of a vehicle is from its engine, transmission, and wheels, which produce sounds at pitches that are directly dependent on road speed and gear selection. In every case, the use of an appropriate class of transformations will ensure that each reference pattern can serve as a model for a wide class of similar, but transformed, patterns. This effective pattern reuse greatly reduces the number of reference patterns that must be used.

In pattern recognition theory, researchers have shown [52, 56] that, for every pattern classification problem, there is an optimal classifier that will, on a statistical basis, correctly determine the class of unknown patterns a higher percentage of the time than will any other classifier. This classifier is known as the *Bayes classifier*. The Bayes classifier is based on an assumed perfect knowledge of the probability density function of each class in pattern space (that is, given an arbitrary pattern, we are assumed to know the probability that it is in each class). Since we do not usually have this detailed level of knowledge, most classifiers are decidedly sub-Bayesian in their performance. Notice that, although a Bayes classifier has optimal performance, it may not be perfect. The performance of the Bayes classifier is determined by how much overlap exists between the classes. In other words, given the pattern data provided, can a particular unknown pattern belong to more than one class? For example, if we are classifying speech by means of a 2-dimensional spatiotemporal pattern $\mathbf{u}(t)$ that gives us the total sound power level, and the frequency of the loudest speech component at time t, it may not be possible to classify the last few hundred milliseconds of speech as being associated unambiguously with one particular word. Even if we are given a high quality 128–channel frequency spectrum and allow for pitch and time–warp transformations, there may still be ambiguous words, at least over the time interval $[t - a, t]$ in which the classifier is operating.

Given a training set that is a sufficiently comprehensive statistical sample of the entire pattern environment to be encountered during operation of the classifier, the nearest matched filter classifier can be shown to have near-Bayesian performance (my 1987 paper [112] demonstrates this for the case where $\mathscr{C}$ is the set of time translations). In particular, the average error rate R of the nearest matched filter classifier (the average fraction of the time that a pattern will be misclassified) is provided by the following theorem from the 1987 paper.

■ **RESULT 6.1.1** *Given a sufficiently statistically comprehensive training set P, a nearest matched filter classifier based on P will have an error rate R that satisfies the Cover and Hart inequality*

$$R^* \leq R \leq R^* \left(2 - \frac{M}{M-1} R^* \right), \tag{6.6}$$

where R^* is the error rate of the Bayes classifier. ■

This theorem establishes that, in the worst case, the error rate of the ideal nearest matched filter classifier will be less than twice the error rate of the Bayes classifier. Since, for most pattern classification problems of interest, the Bayes classifier error rate is fairly low (often well under 5 percent), we can hope to achieve good performance with the nearest matched filter classifier, assuming that we can build one with a sufficiently rich training set, which we will define as a training set containing an example that is close to every input pattern that is entered into the classifier.

The nearest matched filter classifier has one problem, and two advantages. The problem is that we may require an enormous training set; this requirement may make the potential physical size of the implementation impossibly large and computationally burdensome (since all N of the $H_{v_k}(\mathbf{u}, t)$ integrals must be computed in parallel). The advantages are that the classifier is capable of near-Bayesian performance, and that the individual matched filters are insensitive to noise. This latter advantage is particularly important if all of the matched filters are using the same weighting function (as opposed to weighting functions that merely have the same time integral), since Equation 6.5 shows that all of the matched filters will then react the same to additive noise. Thus, since the decision process is a relative comparison of the matched filter outputs, the classifier output will be especially insensitive to additive noise. The combination of guaranteed high classification accuracy (given our ability and willingness to implement a sufficient training set) and additive noise insensitivity make the nearest matched filter classifier an interesting candidate for solving spatiotemporal classification problems.

Finally, because the windowing function limits the consideration of the incoming spatiotemporal pattern to the time interval $[t-a, t]$, the nearest matched filter classifier can carry out only the first local-in-time stage of spatiotemporal pattern recognition. For many problems, local-in-time classification is not sufficient. Often, to do a good job of classification, we must exploit context information that we can obtain only by considering longer periods of time. One way to do this is to change the output of the nearest matched filter classifier to provide the identities and filter output values for all of the filters that have reasonably low outputs, not just the single lowest one. These selected matched filter output values can then be used as inputs to a process that combines these outputs with statistical context information, to disambiguate ambiguous classifications, and to decide exactly when a pattern actually appeared in the input. Because such a postprocessing operation is often essential if adequate performance is to be

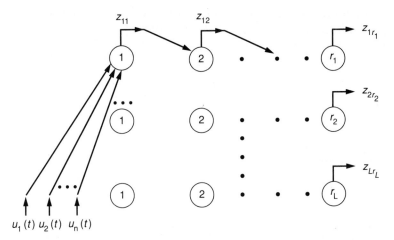

$$u_1(t)\ u_2(t)\ u_n(t)$$

Fig. 6.4. • Architecture of the spatiotemporal pattern recognizer neural network. The input to the network is a spatiotemporal pattern $\mathbf{u}(t)$; the output is the spatiotemporal pattern $(z_{1r_1}(t), z_{2r_2}(t), \ldots, z_{Lr_L}(t))$.

achieved, the nearest matched filter classifier should really be thought of as just a front end for a complete classifier.

SPATIOTEMPORAL PATTERN RECOGNIZER NETWORK   In this subsection we will discuss a neural network called the *spatiotemporal pattern recognizer* that approximately implements a type of nearest matched filter classifier. The class of spatiotemporal warping transformations $\mathscr{C}$ that we wish to be insensitive to is the set of time warps $\theta(t)$ for which $0.5 \leq d\theta/dt \leq 2.0$. The weighting functions used shall have time windows equal in length to the time duration of the pattern to which each is assigned (but shall have total time integrals of 1.0). In light of the fact (as discussed above) that a nearest matched filter classifier usually will be used as the front end portion of a complete classifier, it will be assumed that the spatiotemporal pattern recognizer neural network will provide the back end of the classifier with the raw time–varying matched filter output for each of the L reference pattern filters implemented by the network. Using this data, the downstream system may be able to carry out context-exploitation operations.

The architecture of the spatiotemporal pattern recognizer neural network is shown in Figure 6.4. It consists of L rows of processing elements, where each row approximately implements the function of a generalized matched filter based on a specific spatiotemporal example pattern. We shall assume that row i implements the matched filter function for training set reference pattern $\mathbf{v}_i$.

In Figure 6.5, the operation of a representative processing element in the network is illustrated. The particular processing element shown in Figure 6.5 is the ith processing element of row l of the network. The output signal of this processing element is $z_{li}(t)$. The processing element receives inputs from all of the lower–numbered processing elements in its row (that is, those to its left), as well as from all n channels of the spatiotemporal input pattern $\mathbf{u}$ that is to be classified. The transfer function equation for this processing element is given by

$$z_{li} = U(x_{li}(t) - \sigma_{li}), \tag{6.7}$$

where

$$x_{li}(t) = \alpha_{li} \left(-c_{li}\, x_{li}(t-1) + d_{li}\, U \left([\psi_{li} - |\mathbf{v}_{li} - \mathbf{u}(t)|]\, z_{l(i-1)}(t-1) \right) \right), \tag{6.8}$$

$$0 \le x_{li}(t) \le 1,$$

$$z_{l0}(t) \equiv 1,$$

$$U(\zeta) = \begin{cases} 1 & \text{if } \zeta > 0 \\ 0 & \text{if } \zeta \le 0, \end{cases} \tag{6.9}$$

$$\tag{6.10}$$

and

$$\alpha_{li}(\xi) = \begin{cases} \xi & \text{if } \xi \ge 0 \\ \phi_{li}\, \xi & \text{if } \xi < 0, \end{cases} \tag{6.11}$$

and where $\mathbf{v}_{li}$ is a constant vector, and $c_{li}, d_{li}, \sigma_{li}, \psi_{li}$, and ϕ_{li} are positive constants, with $c_{li}, \phi_{li} < 1$.

Although this transfer function appears complicated, the concept behind it is simple. The basic idea is that the output of the final processing element of one row of the spatiotemporal pattern recognizer network should be essentially a binary indicator of whether or not ($z_{lr_l} = 1$ or 0) the spatiotemporal pattern $\mathbf{u}$ has just completed approximately traversing the path in space defined by the spatiotemporal example pattern $\mathbf{v}_l$ — in the proper direction, and at a speed that was within selected time–warp limits of the speed of $\mathbf{v}_l$ at each point in its trajectory. In other words, the recent behavior of the pattern $\mathbf{u}$ has closely matched that of a suitably time–warped version of the pattern $\mathbf{v}_l$. Given that we can establish these claims, then the output z_{lr_l} will be a binary indicator of the event of having $H_{\mathbf{v}_l}(\mathbf{u}, t)$ take on a suitably small value. The operation of row l of the spatiotemporal pattern recognizer network is now described in terms of Equations 6.7 and 6.8.

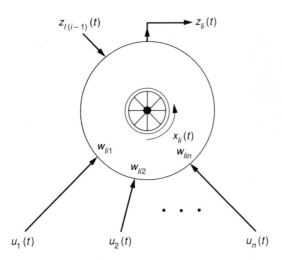

Fig. 6.5. • Spatiotemporal pattern recognizer processing element. The processing element receives input from the previous processing element in its row, as well as from the pattern $\mathbf{u}(t)$; these inputs cause a braked flywheel within the unit to spin up. The output z_{li} of the unit is 1 if the flywheel is spinning faster than threshold σ_{li}; otherwise, the output is 0.

As shown in Figure 6.5, each of the processing elements in this network has the equivalent of a small flywheel inside it. The speed of this flywheel is the quantity $x_{li}(t)$. The time variable t is an integer variable in this network. The increment of time corresponding to each unit increase in t is chosen to be much less than the Nyquist sampling period required by the most rapidly changing component of $\mathbf{u}, \mathbf{v}_1, \mathbf{v}_2, \ldots,$ and $\mathbf{v}_L$. By choosing a sufficiently small time increment, we can ensure that the input pattern and the example pattern will never change much over this small increment of time. The constants c_{li}, d_{li}, and ϕ_{li}, which determine the flywheel dynamics, are set such that they are matched to the typical range of change rates of the $\mathbf{u}$ and $\mathbf{v}$ patterns.

To understand the behavior of the flywheel within each processing element, let us consider what will happen in Equations 6.7 and 6.8 if the input pattern $\mathbf{u}$ traverses a trajectory close to that of the pattern $\mathbf{v}_l$. As shown in Figure 6.6, we choose the weight vectors $\mathbf{v}_{li}$ of the processing elements of row l to be the positions of the pattern vector $\mathbf{v}_l(t)$ every 10 time units or so throughout its time duration. The time increment is assumed to be so small that, even if we sample the position of $\mathbf{v}_l(t)$ every tenth time unit, the samples will change very little from one sampling to the next. We choose to take a sample approximately every 10 time units so that Equation 6.8 will properly function as a flywheel equation (see Section 3.5). Once the samples $\mathbf{v}_{l1}, \mathbf{v}_{l2}, \ldots, \mathbf{v}_{lr_l}$ have been selected, spheres are then positioned around each of these weight vectors to form a sort of bumpy cylinder surrounding the trajectory v_l (see Figure 6.6). The individual radii of these spheres ($\psi_{l1}, \psi_{l2}, \ldots, \psi_{lr_l}$, respectively) are chosen such that the minimum

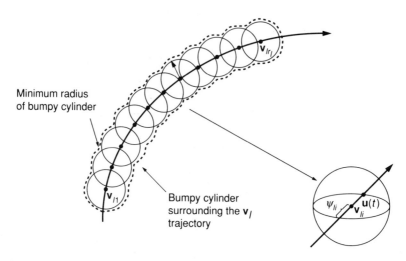

Minimum radius
of bumpy cylinder

Bumpy cylinder
surrounding the $\mathbf{v}_l$
trajectory

Fig. 6.6. • Activator spheres for the example pattern $\mathbf{v}_l$. If the pattern $\mathbf{u}(t)$ enters into a sphere of radius ψ_{li} surrounding the example pattern sample $\mathbf{v}_{li}$, then the quantity $[\psi_{li} - |\mathbf{v}_{li} - \mathbf{u}(t)|]$ becomes positive. If $\mathbf{u}(t)$ has also just finished traversing the spheres $(\mathbf{v}_{l1}, \psi_{l1}), (\mathbf{v}_{l2}, \psi_{l2}), \ldots,$ and $(\mathbf{v}_{l(i-1)}, \psi_{l(i-1)})$ in the proper order and within the time–warp speed ratio limits, then the x_{li} flywheel will begin to spin up. If it spins up far enough (to a speed greater than σ_{li}), then z_{li} will become 1. This process is continued to the end processing element of row l, thus implementing the matched filter function.

distance from the $\mathbf{v}_l$ trajectory to a point outside of the union of the spheres is greater than some selected minimum value. This ensures that any $\mathbf{u}$ trajectory that approximately follows $\mathbf{v}_l$ to within this distance will cause the z_{lr_l} output to be equal to 1 at the point where $\mathbf{u}(t)$ traverses the $\mathbf{v}_{lr_l}$ sphere.

As the trajectory $\mathbf{u}(t)$ (again, assumed to be similar in the recent past to the example trajectory $\mathbf{v}_l$) enters the $\mathbf{v}_{li}$ sphere (of radius ψ_{li}), the $[\psi_{li} - |\mathbf{v}_{li} - \mathbf{u}(t)|]$ portion of the argument of the unit step function in Equation 6.8 will become positive (outside the sphere, it is negative). Assuming that the quantity x_{li} is currently at a low value (x_{li} is hard-limited between 0 and 1), the value of x_{li} will increase rapidly (assuming that $z_{l(i-1)} = 1$ and that the constants c_{li} and d_{li} have been chosen properly). The behavior of x_{li} under these circumstances is shown in Figure 6.7. As $\mathbf{u}$ enters the sphere, the value of x_{li} rises rapidly (in accordance with the time constant $1/c_{li}$), until it quickly hard limits at 1. It maintains this value of 1 until $\mathbf{u}$ leaves the sphere, at which time it begins to decay exponentially with time constant ϕ_{li}/c_{li}. Notice that the time constant for activation is different from the time constant for decay; this is because of the form of the *attack function* α_{li}, as shown in Figure 6.8. The attack function lets the flywheel speed x_{li} spin up rapidly as $\mathbf{u}$ enters the sphere, and then causes the flywheel to spin down more slowly after $\mathbf{u}$ leaves the sphere. We can always assume that the flywheel speed x_{li} is small as $\mathbf{u}$ enters the sphere, because we assume that $\mathbf{u}$ will not "loop back" to this sphere, once it has left it, until after

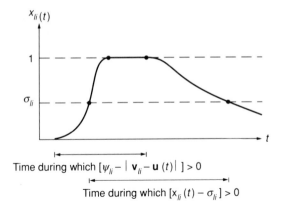

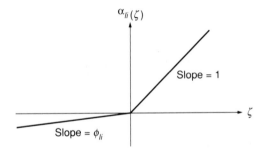

Fig. 6.7. • Behavior of the function $x_{li}(t)$ as **u** passes through the $\mathbf{v}_{li}$ sphere of radius ψ_{li} (assuming that **u** previously passed through the earlier spheres of the row in the proper order and within the proper speed range, thus ensuring that $z_{l(i-1)} = 1$).

Fig. 6.8. • The attack function α_{li}. This function ensures that the flywheel takes longer to spin down than it does to spin up.

this unit's flywheel has spun down considerably. The constant σ_{li}, along with the constants ϕ_{li} and c_{li}, determine the length of time required for the flywheel to spin up to a speed where the processing element output signal z_{li} can potentially go to the value 1, as well as the length of time z_{li} will remain at this value after **u** leaves the sphere.

As shown by Equation 6.7, two things must happen before the value of z_{li} can become 1. First, the flywheel speed x_{li} must be greater than the speed threshold σ_{li}; this ensures that **u** has entered the $\mathbf{v}_{li}$ sphere and has remained within it for a sufficiently long time. Second, $z_{l(i-1)}$ at the previous time increment $(t-1)$ must also have been equal to 1. This condition means that **u** is within the $\mathbf{v}_{l(i-1)}$ sphere, or has just left that sphere in the recent past. Also, while it was in that previous sphere, the $z_{l(i-2)}$ input had also been 1. Thus, Equations 6.7 and 6.8 are recursive formulas that demand, through a chain of sequential steps, that **u** already has traversed the spheres around $\mathbf{v}_{l1}, \mathbf{v}_{l2}, \ldots, \mathbf{v}_{l(i-1)}$ and has now penetrated the sphere around $\mathbf{v}_{li}$. All of this must happen before z_{li} will attain the value 1. So, as previously claimed, z_{lr_l} can become equal to 1 if and only if $\mathbf{u}$ has closely followed the entire trajectory of $\mathbf{v}_l$ in the most recently passed increments of time.

Notice that, in Figure 6.7, the rise and fall of x_{li} as a function of time will always follow approximately the same rise and decay curves (again, assuming that x_{li} starts off at a very low value). This is true because the second term of the right side of Equation 6.8 provides a "flywheel driving torque" that is equal to d_{li} whenever $\mathbf{u}$ is within the $\mathbf{v}_{li}$ sphere (that is, during spin up of the flywheel) and is 0 after $\mathbf{u}$ leaves the sphere (during spin down). Thus, the time delay between entry of $\mathbf{u}$ into the $\mathbf{v}_{li}$ sphere, and the point at which x_{li} exceeds σ_{li}, is fairly constant. Similarly, the period of time between the beginning of spin down and the point when x_{li} reaches σ_{li} is always the same. Thus, the transit time of $\mathbf{u}$ through the sphere $\mathbf{v}_{li}$ must be longer than the minimum spin up time in order for x_{li} to reach the Equation 6.7 threshold of σ_{li}. This effectively sets an upper limit on the time warp speed $d\theta/dt$. A lower limit is established by the subtle fact that z_{li} must continue to be 1 essentially throughout the transit of $\mathbf{u}$ through the sphere around $\mathbf{v}_{l(iti)}$ (see Exercise 6.1.6). In essence, $\mathbf{u}$'s average speed through the next sphere must be fast enough that $z_{l(i+2)}$ can be activated before the "tail" of x_{li} reaches σ_{li}, thus extinguishing z_{li} and causing $x_{l(i+1)}$ to begin to spin down over a fixed time course. If $z_{l(i+2)}$ does not become active before $z_{l(i+1)}$ is extinguished, the chain will be broken.

So, each row of the spatiotemporal pattern recognizer neural network acts as a detector for time warped (within limits) approximations of a single pattern $\mathbf{v}_l$. By selecting the adjustable constants correctly, we can set the allowable limits of time warping and spatial approximation for each example pattern. This non-cued classifier is suitable for applications such as continuous speech recognition, where the placement of the patterns to be sensed in the time series is arbitrary and unpredictable.

Although the spatiotemporal pattern recognizer network has considerable capability, it suffers from the lack of a learning law (although, in actual practice, configuring the network is not as difficult as it might seem to be). A simpler version of this network, which is capable of using Kosko/Klopf learning (see Section 3.6), has been defined [112]. However, this simplified network does not have all of the capabilities and the robustness of the spatiotemporal pattern recognizer network defined here.

In conclusion, the spatiotemporal pattern recognizer network can function as an almost ideal local–in–time front end for a global–in–time pattern recognition system. Each row of the network functions approximately as a binarized generalized multi–dimensional matched filter for a particular example spatiotemporal pattern $\mathbf{v}_l$. As with the nearest matched filter classifier, the number of rows required to solve a particular problem may be enormous (ways of reducing this inherent redundancy are being investigated).

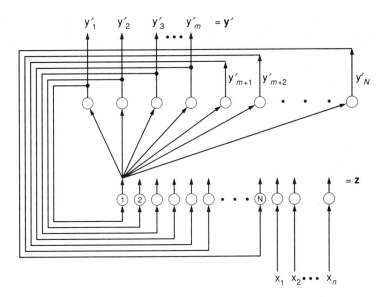

Fig. 6.9. • Architecture of the recurrent backpropagation network. The network consists of a single functional layer of N processing elements. Time (t) moves forward in discrete integer steps. The outputs of the N processing elements at time $t-1$ are fed back to all N units as inputs at time t. Each of the N units also receives n external–world inputs (the components of the vector $\mathbf{x}(t-1)$) and a bias input (always 1.0 — not shown) at time t. The outputs of the network at time t consists of the output signals of the first m processing elements — which form the components of the network output vector $\mathbf{y}'(t)$.

6.1.2 Recurrent Backpropagation Neural Network

This subsection discusses the *recurrent backpropagation network*. This network is a spatiotemporal generalization of the backpropagation network of Section 5.3. The recurrent backpropagation network was introduced in 1986 by David Rumelhart, Geoffrey Hinton, and Ronald Williams [203] and was later substantially improved and expanded upon by Luis Almeda [6], Ronald Williams and David Zipser [239], and Fernando Pineda [189].

RECURRENT BACKPROPAGATION NETWORK ARCHITECTURE   The topology of the recurrent backpropagation network is described in Figure 6.9. The network consists of a single layer of N functional units. A layer of fanout units serves to distribute both the fed back output signals of the N output units, as well as to distribute the components $x_1(t-1), x_2(t-1), \ldots, x_n(t-1)$ of the input vector $\mathbf{x}(t-1)$ (the input vector used during the network's operation at time t is latched into the fanout units at time $t-1$ along with the fed back processing element output signals from time increment $t-1$). Each of the N processing elements of the functional layer also receives a bias input, which we shall label as $x_0(t-1)$, where $x_0(t) \equiv 1.0$ for all values of t (this bias input is not shown in Figure 6.9).

The outputs of the network at time t are the outputs $y'_1(t), y'_2(t), \ldots, y'_m(t)$ of the first m processing elements of the functional layer of the network. The output signals of the remaining units are $y'_{(m+1)}(t), y'_{(m+2)}(t), \ldots, y'_N(t)$. To simplify the notation, we define

$$z_j(t) = \begin{cases} x_j(t) & \text{if } 0 \le j \le n \\ y'_{(j-n)}(t) & \text{if } (n+1) \le j \le L \end{cases} \qquad \text{(6.12)}$$

where $j = 0, 1, 2, \ldots, L$, and $L = N + n$. For convenience we shall assume that time always begins at $t = 0$.

The scheduling of the recurrent backpropagation network involves two passes of operation of the network during every integer time step. The first pass is the *output calculation* pass. During this pass, on time step t, processing element i calculates its output signal $y_i(t)$ by means of the formula

$$y'_i(t) = s_i(I_i(t)) \qquad\qquad i = 1, 2, \ldots, N, \qquad \text{(6.13)}$$

where

$$I_i(t) = \sum_{j=0}^{L} w_{ij}\, z_j(t-1), \qquad \text{(6.14)}$$

and where each of the functions $s_i(u)$ is bounded and has a continuous derivative.

The second pass of the network (the *training* pass) is when the weights of the network are updated. This pass will be described later, after the learning law used by the network has been derived. To provide needed background for this derivation, the overall problem that the recurrent backpropagation network is designed to solve is described first.

As discussed in Section 5.3, the backpropagation network is a mapping network that can be used to approximate a function $f : A \subset \mathbf{R}^n \longrightarrow \mathbf{R}^m$. The recurrent backpropagation network carries out a similar function, only, instead of implementing a spatial mapping that maps a point $\mathbf{x}$ into a point $\mathbf{y}$, it approximates a *spatiotemporal mapping* that maps a spatiotemporal function $\mathbf{x}$ into a spatiotemporal function $\mathbf{y}$. This will now be made precise.

To see what the recurrent backpropagation network does, examine its activities during a complete sequence of operation. Let the input to and output from the system at time t be $\mathbf{x}(t-1)$ and $\mathbf{y}'(t)$, respectively. We shall assume that the system starts operation at $t = 1$. Initial values for the internal states of the system at time $t = 0$ are uniquely defined by the initial values of the output signals (in other words, by the vector $\mathbf{y}'(0)$). The system runs forward in time until some arbitrary stopping time t_{stop} is reached. During each of these "runs" of the system the input sequence $\{\mathbf{x}(0), \mathbf{x}(1), \mathbf{x}(2), \ldots, \mathbf{x}(t_{\text{stop}} - 1)\}$ is provided to the system. From the initial state of the system ($\mathbf{y}'(0)$), and this sequence of $\mathbf{x}(t)$ inputs, the system produces outputs $\{\mathbf{y}'(1), \mathbf{y}'(2), \ldots, \mathbf{y}'(t_{\text{stop}})\}$. Clearly then, the overall purpose of the system on each run is to map the set

$$\mathbf{x} \equiv \{\mathbf{y}'(0), \{\mathbf{x}(0), \mathbf{x}(1), \mathbf{x}(2), \ldots, \mathbf{x}(t_{\text{stop}} - 1)\}\}$$

into the set of m-dimensional vectors

$$\mathbf{y}' \equiv \{\mathbf{y}'(1), \mathbf{y}'(2), \ldots, \mathbf{y}'(t_{\text{stop}})\}.$$

Thus, we can view the operation of such a spatiotemporal system as performing a mapping from a set consisting of the initial system state and a set of input values provided over the run to a set consisting of the output states produced by the system over the run. The confusing thing about this picture is that in many practical instances (such as most control systems) the $\mathbf{x}(t)$ inputs are functionally dependent upon earlier $\mathbf{y}'(t)$ outputs. The key observation is that *this doesn't matter*. The only effect this has is to limit the range of possibilities for the $\mathbf{x}(t)$ sequences that the system will see. We are only concerned with what the system does when a particular sequence of $\mathbf{x}(t)$ inputs is presented (given a certain initial state of the system). We don't care how those inputs arose.

A control system or any other practical spatiotemporal system will, for our purposes, be assumed to operate in an environment that is statistically stable. In other words, it is assumed that the probability of seeing a particular initial value and input data sequence (in other words, a particular $\mathbf{x}$) is given by a fixed probability density function $\rho(\mathbf{x})$.

In most situations the range of possible $\mathbf{x}$ sets that the recurrent backpropagation network could encounter is extremely broad. Let us define the *input space A* of the network to be the set consisting of all possible sets $\mathbf{x}$ (all those of non-zero probability). Conceptually, the $\mathbf{x}$ sets can be thought of as *points* in the space A. Similarly, we can view the $\mathbf{y}'$ sets as points in an *output space B*.

Given these definitions and concepts, we can now look at the overall purpose of the recurrent backpropagation network. That purpose is to approximate a *spatiotemporal mapping* $f : A \longrightarrow B$, in the most accurate possible manner, given that the $\mathbf{x}$ points are chosen randomly from A in accordance with the probability density function $\rho(\mathbf{x})$.

Unlike the recurrent backpropagation network (which is functioning as an approximation to f), the output of the mapping f is a set of the form

$$\mathbf{y} \equiv \{\mathbf{y}(1), \mathbf{y}(2), \ldots, \mathbf{y}(t_{\text{stop}})\}.$$

Thus, as with the backpropagation neural network, our goal is to minimize the average error between $\mathbf{y}'$ and $\mathbf{y} = f(\mathbf{x})$, where the average is weighted by the probability density function $\rho(\mathbf{x})$ used to select the $\mathbf{x}$ inputs to both systems.

The error calculation procedure for the recurrent backpropagation network is similar to that used with the backpropagation network, but with one important difference: not all correct output signals are known. In the case of recurrent backpropagation we assume that with each training run example $\mathbf{x}$ we are also given information concerning some of the correct values of outputs of the network at various points during the run. Specifically, we assume that at each time t, $1 \leq t \leq t_{\text{stop}}$ during a training run we are given a set $U(t)$ of integers lying in the range from 1 to m, inclusive, such that the correct output value $y_k(t)$ for unit k at time t is given for each $k \in U(t)$. It is perfectly acceptable to have $U(t)$ be the empty set at some times t during the training run. However, for there to be useful training, $U(t)$ must be non-empty at at least one time t during training.

Given the sets $U(t)$, and the correct $y_k(t)$ values for each $k \in U(t)$, then we define the mean squared error $F(\mathbf{w})$ of the recurrent backpropagation network to be

$$
F(\mathbf{w}) = \mathrm{E}\left[\left(\frac{1}{\sum_{t=1}^{t_{\text{stop}}} \#U(t)} \right) \sum_{t=1}^{t_{\text{stop}}} \sum_{k \in U(t)} [y_k(t) - y_k'(t)]^2 \right],
$$

where $\mathbf{w}$ is the weight vector of the network, $\#U(t) = $ the number of elements in $U(t)$ ($\#U(t) = 0$ if $U(t)$ is empty), and E[ ] is the expectation or averaging operator (the averaging is done over an unboundedly large number of input examples chosen randomly with respect to ρ). Note that the entire sum is divided by the the total number of error terms used. Thus, we are measuring the average squared error per output for which the correct output is given. This quantity is then averaged over the entire input space by the expectation operator. Again, as with backpropagation, the mean squared error depends only on the weights. Naturally, for this dependency to hold it must be assumed that the weights are fixed throughout the evaluation of network performance (an assumption which we will initially make, but later relax, in exact analogy with the Widrow learning law variant in Chapter 3 and the backpropagation jump-every-time generalized delta learning law derivation in Chapter 5).

RECURRENT BACKPROPAGATION NETWORK LEARNING LAW   We now examine how we can iteratively lower the mean squared error of the network. Obviously, as with the ADALINE and the backpropagation network, we want to do this by calculating the gradient of F with respect to the weight vector $\mathbf{w}$ (using batching) and then making a gradient descent using a finite jump. As with these earlier derivations, we will proceed to calculate the gradient by simply taking the gradient operator inside the expectation operator (the proof that we can do this is presumably the same as the proof for the backpropagation network, but I have not verified this). Thus, we get

$$
\begin{aligned}
\frac{\partial F(\mathbf{w})}{\partial w_{ij}} &= \mathrm{E}\left[\left(\frac{1}{\sum_{t=1}^{t_{\text{stop}}} \#U(t)} \right) \sum_{t=1}^{t_{\text{stop}}} \sum_{k \in U(t)} \frac{\partial [y_k(t) - y_k'(t)]^2}{\partial w_{ij}} \right] \\
&= \mathrm{E}\left[\left(\frac{1}{\sum_{t=1}^{t_{\text{stop}}} \#U(t)} \right) \sum_{t=1}^{t_{\text{stop}}} \sum_{k \in U(t)} 2\,[y_k(t) - y_k'(t)] \frac{\partial y_k'(t)}{\partial w_{ij}} \right].
\end{aligned} \quad \textbf{(6.15)}
$$

So, we need to calculate $\frac{\partial y_k'(t)}{\partial w_{ij}}$.

$$\frac{\partial y_k'(t)}{\partial w_{ij}} = \frac{\partial}{\partial w_{ij}} s_k \left(\sum_{l=0}^{L} w_{kl} \, z_l(t-1) \right)$$

$$= s_k'(I_k(t)) \left(\sum_{l=0}^{L} \frac{\partial}{\partial w_{ij}} [w_{kl} \, z_l(t-1)] \right)$$

$$= s_k'(I_k(t)) \left(\sum_{l=0}^{L} \left[\delta_{ik} \, \delta_{jl} \, z_l(t-1) + w_{kl} \frac{\partial z_l(t-1)}{\partial w_{ij}} \right] \right)$$

$$= s_k'(I_k(t)) \left([\delta_{ik} \, z_j(t-1)] + \sum_{p=1}^{N} \left[w_{k(p+n)} \frac{\partial y_p'(t-1)}{\partial w_{ij}} \right] \right), \quad \textbf{(6.16)}$$

where s_k' is the first derivative of s_k, and where δ_{ik} is the Kronecker delta ($\delta_{\alpha\beta} = 1$ if $\alpha = \beta$; else $\delta_{\alpha\beta} = 0$). Thus, if we let

$$r_{kij}(t) = \frac{\partial y_k'(t)}{\partial w_{ij}}, \quad \textbf{(6.17)}$$

then we can write Equation 6.16 as the recursive formula

$$r_{kij}(t) = s_k'(I_k(t)) \left([\delta_{ik} \, z_j(t-1)] + \sum_{p=1}^{N} [w_{k(p+n)} \, r_{kij}(t-1)] \right). \quad \textbf{(6.18)}$$

Notice that

$$r_{kij}(0) = 0, \quad \textbf{(6.19)}$$

since the initial value $y_k'(0)$ cannot depend upon w_{ij}.

At the end of each run (after all of the $z_l(t-1)$ values are known), the recursion formula of Equation 6.18 can be solved, using Equation 6.19 to provide the initial condition. The solutions to these equation then provide the $\frac{\partial y_k'(t)}{\partial w_{ij}}$ values required by Equations 6.14 and 6.15 for the calculation of the gradient. Naturally, in order to adequately approximate the expectation operator we must average over a large number of runs, where the $\mathbf{x}$ initial value and input sequence examples are chosen randomly in accordance with p.

Once we have batched up an adequate number of runs to accurately estimate $\nabla_{\mathbf{w}} F(\mathbf{w})$, then we apply the traditional learning law

$$\mathbf{w}^{\text{new}} = \mathbf{w}^{\text{old}} - \alpha \nabla_{\mathbf{w}} F(\mathbf{w}), \quad \textbf{(6.20)}$$

where, as usual, α is the learning rate constant. The need to batch up the results from a number of runs before modifying the weights makes this learning law very slow, even compared with the batching version of the backpropagation generalized delta rule. This is because each learning trial of the backpropagation network consists of only one data vector input and output, whereas each learning run of the recurrent backpropagation network consists of a whole sequence of data vector inputs and outputs. Clearly, the need to solve the recursive equation (Equation 6.18) adds even more computational burden to recurrent backpropagation.

Both the Widrow learning law and the jump-every-time version of the generalized delta rule involve a process whereby the network weight vector is modified on each input/output cycle. A similar approach can be used with recurrent backpropagation. In fact, there are two versions: jump on every time step for which training data is available, and jump at the end of each run. Each of these is implemented in the obvious way, namely, by simply replacing $\frac{\partial F(\mathbf{w})}{\partial w_{ij}}$ (the ijth component of $\nabla_\mathbf{w} F(\mathbf{w})$) in Equation 6.20 with

$$\frac{1}{\#U(t)} \sum_{k \in U(t)} 2[y_k(t) - y_k'(t)]\frac{\partial y_k'(t)}{\partial w_{ij}},$$

or with

$$\frac{1}{\sum_{t=1}^{t_{\text{stop}}} \#U(t)} \sum_{t=1}^{t_{\text{stop}}} \sum_{k \in U(t)} 2[y_k(t) - y_k'(t)]\frac{\partial y_k'(t)}{\partial w_{ij}},$$

respectively.

Another variant of the recurrent backpropagation learning law is the *teacher-forced learning law* introduced by Ronald Williams and David Zipser [239]. This variant is like the jump-every-time-step version, except for two changes. First, all of the correct output values $y_k(t)$ that we are given for training are used in the recursion equation (Equation 6.18) in place of the corresponding $y_k'(t)$ values. Second, after each weight jump the $r_{kij}(t)$ ($=\frac{\partial y_k'(t)}{\partial w_{ij}}$) value used to compute the jump is set to 0. Williams and Zipser report that, at least for some problems, the teacher forced learning law seems to converge to a useful solution faster than the original learning law or the two other variants. However, the recurrent backpropagation network is still at an early stage of development, and so it would be wise to try all of the learning law variants on each problem.

It is worth noting that the above derivation assumes that the inputs to the network do not depend upon the weight values. For many practical problems, such as in control, this assumption will be false because of the fact that the input is derived from the output (for example, by a plant that takes control signal outputs from the network, which definitely depend on the weights, and produces sensor inputs to the network — which therefore also depend upon the weights). Thus, in using the recurrent backpropagation network this limitation must always be kept in mind. However, this isn't to say that the method is unusable in these cases. Often the dependence of the input on the weights is small; in which case the method may still work. Besides this dependency problem, the form of the mean squared error function introduces two additional problems. The discussion of these two major flaws finishes off the section.

PROBLEMS WITH THE RECURRENT BACKPROPAGATION ERROR FUNCTION
The definition of mean squared error $F(\mathbf{w})$ that is used with the recurrent back-propagation network has two significant problems associated with it. First, because we typically only know a few of the correct output values on each run (as opposed to backpropagation, where we know them all), the error measurement on each single run will be imprecise and it will require a large number of runs to accumulate enough performance data to accurately assess the network's overall performance. Thus, just like training, testing such a network can be a major computational challenge.

Second, and more serious, for many systems (most control systems, for example) the inputs to the system at time t depend upon the outputs at earlier times. In this situation if the network and the mapping it is only imperfectly approximating are given the same inputs initially in a run, the later inputs will diverge from one another because of the differences in the input/output behavior between the two systems. What this means is that comparing the output errors for *the same input sequences* (which is exactly what our mean squared error function does) is uninteresting — since in real life the mapping and its approximation could never have the same inputs. A way of overcoming this deficiency has been discovered. It is based upon a control theory concept called *model-based control*. We now briefly describe this idea. In this concept the functional layer of the recurrent backpropagation network is split into two subsets. The weights of the network are arranged so that all of the weights from the external inputs to the units of the second subset are permanently set to 0, as are the weights on the recurrent connections from the second subset to the first subset. Some of the weights on the recurrent connections from the first subset to the second subset are usually also permanently set to 0 — see below. Some of the output units are in the second subset and some are in the first subset (those in the first subset are the units that feed output from the first subset to the second). The first subset takes the external input and processes it and then sends it on to the second subset, which then creates the overall output of the system (which, therefore, consists of the signals from those output units that happen to be in the second subset). The trick used in model-based control is to train the overall network input/output function to implement a particular constant mapping (in other words, $\mathbf{x}(t) = \mathbf{y}'(t) = \mathbf{c}$ (where, in this case, $\mathbf{y}'(t)$ is made up of the set of output signals from output units belonging to the second subset). The network is trained in two stages.

The first stage of training concentrates only upon the second subset of the network. The output signals that originate in output units belonging to the first subset (in other words, the output signals of those first subset units whose recurrent connections to second subset units have non-zero weights) are identified with (and set to the values of) the control inputs to the plant being controlled. The $\mathbf{y}'(t)$ outputs of the network are identified with the sensor outputs of the plant. Regardless of the source of the control inputs (whether it be the first subset of the network — operation in this mode is called *bootstrapping*; see [177] for an example of this — or an existing controller that we want to improve upon) we simply want to use the second subset of the network to accurately model the plant's spatiotemporal input/output behavior (notice that both the first and second subsets can have any number of recurrent connections that do not connect to the other subset).

Once the second subset is performing accurately as a plant model we then freeze all of its weights and begin training the first subset (this is the second stage of training). This second training stage is carried out in the ordinary recurrent backpropagation manner (as described earlier); where the only "correct output values" used during this second stage of training are the desired $\mathbf{y}(t)$ sensor output signals that correspond to our goals for the plant's correct operation. As mentioned above, we assume that these desired sensor output values are to be held constant throughout each run (the other sensor outputs — consisting of signals in recurrent connections from units that do not contribute to $\mathbf{y}'(t)$ — *can* vary). For example, if the plant is a rolling mill we might specify that the thickness of the steel sheet (say, output signal $y_1'(t)$) should always be exactly 3.0000 mm (in other words, $y_1(t) = 3.0000$ for $t = 1, 2, \ldots, t_{\text{stop}}$). The controller portion of the network (the first subset) is trained to do the best possible job of meeting our plant performance goals, as expressed in terms of errors in the plant model sensor output readings. The net result of the model-based approach is the avoidance of a mismatch between the input sequence processing behavior of our neural network approximation to the system and the system itself. This is accomplished by formally considering as external only those sensor variables that are to be held constant as the outputs (and inputs!) of the network. All other "output" signals are simply considered to be internally fed back recurrent signals that are of no external importance. Thus, the spatiotemporal mapping that this network is trying to implement (at least during the second stage of training) is a *constant* mapping for which the input and desired output never change. This neatly avoids the problems associated with trying to learn a mapping for which the output can be modified by the input.

No general theory of the approximation of spatiotemporal mappings (either for discrete time or continuous time) yet exists. However, the issues discussed above in connection with the recurrent backpropagation neural network will probably be part of such a theory, when it comes along. The enlightening book *Mathematical Theories of Nonlinear Systems* by Stephen Banks [19] offers some additional perspectives on spatiotemporal mapping approximation from the standpoint of nonlinear control theory. This book is highly recommended to all readers who have studied both mathematics and control theory.

In conclusion, the recurrent backpropagation network is designed to approximate spatiotemporal mappings, much as the backpropagation network approximates spatial mappings. In general, recurrent backpropagation networks lack the weight symmetries of ordinary backpropagation networks, and so it may well turn out that the effective information storage per weight will be much higher (see Exercise 6.1.7 and Exercises 5.3.2 and 5.3.3). Thus, a recurrent network may be able to "do a lot more" than a backpropagation network with the same number of weights. Early experience suggests this intuitive notion is correct, but no theory confirming this idea yet exists.

Exercises

6.1.1. Demonstrate that, if a spatiotemporal pattern $x(t)$ (in other words, $x :$ $(-\infty, +\infty) \longrightarrow R^n$) is transformed by a time warp into a spatiotemporal pattern $x(\theta(t))$ (in other words, $x(\theta) : [(-\infty, +\infty)] \longrightarrow R^n$), then the ratio of the speed at which this new pattern will traverse the original pattern's path in R^n to the original speed will be $\frac{d\theta}{dt}$ at each pair of equivalent times..

6.1.2. Demonstrate that the distance measurement D (defined by Equation 6.1) is well defined for all pairs of spatiotemporal patterns u and v (in other words, show that the improper integral in Equation 6.1 will always converge).

6.1.3. Using the definition of the distance measurement D given by Equation 6.1, demonstrate that D has the properties **I, II, III, IV** given by Equation 6.2.

6.1.4. To give us the capability to "chop off" a spatiotemporal pattern so as to make it equal to the 0 vector outside an interval $[t_0, t_1]$, it is handy to have a multiplicative scalar weighting function that is exactly equal to 1 in the interval $[t_0 + \Delta, t_1 - \Delta]$ and is exactly equal to 0 outside the interval $[t_0, t_1]$ (where Δ is a small positive number). Construct such a function by starting with the function

$$g(t) = \begin{cases} e^{-(1/x^2)} & \text{for } x > 0 \\ 0 & \text{for } x \leq 0. \end{cases}$$

[Hint: translate g appropriately, take a second copy of this translated function with time t replaced by $-t$, multiply these two functions together, integrate the resulting function, scale and translate this function (which is a smooth step function), and finally translate and subtract two of these smooth step functions (one based on t and the other based on $-t$) to achieve the final desired result.]

6.1.5. Show that $H_v(u, t)$ can be written as $G(\mu_t u, \mu_t v)$, where the class $\mathscr{C}$ of spatiotemporal warps used in H and G are the same, and where $\mu_t(\tau) = \mu(\tau - t)$.

6.1.6. Show that the forms of Equations 6.7 and 6.8 imply that there exists a lower bound on the time warp speed $d\theta/dt$.

6.1.7. Show that, in general, the recurrent backpropagation network does not have any weight permutations that leave its spatiotemporal mapping function unchanged. Interpret this fact in terms of the ratio of information content per weight (for quantized weights) for the recurrent backpropagation network compared to a backpropagation network (having K weight permutations that leave its input/output function unchanged) with the same number of weights quantized to the same levels in both networks (see Exercises 5.3.2 and 5.3.3).

6.1.8. A recurrent backpropagation network has only one external input ($x_1(t)$) and one external output ($y_1(t)$). Each run of the network lasts exactly $t_{\text{stop}} = n$ time steps. During a each run the external inputs are $x_1(0), x_1(1), x_1(2), \ldots, x_1(n-1)$. Design the network and arrange the s_i functions and weights so that the output of the network at time t_{stop} (i.e., $y_1(t_{\text{stop}})$) will be equal to the sum $\sum_{k=0}^{(n-1)} u_k \, x_1(k)$. This demonstrates that the recurrent backpropagation network can implement the function of an ADALINE if the n inputs are spread out in time.

6.1.9. Demonstrate that the recurrent backpropagation network can implement the equivalent of any backpropagation network (no matter how many hidden layers are used), where the backpropagation network input vector $\mathbf{x}$ is delivered to the recurrent backpropagation network at time step 1 (in other words, as input vector $\mathbf{x}(0)$) and the network produces the same output $\mathbf{y}'$ as the backpropagation network at time t_{stop}. Determine the minimum possible value of t_{stop} for the emulation of a backpropagation architecture with one hidden layer.

6.1.10. Carefully explain why the recurrent backpropagation network error function would not make sense if the spatiotemporal mapping being approximated had an input sequence that depended strongly on past outputs and if the network approximation of the mapping is poor. Give an example of a specific real-world situation where this problem would occur and another where it would not occur.

6.2 Stochastic Networks

This section discusses neural networks that use noise processes in their operation. Typically, such networks have an energy or performance function associated with them. The noise process is used in an (often successful) attempt to reach a global minimum of this function, rather than getting stuck in a local minimum (as with the Hopfield and BAM networks of Chapter 4).

   We begin with a general discussion of the simulated annealing technique for finding a global minimum of a function. We then discuss Boltzmann machine networks, which utilize the simulated annealing technique.

6.2.1 Finding Global Minima by Simulated Annealing

The basic concept of simulated annealing arose from an analogy with metallurgical annealing. In *metallurgical annealing*, a body of metal is heated to near its melting point and is then slowly cooled back down to room temperature (in contrast to *quenching* in which the metal is rapidly cooled). The idea of annealing is that dislocations and other crystal lattice disruptions can be eliminated by thermal agitation at high temperature, and the formation of new dislocations can be prevented by slowly cooling the metal, which gives it time to repair any dislocations that occur as the temperature drops. The essence of this process is that the global energy function of the metal will eventually reach an absolute minimum value. If the temperature is dropped too quickly, the energy of the metallic lattice will be much higher than this minimum because lattice dislocations (that would otherwise eventually disappear due to thermal agitation) get frozen into the metal.

The amazing thing about annealing is that the statistical process of thermal agitation inevitably leads to approximately the same low energy state. This result has dependence on neither the initial condition of the metal, nor any of the details of the statistical annealing process. The mathematical concept of *simulated annealing* derives from an analogy with this physical behavior.

The fundamental mathematical idea on which simulated annealing is based was discovered by Nicholas Metropolis, Arianna Rosenbluth, Marshall Rosenbluth, Augusta Teller and Edward Teller in 1953 [170]. Their interest was the use of Monte Carlo methods for investigating such properties as equations of state for substances consisting of interacting individual molecules. The crucial observation of this paper was that the global process of minimizing the energy of the system (which occurs in physical systems because of statistical energy transfer via mechanical molecular interactions) can be boiled down to a simple localized process of energy modification. As with many other great discoveries in physics, the idea that Metropolis and his colleagues devised was truly a stroke of genius (although they gave an intuitive reason why it should be sensible). The basic idea is to provisionally change a single randomly selected part of the system at a time. If this change results in a lower overall global system energy, then the change is "accepted" and allowed to stand. If the change results in an increase in the global energy of the system, then this change is accepted with probability p given by

$$p = \exp\left(\frac{-\Delta E}{T}\right), \tag{6.21}$$

where $\Delta E = E^{\text{new}} - E^{\text{old}}$ is the change in energy and T is the system "temperature" (in appropriate units). We shall hereafter refer to this prescription as the MR_2T_2 algorithm. In its original form, the MR_2T_2 algorithm was used strictly to calculate physical properties (such as pressure, magnetization, etc.) for systems at equilibrium at a fixed temperature. In 1982, Scott Kirkpatrick, Charles Gelatt, and M. P. Vecchi [135], and V. Çerny [36, 37], independently developed the concept of using the MR_2T_2 algorithm with a slowly decreasing temperature to simulate the process of annealing in metals. Although this method was intended strictly as a mathematical optimization technique, Kirkpatrick and his

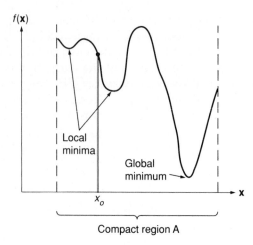

Fig. 6.10. • Finding the global minimum of a function.

colleagues used data from experimental studies in physical chemistry and metallurgy to derive the *cooling schedule* to be used for lowering the temperature. From the very outset, it was realized that simulated annealing represented a major breakthrough in optimization.

The mathematical theory of simulated annealing was later developed by Stewart Geman and Donald Geman [84] (see the excellent book *Simulated Annealing and Boltzmann Machines* by Emile Aarts and Jan Korst [1] for a more complete discussion).

A classical problem in mathematical optimization is to find the global minimum of a function $f(\mathbf{x})$ on a compact region A. As shown in Figure 6.10, this problem cannot typically be solved by gradient descent methods. If gradient descent is used, the solution will typically be a local minimum of the function and not a global minimum (a function may have more than one global minimum, e.g., the error function of the backpropagation neural network—see Section 5.3). The simulated annealing procedure discussed in this subsection is a stochastic search process which has been found to be quite effective for finding the global minima of functions [83].

For the purposes of this section, we will only consider simulated annealing as it is applied to problems in *combinatorial optimization*. A combinatorial optimization problem is one in which a real-valued function $f(\mathbf{x})$ of a binary vector $\mathbf{x}$ is to be minimized. The simulated annealing approach to the solution of this problem is encapsulated in the following procedure:

1. Randomly select an initial vector $\mathbf{x}$. Select a large value for the initial temperature T. Choose the initial value of T such that $\exp(\frac{-\Delta}{T}) \geq 0.999$ for all energy changes Δ (see Step 3 below for the definition of Δ).

2. Select a component x_i of $\mathbf{x}$ uniformly at random.

3. Let the vector $\mathbf{x}'$ be the same as $\mathbf{x}$, except that the value of component x_i is changed (from a 0 to a 1 or from a 1 to a 0, as appropriate). Then, let $\Delta = f(\mathbf{x}') - f(\mathbf{x})$.

4. If Δ is < 0, then let $\mathbf{x} = \mathbf{x}'$, and go to Step 6.

5. If $\Delta \geq 0$, then set $\mathbf{x} = \mathbf{x}'$ with probability $\exp(\frac{-\Delta}{T})$. In other words, select a random number ξ between 0 and 1 using a uniform probability density function. If ξ is $< \exp(\frac{-\Delta}{T})$, then set $\mathbf{x} = \mathbf{x}'$, else leave $\mathbf{x}$ alone.

6. If M successful changes in $\mathbf{x}$ (changes for which the value of f dropped) or N total changes in $\mathbf{x}$ have occurred since the last change in temperature, then set the value of T to αT. M is typically an order of magnitude smaller than N and α is typically a constant — typically between 0.8 and 0.9999.

7. If the minimum value of f has not decreased more than ϵ (a small constant) in the last L (a constant much larger than N) iterations, then stop; otherwise go to Step 2.

The mathematical proofs that have been offered for the simulated annealing process all demand that an infinite number of provisional changes to $\mathbf{x}$ be tested. Obviously, this is ridiculous, since there are only a finite number of possible values for $\mathbf{x}$. Given these facts, why should simulated annealing be so interesting? The answer stems from the fact that the practical results that are obtained with the above finite version of the algorithm are typically excellent. For reasonably well-behaved functions, the number of cycles needed to converge to a value of f close to a global minimum is surprisingly small. For example, in the famous Traveling Sales Problem, we are given K cities, and we wish to find the shortest tour that visits all of the cities exactly once and return to the starting point. This problem, for which there are a total of $K!/(2K)$ possible different tours that would have to be checked in an exhaustive search, can often be approximately solved with simulated annealing in a number of steps equal to a small power of K. The approximate solution obtained by using simulated annealing is often within a few percent of the optimum. (It is interesting to note that the actual optimum cannot be determined by any method for problems with more than a few tens of cities). The next subsection considers the application of simulated annealing to the Hopfield network. This yields a new, stochastic, neural network called the *Boltzmann machine*.

6.2.2 The Boltzmann Machine Network

The Boltzmann machine is simply a discrete time Hopfield network in which the processing element transfer function (Equation 4.28) is modified to use the simulated annealing procedure.

The processing element transfer function of the Boltzmann machine is given by

$$x_i^{\text{new}} = \begin{cases} -x_i^{\text{old}} & \text{if } \Delta H < 0 \\ -x_i^{\text{old}} & \text{if } \Delta H \geq 0 \text{ and } \xi < \exp\left(\frac{-\Delta H}{T}\right) \\ x_i^{\text{old}} & \text{otherwise,} \end{cases} \tag{6.22}$$

where

$$\Delta H = 4\, x_i^{\text{old}} \left[\sum_{j=1}^{n} w_{ij} x_j^{\text{old}} - T_i \right], \tag{6.23}$$

T = temperature,

ξ = a random number between 0 and 1 chosen by means of a uniform probability density function.

As in the Hopfield network, only one processing element is updated at a time. This processing element is chosen at random by a *scheduling unit* processing element (see Figure 4.7 for a diagram of the Hopfield network). The scheduling unit selects the processing element to be updated uniformly at random and notifies it by sending a message that includes the number of that unit (from 1 to n) and the current temperature T. The unit then updates its state in accordance with the transfer function of Equation 6.22. Following this, the scheduling unit then selects the next processing element for update, and so on.

As with the simulated annealing procedure described in the previous subsection, the temperature is lowered when either the energy has dropped quite a bit, or when a sufficiently large number of updates has occurred. The stopping criterion for the Boltzmann machine is usually taken to be the same as that for the simulated annealing procedure. Unlike the Hopfield network, which is guaranteed to converge to a local minimum of the energy function H in a finite number of update steps, the Boltzmann machine may or may not converge to a final stable state. However, although convergence is not guaranteed, the state achieved by the Boltzmann machine at the point where the stopping criterion ends its operation is usually very close to the global minimum of H. Note that the Boltzmann machine is a legal neural network, since the scheduling unit (which receives inputs from all the other units) can compute the value of the energy change function locally (see Exercises 6.2.1 and 6.2.2).

The Boltzmann machine was invented by Geoffrey Hinton, Terrence Sejnowski and David Ackley in 1984 [120] (also see [7, 26, 126]). The definition given above is considerably simpler (and more consistent with simulated annealing) than their original 1984 definition. The original Boltzmann machine was, at least vaguely, conceived as a biological neural model. Thus, it used what the originators considered a more biologically plausible transfer function than that presented in Equation 6.23. However, for engineering purposes, the formulation given above is believed to be superior.

Again, as with simulated annealing, it can be rigorously established that the Boltzmann machine will probabilistically converge to a global minimum of its energy function. However, as with the proof that simulated annealing converges in probability to a global minimum, this proof relies on the use of an infinite number of provisional updates, thus invalidating its applicability to practical situations. However, notwithstanding the lack of a mathematical proof of convergence in finite time, the Boltzmann machine has been shown to be generally effective for locating a state with very low energy (close to a global minimum). The Boltzmann machine can be quite useful for solving certain types of combinatorial optimization problems. These include the Traveling Sales Problem, the Max Cut Problem, the Graph Coloring Problem, and the Job Shop Problem [1].

Other types of stochastic neural networks have been defined. For example, *genetic* neural networks utilize random modifications of weights or adaptive coefficients as a learning mechanism. Following weight modification, the "fitness" of the network is reevaluated to decide whether the weight "mutation" deserves to survive or not. Elaborate schemes for genetic weight modification have been developed [2] to control this "evolutionary process." Genetic networks have shown considerable promise, and this continues to be an active area of research. *Random population* networks, which involve groups of processing elements firing randomly in accordance with a local firing frequency model, have also been studied [157].

In conclusion, the Monte Carlo probability method (upon which all stochastic networks are essentially based) holds out the possibility of exploring an enormous range of alternative configurations in a reasonably small amount of time. With the addition of the MR_2T_2 algorithm and the simulated annealing procedure, the power of the Monte Carlo method has been extended enormously. Stochastic neural networks promise to remain a central element in the future of neurocomputing.

Exercises

6.2.1. Derive Equation 6.23 from Equation 4.35, using the assumption that the new state being considered for processing element i is $-x_i^{old}$.

6.2.2. Demonstrate that processing element i has all of the information necessary to implement its transfer function (Equation 6.22) in a Boltzmann machine. In particular, demonstrate that it can calculate ΔH, given by Equation 6.23.

6.2.3. Define a Boltzmann machine with 5 processing elements and run it until it reaches equilibrium. Did the network energy function reach a global minimum?

6.2.4. Explain in detail how simulated annealing could be used to solve the Traveling Sales Problem.

6.3 Hierarchical Networks

The neural networks studied so far in this book are either essentially single layer networks or multilayer networks with massive interconnection between layers. The GMDH network is not an exception to this because each layer starts out with every allowable connection from the previous layer. In this section, we study networks (and network principles) that are directed toward networks with sparse and localized connectivity between layers. Such networks are termed *hierarchical networks*. The basic idea of hierarchical networks is to have processing elements on each layer of the network only receive connections from a restricted localized subset of the previous layer's processing elements. This implies that each processing element can only act upon partial information — namely, the set of input signals that it can "see."

The advantage of a hierarchical neural network structure is that the processing elements of each layer only have to concern themselves with the processing of a limited amount of information. The total global situation is then pieced together as one ascends from one hierarchical layer to the next. This approach has two major benefits. First, the processing elements at each layer need only concern themselves with the relatively simple situation described by their input connection signals (which make up only a tiny fraction of the total input coming to the layer from the previous layer). Second, hierarchical networks can typically function with a spectacularly smaller number of processing elements than would be required by a network that would deal with the entire input as a single unit (rather than first breaking it up into small pieces). By processing the input information one step at a time, hierarchical networks can provide capabilities that would otherwise be impossible to deliver. Naturally, hierarchical networks are only appropriate in those situations where the inputs to the network have low-level, intermediate-level, and high-level structures that can be consistently related to one another, as images or sounds from outdoor scenes. Random data, for example, does not have such structure.

This section starts with a discussion of the original hierarchical neural network: the neocognitron. The issue of representation codes for hierarchical neural network layers, (*combinatorial hypercompression*) is then discussed. Finally, the last subsection describes a hierarchical network technique for attentional focusing.

The networks discussed in this section are at an early stage of development. However, they represent an important future theme. The class of hierarchical neural networks may well become a primary focus of neurocomputing over the next few decades.

6.3.1 Neocognitron Network

The *neocognitron* neural network was developed by Kunihiko Fukushima with the assistance of Sei Miyake and Takayuki Ito over the years 1980 to 1988 [69, 71, 72, 74]. It was developed as a follow-on to the earlier *cognitron* neural network developed by Fukushima between 1969 and 1981 [73, 75, 76, 77].

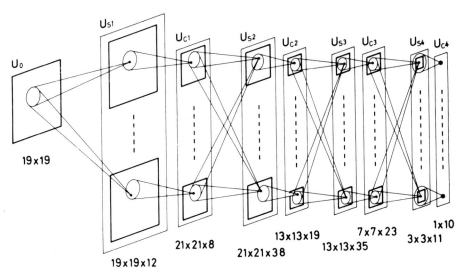

U_{s1}

U_{c1} U_{s2} U_{c2} U_{s3} U_{c3} U_{s4} U_{c4}

U_0

19x19

19x19x12   21x21x8   21x21x38   13x13x19   13x13x35   7x7x23   3x3x11   1x10

Fig. 6.11. • Hierarchical network structure of the neocognitron. The numerals at the bottoms of the sublayers show the total numbers of processing elements in each sublayer of the network.

The neocognitron neural network is the only well studied hierarchical neural network as of this writing. It represents one of the crowning achievements of neurocomputing to date.

Not only is the neocognitron the archetypical hierarchical neural network, it is also the largest and most complicated neural network yet developed. This complexity makes it difficult to describe in an exposition of reasonable length (an exercise that would be largely pointless anyway, since Fukushima's own expository descriptions of the network [69, 72] are so lucid). So, instead of a detailed exposition, this subsection will concentrate on a functional description of the network and the design principles employed.

The basic function of the neocognitron is to act as a pattern recognition network for spatial images (in particular, binary images of alphanumeric characters). The input image is a low-resolution character image (such as the examples shown later in Figure 6.20). The operational goal of the network is to identify the character present in the input image. The network is typically trained and tested using a small set of characters (such as the numerals 0 through 9).

Fukushima has explored neocognitron networks of various sizes and configurations (each with slight differences in its principles of operation); here we shall focus on a single configuration — that described in Fukushima's 1988 paper summarizing his work on the neocognitron [69].

The architecture of the neocognitron neural network is shown in schematic form in Figure 6.11. The network consists of 156 separate and distinct slabs (ranging in size from 441 processing elements to 1 processing element) arranged in groups forming a total of four "layers" (as with backpropagation, we shall misuse this term, since each of these layers actually consists of many individual slabs). The network contains a total of 50,732 processing elements and over 14 million connections.

As shown in Figure 6.11, the first layer consists of 20 slabs organized into two sublayers. The first sublayer consists of 12 two-dimensional slabs in the form of 19 × 19 square arrays of processing elements. Each of the processing elements on these slabs is of a type designated by Fukushima as "S" (for simple[5]). Each of these processing elements receives inputs from a 3 × 3 array of pixels in the 19 × 19 input image. The center of the group of 9 pixels that supply input to a particular processing element on one of the 12 slabs corresponds geometrically to the relative position of the processing element in the slab. In other words, the location of the pixels on the input image that supply input to a particular processing element on one of the 12 slabs of the first sublayer is proportional to the geometrical position of that processing element on its slab. Note that these slabs are the same size as the input image.

The processing elements on each of the 12 slabs of the first sublayer are identical. They all have the same transfer function *and* the same weights. In other words, each of the 12 slabs on the first sublayer implements a particular *local feature analysis* operation at each location in the input image. The processing elements on each one of these slabs are are "tuned" to a specific spatial pattern feature (such as a vertical edge, a horizontal line end, etc.). Examples of these 3 × 3 weight sets are shown in Figure 6.12. Note that there are 12 weight patterns, corresponding to the 12 slabs of the first sublayer.

The neocognitron can be trained using either supervised training or self-organization. The training methods used with the neocognitron will be discussed later. For now, we shall merely discuss the structure and function of the network after training.

The 12 weight patterns shown in Figure 6.12 are designed to detect line segments at various orientations. The two patterns on the top row of the array of Figure 6.12 are intended to detect horizontal (the left top weight pattern) and vertical (the right top weight pattern) lines. Similarly, the pair of weight patterns on the fourth row are designed to detect 45 degree angle lines. Earlier versions of the neocognitron had difficulty with lines lying between the four vertical, horizontal, and oblique orientations. To help solve this problem, Fukushima devised the idea of having pairs of features for measuring such lines. These pairs of weight patterns are indicated by the connecting lines in Figure 6.12. The two patterns on rows 2 and 3 of the left column of weight patterns are designed to detect lines at a clockwise azimuth from vertical of approximately 67.5 degrees. The two detectors in rows 5 and 6 of column 1 are designed to detect lines at an azimuth of approximately 22.5 degrees. The top and bottom

---

[5] Actually, all first sublayer slabs of all layers also contain type V processing elements; but these are not important for this part of the discussion. The type V processing elements will be discussed later in this subsection.

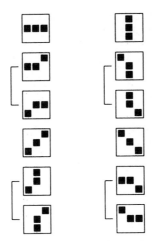

Fig. 6.12. • Weight patterns of the 12 slabs of layer U_{S1}. The pairs of patterns connected by lines indicate that the outputs of the corresponding S-planes are joined together and converge to a single C-plane at U_{C1}.

pairs of weights in the right column of Figure 6.12 are designed to detect lines at azimuths of approximately 157.5 degrees, and 112.5 degrees, respectively. Thus, the 12 slabs of the first sublayer of the network form a set of eight local line orientation detectors that are organized at increments of 22.5 degrees. The type "S" processing elements that utilize these weights have transfer functions that cause the processing element to become active only if two conditions are met:

1. The pattern within the receptive field must have active pixels where the weight values are high. This ensures that only processing elements that are well aligned with appropriate elements of the incoming character image will respond.

2. There must not be more than a small fraction of other activity within the receptive field compared with that within the areas in which the weights are high. This ensures that a processing element will not respond to an incoming pattern simply because a piece of the pattern matches its weight pattern well. For example, if the weight pattern of the processing element is tuned to vertical line segments, and an area with all pixel brightnesses high is entered, the processing element should not respond because the overall match between the incoming receptive field pattern and the weight pattern is not very good.

One might wonder why Fukushima decided to use this vector dot product based approach, instead of using euclidean distance or some other matching scheme that does not suffer from the problems of a vector dot product approach. The reason is that the neocognitron is as much intended to be a suggestive

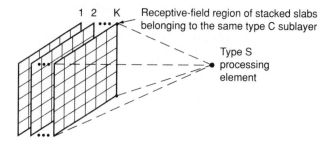

Fig. 6.13. ● Each type S processing element's receptive field on layers 2, 3, and 4 is a rectangular region cutting through all of the slabs of the previous sublayer. In this case, a 5 × 5 region is shown. This is called a *core sample* (see Figure 6.14).

biological neural model as it is an engineering pattern recognition system, and there is widespread belief that neurons can compute dot products.

Once the processing elements of the first sublayer have responded to the input image, their output signals are then sent to the appropriate slabs of the second sublayer. This sublayer consists of a total of eight slabs, each of which is arranged as a 21 × 21 two-dimensional array of processing elements. These processing elements are of type "C" (for *complex*). Each processing element has a 3 × 3 receptive field positioned within the slab(s) that provides input to the processing element's slab.

As noted above, four of the 12 slabs of the first sublayer provide output signals that indicate the places in the input image where lines of a particular orientation occur. The other 8 slabs operate in pairs to detect lines that lie between the 4 major line directions. Each of the singular line direction detector slabs provides output to one of the slabs of the next sublayer. Each pair of intermediate line detector slabs on the first sublayer jointly provide outputs to a single slab of the second sublayer (in other words, these C processing elements have *two* 3×3 receptive field inputs). Thus, the 8 slabs of the second sublayer are each accumulating information about line activity at a particular line orientation throughout the input image.

The type C processing elements of the second sublayer have fixed input weights (which are highest at the middle of their receptive field and fall off towards the edges). The job of these weights is to respond to any type S processing elements within their receptive field that are emitting a high output signal. Except for the different weighting factors at different positions within the receptive field, it makes no difference where within this receptive field the active S processing element(s) happens to lie. This means that if the input character is modified or distorted slightly (thus slightly changing the positions of the highly responding processing elements of the slabs of the first sublayer), the response of the type C processing elements on the second sublayer will not change much. This introduces a *slop factor* (this is my term, not Fukushima's) into the system by making the responses of the type C sublayer processing elements insensitive

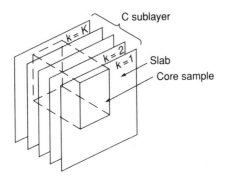

Fig. 6.14. • Each type-S processing element on layers 2, 3 and 4 has a receptive field that consists of a *core sample* of all of the slabs of the previous (type-C) sublayer stacked up on top of one another.

to small changes and distortions in the input pattern. This feature significantly increases the robustness of the neocognitron.

Thus, as described above, the first layer of the network consists of an initial sublayer that dissects the input character into line segments of (effectively) 8 different orientations. The second sublayer re-expresses the responses of the slabs of the first sublayer by combining nearby responses and introducing an insensitivity to small character shifts and distortions.

The basic structure defined by the first layer of the network (namely, a sublayer of slabs with type S processing elements followed by a sublayer of slabs with type C processing elements) is repeated on all the subsequent layers of the network. However, the sizes and numbers of slabs change, as illustrated in Figure 6.11.

On the first sublayer of the first layer, the receptive field of each processing element merely consisted of a rectangular set of pixel intensity values of the input image. The receptive fields of the processing elements of the slabs of the first sublayer of the second layer again consist of rectangular arrays, but these arrays receive 5×5 sets of processing element output signals from *all* 8 slabs of the second sublayer of the first layer. In other words, the receptive field of each processing element on each slab of the first sublayer of the second layer consists of a *core sample*, as shown in Figures 6.13 and 6.14. This allows each such processing element to develop a response that combines the feature responses of the individual slabs of the previous sublayer. Notice that this is a different type of connectivity than that used between the first and second sublayers of each layer — where the goal is simply to combine detectors that are looking for nearby expressions of the same feature and to introduce a slop factor. The connectivity between and within the layers continues in this pattern up through layer 4, where the final sublayer of the network consists of 10 slabs having one processing element each. These slabs correspond to the 10 numerals 0 through 9 that the neocognitron is configured to recognize. When a 0 is entered into the system, one of these ten output units will normally respond at

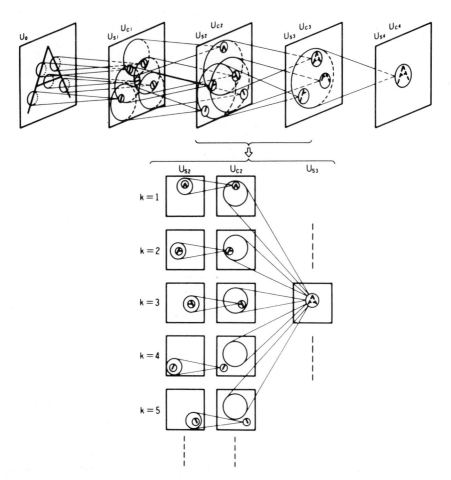

Fig. 6.15. • Illustration of the process of pattern recognition in the neocognitron.

a level significantly higher than the other 9. This 1–out–of–N code represents the classification output of the network.

Figure 6.15 illustrates some of the details of how the neocognitron operates. In essence, at each successive layer of the network the input image is locally analyzed within a receptive field neighborhood that effectively (in terms of the set of original image pixels to which it is indirectly connected) grows larger and larger; until finally at the second sublayer of layer 4, the entire input character is classified. Figure 6.16 illustrates the operation of the network for an input image of the numeral "2". The responses of the second sublayer of each layer are shown. Figure 6.17 illustrates a variety of text characters that were correctly classified by the network. Clearly, the neocognitron is insensitive to scale change, shift in position, distortion, and shot noise.

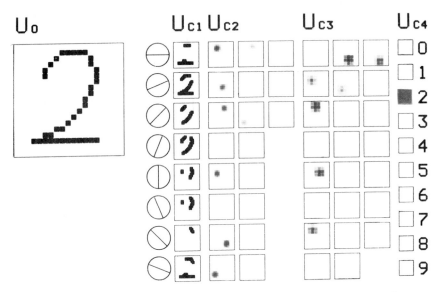

Fig. 6.16. • An example of the response of the type C processing elements in a neocognitron network trained to recognize handwritten numerals.

As mentioned at the beginning of this subsection, training of the neocognitron can be carried out using a supervised training regime or through self-organization. The supervised training approach involves the use of indirect inputs to the type S sublayers. Each of the 12 slabs of the first sublayer are presented with one of the patterns shown in Figure 6.12. The pattern used during training is the same as the weight pattern that is desired on that slab after training. Similar indirect inputs (of more complicated patterns) are made to the first layer slabs of layers 2, 3 and 4. Training of each subsequent layer does not begin until the training of the previous layer has finished. As each training pattern is entered into the input image, the lower layers respond to this pattern and then provide an input to the layer currently being trained. In addition to this input, Fukushima manually selects a set of processing elements (a maximum of one per slab) at the positions of crucial features in the input image that he wants those slabs to become sensitive to. For the slabs of the first layer, the input pattern (one of the 3 × 3 weight patterns of Figure 6.12) is placed in the exact center of the input image. The middle processing element on the slab that is to become sensitized to this pattern is then selected for training. The processing elements selected for learning on each training trial on layers 2, 3 and 4 are located at the positions of crucial features in the input image, and are thus not necessarily located in the center of their slab.

Figures 6.18, 6.19, and 6.20 show training patterns used to train the first sublayer of layers 2, 3 and 4. The patterns for the second sublayer were again centered in the image, and the center processing elements of the appropriate slab(s) were activated. The processing element(s) selected for activation when

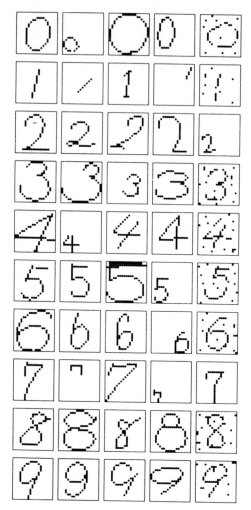

Fig. 6.17. • Some example of deformed input patterns which the neocognitron recognized correctly.

training the first sublayer of layer 3 are shown by x's in Figure 6.19. For the sublayer of layer 4, the central processing element in the appropriate 3 × 3 slab was again used.

An unusual feature of the neocognitron training process is its *weight sharing mechanism*. This mechanism is arranged so that whenever a processing element on a slab has its weights modified (at most one processing element on each slab can modify its weights on each training trial), all of the processing elements of the slab immediately adopt these new weights. This is how all of the processing elements of the slab end up having the same weights. Fukushima does not specify a legal neural network mechanism for accomplishing this weight sharing.

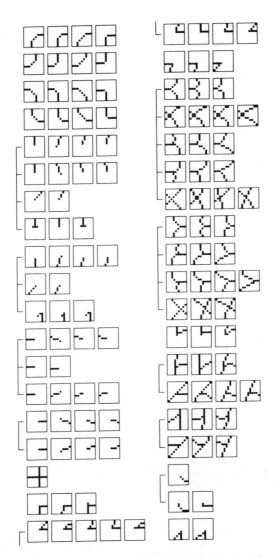

Fig. 6.18. ● Training patterns used to train the 38 slabs of layer U_{S2}.

In the self-organization mode (which yields a network that has lower classification accuracy than when the supervised training approach described above
is used), a competition mechanism is used to select the processing elements
that will have their weights modified. The first part of the competition involves
competition between type S processing elements that all lie within the same
core sample (defined now in terms of the stack of all S slabs of a given layer)
on the basis of their output signal levels in response to the input pattern. The
winners from these competitions then compete with other processing elements
on their slab that have won similar core sample competitions (if any) for the

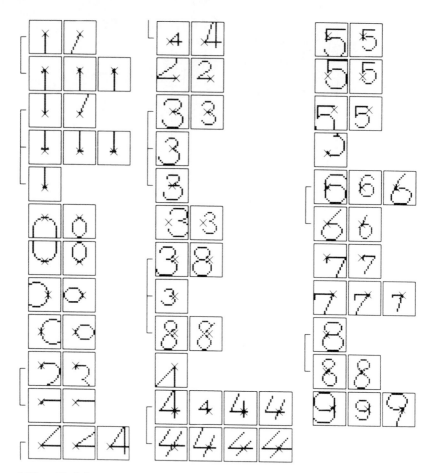

Fig. 6.19. • Training patterns used to train the 35 slabs of layer U_{S3}. Receptive field centers of the seed-units are marked by crosses in the figure.

right to be the single processing element on their slab that has its weight modified on this training cycle. In self-organization training, the network is simply presented with a large number of character examples. The network is not told which numeral each example corresponds to. Nonetheless, the network often becomes a good classifier. Each of the processing elements on the top sublayer comes to represent one of the numerals. Thus, when we enter an image of any numeral between 0 and 9 into the network, the end result is that one of the 10 highest sublayer units responds at a higher level than all of the others. This unit can then be interpreted as a detector for this particular numeral. The self-organizing neocognitron, while not as good as the supervised learning neocognitron, nonetheless displays reasonable classification accuracy. For example, it will correctly classify most examples of the type shown in Figure 6.17.

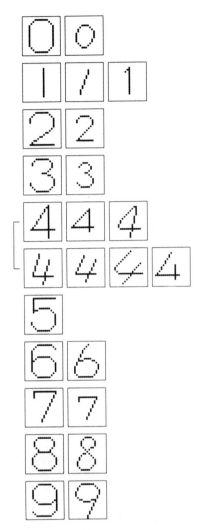

Fig. 6.20. • Training patterns used to train the 11 slabs of layer U_{S4}.

The learning law used (for both supervised training and self-organization) could be called the *Pinnocchio learning law* (this is my term, not Fukushima's). This learning law, which is similar to Hebb learning, has the unusual property that the weight vector of each type S processing element keeps growing longer and longer as the training process continues (much as the character Pinnocchio's nose continued to grow in the Walt Disney movie). The growth of this (excitatory) weight vector is counteracted by a similar unbounded growth in a single inhibitory weight (the weight on the input from the type V processing element associated with each type S processing element — see Figure 6.21). If Pinnocchio learning is continued indefinitely, the weights will grow to impossibly large magnitudes. However, much as with the cartoon character, the training process is ended once the system has learned the desired lessons.

In 1987, Todd Gutschow and I experimented with a neocognitron architecture in which Pinnocchio learning is replaced with a modification of Kohonen learning, the modification being that the competition process is now carried out across core samples and then across slabs to select at most a single winning processing element per slab, which then gets to modify its weight in accordance with Kohonen learning. This scheme seemed to work rather well, although most of the experiments were carried out with a single layer.

In conclusion, the neocognitron provides us with a starting point for the development of hierarchical neural networks. The next subsection discusses a different subject: schemes for efficiently representing information in neural networks.

6.3.2 Combinatorial Hypercompression

This subsection explores certain aspects of the issue of how information can be represented within hierarchical neural networks. In particular, a coding scheme called *combinatorial hypercompression* that offers the information density advantages of dense binary number codes, and yet fits within the natural capabilities of neurocomputing systems, is examined. The concept of combinatorial hypercompression was introduced in a paper that I wrote in 1987 [111].

As in the neocognitron, information within a layer of a hierarchical network is often expressed by means of one or more competition processes by which a set of "winning" processing elements that best represent the inputs to the network is selected. The winning units (a tiny minority of the total set of processing elements at a particular layer—most of which are inactive at any time) will typically have output signals that span some range of values (with the currently inactive units having essentially 0 output). In this subsection we shall only concern ourselves with *active* and *inactive* units (in other words, units that will be assumed to have binary states), and we shall not be concerned with the fact that the active units can have graded signal values. The issue we explore here is how such a competitive system can be used to efficiently code information. As discussed earlier in Section 4.5, such systems can form sparse codes. This subsection explores this theme further.

INFORMATION CODING SCHEMES   In traditional algorithmic computing systems, information is represented in the form of n-bit words in which each bit can be filled with either a 0 or a 1. Such representations are universal, and can be used to efficiently store essentially any type of data.

This subsection explores a means to allow neurocomputing systems to develop representational codes that have the potential for storing information with an efficiency comparable to that achieved in programmed computing systems.

In many neurocomputing systems, at least some of the information in the network is represented by means of a 1-out-of-N code. For example, in Terrence Sejnowski and Charles Rosenberg's now classic NETtalk speech synthesis

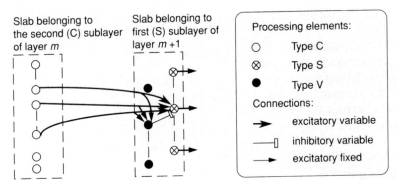

Fig. 6.21. • Connections converging to a feature-extracting type S processing element.

backpropagation network [206] (see Section 9.4), each of the 7 input characters was represented by means of a 1-out-of-29 code. While certainly not all information representation codes used in neurocomputing are 1-out-of-N codes, this is a common situation.

The main points of this subsection are as follows:

- 1-out-of-N codes are weak when compared with any-out-of-N binary codes
- no good method has yet been identified for using any-out-of-N codes in neurocomputing
- K-out-of-N codes are almost as combinatorially powerful as any-out-of-N codes when K is a reasonable fraction of N.
- Evidence is presented that useful K-out-of-N codes may be implemented within neurocomputing systems using standard neural network mechanisms

INFORMATION REPRESENTATION BY MEANS OF BINARY CODES   A binary word with N bits in which any bit may be set to either 0 or 1 can convey N bits of information. Such an information representation code will be called an *any-out-of-N* code. As discussed earlier, a *1-out-of-N* code is an N-bit binary word in which only one of the bits is set to 1 and the others are set to 0. A *K-out-of-N* code is one in which K bits are set to 1 and the other $N - K$ are set to 0. The total number of codewords available in each of these codes is 2^N, N, and $C(N, K)$, respectively (where $C(N, K)$ is the number of combinations of N things taken K at a time $= N!/[(N - K)!K!])$.

The information capacity (measured in bits) of an individual codeword in a code is equal to the logarithm to the base 2 of the number of ways in which the codeword can be chosen (assuming that the codewords are equiprobable). Thus, in the cases of any-out-of-N, K-out-of-N, and 1-out-of-N codes, the information content per codeword is, respectively: N, $\log_2 C(N, K)$, and $\log_2 N$. As K goes from 1 up to a significant fraction of N the information content (in bits per codeword) of each codeword goes up in a roughly linear fashion (see Exercise 6.3.3).

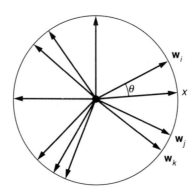

Fig. 6.22. • K-nearest neighbor classification

For example, a 1-out-of-N code codeword with $N = 1000$ can represent about 10 bits of information. This is enough to assign a unique codeword to each member of the United States Congress. A K-out-of-N code codeword with $N = 1000$ and $K = 50$ can represent 282 bits of information. This is enough to assign a unique codeword to each atom in the universe. In both cases, a total of 1000 bits must be implemented. Thus, the information representation advantages of K-out-of-N codes verses 1-out-of-N codes are obviously worth pursuing.

COMBINATORIAL HYPERCOMPRESSION   A general-purpose method for implementing a K-out-of-N code is now described. The purpose of the code is to represent data that is being input into a neurocomputing system or into a subset of a neurocomputing system. The incoming data is assumed to be a unit vector **x** from n-dimensional euclidean space $\mathbf{R}^n$ that is a random sample of the class of all input data vectors. The set of all possible input data vectors is assumed to be determined statistically by a probability density function ρ on the unit sphere (in other words, for the purposes of this discussion we shall assume that the input data vectors are normalized).

The basic idea behind *combinatorial hypercompression* is to use a neural network K-nearest neighbor classifier to select the nearest K-out-of-N templates. This is illustrated in Figure 6.22 for the case $K = 3$.

The neural network we shall use here consists of N linear combiner processing elements having unit length weight vectors $\mathbf{w}_1, \mathbf{w}_2, \ldots, \mathbf{w}_N$. These processing elements have initial transfer functions given by:

$$z_i = \sum_{j=1}^{n} w_{ij} x_j = \mathbf{w}_i \cdot \mathbf{x}. \tag{6.24}$$

In the case where $K = 1$, we would simply choose (by means of a competitive interaction between the N processing elements) the smallest index i for which $z_i \geq z_j$ for all j, $j = 1, 2, \ldots, N$. The processing elements would then go into a final stable state (by invoking a different transfer function) in which all processing elements would be set to 0 except the one with the closest matching weight, which would be set to 1.

Note that in this 1-out-of-N case, as in a Kohonen layer (see Section 3.4), each processing element has a *win region* on the sphere associated with it. Whenever an **x** is in this win region, it is closer to this processing element's weight vector than to that of any other, and will thus cause this processing element to win the competition.

In the case $K > 1$, the idea is the same as in the $K = 1$ case, except the nearest $\mathbf{w}_i$ is determined first (in accordance with the prescription given above) and then eliminated from the list of candidate processing elements. Then, the second-nearest neighbor $\mathbf{w}_j$ is determined from among the remaining $N - 1$ weight vectors, and so on. Figure 6.22 shows the three nearest neighbors to the normalized input data vector **x**. The outputs of the system are the N final processing element output signal values, among which K are equal to 1 and $N - K$ are equal to 0. Where a workable code of this type can be developed, its use can achieve *combinatorial hypercompression* of the input data vectors. Clearly, the effectiveness of such a code depends on the proper selection of the $\mathbf{w}_i$ vectors. This issue is explored next.

THE EXISTENCE OF COMBINATORIAL HYPERCOMPRESSION CODES   A difficulty with the above scheme is the selection of the weight vectors. In order for a particular selection of weight vectors to function as the basis for a combinatorial hypercompression code, they must meet the following requirements:

1. Most of the $C(N, K)$ K-nearest neighbor win regions (a K-nearest neighbor win region is defined as the set of points **x** on the sphere for which a particular set of K $\mathbf{w}_i$ vectors are the K closest among the total set of N $\mathbf{w}_i$ vectors) must be non-empty. Note that, by definition, the win regions are automatically disjoint. A code for which most of the codewords never get used has little value.

2. Non-empty K-nearest neighbor win regions are approximately equiprobable with respect to random **x** input vectors chosen in accordance with ρ. This ensures that the full combinatorial diversity of the code is available by avoiding situations where a few codes get used most of the time (which greatly decreases their information content).

3. The union of the K-nearest neighbor win regions equals the portion of the sphere for which $\rho > 0$. This ensures that all inputs can be represented.

These requirements ensure that the code will be usable as a means for representing input data vectors. Thus, the basic questions concerning the existence of combinatorial hypercompression codes are:

1. Under what set of conditions on ρ does a suitable set of N $\mathbf{w}_i$ vectors exist?

2. Assuming that a usable set of $\mathbf{w}_i$ vectors exists, can an adaptation law be developed so that such a set will self-organize in response to a long series of **x** data vector inputs?

Although the answers to both of these questions are, in general, unknown, the answer to the first question is known in the case of uniform ρ on the whole sphere. In this case we can choose the $\mathbf{w}_i$ vectors to be a set of orthonormal basis vectors (see Exercise 6.3.4). For this set of orthonormal vectors (and for any fixed K, $1 \leq K \leq N$) all of the $C(N, K)$ win regions exist, are equiprobable, and have a union that is equal to the whole sphere. This example gives us hope that combinatorial hypercompression codes may be possible in more general cases.

With respect to hierarchical networks, it would be ideal if the processing elements that viewed a particular subset of inputs on a previous layer could together yield a K-out-of-N code for their portion of the input. This would allow a large diversity of different inputs to be coded appropriately. Each individual area of the input region could then be coded in terms of its local structure. These codes could then be combined with each other at later stages of processing. If combinatorial hypercompression codes can be found, then the required competition process can be based upon a simple distance or angle comparison operation — the kind of operation that neural networks can carry out with ease.

6.3.3 Attention Mechanisms: Segmentation and Object Isolation

This subsection describes yet another potential advantage of hierarchical networks — the ability to deal with patterns in which the objects of interest are embedded in a larger milieu. For example, instead of an image containing a single character, we might be presented with an image containing several characters — some of which overlap. Alternatively, we may be given a time-varying spectral representation for a soundstream in which a speech signal is mixed with background traffic noise. In both of these instances, we would like to have an *attentional mechanism* that would allow us to locate and identify objects of interest embedded in a larger pattern.

In this subsection we will discuss an attention mechanism developed by Kunihiko Fukushima. This mechanism, which is implemented using a modified neocognitron network, allows the network to focus attention on individual characters in a multi-character image [68].

FUKUSHIMA'S ACTIVATION SOURCE BACKTRACKING METHOD   For the purposes of this discussion, we will concentrate on binary images containing alphanumeric characters to be located and classified. The images are otherwise blank, except possibly for a shot noise process. As discussed briefly in Section 6.1, the characters in such an image can suffer from both obscuration and interference. *Obscuration* would correspond to a situation where some of the shot noise is present in the vicinity of the character. This will have the effect of making the location and classification process more difficult. *Interference* will occur wherever two characters are juxtaposed in close proximity. In such a situation, we have the additional problem of ignoring the interfering character(s). As has been demonstrated by Fukushima, the neocognitron can be modified to carry

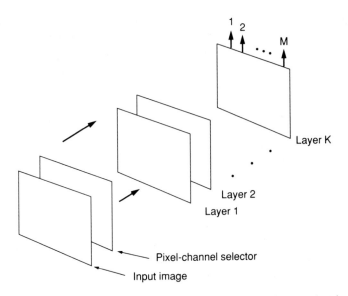

Fig. 6.23. • Neocognitron network equipped with backtracking mechanism and pixel channel selector. The input image may now contain multiple characters, each of which will be attended to in sequence.

out an attentional focusing process that locates characters at arbitrary positions in the image and overcomes the problems of obscuration and interference. The general approach used in this neural network is now described.

Figure 6.23 shows the neocognitron network equipped with the additional machinery required to implement the attentional focusing mechanism. As can be seen, the only visible change from the basic neocognitron is the addition of a pixel channel selector that lies between the input image and the first layer of the network. This selector is equipped with an attenuator for each of the pixel signals of the input image. These signals traverse the selector, and are then distributed to layer 1 as described in Subsection 6.3.1. The channel selector can be set up to allow any designated subset of pixels to pass through it unaffected. However, the pixels that are not designated are blocked. The pixel value sent on to layer 1 for these blocked pixels is always 0 (meaning there is no character energy in this pixel) — no matter what the actual pixel value of the original image was.

Clearly, if we know which pixel channels to select, the pixel channel selector can be used to produce an image in which only one character appears. The manner in which this designated set of pixels is determined is now described.

The first step in the operation of the augmented neocognitron is to set the pixel channel selector to pass all pixels (this is done via signals that go from layer 1 to the pixel channel selector). As each of the characters in the image impinges upon layer 1 of the network, the appropriate local feature detectors are activated. These detector outputs subsequently activate the detectors on layer 2, and so forth, until finally the class detection units of the top layer of the network produce their output signals (there will typically be more than one output signal because characters of different classes are usually present in the input image). To carry out the attentional focusing process, the network has been augmented with additional processing elements that implement a *source backtracking* function; this function is illustrated in Figure 6.24. The first step is to identify (by a competitive process) the most highly active class indicator output on the second sublayer of the highest layer of the network. In the case of Figure 6.24, this output corresponds to the letter "A" (two of which are present in the input image). The backtracking mechanism next identifies the process-ing elements on the second-to-highest layer that cause the "A" class detector to become active. This is easy to do by simply providing reciprocal connections backwards from each processing element on each sublayer to the processing elements of the previous layer which feed it with inputs. The backtracking mechanism shuts down all of the processing elements that were not involved in causing the "A detector" to become highly active. Thus, as shown in Figure 6.24, the units corresponding to the "B" character are shut down. A new fea-ture of this modified neocognitron is that there are now reciprocally symmetric connections *within* each sublayer that link together processing elements that are simultaneously active during training (which is carried out using only images with a single character in them). These symmetric intra-slab connections cause the units activated by a single character to form a group. Thus, as shown in Figure 6.24, the processing elements associated with one of the "A" characters in the input image (shown as group A_1) is a separate subset of processing ele-ments from the group (A_2) associated with the other character "A" in the initial input image.

An additional competition mechanism (that only operates after clearly ex-traneous processing elements, such as those associated with the character "B", are shut down) now comes into play. This competition mechanism operates between still-active groups representing the same character, and only one of the groups can win. At the end of this competition process on each sublayer, only one group of processing elements remains active — namely, those activated by a single character in the original input image. This backtracking process con-tinues downward, sublayer by sublayer, until the first sublayer of the network is reached. At this point, the pixels responsible for activating the processing ele-ments that remain active at the end of the competition process are identified by backtracking to the pixel channel selector. The channel selector then continues to allow these designated pixels to get through and blocks all of the other pixels of the image. The entire neocognitron network from layer 1 to the top layer is then reset, and this edited image is entered. If everything has worked correctly[6], the pattern class detector associated with the pattern "A" should now have a high

---

[6] The actual mechanism proposed by Fukushima does not work exactly as described here, but the effect is equivalent.

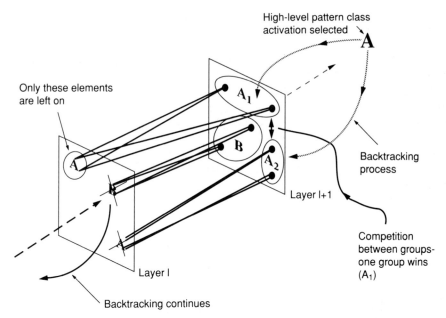

High-level pattern class
activation selected

A

Only these elements
are left on

A_1

B

A_2

Backtracking
process

Layer I+1

Competition
between groups-
one group wins
(A_1)

Layer I

Backtracking continues

Fig. 6.24. • Attentional focusing by backtracking.

output level (see Figure 6.24), and all of the other detectors should have low output levels. This can be thought of as a validity test of the segmentation of the input pattern.

In order to provide the ability to automatically scan the entire image for characters, Fukushima arranges for processing elements that win the competition during the backtracking phase to become "fatigued." Thus, following the testing of the provisional image segmentation (if the testing failed, there was no remedy in Fukushima's initial system), the entire image is once again entered into the system. The winners of the recent backtracking competition are now less able to respond to their particular pattern because of fatigue. The net result is that a different pattern identity output will become the largest, and the backtracking and image segmentation process will proceed for it (except in the case where more "A"s may be present that still cause the "A" detector to have maximal output, in which case backtracking will correctly locate these other characters, since the fatigued groups can no longer win the backtracking group competitions).

This process continues until all of the characters have been discovered. Notice that, as the pixels corresponding to each character are identified and designated, this provides information about the location of the character in the image — which might be useful for other purposes. This process of full image input, bottom-up classification, high level identity selection, backtracking, image segmentation, and segmentation verification is repeated over and over again as the image is analyzed. Thus, image pattern recognition with such an attentional mechanism becomes a "rhythmic process."

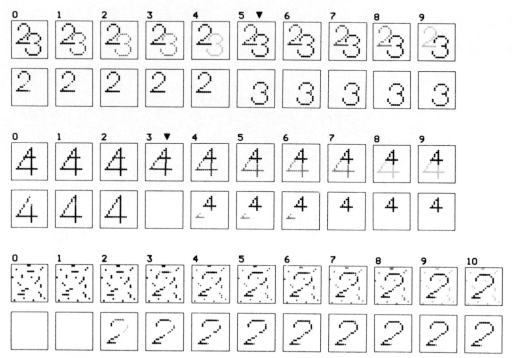

Fig. 6.25. • Examples of multiple character images successfully processed by the augmented neocognitron. The throughput of the "pixel channel selector" is illustrated for the processing of three images. Fukushima's system does not function exactly like the system described in the text.

In conclusion, Fukushima has demonstrated a system which has remarkable capabilities for locating characters within an image and overcoming problems connected with obscuration and interference. Some examples of images in which every character was correctly located and identified are provided in Figure 6.25.

Notice that, in one of the cases presented in Figure 6.25, the network was able to "complete" an incomplete character. This is an extremely useful byproduct of the attentional focusing mechanism in that it allows us to deal more effectively with obscuration. The neocognitron augmented with the backtracking attentional focusing mechanism represents an exciting new direction in neurocomputing. Perhaps someday these capabilities can be extended to the case of more general, grey-scale imagery with far larger numbers of objects of interest.

Exercises

6.3.1. Explain how the features shown in Figure 6.12 can be used to locate oriented lines in input images supplied to the neocognitron.

6.3.2. Conjecture in detail as to how the neocognitron would assemble a capital "A" letter image, starting at the first layer and moving to the top layer.

6.3.3. Demonstrate that, as a crude approximation, the number of bits per codeword (the codewords are assumed to be equiprobable) in a K-out-of-N code goes up roughly linearly with K.

6.3.4. Show that, for a uniform probability density function on a sphere centered on the origin, the vectors of an orthonormal basis will work as a combinatorial hypercompression vector set for any K between 1 and the dimensionality of the space.

6.3.5. How might Fukushima's attention mechanism be used with grey-scale (non-binary) images? [Hint: Suggest a method for determining what is background and what is an object of interest.]

This chapter ends our discussion of neural network architecture and theory. In the next two chapters, neurosoftware and neurocomputer design are discussed.

7

Neurosoftware: Descriptions of Neural Network Structure

This chapter presents a discussion of languages that are designed to describe neural network architectures. The coded description of a neural network in such a language is called *neurosoftware*. The discussion of neurosoftware in this chapter is primarily directed towards its use with digital electronic neurocomputer coprocessors operating as process servers to host digital computers. However, there are other potential uses for neurosoftware. For example, researchers could provide neurosoftware descriptions of their neural network architectures in their papers (which would make it easy to reproduce and verify their results — something that is often difficult today). Another use of neurosoftware would be to allow the easy running of a neural network on an ordinary computer by means of compilation and creation of a linkable object module, much in the manner of ordinary software.

The chapter begins with a general overview of neurosoftware. This is followed by a discussion of the interfaces between the software running on a host computer and the neurosoftware running on a neurocomputer coprocessor or process server. To provide a detailed description of a specific neurosoftware language, we then present the AXON language. Finally, two specific examples of AXON code (the AXON descriptions of the backpropagation and counterpropagation networks) are presented. The AXON language is used for the examples presented in this chapter because it is the only neurosoftware language with which I am familiar.

7.1 Neurosoftware: Coded Descriptions of Neural Network Structure

This section begins with a general discussion of neurosoftware and then reviews some of the requirements that neurosoftware languages should satisfy.

The idea that formal languages should be invented for the express purpose of describing the functional structure of neural networks was first explicitly proposed by David Zipser [247]. As with so many other good ideas, the concept of a neurosoftware language now seems obvious and trivial. However, given the state of the field at the time, Zipser's concept was a major breakthrough.

The main appeal of neurosoftware languages for describing neural networks is that the structure common to all neural networks can be built into the language. Thus, such a language might offer a significant increase in ease of use and efficiency of expression over, say, descriptions written in a language optimized for expressing algorithms (such as C, LISP, FORTRAN, or BASIC[1]). As we shall see, these advantages can, in fact, be realized.

Neurosoftware languages are typically built around a model of neural networks (such as the AXON model presented in Chapter 2). By building the language around a model the user is freed from having to repeatedly express the structural knowledge contained within the model. The use of a model also simplifies the editing and modification of a network, since only the specific changes themselves need to be addressed, and not the side effects of those changes (as is often required with software implementations). In fact, neural network languages lend themselves to object–oriented methods that are now being used to address the deficiencies of traditional software development.

Most of the extant neurosoftware languages (such as Zipser's P3 system [247]) are built on a restrictive model — such as assuming that every network is constructed of layers of affine combiners with activation functions on their outputs (as in the backpropagation network). However, a few languages (such as AXON and Candela [139]) are built around very general models.

---

[1] In 1968 I wrote a paper, entitled "The Brain as a Digraph", which described the results of some work applying mathematical graph theory to neural networks. After some polishing, I submitted the paper to *Mathematical Biosciences*. In addition to the main discussion about applying graph theory, the paper also contained a description (in BASIC) of a neural network that embodied some of these graph theory ideas. A few weeks later I got a very kind letter back from Richard Bellman (who, at the time, was Editor in Chief of *Mathematical Biosciences* and about 40 other journals) gently explaining that my graph theory idea was both trivial and well known. Further, he firmly stated that even if I could salvage the rest of the paper (which I couldn't), the BASIC coded neural network had to go. This episode led to two changes. First, I began studying the literature of neural networks much more thoroughly and carefully. Second, apparently as part of a psychological blocking process caused by my extreme sense of embarrassment over this episode, I have never since written another neural network in BASIC.

Besides the neurosoftware approach discussed in this chapter, there is another popular way to describe a neural network, namely, using an *environment*. Clearly, to provide a complete description of an episodically updated neural network the user must provide an unambiguous description of the processing element transfer functions, the connections, and the scheduling functions. An environment is a computer menu-based and/or graphical icon-based system that provides a means for the user to enter the required data. Several neural network description environments have been built, many of them predating the invention of the formal neurosoftware language concept. For example, Todd Gutschow and I developed the ANSE (Artificial Neural System Environment) at TRW, Inc. during 1983 – 1985 (see Section 8.5 for a description of the ANSE environment). Several of these environments provide a graphical display of the design being created — which can help make the design process much easier.

Although environments are an attractive idea, they currently suffer from the deficiency that their final output is a data file that is machine-readable, but not human-readable. Perhaps someday advanced environments will provide for the automatic generation of a nicely structured neurosoftware description of the network as the final output of the design process. The ability to go backwards from the neurosoftware description to a graphics representation would also be important. Such tools would provide the perusing, portability, printability, paper and pen editing, and correctness checking advantages of code listings along with the intuitive advantages of graphics visualization. A run-time development environment could provide the user (via a computer graphics artificial reality) with an ability to 'visually inspect' the network as it runs, to help in diagnosing its behavior (a system of this type was actually built several years ago — see Section 8.5).

In the next section the way in which neurosoftware languages interact operationally with neurocomputers is described.

7.2 Software Interfaces Between Computers and Neurocomputers

In this section we discuss the manner in which a neural network can be called from software running on the host computer. The compilation of neurosoftware into a form that can be loaded into a neurocomputer is also described. The presentation is based on the approach used in the majority of neurocomputers currently in use.

Neural networks used in the solution of a problem are often implemented on a neurocomputer coprocessor that functions as a process server for the host computer (such coprocessors typically offer a speedup of from two to three orders of magnitude compared to an implementation of the same neural network in software on the host computer). Whenever a particular network is needed, it is called from the software on the host computer, much in the manner of a subroutine. By means of this coprocessor approach, neural networks can be employed as adjuncts to ordinary programmed computing. This approach allows the best features of programmed computing and neurocomputing to be combined [2].

Given a text file containing a neurosoftware language description of a neural network, the first step is *compilation* of this file into a *package*. This process simply involves invoking a compiler, which is a software tool that typically runs on the host computer (although it could run on the neurocomputer instead). The compiler requires only the name of the source code file and the desired name for the package file that it will produce. The compiler then compiles the neurosoftware source code into the neurosoftware package.

A neurosoftware package is typically the description of an entire class of neural networks, not just a single network. For example, if we compile the AXON description of the backpropagation network given in Section 7.4, we get a neurosoftware package that includes *all* three-layer backpropagation networks that use the jump-every-time generalized delta rule learning law (see Section 5.3) — with any set of network constants (e.g., learning rates for the hidden and output layers), any number of input/hidden/output units, and so on. The ability of a single package to describe an entire class of networks makes each package more useful and reduces the number of compilations that must be carried out (except, of course, during development).

Given a neurosoftware package (most neurocomputers are shipped with a variety of precompiled and optimized packages for all of the most popular neural networks), the next step in the process of using the neural network is to *load* the network into the neurocomputer. This involves two steps. First, a data structure is created that specifies all of the parameters needed to precisely describe the network to be loaded. These parameters include constants such as the number of processing elements on each layer of the network, the learning rates to be used on each layer, and any details regarding particular optional connection patterns to be used (for example, connecting the input units of a network to the output units of a network, as well as to the hidden units). Once this data structure has been defined a *LoadNet* command[3] is invoked from the user's software.

The *LoadNet* command requires the user to provide three things: the parameter data, the name of the file in the host computer mass memory that contains the neurosoftware package to be loaded, and a *NET_ID* character string tag that

---

[2] The idea that a neurocomputer is only used for running neural networks is rapidly becoming obsolete (although this will be ignored here to avoid confusion). The trend is for both ordinary software (most neurocomputers also have software compilers) and neural networks to be run on neurocomputers (to achieve maximum execution speed). However, the software interfaces between the user software and the neural networks do not change much from those presented in this section.

[3] LoadNet and the other software interface commands discussed in this chapter are all part of HNC's User Interface Subroutine Library (UISL, pronounced "weasel").

will be used as the identifier for this network in future commands to the neuro-computer. Having a unique tag is important because multiple neural networks are typically co-resident on the neurocomputer at any time and the tags provide a means for specifying to which network a particular command is to apply. The invocation of the *LoadNet* command causes the neurosoftware package to be *elaborated* or *instantiated* into the specific neural network architecture which is desired by the user. Following the execution of the *LoadNet* command, the network is ready for use.

Once a network is loaded into the neurocomputer, several commands can be used to control its activity. One of the first that is often used is the *PutCts* ("put constants") command. This command allows run-time constants such as a learning on/off switch, learning rates, momentum constants, user-set thresholds, etc. to be set. These can be modified at any time, and as often as desired.

Once the network has been loaded into the neurocomputer and the run-time constants have been properly set, the next step is to provide input to the network. This is typically done using a *PutSts* ("Put States") command, which puts a specified set of input values into the processing elements of the network designated in the command (typically, but not necessarily, these are input units). *PutSts* can also be used to initialize particular processing elements to desired starting states. The *PutWts* ("Put Weights") command is used to set specified weights to specified values.

The *GetWts* ("Get Weights") and *GetSts* ("Get States") commands allow the current weight values and, respectively, processing element output state values specified in the commands to be retrieved from the neurocomputer memory. These commands allow the host software to monitor network activity and status.

To actually run the neural network the *IterNet* ("Iterate Network") command is used. This command causes the network scheduling function to be activated. The number of time steps that the network runs will depend upon the form of the scheduling function. Sometimes (as in the case of the back-propagation network presented in the next two sections) the network simply goes through one cycle of operation (for example, one forward pass followed by one backward pass). Other networks may run continuously. The scheduling function can also set flags or semaphores in the neurocomputer memory to indicate network status. These flags can then be read by the host computer via a *GetSts* command.

At the end of host processing the *SaveNet* ("Save Network") command can be used to save the neural network in the exact state it is in at the end of its last iteration. This command transfers the specified network from the neurocomputer into a data file on the host computer (the name of this file is specified in the command). This data file can later be loaded back into the neurocomputer using a *LoadNet* command. The network will then be restored to *exactly* the same state it was in when it was saved. A *FreeNet* ("Free Network") command purges a specified network from the neurocomputer without saving it.

Finally, the *LoadNcp* ("Load Neurocomputer") command is used immediately after host software begins running to prepare the neurocomputer for the reception of commands. *FreeNcp* ("Free Neurocomputer") is used to deallocate the neurocomputer just before host software execution ends.

The HNC UISL system is based upon the interaction protocol concept that the neurocomputer shall be completely passive. The neurocomputer only responds to commands from the host computer software; it never generates any actions itself. For example, once an *IterNet* command has been executed the neurocomputer simply waits for the next command. It does not notify the host computer after the running of the neural network has been completed. This approach obviates the need for the user to develop interrupt handlers and other complex interface support software. It also enables the host computer to proceed with further processing immediately after issuing each UISL command, since there is never a need to wait for a delayed response from the neurocomputer (responses from commands that require data transfer from the neurocomputer to the host computer — such as GetSts — are produced immediately). Thus, the host computer is not hung up while the neurocomputer performs its tasks. In the event that the results of neurocomputer processing are needed immediately after they are generated (such as in a control application, where time latency of response is critical), the host software can simply poll the neurocomputer every few hundred microseconds to see if processing has finished. Each of these polling operations takes only a few host computer cycles to complete. Thus, this "we'll call you, don't call us" protocol can be used even in demanding real-time applications.

In summary, by use of a small set of simple commands we can configure and load neural networks into the neurocomputer and can insert and extract states, weights, and constants. By use of *NET_ID* tags any number of neural networks can be independently loaded, accessed, and controlled (up to the memory capacity of the neurocomputer). This is important because many real-world applications require the use of multiple neural networks.

Given this brief overview of how networks expressed in neurosoftware are used, the AXON language is described next.

Exercises

7.2.1. Devise a sequence of UISL commands for loading a backpropagation network package, initializing its weights, setting its learning flag and learning rates, and carrying out a sequence of 1000 training trials on examples $(\mathbf{x}_1, \mathbf{y}_1), (\mathbf{x}_2, \mathbf{y}_2), \ldots, (\mathbf{x}_{1000}, \mathbf{y}_{1000})$. Do not worry about the detailed arguments that need to be passed, merely construct the command flow.

7.2.2. Describe in a detailed drawing how a system for displaying a neural network structure on a computer graphics screen might work. Specifically, indicate how the processing elements and connections would be displayed and indicate how weight values and other local memory values might be shown. How might the real-time dynamic behavior of the neural network be displayed?

7.2.3. Assume that a neurosoftware language compiler on a supercomputer produces an implementation of a network in the form of a subroutine that could be linked in with other code. Compare and contrast the characteristics of such a scheme with those of an attached neurocomputer coprocessor with the characteristics mentioned in this section. Ignoring issues related to implementation efficiency or cost, what would be the advantages and disadvantages of each of these implementation approaches.

7.2.4. An exotic neural network running on a neurocomputer has just completed a training program (using reinforcement learning) during which it developed a method for controlling the temperature and voltage of a special electrochemical cell in which cold nuclear fusion is reliably produced. Following this successful training session the weight values are stored in a file in the mass memory of the host computer. These weights are potentially of enormous value and you want to establish a legal position that would exclude others from using these weights without paying you. How would you go about securing such a position? For example, could you patent the weights? Could you copyright them? How would you go about patenting or copyrighting these weights? Should you simply hold them confidential as trade secrets? Finally, if someone did the same training run, but with a different set of random starting weights, and found another viable set of weights, what action could you take against them?

7.3 AXON Language

This section provides an introduction to the AXON neural network description language. AXON's syntax is based upon that of the C programming language. It will be assumed in this section that the reader has at least basic familiarity with C. Readers without this background might want to scan a C primer or manual before proceeding.

7.3.1 AXON Structure

As discussed in Chapter 2, to describe a neural network completely (using the AXON model) we must supply the following information:

- *Slabs* — The number of distinct slabs or layers is specified.
- *Processing element transfer functions* — For each slab or layer in the network the classes of inputs to each processing element are specified, the transfer function is defined, the organization of processing element local memory is

specified (including both weights and other data values), and the type of the output signal is specified.

- *Connections* — The connection fascicles are specified in terms of their class numbers, domains of origin and destination, and selection functions.
- *Scheduling function* — The procedure for updating the slabs of the network in the proper order, and with the proper scheduling processing element control signals ("activate" signals), is specified.

As we shall now see, AXON has constructs that incorporate all of the structural knowledge of the AXON model. Essentially, all we must do is fill in the information listed above (although not exactly in this order).

AXON code describing a neural network is divided into five "blocks". These are listed, in order, below:

- Parameter Definition Block
- Processing Element and Slab Definition Block
- Network Creation and Connection Definition Block
- Scheduling Function Block
- Function Definition Block

We shall describe these blocks, in order. The AXON description of the generic three-layer backpropagation neural network presented in the next section is used as a source of examples. You will find it useful to refer to this integrated code while reading the remainder of this section. Before beginning the discussion of the five code blocks, the reserved names of AXON, identifier conventions, and the scope concept are reviewed.

KEYWORDS, BUILT-IN FUNCTIONS, AND AXON MATHEMATICAL LIBRARY FUNCTIONS   Table 7.1 lists the reserved keywords used in AXON statements. These are reserved for the specific purposes they serve in the AXON language and may not be otherwise used in AXON code. In addition to these keywords, the names of the built-in AXON functions (which are listed in Table 7.2) and of the AXON mathematical function library routines (these are listed in Table 7.3) are also reserved.

In AXON, each keyword, function or variable identifier, or constant identifier must be delimited by white space, a non-keyword operator, or punctuation. White space used inside a string constant or character constant is not seen by the compiler as a delimiter, but it is treated as such inside any other type of atom.

Keywords, built-in function names, and AXON mathematical function library names may appear in either all lowercase or all uppercase letters, but not mixed uppercase and lowercase letters. In the AXON examples presented in the next section, keyword references are noted in all lowercase letters.

IDENTIFIERS   The term *identifier* refers to the names assigned to variables, constants, or types. Identifiers may consist of letters and numbers, but they must start with a letter and must not be an AXON keyword or reserved AXON

block	break	build	case	char
class	connect	continue	create	data
default	disconnect	do	domain	else
elseif	end	enum	external	for
from	function	global	goto	if
in	include	init	input	integer
is	list	local	memory	net
of	operate	pe	random	real
record	repeat	return	selection	show
signal	sizeof	slab	state	static
then	transfer	type	union	unsigned
until	update	using	void	weight
when	while			

Table 7.1. Reserved statement keywords of AXON. These keywords may not be used for any other purpose than that specified in the definition of the language.

copy_domain()	count()	empty_domain()	free_domain()	free_mem()
full()	full_domain()	get_mem()	member_cnt()	one_to_one(
pe_index(PE)	show()			

Table 7.2. Reserved built-in function names of AXON. These names may not be used for any other purpose.

asin()	acos()	atan()	atan2(,)	atanh()
ceil()	cos()	cosh()	exp()	fabsf()
floor()	fmodf()	frand()	log()	log2( )
log10( )	pow(,)	round( )	logistic()	sinh( )
sin( )	sqrt( )	tan( )	anh( )	trunc( )
rand()	srand()	fsrand()	ldiv(, ,)	labs()
div(, ,)	abs( )			

Table 7.3. Reserved AXON mathematical function library names. These names may not be used for any other purpose.

built-in or mathematical library function name. The underscore '_' is considered a letter and is used frequently to merge several words or abbreviations into an easily recognized one-word identifier. The allowable length of identifiers exceeds all common usage. For example, Brute_4ce and i_like_AXON are acceptable, but return (a reserved AXON keyword) and 4_the_money (begins with a nonletter) are not.

SCOPE   An AXON identifier is visible only within a certain region of an AXON module, ranging from a small portion of the module to the entire module. The term *module* refers to a body of AXON source code that completely describes a neural network. In other words, a module is the neurosoftware analog of a *program* or *procedure* in programmed computing. The region of applicability of the identifier within the module is called the identifier's *scope*.

In decreasing order of visibility, the three categories of identifier scope are: module scope, function scope, and block scope.

- *Module scope* — When the declaration of an identifier occurs inside the Parameter Definition Block (see Section 7.3.2), the identifier is said to have *module scope*. Identifiers with module scope can be used anywhere within the module.
- *Function scope* — When the identifier is declared within a function of the Function Definition Block (see Section 7.3.6), the identifier is said to have *function scope*. Such identifiers apply from the point of the declaration statement to the end of the function. Labels for GOTO statements (yes, AXON has a GOTO statement — see Table 7.1) have function scope within the entire function statement, not just from the point of declaration.
- *Block scope* — When the identifier is declared within the interior of a block other than the Parameter Definition and Function Definition Blocks (see Sections 7.3.3 through 7.3.5), the identifier is said to have *block scope*. Such identifiers apply from the point of the declaration statement to the end of that block.

The five code blocks that make up an AXON program are now described using the AXON description of a three-layer backpropagation network as an example.

7.3.2 Parameter Definition Block
The Parameter Definition block of the three layer backpropagation neural network (see Section 7.4 for the complete code listing) is given by:

```
type record tCtsBpn is
    record lt is
            integer:32  iCnt;
            integer:32  hCnt;
            integer:32  oCnt;
            integer:32  RandomSeed;
```

```
        real:32     InitWeightMax;
        integer:32  ConnectInputs;
    end lt;
    record rt is
        real:32     HiddenAlpha;
        real:32     OutputAlpha;
        real:32     HiddenBeta;
        real:32     OutputBeta;
        integer:32  BatchSize;
        integer:32  LinearOutput;
        integer:32  LearnFlag;
    end rt;
end tCtsBpn;


type enum tPass is
    FORWARD, BACKWARD, FINAL
end enum tPass;


integer:32 HidSunCnt;
integer:32 HidPltCnt;
integer:32 OutSunCnt;
integer:32 OutPltCnt;
```

This code block defines the network parameters that are used in later blocks to set up and control the network. These constants will be supplied to the network by the LoadNet and PutCts UISL routines. There are two basic types of parameters defined in this block: load-time parameters (such as the numbers of input, output, and hidden layer units) belonging to the "lt" subrecord and run-time parameters (such as the learning rates to be used by the hidden and output planets and a learn/no learn Boolean switch) belonging to the "rt" subrecord. The entire set of network parameters (including both the load-time parameters and an initial set of run-time parameters) are provided in the LoadNet UISL call that loads the network into the neurocomputer. After the network is loaded into the neurocomputer, PutCts calls can be made at any time to specify new values of the run-time parameters (the load-time parameters are forever frozen at load time).

In general, the load-time parameters determine the size and configuration of the network (which is why they can only be specified at load-time, when the network is being elaborated), whereas run-time parameters are used to control the operation of the network (and can therefore be changed at any time after loading).

In the backpropagation network Parameter Definition block listing given above, the entire network parameter record is defined to be of type *tCtsBpn* (see any C language manual for a discussion of records — the same construct is used here). Records of this type are comprised of two subrecords called *lt* ("load time") and *rt* ("run time"). As discussed already, subrecord lt contains the parameters needed to configure and set up the network. For example, *iCnt*, *hCnt*, and *oCnt* define the number of input, hidden, and output units the network will have. *RandomSeed* defines the seed for the random number generator that will be used to generate the initial random weights of the network and *InitWeight-Max* defines the maximum magnitude these uniformly randomly chosen weights should have. The *ConnectInputs* parameter determines whether (ConnectInputs = 1) or not (ConnectInputs = 0) the inputs to the network will be supplied directly to the output units (in addition to the hidden layer). These parameters illustrate the subtle issues that must be addressed in the design of neurosoftware. Creating a neural network description that can actually be compiled and run is much more challenging than simply writing down some equations (as we did for backpropagation in Chapter 5).

After the network constants record type tCtsBpn is defined the enumeration type variable *tPass* and four module scope variables are defined. These variables will be used in multiple blocks later in the code. Exercises 7.3.1 and 7.3.2 address additional features of the Parameter Definition block.

7.3.3 Processing Element and Slab Definition Block
The Processing Element and Slab Definition block of the AXON description of the three-layer backpropagation neural network is given here:

```
net Bpn(tCtsBpn Cts) is

    pe PeIn is
        state is real:32 x;
    end PeIn;

    pe PeHidPlt is
        state is real:32 xw;
        transfer function is HiddenPlanetXfer(tPass);
        input class list is F1, F2;
            signal of F1 is real:32 x;
            signal of F2 is real:32 HiddenError;
        local memory is
            weight of F1 is real:32 w;
    end PeHidPlt;

    pe PeHidSun is
        state is real:32 z;
        transfer function is HiddenSunXfer(tPass);
        input class list is F3, F4;
            signal of F3 is real:32 zw;
            signal of F4 is real:32 ew;
        local memory is
```

```
            data is real:32 I;
    end PeHidSun;

    pe PeOutPlt is
        state is real:32 zw_or_ew;
        transfer function is OutputPlanetXfer(tPass);
        input class list is F5, F6;
            signal of F5 is real:32 z;
            signal of F6 is real:32 OutputError;
        local memory is
            weight of F5 is real:32 w;
    end PeOutPlt;

    pe PeOutSun is
        state is real:32 y';
        transfer function is OutputSunXfer(tPass);
        input class list is F7, F8;
            signal of F7 is real:32 zw;
            signal of F8 is real:32 y;
        local memory is
            data is real:32 I;
            data is real:32 tmp;
    end PeOutSun;

    slab is PeIn      SlabOne[1];
    slab is PeIn      SlabTrn[OutSunCnt];
    slab is PeHidSun SlabHidSun[HidSunCnt];
    slab is PeIn      SlabIn[Cts.lt.iCnt];
    slab is PeOutSun SlabOutSun[OutSunCnt];
    slab is PeHidPlt SlabHidPlt[HidPltCnt];
    slab is PeOutPlt SlabOutPlt[OutPltCnt];

    create  function is BpnSetup();
    operate function is BpnRun();
end net Bpn;
```

This code block carries out several functions. However, its overall function is to name the neural network being defined and declare the network's ingredients completely. The manner in which it carries out this function is now described.

The opening and closing of the block are the statements *net Bpn(tCtsBpn Cts) is* and *end net Bpn*. Between these statements all of the network's elements are specified in terms of quantities that are named, but not defined, in this block (they are defined in the subsequent blocks). Note that the network parameters record is called simply *Cts*. It is of type *tCtsBpn*.

The first (and largest) set of statements are *processing element definition statements*. These statements begin by declaring the name of the type of processing element they are defining. Then the mathematical type and generic symbolic variable name (i.e., without a processing element number index) of the processing element state (output signal) are defined. The transfer function of the processing element is then named, followed by a list of the connection input classes that processing elements of this type will accept. The mathematical types of the signals in each of these input classes are then defined. A generic mathematical symbol designating the input signal of each input class is also provided.

Following the input class specification the local memory structure of this type of processing element is specified. The mathematical type of the weights associated with each input class having weights is then specified, as is a generic symbol for these weights. Following definition of the weights, the local memory data values are defined. Unlike weights (the number of which can vary from processing element to processing element on a slab, depending on how many inputs of that type each processing element receives), the number of data values per processing element is fixed. Since processing elements are defined by their input classes, transfer function, local memory, and output signal this completes the definition of the processing elements. Note that, just as in Section 5.3, input units, hidden suns, hidden planets, output suns and output planets are defined in the code block above.

After the processing elements are defined the slabs can be declared. Basically, all the *slab is* statements have to do is declare the type of processing element from which the slab is constructed and declare how large the slab is. These steps are accomplished by naming the processing element type to be used (by invoking one of the names defined immediately above), then naming the slab and giving its size in brackets. Note that *SlabOne* has only one processing element. This slab is used to provide the 1.0 bias input to the bias planets of the hidden and output rows. The manner in which this slab is used will be described. Note that the size of the hidden planets slab is (Cts.lt.iCnt+1)(Cts.lt.hCnt), since each of the Cts.lt.hCnt hidden layer units needs Cts.lt.iCnt+1 planets. The derived constants *HidSunCnt, HidPltCnt, OutSunCnt* and *OutPltCnt* are defined in the Network Creation and Connection Definition block.

Following the definitions of the slabs, the names of the network's *create function* and *operate function* are declared. The create function builds the network by creating the slabs and then creating the connections (see the next subsection for details).

The operate function is the AXON name for the network scheduling function. It is described following the create function.

7.3.4 Network Creation and Connection Definition Block

The Network Creation and Connection Definition block of the AXON description of the three-layer backpropagation neural network is given here:

```
create function BpnSetup() is

    domain          OneAndInput;
    domain          OneAndHidden;
    domain PeHidPlt HPdomain;
    domain PeOutPlt OPdomain;

    integer:32 iPe;
    integer:32 OutPltPerSun;
    integer:32 HidPltPerSun;

    if Cts.lt.iCnt < 1 then      // Check if input size is reasonable.
        Bpn.error = -101;
        return;
    end;

    if Cts.lt.hCnt < 0 then      // Check if hidden slab size is reasonable
        Bpn.error = -102;
        return;
    end;

    if Cts.lt.oCnt < 1 then      // Check if output size is reasonable.
        Bpn.error = -103;
        return;
    end;

    HidSunCnt = Cts.lt.hCnt;
    OutSunCnt = Cts.lt.oCnt;

    HidPltPerSun = Cts.lt.iCnt + 1;
    HidPltCnt    = HidSunCnt * HidPltPerSun;

    if Cts.lt.ConnectInputs <> 0 then
        OutPltPerSun = Cts.lt.hCnt + Cts.lt.iCnt + 1;
    else
        OutPltPerSun = Cts.lt.hCnt + 1;
    end;

    OutPltCnt = OutSunCnt * OutPltPerSun;

    build Bpn;                       // Create the network data structures.

    OneAndInput = SlabOne + SlabIn;

    iPe = 0;
```

```
for _Pe in SlabHidSun do
    HPdomain = SlabHidPlt[iPe:iPe + HidPltPerSun - 1:1];
    connect class F1 of HPdomain from OneAndInput using one_to_one();
    connect class F2 of HPdomain from _Pe using full();
    connect class F3 of _Pe from HPdomain using full();
    iPe += HidPltPerSun;
end;

if Cts.lt.ConnectInputs <> 0 then
    OneAndHidden = SlabOne + SlabHidSun + SlabIn;
else
    OneAndHidden = SlabOne + SlabHidSun;
end;

iPe = 0;
for _Pe in SlabOutSun do
    OPdomain = SlabOutPlt[iPe + 1:iPe + HidSunCnt:1];
    connect class F4 of SlabHidSun from OPdomain using one_to_one();
    OPdomain = SlabOutPlt[iPe:iPe + OutPltPerSun - 1:1];
    connect class F5 of OPdomain from OneAndHidden using one_to_one();
    connect class F6 of OPdomain from _Pe using full();
    connect class F7 of _Pe from OPdomain using full();
    iPe += OutPltPerSun;
end;

connect class F8 of SlabOutSun from SlabTrn using one_to_one();

fsrand(Cts.lt.RandomSeed);

for _Pe in SlabHidPlt do
    for Icn in _Pe.F1 do
        Icn.w = ((2 * frand()) - 1) * Cts.lt.InitWeightMax;
    end;
end;

for _Pe in SlabOutPlt do
    for Icn in _Pe.F5 do
        Icn.w = ((2 * frand()) - 1) * Cts.lt.InitWeightMax;
    end;
end;

    SlabOne[0].x = 1.0;
end BpnSetup;
```

The primary function of this code block is to define the create function *BpnSetup* that specifies how the network is to be constructed. Construction of the connections is a major part of this network creation process. The individual steps are now described.

The first two elements of code are the domain definitions and the definitions of some auxiliary variables. As discussed in Chapter 2, domains are constructed from unions, intersections, and set differences of slices and other domains. In this case the first two domains declared are simply the unions of two entire slabs (namely, the bias slab and the input and hidden sun slabs, respectively). The *domain* statements simply declare these names. Their actual definitions are provided later in the block. The third and fourth domains (*HPdomain* and *OPdomain*, respectively) are then declared to be subsets of the set of all hidden planet processing elements and the set of all output planet processing elements, respectively.

Following the type declarations of local variables *iPe*, *OutPltPerSun*, and *HidPltPerSun* some tests are carried out on the input variables. These tests are designed to ensure that the values of these parameters are within valid ranges. For example, if *Cts.lt.iCnt*= -12 this would indicate that there are -12 inputs to the network, which is clearly ridiculous. While the three tests provided in the code block above by no means represent an exhaustive check of the network parameter values, they demonstrate the point that AXON supports such checking. Note that, if a test fails, the variable *Bpn.error* is set to a negative value. This automatically causes the UISL to return an exception to the calling routine (typically *LoadNet*) that caused the error. The attempt to load the network is aborted automatically. AXON provides the variable *.error* and the associated automatic exception handling as a built-in feature for every network name (in this case *Bpn*). This feature allows the development of highly robust systems that are virtually crashproof. Even if faulty values are transmitted to the neurocomputer, it will not hang or drop off line (assuming the user actually provides the required error checking). User-developed error handling routines on the host computer can then reestablish normal system operation. As in the above code block, the value of *[netname].error* can be set to different negative values to indicate the nature of the error to the error handling routine (positive values of *[netname].error* are reserved for use by the UISL system).

Following the code for parameter error checking, the network connections are built. The building of the network is activated by the *build Bpn* statement. Connection building is both the most powerful and the most arcane of AXON's features. Skilled AXON users can rapidly and surely construct connections for even the most complicated networks, but the novice is often overwhelmed. To understand this portion of the language, let us analyze the first connection statement set in detail. The relevant code from the preceding block is reproduced here:

```
OneAndInput = SlabOne + SlabIn;

iPe = 0;
for _Pe in SlabHidSun do
    HPdomain = SlabHidPlt[iPe:iPe + HidPltPerSun - 1:1];
```

```
    connect class F1 of HPdomain from OneAndInput using one_to_one();
    connect class F2 of HPdomain from _Pe using full();
    connect class F3 of _Pe from HPdomain using full();
    iPe += HidPltPerSun;
end;
```

The first line carries out the construction of the domain *OneAndInput* as the union of all processing elements of *SlabOne* and *SlabIn* (the bias and input slabs). Note the overloading of the "+" operator. Next, the processing element index *iPe* is set to 0. Then, for each processing elements in the hidden sun slab the following steps are carried out. First, domain *HPdomain* is set equal to the hidden planet slab slice starting at planet *iPe* and going to *iPe + HidPltPerSun-1* in steps of one processing element. Since *HidPltPerSun* was defined earlier in the code to be the number of hidden planets per hidden sun (calculated from *Cts.lt.iCnt* and *Cts.lt.hCnt*), this simply means that we are defining *HPdomain* to be the planets associated with the first sun of the hidden layer.

The first connect statement then builds connections of hidden planet input class *F1* by forming connections from the domain *OneAndInput* to *HPdomain* (the planets of the first hidden sun) using the (built-in) selection function *one_to_one()*. The selection function *one_to_one()* simply connects the bias unit of *OneAndInput* to the first planet of *HPdomain*, the first input unit of slab *SlabIn* to the second planet of *HPdomain*, and so on, until all of the inputs are connected. In other words, *one_to_one()* connects the first processing element of the source domain to the first processing element of the target domain, the second to the second, and so on; until one domain runs out of processing elements. In this case, both domains have exactly the same number of processing elements. Note that processing element indices always start at 0 in AXON.

The second connect statement forms connections to the planets of *HPdomain* from their sun (these are used during the backward pass to transmit the δ_{li} error back to the planets). These connections belong to input class *F2*.

The final connect statement forms the connections that take the outputs of the planets of *HPdomain* to their sun (these carry the weighted input values to the sun on the forward pass). Note that both of these connect statements use the built-in selection function *full()*. In the first connection statement *full()* connects each element of *HPdomain* from *_Pe*. In the second connect statement, *full()* connects *_Pe* from all of the planets of *HPdomain*. In short, *full()* provides each processing element in the target domain with a connection from each processing element in the source domain.

After the connections are established for the planets of the first hidden sun the hidden planet starting index *iPe* is incremented by *HidPltPerSun* and the connections for the planets of the second hidden sun are then established, and so on, until all of the hidden planets are wired up.

The other connection statements of the above code block are left to you to unravel.

Although AXON connection statements seem cumbersome at first, with a little practice they become second nature. The experienced AXON user can both write and read complex networks easily and quickly. Notice that details such as the slab sizes are suppressed in the statements presented above. This network size information was already supplied in the previous code block.

Following the last of the connect statements the planet weights are initialized to random values. Finally, the output signal of the single processing element of the bias slab is set to 1.0. Since its value is never updated or modified by any of the subsequent processing this output signal remains at 1.0 indefinitely.

7.3.5 Scheduling Function Block

The Scheduling Function block of the AXON description of the three-layer backpropagation neural network is given here:

```
operate function BpnRun() is

    /* FORWARD PASS */
    update SlabHidPlt(FORWARD);
    update SlabHidSun(FORWARD);
    update SlabOutPlt(FORWARD);
    update SlabOutSun(FORWARD);

    /* BACKWARD PASS */
    if Cts.rt.LearnFlag <> 0 then
        update SlabOutSun(BACKWARD);
        update SlabOutPlt(BACKWARD);
        update SlabHidSun(BACKWARD);
        update SlabHidPlt(BACKWARD);
        update SlabOutSun(FINAL);
    end;

end BpnRun;
```

The network scheduling function *BpnRun()* (known in AXON terminology as an *operate function*) consists of *update* statements that cause all of the processing elements of the slab being updated to have an "activate" input sent to them, thus activating their episodic transfer functions. The specific actions taken by the transfer functions when they receive these activate inputs are defined in the next code block.

The operate function of the network is itself activated every time an *IterNet* UISL command is sent to the network. In the case of this backpropagation network a call to IterNet causes a forward pass (updating of hidden planets, hidden suns, output planets, and output suns, in order) and, if Cts.rt.LearnFlag is unequal to zero, a backward pass (updating of the output suns to produce raw output errors, feedback of those errors to the output planets for weight modification calculations, feedback of the output sun error-weighted old output planet weights to the hidden suns, feedback of the hidden sun derived errors to the hidden planets for weight modification), and finally, the output sun output signals are restored to the original y_i' output signal values that they had following the forward pass (recall that these outputs were used to transmit the errors back to the hidden layer during the backward pass). This last step is the *FINAL* pass. This is precisely the sequence of events defined in Section 5.3. The AXON code expression of the backpropagation network scheduling function is about as neat and trim as one could wish.

7.3.6 Function Definition Block

The Function Definition block of the AXON description of the three-layer back-propagation neural network is given next. This block is primarily used to define the transfer functions used in the processing element type definitions, although other functions used in the code are sometimes included.

```
transfer function HiddenPlanetXfer(tPass pass) is
    case pass of
        when FORWARD:
            for Icn in this_pe.F1 do
                this_pe.xw = Icn.x * Icn.w;
            end;
        when BACKWARD:
            for IcnF1 in this_pe.F1, IcnF2 in this_pe.F2 do
                IcnF1.w += Cts.rt.HiddenAlpha * IcnF2.HiddenError * IcnF1.z;
            end;
    end case;
end HiddenPlanetXfer;

transfer function HiddenSunXfer(tPass pass) is
    real:32 error;
    case pass of
        when FORWARD:
            this_pe.I = 0.0;
            for _Icn in this_pe.F3 do
                this_pe.I += _Icn.zw;
            end;
            this_pe.z = logistic(this_pe.I);
        when BACKWARD:
            error = 0.0;
            for Icn in this_pe.F4 do
                error += Icn.ew;
            end;
            this_pe.z  = (1.0 - this_pe.z) * this_pe.z * error;
    end case;
end HiddenSunXfer;

transfer function OutputPlanetXfer(tPass pass) is
```

```
case pass of
    when FORWARD:
        for Icn in this_pe.F5 do
            this_pe.zw_or_ew = Icn.z * Icn.w;
        end;
    when BACKWARD:
        for IcnF5 in this_pe.F5, IcnF6 in this_pe.F6 do
            this_pe.zw_or_ew = IcnF5.w * IcnF6.OutputError;
            IcnF5.w += Cts.rt.OutputAlpha * IcnF6.OutputError * IcnF5.z
        end;
    end case;
end OutputPlanetXfer;


transfer function OutputSunXfer(tPass pass) is
    case pass of
        when FORWARD:
            this_pe.I = 0.0;
            for Icn in this_pe.F7 do
                this_pe.I += Icn.zw;
            end;
            if Cts.rt.LinearOutput == 0 then
                this_pe.z = logistic(this_pe.I);
            else
                this_pe.z = this_pe.I;
            end;
        when BACKWARD:
            this_pe.tmp = this_pe.z;
            for Icn in this_pe.F8 do
                this_pe.z = Icn.y - this_pe.z;
            end;
            if Cts.rt.LinearOutput == 0 then
                this_pe.z *= (1.0 - this_pe.tmp) * this_pe.tmp;
            end;
        when FINAL:
            this_pe.z = this_pe.tmp;
    end case;
end OutputSunXfer;
```

These processing element transfer functions are defined in terms of connections (*Icn* — 'Interconnection' — is the generic AXON identifier for a connection) belonging to particular input classes. Powerful statements such as "*for Icn in this_pe.F7 do*" (i.e., "for all connections Icn to this processing element of input class *F7* do the following:") make the job of transfer function writing easy. Exercise 7.3.4 considers one of the statements of the above code block in more detail.

It is important to note that while AXON is a useful language, it is not without flaw. For example, one of its failings is the rigid runtime/loadtime structure of its parameter definition blocks. (See the next section.) Also, the definition of domain does not include all of the domain structure spelled out in Chapter 2. Finally, the weight indexing scheme used in AXON (this scheme is not discussed in this chapter) is idiosyncratic and makes it difficult to specify which weights belong to which processing element.

Exercises

7.3.1. Why would we want to connect the inputs to the output units in a backpropagation neural network?

7.3.2. Speculate as to what the *LinearOutput* and *LearnFlag* run-time parameters of the *tCtsBpn* record are used for.

7.3.3. Describe the function of the following AXON code block in detail.

```
if Cts.lt.ConnectInputs <> 0 then
    OneAndHidden = SlabOne + SlabHidSun + SlabIn;
else
    OneAndHidden = SlabOne + SlabHidSun;
end;
iPe = 0;
for _Pe in SlabOutSun do
    OPdomain = SlabOutPlt[iPe + 1:iPe + HidSunCnt:1];
    connect class F4 of SlabHidSun from OPdomain using one_to_one();
    OPdomain = SlabOutPlt[iPe:iPe + OutPltPerSun - 1:1];
    connect class F5 of OPdomain from OneAndHidden using one_to_one
    connect class F6 of OPdomain from _Pe using full();
    connect class F7 of _Pe from OPdomain using full();
    iPe += OutPltPerSun;
end;
```

7.3.4. Devise a set of domain definitions and connection statements for the linear associator. Make up appropriate slab names.

7.3.5. Explain the *OutputSunXfer(tPass pass)* output sun transfer function in detail.

7.3.6. Explain why a *FINAL* pass is necessary in the AXON description of the three-layer backpropagation network. Refer to the equations of Section 5.3 to justify your answer. Would a FINAL pass be needed in a four layer backpropagation network?

7.4 AXON Examples

This Section presents two examples of neural network architectures (backprop-agation and counterpropagation — see Chapter 5) written in AXON. The back-propagation network is the same one dissected in the last section. The coun-terpropagation network is presented to allow the reader to apply their AXON understanding to an entirely different network (see Exercises 7.4.1 through 7.4.5 below).

7.4.1 Backpropagation

This subsection presents an AXON description of a three-row backpropagation neural network.

```
/* BEGIN PARAMETER DEFINITION BLOCK */

type record tCtsBpn is
    record lt is
        integer:32 iCnt;
        integer:32 hCnt;
        integer:32 oCnt;
        integer:32 RandomSeed;
        real:32    InitWeightMax;
        integer:32 ConnectInputs;
    end lt;
    record rt is
        real:32    HiddenAlpha;
        real:32    OutputAlpha;
        real:32    HiddenBeta;
        real:32    OutputBeta;
        integer:32 BatchSize;
        integer:32 LinearOutput;
        integer:32 LearnFlag;
    end rt;
end tCtsBpn;

type enum tPass is
    FORWARD, BACKWARD, FINAL
end enum tPass;

integer:32 HidSunCnt;
integer:32 HidPltCnt;
integer:32 OutSunCnt;
integer:32 OutPltCnt;

/* END PARAMETER DEFINITION BLOCK */
```

```
/* BEGIN PE AND SLAB DEFINITION BLOCK */

net Bpn(tCtsBpn Cts) is

    pe PeIn is
        state is real:32 x;
    end PeIn;

    pe PeHidPlt is
        state is real:32 xw;
        transfer function is HiddenPlanetXfer(tPass);
        input class list is F1, F2;
            signal of F1 is real:32 x;
            signal of F2 is real:32 HiddenError;
        local memory is
            weight of F1 is real:32 w;
    end PeHidPlt;

    pe PeHidSun is
        state is real:32 z;
        transfer function is HiddenSunXfer(tPass);
        input class list is F3, F4;
            signal of F3 is real:32 zw;
            signal of F4 is real:32 ew;
        local memory is
            data is real:32 I;
    end PeHidSun;

    pe PeOutPlt is
        state is real:32 zw_or_ew;
        transfer function is OutputPlanetXfer(tPass);
        input class list is F5, F6;
            signal of F5 is real:32 z;
            signal of F6 is real:32 OutputError;
        local memory is
            weight of F5 is real:32 w;
    end PeOutPlt;

    pe PeOutSun is
        state is real:32 y';
        transfer function is OutputSunXfer(tPass);
        input class list is F7, F8;
            signal of F7 is real:32 zw;
            signal of F8 is real:32 y;
```

```
        local memory is
            data is real:32 I;
            data is real:32 tmp;
    end PeOutSun;

    slab is PeIn     SlabOne[1];
    slab is PeIn     SlabTrn[OutSunCnt];
    slab is PeHidSun SlabHidSun[HidSunCnt];
    slab is PeIn     SlabIn[Cts.lt.iCnt];
    slab is PeOutSun SlabOutSun[OutSunCnt];
    slab is PeHidPlt SlabHidPlt[HidPltCnt];
    slab is PeOutPlt SlabOutPlt[OutPltCnt];

    create  function is BpnSetup();
    operate function is BpnRun();
end net Bpn;

/* END PE AND SLAB DEFINITION BLOCK */

/* BEGIN NETWORK CREATION AND CONNECTION DEFINITION BLOCK */

create function BpnSetup() is

    domain          OneAndInput;
    domain          OneAndHidden;
    domain PeHidPlt HPdomain;
    domain PeOutPlt OPdomain;

    integer:32 iPe;
    integer:32 OutPltPerSun;
    integer:32 HidPltPerSun;

    if Cts.lt.iCnt < 1 then // Check if input size is reasonable.
        Bpn.error = -101;
        return;
    end;

    if Cts.lt.hCnt < 0 then // Check if hidden slab size is reasonable.
        Bpn.error = -102;
        return;
    end;

    if Cts.lt.oCnt < 1 then // Check if output size is reasonable.
        Bpn.error = -103;
        return;
```

```
end;

HidSunCnt = Cts.lt.hCnt;
OutSunCnt = Cts.lt.oCnt;

HidPltPerSun = Cts.lt.iCnt + 1;
HidPltCnt    = HidSunCnt * HidPltPerSun;

if Cts.lt.ConnectInputs <> 0 then
    OutPltPerSun = Cts.lt.hCnt + Cts.lt.iCnt + 1;
else
    OutPltPerSun = Cts.lt.hCnt + 1;
end;

OutPltCnt = OutSunCnt * OutPltPerSun;

build Bpn;   // Create the network data structures.

OneAndInput = SlabOne + SlabIn;

iPe = 0;
for _Pe in SlabHidSun do
    HPdomain = SlabHidPlt[iPe:iPe + HidPltPerSun - 1:1];
    connect class F1 of HPdomain from OneAndInput using one_to_one();
    connect class F2 of HPdomain from _Pe using full();
    connect class F3 of _Pe from HPdomain using full();
    iPe += HidPltPerSun;
end;

if Cts.lt.ConnectInputs <> 0 then
    OneAndHidden = SlabOne + SlabHidSun + SlabIn;
else
    OneAndHidden = SlabOne + SlabHidSun;
end;

iPe = 0;
for _Pe in SlabOutSun do
    OPdomain = SlabOutPlt[iPe + 1:iPe + HidSunCnt:1];
    connect class F4 of SlabHidSun from OPdomain using one_to_one();
    OPdomain = SlabOutPlt[iPe:iPe + OutPltPerSun - 1:1];
    connect class F5 of OPdomain from OneAndHidden using one_to_one();
    connect class F6 of OPdomain from _Pe using full();
    connect class F7 of _Pe from OPdomain using full();
    iPe += OutPltPerSun;
end;
```

```
    connect class F8 of SlabOutSun from SlabTrn using one_to_one();

    fsrand(Cts.lt.RandomSeed);

    for _Pe in SlabHidPlt do
        for Icn in _Pe.F1 do
            Icn.w = ((2 * frand()) - 1) * Cts.lt.InitWeightMax;
        end;
    end;

    for _Pe in SlabOutPlt do
        for Icn in _Pe.F5 do
            Icn.w = ((2 * frand()) - 1) * Cts.lt.InitWeightMax;
        end;
    end;

    SlabOne[0].x = 1.0;
end BpnSetup;

/* END NETWORK CREATION AND CONNECTION DEFINITION BLOCK */

/* BEGIN SCHEDULING FUNCTION BLOCK */

operate function BpnRun() is

    /* FORWARD PASS */
    update SlabHidPlt(FORWARD);
    update SlabHidSun(FORWARD);
    update SlabOutPlt(FORWARD);
    update SlabOutSun(FORWARD);

    /* BACKWARD PASS */
    if Cts.rt.LearnFlag <> 0 then
        update SlabOutSun(BACKWARD);
        update SlabOutPlt(BACKWARD);
        update SlabHidSun(BACKWARD);
        update SlabHidPlt(BACKWARD);
        update SlabOutSun(FINAL);
    end;

end BpnRun;


/* END SCHEDULING FUNCTION BLOCK */
```

```
/* BEGIN FUNCTION DEFINITION BLOCK */

transfer function HiddenPlanetXfer(tPass pass) is
    case pass of
        when FORWARD:
            for Icn in this_pe.F1 do
                this_pe.xw = Icn.x * Icn.w;
            end;
        when BACKWARD:
            for IcnF1 in this_pe.F1, IcnF2 in this_pe.F2 do
                IcnF1.w += Cts.rt.HiddenAlpha * IcnF2.HiddenError * IcnF1.z;
            end;
    end case;
end HiddenPlanetXfer;


transfer function HiddenSunXfer(tPass pass) is real:32 error;
    case pass of
        when FORWARD:
            this_pe.I = 0.0;
            for _Icn in this_pe.F3 do
                this_pe.I += _Icn.zw;
            end;
            this_pe.z = logistic(this_pe.I);
        when BACKWARD:
            error = 0.0;
            for Icn in this_pe.F4 do
                error += Icn.ew;
            end;
            this_pe.z  = (1.0 - this_pe.z) * this_pe.z * error;
    end case;
end HiddenSunXfer;

transfer function OutputPlanetXfer(tPass pass) is
    case pass of
        when FORWARD:
            for Icn in this_pe.F5 do
                this_pe.zw_or_ew = Icn.z * Icn.w;
            end;
        when BACKWARD:
            for IcnF5 in this_pe.F5, IcnF6 in this_pe.F6 do
                this_pe.zw_or_ew = IcnF5.w * IcnF6.OutputError;
                IcnF5.w += Cts.rt.OutputAlpha * IcnF6.OutputError * IcnF5.z;
            end;
```

```
        end case;
end OutputPlanetXfer;


transfer function OutputSunXfer(tPass pass) is
    case pass of
        when FORWARD:
            this_pe.I = 0.0;
            for Icn in this_pe.F7 do
                this_pe.I += Icn.zw;
            end;
            if Cts.rt.LinearOutput == 0 then
                this_pe.z = logistic(this_pe.I);
            else
                this_pe.z = this_pe.I;
            end;
        when BACKWARD:
            this_pe.tmp = this_pe.z;
            for Icn in this_pe.F8 do
                this_pe.z = Icn.y - this_pe.z;
            end;
            if Cts.rt.LinearOutput == 0 then
                this_pe.z *= (1.0 - this_pe.tmp) * this_pe.tmp;
            end;
        when FINAL:
            this_pe.z = this_pe.tmp;
    end case;
end OutputSunXfer;


/* END FUNCTION DEFINITION BLOCK */
```

7.4.2 Counterpropagation

This subsection presents a version of the counterpropagation neural network of Chapter 5 described in AXON. Less annotation is provided so that the reader will have to identify the code blocks. This will reinforce the learning of the previous section.

```
// Counterpropagation

type record tCtsCpn is
    record LoadTime is
        integer:32   InputSize;
        integer:32   GrossbergSize;
        integer:32   KohonenSize;
        integer:32   RandomSeed;
```

```
            real:32     InitWtMin;
            real:32     InitWtMax;
        end lt;
        record RunTime is
            real:32     Alpha;
            real:32     Beta;
            real:32     a;
            real:32     b;
            real:32     c;
            real:32     d;
            real:32     r;
            real:32     T;
            real:32     Reject;
            integer:32  Winners;
            integer:8   StatsFlag;
            integer:8   CountFlag;
            integer:8   LearnFlag;
            integer:8   WinRatioFlag;
        end rt;
end tCtsCpn;


type enum is
    PASS1, PASS2, PASS3, PASS4, PASS5, PASS6
end tPassCpn;


type real:32     tStsCpn;
type real:32     tWtsCpn;
type integer:32  tStsMinCpn;
type integer:32  tStsCntCpn;


type record rStsMminCpn is
    real:32 MinDistance;
    real:32 MinValue;
end tStsMminCpn;


type enum is
    INVALID_IN_SIZE  = -101,
    INVALID_KOH_SIZE = -102,
    INVALID_GSB_SIZE = -103
end tErrorCpn;



net Cpn(tCtsCpn Cts) is
    pe PeInCpn is
        state is tStsCpn x;
```

```
end;

pe PeKohCpn  is
    state is tStsCpn z;
    transfer function is KohXfer(tPassCpn);
    input class list is FromIn, FromMin, FromMmin, FromSum;
        signal of FromIn   is tStsCpn      x;
        signal of FromMin  is tStsMinCpn  MinPeIdx;
        signal of FromMmin is tStsMminCpn Mmin;
        signal of FromSum  is tStsCpn      Sum;
    local memory is
        weight of FromIn is tWtsCpn w;
        data is real:32 d;
        data is real:32 p;
        data is real:32 b;
        data is real:32 tp;
end;

pe PeGsbCpn  is
    state is tStsCpn y;
    transfer function is GsbXfer(tPassCpn);
    input class list is FromKoh, FromTrn;
        signal of FromKoh is tStsCpn z;
        signal of FromTrn is tStsCpn t;
    local memory is
        weight of FromKoh is tWtsCpn u;
end;

pe PeMinCpn is
    state is tStsMinCpn MinPeIdx;
    transfer function is MinXfer();
    input class list is FromKoh;
        signal of FromKoh is tStsCpn z;
    local memory is
        data is integer:32 UnbiasedWinner;
        data is integer:32 cSame;
        data is integer:32 cTotal;
        data is real:32    PercentSame;
end;

pe PeMminCpn is
    state is tStsMminCpn MultiMin;
    transfer function is MminXfer();
    input class list is FromKoh;
        signal of FromKoh is tStsCpn z;
```

```
       end;

   pe PeSumCpn is
       state is tStsCpn Sum;
       transfer function is SumXfer();
       input class list is FromKoh;
           signal of FromKoh is tStsCpn z;
   end;

   pe PeStatCpn is
       state is tStsCpn Stat;
       transfer function is StatXfer();
       input class list is FromGsb, FromTrn;
           signal of FromGsb is tStsCpn y;
           signal of FromTrn is tStsCpn t;
       local memory is
           data is real:32 Sum;
           data is real:32 cIter;
   end;

   pe PeCntCpn is
       state is tStsCntCpn Count;
       transfer function is CntXfer();
       input class list is FromKoh;
           signal of FromKoh is tStsCpn z;
   end;

   slab is PeInCpn    SlabInCpn[Cts.lt.InputSize];
   slab is PeKohCpn   SlabKohCpn[Cts.lt.KohonenSize];
   slab is PeGsbCpn   SlabGsbCpn[Cts.lt.GrossbergSize];
   slab is PeInCpn    SlabTrnCpn[Cts.lt.GrossbergSize];
   slab is PeMinCpn   SlabMinCpn[1];
   slab is PeMminCpn  SlabMminCpn[1];
   slab is PeSumCpn   SlabSumCpn[1];
   slab is PeStatCpn  SlabStatCpn[2];
   slab is PeCntCpn   SlabCntCpn[1];

   create  function is CpnSetup();
   operate function is CpnRun();
end;

create function CpnSetup() is
    if Cts.lt.InputSize < 1 then
        Cpn.error = INVALID_IN_SIZE;
        return;
```

```
end;

if Cts.lt.KohonenSize < 1 then
    Cpn.error = INVALID_KOH_SIZE;
    return;
end;

if Cts.lt.GrossbergSize < 1 then
    Cpn.error = INVALID_GSB_SIZE;
    return;
end;

build Cpn;

connect class FromIn    of SlabKohCpn from SlabInCpn    using full();
connect class FromMin   of SlabKohCpn from SlabMinCpn   using full();
connect class FromMmin  of SlabKohCpn from SlabMminCpn  using full();
connect class FromSum   of SlabKohCpn from SlabSumCpn   using full();

connect class FromKoh of SlabGsbCpn from SlabKohCpn using full();
connect class FromTrn of SlabGsbCpn from SlabTrnCpn using one_to_one();

connect class FromKoh of SlabMinCpn  from SlabKohCpn using full();
connect class FromKoh of SlabMminCpn from SlabKohCpn using full();
connect class FromKoh of SlabSumCpn  from SlabKohCpn using full();
connect class FromKoh of SlabCntCpn  from SlabKohCpn using full();

connect class FromGsb of SlabStatCpn from SlabGsbCpn using full();
connect class FromTrn of SlabStatCpn from SlabTrnCpn using full();

fsrand(Cts.lt.RandomSeed);

for Pe_ in SlabKohCpn do
    Pe_.b  = 0.0;
    Pe_.p  = 1.0 / Cts.lt.KohonenSize;
    Pe_.tp = Pe_.p;
    for Icn in Pe_.FromIn do
        Icn.w = (Cts.lt.InitWtMax - Cts.lt.InitWtMin) * frand()
                + Cts.lt.InitWtMin;
    end;
end;

for Pe_ in SlabGsbCpn do
    for Icn in Pe_.FromKoh do
        Icn.u = (Cts.lt.InitWtMax - Cts.lt.InitWtMin) * frand()
```

```
                             + Cts.lt.InitWtMin;
         end;
    end;

    SlabStatCpn[0].Sum   = 0.0;
    SlabStatCpn[0].cIter = 0.0;

    SlabStatCpn[1].Sum   = 0.0;
    SlabStatCpn[1].cIter = 0.0;

    SlabMinCpn[0].cSame  = 0.0;
    SlabMinCpn[0].cTotal = 0.0;
end;



operate function CpnRun() is

    update SlabKohCpn(PASS1);

    if Cts.rt.LearnFlag <> 0 then
        update SlabMinCpn(PASS1);
        update SlabKohCpn(PASS2);
        update SlabGsbCpn(PASS2);
        update SlabKohCpn(PASS3);
        update SlabMinCpn(PASS2);
        update SlabKohCpn(PASS4);
    elseif Cts.rt.CountFlag <> 0 then
        update SlabCntCpn();
    elseif Cts.rt.Winners == 1 then
        update SlabMinCpn(PASS1);
        update SlabKohCpn(PASS2);
        update SlabGsbCpn(PASS1);
    else
        update SlabMminCpn();
        update SlabKohCpn(PASS5);
        update SlabSumCpn();
        update SlabKohCpn(PASS6);
        update SlabGsbCpn(PASS1);
    end;

    if Cts.rt.StatsFlag <> 0 then
        update SlabStatCpn();
    end;
end;
```

```
transfer function KohXfer(tPassCpn Pass) is
    integer:32 pe_index();
    real:32 Scale;

    case Pass of
        when PASS1:
            this_pe.z = 0.0;
            for Icn in this_pe.FromIn do
                this_pe.z += (Icn.x - Icn.w) * (Icn.x - Icn.w);
            end;
            this_pe.z = sqrt(this_pe.z);
            this_pe.d = this_pe.z;
        when PASS2:
            for Icn in this_pe.FromMin do
                if pe_index(this_pe) == Icn.MinPeIdx then
                    this_pe.z = 1.0;
                else
                    this_pe.z = 0.0;
                end;
            end;
        when PASS3:
            if this_pe.p < Cts.rt.T then
                this_pe.z = Cts.rt.d;
            else
                this_pe.z = this_pe.d - this_pe.b;
            end;
        when PASS4:
            for Icn in this_pe.FromMin do
                if pe_index(this_pe) == Icn.MinPeIdx then
                    this_pe.p += Cts.rt.b * (1.0 - this_pe.p);
                    Scale = Cts.rt.Alpha;
                else
                    this_pe.p += Cts.rt.b * (0.0 - this_pe.p);
                    Scale = Cts.rt.Beta;
                end;
            end;
            this_pe.b = Cts.rt.c * (this_pe.tp - this_pe.p);
            if Scale <> 0.0 then
                for Icn in this_pe.FromIn do
                    Icn.w += Scale * (Icn.x - Icn.w);
                end;
            end;
        when PASS5:
            for Icn in this_pe.FromMmin do
```

```
                if this_pe.z <= Icn.Mmin.MinValue then
                    if Icn.Mmin.MinDistance == 0.0 then
                        if this_pe.z == 0.0 then
                            this_pe.z = 1.0;
                        else
                            this_pe.z = 0.0;
                        end;
                    else
                        this_pe.z = Icn.Mmin.MinDistance / this_pe.z;
                        if Cts.rt.r <> 1.0 then
                            this_pe.z = pow(this_pe.z, Cts.rt.r);
                        end;
                    end;
                else
                    this_pe.z = 0.0;
                end;
            end;
        when PASS6:
            for Icn in this_pe.FromSum do
                this_pe.z = this_pe.z / Icn.Sum;
            end;
    end;
end;


transfer function GsbXfer(tPassCpn Pass) is
    this_pe.y = 0.0;
    for Icn in this_pe.FromKoh do
        this_pe.y += Icn.z * Icn.u;
    end;
    if Pass == PASS2 then
        for IcnTrn in this_pe.FromTrn do
            for IcnKoh in this_pe.FromKoh do
                if IcnKoh.z == 1.0 then
                    IcnKoh.u += Cts.rt.a * (IcnTrn.t - IcnKoh.u );
                end;
            end;
        end;
    end;
end;


transfer function MinXfer( tPassCpn Pass) is
    tStsCpn MinVal;
    integer:32 pe_index();
```

```
    for Icn in this_pe.FromKoh do
        MinVal = Icn.z;
        this_pe.MinPeIdx = pe_index(Icn.from_pe);
        break;
    end;
    for Icn in this_pe.FromKoh do
        if Icn.z < MinVal then
            MinVal = Icn.z;
            this_pe.MinPeIdx = pe_index(Icn.from_pe);
        end;
    end;
    if (Cts.rt.Reject >= 0) && (MinVal > Cts.rt.Reject) then
        this_pe.MinPeIdx = -1;
    end;
    if Pass == PASS1 then
        this_pe.UnbiasedWinner = this_pe.MinPeIdx;
    elseif Cts.rt.WinRatioFlag <> 0 then
        this_pe.cTotal++;
        if this_pe.UnbiasedWinner == this_pe.MinPeIdx then
            this_pe.cSame++;
        end;
        this_pe.PercentSame = (real:32) this_pe.cSame / this_pe.cTotal;
    end;
end;


transfer function MminXfer() is
    tStsCpn     MinVal;
    tStsCpn     Floor;
    tStsCpn     NotMin;
    integer:32 cOccur;
    integer:32 cWinners;

    for Icn in this_pe.FromKoh do
        MinVal = Icn.z;
        NotMin = Icn.z;
        break;
    end;
    cOccur = 0;
    for Icn in this_pe.FromKoh do
        if Icn.z < MinVal then
            MinVal = Icn.z;
            cOccur = 1;
        elseif Icn.z == MinVal then
            cOccur++;
```

```
                else
                    NotMin = Icn.z;
                end;
        end;
    cWinners = cOccur;
    this_pe.MultiMin.MinDistance = MinVal;
    while cWinners < Cts.rt.Winners do
        cOccur = 0;
        Floor  = MinVal;
        MinVal = NotMin;
        for Icn in this_pe.FromKoh do
            if (Icn.z > Floor) && (Icn.z < MinVal) then
                MinVal = Icn.z;
                cOccur = 1;
            elseif Icn.z == MinVal then
                cOccur++;
            else
                NotMin = Icn.z;
            end;
        end;
        cWinners += cOccur;
        if (Cts.rt.Reject >= 0) && (MinVal > Cts.rt.Reject) then
            MinVal = Cts.rt.Reject;
            break;
        end;
    end;
    this_pe.MultiMin.MinValue = MinVal;
end;


transfer function SumXfer() is
    this_pe.Sum = 0.0;
    for Icn in this_pe.FromKoh do
        this_pe.Sum += Icn.z;
    end;
end;


transfer function StatXfer() is
    real:64    fabs(real:64);
    integer:32 pe_index();

    this_pe.cIter += 1.0;
    if pe_index(this_pe) == 0 then
        for IcnGsb in this_pe.FromGsb, IcnTrn in this_pe.FromTrn do
```

```
            this_pe.Sum  += (IcnTrn.t - IcnGsb.y) * (IcnTrn.t - IcnGsb.y)
        end;
    else
        for IcnGsb in this_pe.FromGsb, IcnTrn in this_pe.FromTrn do
            this_pe.Sum += fabs(IcnTrn.t - IcnGsb.y);
        end;
    end;
    this_pe.Stat = this_pe.Sum  / this_pe.cIter;
end;


transfer function CntXfer() is
    this_pe.Count = 0;
    for Icn in this_pe.FromKoh do
        if Icn.z <= Cts.rt.Reject then
            this_pe.Count++;
        end;
    end;
end;
```

Exercises

7.4.1. Identify and explain in detail the Parameter Definition block of the AXON description of the counterpropagation network.

7.4.2. Identify and explain in detail the Processing Element and Slab Definition block of the AXON description of the counterpropagation network.

7.4.3. Identify and explain in detail the Network Creation and Connection Definition block of the AXON description of the counterpropagation network.

7.4.4. Identify and explain in detail the Scheduling Function block of the AXON description of the counterpropagation network.

7.4.5. Identify and explain in detail the Function Definition block of the AXON description of the counterpropagation network.

7.4.6. Develop an AXON description of the discrete-time Hopfield neural network.

8

Neurocomputers: Machines for Implementing Neural Networks

The progress of neurocomputing is inexorably tied to progress in neurocomputer design. Historically, the first real-world applications of neurocomputing only became possible with the advent of sufficiently powerful implementation hardware. Most future applications will likely require ever more powerful neurocomputers. This chapter discusses the principles of neurocomputer design (and related issues) as well as providing descriptions of some existing neurocomputers.

The goal of this chapter is to present an overview of neurocomputer design that provides sufficient background for reading the literature. Thus, it is not meant to provide a definitive exposition of the state of the art. In fact, the neurocomputer examples presented in the chapter are all relatively ancient. Nonetheless, they illustrate some basic themes that remain at the heart of neurocomputer design practice.

The chapter begins with a discussion of methods for attaching neurocomputers to computers, the definitions of some neurocomputer performance measures, and a description of some attributes that can be used to create a neurocomputer taxonomy. This is followed by a general discussion of neurocomputers. Design principles of analog and hybrid neurocomputers are then discussed, followed by a description of the designs of some existing analog and hybrid neurocomputers. Discussions of design principles for digital neurocomputers and existing examples of such machines complete the chapter.

Neurocomputer design is a lively research topic. Over 100 different neurocomputer designs have already been built, and some of these are available as commercial products. Neurocomputer designers are exploring the use of virtually every known computing hardware idea, including digital, analog, and hybrid approaches using electronic, optical, acoustic, mechanical, and chemical technologies and combinations of these technologies. Notwithstanding the diversity of approaches being explored, neurocomputers intended for use in real-world applications are likely to continue to be employed as computer coprocessors, at least for the foreseeable future, because of the continued dominance of programmed computing[1]. This will probably work to the advantage of neurocomputing, since the functional requirements that coprocessors must satisfy are much less stringent than are those imposed on host computers. This simplicity allows neurocomputer designers to concentrate their efforts on faster neural network execution. They will spend little time worrying about hardware interfaces, input/output control, and so on, although software interfaces and user interfaces must still be carefully attended to. It could even come to pass that exotic new information processing hardware technologies will routinely make their debut in neurocomputers because of the development cost savings associated with this simplicity factor.

Eventually, there may even be stand-alone neurocomputers. Such devices would have all input, processing, and output carried out by neurocomputing elements. Perhaps the first of these machines will be microneurocomputers for use in toys or appliances.

8.1 Neurocomputer Fundamentals

This section discusses three fundamental topics: methods for attaching neurocomputers to host computers, neurocomputer performance measures, and a taxonomy for neurocomputers. These provide a concrete basis for the discussion of neurocomputer design that follows.

8.1.1 Neurocomputers as Computer Coprocessors

Neurocomputers (both production models and experimental units) are typically attached as slave coprocessors to a host programmed computer.[2] Three methods

---

[1] However, a growing trend in neurocomputer design is to use the host computer merely as an input/output server. In other words, it is becoming common for people to most of the software for solving a problem onto the neurocomputer — along with the neurosoftware. Hosting this software on the neurocomputer is possible because of the availability of programmed computing language compilers for neurocomputers and simple methodologies (such as slightly altered versions of the UISL commands described in Section 7.2) for controlling the interactions between the software and the neurosoftware. The net result of this trend is the emergence of general-purpose *process servers* that are designed to run both software and neurosoftware.

[2] For the discussion in this section, we will assume that the host computer/neurocomputer software interface and communications protocol being used are similar to those described in Section 7.2.

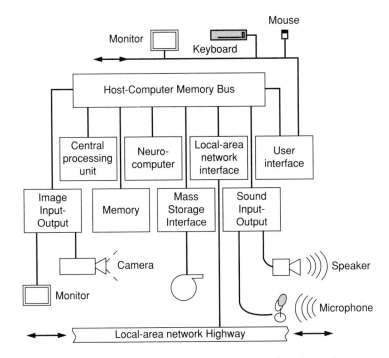

Fig. 8.1. • Attachment of a neurocomputer coprocessor directly to the memory bus or backplane of the host computer. This method allows close coupling of the neurocomputer to the host, but bus loading can be a problem.

for attaching a neurocomputer to a host computer have been defined. These are illustrated in Figures 8.1, 8.2, and 8.3.

The first method is to install the neurocomputer as a memory-mapped device on the bus or backplane of the computer (see Figure 8.1). This method has the advantage that it couples the neurocomputer as closely as possible to the host computer. Calling the neurocomputer from software is easy, because the neurocomputer can be accessed as a memory mapped device by the driver software (in other words, the neurocomputer occupies addresses in the memory space of the computer and can be accessed directly from the host Central Processing Unit (*CPU*) software by means of data transfers to and from those addresses). The neurocomputer can also take direct advantage of host resources such as mass storage devices, other memory-bus attached coprocessors such as image or sound input/output devices, and pointing and picking devices. A disadvantage of this scheme is that any memory bus activity in support of the neurocomputer subtracts directly from the host processor's access to the bus.

In the scheme of Figure 8.2, the neurocomputer is attached as a peripheral device using a standard peripheral interface (such as SCSI, RS-232, or DRV-11). This peripheral interface approach has the advantage that the neurocomputer hardware can attach to any computer that has the standard interface used by the neurocomputer. Thus, the neurocomputer can be ported from one type of host

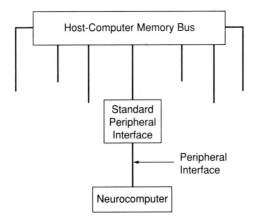

Fig. 8.2. • Attachment of a neurocomputer coprocessor to the host computer via a peripheral interface. This method involves a high host computer bus loading, as with direct attachment.

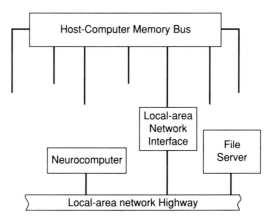

Fig. 8.3. • Attachment of a neurocomputer coprocessor to a host computer via a local area network. This method allows the neurocomputer to access memory servers and other outboard devices with no host computer loading.

computer to another relatively easily. However, this scheme has the same bus loading problems as does the bus-attached neurocomputer. It also suffers from the reduced bandwidth of the peripheral interface, as compared with direct bus mounting.

Figure 8.3 depicts a third option for attaching a neurocomputer coprocessor to a host computer. In this scheme, the neurocomputer sits with other peripherals, coprocessors, process servers, and file servers on a high-bandwidth Local Area Network (*LAN*). Examples of high-bandwidth LANs include the Ethernet, AppleTalk, and Cheapernet. This scheme has the advantage that the neurocomputer can interact directly with other peripherals and coprocessors on the LAN (such as image input/output devices, sound input/output devices, file servers, data base machines, etc.) without loading the host computer's bus. This can significantly decrease the loading that the neurocomputer imposes on the host computer, as well as greatly increase the number and variety of information processing resources with which the neurocomputer can interact directly. This approach might also allow one neurocomputer to run networks for multiple hosts on a time-multiplexed basis. A neurocomputer of this kind might be thought of as a process server. In fact, as mentioned previously, there is a trend to build neurocomputers that can run both software and neurosoftware — these could definitely be thought of as process servers. In this instance, the host computer is reduced to acting as little more than a control port and input/output device.

The software required for a LAN connection scheme is much simpler than that required to attach a neurocomputer via a peripheral interface, since LAN interfaces operate at a much higher software level (most peripheral interfaces merely support word transfer protocols, whereas LAN software typically supports complete file and message transfers). This higher level software can save significant development cost (compared to the low-level software typically associated with the peripheral interface and bus mounting approaches), and can increase the portability of the LAN neurocomputer interface software drivers from one host computer type to another.

In general, for small computers the host memory bus neurocomputer attachment approach is probably best. For larger computers LAN attachment is probably best.

Finally, with respect to the manner in which neurocomputers are treated as coprocessors, there is the issue of interface protocols for interaction of a neurocomputer with its host computer. As pointed out in Chapter 7, the currently dominant choice is the "Don't call us, we'll call you" protocol in which the neurocomputer acts only when it is directed to act; the neurocomputer never initiates calls to the host computer, no matter what. This protocol, which is ideal for a slave processor, is simple and easy to manage, since communications conflicts and Byzantine interface specifications are neatly avoided. However, as mentioned above, the trend is for neurocomputers to move in the direction of becoming process servers. If this trend continues the currently dominant interface protocol may have to become more complicated.

8.1.2 Performance Measures

A number of neurocomputer performance measures that have been found to be useful in assessing capabilities and costs are presented in the following descriptive paragraphs.

CAPACITY   There are two measures of *capacity* (although often they cannot be separated from one another). The first concerns the sizes of specified types of networks that can be implemented by the neurocomputer. The second measure of capacity is the total number of networks of specified types and sizes that can

be stored ready for immediate use within the neurocomputer. This second capacity is important, since most applications of neurocomputing require multiple
networks, and since loading networks into a neurocomputer over an interface
is usually a time-consuming process. Since many simple neural networks have
processing elements that require one real floating-point weight per connection,
one floating-point value as the output signal of the processing element, and, at
most, a small number of other local memory values, it has become customary
to rate capacity in terms of these sorts of processing elements and connections.
Each processing element output signal is assumed to require storage of one or a
small number of real floating-point numbers, and each connection is assumed to
require storage of one real floating-point weight. Most often, capacity is rated
in terms of the numbers for backpropagation networks (although the same numbers are approximately correct for a variety of other networks).

SPEED   *Speed* is rated by how quickly (measured in elapsed real time) a specified network of a specified size can be moved forward in "network time" (as
defined by the equations of the processing elements of the network) by one
(discrete or continuous) unit time step. In other words, speed is determined
by how quickly the network processing elements can all be either updated by
one time step (for episodically updated networks), or moved forward in time
either by one time unit (for continuously updated networks) or by the time it
takes to allow the network to undergo one complete cycle (for example, as in
backpropagation, where each cycle consists of a forward pass to produce y' and
a backward pass to adjust the weights — see Section 5.3). Commercial neurocomputers are typically benchmarked using a large backpropagation network
of a stated number of layers and processing elements per layer. So that the
speed measurement can be normalized, the total number of connections that
can be updated in 1 second is often used as the speed measurement. This value
expresses the speed of the machine in units that can then be applied to a broad
range of backpropagation network sizes (although, for very small networks, the
overhead associated with starting and stopping the updating of each processing
element and each layer usually will significantly erode the stated values — which
are typically determined for extremely large networks). It is customary to provide two speed measurements — one for the forward pass alone, and one for
the combined forward and backward passes. In establishing connections-per-
second speed numbers by using backpropagation, we count only the forward
connections going between rows.

COST   *Cost* is one of the most difficult performance measures to determine in
a fair and accurate way. Further, there are legitimately different approaches
to cost measurement. The measurement approach that most comprehensively
incorporates all of the costs involved is the calculation of the *delivered capability cost*. Given a neural network of a certain type and size that is activated
from software, the delivered capability cost is the total cost of running that
network through some stated number of update iterations. This cost should
include the purchase price of the neurocomputer (including any taxes); the cost

of any required software, prepackaged neurosoftware, neurosoftware languages, cables, LAN hardware, and so on; and neurocomputer system administration costs. Maintenance costs must also be incorporated over the useful life of the machine. The running time of the neural network for which the delivered capability cost is to be measured is then divided by the total estimated running time (the time during which the neurocomputer will actually be running neural networks) over the useful life of the machine. The total cost of the neurocomputer is then multiplied by this fraction to obtain the estimated delivered capability cost for that network. The delivered capability cost has the advantage of incorporating the initial cost, the projected maintenance cost, and any cost savings introduced by having multiple users. It reflects the total actual cost of the delivered capability.

ACCURACY   *Accuracy* is a neurocomputer capability performance measure that assesses the numerical accuracy of the machine in terms of the needs of certain specified networks. The measure is typically binary. Either the neurocomputer can implement a particular specified neural network to the necessary degree of accuracy, or it cannot do so. For example, if a neurocomputer is limited to 8 bits of numerical accuracy, it will not be able to run a backpropagation network during training. Accuracy is a special case of generality. However, it is often of such importance that it is considered separately.

GENERALITY   Some neurocomputers are suitable for implementing only certain neural network architectures. Other neurocomputers can implement essentially any architecture. Given a specific list of architectures, *generality* is the binary measurement of whether the neurocomputer can or cannot implement those network types.

SOFTWARE INTERFACE PROVISIONS   For software programs to be able to call neural networks as "subroutines," it is necessary to have software routines that can be linked in with the user software and then called whenever needed to control the neurocomputer. The simplicity and ease of use of these *software interface provisions* are of great importance. Qualitative, subjective, evaluation of the ease of use of a particular set of software interface provisions can be carried out by means of relative testing.

CONFIGURATION PROVISIONS   For a neurocomputer to be used, it must be configured to run the desired neural networks. There are two basic approaches to this problem. First, most of the commonly used neural networks should be available in highly efficient (in other words, microcoded or otherwise optimized) pre-packaged form. This coding efficiency ensures that the networks used most often execute at maximum possible speed on the hardware. For modification of standard networks or for designing other neural networks, it is essential to have provisions for compiling and running neurosoftware (neural network description language) descriptions of those networks. As with software interface provisions, *configuration provisions* are best judged on a relative-merit basis. The availability of a general-purpose neural network description language capable of describing a large percentage of neural network architectures efficiently (such as AXON) for use with the neurocomputer is an important consideration.

8.1.3 Taxonomy

Attributes that can be used in the construction of a neurocomputer taxonomy are presented next. These attributes can be used to place any neurocomputer into a unique taxonomic category. Surprisingly, examples of neurocomputers in most of the resulting categories have already been built.

CONTINUOUS VERSUS EPISODIC UPDATING   Some neurocomputers update the states of their processing elements *continuously* in time. Others carry out these updates *episodically*. To date, these two categories have been mutually exclusive. However, there is no reason why a neurocomputer could not employ both approaches: some processing elements could be updated continuously, and others could be updated episodically. Thus, there are three possible ratings for neurocomputers in this category: purely continuous updating, purely episodic, or a combination of the two.

ANALOG, DIGITAL, AND HYBRID NEUROCOMPUTERS   Neurocomputers can also be categorized on the basis of the method used to express the output signals of the processing elements and other values within the network. There are three possibilities. First, the quantities could be *analog*, meaning that they can take on any value in a continuous range of values. For example, the output signal of a processing element might be expressed as a voltage going from 0 to 5 volts. Another approach is to code the various quantities used within the neurocomputer in terms of numbers expressed as *digital* values. Such codes have the advantage that they can be stored, transmitted and manipulated using highly reliable binary physical phenomena. They suffer from the disadvantage that the amount of hardware required to process information represented digitally is typically larger than that needed for analog representations. However, the mathematical accuracy and dynamic range that can be achieved with digital codes is much higher than that that can be achieved with analog codes. This difference can be significant because the accuracy and dynamic range requirements of neural network architectures are not well understood yet. Therefore, it is best to err on the side of too much accuracy and dynamic range. *Hybrid* neurocomputers are those that contain both analog and digital elements. For example, an electro-optical system might be used to carry out analog multiplication and summing, followed by an analog-to-digital (A/D) converter connected to digital logic. Hybrid neurocomputers can take advantage of the best parts of analog and digital information processing schemes. For the purposes of this chapter, all number representations (whether analog or digital) shall be thought of as being ultimately represented in a floating point format. In other words, each number shall have the form

$$(2 * a_0 - 1) * a_1.a_2a_3a_4 \ldots a_{(n-1)} * 2^{b_1b_2b_3\ldots b_k},$$

where $(2 * a_0 - 1) * a_1.a_2a_3a_4 \ldots a_{(n-1)}$ is an n-bit signed binary decimal number (with $a_1 = 1$, unless all the a_i, $i = 1, 2, \ldots, (n-1)$ are 0, in which case a_1 is set to 0) and $b_1b_2b_3 \ldots b_k$ is a k-bit 2's-complement binary number. The *accuracy* of this floating point number is the number of bits (n) used to represent the number's *mantissa* $(2 * a_0 - 1) * a_1.a_2a_3a_4 \ldots a_{(n-1)}$. The *dynamic range* of this floating point number is $\pm 2^{-2^{k-1}}$ to $\pm 2^{2^{k-1}-1}$, or (alternatively put), 2^k *octaves* (where an octave is a power of 2). We shall also use the term *accuracy* to indicate the multiplicative uncertainty in a value. Specifically, given a value u that approximates some fixed, but unknown, value v; if k is the smallest integer for which we are certain that $(1 - 2^{-(k-1)})v \le u \le (1 + 2^{-(k-1)})v$, then we say that the *accuracy* of u is k *bits*. Integer numbers shall be thought of as being represented as floating point numbers.[3] Analog numbers associated with physical hardware (which theoretically have infinite precision — in other words, bits of resolution) always have finite accuracy and dynamic range because of the presence of thermal and quantum noise.[4]

FULLY IMPLEMENTED VERSUS VIRTUAL NEUROCOMPUTERS   Some neurocomputers have a dedicated piece of hardware for each processing element and connection of each neural network that they implement. Such neurocomputers are called *fully implemented*, meaning that they provide dedicated hardware for all of the neural network's functions. *Virtual neurocomputers*, on the other hand, time multiplex the hardware used to implement processing elements and/or connections. Since most neurocomputers are constructed out of electronic or optical hardware, and since this hardware is typically able to function at extremely high speeds, time multiplexing allows a number of virtual network elements to share the capability of this hardware and yet often to achieve adequate overall network updating speed.

In virtual neurocomputers, the processing elements or connections that are not currently using the hardware sit in a memory structure of one sort or another waiting their turn to use the hardware. Thus, although virtual neurocomputers are able to share hardware elements among multiple virtual processing

---

[3] Some neurocomputers use *fixed point arithmetic*, in which the possible error of each number is equal to an additive uncertainty, not a fixed multiplicative uncertainty Thus, for such a system the accuracy of a fixed point number varies with its value. For example, if an 8-bit fixed point positive number is equal to 1, then its potential error is $\pm 1/2$, and so it has an accuracy of 2 bits (an uncertainty of 0.5 on a value of 1.0). If the number is 250, then its accuracy is almost 9 bits (an uncertainty of 0.5 on a value of 250). To avoid these complications, we shall not discuss fixed-point numbers in this book.

[4] *Accuracy* is the measure of how small a fractional change in a quantity we can correctly resolve. *Precision* is an expression of how small a fractional change in a quantity we can represent — whether it is correct or not. Thus, accuracy is the portion of representational precision that we can use. Since accuracy is the only thing that concerns us, we will ignore precision.

elements and/or connections, additional hardware expense is incurred to provide the mechanism for temporarily storing the dormant states of the processing
elements and/or connections not currently being used or updated, as well as the
hardware needed to switch these in and out of the functional portions of the
machine. Notwithstanding the additional complication incurred, virtual neurocomputers are the most common type. The tendency in present commercial
neurocomputer design is to use extremely powerful and expensive processing
resources, but then to multiplex their use over populations of hundreds, thousands, or even millions of virtual processing elements.

IMPLEMENTATION TECHNOLOGY   Neurocomputers can be built from electronic hardware, optical hardware or both (other technologies, such as chemical,
acoustic, and mechanical can also be used — but we shall ignore these for now[5]).
Today, however, the only practical information processing hardware technology
is electronics. This may change in future years as electro-optical and optical
components reach a level of maturity that would allow their use in commercial
products. One of the main lessons of the experimental neurocomputer designs
demonstrated to date is that each of the hardware technologies has its domain
of superiority. However, an immense cost is incurred in developing a hardware technology to the point where its use for practical applications is feasible.
The performance or cost savings benefit offered by such a technology must be
significantly beyond that possible with incremental improvements of existing
technologies if such investments are to be sensible.

All currently available large-scale information processing systems are based
on digital electronic technology. Research and development investments of
hundreds of billions of (current) dollars over the last half-century have been
required to bring this technology to its current state of development. It is reasonable to expect that any technology hoping to supplant, or even to successfully
compete with, digital electronics would require a comparable investment over
a comparable period of time. The motivation for such an enormous commitment of resources is unlikely to emerge. What is much more likely to happen
is that analog electronic approaches, as well as analog and digital optical and
electro-optical hardware, will be created out of building blocks developed by the
existing digital electronics industry. For example, Carver Mead has built *analog* VLSI chips using a Complementary Metal Oxide Semiconductor (CMOS)
digital VLSI process [169]. He does this by utilizing a microcell, built out of
digital transistors, that functions as a nonlinear "resistor." The "resistance" of
this "device" can be controlled much more accurately than can the resistance of
a lithographically deposited resistor. In other words, its resistance is insensitive
to the normal CMOS process variations that occur across the chip and across
the wafer (this insensitivity is achieved by using a self-compensating design —
much as in the design of an analog integrated circuit operational amplifier).

---

[5] Note: An electrochemical neurocomputer component is discussed in Section 8.2.

Mead's point is that the transistors used in digital logic are still just transistors, and can be used to carry out many analog functions — particularly when they are operated in a non-binary-switching mode.[6]

Other examples of digital VLSI processing technology being used to implement non-standard functions include liquid crystal spatial light modulators (used commercially as miniature flat television screens and portable computer displays) and quantum well digital/optical switching devices. Another major innovation has been microchannel plate technology. Microchannel plates are relatively inexpensive devices that can carry out linear or nonlinear light amplification while accurately maintaining the spatial distribution of the light.

Both liquid crystal spatial light modulators and microchannel plate image intensifiers[7] have benefitted greatly from the large-scale production of these devices (the former for consumer television products and the latter for military night vision goggles).

Exercises

8.1.1. A fast computer with a 32K-word cache memory is able to carry out 80 million floating point operations per second (MFLOPS) when the data that is used resides in the cache memory (if these terms are not familiar, then read an introductory book on computer architecture before solving this problem). The main memory of this machine is 16M-words long and has a cycle time of 100ns. We want to use this machine to compute 100,000 weighted sums, where each weighted sum has 200 terms, and where each term consists of the product of a real data value and a real weight value. The same 200 data values are used in each weighted sum, but the weights are different. In the beginning, all of the data values and weight values are stored in the main memory. How many seconds will it take to calculate all 100,000 weighted sums? How would you change the design of the computer to improve its performance on this task?

8.1.2. Explain in detail how the division of two floating point numbers can be carried out at high speed using only a floating point multiplier and a floating point adder/ALU. In other words, devise an efficient method for computing the quotient of two numbers using only addition, subtraction, multiplication, and simple logical operations such as comparison tests.

---

[6] Carver Mead's exceptionally well written book *Analog VLSI and Neural Systems* [169] is must-read material for anyone studying neurocomputing.

[7] See [66] for an excellent review of the properties of both liquid crystal spatial light modulators and microchannel plate image intensifiers

8.1.3. A new type of memory device[8] takes the form of a regular 2-dimensional grid of points with an inter-point spacing of 15nm in both dimensions laid out on a polished silicon wafer. Each point represents 1 bit of information. If a point is undisturbed, it represents a 0. If we create a crater in the silicon surface at the position of a point (by stabbing it with a super-sharp tungsten needle), then the point represents a 1. Clearly, this is a Write Once Read Many (WORM) type memory (unless a scheme for "healing" the craters can be developed). Calculate the information storage density of this memory device in bits per square centimeter of silicon area. How does this compare with the storage density of electronic RAM memories? Propose a method for reading the data out of the memory once it has been entered.

8.1.4. If, in the silicon memory of the previous exercise, each crater is a hemisphere of 4nm radius, approximately how many silicon atoms are displaced during the formation of one crater?

8.1.5. The year is 2565. A popular bioengineered house plant (known as the *perfume plant*) is equipped with a simple light-powered nervous system (an *excitonic brain*) that allows it to crudely understand a small repertoire of simple spoken commands (each command must be preceded by the words "your plantship" to avoid inadvertent activation). A plant of this type can respond to requests from its owners to synthesize and release a variety of odors that can set the "mood" of the house. The connections in the plant's nervous system consist of filaments of chlorophyll-containing proteins arranged single-file in a filament, like beads on a string. The proteins on the input end of the connection contain chlorophyll tuned to blue light and those on the output end of the connection contain chlorophyll tuned to red light. The proteins in between gradually and monotonically shade from blue to red along the filament (except in the intermediate green band, where there is a major jump in wavelength between two adjacent proteins — there are no green-absorbing chlorophylls, which is why plants reflect green light). A binary signal (much like an animal nerve impulse) is entered into the input end of the filament by means of a blue-light-energy-equivalent *exciton* (an exciton is an excited electron-proton pair, not linked as a hydrogen atom, that can move through and between certain types of closely spaced molecules). This exciton then hops from protein to protein along the filament, losing a small amount of energy at each step. Eventually, it emerges at the output end of the filament, ready to activate a receiving molecule with its remaining energy. Excitons are potentially interesting as information transmission units because a single exciton can reliably transmit a binary signal. They are reliable because they

---

[8] The memory described in Exercise 3 was built by Calvin Quate several years ago [194].

are very energetic; and yet they do not "leak away" and they do not harm the molecules used in transmission. The exciton generally moves along the filament in the desired direction (in other words, from the input end to the output end) because at each stage of exciton absorption and reemission (on average, these chlorophyll-containing proteins reemit the exciton 5ps after they absorb it — they almost never capture it), the exciton loses energy and cannot go backwards to the higher-energy proteins earlier in the chain (except when tunneling occurs — which is statistically unlikely).[9] Let us assume that, at each protein of the chain that absorbs and then reemits the exciton, the probabilities of the exciton jumping two proteins backward, one protein backward, one protein forward, two proteins forward, and three proteins forward are, respectively, 1%, 5%, 70%, 23% and 1%. We further assume that adjacent proteins in the filament are spaced 10 nm apart, and that the exciton jumps every 5 ps. Each jump takes place at 1/2 the speed of light. Given this situation, what will be the average speed of the exciton moving down the filament?

8.1.6. If an exciton moving in one of the "chlorophyll wire" connections of the previous exercise loses 2×10^{-23}[10] joules in jumping from one protein to the next (except for a single pair of adjacent "green gap" proteins where, between one protein and the next, the chlorophyll energy drops from the equivalent of a 500nm wavelength photon to that of a 600nm photon), calculate the maximum possible length of such a connection in meters, assuming that the input and output excitons are at the energies of 400nm and 800nm photons, respectively.

---

[9] Plants use relatively large 2-dimensional arrays of such proteins to form a "chlorophyll antenna" around a special chlorophyll-containing protein that can use the exciton (or a photon, if it gets lucky and gets hit by one) to separate an electron from a proton, thus creating a mobile charge. This charge is then transferred to a sequence of other molecules — supplying the energy for splitting water into hydrogen and oxygen and carbon dioxide into carbon and oxygen. Most of the oxygen gets released to the atmosphere and the hydrogen and carbon are combined to form sugar (these products then keep those of us who aren't plants going). The chlorophyll antenna acts to efficiently absorb photons over a large area. The energy from each photon that is absorbed by the antenna is converted to an exciton, which then bounces around from protein to protein inside the antenna until it is finally captured and used by the special charge-separating protein. Apparently, some plants have disk-shaped chlorophyll antennae that have proteins that go from blue at the outer circumference to red at the center. Such antennae efficiently transport captured light energy radially inward towards the center of the disk, where the special charge separating protein is located [43]. It is from the design of this natural system that I got the idea for the exciton filament connections.

[10] This level of energy loss between adjacent proteins is quite ambitious and may not be achievable. Nonetheless, it will set a good upper limit on what can be achieved.

8.2 Analog and Hybrid Neurocomputer Design Fundamentals

This section surveys the fundamental principles behind the design of analog and hybrid neurocomputers. As with all neurocomputers, the primary processing task of an analog or hybrid neurocomputer (other than host computer interface, which is ignored in the remainder of the chapter) is the transfer function processing that occurs within the processing elements of the network. This processing is discussed in this section, with particular attention to the problems of implementing these functions in either purely analog hardware, or in combination with analog and digital hardware.

8.2.1 Overview

Analog and hybrid neurocomputers are distinguished by the fact that they are almost always restricted in their generality. One of the reasons for this is that analog computation is typically carried out using some fundamental physical principle (such as the linear attenuation of light intensity by the transmissivity of an optical medium, or the linear attenuation of voltage by an electrical resistor) that, by its nature, is rigid and unchangeable. Another restriction to generality is the fact that analog components are often difficult to time multiplex, thereby strongly favoring hard-wired, fully implemented designs. However, as we shall see, these generalizations are not by any means universal.

The primary perceived advantage of analog processing is the ability to carry out arithmetic operations in potentially inexpensive hardware. The word "potentially" is crucial. For example, there are a number of neurocomputers that have been built with programmable volume hologram elements [88, 27, 193, 192, 191]. These machines are often touted as potentially inexpensive because they are built mainly out of a "chunk of glass;" however, in the current embodiments, the chunk of glass that is used is often an exotic electro-optic crystal worth its mass in gold.

Unlike digital computation, analog computation using physical principles allows little design flexibility. Only those mathematical functions that are found in the physical constitutive relationships of materials are available for use. Although new human-made materials (such as strained-lattice layered semiconductors) allow some tailoring of these relationships, the range of achievable mathematical forms is still limited. Processing elements containing extensive logical processing, complicated learning laws, or difficult activation functions cannot typically be implemented economically using analog components. Therefore, analog and hybrid neurocomputers are usually best suited for the implementation of simple neural networks or network elements. The attractiveness of hybrid neurocomputers is that the processing that requires n^2 operations (where n is the number of data inputs) — which tends not to be computationally demanding (such as computing a vector dot product) — can sometimes be carried out using analog components. Sometimes, the output of this analog input connection processing is then used in additional analog circuitry to implement the remainder of the processing element transfer function (see [169] for examples of this). However, the transfer function is sometimes too complicated to implement in analog circuitry — in this case a hybrid approach in which the more complicated transfer function processing (which tends to be of order n) would be implemented digitally might be used. For networks for which such an approach is sensible, the advantages of both analog and digital computation can be exploited.

One of the problems that constantly plagues analog computation is its inherently low accuracy. Analog computation with accuracy exceeding 8 bits is usually not possible. Even attaining 6 bits of accuracy is difficult, although large dynamic ranges can often be achieved. Although this level of accuracy is quite acceptable for some neural networks, it certainly is not applicable to many of them. For example, the backpropagation network requires more than 6 bits of computation accuracy in order to work its way down the shallow slopes of its error surface.

The difficulty of achieving even moderate accuracy with analog computations is easy to illustrate. Typical resistors used in electronic circuits have values that can vary by as much as ±20% from their rated value and still be within tolerance, and even this accuracy is degraded significantly by changes in temperature. Thus, ordinary resistors have a numerical accuracy of roughly *3 bits*. Expensive high-accuracy resistors (1% tolerance) can only achieve 6 or 7 bits of accuracy. Naturally, the dynamic range of such components is often extremely large. For example, common resistors are available in values spanning roughly 27 octaves of dynamic range (1 Ω to 100 MΩ). However, the usefulness of dynamic range is frequently limited since, most of the time, analog components are used to compute weighted sums, euclidean distances, or other simple arithmetic functions of inputs and weights (the final accuracy of each of which depends on the *accuracy* of the operands, and not on dynamic range).

Many of the calculations carried out in processing elements entail a loss of accuracy. For example, as shown in Figure 8.4, carrying out a weighted sum calculation entails a loss of almost exactly 1 bit of accuracy (at least when all of the operands start out with 4 bits or more), regardless of the number of terms. The impact of this accuracy loss varies greatly depending upon the type of neural network being implemented.[11] Binary or bipolar networks, such as the Hopfield network or the BAM, are typically somewhat more tolerant of lower accuracy than are networks such as backpropagation and counterpropagation (see Exercise 8.2.1). Also, in general, accuracy is more important in neural networks during learning than it is after learning. For example, many mapping networks can function reasonably well in the feedforward mode with from 8 to 16 bits of numerical accuracy, whereas some of the same networks require 16 to 24 bits of accuracy for learning.

---

[11] For example, some of the neural networks implemented on Carver Mead's analog VLSI chips are quite insensitive to such accuracy losses [169].

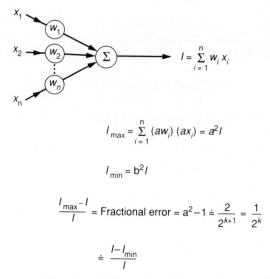

$$I = \sum_{i=1}^{n} w_i x_i$$

$$I_{max} = \sum_{i=1}^{n} (aw_i)(ax_i) = a^2 I$$

$$I_{min} = b^2 I$$

$$\frac{I_{max} - I}{I} = \text{Fractional error} = a^2 - 1 \doteq \frac{2}{2^{k+1}} = \frac{1}{2^k}$$

$$\doteq \frac{I - I_{min}}{I}$$

Fig. 8.4. • Loss of accuracy in weighted sum calculations. Assuming that each of the x_i input values and each of the w_i weight values is represented with k bits of accuracy, then if we let $a \equiv 1 + (1/2^{k+1})$ and $b \equiv 1 - (1/2^{k+1})$, then the above argument shows that the weighted sum has an accuracy almost exactly 1 bit less than the accuracies of its factors, regardless of how many terms the weighted sum has. In other words, preforming a weighted sum reduces accuracy by 1 bit.

Biological information processing systems avoid many of the problems of analog computation by using binary pulse coded signals.[12] Such pulse coding schemes have the potential for high accuracy (perhaps as much as 10 bits), but not enough is yet known to comment intelligently about this.

In addition to pulse coding, animal homeostatic systems provide a stable and unchanging physical and chemical environment for each neuron. A crude electronic analogy to the brain would be a neurocomputer in which each transistor would have its own dedicated high-accuracy voltage regulator and its own temperature-controlled chamber. Given the stability of such a scheme, it seems

---

[12] Although it has been known for about a century that nerve cells signal one another using sequences of (pairwise indistinguishable) pulses, the modulation (in other words, information coding) schemes that are used are still not understood in detail. One scheme that is known to be used is pulse frequency modulation; in which the signals to be sent range continuously between a smallest value to a largest value and these are coded by pulse frequencies ranging from some minimum to some maximum. Another information coding scheme that is apparently used in brains (possibly for implementing some attention mechanisms [89, 219]) is *phase coding*. In such a code the relative phases of individual pulses in the axons of different neurons are used to convey information to a neuron that receives one or more collateral from each axon as input.

reasonable to suppose that perhaps the "analog" portion of each cell (for example, the dendritic tree) might also achieve high accuracy (perhaps as high as 10 bits). Biological components have the added advantage that their "analog values" are apparently adaptively adjustable (at least over a limited range). Thus, unlike the electronic components used in analog neurocomputers (only a small fraction of which are typically adjustable or adaptive), it is likely that many parts of neurons adaptively adjust themselves in response to the local information environment.

If the above speculations are correct, brains can be thought of as hybrid processors built from digital and analog components that are capable of achieving relatively high accuracy over a limited dynamic range. In contrast, most analog computing elements developed by human technologists have the opposite characteristic of being low in accuracy, but of having a very large dynamic range potential. Thus, it would seem to be erroneous to draw analogies between biological information processing systems and human-constructed analog neurocomputing devices. However, as Christoph Koch and his associates have demonstrated [138], such analogies, if carefully drawn, can sometimes be both reasonable and interesting, as well as potentially useful.

Finally, apropos the comparison of nerve networks and neural networks, the fact that brains use binary signals (modulated by pulse frequency and phase) is a crucial observation. It means that the analog components of neurons are typically (but not always) dealing with information that arrives in the form of a sequence of pulses that are individually indistinguishable from one another. This use of discrete signalling begs the question of whether these components should really be called analog at all, and, if they should be, how they are related to the sorts of simple electronic, optical, and electro-optical analog components familiar to engineers (see [61, 3, 42, 169] for discussions of electronic circuits that are more "neuron-like"). Since we know very little about how neurons interact with one another in vivo, the usefulness of thinking of neurons as "analog" components cannot yet be evaluated.

One of the long-term goals of neurocomputing is to exploit the principles of information processing used in brains. However, based on the progress neuroscience has made over the past century, I believe it will require between 100 and 300 more years to achieve an initial e first order understanding of how all of the structures of the human brain work. Thus, the flow of ideas from neuroscience to neurocomputing will most likely be a trickle rather than a flood.[13]

---

[13] Neuroscience researchers have recently given neurocomputing a fundamentally new idea that may bear fruit. The idea is to use phase locking between processing elements that each function as a kind of non-linear oscillator as a way of momentarily linking groups of processing elements into constellations. Such constellations might be used, for example, to bind a collection of attributes or features that describe or represent a single object. This might someday lead to a class of *attentional neurocomputers* that could locate objects with arbitrarily specified combinations of attributes in a scene (visual or auditory). See [103] for further details.

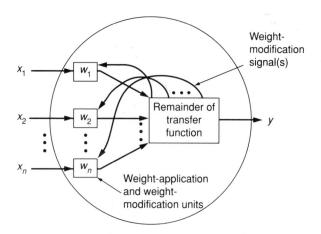

Fig. 8.5. • Simplified type of processing element. Many neural networks rely on weighted sum inputs and on learning laws that can be applied locally at the point where the weight is applied to the input signal. This scheme allows considerable simplification of the hardware used to implement the network, and opens up the opportunity for distributing the weight application and weight change mechanisms in separated units.

We will now consider the design of analog and hybrid neurocomputers. One of the enticing characteristics of analog computational elements is the potential for achieving a high level of integration. For example, an analog optical vector-matrix multiplier typically has an input that comes from a spatial light modulator containing a large number of components. This matrix attenuator or holographic redirector typically consists of a large, dense array of light interaction elements. The output is formed by a linear detector array consisting of a large number of detector elements, often in monolithic form. Such a high level of integration often translates into reduced size, mass, power, and cost. There may well be some types of neural network, such as the Hopfield network or the BAM, that can be usefully implemented in such analog hardware, As we will see in the next section, some small experimental analog neurocomputers have already been successfully demonstrated.

8.2.2 Primacy of Input Processing and Weight Modification

Most neural networks have processing elements with significant numbers of inputs. For the purposes of our discussion, we shall assume that these inputs are to be combined in one or more weighted sums in which most of the weights are to be adjusted in accordance with some learning law that can be implemented locally at the point where the weight is stored (using inputs from the main transfer function of the processing element). This situation is illustrated in Figure 8.5.

Even greater simplification is often possible. This is true particularly in the case where the weights only need to be programmable and on-line learning is not necessary. In Figure 8.6, each of the incoming signals, $x_1, x_2, \ldots, x_n$,

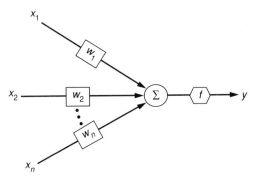

Fig. 8.6. • Further simplified processing element. Many types of neural networks (or portions of networks) have the property that their processing element transfer functions consist of simply a weighted summation followed by the application of a simple function to yield their output signal. This form allows considerable simplification of the hardware implementations of such networks. It is even possible for the weight units to incorporate weight modification, often using a signal broadcast from the output signal generation function to all of the weight units (as with each sun and its planets in the backpropagation network).

is multiplied by its corresponding weight w_1, w_2, ..., w_n, respectively. These products are then sent off to a summer (the circular unit labeled Σ); which yields the total input intensity for this weighted sum. The input intensity is then used by the remainder of the transfer function in computing the overall output signal of the processing element. Several types of neural network architecture (or portions of such architectures) use this scheme when they are operated in the feed-forward, non-learning mode. Examples include backpropagation networks, counterpropagation networks and the neocognitron. As in Figure 8.5, it is even possible in the simplified case of Figure 8.6 for the remainder of the transfer function to supply weight modification signals to the weight units that will allow the weight units to modify their individual weights.

In processing elements of this type, the overwhelming majority of the processing load involves the multiplication of the input signals by the weights, the summation of these weighted inputs, and the adaptive modification of the weights. The remainder of the transfer function is often very small and simple in comparison to these operations. Thus, the processing of the inputs to yield the input intensity and the weight modification often make up the primary processing load of the processing element. Thus, it is input processing and weight modification that typically lie at the focus of attempts to apply analog computational hardware to neurocomputing. Figures 8.7 through 8.10 illustrate three analog hardware approaches to input processing and weight modification.

Figure 8.7 illustrates how a floating gate field effect transistor (FET) can be used as a weight storage, weight application, and weight modification unit. The transistor is constructed on a p-doped silicon substrate. Source and drain tubs are built into the substrate, and a stack of two gates is built on top of the region

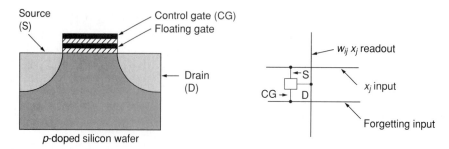

Fig. 8.7. • A floating gate field effect transistor modifiable analog weight implementation. This is a transistor similar to those commonly used in Electronically Erasable Programmable Read Only Memories (*EEPROMs*).

between the source and drain. The first layer of the stack immediately above the substrate is a thin oxide layer. Above this is a metal gate (the *floating gate*) that is insulated from all other structures by an oxide insulator below it and an oxide insulator above it. Finally, another metal gate (the *control gate*) is placed on top of the stack.

Whenever the source and drain are simultaneously raised to a sufficiently high voltage relative to the control gate, electrons will tunnel through the thin oxide layer between the substrate and the floating gate and will get trapped in the floating gate, creating a body of trapped charge. The number of electrons that tunnel through from the substrate to the floating gate depends mostly on the voltage to which the source and drain are raised (relative to the control gate) and the duration of this raised voltage. The floating gate simply integrates the total charge transferred. The charge transferred to the floating gate cannot leak away because the band gaps of the oxide insulators above it and below it are higher than that of the trapped electrons in the floating gate. Normal operating voltages between the source, control gate, and drain are low and are not sufficient to cause any significant lowering of these barriers. In fact, in well designed floating gate transistors the charge can be stored reliably in the floating gate for 10 years or more. The charged floating gate acts as any other field effect transistor gate does. If its voltage relative to the substrate is above the level at which pinchoff occurs and below the voltage at which saturation occurs (assuming the device is designed to turn on with increased voltage — some FETs work differently), the amount of current that flows from the source to the drain will be an approximately linear function of the voltage applied across these contacts. The constant of proportionality in this approximately linear relationship is controlled by the amount of charge stored in the floating gate. Thus, the floating gate transistor can implement a weighting operation. Applying a high reverse voltage to the control gate (relative to the substrate) causes the charge trapped in the floating gate to migrate back into the substrate — thus erasing the weight value.

By the above discussion, the weight w_{ij} implemented by the transistor is determined by the charge stored in the floating gate. Unfortunately, the relationship between stored charge and the weight value is nonlinear. However, the effect of this weight on the current flowing from the transistor's source to its drain is roughly a linear multiplication, assuming that the source to drain voltage is small (below the *saturation voltage*). This voltage range between pinchoff (the point at which the device no longer conducts current from source to drain) and saturation is known as the *linear* operating region of the device.

Thus, if the source to drain voltage is in the linear operating range the current passing through the transistor can be approximately expressed as $w_{ij}x_j$, where w_{ij} is the effective weight of the transistor (due to the amount of charge trapped in its floating gate) and x_j is the source to drain voltage. The currents $w_{i1}x_1$, $w_{i2}x_2$, ..., and $w_{in}x_n$ can then be summed (via Kirchhoff's law of current addition) by the $w_{ij}x_j$ readout line shown in Figure 8.7. The net result is the performance of the weighted sum by the weight transistors of processing element i (arranged as a column, all attached to the $w_{ij}x_j$ readout line) and the $w_{ij}x_j$ readout line. The $w_{ij}x_j$ readout line is kept at a zero voltage to ensure that Kirchhoff's current summation law is obeyed.

Because a floating gate FET weighting unit must be operated in the linear region, the range of input (source to drain) voltages (which must be non-negative) that can be used is quite limited. Further, the range of weights that can be implemented is also limited. These weights are all positive and all lie in a narrow range. Note that to achieve even limited four-quadrant multiplication (in other words, multiplication of an input voltage between, say -1 and $+1$, with a weight lying in the same range), four FETs must be used (one each for the $++$, $+-$, $-+$, and $--$ product calculations). Unfortunately, if this scheme is used we must have two separate output lines (one for the two "positive" output signals and one for the two "negative" output signals—which actually turn out to be positive currents). A example of an MNOS-CCD neurocomputer chip based on this design is presented in the next section.

If we only wanted one output line, then we would need to use both positive (p-transistor) and negative (n-transistor) current flow transistors. Unfortunately, such "opposite polarity" FETs do not have the same current ranges (in other words, range of effective weight multipliers) as those discussed above, and so the outputs of a positive weighting unit and a negative weighting unit (both operating on the same positive or negative input voltage) cannot simply be summed together via Kirchhoff's law (assuming both transistors are the same size). One way to deal with this problem is to build the p-transistors with wider gate channels (leaving the length of the electrical path across the channel constant). In the case of a typical CMOS process, the p-transistor gate widths must be increased in the ratio of $\frac{20}{7}$ over the n-transistor gate widths to achieve current parity [132]. These weight range and polarity difficulties, which represent a significant limitation, apply to essentially all analog input processing schemes that are based on direct weight application using individual transistors. Schemes in which a floating gate FET is used simply as a weight storage device, with the weight application being carried out using another analog circuit such as a Gilbert multiplier [169], show much greater promise than schemes where a single FET carries out both weight storage and weight application. A neurocomputer chip based on this idea was developed in 1989 by David Andes and his associates [122]. Also see [60] for a description of a neurocomputer chip that uses weight storage capacitors that are frequently refreshed from a digital memory using a 12-bit D/A (digital to analog) converter. This approach has the advantage that the weight stored on the capacitor can be either positive or negative and can be set to about 10 bits of accuracy over a considerable range of values.

The floating gate FET can be used in a learning mode, with increases in charge arranged by coincident inputs along the input and output lines, much as in the manner of Hebb learning. Trapped charge can also be removed from the floating gate (to implement a "forgetting" or "anti-Hebb" learning operation) if the control gate voltage is increased sufficiently to allow the charges trapped in the floating gate to escape to the substrate. However, this is usually not as controllable as the planting of charge in the floating gate — the charge tends to leave all at once when the barrier voltage is reached. Thus, the most natural use of the floating gate FET is in a neurocomputer in which the weights are written once and are then left unchanged for a considerable period of time, or where a learning law is used that never decreases a weight value. Any time it is desired to erase all of the weights, the control gate "forget lines" (see Figure 8.7) are simply raised to a high voltage.

Figure 8.8 illustrates how the linear physical effect of optical transmissivity can be used to implement weight units. One of the advantages of this approach is that each variable transmissivity segment can be as small as a few square micrometers. For example, photographic film designed for spectroscopy can be used to build transmissive masks with weight segment areas of approximately 100 square microns each (10 microns on a side). Although such weights are limited in dynamic range, their accuracy is good (between 9 and 12 bits). A single 10 cm × 10 cm piece of film is capable of implementing 100,000,000 weights at a materials cost of approximately $10. This is a cost of 100 nanodollars per weight. For comparison, most digital electronic neurocomputers store weights using Dynamic Random Access Memory *DRAM* devices. DRAMs currently cost approximately $100 per megabyte, or 143,000 nanodollars per 12 bit weight — about 1000 times the cost of film. A RAM memory for 100,000,000 12-bit weights would require a circuit board approximately the same size as the 10 cm × 10 cm film (assuming planar mounted 16 Mbit DRAMS). This example illustrates the density parity and cost savings potential of the optical approach. Volume holograms, if they can be made less expensively than today, are also an attractive possibility, because their potential weight storage capacity is even greater than that of film.

Figure 8.9 illustrates how the scheme of Figure 8.8 can be used with a large planar array of transmissivity segments (such as might be implemented with film). In this design, each of the *n* emitters (which are mounted in a vertical

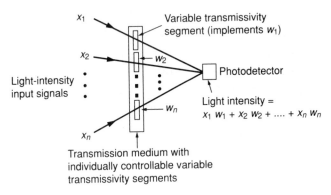

x_1

Variable transmissivity
segment (implements w_1)

x_2

w_2

Photodetector

Light-intensity
input signals

Light intensity =
$x_1\,w_1 + x_2\,w_2 + \ldots + x_n\,w_n$

w_n

x_n

Transmission medium with
individually controllable variable
transmissivity segments

Fig. **8.8.** ● Use of optical transmissivity as a weighting mechanism. In this scheme beams of light of intensity $x_1, x_2, \ldots, x_n$ impinge on transmissivity mask segments having transmissivities proportional to weights $w_1, w_2, \ldots, w_n$, respectively. As each beam passes through its segment, it is multiplicatively attenuated by the corresponding weight. The resulting light beams all fall on a single photodetector, which sums their intensities to yield an overall intensity signal I equal to $w_1x_1 + w_2x_2 + \ldots + w_nx_n$. A variety of materials and hardware designs for implementing variable transmissivity segments have been developed. Several of these involve the use of liquid crystal "spatial light modulators" developed for commercial electro-optic products such as miniature pocket television sets and portable computer displays.

array) has its light uniformly sprayed out horizontally by use of baffles and an anamorphic lens (such as a cylinder lens that spreads light in one dimension but not in the other). Thus, the light from the first emitter (which has intensity x_1) uniformly illuminates the first row of the 2-dimensional transmissivity segment array (often referred to as a *mask*). The light from the second emitter (of intensity x_2) uniformly illuminates the second row, and so on.

Each column of the mask contains the weights of the inputs to a single processing element. The product of each incoming signal and the corresponding transmissivity weight is then represented by the intensity of the light emanating from each weight segment of the column (optical attenuation is an accurately linear multiplication phenomenon). These intensities are then combined, by means of additional baffles and a horizontal anamorphic lens, to fall on each of the detectors of the detector array. Each detector sums the total light transmission through the weight segments of one column of the mask. In Figure 8.9 there are three emitters (transmitting signals x_1, x_2, and x_3) and four detectors (receiving the signals $w_{11}x_1 + w_{12}x_2 + w_{13}x_3$, $w_{21}x_1 + w_{22}x_2 + w_{23}x_3$, $w_{31}x_1 + w_{32}x_2 + w_{33}x_3$, and $w_{41}x_1 + w_{42}x_2 + w_{43}x_3$, respectively). This scheme utilizes only as many emitters as there are inputs per processing element and only as many detectors as there are processing elements, which keeps cost low. However, the number of weights is the product of the number of input signals and the number of processing elements, which is high. Clearly, by keeping the

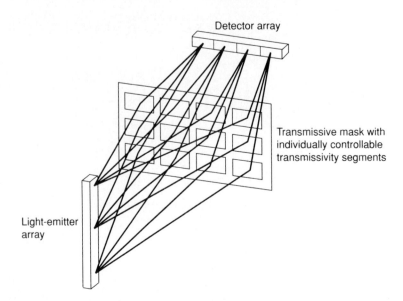

Fig. 8.9. • A phototransmissive array weight application unit. This array functions as a multiple processing element version of the arrangement in Figure 8.8. Each column of the array corresponds to one complete input processing system as in Figure 8.8. Only one emitter is used for each signal x_i. The output of each such emitter is fanned out horizontally to uniformly illuminate its corresponding row of the transmissivity mask. Each photodetector in the horizontal photodetector array sums the output intensities of the transmissivity segments of its corresponding column of the mask. Only positive weights with magnitudes less than 1.0 can be implemented by this scheme, and only positive input signals can be used (the use of coherent light, where both phase rotation and amplitude attenuation can be employed, can increase the utility of this scheme, but the requirements for alignment accuracy increase dramatically).

per weight cost low (such as by using film) a great overall cost advantage can be realized, since there are so many weights.

Figure 8.10 shows yet another approach to analog input processing. Ohm's law is used to convert input voltages to weighted currents, which are then summed by means of Kirchhoff's current addition law. Note that a very large resistor yields a weight of approximately 0, whereas a very small resistor yields a weight near 1. The weights have a value less than approximately 1 (in other words, resistances greater than 1Ω) to prevent excessive current and the resulting meltdown of the resistor and other circuit elements due to I^2R Ohmic heating.

As briefly mentioned in Chapter 1, both the *Snark* neurocomputer (built in 1951) and the *Perceptron Mark I* neurocomputer (built in 1957/58) used resistive circuits for implementing their weights. As shown in Figure 1.5, the Perceptron had 512 motor-driven potentiometers that functioned as variable-resistance weight units. The potentiometer drive motors were activated

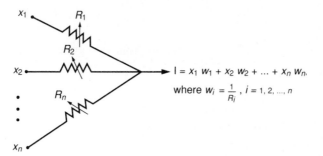

$$I = x_1 \, w_1 + x_2 \, w_2 + \dots + x_n \, w_n,$$

$$\text{where } w_i = \frac{1}{R_i} \, , \, i = 1, 2, \dots, n$$

Fig. 8.10. • Resistive circuit for implementing weights. In this approach, variable resistors are used to implement positive weights. The weights are applied using the physical principle embodied in Ohm's law ($V = IR$). The resulting currents are then summed in accordance with Kirchhoff's law to yield the output current I. In this instance, each input signal x_i is expressed as a voltage. The output terminal of the device (which carries away the total input intensity current I) is held at 0 volts. Thus, the voltage drop across each resistor is exactly its respective x_i input signal. The current flowing through each resistor is thus equal to this voltage drop divided by the resistance of the resistor. If we set each resistance to the inverse of the corresponding desired weight value w_i, then the current flowing through the ith resistor is $w_i x_i$. By simply connecting these output terminals together these currents are summed to yield intensity I.

by electrical error signals to modify the weight values. In this way Rosenblatt learning (in other words, the Perceptron learning law) was implemented in real time.

Another successful neurocomputer that used resistive weights was Bernard Widrow's ADALINE. ADALINE, and its big sister MADALINE (Multiple ADA-LINE), used a type of electronically adjustable resistor called a *memistor* (see Figure 8.11). The memistor is a miniature electrochemical cell in which copper is plated onto a carbon rod substrate from a copper sulfate solution (or from the rod back into solution) in response to a DC electric current into or out of a third electrode wetted by the electrolyte solution. The other two terminals of the device were used with AC signals to employ the resistance of the carbon substrate and its copper coating as a weight in the neurocomputer. The ADALINE and MADALINE were the world's first commercial neurocomputers (see [237] for further details). The Memistor Corporation, founded and managed by Bernard Widrow, offered these machines (as well as individual memistor components) for commercial sale between 1962 and 1965. Figure 8.12 shows photographs of a production memistor with and without its protective metal can. Figure 8.13 is an advertising brochure for the memistors. Clearly, the Memistor Corporation was far ahead of its time.

In summary, none of the simple analog hardware approaches to weight implementation (which mostly use attenuators or limited gain amplifiers of one sort or another) can achieve high accuracy, nor can any of these schemes deal with large dynamic ranges of input or weight values. Since many neural

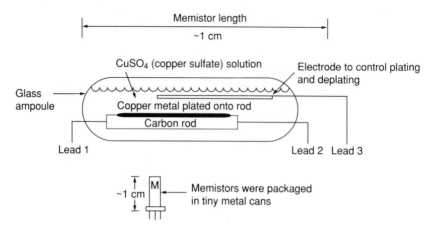

Fig. 8.11. • The memistor. A variable resistance electrochemical cell that was used as a weight unit in Bernard Widrow's ADALINE and MADALINE neurocomputers (which were sold commercially from 1962 to 1965). A DC voltage applied between lead 3 and the zero voltage level of leads 2 and 3 (which have AC applied to them) causes electrochemical plating (unplating) of copper from (to) the copper sulfate solution within the glass vial to (from) the carbon rod. An AC signal across leads 1 and 2 (which has no plating or unplating effect) is used to read out the resistance. Production memistors were cycled 1000+ times from maximum to minimum resistance without any sign of degradation. Full-scale weight change from minimum to maximum, or vice versa, required approximately 15 seconds.

network architectures require more accuracy and dynamic range than are offered by these hardware approaches, these are serious limitations. The technological challenge is to find applications for which the limited capabilities of these components can be tolerated. If these can be found, then the potentially significant cost savings of analog input processing can be realized. Naturally, it may also be possible to improve the characteristics of these analog devices, particularly by combining a number of simple, imperfect devices to create more accurate compound devices (which is the theme that has been pursued by Carver Mead [169]. However, these compound devices are much larger than the simple devices, and a careful examination of the tradeoff of using such a compound device analog implementation verses using a digital implementation should always be carried out.

8.2.3 Transfer Function Implementation

Following the calculation of the input intensity weighted sums (assuming that the neural networks to be implemented are of a suitably simple variety) and the handling of the weight modification operations (if any), the next step is the implementation of the remainder of the transfer function. In other words, we need to implement the portion of the transfer function not concerned with weight application, weight modification, or total input intensity calculations.

Fig. 8.12. • Photographs of a production model memistor with (left) and without (right) its protective metal can. This three terminal device is approximately 1 cm high (not including the leads). The two metallic electrodes and the single carbon electrode can be seen inside the glass envelope in the right hand photo. The liquid inside the glass is a water/copper sulfate solution.

For the simple neural networks under consideration here the remainder of the transfer function often involves little more than the calculation of the value of a nonlinear function of a single input intensity, as in backpropagation network suns. Other common operations include the calculation of derivatives or fading window integrals, or the addition of terms that depend upon previous state values.

Two general approaches to implementing the remainder of the transfer function have emerged. One is to digitize the analog input intensity signal(s) and then simply carry out the remainder of the transfer function processing digitally. Following this processing, the output signal can then be put through a digital to analog converter and reissued as an analog signal. This method is appropriate where either the remainder of the transfer function is very complicated (and therefore is difficult to implement correctly in analog hardware), or where the digital hardware is so much faster than the analog hardware that it can be time multiplexed across many processing elements; thereby saving considerable cost. The second approach to transfer function implementation is to use analog processing exclusively. This approach is only appropriate where an analog

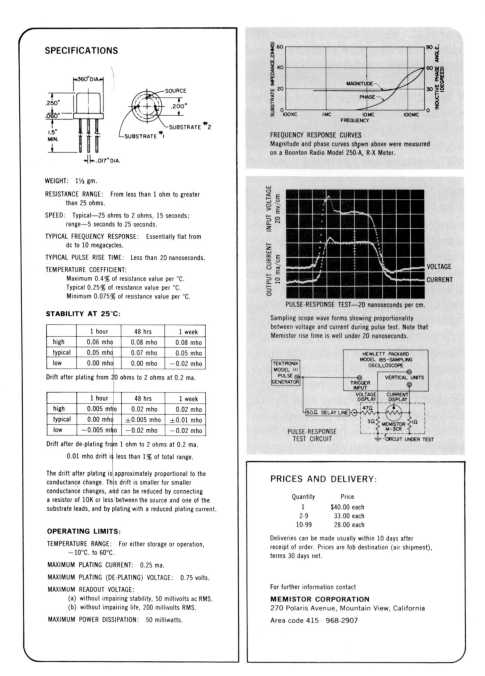

Fig. 8.13. • Specification sheet from a 1965 memistor brochure. Memistors were touted as *liquid state devices* (a takeoff on the then-new term *solid state device*). Over 1000 memistors were sold by the Memistor Corporation. This brochure conveys the spirit of neurocomputing during its brief surge forward 25 years ago. Courtesy of Dr. Bernard Widrow.

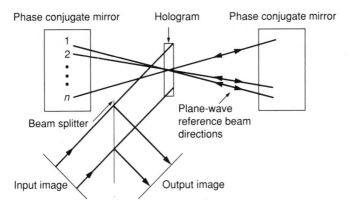

Fig. 8.15. • Optical neurocomputer. This neurocomputer utilizes optical input, optical output, and entirely optical processing components.

column i position. Thus, this neurocomputer is capable of implementing the three weight values required by the simple Hopfield network that Farhat and his associates were working with. The neurocomputer operates episodically. At the end of each cycle the current state of the network (either the state that existed at the end of the last updating cycle or an initial state entered by the user using a switch panel) is displayed on an array of LEDs on an external state display, which is part of the neurocomputer control panel (this allows convenient human monitoring of the behavior of the system). When the GO button on the neurocomputer control panel is pushed, this state is sent to the LEDs of the emitter array, and the analog components of the neurocomputer then proceed to compute the next network state. This process takes approximately 60ms. This speed is slow primarily because of the audio–grade operational amplifiers used in the system.

This electro-optical neurocomputer was shown to be capable of successfully implementing simple Hopfield neural networks with weight values restricted to the set $\{-1, 0, +1\}$. It performed identically to the same network implemented in software running on a general-purpose computer.

8.3.2 Optical Neurocomputer

In 1985, Bernard Soffer and his colleagues G. Dunning, Yuri Owechko, and E. Marom developed the world's first all-optical neurocomputer [59]. The input to this neurocomputer is an optical image, all of the processing within the neurocomputer takes place entirely in optical components, and the output from the neurocomputer is an optical image. The design of this machine is illustrated in Figure 8.15.

The input to the optical neurocomputer is an image imposed on a coherent beam of light. In other words, a coherent plane-wave beam of light is amplitude modulated so that its cross-section has an amplitude distribution density proportional to the (x, y) gray scale density of the image. As shown in Figure 8.15, this input image is introduced into the system at a 45 degree angle. The image first passes through a beam splitter which attenuates it by 50%. This beam splitter has no utility relative to the input image. It is used to turn the output image 90 degrees so that it can be independently sensed. After passing through the beam splitter, the input image impinges on the hologram. The hologram has been programmed with n images of different objects. To make the discussion concrete, let us assume that the objects stored in the hologram are pictures of people's faces. For each person's face image, a different plane wave reference beam is used (in their original experiment Soffer and his colleagues used two images and two reference beams). As shown in Figure 8.15, the reference beam for the first face image to be stored approaches the hologram from a particular angle. The reference beam for the second face image to be stored approaches the hologram from a slightly different angle, and so on for each of the n images. Thus, each image is stored using a plane-wave reference beam that approaches the hologram from an angle that is different from all of the other reference beams.

To fix ideas, let us imagine that the input image is of a person's face. The goal is to determine which of the stored face images most closely matches that of the face of the input image. The matching function is merely the correlation between the input image and each of the stored example images. This function can be expressed as follows:

$$C_i = \mathbf{x} \cdot \mathbf{w_i}, \tag{8.1}$$

where the vector $\mathbf{x}$ is the input image expressed as a rasterized vector, and where $\mathbf{w}_i$ is the ith stored reference image, again expressed as a rasterized vector. The stored image that has the largest C_i is the closest match (all of the stored images, reference beams, and input images are artificially forced to have unit magnitude as rasterized image vectors; in other words, $|\mathbf{x}| = |\mathbf{w}_i| = 1$). The quantity C_i is a measure of how closely the input image matches the ith reference image. One of the remarkable things about holograms is that they can essentially calculate these correlations instantaneously for a large number of reference images [27].

When the input image impinges on the hologram, it has a level of correlation C_i with each of the reference images. The key principle used in this neurocomputer is the fact that the input image will reconstruct the reference beam of each of the stored reference images as it impinges on the hologram (all of the reference images were entered along the same path as the input image). However, the intensity of each of these reconstructed reference beams — which each move in their own separate direction — is proportional to C_i [88]. Thus, to find a reference image that best matches the input image, we need only discover which of these reconstructed reference beams is the strongest. That is the function of the remainder of the neurocomputer hardware.

Once all of the reference beams have been reconstructed, each at its intensity level proportional to C_i, these reference beams (which originally impinged on the hologram from left to right during storage of the reference images) now proceed together to the right from the hologram towards the phase conjugate mirror shown in Figure 8.15. The phase conjugate mirror has the property that it essentially reverses time for optical waves entering the mirror [59]. In other words, the plane waves that enter the phase conjugate mirror are simply reversed and returned exactly in the direction they came without any dispersion or change (a phase conjugate mirror acts essentially as a time reversal). However, the amplitudes of these waves are amplified by the phase conjugate mirror. The amount of amplification is directly proportional to the intensity of the plane wave. Thus, the strongest plane wave (the one with the highest C_i) gets amplified more than all the others. Thus, the plane waves that return to the hologram (and largely pass through it) have had their relative intensities modified. The strongest of these plane wave reference beams is now even stronger than all the others. As these reference beams impinge on the left phase conjugate mirror, this phenomenon of differential amplification occurs again, leading to further enhancement of the intensity of the brightest plane wave reference beam (the one corresponding to the closest matching stored image).

Another aspect of this neurocomputer design is a limited total resonant optical cavity power. In other words, the total amount of optical power in the reference beams bouncing back and forth between the phase conjugate mirrors is fixed. Thus, as the strongest plane wave reference beam is differentially intensified relative to the other reference beams, the total amount of intensity shared by all of the beams is fixed. Thus, the initially strongest reference beam eventually captures all of the available intensity, and the other plane wave reference beams are extinguished. Clearly, this beam selection behavior is a winner-take-all competition process essentially the same as that used in a Kohonen layer.

Following the extinction of all but the dominant plane wave reference beam, every time this beam passes through the hologram, the reference image to which it corresponds is reproduced. In fact, as it passes through the hologram from right to left, this image is directed back exactly in the direction of the input image and the beam splitter. The beam splitter takes half of this output image and deflects it 90 degrees so that it can be viewed in isolation. This output image is nothing but a reconstruction of the stored face image that most closely matches the input face image. Thus, at least in the sense of the matching criterion of Equation 8.1, this optical neurocomputer functions (at least for normalized patterns) as a nearest-neighbor classifier — a function that is basic to several neural network architectures, such as counterpropagation and the Kohonen self-organizing map.

A disadvantage of this design is its surprisingly slow speed. Currently available phase conjugate mirrors operate with time constants measured in hundreds of milliseconds. An incoming reference beam must shine on the phase conjugate mirror for a long time before the mirror begins to function. This is because most phase conjugate mirrors are crystals in which electric charges must be redistributed across considerable distances (on the order of micrometers) before the desired diffraction pattern that can accomplish phase conjugation is produced [59]. The fact that all-optical neurocomputers would be the slowest of all neurocomputers was not anticipated. Considerable advancement in materials and techniques must be made before such devices become suitable for practical application.

In conclusion, the work of Soffer and his colleagues proves that all-optical neurocomputers can be built.

8.3.3 MNOS/CCD Electronic Neurocomputer Chip

In 1986, Jay P. Sage and his associates, Karl Thompson and Richard Withers developed a neurocomputer chip based on Metal Nitride Oxide Semiconductor (*MNOS*) floating gate transistor technology [205]. This chip utilized analog weights stored in MNOS floating gate transistors to implement a simple Hopfield-type neural network. Besides the use of floating gate transistors to store electrically modifiable non-volatile weights, the chip also utilized Charge Coupled Device (*CCD*) technology. The design of this neurocomputer chip is shown in Figure 8.16. Each of the 13 processing element units along the bottom of the chip produces an output voltage that is either $+1$ or -1. In actuality, there are two lines running from each processing element because these two possible output signals are coded differentially. In other words, one of the lines has a signal at a fixed voltage level, and the other has a voltage of 0. Bringing one of the lines to high voltage is the code for a $+1$ output signal, and bringing the other line to high voltage is the code for a -1 output signal. To simplify the presentation, only the action of the $+1$ line will be discussed initially. Following this, the rest of the picture will be filled in.

Each of the output signal lines from the processing elements is looped around and connected to its own horizontal distribution line, as shown in Figure 8.16. Each processing element is also equipped with two vertical lines (again, one for positive signals and the other for negative—only the positive one is shown in Figure 8.16) that collect and sum the weight unit inputs to their processing element. We will now examine the effect of the positive output of one of the processing elements on the positive weighting component of one of the weight application units.

The weight units of this chip are as depicted in Figure 8.17. Each weight unit consists of four CCD gates with an MNOS floating gate transistor stuck in the middle. The operation of this weight unit is illustrated in Figure 8.18. The first step of operation is illustrated in line A. In this step, gate G is turned off to raise its potential barrier and to seal off the output summing line contact I_i from the rest of the device. In the next step, illustrated in line B, the voltage of input S is raised to a high level. Input S is connected to all of the weight units of the entire chip. The sequence of events described here occurs simultaneously (in other words, in parallel) at all of the weight units of the chip.

The gate labelled P_j in Figure 8.18 is connected to the positive output of the jth processing element (the weighting unit shown in Figures 8.17 and 8.18 belongs to processing element i and implements the weight w_{ij}). If P_j is 0, the potential barrier of gate P_j is so large (the opposite of the case shown in Figure

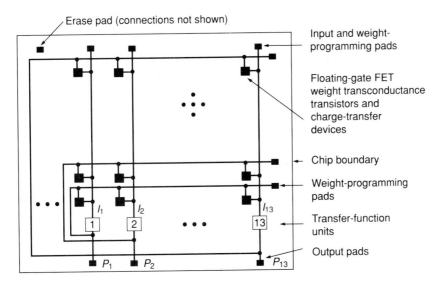

Fig. 8.16. • MNOS/CCD electronic neurocomputer chip. This device consists of a 13 × 13 array of externally adjustable weight application units along with 13 processing elements.

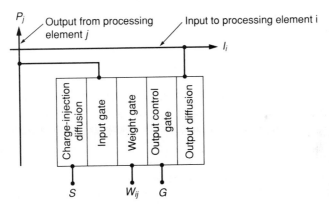

Fig. 8.17. • A single MNOS/CCD weight application unit. This unit receives the output P_j from processing element j and applies weight w_{ij} to it. The resulting output (a charge packet) is added to the input sum I_i of processing element i. The weight w_{ij} is programmed externally by raising the P_j and I_i leads to an appropriately high level (after previously erasing the floating gate).

8.18 — where P_j is 1) that no charge can be transferred to the silicon beneath floating gate w_{ij}. Thus, in this case, the weight unit contributes no charge to output line I_i. If P_j is set to the standardized high-voltage level that indicates the output signal is a +1 (the case shown in Figure 8.18), then the barrier on this gate is lowered to a fixed and repeatably accurate level, as illustrated in

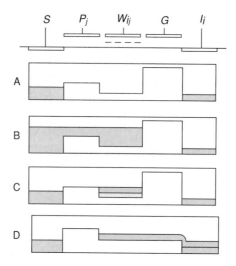

Fig. 8.18. • Operating sequence of a single MNOS/CCD weight application unit.

line B. In this case, the charge from gate S will spill over through gate P_j into the MNOS transistor structure under gate G. Gate w_{ij} has a potential that is produced by the charge stored in the silicon nitride floating gate of the w_{ij} MNOS FET transistor element. The amount of charge that flows into the w_{ij} gate is controlled by the voltage potential created by this trapped charge. As illustrated in line B, the depth of this well can be varied somewhat by varying the amount of trapped charge. The amount of this variation is the amount by which the weight w_{ij} can be changed.

The next step is illustrated in line C. In this step, the voltage applied to gate S is reduced significantly to a value below the potential barrier of gate P_j. Any excess charge in the w_{ij} gate beyond the level of P_j voltage drains back into gate S – leaving a perfectly measured packet of charge in gate w_{ij} that is related to the charge trapped in the floating gate (in actuality, an additional control voltage is simultaneously applied to the control gates of all of the MNOS w_{ij} floating gates — see Figure 8.7). Finally, as illustrated in line D of Figure 8.18, the voltage on gate G is decreased significantly, which causes the charge packet trapped in gate w_{ij} to drain into the output line I_i. During this process, the output line I_i is isolated from all outside connections. As weight units drain charge into it, a high-impedance detector is used to measure the change in its total charge, which is the sum of the charges in the w_{ij} floating gate charge packets of all of the weight units associated with that particular processing element input line.

The amount of charge transferred to the processing element input line I_i from the w_{ij} weight unit is, in fact, determined mostly by the control voltage previously applied to the control gate of the MNOS floating gate structure and is only slightly influenced by the trapped charge corresponding to w_{ij}. Thus,

S	P_j	W_{ij}^{++}	G	I_i^+
S	P_j	W_{ij}^{+-}	G	I_i^-
S	N_j	W_{ij}^{-+}	G	I_i^+
S	N_j	W_{ij}^{--}	G	I_i^-

Fig. 8.19. • Complete (quad) weight application unit (top view). This unit is capably of dealing with both $+1$ and -1 inputs, and with both positive and negative weights.

the question of how this scheme can actually compute a weighted sum arises. This question is now addressed in terms of an explanation of the operation of the entire weight unit.

The design of the complete weight unit is illustrated schematically in Figure 8.19. It consists of four of the units illustrated in Figures 8.17 and 8.18. All four of these units share the same S, C, and G inputs. The top two units have their input signal gates connected to P_j (the processing element output signal line corresponding to a $+1$ output). The bottom two weight units have this gate connected to N_j (the second output line from processing element j, which has high voltage applied when the output signal of the processing element is to be -1). The outputs of the first and third weight units are connected to the positive vertical input line running to processing element i (carrying the charge summation signal that we will designate by I_i^+). The second and fourth weight units are connected to the vertical processing element input charge summation line that carries the combined negative input signals to the processing elements (the summation signal in this line shall be designated as I_i^-). Notice that the weights in the four weight units (one through four) described above are designated w_{ij}^{++}, w_{ij}^{+-}, w_{ij}^{-+}, and w_{ij}^{--}, respectively. With this scheme, bipolar processing element output signals can be multiplied by any arbitrary weight (positive or negative) with magnitude less than a fixed upper limit. Notice that, with this scheme, the effects of the MNOS gate control signals are eliminated. Regardless of whether the output signal of the processing element j is positive or negative, the same amount of control-gate-determined-charge will be deposited equally to both the I_i^+ and I_i^- lines. Since the processing element merely subtracts the charge in the I_i^- line from that in the I_i^+ line to make its final decision on whether to have a $+1$ or -1 output, the excess (and equal) charges created by the control voltages cancel one another out, thus leaving the final decision to the comparison of the correct positive and negative weighted sums — which is what is called for in a Hopfield network with zero thresholds.

In the end, this MNOS/CCD neurocomputer chip (with 13 processing elements) was successfully able to implement the Hopfield network. Programming of the w_{ij} weights was done by transferring a measured charge packet to the substrate region beneath the silicon nitride floating gate structure (by using techniques similar to those illustrated in Figure 8.18, lines *A*, *B*, and *C*) and then applying a very high voltage ($\approx$ 35 V between the substrate and the control gate) to cause this charge packet to tunnel through the thin oxide layer into the silicon nitride floating gate, where it is trapped. Clearly, the weight units used in this design can be utilized for implementing many different neural network architectures. In fact, Sage and his colleagues have demonstrated the use of this weight unit design to implement neural networks that require on-line learning (unlike the Hopfield network, which simply uses pre-calculated weights).

Exercises

8.3.1. What types of light emitters (for example, incandescent bulbs, light emitting diodes, and laser diodes) would be useful as light sources for the analog weight application scheme used in the electro-optic neurocomputer example presented in Subsection 8.3.1? Explicitly state the requirements that would be important for such an emitter and then evaluate each candidate light production technology in terms of its ability to meet these requirements.

8.3.2. Color CCD imaging chips are used in most hand-held video camcorders. Provide an overview of how these devices work, including how the colors are separated and how the chip is interfaced with video circuitry. What are the characteristics of these devices in terms of both their optical and electronic specifications? Describe the "electronic shutter" feature frequently implemented with such chips. What does this feature do and how does it work? [Hint: consult a recent technical review paper on Color CCD imaging devices.]

8.3.3. Is the floating gate structure of the MNOS/CCD neurocomputer chip of Subsection 8.3.3 used in the same way as that of the floating gate FET described in Section 8.2? Explain your answer in terms of the weight application process used in each case.

8.3.4. Why would the refractive index of a phase conjugate mirror crystal (such as that used in the optical neurocomputer of Section 8.3.2) change locally when charge is moved to new positions? Explain your answer in terms of the physical constituative relations for a specific crystal material that exhibits this behavior. [Hint: consult a text on electro-optic crystals.]

8.3.5. If the electro-optical neurocomputer of Section 8.3.1 were equipped with two liquid crystal spatial light modulators (instead of film transmissivity masks) then the weights could be modified during operation. How would such spatial light modulators be configured to replace the film masks (give all the intimate details, such as whether polarizers will be required, and if so, how they will be oriented)? How fast could such masks be modified? How many grey-scale transmissivity levels could be achieved? [Hint: consult a recent review paper on liquid crystal display devices.]

8.4 Digital Neurocomputer Design Fundamentals

Digital neurocomputers benefit from the legacy of the most advanced human technology: digital information processing. Digital neurocomputer designers have at their disposal a vast armamentarium of digital hardware technologies, digital design techniques and tools, and digital information processing methodologies. To keep the exposition of this section reasonably short, only digital implementations of episodically updated neural networks will be considered.

8.4.1 Overview

Digital neurocomputers can be built either as hard-wired machines capable of implementing only a limited set of neural network architectures, or as flexible, reconfigurable machines that can run a wide variety of neural network architectures. For those applications where running multiple network types is important, reconfigurability is essential. However, hardware designed expressly for running a specific network architecture can sometimes be more efficient. One of the main discoveries of digital neurocomputer design to date is the fact that for a broad class of popular neural networks, considerable reconfigurability can be achieved with almost no loss in performance over a completely hard-wired design. This unexpected property is primarily due to the fact that the majority of the processing required in many types of neural network architecture involves a small set of standard processing procedures such as weighted sum calculations or euclidean distance calculations. Thus, a digital neurocomputer design with provisions for carrying out these operations at high speed and with high efficiency will often be able to implement a number of neural networks well.

Digital neurocomputer design is in its infancy. However, evidence to date suggests that most digital neurocomputers can be designed using existing digital hardware elements that were originally developed for use in ordinary computers. All digital hardware design involves two major considerations: the capabilities of the hardware components that are available for use, and the performance requirements that the neurocomputer must satisfy (including cost, speed, generality, and accuracy). Today's digital hardware components are electronic. They include general-purpose custom, semi-custom and gate array chips, memory chips, arithmetic chips, address generators, and I/O controllers. Digital neurocomputer designs intended for use in the next few years must be designed using these elements. This section and the next section will concentrate on digital neurocomputer design with these sorts of hardware elements. However, as new hardware elements (such as durable and low-cost ferroelectric memories or affordable, high-speed digital optical components) become available, new design approaches will become possible. For example, if a planar sheet of quantum well material reliably implementing a two-dimensional array (8192 × 8192) of binary optical switches becomes available at reasonable cost, entirely new approaches to neurocomputer design will become possible. Since it is not possible to accurately forecast which types of digital processing components (beyond those that are simple extensions of the familiar existing electronic components) will become available in the future, the possible use of such components in neurocomputer design will not be considered here. Suffice it to say that the future of digital hardware in neurocomputing appears to be extremely bright.

Finally, digital neurocomputers capable of utilizing neurosoftware provide the potential advantage of allowing users to port neural network designs easily from machine to machine and from hardware generation to hardware generation. As with programmed computing and software, much of the expense of developing neurocomputing applications is incurred in selection and refinement of the neural network architectures that are used. Thus, it would appear to be of significant benefit to be able to port an application solution from one neurocomputer to another. This will be the payoff of standardized neurosoftware languages and high-efficiency neurocomputers that can use them. However, as of yet, neurosoftware languages have not reached a sufficient level of development maturity and standardization to make this possible.

8.4.2 Fully Implemented Design Approaches

Fully implemented digital neurocomputers might not, at first, seem to make sense. For example, it would seem wasteful to have a separate parallel digital data path extending from each processing element to each of the other processing elements to which it sends its output signal. Logically, such a design would be better implemented using some sort of digital bus lines shared by multiple processing elements — particularly because bus speeds often exceed the processing speed of existing silicon systems (for example, high-speed busses can run at hundreds or even thousands of megabits per second, whereas digital processors typically operate at slower speeds). However, there is another possibility: serial transmission across a single line (either an electrical wire that fans out into copies or an optical beam that is split and directed by a hologram). Fully implemented designs such as these can probably be built, particularly if the connections are laid out in some kind of orderly pattern such as in a rectangular grid. Nonetheless, problems exist with this approach. The largest problem is one that all electronic digital systems share—namely that of limited fan-out (in other words, drive) capability (this characteristic is not shared by optical systems, in which the fanout can be much higher); a single electronic digital transistor output signal can normally only drive approximately 2 to 10 similar devices. This limitation is complicated because it involves not only the drive power of the transistor, but also the capacitance of the intervening wires and the required speed. The only way to bypass this restriction is to use either signal buffers (which can multiply the fan-out capability of a drive transistor, but at the price of one or more lost clock cycles) or drive transistors (which occupy large areas on silicon and dissipate substantial amounts of power).

One of the most important issues relative to fully implemented digital neurocomputers is cost. To evaluate cost, it is essential to know the updating speed required by each neural network architecture be run on the neurocomputer. For many fully implemented neurocomputer applications, the speed of updating the entire network is limited not by the hardware design, but by the availability of data to be processed (although this may not be true during training). For example, if a neurocomputer will be used in a real-time image analysis application, it must be remembered that the frame rates of most imaging systems (television systems, video storage and retrieval systems, and so on) are quite limited (typically 30 Hz to 60 Hz). Given the fact that a fully implemented neurocomputer used for such an application will be dealing with all of the channels of the image, subimage or derived feature set in parallel, the neurocomputer need not go any faster than the rate at which the data can be supplied (except during training, where direct access memory banks can be used to provide the training set data to the neurocomputer at extremely high speed).

To illustrate this point, imagine that we are carrying out some sort of pattern recognition function on high-resolution (1024×1024 pixels) monochrome imagery. Further, imagine that we are analyzing this image using overlapping blocks of 128×128 pixels each. Each image will be assumed to provide 400 (overlapping) subimage blocks, each of which will be analyzed in sequence using a single time-multiplexed, but fully implemented, neurocomputer. The images shall be assumed to arrive at a frame rate of 30 Hz. Thus, the neurocomputer must deal with 1200 blocks per second; which allows 83 μs per block. If we assume that the fully implemented digital neurocomputer can completely carry out its input/analyze/output function in 1 microsecond (this would correspond to a fairly complex neural network architecture), then the fully implemented digital neurocomputer design is an overkill by almost two orders of magnitude. Processing of 30 Hz frame rate high-resolution imagery is considered to be one of the most challenging processing tasks known. Even so, a fully-implemented neurocomputer design assigned to carry out this task is simply too fast, and thus, too expensive. A virtual neurocomputer design capable of carrying out the same processing at the required speed, but costing one-tenth as much, could probably be designed. Notice that the cost would probably not drop by two orders of magnitude, because virtual neurocomputer designs require time-multiplexing controls and other accessories that reduce efficiency somewhat. Thus, whenever a fully implemented digital neurocomputer design is under consideration, the question of cost effectiveness should be examined carefully.

There is an interesting psychosocial phenomenon connected with fully implemented neurocomputer design — namely, the tendency for some technologists to view such designs as somehow being more "natural," "elegant," or "esthetically correct" than virtual designs. This naive chauvinism seems to be fueled by assumed analogies between neurocomputer design and biological design. As discussed earlier, such analogies are specious.[14]   As with any other subject in technology, neurocomputer designs are best judged on the basis of objective engineering criteria such as cost, speed, capacity, generality, and accuracy.

Notwithstanding the above comments regarding the frequent inappropriateness of fully implemented digital neurocomputer designs, there are definitely occasions where such designs are both appropriate and highly cost effective. These situations are often associated with an extremely demanding real-world signal environment (such as electronic warfare, cryptography, and the study of high-speed chemical and physical processes). In such situations, the absolute utmost possible speed must be achieved. It is in applications such as these that fully implemented digital neurocomputer designs make sense, since these designs will allow the maximum speed of the digital hardware to be reflected in the update rate of the neural network architecture implemented.

Another area of application where fully implemented designs may sometimes be justified is where a large neural network must be exposed to an extremely high volume of training data over a short physical time interval. This situation frequently arises in situations where the entire network needs to be trained in one piece on the data (in other words, the network cannot be broken up into different pieces which can be trained separately on larger numbers of virtual neurocomputers running at slower absolute speeds). Although it is not yet clear how important this class of applications will be, there is no question that one of the factors that has enabled neurocomputing to solve real world problems has been the ability of these machines to carry out training processes within a few hours that, in the past, would have required months or even years of computer time to accomplish.

-----

[14] It might very well turn out that some brain structures employ virtual designs. For example, a portion of a brain nucleus might be loaded with processing instructions from memory storage in another brain area that configures the nucleus to carry out a specific type of processing function. If such structures exist,they would be sequentially reconfigured to implement multiple virtual networks (these might be, for example, networks for controlling brain resources for carrying out specific types of thought processes). If this speculation turns out to be true, then it might someday be *virtual* neurocomputers that become the esthetic ideal! Clearly, given our abject ignorance of how brains operate, any chauvinism based on analogies between the designs of neurocomputers and brains is ridiculous.

In summary, fully implemented digital neurocomputers are more likely to use 1-bit serial transmissions of information than n-bit parallel transmissions (particularly in electronic hardware where the number of physical wires that can be constructed is quite limited). Further, such neurocomputers make sense only in situations where the highest possible updating rate of neural network architectures is required (such as in exotic defense applications and in situations where extremely fast training of a network must be accomplished). Because of the limited range of applicability of fully implemented digital neurocomputers, such machines may not appear as commercial products for a while.

8.4.3 Virtual Design Approaches

Virtual digital neurocomputer design revolves around the observation that (at least with today's technology) arithmetic processing is comparatively expensive and memory is comparatively inexpensive. Thus, to minimize cost in a digital neurocomputer design, one uses the minimum amount of arithmetic processing capability needed to meet the requirements imposed by the proposed applications. Once this processing capability has been determined, mechanisms for multiplexing the available processing resources across the processing elements of the neural networks to be run must then be devised. The design of such multiplexing schemes is the primary challenge of virtual neurocomputer design. Another important consideration is generality. Since almost all applications of neural networks require extreme generality in both transfer function definition and connection configuration, the achievement of maximum generality is often of crucial importance.

Because of the limited supply of processing resources, it is essential that the processing load of an arbitrary neural network to be run on the neurocomputer be spread evenly across the available processors to ensure efficient utilization of these resources. The common problem with respect to this issue is that a small number of processing resources will be loaded to 100% of capacity, while other processing resources are using only a small portion of their capacity. The net result of this situation is that the neurocomputer runs slower than it could because many of the available processing cycles are not being utilized.

One of the most important discoveries of neurocomputing is that almost all neural network architectures (because of the locality of processing and the fact that each processing element can have only a single output signal) can be partitioned into an arbitrarily large number of separate processing tasks (at least up to the number of processing elements) where the average processing load of each task is approximately equal. Each processing task is responsible for the updating of a subset of processing elements (assumed fixed) that are assigned to that task. The processing task is assumed to have storage available for all of the local memory values and transfer function definitions of the processing elements assigned to it. The only interprocess communication that is required is the sharing of processing element output signal values and scheduling function coordination information. The term *equipartitioning* will be used to denote this process of dividing a neural network architecture into a given number of pieces, each of which has essentially the same average processing requirement (as measured relative to a particular type of processing resource). This property can be used to partition an arbitrary neural network into n parts, each of which might then be implemented by a single processor of a neurocomputer with n processors. Partitioning is theoretically possible with all neural networks in which the processing load of each processing element is approximately constant over time. If this constancy condition is violated, then fixed equipartitioning is no longer possible, and implementation efficiency may suffer. Unfortunately, although equipartitioning is known to be possible, no general method for carrying it out (such as for arbitrary AXON code) is known.

The achievement of generality in a virtual digital neurocomputer design is primarily a function of the generality of the individual processors used in the design. The best approach seems to be to design the neurocomputer with a specific set of neural networks that must be run with maximum efficiency in mind. However, provisions for implementing arbitrary transfer functions should be incorporated. Such a general neurocomputer might well be able to run essentially all types of neural networks, although its efficiency will probably only be high on the particular group of network types for which it is optimized. This approach combines the benefits of generality with many of the advantages of specialization.

An important aspect of virtual digital neurocomputer design is that the only information (other than scheduling function coordination data) that needs to be communicated between the n processors are updates to the states of the processing elements. To carry out updating of the processing elements that have been assigned to it, the individual processor needs to know the output signal values of those processing elements that send connections to the processing elements assigned to that processor for updating (as discussed above, this assignment is assumed to be permanent during the time that the network is being run). Thus, each processing resource must maintain a *state table* that contains the current state values needed by that processing resource.

Clearly, as each processing element is updated, its new state value must be transmitted to all of the processing resources that require that value. While there are many techniques by which this transmission operation could be accomplished, perhaps the simplest is to use a broadcast structure in which each processing element state update is simply broadcast simultaneously to all of the processing resources of the neurocomputer. Each of these resources can decide (based on the processing element ID tag that is transmitted with the update) whether or not it needs this update for its state table. Because the total number of states in any given neural network is typically small (the number of states is exactly equal to the number of processing elements in the network — which is typically much smaller than the number of weights and other local memory values), it is often easiest simply to provide each processing resource with a complete state table for the entire network.

An example of an electronic broadcast structure is discussed in Section 8.5 in connection with the description of the design of the Mark III neurocomputer. Electronic broadcast structures have the limitation that the number of processing resources must be less than the fan-out capability of a single bus line drive transistor — which can be rather low (16 to 32 is typical). Pipelined and multistage driver transmission structures can eliminate this restriction, but introduce other problems such as failure sensitivity, delay, and hardware complexity. Electro-optical broadcast structures show promise of being able to handle fanouts of 1000 or more at extremely high speeds.

Although the selective reception of updates (limiting the accepted updates to those actually needed by a processing resource) introduces additional hardware complexity, it has the advantage of reducing the total number of updates per second that must be posted in each processing resource's state table. Since the number of state updates per second produced by the entire neurocomputer can be much higher than the normal operating speed of each processor individually, there is a potential speed mismatch between the aggregate rate of update transmission on the broadcast structure and the feasible rate of state updating on each processing resource.

One solution to this speed mismatch problem is to use high speed memory technology for the state table that can accept updates at the required rate. However, this option is not always available, since the speed may simply be too great for any existing memory technology, or the cost of the required high-speed memory devices may be so high as to make this approach undesirable. Another approach is to use a *filter* device on the receive portion of each processing resource's broadcast structure terminal. This filter simply checks the processing element number of each of the updates to see whether that update is needed by the associated processing resource. If it is needed, then the update is put into a First-In-First-Out (*FIFO*) buffer from which it can be retrieved by the state table update mechanism of the processing resource. For many (but certainly not all) types of neural networks, such a filter can allow a speed mismatch of an order of magnitude or more to exist between the bus transmission rate and the state table updating mechanism. This filtering scheme would seem to work best in situations where the processing elements being updated by each processing resource only receive inputs from a limited subset of the processing elements of the entire network (such as in hierarchical neural networks — see Section 6.3). Since the use of hierarchical networks will probably increase, filtering may become important in the design of digital virtual neurocomputers. However, many of the currently popular neural networks, such as backpropagation, have architectures for which filtering is of little or no value.

When discussing state transmissions, it is important to remember that processing element output signals can be of arbitrary mathematical type. Thus, although a neurocomputer may be designed to transmit many commonly encountered state types as single digital words, provisions must be made for multi-word transmission. Naturally, similar provisions must be made for handling weights and other local memory values, which can also be of arbitrary mathematical types.

Finally, ease of use must be a primary concern in any neurocomputer design. The user interface provisions that allow users working on a host computer to call neural networks effortlessly from their software is a crucial issue. The ability to quickly compile neurosoftware and load the resulting neural network into the neurocomputer is also essential. Diagnostic tools for monitoring the activity of the network during execution can also be quite valuable.

Exercises

8.4.1. The processing resources of a particular digital neurocomputer consist of a floating point multiplier and a floating point adder/arithmetic logic unit (which can add numbers and carry out various comparison operations). A particular neural network being implemented on this neurocomputer has processing elements which need to calculate the quantity

$$\frac{1}{\log(1 + u^4)}$$

for values of u between -10 and $+10$. Devise a method for using the resources of this neurocomputer to carry out the calculation of this function.

8.4.2. The only numerical quantities used in a particular fully implemented neurocomputer happen to be integers between 0 and 15. These quantities are represented as 4-bit binary numbers, which are transmitted between functional elements of the neurocomputer as serial bit strings on single wires. Each functional element of the neurocomputer receives a global system clock signal that consists of pulses in phase with the bits being serially transmitted. These elements also receive a global "start" pulse in phase with the first bit of the strings being transmitted (to indicate start of transmission). An adder for use in this neurocomputer takes two incoming bit strings and adds them together. The output of the adder is a serial bit stream 4 bits in length that is the hexadecimal code for the minimum of the sum of the two incoming numbers and 15. Develop a detailed (gate-level) design for such an adder, keeping the gate count of the design as small as possible. [Hint: consult a book or survey paper on serial digital processor design.]

8.4.3. Develop a detailed (gate-level) design for a multiplier for the neurocomputer of the previous problem. The output of the multiplier should be the minimum of the product of the 2-bit strings and 15. Keep the gate count of this design as small as possible.

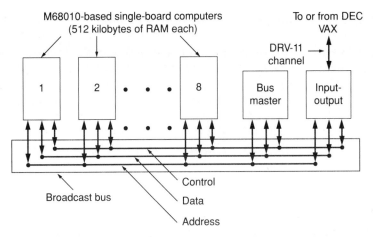

Fig. 8.20. • The Mark III neurocomputer. This machine consisted of 8 Motorola 68010 based single board computers mounted on a broadcast bus backplane. The Mark III functioned as a coprocessor to a Digital Equipment Corporation MicroVAX host computer.

8.5 Digital Neurocomputer Design Examples

In this section, three examples of digital neurocomputer designs are presented. These examples illustrate the diversity of approaches that have been used in designing digital electronic neurocomputers. The two neurocomputers described (the Mark III and Mark IV) were originally developed by Todd Gutschow and I at TRW, Inc. (with a major contribution to the Mark III by Robert Kuczewski). Both of these machines were subsequently improved by a team led by Michael Myers and including Robert Kuczewski and William Crawford. These examples were chosen because of my personal familiarity with their designs and because they were contemporary with the examples presented in Section 8.3.

8.5.1 Mark III Neurocomputer

The Mark III was built at TRW, Inc., during 1984 and 1985 using a design that I had conceived (but had not built) in 1982 at Motorola, Inc. The 1982 design was based on the use of a number of Zilog Z8000-based single board computers, each equipped with 32K bytes of DRAM. These 16-bit single board computers, which ran at an anemic clock speed of 4 MHz, were nonetheless remarkably capable for their day.

By 1984, it was possible to substitute Motorola M68010-based boards running at 12 MHz, with 512K bytes of DRAM memory each. As shown in Figure 8.20, the Mark III used eight of these single-board computers. Each of the single-board computers was in the form of a standard VME bus circuit board (approximately 16 cm × 24 cm). These boards were plugged into a modified VME bus backplane cardcage rack along with a bus master card and an input/output interface card that connected the neurocomputer to a host Digital Equipment Corporation MicroVAX computer through a DRV-11 high-speed channel. The VME bus was converted to a broadcast bus by modifying each of the single board computers and adding a custom VME bus board (not shown in Figure 8.20) that controlled the access of each of the eight single-board computers to the bus. To allow broadcast operation, all eight single-board computers had their bus addresses set to the same values. Thus, with all of the single-board computers set to the same block of addresses, a transmission on the bus to a memory location within this address block would be received by all eight single-board computers simultaneously. This had the effect of increasing the effective bus bandwidth for broadcast transmissions by approximately a factor of 8. For the purposes of loading and unloading software, weights, states, and so on, into and out of the single-board computers from the VAX, the custom bus controller could be used to arrange for each of the boards to have exclusive access to the bus so that it could communicate with the VAX through the Input/Output interface card. The VME bus provided a 32-bit data path, of which 16 bits were used by the 16-bit single-board computers. The Input/Output interface was also a 16-bit device, as was the Q-Bus of the DEC MicroVAX host computer that was used. The original Mark III had a capacity of approximately 8000 processing elements and 480,000 connections, but it could only implement one neural network at a time. It had a speed of 380,000 connections per second for a large instar network using Grossberg learning (see Section 3.5).

The Mark III neurocomputer had an extensive software support environment that operated on the MicroVAX. This environment included a menu- and graphics-based neural network specification capability that allowed neural networks that fit within the model used by the environment (a difference equation model described in the next subsection) to be entered. After a network was specified, a compiler would chop it into eight equal pieces and translate it into a software and data load that would be sent to each of the eight single-board computers. A portion of the compiler, called the *leveler*, was responsible for equipartitioning of the network so that each of the single board computers had the same processing load.

The environment used with the Mark III (called the Artificial Neural Systems Environment, *ANSE*) assumed that each processing element in the network was to be updated on each time step. Thus, the job of each of the single board computers was to update all of the processing elements it was assigned to implement by one time step. Once a neural network was described by use of the ANSE and loaded into the Mark III, it could be called from user software as a subroutine, using a crude type of user interface. However, only one neural network at a time could be loaded into the Mark III.

Once all of the eight boards had updated their processing elements by one time step, each board would broadcast all of its updated state values on the bus. At the end of these eight broadcasts, each board would have a completely updated copy of the state table for the entire network. Following this update sharing, the eight boards would begin the next time iteration of updating. During the broadcasting of the updates, the input/output interface board could be used to read these updates passively and send them to the host computer. This allowed the states of the processing elements of the network to be displayed graphically on a host computer terminal (using a color temperature scale code) during network operation. This display capability proved to be quite useful for understanding the operation of a network in a particular application, and for diagnosing problems.

The Mark III not only demonstrated the utility of a broadcast bus oriented neurocomputer design, but also provided a useful research tool for exploring applications of neurocomputing. The initial version of the Mark III (the version described here) was subsequently turned into a commercial product by Michael Myers and his team, and was sold to a number of research organizations for use in application studies. The original Mark III also served another purpose — as a testbed for ideas that would later be incorporated into the Mark IV.

8.5.2 Mark IV Neurocomputer

In 1984, Todd Gutschow and I began a major neurocomputer design and development project at TRW, Inc., under funding from the Defense Science Office of the Defense Advanced Research Projects Agency (DARPA). The purpose of the project was to explore a number of ideas for parallelizing the implementation of neural networks within an individual processing resource (unlike the Mark III project, which had as its primary goal the development of a multiple processing resource neurocomputer). The result was the Mark IV neurocomputer. In a sense, the Mark IV can be thought of as a single processing resource that could be used in parallel with many additional identical processing resources to build an even larger neurocomputer.

The design study for the Mark IV was carried out during 1984 and early 1985. Phyllis Li carried out a number of hardware trade-off analyses during the summer of 1985. Construction of the machine began in the fall of 1985 and it became operational a year later.

To validate the design, we modified the software of each of the processing resources (M68010 single board computers) of the Mark III neurocomputer to emulate the Mark IV design. Although there were small differences between the modified Mark III processing resource software and the Mark IV design, the Mark IV design concept was validated.

The design of the Mark IV is shown in Figure 8.21. Again, the goal was to parallelize as many of the functions involved in updating a processing element as possible. Additional options for parallelization — principally, the parallelization of individual functions in the updating process — were deliberately not pursued. Again, as with the Mark III, it was assumed that all of the processing

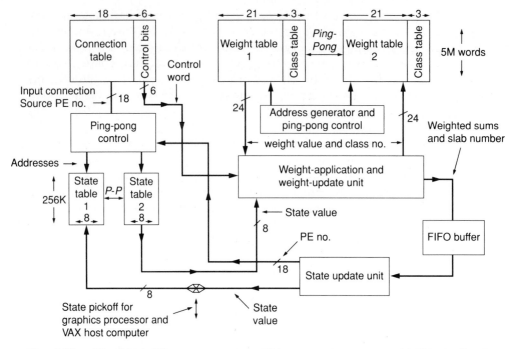

Fig. 8.21. • The Mark IV neurocomputer. This neurocomputer was highly pipelined. It had a capacity of 250,000 processing elements and 5,500,000 connections, and a speed of 5 million connections per second (with learning) for any neural network it could implement. The Mark IV was constructed out of signal processing building blocks (memories, multipliers, adders, and barrel shifters), TTL logic parts, and memory parts.

elements being implemented by the Mark IV were to be updated episodically, with all processing elements being updated on each time step.[15]

To facilitate the design of the Mark III and the Mark IV, we had to develop a general description of the class of neural networks that would be implemented by these machines. Our intention was to encompass as broad a class of networks as possible, while restricting the mathematical operations to be carried out sufficiently to allow the hardware available in 1985 to carry them out efficiently. One of the important advancements since the original Mark III and Mark IV development has been the capability to design neurocomputers capable of running essentially *any* type of neural network (subject to the capacity limitations

---

[15] Episodic updating does not, in general, imply that each processing element of the network gets updated at each time step (although when a slab is updated, all of the processing elements of that slab are updated together). In fact, the scheduling function of an episodically updated network can update the slabs of the network according to any desired schedule — see Chapter 2 for details.

of the machine). However, these more modern neurocomputers still have the restriction that only certain types of networks will run efficiently.

The neural networks in use in 1984 included the neocognitron, brain state in a box, linear associator, and an early type of spatiotemporal pattern recognizer network (the Hopfield network, backpropagation, counterpropagation, and the self-organizing map were not widely promulgated or did not exist at that time). Thus, it was this set of networks that we attempted to implement efficiently on the Mark III and Mark IV.

Like the Mark III, the Mark IV was designed to have a single neural network loaded into it at any given time. The network could have as many as eight layers or slabs, and each processing element could have as many as four input classes. Each of the processing elements on each of the slabs was assumed to have a transfer function that could be written in the following functional form:

$$x_i^{\text{new}} = F(x_i^{\text{old}}, I_i^1, I_i^2, I_i^3, I_i^4, \Gamma_1, \Gamma_2), \tag{8.2}$$

$$w_k^{\text{new}}(i, j) = w_k^{\text{old}}(i, j) + G_k(w_k^{\text{old}}(i, j), x_i^{\text{old}}, x_{m(i,j)}^{\text{old}}), \qquad k = 1, 2, 3, 4, \tag{8.3}$$

with

$$I_i^k = \sum_{j=M_{k-1}(i)+1}^{M_k(i)} w_k^{\text{old}}(i, j) \, f_k(x_{m(i,j)}^{\text{old}}), \qquad k = 1, 2, 3, 4, \tag{8.4}$$

where

$$
\begin{aligned}
x_i(t) &= \text{output signal from processing element number } i, \ i = 1, 2, \ldots, N; \\
x_i(t) &= \text{external signal input } i \text{ to system, } i = N+1, N+2, \ldots, N'; \\
x_i(t) &\geq 0, i = 1, 2, \ldots, N'; \\
m(i, j) &= \text{number of the processing element output signal (or external signal)} \\
&\quad \text{that forms the } j\text{th input to processing element } i, \text{ clearly,} \\
&\quad 1 \leq m(i, j) \leq N'; \\
w_k(i, j) &= \text{weight associated with } j\text{th input} \\
&\quad \text{to processing element } i, k \text{ denotes the class number of the input;} \\
M_k(i) - M_{k-1}(i) &= \text{number of inputs of class } k \text{ to processing element } i; \\
M_0(i) &\equiv 0; \\
M_4(i) &= \text{total number of inputs to processing element } i; \\
f_k &= \text{preweighting function for inputs of class } k; \\
\Gamma_1, \Gamma_2 &= \text{global signals 1 and 2 (from outside the system);} \\
F &= \text{processing element update function;} \\
G_k &= \text{weight update (learning law) function for inputs of} \\
&\quad \text{type } k, k = 1, 2, 3, 4;
\end{aligned}
$$

Although these functional forms may seem restrictive, they are actually capable of implementing a broad range of neural network architectures (although using this capability often requires quite a bit of algebraic manipulation). Naturally, each of the up to eight slabs could have its own separate set of these equations for its processing elements.

Although the forms of Equations 8.2, 8.3, and 8.4 are fairly general, the numerical accuracy of the arithmetic used to compute each of these equations was quite low. For example, all of the processing element states x_i were assumed to be expressible as an 8-bit fixed-point number. Similarly, all of the weights $w(i, j)$ (the weight associated with the jth input to processing element i) were coded as 21-bit fixed-point numbers. Beyond these, there were additional simplifications. For example, in the calculation of the function $G_k(w(i, j), x_i, x_{m(i,j)})$, the value of $w(i, j)$ is truncated and only the 8 most significant bits are used. Similarly, only the 4 most significant bits of x_i and $x_{m(i,j)}$ are used in this calculation. By means of these truncations, the function G could be viewed as a scalar function of a 16-bit variable. Thus, this function could be implemented with a lookup table having 64K 21-bit entries. For maximum generality, the lookup table was given 24 bits of output accuracy. To accommodate a variety of neural network architectures, the selection of the 16 bits of the values I_i^k (out of a total of 21 bits that were used in accumulating these sums) that were used in Equation 8.2 could be controlled by use of a variable-shift barrel shifter. The Mark IV ANSE compiler could control this shift operation by entering the desired number of bits of shift for each input class into registers within the machine during the set-up process. All loading and reading of tables, memories, registers, and switches by the host MicroVAX computer was carried out on a Direct Memory Access (DMA) basis through a DRV-11 interface. Processing element state values could be monitored during operation of the machine via a second DRV-11 interface (this was connected to the hexagonal point shown in Figure 8.21).

The design of the Mark IV neurocomputer is illustrated in Figure 8.21. Equations 8.3 and 8.4 were implemented in the weight application and weight update unit. The Mark IV was a highly pipelined architecture in which operation of all of Equations 8.2, 8.3, and 8.4 occurred simultaneously on each clock cycle. The operation of the Mark IV is now described.

The main memory of the Mark IV consisted of the three large sequentially addressed memories shown at the top of Figure 8.21. Each of these memories could store 5.5M 24-bit words and could read or write one word per clock cycle (200 ns). One complete pass through these memory tables constitutes one time cycle of updating for the entire neural network. The connection table was always read from top to bottom. This table contains the addresses of the processing elements that supply the input signals for each of the input connections in the network. The connections are ordered in sequence beginning with the first connection of class number 1 of the first processing element of the first slab and ending with the last connection of the highest-used class (potentially class number 4) of the highest-numbered processing element of the highest-numbered slab. The Mark IV was capable of implementing as many as 262,144 processing elements and 5.5M connections.

We shall now describe the Mark IV's operation in terms of the events that occurred on each clock cycle between the emission of the first word in the connection table and the emission of the last word in the connection table (that was used for the particular network being run). At the beginning and end of each pass through the connection table, a number of housecleaning functions were carried out that required a small number of cycles. Except for these housecleaning functions (which will be ignored here), the Mark IV was able to process one connection every 200 ns. In other words, it had a sustained speed of 5 million connections per second. The speed of the Mark IV was a fixed 5 million connections per second, whether or not learning was taking place.

Each update of each processing element followed the same sequence of processing. This involved reading a sequence of words from the connection table that describe the inputs to the processing element. This processing sequence will now be described.

The first word emitted by the connection table during the updating of a particular processing element contained the processing element number of the processing element to be updated. This processing element number was given by the first 18 bits of the 24-bit connection table output word. The last 6 bits of each of these words was a control word that was used to control various aspects of the Mark IV's operation (some of which will be described below). The 18-bit processing element number (an integer index for each of the up to 256K processing elements) was fed through the ping-pong control shown in Figure 8.21 to whichever of the state tables was currently in the read mode. The two state tables ping-ponged back and forth, each alternately being a read-only memory and then a write-only memory. The read-only memory (shown on the right in Figure 8.21) contains the state values from the previous round of updating. The state table in the write mode during a particular cycle through the connection table was used to record the new state values of the processing elements of the networks. At the end of each cycle through the connection table, the roles of these tables change and the formerly new values become the old values. As we will see, the weight tables in the upper-center and upper-right portions of Figure 8.21 also ping-pong back and forth and alternate read-only and write-only functions.

The 18-bit processing element number identifier of the processing element to be updated is sent to the read state table, and the old state value (from the last update) is read out and sent to the weight unit. Responding to the 6-bit control word command sent from the connection table, the weight unit takes this processing element state value and stores it in a special register. This state value was also sent on from the weight unit to the FIFO buffer. Following the readout of the state of the processing element being updated, the states of each of the processing elements supplying input signals to this processing element are then read out in order of connection sequence, starting with the first connection of class 1 and ending with the last connection of the highest class of connections used (maximum 4). Each time a processing element number was read out of the connection table, the corresponding weight was read out of weight table 1 (at least on this pass through the connection table — on the next pass, the weights will be read from weight table 2). Given these values, the weight unit can then implement Equations 8.3 and 8.4. Each weight value that was read in from weight table 1 contains 3 bits of information regarding the class of the input and other information.

As the weight unit completes each of the weighted sums given by Equation 8.4, these sums are sequentially loaded into the FIFO buffer (which has 24 bits of width — some of which are used as control bits to pass control information from the connection table through the weight unit and into the state update unit). The state update unit implemented Equation 8.2. This unit consists of a 16-bit Texas Instruments TMS32020 digital signal processing chip (a general purpose processor) along with a 64K-word Static Random Access Memory ($SRAM$) and an input/output unit. When each processing element output state was to be updated, the state update unit read the five required values (x_i^{old}, I_i^1, I_i^2, I_i^3, and I_i^4) from the FIFO buffer. The values Γ_1 and Γ_2 (there are up to two such values per slab) are both generated and stored within the state update unit.

The state update unit can use any user-specified function F for implementing the state updates. The output of the state update unit was a new 8-bit state value for the processing element; this value was sent to the write-only state table to be recorded. Notice that the state update unit also sends the 18-bit address of the newly updated processing element to the ping-pong control so that the state can be recorded in the proper location. This address was generated sequentially by an address generator, since each of the processing elements in the network was updated in order of its processing element number.

As each of the weights was updated by the weight unit in accordance with Equation 8.3, the revised weight values were sent to weight table 2. The address generator and ping-pong control were responsible for generating the read and write addresses for weight table 1 and weight table 2. Following a complete pass through the connection table, the weight tables ping-pong and reverse read-only and write-only roles. The new weight values from the previous cycle then become the old weight values of the next cycle. The weight values from two cycles ago are then overwritten.

As mentioned earlier, the Mark IV was designed to be a node of a larger neurocomputer (which was never intended to be constructed). This larger neurocomputer would consist of many Mark IV nodes on a fast broadcast bus structure (much like the Mark III). Each bus transmission of a node would be constructed from the state value output of the state update unit, which could be intercepted at the point shown by a hexagon at the bottom left of Figure 8.21 and sent to the broadcast transmission subsystem. The filter structure (recall the discussion of filtering in Section 8.4) would select needed state updates from the broadcast bus and put them in a FIFO structure from which they would be taken and subsequently inserted into the write-only state table — again via the hexagon tap point in Figure 8.21. In the Mark IV design study, it was determined that as many as 1,000 Mark IV nodes could be connected via an optical broadcast bus structure. Thus, a full-scale neurocomputer based on this idea would have had approximately 1,000 times the capability of the Mark IV. Of course, the cost of such a system would have been prohibitive. However, as silicon hardware technology advances and the cost of implementing large designs decreases, this multi-Mark IV design approach (with improvements) might well provide a model for large neurocomputers that can fully exploit the capabilities of advanced digital hardware.

As with the Mark III, the Mark IV used the ANSE environment for specifying the neural network to be implemented. That neural network could then be called on the Mark IV from user software on the DEC MicroVAX through a primitive user interface. Physically, the Mark IV occupied two standard 0.5 meter wide equipment racks that were each 1.7 meters tall and approximately 0.6 meters deep giving a total volume of approximately 1 cubic meter. The Mark IV had a mass of approximately 200 kg and drew approximately 1.3 kW of power (including the power used for the many cooling fans).

An interesting feature of the Mark IV neurocomputer (which will probably be found in many research neurocomputers in the future) was an ultra high-speed graphics display facility for monitoring the activity of the neural network being implemented on the Mark IV. Earlier experimental work that I carried out at Motorola and work that Todd Gutschow and and I had carried out on the Mark I and Mark II software-based neural network implementation packages at TRW, convinced us of the need to monitor the output signals of the processing elements of a network in real time. As indicated in Subsection 8.5.1, the Mark III was set up so that the VAX computer would get all of the processing element state values as part of the broadcast transmission of those values after every update cycle. These transmissions allowed the state values to be displayed on a VAX color graphics terminal in real time. The earlier Motorola system and the Mark I and Mark II were also able to display the state of the processing element output signals graphically in real time, since these systems were implemented in software and ran at an extremely slow speed. Even the Mark III was slow enough so that a standard graphics terminal could keep up with the updates for most networks. The Mark IV, however, could update as many as 250,000 elements per second — and this was too high a rate for the host computer and an attached graphic terminal to handle. Nonetheless, we felt that the real-time observation of network performance was essential.

To solve this problem, we used a stand-alone ultra-high-speed graphics monitoring system connected to the Mark IV. The basic idea behind this graphics monitoring system was a concept we called *The Wall*. The idea was to think of the processing elements of the neural networks being implemented as being represented by small squares (all the same size) organized into 1-dimensional or 2-dimensional slabs, with all of these structures being placed on a 2-dimensional surface, such as the wall of a room. The 8-bit output signal level of each processing element was coded by one of 16 colors — each color representing an interval of 16 levels of output signal value. The colors ranged from dark blue (indicating a low output signal) to bright red (indicating the highest possible output signal). With some experimentation, we were able to develop a color "temperature scale" that was visually quite satisfactory. The purpose of the graphics display system was to provide three movable viewports for viewing The Wall in real time. The graphics display hardware consisted of a 32-bit Motorola M68020-based VME single-board computer with 1 M byte of memory and two DRV-11 VME bus interface boards, all mounted in a VME backplane rack. One of the interfaces was connected to a DRV-11 output port on the Mark IV that was able to tap all of the processing element state updates produced by the state-update unit as they were transmitted to the write-only state table (in other words, they were extracted at the point marked with a hexagon in the bottom left of Figure 8.21). The Mark IV also provided a separate DRV-11 interface to the host VAX computer, as in the Mark III design. The other DRV-11 VME card was used to send transmissions from the M68020 single-board computer to a high-speed graphics processor that drove a (1280 × 1024 pixel) high-resolution, full-color (256 colors drawn from a palette of over 1 million colors), 60 Hz refresh rate, non-interlaced, graphics monitor. The graphics processor had a digitizer mouse interface that would allow mouse commands to be transmitted back through the DRV-11 channel to the M68020 single-board computer. The output display system was entirely mouse driven. The user could designate any one of the three viewport windows and could cause the window to pan and zoom over The Wall. Zoom values were powers of 2 and when the viewport zoomed out so far that individual processing elements dropped below the one color pixel size, then multiple processing element output signals would be averaged together to yield a convincing blended value. By this means, a viewport could be zoomed out to see the entire Wall or zoomed in to where each processing element occupied a square area approximately 25 pixels on a side.

The ability to position each of the three viewports separately and independently allowed various aspects of the network's behavior to be monitored simultaneously. The M68020 single-board computer and the graphics processor were capable of creating between 10 and 30 *new* frames per second (the display had a non-interlaced refresh rate of 60 Hz for whatever frame was currently being displayed). The slower frame creation rates corresponded to situations where output signal averaging was required. Recall that this system was built in 1986.

The output graphics system of the Mark IV neurocomputer was absolutely delightful to operate. It allowed the operator to peer into the artificial universe of The Wall, and to see the neural network operating in full real time. At the update rate of 5 million connection per second, some small networks would update faster than the frame creation rate of the graphics output system. However, in this case the system would simply skip updates, and would display every second or third update value. However, for most networks of interest in applications, the total network update rate was less than 30 Hz and all updates could be displayed. The value of this tool for experimental research in neural network architectures and neural network applications cannot be overestimated. Although such systems will probably always be somewhat expensive, the expense is clearly justified for applications development and research, where being able to clearly see what the neural network is doing is essential. With the ever-decreasing cost of processing power, and the widespread demand for high-resolution, high-speed graphics capability (CAD, entertainment, and so on), the cost of such subsystems will probably soon be affordable for almost all users.

A great deal was learned from the Mark IV. Design ideas pioneered in the Mark IV are now found in most digital virtual electronic neurocomputers.

Exercises

8.5.1. The basic idea of connecting a number of single-board neurocomputers together using a broadcast bus (as in the Mark III) can potentially be applied to many different neurocomputers. What are the advantages and disadvantages of this approach compared to other approaches such as the pipelined processor approach of the Mark IV? How does the performance-to-price ratio of such a multi-board neurocomputer compare with the ratio for a single-board neurocomputer?

8.5.2. Taking the situation in Exercise 8.5.1 one step further, let us assume that we are going to freeze the hardware technology to be used in each new generation of single-board neurocomputers every three years. In other words, every three years we will take the most advanced versions of the hardware elements that we need (those that will be available for volume production in 12 months) and use them to design the next-generation single-board neurocomputer (which is then offered for sale 12 months after the technology freeze). At the time the single-board neurocomputer is introduced for sale we begin work on a Mark III - type neurocomputer based on this single-board neurocomputer (but having 10 times the performance of the single-board system). Development of this multi-board system requires 18 months, at which point the multi-board system is offered for sale. Thus, the multi-board system enters the market 18 months before the next-generation single-board neurocomputer (offering the same performance as the multi-board system, but at a much lower price) will be introduced. Comment on the marketing and sales characteristics of such a product (the multi-board neurocomputer). Will this be an attractive product? What types of customers might want to buy it?

8.5.3. The Mark IV neurocomputer provides an even more extreme example than the Mark III of how the technology at any given time can be used to achieve substantially greater performance than a single-board neurocomputer built from the same generation of technology. Given the assumptions of Exercise 8.5.2, let us assume that a multi-node Mark

IV - type neurocomputer can achieve 100 times the performance of a single-board neurocomputer based on the same generation of hardware technology (although it will take a lot of hardware to do this, and the resulting machine will probably cost over 100 times the cost of a single-board system). We assume that it takes three years to develop this multi-node Mark IV - type system after the technology freeze (as opposed to one year for the single-board neurocomputer and 30 months for the multiple-board, Mark III - type neurocomputer). Comment on the sales and marketing characteristics of such a multi-node Mark IV - type product. What would be your reaction to a just-introduced product built out of technology that was first sold two years earlier (in other words, which developers began designing into their products three years earlier)? What types of customers might want to buy such a product? What potential impact might parts cost reductions due to technology maturation have on the price of the product? In other words, how much might the prices of the parts used in the product be expected to drop in the three years since those parts were first sampled, and how much impact will this drop have on the sales price of the product? Speculate as to why neurocomputers of the Mark III and Mark IV types are not currently offered for sale.

8.5.4. Develop a conceptual design for an optical broadcast bus to be used with a multi-node Mark IV - type neurocomputer. First, develop a list of requirements that the bus must meet, and then design a bus that meets these requirements.

8.5.5. Given a neurocomputer application that is not price sensitive and that will require the largest possible multi-node Mark IV - type neurocomputer, what factors would limit the ultimate size of such a machine? How might such a system be packaged?

In conclusion, neurocomputer design is only in its infancy. The prospects for analog neurocomputers and for neurocomputers built out of exotic hardware technologies with no market pull are currently difficult to assess, although analog, digital, and hybrid silicon chips may be important for certain specialized applications. Digital virtual electronic neurocomputers will probably continue to dominate neurocomputing, with combined neurocomputing/programmed computing process servers becoming more important. Eventually, many computers may be designed so that they can efficiently implement both algorithms and neural networks — thus broadening the potential base of neurocomputing applications and bringing neurocomputing into the mainstream of information processing.

9

Neurocomputing Applications: Sensor Processing, Control, and Data Analysis

Unlike mathematics and science, which, respectively, pursue pure beauty and an understanding of nature, technology pursues the development of useful things. Thus, it is in its *application* to real-world problems that the real worth of neurocomputing technology must be measured.

This chapter begins with a section discussing applications engineering. The remaining three sections then discuss applications of neurocomputing to sensor processing, control, and data analysis.

Because the solution of real problems always involves an enormous amount of domain-specific knowledge (along with proprietary and/or classified information), it is not possible to treat real applications in an introductory textbook. Therefore, the applications examples presented in this chapter focus upon "toy problems" that can be described and understood with little domain knowledge. In almost all cases, it is the principles used in solving these toy problems that are the focus of attention. These principles can often be used in solving real problems, even though the solutions to the toy problems may be of no practical value.

9.1 Neurocomputing Applications Engineering

As with almost all new technologies, neurocomputing is just one new tool in an already well-equipped toolbox. If neurocomputing is to realize its economic potential, it will be necessary to blend neurocomputing techniques with other existing techniques. Thus, we must constantly ask ourselves how we can most effectively combine neurocomputing with other technological ingredients.

This section discusses two of the key issues of neurocomputing applications engineering: problem solving methodologies and functional specification development. These issues relate primarily to the initial process of defining a neurocomputing application. If this initial process is successful, then the methodologies presented in the Appendix can be employed to analyze the proposed application, develop a business plan for the proposed project, and (if the business plan demonstrates the desirability of the project and leads to the allocation of the necessary resources) plan and manage the resulting development process.

9.1.1 Solving Problems with Neurocomputing

The most important ingredient in the conception and development of any new product, process, or problem solution is domain knowledge. Someone who is going to develop a neural network controlled chemical reactor to produce a polytetrafluoroethylene plastic powder having an extremely narrow molecular weight distribution had better know a great deal about polymer chemistry and plastics manufacturing. Similarly, someone who is going to develop a new system for rating the credit-worthiness of mortgage borrowers should be intimately familiar with finance and mortgage banking. Experience to date suggests that the most useful neurocomputing applications will flow from the work of domain experts in the area of application who are also familiar with neurocomputing, or from situations where domain experts are in charge of the development project and the neurocomputing expertise is applied at their direction. This idea of putting domain expertise ahead of technical expertise runs somewhat counter to the recent trend in the organization of technological education — namely, the segregation of technology into largely isolated topics. In industry, technologists must often become well versed in a variety of specialized areas, not all of which belong to the same technological discipline. Fortunately, neurocomputing is a subject that almost all technologists (and many others) can readily learn (unlike bioengineering and information theory, which often require years of study of the relevant scientific or mathematical underpinnings of the subject).

Because of the central importance of detailed domain knowledge in the conception and development of neurocomputing applications, we will assume that each technologist working on the project either personally has, or is being directed by someone who has, a comprehensive understanding of the domain for which the application is intended.

Because neurocomputing offers at least a few capabilities that are fundamentally new, there will be some situations in which the entire design of the system revolves around the system's neurocomputing components. In other instances, however, the neurocomputing components of a system will simply serve as performance enhancement replacements for existing system elements or for elements that would otherwise be built using non-neurocomputing approaches.

The primary problem solving methodology for neurocomputing is to "work in reverse." We start by constructing a list of neural networks that are sufficiently understood to be useful for solving real world problems. This list (see Exercise

9.1.1) describes the functional capabilities of each network and specifies the type and quantity of data that must be available for training and testing the network. We also construct an exhaustive list of the operational functions involved in our particular application domain. For example, if the application domain is plastics extrusion, this list might contain the following entries:

- Marketing and sales
- Plastic pellet ordering and receiving
- Plastic pellet storage and intrafactory transport
- Plastic pellet dehumidification and alloying
- Additive mixing
- Extruder control
- Die heating control
- Product cooling
- Fly cutting and finishing
- Packaging
- Shipment, transportation, and billing
- Planning and management

In this example, there are probably candidate neurocomputing applications in each operational area of a plastic extrusion enterprise. We discover these applications by taking the list of neurocomputing capabilities and the list of operational functions and trying to match problems and opportunities identified in the latter with capabilities offered by the former.

Bringing those who are closest to the day-to-day operations into the discussions about possible applications is crucial. For example, one could go from department to department, talking with specialists in each area about their problems and their operational procedures. Your general domain expertise, combined with their specialized in-depth understanding of the operational realities, can often yield a comprehensive assessment of the potential value of applying neurocomputing technology to a particular problem. Sometimes, no project worthy of further consideration will be discovered. Nonetheless, this discussion survey is still a valuable exercise because it gives assurance that a thorough search for ways to exploit the technology has been conducted.

The importance of enlisting the aid of operational personnel in the definition of the application concept, as well as in its evaluation, cannot be overemphasized. However, it must be borne in mind that such individuals are typically not technologists, and they may not view the world in technical terms. Nonetheless, they are the people who will use or purchase the end result of the application project, and their operational expertise is often a key ingredient in the project's success. The time and effort spent communicating with end users will almost always pay large dividends.

In conclusion, the primary methodology for applying neurocomputing is to work in reverse. The domain expert technologist (who is also knowledgeable in neurocomputing) constructs a list of neural networks which describes each network's problem solving capabilities and training requirements. A list of operational functions (or product categories) is then developed, and applications in each of these areas are considered (with strong end-user involvement throughout the process). Candidate applications that emerge from this process are then evaluated further (see the next subsection).

9.1.2 Functional Specification Development

Once a candidate neurocomputing application is discovered, the next step is to define it precisely. This step is essential, since trying to solve a problem that has not been precisely defined is like trying to nail Jell-o to the wall. The means by which a problem is defined is via a short, but formal, document called the *functional specification* (the United States Department of Defense, which manages the world's largest technological activity, terms this the *Level A Specification* or simply the *A Spec.*).[1] The functional specification is a mechanism to allow technologists who are not domain experts to work on an application project. The technologists design and develop a working system that meets the requirements set down in the functional specification. Thus, the functional specification is perhaps the most important document of any application project.

The functional specification is drawn up and then iteratively improved and critiqued by both the technologist and the group of cooperating end users. The advice and critique of highly experienced, neurocomputing-knowledgeable technologists is also important, as they will help to validate the application concept from a technical perspective, as well as to evaluate it from a feasibility and doability standpoint. Senior technologists with many years of experience in a particular area often have an almost uncanny ability to accurately size up a proposed project and to accurately estimate the labor, materials, and time that will be required to carry it out. Enlisting the aid of such individuals is well worth whatever price you have to pay. Typically, the most useful advice is provided by those who have risen through the ranks of project management to a position where they are managing large projects. Getting access to such people is often difficult, but any help that you can get from them will usually be worth the effort.

The best way to view the functional specification is as a contract. Once it is complete, it is a statement from the end users to the technologists on the project that if they are successful in developing the capability or product

---

[1] The A Spec. describes the end user problem to be solved and provides end user requirements that the final system must satisfy. There are also B and C Specs., which are produced by the technologists who are developing the system. The *B Spec.* describes the top-level design of the system to be built and is reviewed at a *Preliminary Design Review (PDR)*. If it passes this review, the problems identified during the PDR are corrected, and a detailed design is then produced. This detailed design is described in the *C Spec.*, which is reviewed at the *Critical Design Review (CDR)*. After the C Spec. passes CDR, the identified problems are fixed and the system is built.

described in the functional specification, then the end users will accept the resulting item with great enthusiasm. The functional specification is a statement by the technologists involved in the project that the application represents a reasonable and achievable technological goal.

The functional specification should be written along the lines of the following outline:

1. *Description* — Brief description of the capability or product that is to be developed

2. *System Interface Requirements* — Requirements for interfacing the capability or product with other systems

3. *Human Interface Requirements* — Requirements or constraints regarding the interface between the proposed developed item and humans, including any safety or failsafe requirements

4. *Performance Requirements* — Requirements on the overall performance of the system; these requirements might include:

   (a) Accuracy

   (b) Speed

   (c) Reliability

   (d) Size

   (e) Mass

5. *Economic Requirements* — Requirements regarding recurring cost, appearance, similarity to other products or systems, and so on

6. *Development Project Requirements* — Constraints that must or should be honored by the development project; these constraints might include nonrecurring cost bounds, unusual environmental restrictions, schedule constraints, restrictions on material sources or subcontractors, security restrictions, and proprietary restrictions

The technologist working with the end users should construct an initial draft of the functional specification. The entire functional specification is rarely longer than 10 pages (unless the project is unusually large), and is usually only two or three pages. The draft functional specification is then reviewed and improved by the end users, the project leader, and advisory technologists. It is a good idea to test the functional specification by having technologists without domain knowledge critique it. Such critiques can often identify missing or incomplete information, as well as provide an assessment of the readability and understandability of the entire document.

Once the functional specification has been completed, the decision of whether or not to go forward with the project must be made. This decision should be made in two steps. First, get all of the people who would be involved in the project or who would use its output into one room and, together, make a *go/no-go* decision. If the decision is to *go*, then the next step is to write a *business plan* for the proposed project.[2] A business plan is a tool for evaluating *any* candidate project (not just a business). In a sense, the functional specification serves as an initial filter for candidate application concepts. Typically, only a small fraction of the functional specifications that are written ever turn into actual projects. The process of writing the functional specification usually identifies problems that make the initial concept uninteresting or infeasible.

In conclusion, neurocomputing applications are much like other technology applications. However, because neurocomputing offers new capabilities, it may sometimes become the driving element in a design. The remainder of this chapter concentrates on describing the applications of neurocomputing to toy problems. Again, bear in mind that these problems are presented mostly to illustrate methods by which neurocomputing can be applied, as well as to illustrate specific techniques that are applicable across a much broader range of real-world problems.

Exercises

9.1.1. To support your own future applications work, form a list of all of the neural network architectures described in this book. For each architecture, develop a detailed, but concise, description of its functional capabilities and the type and quantity of data that must be made available for training and testing.

9.1.2. Create an operational functions list for an organizational element with which you have been personally involved.

9.1.3. Write a complete functional specification for a new product in a field in which you have domain knowledge.

9.1.4. Besides working closely with end users and developing a good functional specification, one must face *institutional factors* that will also affect the project. Institutional factors are issues, arising outside of the group of end users and project performers, that could significantly impact the project. Create a detailed outline for a report examining the institutional factors connected with a project to install 25,000 nuclear fusion power plants along the coasts of the populated continents of Earth. These power plants would make electricity, desalinate seawater, and produce their own fuel from seawater. They would utilize a large number of neural networks to actively stabilize the magnetically contained, but otherwise unstable, thermonuclear plasma. The fusion reactors are inherently incapable of exploding, and release approximately one millionth the amount of radioactivity into the environment as a coal–fired plant with equivalent power output (coal has an appreciable amount of

---

[2] Business plans are discussed in Section A.1 of the Appendix.

radioactive material in it). However, these fusion plants must be abandoned after 5 years and left to radioactively "cool down" for 100 years — at which time the plant materials can be safely recycled.

9.2 Sensor Processing

From the earliest days of neurocomputing, neural networks have been recognized as being unusually well suited for solving problems in sensor processing. By *sensor processing*, we primarily mean pattern recognition, although other functions such as filtering and sensor data compression are also important application areas.

Although there are some exceptions, sensor processing problems tend to involve one of two different classes of sensor data: images and time series. For the purposes of this paper, all images and time series will be assumed to be digitally sampled at regular discrete spatial and time intervals, respectively. Each of the examples presented will require only a minimal amount of background information to be appreciated.

9.2.1 Character Recognizer

The problem of automatically recognizing characters in printed or hand-written material has been studied for decades [100, 132].

A number of technical and market successes have been achieved in character recognition. For example, the United States Postal Service uses character recognizers extensively for reading printed addresses on letters. Banks utilize character recognition machines for reading the numerical amounts of checks. Commercial character recognition systems for use with document scanners attached to personal computers are also available.[3]

We shall now look at an example of a simple character recognizer based on a neural network. The character recognition problem to be solved is the classification of single numerals written by hand on a digitizer tablet. The set up is shown in Figure 9.1. The goal is to be able to classify single numerals (0 through 9, inclusive) that are drawn on a digitizer tablet with an electronic pen. The user of the system can draw the character any size and it may be located anywhere within the active area of the digitizer tablet. Once the user has drawn a numeral on the digitizer tablet, he or she pushes a small button on the pen, which activates the recognition process.

---

[3] In character recognition, there are two important performance measures: *acceptance rate* and *substitution rate*. The acceptance rate is the number of characters per million that the system accepts as readable. The substitution rate is the number of characters per million accepted characters that the system classifies incorrectly. Both of these rates are measured by testing the system on huge volumes of text drawn at random from the environment in which the system is expected to operate.

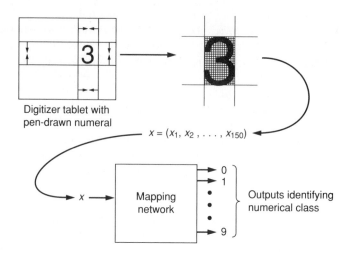

Fig. 9.1. • Character recognition system. The user forms a character (a numeral from 0 to 9) by writing on a digitizer tablet with a special pen. The system then recognizes the character and prints it on the screen of the host computer.

The product of the character input process is a high-resolution image (approximately 2048×2048 pixels), with all of the pixels equal to 0 except those belonging to the 1-pixel-wide line corresponding to the pen-drawn numeral. (The time history of the pen's movement is not retained — only the resulting character image.) The first step in the processing is to start a vertical line at the left edge of the image and move it to the right until it touches the leftmost pixel of the character. Another vertical line is then started at the right edge of the image and moved left until it touches the character. Horizontal lines are then moved down from the top of the image and up from the bottom of the image to vertically bracket the numeral. These lines are shown in Figure 9.1. The net result of this first step is to place a rectangular box around the numeral.

Following the placement of the box around the numeral, the next step is to divide this box into 150 equal area sub-boxes. Then, the box is divided into 10 equal-width columns and 15 equal-width rows, as shown in Figure 9.1. Next, it is determined whether or not the character line goes through each of the 150 sub-boxes. A binary vector $\mathbf{x}$ is used to record the results of these determinations. If the numeral line (or lines, in cases of retraces) passes through the ith box, then x_i is set to 1; otherwise, x_i is left set at 0. In this way, the 150-dimensional vector $\mathbf{x}$ is used to code the spatial form of the character. Note that, if exactly the same character were drawn at a different location or at a different scale on the digitizer tablet, then the vector $\mathbf{x}$ would be approximately the same. Thus, this method of coding the spatial form of the character automatically provides shift and scale change insensitivity.

After the $\mathbf{x}$ vector has been constructed, it is submitted to a mapping network (such as backpropagation or counterpropagation) for classification. The network has 150 inputs for the components of $\mathbf{x}$, and 10 outputs (one each for the numerals 0 through 9). The 10 network outputs supply a 1-out-of-N code that indicates which of the numerals the vector **x** represents. For example, in the situation illustrated in Figure 9.1, the fourth output of mapping network (the one corresponding to the numeral "3") would be expected to have an output of 1, and all of the other outputs would be expected to be 0. In a situation where the network is uncertain about the classification of the numeral, the outputs might deviate significantly from this pure 0–or–1 code. In this instance, we would typically take the largest output as the correct class of the numeral, except in situations where the mapping network would be able to indicate an uncertainty that **x** represents any valid numeral, in which case all of the outputs would have low values.

The training of such a character recognition network is accomplished by means of supervised training on examples of known characters. A typical method for generating such a training set is to have a computer prompt the input of each character by asking the human training participant to form a particular numeral on the digitizer tablet and to push the input button when the numeral desired by the computer has been completed. This approach involves a minimum of programming and allows a large training set to be produced in a semi-automatic manner in a short period of time.

A system of this type built in 1987 at HNC, Inc., utilized 1200 training examples (numerals) gathered from 12 different people. When tested on a large number of examples from over 50 people, this system achieved an acceptance rate of approximately 95%, and a substitution rate of less than 5%. The development of this system was carried out in less than 1 month by a single person.

9.2.2 Cottrell/Munro/Zipser Technique

The Cottrell/Munro/Zipser technique is a general-purpose neurocomputing technique that was developed in 1986 by Garrison Cottrell, Paul Munro, and David Zipser. To understand the technique, it will be useful to start by first considering their image compression experiments. The general principle will then be extracted from this context.

The problem that Cottrell, Munro, and Zipser set out to investigate was that of *image compression*. Image compression is the problem of coding image data to reduce the amount of data that must be sent to transmit the image from one location to another (where it is reconstructed) over an information channel. Image compression is possible because nearby pixels in images are often highly correlated, which allows these local statistical relationships to be exploited.

The Cottrell/Munro/Zipser image compression system is illustrated in Figure 9.2. As shown in the upper left corner of Figure 9.2, a high-resolution image is sampled in 8 × 8 blocks, each containing 64 pixels. The image is panchromatic and each pixel has a gray scale consisting of 256 levels ranging from 0 (completely dark) to 255 (completely light). The intensity of each of the 64 pixels is coded as an 8-bit number x_i. By *rasterization* (the process of ordering the pixels into a linear list by taking the first row of pixels first, the second row of pixels second, and so on), the 64 pixel intensities are formed into the

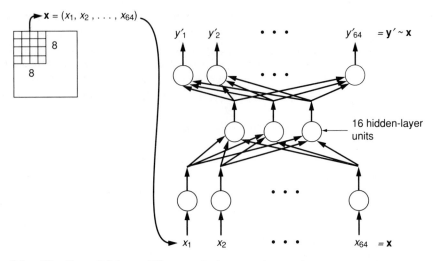

Fig. 9.2. • The Cottrell/Munro/Zipser technique. This technique uses a backpropagation network with fewer hidden units than input or output units. The goal is to learn the identity mapping for some arbitrary input data environment. The network is forced to discover a set of good hidden layer weight vectors (that is, affine features) for representing the input data without throwing away information. The output layer uses these feature outputs (the outputs of the hidden layer units) to attempt to reconstruct the input pattern. The technique yields a set of features that have the capability to represent the input data vector in a more compact or *compressed* form, while losing as little information about the input vector as possible.

vector $\mathbf{x}$. To carry out image compression, Cottrell, Munro, and Zipser utilized a three-layer backpropagation network with 64 inputs, 64 outputs, and 16 hidden layer units (see Figure 9.2). The inputs to the network are the components of $\mathbf{x}$. The outputs of the network are 64 values that, if everything is working perfectly, will be exactly the same as the pixel values in $\mathbf{x}$.

The hidden layer of the Cottrell/Munro/Zipser network contains 16 units.[4] These hidden units are responsible for taking the 64 input values and somehow reexpressing them as only 16 numbers — from which the entire original set of 64 numbers is to be reconstructed by the output layer. The use of the system for image compression now becomes clear. The bottom two rows of the Cottrell/Munro/Zipser network are located at the transmission point. As each block of 64 pixels is entered into the network, the hidden layer then produces a set of 16 values (which are also quantized to 8 bits of resolution). These 16 values are then transmitted over the information channel. On the receiving end, where the top layer of the network is located, the 16 hidden layer output

---

[4] Note: the 8×8 pixel array and 16 hidden unit configuration is just typical; Cottrell, Munro, and Zipser experimented with several different configurations.

values are then inserted into the output units of the top layer to reconstruct the 64 pixel values of the block. With this scheme, the number of bits that must be transmitted per block is reduced by a factor of 4 (from 64 bytes to 16 bytes). Naturally, the output of the network will not always be identical to the input, but the performance of the system is remarkably good. (The network's performance is comparable to that of other fixed–transform image compression systems.)

The training of the Cottrell/Munro/Zipser network is carried out using imagery that is statistically representative of that which will be encountered in operational service. For each image, blocks of pixels are entered into the network, starting at the upper left corner of the image and moving the block rightward one pixel at a time (until the end of the row is reached, at which point the block is reset to the left of the image and moved down one pixel). Using this scheme, each image (assumed to be 512×512 or larger) can supply hundreds of thousands of training examples.

As each training example is generated, it is entered into the bottom of the network as input and used as the correct output by the output layer of the network. Thus, the Cottrell/Munro/Zipser network is, in a sense, a self-organizing network. The training process is continued until the network's mean-squared error F (as measured using examples not employed during training) seems to stabilize at a reasonably low value.

Once training has been completed, the system is then ready for operational use. During operational use, the blocks are usually chosen so that they do not overlap and so that they tile the image completely. In other words, the blocks are located at 8 pixel intervals, both horizontally and vertically across the entire image. As each block is entered into the network, the corresponding 16 byte signal is transmitted and then decoded on the receiving end to approximately reconstruct the block. This block is then inserted into the received image at the proper location. Following transmission of all of the blocks, the received image can then be viewed and evaluated.

Cottrell, Munro, and Zipser discovered two interesting facts about the reconstructed images. First, the subjective quality level[5] of the images produced by the Cottrell/Munro/Zipser technique is comparable to that of images produced by other image compression schemes having the same bandwidth reduction; therefore, the performance of the Cottrell/Munro/Zipser technique is on a par with that of other similar image compression techniques. Second, Cottrell, Munro, and Zipser demonstrated that the performance of the system degrades for images that are not statistically consistent with those used for training (as would be expected). For example, Cottrell, Munro, and Zipser used images of groups of people indoors for training. When they then tested the system on similar images, the performance was quite good. However, when they tested

---

[5] Currently, the only way to measure the quality of an image is with double-blind human evaluation — no satisfactory automated technique exists.

the system on images of automobiles, a number of easily noticeable artifacts were produced, such as strange spurs or spikes on chromium-metal-plated parts of the automobile.

Like the character recognition system of the previous subsection, the Cottrell/Munro/Zipser image compression system was developed in an amazingly short time (a few weeks). Previous image compression systems required many months or even years to develop. Additionally, neither Cottrell, Munro, nor Zipser had an extensive background in image compression. This illustrates yet another aspect of neurocomputing applications: the only important expertise is that associated with writing a good systems specification and devising a clever way to exploit the power of the neural network(s) involved. In-depth technical knowledge of the particular area of information processing being considered is typically not necessary; although a general knowledge of the area is often required. Thus, in this sense, neurocomputing places a higher premium on domain knowledge and network use cleverness than on deep technical understanding.

In the future, most neural-network-based information processing systems may routinely carry out operations that no human understands in detail on an algorithmic basis. It may even turn out that the study of algorithms will become less and less important, and will eventually evolve into an obscure academic pursuit (much like the study of taxonomy in biology — a subject that once occupied almost the entire field). Although such thoughts are heretical today, such an evolution is certainly not out of the question. Given the tools to develop systems that find their own algorithms, and given those tools necessary to test and understand the development of such systems, neurocomputing may well eliminate the practical need to understand the intricate details involved in the algorithm itself. Even if this does not occur, at least the advent of neurocomputing will have stimulated us to seriously consider such possibilities.

The Cottrell/Munro/Zipser image compression system cleverly employs the idea that, if the hidden layer is smaller than the input and output layer, then the input data must somehow be "squeezed" down to a more compact representation on the hidden layer, and then re-expanded on the output layer. This squeeze play forces the network to develop an efficient set of *hidden layer features* (hidden layer unit weight vectors) that define affine combinations of the input values that contain statistically meaningful information that will be useful in reconstructing those values. This principle of using the mean-squared error minimization characteristic of the backpropagation neural network to force the development of redundancy eliminating features as hidden layer weight vectors is known as the *Cottrell/Munro/Zipser technique.*

The Cottrell/Munro/Zipser technique can actually be used with virtually any kind of data (since the network is self-organizing). In each case, the hidden layer of the network will be forced to find a near-optimal set of features that are expressly tailored to the statistics of the input vectors. These features are, in fact, optimal for the purpose of reconstructing those input vectors. Thus, the overall goal that the system is trying to satisfy is to minimize the loss of information in this compact representation. Thus, the Cottrell/Munro/Zipser technique can be used whenever one faces the situation of having large input vectors for which it is suspected that a much more compact code can be developed. The Cottrell/Munro/Zipser technique can then be used to attempt to find such a code. For some situations, it may be necessary to use more than one hidden layer. If this is done, the representing features are then taken to be those of the smallest hidden layer. However, if this is not the last hidden layer, then the subsequent layers must be included in whatever network is used with these compact features.

The Cottrell/Munro/Zipser technique is often useful for condensing massive vectors containing little information into a much more compact representation that can be used both for storage and for later entry into a neural network as surrogate data. Whenever the technique is used, it is important that the resulting features be carefully tested (by testing the Cottrell/Munro/Zipser network) to verify that the reconstruction accuracy is adequate for the application at hand. Research has been carried out [18, 160] to understand more about the features that are formed by a single hidden layer Cottrell/Munro/Zipser network. This research has demonstrated that the network essentially carries out a *principle component analysis* to find these features. In a principle component analysis (which is a standard technique in statistics, pattern recognition, physics, and other fields), the eigenvalues $\{\lambda_1, \lambda_2, \ldots, \lambda_n\}$ and corresponding unit eigenvectors $\{\sigma_1, \sigma_2, \ldots, \sigma_n\}$, of the $n \times n$ data covariance matrix

$$R = \frac{1}{N} \sum_{k=1}^{N} (\mathbf{x}_k - \bar{\mathbf{x}})(\mathbf{x}_k - \bar{\mathbf{x}})^{\mathrm{T}},$$

(where $\bar{x}$ is the average x vector) are calculated (the eigenvectors are necessarily orthonormal — see Exercise 9.2.3). The eigenvalues that are very small in magnitude (and their associated eigenvectors) are discarded. The r remaining eigenvectors are relabeled in descending order of the magnitudes of their corresponding eigenvalues (that is, largest first). This new reduced set of eigenvectors $\{\sigma_1, \sigma_2, \ldots, \sigma_r\}$ can then be used to represent the $\mathbf{x}$ pattern vectors by calculating the dot product features $\sigma_i \cdot \mathbf{x}$. The vector $\mathbf{x}$ can then be approximately represented by the sum

$$\tilde{\mathbf{x}} = \sum_{i=1}^{r} (\sigma_i \cdot \mathbf{x}) \ \sigma_i.$$

The representational error $\mathbf{x} - \tilde{\mathbf{x}}$ will tend to be small (see Exercise 9.2.4).

It is known that the hidden layer features developed by a one hidden layer Cottrell/Monro/Zipser network tend to lie in the subspace spanned by the set $\{\sigma_1, \sigma_2, \ldots, \sigma_r\}$. When using principal component analysis, it is helpful to view the $\mathbf{x}$ data examples as a cloud of points in n-dimensional euclidean space. Principal component analysis fits the best possible ellipsoid (in a certain mean squared error sense) to this cloud. This is useful since some commonly encountered data sets are approximately ellipsoidal. Further, many of the principal axes (the generalizations of the major and minor axes of a 2-dimensional el-lipse) of this best-fitting ellipsoid are often smashed down to almost 0 length (the half-lengths of these axes are the eigenvalues of R). Thus, we need only to use those r eigenvectors that have reasonable lengths. The vectors $\{\sigma_1, \sigma_2, \ldots, \sigma_r\}$ point along these important principal axes. For all practical purposes, the Cot-trell/Munro/Zipser feature vectors are equivalent to some of these eigenvectors (the number obviously depends on the size of the hidden layer used — several different sizes should be tried). Note that, for all Cottrell/Munro/Zipser sys-tems, only the output signals of the smallest hidden layer need to be transmitted. However, as with the development of all Cottrell/Munro/Zipser compression systems, the performance of the network must be optimized for use with trans-mitted output signals coded with the smallest number of total bits possible. The need to deal with these numerical accuracy issues complicates the design process.

Cottrell/Munro/Zipser networks with multiple hidden layers effectively fit more complicated geometrical forms (more complicated than ellipsoids) to the "data cloud." Thus, such networks have capabilities that exceed those of prin-cipal component analysis. This can be important when the data being analyzed does not have the approximate form of an elliptical cloud. Such data sets are common, and for these the multi-layer Cottrell/Munro/Zipser technique works much better than principal component analysis. Again, as in all applications of this technique, it is crucial to try many different network configurations.

In conclusion, the Cottrell/Munro/Zipser image compression system pro-vides us with a general–purpose technique that can be used in a variety of situations to compress vectors that contain significantly less information than data. The experiments of Cottrell, Munro, and Zipser also illustrate the central role of the clever use of neural networks in neurocomputing applications.

COUNTERPROPAGATION VECTOR QUANTIZER   The first data compression system we will discuss is based on a prototype mapping network. This system, which I developed in early 1987 [108], is shown in Figure 9.3. Similar systems were developed at other places at about the same time. The system is based upon the concept of *vector quantization*[?, ?]. A vector $\mathbf{x}$, consisting of components with essentially analog values (for example, pixel grey-scale intensity values), is to be transmitted to a remote location. The space of all $\mathbf{x}$ vectors has been divided into 2^N equiprobable disjoint subsets by use of a counterpropagation network (employing conscience learning) with 2^N Kohonen units (see Sections 3.4 and 5.5). Each equiprobable subset ($\mathbf{w}_i$ weight vector win region) is indexed by a unique number i lying between 0 and $2^N - 1$. In other words, each Kohonen layer weight vector is assigned an N-bit binary vector tag equal to the index of its processing element on the Kohonen layer, minus one.

Let us assume that subset i contains the vector $\mathbf{x}$ to be transmitted. Instead of transmitting $\mathbf{x}$, we simply send the number i across our information channel. Clearly, this requires N bits of information (the N bit number described above). On the receiving end, the decoder has a table of weight vectors $\mathbf{w}_0, \mathbf{w}_1, \ldots, \mathbf{w}_{2^N-1}$, each defining its respective equiprobable subset. The decoder then emits the vector w_i as a substitute for the original vector x. Thus, the error made by the system is the distance between the vector x and the subset representation vector w_i.

Vector quantizer bandwidth compression systems have a number of good characteristics. First, the subsets are equiprobable and are thus adjusted to the statistics of the x vectors. This fact makes the transmitted codewords equiprobable, which is a property of any good code. Second, they can be applied to virtually any type of data that is analog in character. Digital data such as character strings cannot be transmitted using this system because small changes in the numerical value of a character lead to enormous changes in meaning. Third, vector quantizer systems tend to degrade gracefully as the number N is reduced. This offers the possibility of building systems with high compression ratios in situations where transmission fidelity can be sacrificed.

Traditional vector quantizers typically utilize algorithms for dividing the space into rectangular blocks with faces oriented along the coordinate planes of the x space. These algorithms do a fairly good job, but the anisotropy of rectangles in high-dimensional spaces makes such regions undesirable (see Section 2.4). For example, if the w_i vector associated with such a rectangular subset is chosen to be the subset's center, then the distance from this point to another point within the subset can range from a small value (for a point near a face of the hyper-rectangle) to very high value (for a point near a vertex of the hyper-rectangle). This geometric nonuniformity makes such rectangular regions less than desirable. However, the ease of deciding which subset a point x lies in is increased significantly by use of rectangular subsets. In fact, with most of the schemes used, the number of the subset to which a point x belongs can be determined by evaluating n simple inequalities, where n is the number of components in the x vectors. As indicated above, neural network techniques for choosing the w_i vectors typically involve use of the counterpropagation network with the conscience mechanism (see Section 3.4).

Although no careful comparison between classical and neural network vector quantizers has yet been carried out, in general, the neural network based systems seem to perform somewhat better (where both have the same number of bits in their transmitted code words).

Hierarchical vector quantizers are multistage data compression systems in which each subsequent stage of the quantizer attempts to correct the errors made by the previous stage. In other words, the second stage of the system reconstructs a vector v_j that is an approximation of $x - w_i$. The third stage of the system will reconstruct a vector u_k that is approximately equal to $x - w_i - v_j$, and so on. Notice that, since each of the sub-codewords of such a hierarchical vector quantizer is independent of the others, considerable combinatorial power is achieved.

In conclusion, prototype mapping networks can be used to implement data compression schemes for analog vector data. Such vector quantizer systems have been successfully used to compress both image and speech data (where the

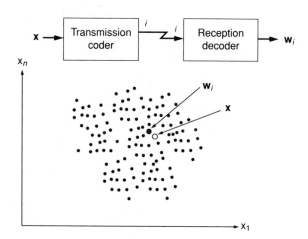

Fig. 9.3. • A counterpropagation-network-based codec for bandwidth compression of analog vector data. The counterpropagation network develops a set of equiprobable weight vectors whose indices then become the code words for the data vectors to be transmitted. This scheme will work only with analog vector data for which a small error in the components will not be a crucial error. The technique has been applied to imagery and to signal data such as coded speech (that is, LPC coded speech).

speech data was coded as LPC vectors [182]). Neural network vector quantizers tend to be easy to develop, do not require much detailed technical knowledge of vector quantization, and seem to exhibit performance comparable to that of classical vector quantization approaches (although relative performance has not yet been carefully quantified).

LOGON IMAGE CODEC   The second approach to compression problems originated with the ideas expressed by Dennis Gabor (who later won the Nobel prize in physics for his 1948 invention of holography) in a 1946 paper with the bold title "Theory of Communication" [79]. In this paper, Gabor proposed a new method for analyzing arbitrary signals: a type of local-in-time frequency analysis. The primary message of Gabor's paper was that the optimal set of basis functions for analyzing signals consists of sinusoidal functions of time multiplied by a Gaussian function of time. The sinusoidal portion of this signal introduces a "waviness," whereas the Gaussian portion of the signal localizes it primarily to a region in time surrounding the time corresponding to the "mean" of the Gaussian. Gabor showed that, for a signal of finite duration, the use of such basis functions minimizes our *joint uncertainty* regarding the product of the effective time duration of the signal times its effective bandwidth. No other set of basis functions has this property. Such Gaussian-weighted sinusoids were dubbed *logon*s (logon is pronounced *low-gone*) by Gabor.

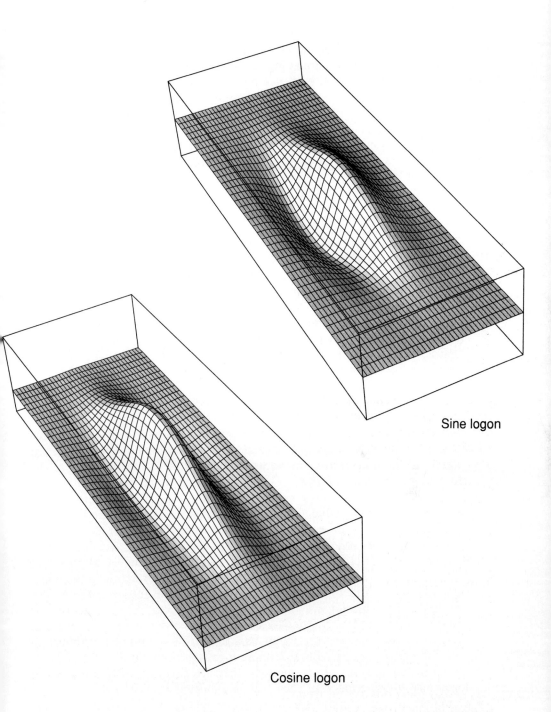

Sine logon

Cosine logon

Fig. 9.4. ● Daugman logon wavelets. Families of these localized spatial frequency functions form a 2-dimensional nonorthogonal basis for general 2-dimensional functions such as images.

In 1980, John Daugman, stimulated by neurophysiological evidence, developed a 2-dimensional version of Gabor's logons [45, 46, 47, 49]. Daugman's development of these 2-dimensional logons represents a classic example of where definitive neurophysiological evidence has been used to develop a neural network with practical utility. One of the hopes of neurocomputing is that such "technology transfers" will continue and accelerate as neuroscience progresses. Typical 2-dimensional logons are shown in Figure 9.4. They are constructed by multiplying a sinusoidal grating function (a washboard surface) times a 2-dimensional Gaussian function. Daugman decided to develop a set of universal 2-dimensional logons that could then be used to analyze arbitrary images. This universal set of 2-dimensional logons has the following characteristics:

- The Gaussians used to define the logons all have a fixed ratio of major axes to minor axes (a ratio of 8:5 is typical).
- Only a small number of discrete major axis lengths are used (typically 5 to 6, with each successively larger set of Gaussians having a major axis length that is twice the major axis length of the next smallest set of Gaussians).
- The sinusoidal grating upon which each logon is built is oriented with its direction of oscillation perpendicular to the major axis of the Gaussian (that is, the projection of the grating onto the minor axis of the Gaussian is a sinusoid, and is constant along the major axis — see Figure 9.4).
- The sinusoidal grating of each logon completes a fixed number of oscillatory cycles (typically 1.5) between the 1 σ points of the minor axis of its Gaussian.
- Two types of logons are used: sine logons and cosine logons. Sine logons have their gratings organized so that the value of the sinusoidal grating (which is biased upward by an additive constant of 1, and therefore ranges from 0 to 2 instead of from -1 to 1) is assumed to have a value of 1 along the major axis of the Gaussian. Cosine logons have their gratings organized so that the value along the major axis is 2 (that is, sine logons are odd functions of the perpendicular distance from their major axis, whereas cosine logons are even functions).
- The logons are oriented at a fixed number of azimuth angles, as measured by the angle between their major axis and some fixed direction on the image plane (typically 3 to 6 different angles, distributed evenly over 0° to 360° are used). For sine logons, the angles are measured from the major axis direction that lies 90° counterclockwise from the direction of increase of the grating as it crosses the major axis. Figure 9.4 contains examples of sine and cosine logons. (Because these logons are self-similar, that is, they are all scaled versions of one another, they are also *wavelets* [153].) A sine logon and a cosine logon of each scale are located at each angle.
- Complete sets of logons (sine and cosine logons of all orientations and scales) are located at regularly spaced points in the image (typically, a rectangular grid of points on 16×16 pixel centers is used).

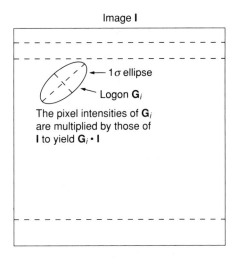

Fig. 9.5. • Dot product of a logon G_i and an image I. The logon is represented as another image — with one amplitude value per pixel. The dot product is the sum of the pixel-by-pixel products of the logon and the image. All of the logon pixels with other than small grey-scale values are located within the one standard deviation (1σ) Gaussian ellipsoid of the logon, which determines the size, aspect ratio, and orientation of the logon.

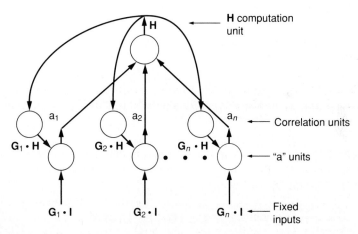

Fig. 9.6. • Daugman's logon coefficient determination neural network. This network uses Widrow learning to quickly determine the logon expansion coefficients for an arbitrary image. The logon set used does not have to be complete.

In mathematical terms, our initial goal is to approximate the image I by means of a linear sum of the logons $\{G_1, G_2, \ldots, G_N\}$ of the above set (the logons and the image I are both treated here as rasterized image vectors). In other words, we would like to find coefficients a_i such that

$$\mathbf{I} \equiv \sum_{i=1}^{N} a_i \mathbf{G}_i. \tag{9.1}$$

Since it will not always be possible to reproduce the image $\mathbf{I}$ exactly as a linear combination of logons, a more realistic goal is to minimize the mean squared error F measured across all n pixels of the image $\mathbf{I}$, where

$$
\begin{aligned}
F(\mathbf{a}) &\equiv \tfrac{1}{n}|\mathbf{I} - \sum_{i=1}^{N} a_i \mathbf{G}_i|^2 \\
&= \tfrac{1}{n}\left[\mathbf{I}^2 - 2\sum_{i=1}^{N} a_i(\mathbf{G}_i \cdot \mathbf{I}) + \left(\sum_{i=1}^{N} a_i \mathbf{G}_i\right) \cdot \left(\sum_{j=1}^{N} a_j \mathbf{G}_j\right)\right] \\
&= \tfrac{1}{n}\left[\mathbf{I}^2 - 2\sum_{i=1}^{N} a_i(\mathbf{G}_i \cdot \mathbf{I}) + \sum_{i=1}^{N}\sum_{j=1}^{N} a_i a_j(\mathbf{G}_i \cdot \mathbf{G}_j)\right],
\end{aligned} \tag{9.2}
$$

and where the dot product of a logon $\mathbf{G}_i$ and an image $\mathbf{I}$ is obtained by means of the operation illustrated in Figure 9.5. The process of calculating the dot product of two logons is identical, since both are image vectors. To minimize the mean squared error, we merely take the gradient of F with respect to the weight vector $\mathbf{a}$. This yields

$$
\begin{aligned}
\nabla F &= -\tfrac{2}{n}\left[\sum_{i=1}^{N}(\mathbf{G}_i \cdot \mathbf{I})\sigma_i - \sum_{i=1}^{N}\left(\sum_{j=1}^{N} a_j \mathbf{G}_j\right) \cdot \mathbf{G}_i \sigma_i\right] \\
&= -\tfrac{2}{n}\sum_{i=1}^{N}\left[\mathbf{G}_i \cdot \mathbf{I} - \left(\sum_{j=1}^{N} a_j \mathbf{G}_j\right) \cdot \mathbf{G}_i\right] \sigma_i,
\end{aligned} \tag{9.3}
$$

where $\{\sigma_1, \sigma_2, \ldots, \sigma_N\}$ is an orthonormal basis for $\mathbf{a}$ space. Thus, if we wish to decrease the mean squared error, all we need to do is move the weight vector $\mathbf{a}$ by a small amount in the direction of $-\nabla F$. Thus, a reasonable learning law for weight a_i is given by

$$a_i^{\text{new}} = a_i^{\text{old}} + \alpha\ (\mathbf{G}_i \cdot \mathbf{I} - \mathbf{G}_i \cdot \mathbf{H}), \tag{9.4}$$

where $\alpha > 0$ is the learning rate constant, and where

$$\mathbf{H} = \sum_{j=1}^{N} a_j^{\text{old}} \mathbf{G}_j \tag{9.5}$$

is the logon approximation to the image $\mathbf{I}$ produced using the weight vector $\mathbf{a}$ produced during the previous weight update. Extensive experimentation with Daugman's logon coefficient determination network has shown that this network usually rapidly converges to a good set of weights.

Assuming that the human visual system employs feature detectors similar to those of other mammals (which have been at least tentatively shown to utilize features similar to logons [190, 164]), then this would imply that we view the world via logon features. In other words, when an image is entered into our visual system, the first few steps of processing are presumably analogous to a logon correlation operation. This operation would be carried out simultaneously across the entire visual field using logons of various orientations and scales (crudely like those described by the above specification, which is based roughly on the parameters of the cat visual system[49]). Whatever subsequent processing takes place is then based upon the outputs of these logon correlation operations. Thus, in some sense, when we look at an image, perhaps all we can see is the logon structure inherent in the image. Given these (presumed) facts, we could then suppose that the most efficient way to render an image for human viewing would be to present it as a combination of logons, since these features feed the human visual system directly, and would therefore be expected to provide the most well-matched representation of the image data. Subjective image quality experiments using logon feature approximations to images suggest that this presumption is operationally useful (even though the detailed neurophysiological processing upon which it is based is not yet understood).

Given these facts, it is clear that an image compression system can be built by using Daugman's network to express the image to be transmitted as the sum of logons. The weight vector **a** can then be coded, transmitted, and used on the receiving end to construct an approximation **H** to the original image **I**. This scheme works well. Daugman has demonstrated almost perfect image reconstruction at a data compression ratio of 3 (on 8-bit grey scale panchromatic images). Compression ratios of up to 8 have been achieved with only minor subjective image degradation [44, 45, 46, 47, 48]. These results were obtained using the original version of the system, as characterized by the above logon set specification. A number of areas of possible improvement for this scheme have been identified (such as locating the logons at less regular positions within the image, decreasing the number of scales used, and vector quantizing or otherwise coding the **a** vectors), and these are expected to yield further improvements in performance. Notice that Daugman's scheme exploits linear superposition, but does not involve orthogonal functions.

In summary, Daugman's 2-dimensional logon image representation scheme is an interesting image compression approach. Its presumed compatibility with the human visual system makes it a natural choice for use in image compression and in other applications such as texture classification.

In the next subsection, we will discuss an application of neural networks to the problem of noise removal from time-series signals.

9.2.3 Noise Removal from Time-Series Signals

The problem of removing unwanted noise from a time-series signal was first addressed over 100 years ago in connection with early telephone systems. The subsequent decades have seen the development of a theory of noise filtering

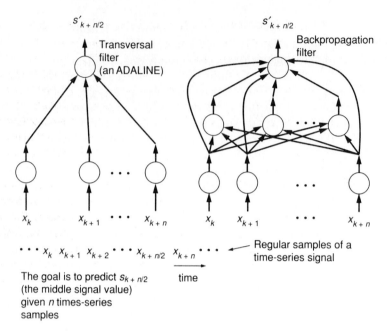

Fig. 9.7. • Noise removal scheme for time series signals. This network is trained to carry out a function that cannot be satisfactorily implemented with ordinary linear signal processing — namely, the removal of strong wideband noise from a *structured* signal.

based upon linear system concepts. By the mid-1970s, linear signal process-ing had advanced to the point where essentially any bandpass filtering function could be implemented in a digital system in which samples of the time series obtained at regular time intervals would be filtered to remove narrowband or out-of-signal-band noise. Comprehensive textbooks describing these and other developments in linear signal processing theory were written in this epoch [185]. At the current time, linear concepts continue to dominate all aspects of signal processing theory and practice. However, the limitations of these linear ap-proaches (which also tend to not be formally compatible with a local in-time signal analysis point of view) are now becoming more apparent. In this sub-section, we will examine a particular signal processing function — namely, the removal of undesirable additive wideband noise from a desired signal.

The situation with which we are concerned is illustrated in Figure 9.7. Reg-ular samples $x_1, x_2, \ldots$ of a time-series signal $x(t)$ are obtained using an analog-to-digital converter. Each of these samples is of the form

$$x_k = s_k + n_k, \tag{9.6}$$

where s_k is the desired signal value, and n_k is added noise or an interfering signal. After some preliminary discussion, we will be interested mostly in the case where n_k is a noise signal that is assumed to be white (that is, its value is uncorrelated between samples and its long-term power spectrum is flat).

What we would like to build is a device that could take samples x_k, x_{k+1}, x_{k+2}..., $x_{k+n/2}$..., x_{k+n} of the time series and produce an estimate of $s_{k+n/2}$ (the value of the uncontaminated signal component of the middle sample of this set of $n + 1$ samples). A traditional linear signal processing approach to the solution of this problem is the non-causal *transversal filter* structure shown on the the left in Figure 9.7. This transversal filter structure (which is just an ADALINE) simply multiplies each of the $n + 1$ time-sample inputs by its respective weight and then adds together the result (along with a bias weight). The output of the filter is the estimate $s'_{k+n/2}$ of $s_{k+n/2}$. Typically, such a filter is trained using characteristic noise-contaminated or interference-contaminated samples for which the correct uncontaminated signal values are known. Thus, during training, the desired output of the ADALINE is known for each set of input samples. As demonstrated by linear signal processing theory [236, 185] this simple transversal filter structure can learn essentially any bandpass filtering function. In other words, to within the frequency resolution corresponding to the number of input samples (also known as the number of "taps"), this structure can be arranged to amplify or attenuate each of the frequency components of the incoming time-series samples by any necessary factor to achieve optimum noise removal.

Given our Fourier way of thinking, the transversal filter would seem to be ideal for noise removal. For example, in the case where the desired signal and the noise do not overlap in frequency (as in the case of human speech signals contaminated with 60 Hz power line hum), the adaptive transversal filter will do an essentially perfect job of eliminating the noise. However, when the signal and noise do overlap significantly in frequency, the process of filtering out the noise will also tend to filter out the signal, thus degrading performance significantly.

In order to achieve better noise–filtering performance than that of a transversal filter, we must specialize our problem somewhat, so we will only consider $\{s_k\}$ signals that are *structured* (in other words, that have a waveform shape that is always qualitatively about the same — like the set of all human EKG signals). Given this situation, the neural network shown on the right side of Figure 9.7 might be able to provide additional noise filtration. Basically, this filter structure is simply a backpropagation network with the same inputs and output as the transversal filter, but with 1 hidden layer added (or more than 1 hidden layer — we will look at only the case of 1 hidden layer here). In this backpropagation network, the connections between the input units and the output unit are retained. The properties of this network are now described.

Clearly, this backpropagation network is a direct generalization of the transversal filter structure (see Exercise 9.2.5). In fact, if all of the output unit weights associated with inputs from the hidden layer are set to 0, then we obtain the exact form of the transversal filter. Thus, if it is optimum to do so, the backpropagation network filter structure can revert to the transversal filter structure by simply setting all of the hidden layer weights to 0. The question is, can this backpropagation network carry out noise filtering more effectively than the transversal filter structure can by using some non-zero hidden layer weights? As we shall see, the answer seems to be yes.

The first thing to note about the backpropagation filter is that it departs radically from linear signal processing theory. Because of the presence of sigmoid nonlinearities in the hidden layer units of the backpropagation filter, the mathematical form of the output signal from the processing element in the top layer of the network will have a nonlinear response to input signals. For example, if we simply multiply each of the input samples by 2.0, the output of the network will not be twice its former value (which would be the case with a transversal filter). This observation points up the need to carefully control the average power level (averaged over a time equal to a small number of network time window widths) of the input signal $x(t)$ being sampled.

Clearly, we cannot analyze the behavior of this filter simply by taking the input signal and expanding it in some sort of function series and then concern ourselves with the form of the resulting series at the output of the network. All of this machinery is now useless, since the nonlinearities of the backpropagation neural network destroy the principle of linear superposition. In fact, none of the theoretical tools available today is capable of analyzing the behavior of this filter structure. The development of such tools and such analyses is a major challenge. Thus, we have to depend upon the results of empirical experiments at least for now (perhaps forever).

To determine whether the backpropagation filter structure has more to offer than the transversal structure, we compare their performance on the same signals. A typical experiment is to train both filters on the same noise contaminated structured signals and then evaluate both filters using novel signals of the same structural type. A typical experiment would involve the use of an EKG (heartbeat) signal gathered from a human or other species admixed with white noise (random noise that has a constant power level at all frequencies and is uncorrelated across samples). Preliminary experiments with signals of this type have indicated that the backpropagation filter structure can remove more noise from the original source signal than the transversal filter structure can. If we divide the desired signal component of the network output by that portion of the output which is *not* the desired signal, this ratio is between 2 and 10 times larger for the backpropagation filter than for the transversal filter — a significant improvement. However, the experiments upon which these numbers are based are preliminary. They are not sufficient to unequivocally and definitively establish the relative performance of these filters.

In principle, there is no reason why we have to stop at one hidden layer in the construction of backpropagation network filter structures. We might just as well use multiple hidden layers (where, again, the input signals are connected directly to the output unit to guarantee that the network is a direct generalization of the transversal filter structure). There is some evidence that backpropagation networks with more than one hidden layer might offer even greater performance for certain types of signals and certain types of noise or interference. One

hypothesis that has been raised regarding the manner in which a backpropagation filter structure can exceed the performance of a transversal filter structure has to do with the idea of *waveform recognition*. As discussed above, the
transversal filter structure is a simple bandpass filtering device. Its linear nature prevents any internal "decision making" based upon the values of the input
time series in different channels (other than the formation of a simple weighted
sum). However, in the backpropagation filter, the hidden layer(s), working in
conjunction with the output layer, can implement a variety of conditional processing operations. In fact (as shown in Section 5.3), in principle, this network
can implement *any* data-dependent decision making process (because every such
process can be expressed as a function of the input variables). Naturally, many
such operations might require more than one hidden layer to implement them
efficiently. Nonetheless, the range of possibilities is enormous. The idea behind
waveform recognition is that some of the typical characteristics of the waveform
might be recognizable even in the face of significant noise contamination. The
network can use these features (such as a spike in an EKG signal, or the lull
between spikes in such a signal) to guess the general form of the signal. This
guess (coded as a hidden layer unit output) can then be used by the output unit
(or by subsequent hidden layer units) to build a better guess as to the correct
signal value. In summary, in a manner that is not yet even dimly understood,
this filter is able to carry out excellent wideband noise removal for structured
signals belonging to the class on which the network was trained (for example,
the class of white noise contaminated EKG signals). Such filters might be called
super transversal, because they subsume the transversal filters.

Given their practical potential, these new backpropagation filtering structures (which were apparently first developed at HNC, Inc., in 1987) are worthy
of extensive theoretical and experimental investigation. Even if a general theory of operation cannot be developed for these networks (because of the loss of
linear superposition and the lack of eigenfunctions), perhaps a general qualitative understanding of their effect on signals can be gained. Whatever the future
holds, there seems to be little doubt that the consideration of such nonlinear signal processing structures will have an enormous impact on the subject of signal
processing, which has been stuck in the linear systems rut for over 40 years.

Exercises

9.2.1. Explain how, in Figure 9.1, the vector **x** might be slightly different if
the exact same numeral were written at different position and/or scales
on the digitizer tablet.

9.2.2. Derive Equation 9.3 from Equation 9.2.

9.2.3. Show that the eigenvectors $\{\sigma_1, \sigma_2, \ldots, \sigma_n\}$ of the covariance matrix $R = \frac{1}{N} \sum_{k=1}^{N} (\mathbf{x}_k - \bar{\mathbf{x}})(\mathbf{x}_k - \bar{\mathbf{x}})^{\mathsf{T}}$ are orthogonal.

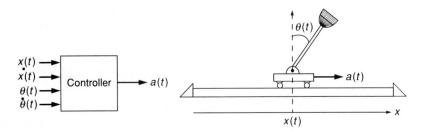

Fig. 9.8. • A cart and broomstick system and system controller. The goal is to build a controller that will keep the broomstick close to vertical and keep the cart close to the center of the track.

9.2.4. Show that the error $|\mathbf{x} - \tilde{\mathbf{x}}|$ introduced by the substitution

$$\tilde{\mathbf{x}} = \sum_{i=1}^{r} (\sigma_i \cdot \mathbf{x}) \ \sigma_i$$

(where the reduced set of unit eigenvectors $\{\sigma_1, \sigma_2, \ldots, \sigma_r\}$ contains those eigenvectors associated with the "large" eigenvalues, ordered in terms of decreasing eigenvalue magnitude) will be small. Explain why this works. Also, suggest a criterion for defining "large."

9.2.5. Show that the backpropagation network of Figure 9.7, with inputs connected to outputs, is a direct generalization of the transversal filter structure of classical linear signal processing.

9.3 Control

Like sensor processing, control seems to be a promising area for neurocomputing applications. This section presents two examples of the application of neurocomputing to control. As is typical of almost all real-world control applications completed to date, both of these examples utilize supervised training. In the future, it is likely that most control applications of neurocomputing will involve a combination of supervised training and reinforcement training. Unfortunately, the development of neural networks that utilize reinforcement training is currently in its infancy. The few networks of this type that exist have not yet been characterized sufficiently well for easy use in practical applications [22].

9.3.1 Vision-Based Broomstick Balancer

Most university control laboratories have a collection of systems that can be used to test new control concepts as well as demonstrate existing concepts. One of the most common of these systems is a *broomstick balancer*. A typical (1-dimensional) system of this type is shown in Figure 9.8. It consists of a cart constrained to roll left or right along a track of finite length. A broomstick is attached to a pivot on top of the cart such that the broomstick can only swing in a vertical plane parallel to the track. At time t, the center of the cart is at a displacement $x(t)$ as measured from the center of the track (where $x = 0$). The broomstick makes an angle $\theta(t)$ at time t, measured clockwise from vertical. Also, an acceleration $a(t)$ operates on the cart, with positive acceleration to the right.

As shown in Figure 9.8, a neural network controller is given the four inputs $x(t), \dot{x}(t), \theta(t), \dot{\theta}(t)$ and is expected to produce the acceleration command $a(t)$ as an output. The design goal is to build a controller that can accelerate the cart left and right so as to keep the broomstick always close to vertical and keep the cart close to the center of the track.

The first neural network broomstick balancer control system was developed by Bernard Widrow in 1962 [220]. This controller was a single ADALINE that was trained with operational control examples supplied by a classical closed loop proportional controller that could do a fair job of keeping the broomstick balanced. As an aside, any controller that can maneuver the cart to keep the broomstick upright can be modified also to keep the cart near the center of the track. The trick is to introduce a small false bias into the θ value that is supplied to the controller. This bias is linearly dependent upon x. It has the effect of making the controller think that the broomstick is tilted slightly toward the center of the track, thus causing the controller to attempt to restore it to vertical. However, the only way that it can accomplish this is by moving the cart farther toward the center of the track than would be necessary simply to balance the broomstick. Such a correction system will cause the cart position to tend toward the center of the track.

Widrow's original broomstick balancer did not prove much since it was trained by an existing automatic control system that could already balance the broomstick fairly well. In fact, construction of an excellent broomstick control system by classical control theory methods is fairly simple.

Twenty-five years after developing his original neural network broomstick balancer, Widrow and his student Viral Tolat devised an improved neural network broomstick balancer control system that added an important new idea to the repertoire of neurocomputing application approaches.

The basic idea of the new Widrow system is to eliminate the x and θ sensors on the cart and broomstick, and to have a human balance the broomstick visually to provide training examples for the network. The input to the network consists of selected rows and columns of two binary images of the broomstick — a current image and one that is 100 ms old. These images, one of which is illustrated in Figure 9.9, are produced by painting the shaft of the broomstick a bright fluorescent color and then filtering the input to a television camera to admit only light at this wavelength. As can be seen in Figure 9.9, the top, middle, and bottom rows of the image, as well as the leftmost and rightmost vertical columns, are supplied to the neural network. The filtered image is thresholded to produce a binary image in which each row and column has at most 1 pixel equal to 1, and all of the other pixels equal to 0. Notice that the location of

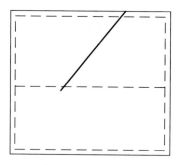

Fig. 9.9. • Image of broomstick showing as dashed lines the rows and columns of the image supplied to the controller network (the network gets the current image and the image from about 100ms ago). This binary image is derived from a camera that is monitoring the cart and broomstick system. Only three rows and two columns of the image are sent to the neural network. These binary vectors each have at most one 1 in them. Whenever the broomstick is approximately straight up and down, it will cross the top row of the image, and its position will be noted by a 1 at the point where it crosses this row. The middle row always has a single 1 in it, indicating the position of the middle of the cart. The two columns at the sides of the image, and the row at the bottom of the image, are normally filled with all 0s, except when the broomstick is either approximately horizontal or hanging down; in which cases the broomstick position will be indicated by a single 1 at the position where the broomstick cuts the row or column.

the pivot point of the broomstick (that is, the position of the cart) is always indicated by the active pixel of the middle row. Similarly, the angle of the broomstick can normally be inferred from the position of the active pixel on the top row compared to that of the active pixel on the middle row. By supplying two images 100 ms apart, the neural network can derive any necessary dynamical information (such as approximations to the time derivatives of x and θ) that it may need. Notice that the leftmost and rightmost columns and the bottom row will not be used unless the broomstick falls over. In the improved version of Widrow's system used in Figure 9.9, the broomstick was mounted at the side of the cart and could swing through the entire 360-degree arc (that is, there is a cliff next to the edge of the track so that the broomstick can hang down below the track). Thus, the only time an active pixel occurs in the leftmost column, rightmost column, or bottom row is when balance of the broomstick has been lost (or not yet achieved).

One of the realities of broomstick balancers is that humans are unable to balance a real broomstick when it is attached to a cart. However, virtually all humans *believe* they *can* balance such a broomstick, even if they have witnessed a succession of other people trying and failing. The sight of a normally rational person making the statement, "Get out of the way; I can do it", after just witnessing four of their co-workers utterly fail to balance the broomstick is quite amusing. We built a full-size broomstick and cart system at HNC and attempted — unsuccessfully — to find someone who could keep it balanced.

Given that a human cannot balance a broomstick on a cart, how can we train a neural network to do so? The answer lies in building a mathematical simulation of the cart, broomstick, and camera system, and then running this simulation in slow motion to train the network. If time is slowed down by a factor of 10 to 100, then humans can easily and accurately balance the broomstick and keep the cart near the center of the track. During such a training run, the accelerations commanded by the human controller are supplied to the neural network as the "desired" output. Given a sufficient period of training (approximately 2 hours at $1/30^{th}$ real time), the network can learn to do a good job of emulating the human operator (I have personally done this experiment). Although I have never personally seen it in action, I am told that a neural network controller can even be taught to erect the broomstick starting with the cart stationary at the center of the track and the broomstick hanging straight down. The technique involves oscillating the cart left and right in phase with the resulting oscillations of the broomstick until finally the cart can be placed underneath the broomstick and normal balancing operation can begin. Given the relative ease with which such a neural network broomstick balancer can be built, it makes a good beginning application for technologists, mathematicians, and scientists interested in applying neurocomputing concepts to control problems.

The modern Widrow broomstick balancing neural network offers several important lessons for control applications of neurocomputing technology. One of these lessons is that, by slowing down time (via a mathematical model of the system to be controlled), a human trainer can often successfully control a system that they might not be able to control if forced to operate in real time. This idea might provide a method for developing neural network training material for systems that might otherwise be uncontrollable using existing control technology. Another lesson of this broomstick balancer is that neural networks can often derive whatever sensor data they need from bulk sources such as imagery. This ability can serve to cut cost and system complexity. Beyond this broomstick balancer, Widrow and his students have explored other control applications, including a truck backer-upper recurrent backpropagation network [177] that is trained via supervised learning based on the position and orientation errors of the truck as it contacts the loading dock.

9.3.2 Automobile Autopilot

A little more than 30 years ago, there was a weekly television broadcast entitled "Science Fiction Theater," which I used to watch religiously. One episode of this series featured an automobile that could drive itself. At the time, I wondered whether such systems would become commonplace in my lifetime. One interesting step in this direction is the control system described below.

The automobile autopilot described in this subsection was developed by John Shepanski and S. Macy in 1987 [208]. Like the image-based broomstick balancer, this control system is trained by a human driver. To make the problem tractable, Shepanski and Macy restricted the driving environment to a two-lane

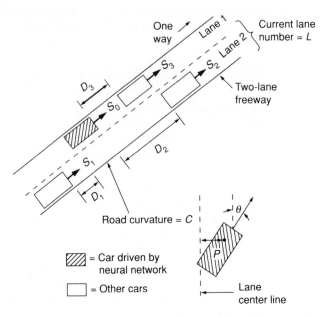

Fig. 9.10. • Automobile autopilot problem definition. This diagram defines the parameters used to describe the position and velocity of the neural network car relative to other cars and relative to the one-way, two-lane roadbed.

freeway roadbed upon which all traffic is moving in the same direction. To make the training and testing process easier, they assumed that each side of the road is equipped with a wide shoulder upon which the car can be driven. This situation is illustrated in Figure 9.10. The neural network driven car can drive in either lane 1 or lane 2 of the freeway. Other cars also drive on the same freeway at various speeds and perform various maneuvers. The other cars are controlled by rational drivers that do not unexpectedly endanger the neural network car or one another. In fact, these cars travel in a preprogrammed manner; therefore, they cannot maneuver out of the way if the neural network car threatens them. Although this lack of response might seem to simplify the problem somewhat, this is not really so, since the occurrence of successful collision avoidance maneuvers is not very common in the real world (most of the time, the car being threatened does not realize it is in danger in time to take effective evasive action). Although the other cars on the road are not able to maneuver to avoid collisions, they are set up so that they will not rear-end the neural network driven car. Thus, the neural network driven car does not have to pay attention to cars behind it in its lane.

A number of variables are associated with this automobile autopilot problem. These are:

- D_1 = distance from the rear bumper of the neural network driven car to the front bumper of the nearest car in the other lane that is next to or behind the neural network driven car.
- D_2 = the distance from front bumper of the neural network driven car to the rear bumper of the nearest car in the other lane that lies ahead of the neural network driven car.
- D_3 = the distance from the front bumper of the neural network driven car to the rear bumper of the nearest car ahead of it in the same lane.
- S_0 = the forward speed of the neural network driven car.
- S_1 = the forward speed of the nearest car in the other lane next to or behind the neural network driven car.
- S_2 = the speed of the nearest car in the other lane ahead of the neural network driven car.
- S_3 = the speed of the nearest car in the same lane ahead of the neural network driven car.
- θ = the angle between the neural network driven car's longitudinal axis and the direction of the center line of the lane in which the neural network driven car is currently driving.
- P = the lateral displacement to the right of the center of the neural network driven car from the center line of the lane the car is in.
- L = the number of the lane (1 or 2) that the neural network car is in.
- C = the road curvature at the point where the neural network driven car is currently located (this value will be 0 for a straight road and will increase to 1 or decrease to -1 for a highly curved road segment).

The overall roadway system is simulated on a color graphics computer and an aerial view of the roadbed and the cars on it is provided to the training driver and to observers. During training, the training driver simply drives the car in accordance with his or her normal driving style. The car is equipped with a speed control, a lane change control, and a steering wheel control. The speed control (which incorporates the functions of both accelerator and brake) is used to maintain adequate separation from the car ahead, to accelerate for passing, and to decelerate after a lane change to avoid a rear-end collision with the car ahead. The lane change command is unusual in that it does not correspond to anything familiar in an ordinary automobile. The idea here is that changing lanes (either from lane 1 to lane 2 or vice versa) can be accomplished as a "canned" maneuver that can be preprogrammed and used whenever it is needed. Using the lane change command will cause the car to move into the other lane, but may not put it in a perfectly centered and stable position in that lane. The steering function takes care of these small misalignments and any other misalignments that might occur during driving.

As the training driver drives the neural network driven car, the two back-propagation networks shown in Figure 9.11 are both trained simultaneously. The top network in Figure 9.11 is responsible for controlling the speed of the

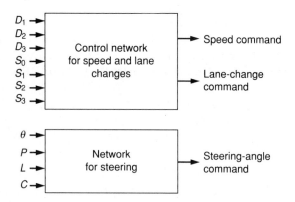

Fig. 9.11. • Automobile autopilot neural networks. One network is responsible for adjusting the speed of the car and for deciding when to change lanes. The other network steers the car down the lane it is in.

car and for commanding lane changes. The bottom network is strictly responsible for steering the car within a lane for the period of time during which the car occupies that lane. When the car switches to the other lane, this network brings the car to the center of that lane, and adjusts the steering angle to keep the car going down the center line of its lane.

During the training process, the first step was to train the network shown at the bottom of Figure 9.11. In other words, the car was taught to steer itself in its lane first. Once the performance of this network reached a fairly high level of accuracy, then the training of the top network of Figure 9.11 began. This training was continued until testing showed that the car could reliably drive in arbitrary traffic without experiencing a collision.

One of the interesting things about this automobile autopilot was its slavish adherence to the driving style of the training driver. If the driver training the system was a "road maniac," then this is how the neural network would drive the car. On the other hand, if the training driver was a conservative, careful driver, the neural network system would be also. This ability to adopt the driving habits of the training driver could be useful in a variety of situations where a system is to be customized to the habits of a particular user.

The neural network automobile autopilot developed by Shepanski and Macy does an excellent job of driving. It can apparently negotiate ordinary traffic indefinitely without suffering a collision. It is able to negotiate twists and turns in the road and to pass other cars when appropriate (if the training driver is in the habit of passing other cars). In short, this is a highly successful experimental control system that operates in a complex enough environment that one could believe that the system could be extended to controlling a real automobile driving on a real freeway.

Exercises

9.3.1. During the discussion of the image-based broomstick balancer, it was stated that devising a control algorithm for this system is simple. Derive such an algorithm, and argue in detail why it should work (or demonstrate, using a simulation, that it does work). [Hint: balance a real broomstick and try to figure out the trick you are using — then derive your algorithm from this.]

9.3.2. Produce a conceptual design for an automobile autopilot for actual use on freeways. What sensors would be required? What would be the likely legal status of such a device? [Hint: compare this with a cruise control.]

9.3.3. Develop a conceptual design for a tooth-flossing machine that would be trained by its user(s). Consider both the required sensors and the mechanical design of the machine. How much would your machine sell for? What do you estimate the sales volume potential to be?

9.4 Data Analysis

Of the application areas to which neurocomputing has so far been applied, those in the area of data analysis seem to be among those having the highest potential for a large early pay-off. The term *data analysis* is usually taken to mean the development of a predictive model or other summary representation of a large body of data (typically, but not always, drawn from a computer database). The ultimate goal of data analysis is usually to extract concentrated value from diffuse and intrinsically less valuable raw data.

In this section we consider three different approaches to data analysis that serve to illustrate the diverse neurocomputing techniques that are being applied to data analysis problems. All of the techniques demonstrated in this section have proven to be of value in solving real-world problems.

9.4.1 Loan Application Scoring

Decades ago, it was realized that the process of deciding whether or not to grant a loan to an applicant (be that applicant an individual or a corporation) is an area of finance where humans consistently demonstrate poor judgement. For example, all too often the decision of a loan officer to grant a loan is influenced by factors such as appearance, friendship, personal chemistry, and blood relationship that have no bearing whatsoever on the creditworthiness of the applicant. Essentially, creditworthiness rating has been shown to be a skill at which virtually no human is expert.

The capability of humans to accurately judge creditworthiness is so poor that even simplistic linear-discriminant techniques yielded a step function increase in profit when these techniques were first applied about 35 years ago. Subsequent improvements in technology have included more sophisticated statistical modeling techniques (such as adaptive binning and factor analysis) and

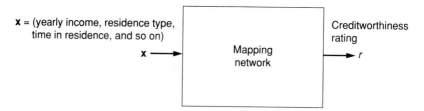

Fig. 9.12. • Loan application scoring neural network. The information presented in the loan application is entered as the input to the network. The network output is a creditworthiness score. Past loans (ones that have been paid back or written off and for which a ground-truth creditworthiness score has been derived) are used as training and testing data.

the use of rules regarding the manner in which the data is to be manipulated and the way in which various statistical tests are to be applied. Decades of technological improvement have yielded creditworthiness tools that can be adapted to almost any credit product for which sufficient relevant statistical data exists. With each of the technological improvements in creditworthiness rating has come a commensurate improvement in profitability. The efficacy of automated creditworthiness evaluation is well understood and appreciated within the financial community. This creates an almost ideal milieu into which advancements offered by neurocomputing technology can be introduced.

The members of the financial community are strict taskmasters. Any proposed improvement to existing creditworthiness systems must offer a significant improvement in profit or ease of use beyond anything currently available, such a system must comply with federal guidelines regarding equal borrowing opportunity, and it must be compatible with the operational structure of the intended user organization. Multiple neural network–based creditworthiness evaluation systems are now in use. If these systems continue to perform as well in an operational setting as they have in early field tests, neurocomputing may quickly become the technology of choice in this application.

Figure 9.12 shows a typical creditworthiness rating or loan application scoring neural network. The vector x (which forms the input to the mapping network that carries out the creditworthiness rating function) is comprised of most of the information on the loan application form (extraneous information, such as the date the application was filled out, is not included in x). As shown in Figure 9.12, the components of x are relevant items such as yearly income, type of residence, length of time lived in current residence, and so on. The output of the mapping network is a creditworthiness rating r. There are many ways to define this rating, but a common choice is to let r be the expected *yield* of the loan (the number of dollars of profit per dollar loaned per year of term). The advantage of the yield is its independence of the amount of the loan and the term of the loan. Unfortunately, many financial institutions operate in such a manner that it is difficult to determine the profit made on a particular loan, so, in practice, other approaches are often used. (Several aspects of the basic system described here can vary from one specific financial institution to another.)

The training of the loan application scoring neural network is carried out using information gathered from past loans that have been completed (either paid back or written off). During training, the application information is coded into the vector **x** and then inserted into the mapping network. The resulting creditworthiness rating "estimate" *r* is then compared to the actual performance on the loan (as determined by the financial records) to yield an error that can then be used for training. Typically, tens of thousands of past loan records are used to train such a network. A similar or larger number of different records are used to test the network before it is put into service.

In summary, loan application scoring is representative of a large class of data analysis applications of neurocomputing (such as bond rating, credit card misuse detection, and so on).

9.4.2 NETtalk

NETtalk was an early demonstration of the capability of the backpropagation neural network. The NETtalk experiment was carried out by Terrence Sejnowski and Charles Rosenberg during the summer of 1985 [206]. Although the initial intention of the experiment was to understand how a neural network could learn to convert English text into English speech, the experiment actually ended up having a far deeper significance.

The basic concept of the NETtalk system is shown in Figure 9.13. NETtalk was based upon the Digital Equipment Corporation DECtalk commercial speech synthesis system. The DECtalk system consists of two elements: a speech synthesis expert system and a sound generator. The expert system (which consists of hundreds of rules painstakingly developed by linguists over decades) converts strings of characters to a sound generation command (essentially a phoneme). The sound generator receives this command and produces the appropriate sound through a loudspeaker. The operation of the DECtalk system is now described.

As shown in Figure 9.13, the text string to be spoken enters the system from the right and moves left one character approximately every 50 ms. The expert system receives seven contiguous characters from this string during each time increment. Its function is to use these seven characters to determine how to pronounce the middle character. In other words, the middle character of the seven character string is what is spoken on each cycle. The three characters on either side of the middle character are simply used as context information to aid in correct pronunciation.

As each character moves through the middle position, it is converted by the expert system into a phoneme sound generation command, which is then executed by the sound generator. Seven letters were chosen because studies have shown that the influence of the fourth and fifth distant letters on the pronunciation of the middle character is statistically small.

To simplify the problem of speech synthesis, the DECtalk system only recognizes 29 valid characters: the 26 alphabetic characters from A to Z, along

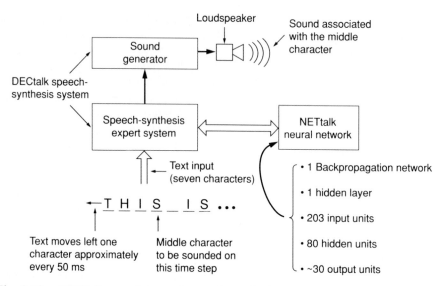

Fig. 9.13. • NETtalk neural network speech synthesizer. The NETtalk backpropagation network is trained by a rule-based expert system element of the DECtalk commercial speech synthesis system. NETtalk is then used to replace that element. The result is a new speech synthesis system that has approximately the same overall performance as the original. In other words, the NETtalk neural network becomes functionally equivalent to an expert system with hundreds of rules. The question then becomes: how are these rules represented within the NETtalk neural network? The answer is: nobody really knows.

with the comma, period, and space (no distinction is made between upper and lower case, and all characters not falling into one of these 29 categories are ignored). The DECtalk expert system contains hundreds of rules and represents a large body of accumulated linguistic knowledge. Among general-purpose speech synthesis systems, DECtalk is considered to be one of the best. Unfortunately, as with all current speech synthesis systems, it speaks English at a fixed cadence (since the character string moves left one character at a fixed interval of approximately 50 ms). Although I personally find DECtalk's speech annoying, it is usually reasonably intelligible.

NETtalk is a neural network that is intended to be a substitute for the DECtalk expert system. In fact, it has exactly the same inputs and outputs as the DECtalk expert system, and it is trained by the DECtalk expert system. The NETtalk network is a backpropagation network having one hidden layer with 80 hidden units. There are 203 inputs to the network (29 for each of the seven characters, which are each entered using a 1-out-of-29 code). The network has approximately 30 output units, which form a 1-out-of-n code for the phoneme sound generation commands.

Sejnowski and Rosenberg trained the NETtalk neural network in stages. At the end of each stage, they connected the network in line as a substitute for the expert system and allowed the sound generator to produce the corresponding sounds. These sounds were then recorded and an audio tape chronicling the process of teaching NETtalk to speak was made. The DECtalk sound generator can be adjusted so that it sounds either like a child or like an adult. To emphasize their point, Sejnowski and Rosenberg selected the child setting. The result is a remarkable audio tape on which the NETtalk network begins by "babbling" and incrementally demonstrates an ever-increasing ability to speak intelligible English. By the end of the training process, the NETtalk network sounds remarkably similar to the DECtalk system (although they are not quite identical).

For the sake of argument, let us claim that, for all practical purposes, the DECtalk expert system and the NETtalk neural network are functionally identical. In other words, if the same seven characters are entered into both subsystems, they will provide exactly the same output (the actual differences that occur in practice are not large enough to alter the following argument). What this assumption implies is that the hundreds of rules in the DECtalk expert system somehow ended up in the NETtalk neural network (they must have, because the two systems are functionally equivalent). The question is: where did the rules go? The simple answer is that nobody really knows (although Rosenberg did learn some things about how the network functions). One can draw some interesting conclusions from this situation.

The first conclusion that can be drawn from NETtalk is that, since the representation of information within the network is in the form of a mathematical transformation, there is no obvious way to reverse the representation formation process and reconstruct a set of high-level rules from the form of this transformation. Given this, it then becomes interesting to ask the question: what if we were forced to decide which of these two representations is probably closer to that used in the human brain — the explicit rule representation scheme of the DECtalk expert system or the implicit rule representation scheme of NETtalk? I suspect that most people would guess the latter. If, in fact, this is a useful analogy, it then brings up the question of the value of neurophysiological knowledge. Might it be that someday neuroscientists will understand the function of each individual neuron in the brain and all of the interactions between these neurons and yet have virtually no knowledge about how information is processed in the brain? Clearly, NETtalk has significant linguistic knowledge embedded within it. It is also clear that we have no in-depth understanding of exactly how all of this knowledge is represented in the network. And yet, we understand the operation of the processing elements of the network and their interactions completely. If, in fact, this analogy does apply to brains, the unraveling of the mysteries of biological information processing may take a lot longer than most people would be willing to guess today, and may require new conceptual and analytical tools that we cannot even dream of yet.

What started out as a demonstration of the gradual accumulation of capability and knowledge by a neural network turned out to be a profoundly important example that helps us better understand the meaning of neurocomputing.

We have discussed the use of neural networks for building predictive models from data and for building expert systems from examples of the application of rules; we will now discuss a technique for building a neural network expert system from knowledge that is implicitly embedded in data.

9.4.3 The Instant Physician

A recent book entitled **The One-Minute Manager** [25] enjoyed considerable success as a result of its encapsulation of basic management principles into a set of terse guidelines. Quick fixes for problems and instantaneous solutions of dilemmas have always been popular in America. In keeping with this theme, the neural network presented in this section performs an instantaneous "one-shot" medical diagnosis and treatment prescription operation for essentially any illness. Although such a neural network might seem to be of questionable value, its performance is surprisingly good and (in other applications) quite adequate for some real-world applications. The Instant Physician[6] was developed by James Anderson (the pioneering associative network researcher and the inventor of the brain state in a box network – see Section 4.4) in 1985 [12, 13].

The basic idea of the Instant Physician is to train a brain state in a box neural network (see Section 4.4) using data obtained directly from medical records (which contain, in an implicit form, substantial knowledge about the practice of medicine). The concept is illustrated in Figure 5.14.

The first step in preparing the Instant Physician is to gather an enormous number of medical records that are statistically representative of the patients who will be treated by the network after training (and who recovered from their illness). For example, it would not be a good idea to train the network on obstetrical case records and then attempt to treat patients with dermatology complaints. Once a large set of appropriate records has been gathered, the next step is to analyze them and create exhaustive lists of symptoms, diagnoses, and treatments. Every symptom seen in any of the records is listed in the list of symptoms. Similarly, every diagnosis and every treatment ever seen in any of the medical records will be listed in those respective lists. Each entry in each list must be posed as a *bipolar question*. In other words, a bipolar question is a question that can be unequivocally answered yes $(+1)$ or no (-1). For each entry in the symptom, diagnosis, and treatment lists, the question to be answered for each new patient is: does this statement apply to this particular patient?

Once these exhaustive lists have been constructed, the next step is to code each medical record as an extremely long vector x (as shown in Figure 9.14). The entries in x are the bipolar answers to the symptom, diagnosis, and treatment

---

[6] "The Instant Physician" is my name for this example. Anderson did not give it a name.

Symptoms	Diagnoses	Treatment
s_1 - headache	d_1 - chronic scumpf	t_1 - asprin
s_2 - temperature 1-2° F high	d_2 - demeaning plebny	t_2 - brain transplant
•	•	•
•	•	•
•	•	•
s_n - plaid skin	d_m - pseudocyesis	t_k - bandage

$$\mathbf{x} = (s_1, s_2, \ldots, s_n, d_1, d_2, \ldots, d_m, t_1, t_2, \ldots, t_k)$$

$$s_i, d_j, t_l \in \{-1, 1\}$$

Fig. 9.14. • Coding of medical records into bipolar vectors. The symptoms, diagnoses, and treatments found in the body of medical records used to train the system are first listed in the form of binary yes/no questions. These questions are then used to describe an arbitrary patient's symptoms, diagnoses, and treatments in a long bipolar vector that records the answers to all of the yes/no questions. The code used is yes = +1 and no = −1. If the answer to any question is not known, a 0 is entered into that component of the vector (0 is used only after training).

questions, in order. For example, in Figure 9.14, if the patient had a headache, then the component s_1 would be set to +1; if the patient did not have a headache, s_1 would be set to −1. For each medical record, all of the components of $\mathbf{x}$ are filled in. In some sense, $\mathbf{x}$ then represents a crude encapsulation of the information in that medical record. It provides an example of relationships between the symptoms, diagnoses, and treatments found in real patients.

After each of the medical records is coded into an $\mathbf{x}$ vector, these vectors are then used to train a brain state in a box network. Notice that for real medical records, the number of symptoms, diagnoses, and treatments (let us call this number N) might easily exceed 1000. So be it. Whatever the length of the $\mathbf{x}$ vectors, we utilize them to train the appropriately configured brain state in a box neural network. This training operation has the effect of creating attractive vertices on the bipolar cube $\{-1, 1\}^n$.

Once all of the data vectors have been entered a sufficient number of times, and the network response to each vector has essentially stabilized, the network weights are frozen. The Instant Physician is then ready to hang out its shingle and begin the practice of rapid medicine. When a patient is brought in to be treated, someone goes through the list of symptoms with the patient and determines whether or not each symptom is displayed by this patient. These +1 and −1 values for the s_i are then entered into an $\mathbf{x}$ vector. However, unlike the training situation, all of the $\mathbf{x}$ entries for diagnosis and treatment (the d_j and t_k) are set to 0 (meaning "don't know"). The $\mathbf{x}$ vector is then ready to be entered into the Instant Physician neural network as its initial state. Once the x vector is entered, the network is run and its state evolves until the final vector x lies at some vertex of the cube. Thus, the resulting x vector (which is considered the output of the Instant Physician) is completely filled with +1 and −1 entries. The diagnosis and treatment for this patient are then simply read from the x vector.

The performance of the Instant Physician is surprisingly good, given its simple construction. In situations where the particular symptoms exhibited by the patient are commonly found in the medical records and the diagnosis and treatment for these symptoms are always the same, the Instant Physician will usually produce exactly this diagnosis and treatment. If the symptoms to be diagnosed and treated are associated with more than one diagnosis and treatment in the medical records used for training, the network will choose those that are most frequently found in the training data. Thus, in a sense, it follows the "weight of evidence." In situations where the symptoms do not match any found in the training medical records, the system will resort to a sort of symptomatic treatment. For example, if s_1 represents "the patient has a headache," t_1 represents "take two aspirin" and $s_1 = +1$, then t_1 will be set to $+1$, more or less regardless of what other symptoms are present. This corresponds to the fact that very often aspirin is prescribed for headache, independent of any other symptoms.

In summary, the Instant Physician provides an example of how a certain type of summary or aggregate knowledge can be automatically extracted from a database containing implicit knowledge. Although the system is admittedly crude, it performs surprisingly well. The Instant Physician technique can be applied to real world problems where a crude summary knowledge would be of value (such as predicting the gross behavior of another company during a competitive procurement).

Exercises

9.4.1. Describe a scheme for setting the yes/no creditworthiness rating threshold for a loan scoring system.

9.4.2. U.S. federal guidelines require that any loan applicant that has an application declined must be told why. Devise a method for determining the reason why a neural network based scoring system gives a particular applicant a low score.

9.4.3. Suggest a method whereby a NETtalk type speech synthesis system could be directly trained by human speakers (instead of by an expert system).

9.4.4. Propose a method for building an Instant Physician type system for predicting the outcome of divorce court cases. Indicate where the necessary training data will come from.

In conclusion, the application of neurocomputing to real-world problems is "where the rubber meets the road." The process of applications engineering provides a methodology for identifying and defining problems to be solved. Once a problem has been identified, a technical approach to solving it can be devised.

Beyond applications engineering and neurocomputing problem solving techniques, there is a need for a methodology for defining, evaluating, planning, and managing development. These are the subjects of the Appendix of this book.

Neurocomputing Projects: Developing New Capabilities that Succeed in the Marketplace

A

This appendix covers the most important subject in technology: how to get things done in the real world. With some improvements in the last few centuries, many of the approaches spelled out here have been in successful use for over three millennia. These were essentially the same methodologies that were used to build the Pyramids, Circus Maximus, the Golden Gate Bridge, and the Boeing 767. Today, these methods are in daily use in technology projects the world over—from the smallest design study to the largest megaproject. In a sense, it is the *organization of work* that is behind essentially all of the major successes of technology. Every technologist, scientist, and mathematician should have a basic understanding of project formulation and evaluation, proposals, project planning, and project management. This knowledge is of significant value, no matter what type of career an individual pursues. The current dearth of technical curricula adequately covering this socially vital material stimulated me to write this appendix.

The appendix consists of three sections. The first section covers a universally applicable project planning and analysis tool—the business plan. The second section briefly discusses proposals. Finally, the third section discusses techniques for planning and managing development projects.

A *business plan* is a document used to thoroughly describe and analyze a project. It includes all aspects of the project, including technical, financial, marketing, sales, institutional and legal issues. In many ways it is a simulation of the project. The business plan is a useful tool whenever a project is being planned and evaluated.

A *proposal* is a plan for carrying out a project that has already been defined by some other organization. The proposal is usually written in response to a *request for proposal* or a *request for quotation* (RFP or RFQ) that describes the work to be accomplished and the constraints (technological, financial, schedule, and others) that the project must be carried out within. RFPs and RFQs should, in principle, be derived from a full business plan (developed by the originating organization) that spells out the overall work to be done and which portions are to be "farmed out" to other organizations.

Once a project is underway, technical personnel are typically responsible for planning and managing the development portion of the project.

Far from being a definitive treatise, this appendix only presents an overview of these project-related topics based on my personal experiences over the past 22 years.[1] These experiences have acquainted me with a set of concepts, general business principles, and practices that I have found useful in planning and performing on technology projects. It is a subset of these concepts, principles, and practices that, along with some personal observations, are briefly (and, thus, incompletely) sketched in this appendix. My hope is that technologists, scientists, and mathematicians who are inexperienced in these matters will find in this encapsulation of my experiences a useful starting point for entry into the real world of organizing, motivating, and managing human beings to accomplish tasks within reasonable time and dollar constraints. Naturally, relevant specialized texts should be consulted for definitive information.

A.1 Business Plan Development

Carrying out any neurocomputing project, whether it be a small single-person research effort that will take two weeks, or the development of a major new neurocomputing-based product, will require an expenditure of resources. Resources may be one person's time for a few weeks or tens of millions of dollars spent over years. Regardless of how large or small a project may be, any expenditure of resources justifies a correspondingly sized planning analysis of the proposed project. For a two-week project, the analysis may only require an hour and may be done on a small computer, or manually using a calculator and a few pieces of paper. For a project involving millions of dollars, the analysis may require months and may require a team of people. The point is that if a project is to succeed, it must be analyzed, planned, and managed properly. This is true regardless of the size of a project, and regardless of the milieu in which it is being carried out.

---

[1] During the past 22 years I have been associated (either as a consultant or as an employee) with a total of 18 different companies (11 small companies, three mid-sized companies, and four large companies). From these experiences I have come to believe that there are three basic ingredients required for a business to have a reasonable probability of success: a practice of keeping the customer at the focus of everything, a good management team, and hard-working employees who are personally committed to the company's success.

Whenever resources are to be expended, an overall plan that justifies and validates the proposed project is essential. This document is often called a *business plan*. The business plan is separate from the detailed *development plan* used to organize and carry out the technical work of the project (development plans are discussed in Section A.3). The business plan puts the project in perspective by analyzing it with respect to all fundamental considerations (considerations that are important in essentially any human enterprise), as well as providing detailed insight into the reasons for carrying out the project (or *not* carrying out the project!) and for determining how the project will fit into the institutional structure(s) in which, and for which, it will be carried out. Because a business plan will reveal some of the problems and flaws in a project, it must typically be modified many times before it is worth executing. Thus, if the business plan is to be useful, time to carry out several iterative improvements and rewrites must be allotted.

This section is organized like a business plan document. The subsections discuss each of the elements of a business plan in the order in which they typically appear in an actual business plan document.

Although the term "business plan" is frequently used to denote the plan for starting a new company, the concept is applicable (and widely applied) to virtually any kind of project. The business plan format described in this section is applicable to both technology projects and entire businesses.

Before delving into the details of the business plan format, it is important to understand the logical flow of the document at the highest level. The business plan is divided into eleven sections:

- Project Definition
- Goals
- Technical Feasibility
- Market Analysis
- Development Plan
- Marketing and Sales Plan
- Production Plan
- Organization and Personnel
- Schedule
- Budget
- Financing and Ownership.

The first two sections of the business plan define the project and explain why it is being pursued (i.e., what the motivations for carrying out the project are). The next two sections verify the overall feasibility of the project. These are followed by three sections that describe how the project will actually be carried out. The subsequent three sections of the plan describe the people who will carry out the project, the organizational structure into which those people will be placed, and the schedule and budget of the project. Finally, the last section of the business plan describes the sources of the resources necessary to carry out the project and identifies who will own the outputs of the project. In essence, the business plan tells someone reading it what the project is, who will care about it, how it will be carried out, who will do the project, who will fund the project, and who will own the outputs of the project. Obviously, these considerations apply to virtually every project that technologists get involved in. They are even more important for neurocomputing projects because there exist so many opportunities to apply this new technology. By developing a short business plan for each of a number of candidate projects, it becomes much easier to decide which projects are worth pursuing.

A.1.1 Project Definition

The first section of any business plan should be a definition of the project. This should start with an overview that explains what the project is in two or three paragraphs. For example, if the plan were for NASA's Apollo Project, the overview could be as simple as:

Develop and demonstrate a system for transporting humans to the surface of the moon and returning them safely to earth.

The purpose of the overview is to give an encapsulated description of the project at the highest possible level. This sets the stage for the more detailed discussion and analysis that follows later in the plan.

After the overview, the basic concept of the project is described in more detail. As with all sections of the business plan, the discussion should stick strictly to the intended content of the section. Discussion of ancillary information such as details of the development plan or marketing and sales information, etc. should be suppressed. The main purpose of this section is to precisely define what it is the project is setting out to do. The goals of the project should be stated and any constraints that the project must live within should be specified. Everything that the project will do and every goal the project will seek to reach should be explained in the project definition.

Finally, the project definition section of the business plan should include a list of precise, but concise, specifications (performance levels, schedule deadlines, product price targets, budgetary limits, etc.) that the project will be expected to meet. Each of the items listed in this subsection should be objectively measurable, so that overall project performance can be graded on the basis of how well the objectives were met. Naturally, it is important to set objectives that can realistically be achieved with reasonably high probability. It is a common, but bad, practice to set project goals that cannot be reached. This is often done with the thought in mind that it will "spur on" project personnel to go farther and do more than they would if less ambitious and attainable goals were set. In reality, all this does is serve to make the project undoable and create an environment in which failure is not only tolerated but fully expected. The mentality associated with this sort of Orwellian "doublethink" environment tends to ripple down through a project. Before long, everyone connected with the project begins to feel that the project plans are a joke, and that everything is careening forward out of control. Setting and requiring adherence to attainable goals has the opposite effect. Accountability and a feeling of accomplishment soon permeate the entire project. As difficult as it may be sometimes to resist setting (or having others impose) unrealistic goals, this absolutely must be resisted. On the other hand, the goals should not be too easy to reach, or productivity and efficiency will drop as people discover that they are not being challenged and stimulated.

A.1.2 Defining Goals

Before beginning any project (whether it be a design study lasting two weeks or the creation of a new company), it is essential that those initiating the project identify both their personal goals and those of the institution(s) involved in the project. By defining these goals, the project can be tailored to better satisfy them.

Identifying goals is not easy. Part of the problem involves stepping back far enough to see the forest for the trees. The personal goals one has in mind in carrying out a project can be difficult to identify. For example, after considerable thought, a person may come to realize that their primary goal in being involved in a particular project is to have an opportunity to gain experience with a certain technology. Such "interest fulfillment" type goals are certainly significant. However, there are many other important issues that should be considered before committing to work on a project, particularly if the project will last a long time or if it will require personal sacrifices. These issues include: job satisfaction, obtaining valuable technical or management experience, spending more time with one's family, getting a promotion, becoming wealthy, travelling, not travelling, having an opportunity to work with a particular mentor, spending more time outdoors, etc. When considering a new project, it is worth the time and effort to sit and reflect on one's own personal goals and write these down as part of the business plan. Neurocomputing projects often require considerable dedication, and this will not be possible if the project does not fit in fairly well with the personal goals of the participants. Talking over the pros and cons of participation in the project with a friend, relative, or spouse can often help sort out these complex tradeoffs.

Beyond personal goals, most projects have strong interaction with one or more institutions. It is essential that the goals of these institutions be identified and stated explicitly in this section of the plan.

During the time of its preparation, and even after the plan is put into effect, a business plan is a living document. Business plans should be carefully reviewed by as many skilled and experienced people as possible. The general rule of business plan preparation is: review, revise, review, revise, review, revise, etc. If a project does not meet the personal and organizational goals set down in this section, then the business plan must be changed, or the project must be abandoned. It is a waste of time and resources to go forward with a project that will not meet the goals of the individuals and institutions involved in the project.

For a large project, it usually takes a long time to get a business plan right. But this is time well spent. This is why most technology businesses start off doing nothing but writing their business plan in the first months of operation. There is no point in spending time or money on a project until the business plan is debugged and judged to be ready for implementation. This idea runs counter to almost every native instinct of technical people (who want to start 'bending metal'). However, not following this path almost guarantees problems and difficulties, and decreases the probability of success dramatically.

A.1.3 Technical Feasibility

In any project, it is essential that the proposed activity be technically feasible. For projects where "proof of principle" examples already exist, this section of the business plan is easy to write. One merely cites references to the prior technical work, and provides an argument for why this is sufficient to prove feasibility of the proposed project.

For projects that are embarking on untrod technical ground, this section of the business plan becomes not only difficult to write, but crucial in attracting the necessary financial support and personnel. In many cases of this type, it is not possible to actually present an airtight feasibility argument. In these situations, the technical feasibility analysis (while retaining that title) actually becomes a *plausibility* argument. The goal of this section is to convince someone who is knowledgeable in the field that the technical approach specified in the project definition can achieve the specified technical goals. In writing this analysis, it is essential to utilize and cite all relevant technical information. The argument should be constructed in a logical, thorough, and rigorous manner.

In writing the technical feasibility section of a business plan, keep the intended audience in mind. This section will primarily be read and evaluated by experts in the field. Therefore, it is perfectly acceptable to utilize equations, technical jargon, diagrams and figures, and to cite references in the literature. Besides providing others with a means for objectively evaluating the project, writing the technical feasibility section is often useful for solidifying and quantifying the thoughts of the project organizer(s).

A.1.4 Market Analysis

Since every project requires the expenditure of resources, it is important to analyze the return that will be obtained from that expenditure. That is the role of market analysis. Market analysis is useful whether the project is a Master's degree thesis or a multi-million dollar hardware development project. The goal in both cases is to determine the benefit that will accrue as a result of carrying out the project.

For projects that do not produce a product, market analysis primarily involves listing all of the payoffs that the project will produce. This section should also list the institutions and individuals who will be interested in the outcome of the project and an assessment of any future benefit that will accrue as a result of the project's successful completion.

If one of the goals of the project is to later have a follow-on project, then all of the known sources of follow-on support, and the type and level of support that they could provide in the event of a successful project conclusion should be estimated. Anticipated time delays associated with such follow-on support should also be noted, since a common problem is that the effect of a successful project is not felt until a considerable time after the project has concluded.

For projects that have as their focus the development of products for sale, the analysis is quite different. The goal here is to realistically quantify the sales volume, revenue potential (and market share potential) of the product as a function of time. The first step is to identify the categories of individuals and institutions who will buy the product (these are called the *market segments*). This often requires quite a bit of thought and a number of exploratory phone calls to gather information and validate assumptions. In addition to talking with a large number of potential customers, one should call upon the advice of experienced members of each of the target market communities to get their opinions on realistic sales potential.

Once the general market segments have been identified, the next step is to characterize the individuals within each segment who will buy the product. This is known as a *buyer analysis*. Again, by using phone calls to potential buyers (and by gathering independent expert opinions) the buyers are profiled and the number of such buyers within each segment that will buy this specific product in each of the next five years is estimated. This forms the sales volume estimate.

Throughout the development of any business plan, the writers should be as objective and unbiased as possible. This goes double for market analysis, where it is very easy to have beliefs overweigh evidence. Listen carefully to what people say and record it accurately.[2] Do not allow your personal enthusiasm or beliefs to color the results. Finally, check with a number of independent sources before drawing conclusions. A market analysis based upon the pontification of one expert is almost always useless.

The next step in the market analysis is to estimate the sales price of the initial product (and any follow-on products) during each of the first five years of operation. These estimates are primarily based upon work done in other sections of the business plan (namely, the Marketing and Sales Plan, Production Plan, and Budget sections). Specifically, the price is determined by adding a profit to the costs of manufacturing, overhead, sales and marketing, and management (expressed on a per unit basis).

Typically, the sales price of an item lies in the range of 1.05 to 10 times its total cost (*cost* is the amount of money it takes to produce the product, including all support personnel costs, overhead, etc.—but not including the costs of sales

---

[2] When gathering market data from potential customers and from experts it is best to work from a carefully prepared list of questions. This will help ensure that you get as many possible opinions on each issue of interest.

and marketing). The 1.05 case would correspond to selling rice to wholesalers in quantities of millions of kilograms. The 10 case would correspond to a situation where staggering sales commissions, heavy advertising expenses, special shipment, etc. would drive the price up. A "pet rock" probably sells for over 10 times its total cost.

Typical high-tech commercial and industrial products which are sold directly by the manufacturer (e.g., by mail, or via an internal sales force) sell for roughly 1.5 to 2.0 times cost. Products in this category that are sold through distributors are typically marked up an additional 20% to 30%. Consumer products typically have an additional 50% to 100% tacked on to the distributor's price by the retail outlet. The total markup from cost to the price at which the organization making the product sells the product is known as the *gross margin*. Most technology projects that develop a product for sale need to achieve a gross margin of at least 50% to be financially sound. Finally, another crude rule of thumb (which is probably wrong as often as it is correct) is that, for electronic products, price equals approximately 10 times parts cost. The rules of thumb presented above should not be used for determining sales price. However, these rules can be used as a "sanity check" to help spot pricing errors.

For large product development projects, professional strategic marketing experts should be utilized. However, the project management and other technologists working on the project should always be involved in market analysis, since they will better be able to spot incorrect assumptions, misplaced emphasis, etc. In other words, market analysis should never be left entirely to marketeers.

After estimating the total unit sales per market segment and the sales price for each of the products in each of the first five years of operation (including the initial product and products that would be developed later), the final step is to use these numbers to calculate the projected revenue per year for the first five years of the product's existence.

The market analysis section of a business plan for a product development project presents the conclusions of the market analysis study. The target market segments are completely described, the numbers of units per year that can be sold to each segment is quantified and justified, and the sales price of each product and its market share[3] are estimated for each year (for the first five years of operation). Just as the technical feasibility section is written to persuade reasonable technical experts in the field, so the market analysis should present a carefully reasoned argument that will convince experienced, unbiased, marketing experts in the field that the analysis is correct. Therefore, the target market identities and the numbers associated with them are not enough. They should be presented as the final conclusions of a carefully reasoned analysis that cites the sources used and provides representative example verbatim quotes of their comments. Remember, a business plan is not a sales document; it is a manifesto designed to convince the reader of the objectively determined worth of

---

[3] *Market share* is the percentage of total annual sales revenue of all companies selling products in this category attributed to this product.

Project Timeline --->	1997	1998	1999	2000	2001
Market Segment 1 (Insurance Co.s)					
Product Sales Into Market Segment 1					
Number of Units Sold (Product A)	8	25	25		
Price Per Unit (Product A)	$500,000	$300,000	$250,000		
Sales Revenue (Product A)	$4,000,000	$7,500,000	$6,250,000		
Number of Units Sold (Product B)			60	70	50
Price Per Unit (Product B)			$100,000	$90,000	$90,000
Sales Revenue (Product B)			$6,000,000	$6,300,000	$4,500,000
Number of Units Sold (Product C)				50	210
Price Per Unit (Product C)				$30,000	$20,000
Sales Revenue (Product C)				$1,500,000	$4,200,000
Sales Revenue (Market Segment 1)	$4,000,000	$7,500,000	$12,250,000	$7,800,000	$8,700,000
Market Segment 2 (Banks)					
Product Sales Into Market Segment 2					
Number of Units Sold (Product A)		38	125		
Price Per Unit (Product A)		$300,000	$250,000		
Sales Revenue (Product A)		$11,400,000	$31,250,000		
Number of Units Sold (Product B)			170	150	100
Price Per Unit (Product B)			$100,000	$90,000	$90,000
Sales Revenue (Product B)			$17,000,000	$13,500,000	$9,000,000
Number of Units Sold (Product C)				480	720
Price Per Unit (Product C)				$30,000	$20,000
Sales Revenue (Product C)				$14,400,000	$14,400,000
Sales Revenue (Market Segment 2)	$0	$11,400,000	$48,250,000	$27,900,000	$23,400,000
Market Segment 3 (Accountants)					
Product Sales Into Market Segment 3					
Number of Units Sold (Product A)					
Price Per Unit (Product A)					
Sales Revenue (Product A)					
Number of Units Sold (Product B)			90	90	
Price Per Unit (Product B)			$100,000	$90,000	
Sales Revenue (Product B)			$9,000,000	$8,100,000	
Number of Units Sold (Product C)				1850	4800
Price Per Unit (Product C)				$30,000	$20,000
Sales Revenue (Product C)				$55,500,000	$96,000,000
Sales Revenue (Market Segment 3)	$0	$0	$9,000,000	$63,600,000	$96,000,000
Total Sales Revenue	$4,000,000	$18,900,000	$69,500,000	$99,300,000	$128,100,000
Cumulative Sales Revenue	$4,000,000	$22,900,000	$92,400,000	$191,700,000	$224,104,800

Fig. A.1. • Typical market analysis summary chart for a product. This format illustrates the sales volume and revenue the project is expected to generate over the first five years. The conclusions presented in this chart are backed up by facts and analyses presented in the Market Analysis section of the business plan.

the project and infect them with enthusiasm. The tone should be logical persuasion based on mounds of factual evidence (including negative evidence), not coercion by bombast, hype, or weasel wording.

A typical market analysis sales volume and revenue summary chart for a product is shown in Figure A.1. Such an analysis should project sales revenue for the first five calendar years of product sales. This analysis should include both the initial product and any follow-on products that will be sold during this five-year time window (these follow-on products should be described). In addition to this analysis, the projected market share should also be estimated.

- Task 1—Prototype System Specification and Design. This task shall develop definitive system specification and system design description documents for the prototype system (which will be used to develop the production model). Detailed discussions concerning desired system specifications and design features shall be held with potential customers located by the Marketing Department. The conclusions drawn from these discussions shall be incorporated into the system specification and the system design.

- Task 2—Software Development and Test. This task shall develop the software for the prototype system. The design of this software shall meet the requirements of the system specification produced in Task 1 and incorporate the relevant elements of the system design produced in Task 1. The software shall be thoroughly and iteratively tested and improved and be ready for integration with the hardware portion of the system no later than 1 October 1997.

- Task 3—Hardware Development and Test. This task shall develop the hardware for the prototype system. The design of this hardware shall meet the requirements of the system specification produced in Task 1 and incorporate the relevant elements of the system design produced in Task 1. The hardware shall be thoroughly and iteratively tested and improved and be ready for integration with the software portion of the system no later than 1 October 1997.

- Task 4—Documentation. This task shall develop a design description document (for internal company use) detailing the design of both the hardware and software of the final system prototypes, as developed in Tasks 2, 3, and 5. A clear and well-organized user's manual (for use by customers testing the prototypes) shall also be developed by this task.

- Task 5—Prototype Integration and Test. This task shall Integrate and iteratively test and improve the hardware developed in Task 3 with the software developed in Task 2. Three copies of the final prototype configuration shall be produced as part of this task for use in further customer testing. These prototypes, which shall be ready no later than 31 January 1998, shall be suitable for use by customer personnel in an office environment. These units must be designed to meet all safety requirements for commercial office equipment. Any testing required to assure compliance with such requirements shall be carried out.

Fig. A.2. • An example development plan statement of work for a product-oriented project business plan. Note that only the highest level of detail is shown. Also note that this statement of work only covers development of the initial prototype.

The totals at the bottom reflect the projected annual revenue for each of the five years.[4]

---

[4] All of the figures of this appendix (in other words, of Sections A.1 and A.3) concern the same project. This project is a new product-oriented business set up to produce a particular class of neurocomputing-based products for use by insurance companies, banks, and accountants.

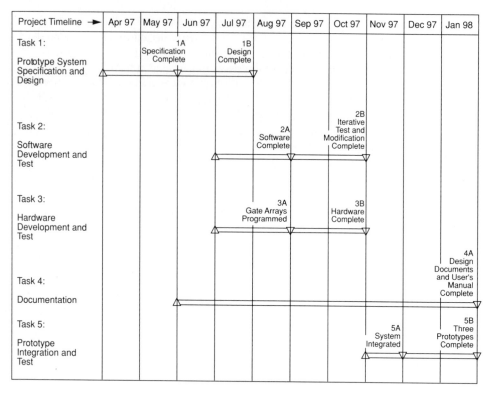

Fig. A.3. • Typical Gantt chart development plan schedule.

A.1.5 Development Plan

The first four sections of the business plan have defined the project, identified the goals of all of the participants, argued for the technical feasibility of the project and analyzed the potential market payoff if the project is successfully completed. With this material as preamble, it is now time to get down to the detailed description of the project itself. In other words, the first four sections define what the project is and what the pay-offs of completing it will be. The remainder of the business plan describes how, by whom, and for whom the project will be carried out.

The purpose of the development plan' section is to explain exactly how the development will be carried out. While this description needs to be complete, it should not be presented in enormous depth. The goal is to simply explain what the project intends to do in sufficient detail that an expert in the field will understand it, and generally agree with it. It is assumed that a detailed development plan is either available or will be constructed immediately after the project begins.

The development plan presentation in the business plan should contain three elements: a statement of work, a schedule with milestones, and a labor hours and material cost budget. These are now described in detail.

The *statement of work* is simply a listing of the tasks that will be carried out during development. For example: detailed product design, prototype software development, prototype hardware development, prototype integration, documentation preparation, and prototype testing. Figure A.2 presents a typical development plan statement of work for a product-oriented project.[5] The statement of work lists the major elements (tasks) of the effort required to carry out the project. Secondary elements (subtasks) such as vendor qualification, test equipment setup, etc. are not usually listed in the summary development plan statement of work presented in the business plan. The reader assumes that (if the project is a large one) each of the large tasks described is composed of a large number of subtasks and subsubtasks that will be fleshed out in the final development plan. However, the high-level development plan presented in the business plan should be pretty much in final form (thus, it may be necessary to work out many of the lower-level details to make sure that the high-level plan is right). Here again, the advice and help of experts with great experience should be sought. This is important because the business plan is not only a description of the project, but also something in the character of a contract. In the business plan, you are telling the readers that this is what you are going to go off and do. If, after the plan is finalized (which can require many drafts), you go off and do something different than what it says in the plan, then the purpose of the plan has been defeated and people monitoring the project will have reason for concern. Thus, the creation of the development plan section should not be thought of as a frivolous matter. In many cases, you will be locked into actually carrying out the development plan you provide in this section (or go through a great deal of trouble to get the plan changed later).

The second part of the development plan section is a description of the schedule across which the various tasks in the statement of work will be conducted. This schedule also identifies critical milestones (typically at intervals of approximately one month or less) that provide binary decision points for objectively measuring the progress of the project.

There are two basic ways to express the schedule of a project: the PERT (Program Evaluation and Review Technique) chart and the "Gantt" chart. However, business plans typically use Gantt charts — which have the advantage of being easily read and understood by anyone (as opposed to the PERT chart, which requires an initiation into the PERT notation and philosophy). A typical Gantt chart schedule for a business plan is shown in Figure A.3. Notice that time runs along the horizontal axis. Time is measured in units of weeks or months (depending on project duration) and major milestones are shown for

---

[5] The statement of work presented in Figure A.2 only covers the first development effort (development of the prototype system) of the project. The other two development activities of this project (see Figure A.7) are the development of the production model (Product A of Figure A.1) and the development of the follow-on products (Product B and Product C of Figure A.1). To keep the exposition simple, these portions of the five-year development plan will be ignored.

each project element at frequent intervals. Notice that each project is shown as starting at an open triangular box and ending at an open triangular box. Further, note that each of the tasks has two parallel lines running between the starting and ending triangles for the task. The milestones are also illustrated as triangles. The open triangles and open lines are traditionally used so that project progress can be indicated by filling in the completed activities with ink (although this is rarely done for the development plan presented in a business plan—the more detailed development plan produced before the project begins is used for tracking project progress—see Section A.3).

A list describing each of the milestones presented on the development plan schedule should be provided. The milestone events need to be "binary" — meaning that the completion of the milestone can be measured in an easy yes-or-no way. Each milestone should be described in sufficient detail so that an objective observer could determine whether the milestone had been met or not. Both qualitative and quantitative measures of performance can be used. For example, a milestone specifying that a monthly report was sent to one of the project's sponsors and approved by them is a good (qualitative) binary milestone. A milestone requiring a circuit to run at 50 MHz with no signal reflections above 10 mV would be also be good (in fact, quantitative milestones are better than qualitative milestones because if the milestone is not reached, the deviation can often be more easily measured. A poor milestone would be "*input/output software 50% complete.*" Since the completion level of software is impossible to measure (except by verifying that a particular software module has successfully passed all of an agreed-upon set of tests), this does not form a good milestone.

Setting project schedules is often one of the most critical factors to the success of a project. It is also a subject in which persons outside the project have a great interest. Frequently, attempts are made to pressure the people writing the business plan into accepting a shorter schedule than is realistic. Regardless of how attractive this may be, it is really not a good idea. Essentially all of the organizations that might have been favorably influenced by this tactic in the past now react very negatively to artificially shortened schedules. Again, preparing a fictionalized business plan, regardless of the motivation, is just a bad idea. It is essential to resist the impulse to get a project started at all costs. In technology, the end absolutely does not justify the means. Technologists can function only if their reputation for credibility and conscientious professional conduct is maintained. Therefore, eschew involvement in projects where the business plan is being written in an unrealistic manner to achieve some near-term goal.

The final portion of the development plan section of the business plan is a listing of the labor hour and materials/equipment rental/travel/other cost budgets by task. A typical example illustrating these budgets for two tasks (and the project totals) is shown in Figure A.4. Notice that the type of labor required in each month is identified (again, for smaller projects, this should be by week). The estimated costs, by month, of the materials, rental equipment, travel, and other items that are to be purchased directly for use in this element of the project are also given. These estimates are briefly justified in the business plan. The hourly cost (including salary, but not overhead) is listed for each of the labor categories used on the project. These hourly costs are then used to estimate the total labor costs. The labor and materials/equipment/travel/other costs from this section are transferred to the budget in the budget section. The development plan should not contain any substantial amount of cushion for unanticipated contingencies (although an allowance for expectable delays and problems should be included).

A.1.6 Marketing and Sales Plan

The marketing and sales plan section of the business plan discusses the interaction of the project with the outside world. For projects that do not produce a product, this section should be used to explain how the results of the project will be communicated and to whom. It should also spell out the strategy for garnering support for the follow-on(s) of the project.

For projects that produce a product that will be purchased by customers (the word *customer* is used here to denote any person or institution that purchases the product), this section must be more elaborate. The marketing and sales plan, in this instance, consists of three parts: the marketing plan, the distribution plan, and the sales plan. The marketing plan describes the means by which the intended customers (who were already characterized in the Market Analysis section of the business plan) will learn of the product and be convinced to buy it. Informing customers of the existence of a product and inducing them to buy it can be accomplished by many means. Typical approaches include: advertising in relevant periodicals, trade show participation, marketing communications/public relations/publicity interfaces with the press, brochures and flyers, direct mail marketing (either using purchased lists or self-accumulated lists), trade journal "bingo cards", general media advertising (national magazines, newspaper, radio, television, etc.), distributors, exploratory telemarketing (using college students, for example), sales telemarketing (by professional sales personnel), direct customer visits, sky writing, etc. The techniques for transmitting information about a product to the target customer bases are well worked out. However, they do require considerable persistence, and are almost always expensive.

The second part of the marketing and sales plan section for a product-type project is the distribution plan. The question here is: how will you get the product from your production facility to the customers? Will you sell it directly to them from the project location (which means that you will have to have sales and technical support staffs), or use distributors (full-service or just sales, direct to customers or to retail outlets) to sell your product? Another approach is to set up a network of district sales and technical support offices to carry out this function. Other options include mail-order sales (where there are essentially no sales personnel, only order takers) and catalog sales (where the product is sold in bulk quantity to the catalog distributor, who then sells it to the

Project Timeline --->	Rate	Apr-97	May-97	Jun-97	Jul-97	Aug-97	Sep-97	Oct-97	Nov-97	Dec-97	Jan-98	TOTALS
Project Element V		Start	1A Prototype Specification Completed	1B Prototype Design Completed	1B Prototype Design Completed / Start	2A Prototype Software Completed		2B Iterative Test & Modif. Completed				
Task 1: Prototype System Specification and Design												
Principal Engineer		170	170	170	80							590
Senior Engineer		510	510	510	510							2040
Engineer		510	510	510	300							1830
Technician		20	20	20	20							80
Material		$200	$200	$3,600	$3,600							$7,600
Rental Equipment		$4,000	$4,000	$4,000	$4,000							$16,000
Travel		$1,500	$1,500	$6,000	$1,000							$10,000
Other		$2,500	$300	$300	$100							$3,200
Task 2: Software Development and Test												
Principal Engineer					90	80	80	50				300
Senior Engineer					340	340	340	340				1360
Engineer					170	340	340	170				1020
Technician					20	20	20	20				80
Material					$100	$300	$300	$300				$1,000
Rental Equipment					$0	$0	$0	$0				$0
Travel					$200	$200	$200	$200				$800
Other					$150	$400	$400	$500				$1,450
TOTALS:												
Labor Hours:												
Total Principal Engineer Labor Hours		170	170	170	170	170	170	170	170	170	170	1700
Total Senior Engineer Labor Hours		510	510	510	1020	1020	1020	1020	1020	780	510	7920
Total Engineer Labor Hours		510	510	510	680	680	680	680	850	620	510	6230
Total Technician Labor Hours		20	20	20	170	170	170	170	170	170	80	1160
Total Labor Hours		1210	1210	1210	2040	2040	2040	2040	2210	1740	1270	17010
Labor Cost:												
Total Principal Engineer Hourly Labor Cost	$35.87	$6,098	$6,098	$6,098	$6,098	$6,098	$6,098	$6,098	$6,098	$6,098	$6,098	$60,979
Total Senior Engineer Hourly Labor Cost	$29.12	$14,851	$14,851	$14,851	$29,702	$29,702	$29,702	$29,702	$29,702	$22,714	$14,851	$230,630
Engineer Hourly Labor Cost	$21.56	$10,996	$10,996	$10,996	$14,661	$14,661	$14,661	$14,661	$18,326	$13,367	$10,996	$134,319
Technician Hourly Labor Cost	$26.81	$536	$536	$536	$4,558	$4,558	$4,558	$4,558	$4,558	$4,558	$2,145	$31,100
Total Labor Cost		$32,481	$32,481	$32,481	$55,019	$55,019	$55,019	$55,019	$58,684	$46,736	$34,090	$457,028
Total Materials Cost		$200	$200	$3,600	$7,700	$6,800	$16,900	$1,300	$14,000	$200	$200	$51,100
Total Rental Equipment Cost		$4,000	$4,000	$4,000	$7,500	$7,500	$7,500	$7,500	$6,000	$6,000	$1,500	$55,500
Total Travel Cost		$1,500	$1,500	$6,000	$1,500	$1,500	$1,500	$9,000	$4,500	$4,500	$1,500	$33,000
Total Other Costs		$2,500	$300	$300	$300	$2,500	$2,500	$2,500	$6,400	$8,500	$1,200	$27,000
Subcontract Costs		$0	$0	$0	$0	$0	$0	$0	$0	$0	$0	$0
Total Cost		$40,681	$38,481	$46,381	$72,019	$73,319	$83,419	$75,319	$89,584	$65,936	$38,490	$623,628

Fig. A.4. • Sample of a portion of a development plan labor and equipment cost budget. This sample shows the budget calculations for two tasks and the totals by month.

actual customers without your involvement). Regardless of which distribution scenario is chosen, there will have to be a technical support capability available for handling technical questions, product malfunctions, and repairs. Resources to manage these activities should be built into the budget section of the business plan.

The final part of the marketing and sales plan is the sales plan. Using the assumptions spelled out in the marketing and distribution discussions, the sales plan quantifies the process that will be used to sell the product. Elements of the sales plan include the types and numbers of sales personnel that will be required, the number of sales per month that each type of salesperson is expected to make, and quantification of other factors such as the number of expected leads (phone calls, bingo cards, advertising responses, exploratory telemarketing calls, etc.) that are anticipated to flow into the operation per month. It is important to realistically estimate the average number of leads that will have to be followed up on in order to make one sale (often this number is 100 or more) and the average elapsed time between the first contact with a lead and the sale (often 3-6 months, or more). These factors will determine how much time and effort will have to be put into each sale.

The marketing and sales plan should be worked out in monthly detail for the first 12 months of project operation, and then yearly for the next four years. This budget is later incorporated into the master project budget (see Section A.1.10).[6] The staffing level (in hours) in each category of personnel should be indicated by month, along with the assumed salaries. In estimating the number sales people required, keep in mind that as new sales employees are brought in, the number of units they can sell per month will start off low and build over a three to four month period to a sustained level as they achieve product and market familiarity. Figure A.5 shows a typical budget that would be used in the marketing and sales plan section of a business plan describing a product-oriented project. Note that the projected sales volume figures are brought over from the Market Analysis section of the business plan (Figure A.1). Having these sales numbers available on the budget allows evaluators to more easily judge the adequacy of the marketing and sales plan. Because of the importance of extensive and relevant experience in developing a marketing and sales plan, technologists without such experience should get appropriate help when writing this section of the business plan.

In preparing a business plan for a large project (three technologist months or more) the use of a personal computer with word processing, spreadsheet, and drawing software is almost mandatory. Smaller project business plans can be done by hand.

If the material in the business plan is considered sensitive or proprietary, an appropriate restrictive legend should be applied in large bold type as a header

---

[6] The Market Analysis, Development Plan, Marketing and Sales Plan, Production Plan, and Financing and Ownership sections of the business plan each contribute a budget like this to the Budget section.

Project Timeline --->		Jan-97	Feb-97	Mar-97	Apr-97	May-97	Jun-97	Jul-97
Product Sales								
(from the Marketing Analysis Section)								
Number of Units Sold (Product A)								
Number of Units Sold (Product B)								
Number of Units Sold (Product C)								
Marketing Personnel								
VP of Marketing Hours					170	170	170	170
VP of Marketing Cost	$35.87				$6,098	$6,098	$6,098	$6,098
Marketing Communications Manager Hours					170	170	170	170
Marketing Communications Manager Cost	$28.42				$4,831	$4,831	$4,831	$4,831
Marketing Assistant Hours					170	170	170	170
Marketing Assistant Cost	$13.91				$2,365	$2,365	$2,365	$2,365
Total Cost of Marketing Personnel					$13,294	$13,294	$13,294	$13,294
Sales Personnel								
VP of Sales Hours								
VP of Sales Cost	$35.87							
Customer Service Manager Hours								
Customer Service Manager Cost	$28.42							
District Sales Manager Hours								
District Sales Manager Cost	$32.15							
Sales Assistant Hours								
Sales Assistant Cost	$13.91							
Total Cost of Sales Personnel								
Marketing and Sales Direct Costs								
Advertising					$6,500	$6,500	$6,500	$6,500
Travel					$3,900	$5,500	$5,500	$3,500
Telecommunications					$2,500	$2,500	$2,500	$2,500
Subcontracts (Artwork, Ads, Photos, Videos)					$15,000	$15,000	$15,000	$25,000
Total Marketing and Sales Direct Costs					$27,900	$29,500	$29,500	$37,500
Total Cost of Marketing and Sales								
Total Cost of Marketing and Sales					$41,194	$42,794	$42,794	$50,794

Fig. A.5. • Five year marketing and sales budget projection for a product-oriented project.

and/or footer to each page. All outside individuals to whom a restricted business plan is to be shown should normally be required to sign a non-disclosure agreement drawn up by an attorney. All business plans involving substantial amounts of time and money should be reviewed by an attorney who is knowledgeable and experienced in the relevant field of activity. Good legal representation can be crucial to the success of a project.

If a business plan is for the start of a business, a competent attorney *must* be consulted, since the release and distribution of the plan in this instance is governed by United States Securities and Exchange Commission rules and by state "Blue Sky" laws.

A.1.7 Production Plan

The production plan section of the business plan describes how the item(s) developed by the project will be produced. Obviously, if the project does not involve development of a tangible product, this section does not apply and should be omitted from the business plan. The main purpose of the production plan section of the business plan is to explain how copies of the developed

Aug-97	Sep-97	Oct-97	Nov-97	Dec-97	1997 TOTALS	1998	1999	2000	2001
3	1	1	1	2	8	63	150		
							320	310	150
								2380	5730
170	170	170	170	170	1530	2080	2080	2080	2080
$6,098	$6,098	$6,098	$6,098	$6,098	$54,881	$74,610	$82,071	$90,278	$99,305
170	170	170	170	170	1530	2080	2080	4160	6240
$4,831	$4,831	$4,831	$4,831	$4,831	$43,483	$59,114	$65,025	$143,055	$236,041
170	170	170	170	1530	1530	2080	2080	4160	4160
$2,365	$2,365	$2,365	$2,365	$2,365	$21,282	$28,933	$31,826	$70,017	$77,019
$13,294	$13,294	$13,294	$13,294	$13,294	$119,646	$162,656	$178,922	$303,350	$412,365
			170	170	340	2080	2080	2080	2080
			$6,098	$6,098	$12,196	$74,610	$82,071	$90,278	$99,305
			170	170	340	2080	2080	4160	6240
			$4,831	$4,831	$9,663	$59,114	$65,025	$143,055	$236,041
			340	340	680	8320	14560	24960	66560
			$10,931	$10,931	$21,862	$267,488	$294,237	$566,406	$1,068,080
			170	170	340	2080	2080	6240	8320
			$2,365	$2,365	$4,729	$28,933	$31,826	$105,026	$154,038
			$21,860	$21,860	$43,721	$401,211	$441,332	$799,738	$1,403,426
$6,500	$6,500	$6,500	$38,000	$38,000	$121,500	$1,250,000	$2,000,000	$3,200,000	$5,120,000
$3,500	$6,500	$7,500	$5,500	$5,500	$46,900	$110,000	$176,000	$281,600	$450,560
$2,500	$2,500	$2,500	$6,000	$6,000	$29,500	$48,000	$76,800	$122,880	$196,608
$25,000	$15,000	$20,000	$20,000	$10,000	$160,000	$250,000	$400,000	$640,000	$1,024,000
$37,500	$30,500	$36,500	$69,500	$59,500	$357,900	$1,858,000	$2,652,800	$4,244,480	$6,791,168
$50,794	$43,794	$49,794	$104,654	$94,654	$521,267	$2,221,867	$3,273,054	$5,347,568	$8,606,959

product will be produced. In other words, the development plan covers the *development* of the product; whereas, the production plan describes in detail *how the product will be produced* in whatever quantities are required. The option of having the product (or components of the product) produced by someone else should be explored. Relying on outside vendors is dangerous, but often necessary, and it is a good idea to try to set up two or more independent sources for key elements of the product that are purchased from vendors.

The processes of development and production are enormously different in most cases. Development involves technologists and other personnel whose expertise lies in the area of creating new products. Production involves technologists and other personnel who are experts at manufacturing already created products. The best situation is where the production personnel are heavily involved in the development of the product so that the manufacturing process considerations can drive the design.

The production plan consists of two parts: the plan for setting up the production capability, and an analysis of the production costs of the product. The production set-up plan should very closely follow the format of the development plan. The tasks involved in designing and setting up the production facility should be identified and listed in a statement of work. The schedule and budget for completing these tasks should then be presented.

The other part of the production plan is an estimate of how much it will cost to produce the product. This estimate assumes that the production facility has been built (although ongoing maintenance and upgrading costs should be amortized across the production run and included here as a monthly charge). The first step in the analysis of individual product production is to develop a list of production steps that will be needed to produce the product. The labor categories, labor hours, labor hourly rates by category, overall labor costs by category, and materials costs can then be estimated for each of these production steps. The goal is to define the cost of producing each item in terms of the direct labor and materials. The price paid by the customer is determined later in the budget portion of the business plan.

A.1.8 Organization and Personnel

The organization and personnel section of the business plan describes the overall functional organization of the project and lists the kinds of people that will be needed. Key project participants who can be identified by name are described in detail and full resumes describing education, experience, and other relevant factors are provided.

The organization of a project can often be best described by presenting what is called an *organization chart*. The organization chart shows the management structure of the project and illustrates the organizational roles and responsibilities of each of the participants. A typical organization chart for a project that is a business is shown in Figure A.6. The organization chart should be accompanied by a text description of how the project chain of command will function and how the checks and balances of the project will be set up. Planned periodic management activities such as weekly or monthly reports, design reviews, progress reviews, and all-hands project team meetings should also be described. The authority and responsibility of each of the managers shown on the organization chart should be clearly delineated.

The organization and personnel section also provides a listing of the labor categories of people that will be required to carry out the project. Staffing charts that show the number of personnel in each of the major categories (top management, sales/marketing/customer service, development, production, support, administration, etc.) should be provided, if these are not obvious from the organization chart. Each of the labor categories required for the project should be completely defined. As mentioned above, key personnel who are already identified should be described in detail, with particular emphasis on relevant past experience and training.

Finally, this section should contain a description of the *hiring plan*, which describes the methodology that will be used to locate, attract, interview, and hire each of the necessary participants (including any contractors and consultants

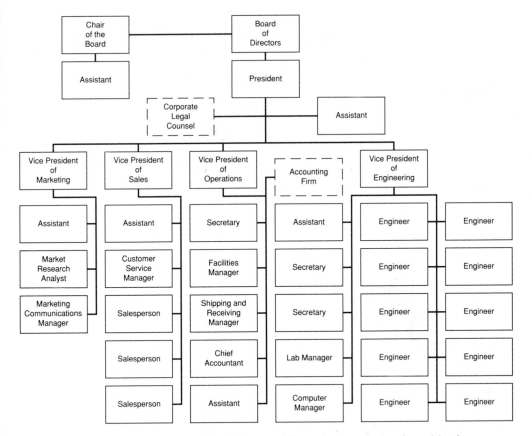

Fig. A.6. • Typical organization chart for a medium-sized product-oriented business.

who will be used).[7] A step-by-step plan for determining the salaries of project personnel can also be quite valuable. As with the rest of the business plan, experienced managers in the field of the project who have been involved in project organization, personnel planning, interviewing, and hiring should be sought out to help write this section. As in marketing and sales, this is an area where the majority of technologists lack the necessary knowledge and experience to do a good job. Obtaining outside expertise is usually very important.

A.1.9 Schedule

The schedule section of the business plan presents the overall schedule of the project, including all of its elements. The schedule (which should, again, be presented as a Gantt chart) consolidates the information contained in the schedules

---

[7] Good consultants and contract employees are expensive. However, their productivity and relevant experience typically make them a bargain. Careful checking of references (at least three) on each prospective consultant and contractor can help avoid hiring the wrong ones.

that appeared in previous sections (development plan, marketing and sales plan, and production plan), as well as adding new information that does not appear anywhere else. Figure A.7 presents a typical project master schedule.

The master project schedule presented in this section should not be very detailed. For example, the entire development activity might be represented by a single bar on this schedule. The main purpose of this schedule is to portray how each of the constituent elements of the project roll out in time relative to one another. The master project schedule allows the coordination of the project to be evaluated.

Besides the scheduled items from previous sections, new items such as the issuance of weekly or monthly technical reports, periodic financial reports, audits, and major project reviews are shown as well. Each of these items deserve a line of its own, even though the item will consist of nothing but triangles (i.e., no open lines between the triangles are typically used). The nature of each of the additional items that appear in the master schedule should be individually defined. For example, if a weekly report is going to be produced, its length and content should be specified. These definitions help avoid misunderstandings later on.

The master project schedule can also be used to show the interaction between this project and other activities outside the project (such as a previous project or a follow-on project). Major events with which the project must interact (such as important conferences, the beginning or ending of a school term, and major project deadlines) should also be shown.

A.1.10 Budget

The budget section of the business plan describes the budget[8] for the entire project. Before discussing the budget section of the business plan, it is important to address the issue of accounting methodologies.

In accounting there are two basic approaches to measuring financial activity:[9] *cash accounting* and *accrual accounting*. In cash accounting, the predicted cash inputs and outputs of the project are determined for each month of the budget, just as in family budget planning. In other words, in cash accounting all incoming cash is entered into the budget when it is actually received. So, for example, if ten product units are shipped in a particular month, the cash receipts from those sales are not entered until 30-90 days later—which is when it would

---

[8] Technically, from an accounting standpoint, the term *budget*, as it is used in this first section of the appendix, is incorrect. The term *cash forecast* is what is actually meant. A *budget* is a profitability analysis using accrual accounting principles.

[9] Most accountants would probably dispute this statement. They would claim that there is one and only one approach to accounting—accrual accounting. While it is true that this is the only system accountants use, two or three billion non-accountants use another system—cash accounting. Because cash accounting (which is what is used in doing a typical family budget) is so natural, familiar, and straightforward it is the scheme that will be used in this section.

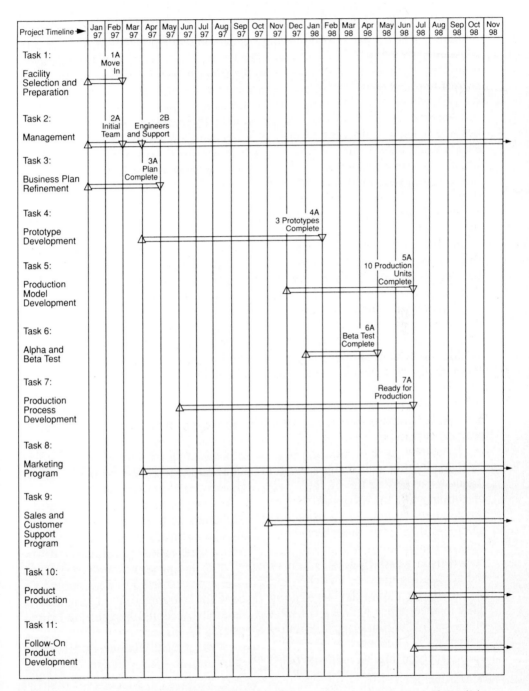

Fig. A.7. • Typical project master schedule. Note that only the highest level of detail is shown.

actually be received (this assumed *receivables delay* must be stated explicitly). Similarly, when a piece of equipment is purchased, the expense for that purchase is not recorded until 30 days afterwards – to reflect the natural delay in billing and payment. Although getting the times of actual receipt and payment correct requires considerable care, it does yield a picture that accurately reflects the cash solvency of the project at the end of each month.

Accrual accounting (which is the system that accountants and almost all businesses use) is different from cash accounting primarily because it records events when they occur, even if the cash impact of the event is delayed somewhat. For example, when a sale is made (i.e., when title is transferred) the income from the sale is recorded immediately, even though the actual cash payment may be delayed for months. Similarly, when a purchased item is received, the expense is recorded immediately, again even though actual cash payment for that item may not occur for a period of time. Because of these differences in the way income and expenses are handled, it is possible for a project to be wildly successful from an accrual standpoint, and yet go bankrupt from a cash standpoint. A typical example of this would be a situation where product sales volume is increasing rapidly. Each month would require a substantial infusion of cash to pay for the production of products for which a corresponding amount of cash was not received during the month (i.e., to pay for the number of products manufactured and shipped this month beyond the number sold in previous months for which payment was received during this month—see Figure A.8). The amount of new cash required each month can be enormous, and this cash has to come from somewhere (sometimes banks will provide *receivables financing* to help with this problem—but often they won't). Many small businesses have gone bankrupt when they were unable to find financing for their rapidly growing expenses.

In general, cash accounting is used in formulating the budget of a business plan (again, this isn't really a budget—technically it is a *cash forecast*). By using cash accounting the budget is relatively easy to formulate and the amount of capital (cash to carry out the project) that the project will require can be quickly determined. By focusing on cash the financial health of the project can be determined (even though many other important measures of performance—such as profitability, which is an accrual accounting quantity, cannot be determined from a cash budget). Unfortunately, once the project is underway all of the accounting must be switched over to the accrual method. This is because essentially all day-to-day accounting (except for extremely small projects) is done in accordance with the *GAAP* (the Generally Accepted Accounting Principles—set by the Financial Accounting Standards Board [65]), or a similar set of principles.[10] Thus, once the project actually starts, an entirely new budget must be produced using accrual practices. Preparation of such a budget is usually

---

[10] The GAAP is the rulebook of accrual accounting. It provides a standardized set of rules that accountants everywhere can follow. Thus, the definition of equipment depreciation in San Diego is the same as the definition in Boston. This standardization of accounting

left to accounting professionals—although, because it plays such an important role in project planning and management, all technologists should have a basic knowledge of finance and accounting.[11]

As with the schedule section, the budget section of the business plan draws most of its data from other sections (such as market analysis, development plan, marketing and sales plan, production plan, organization and personnel, and financing and ownership). The total project budget (cash forecast) is divided into two parts: expenses and income (actually, these are correctly termed *uses of cash* and *sources of cash*). The expenses portion of the budget itemizes the anticipated expenditure by each project activity by month. The income portion itemizes the income by income source by month. A detailed budget should be constructed listing expenses and income by month (or by week for shorter projects) for at least one year (or the full duration of the project if it is shorter than one year). If the project is expected to last more than one year, the expenses by category and income by source should be shown for five years or for the duration of the project, whichever is shorter. If the business plan is for a new company or institution that is intended to go on indefinitely, the budget should project expenses and income for a period of five years.

Figure A.8 shows a typical project budget (only it is correctly labeled as a cash forecast). Such a figure should be accompanied by a detailed explanation of how each of the uses of cash and sources of cash (those which were are not explained in another section) were estimated. Again, it is very easy to miss significant cash use items, and the advice of experienced people should be sought in constructing the budget.

Perhaps the most important part of the cash forecast is the *cash flow* during each month of the project. Cash flow is the net influx (or outgo) of cash during the month. The cumulative total of cash flow from project inception up to the end of the current month is the *cash on hand* at the end of the month. Since many projects are funded by outside sources in episodic payments that occur months apart, this accumulated gain or loss will tend to jump up whenever an infusion of funding occurs, and then be incrementally drawn down as cash outlays are subtracted from the cash provided by this capital investment. This pattern continues until profitable operation is established. Thus, in their early stages, most project budgets take the form of a saw-toothed curve when accumulated gain or loss is plotted as a function of time. It is essential that this curve never approach or go below zero, because this would indicate the bankruptcy of the project.

Besides the cash forecast spreadsheet and explanations of items not covered in previous sections, budget sections for all but the smallest projects should

---

terms and principals is similar to the standardization of the units and procedures of measurement in science and technology.

[11] An excellent book on this subject is *The Complete Guide to Finance and Accounting for Non-Financial Managers* by Steven Finkler [65]. This book is short, concise, and packed with valuable information.

Project Timeline --->	Jan-97	Feb-97	Mar-97	Apr-97	May-97	Jun-97	Jul-97	Aug-97
Project Element V								
Income								
Capital	$2,000,000	$0	$0	$0	$0	$0	$0	$0
Product Sales								
Number of Units Sold (Product A)								
Price Per Unit (Product A)								3
Sales Revenue (Product A)								$500,000
Number of Units Sold (Product B)								$1,500,000
Price Per Unit (Product B)								
Sales Revenue (Product B)								
Number of Units Sold (Product C)								
Price Per Unit (Product C)								
Sales Revenue (Product C)								
Total Sales Revenue								$1,500,000
Expenses								
Marketing and Sales	$0	$0	$0	$41,194	$42,794	$42,794	$50,794	$50,794
Operations	$32,949	$32,949	$32,949	$32,949	$48,183	$48,183	$48,183	$48,183
Product Development	$0	$0	$0	$40,681	$38,481	$46,381	$72,019	$73,319
Product Manufacturing	$0	$0	$0	$0	$0	$9,346	$9,346	$40,186
Capital Equipment	$83,512	$25,800	$25,800	$25,800	$25,800	$25,800	$115,629	$183,337
Total Expenditure	$116,461	$58,749	$58,749	$140,624	$155,258	$172,504	$295,971	$395,819
Net Results								
Net Profit or Loss	($116,461)	($58,749)	($58,749)	($140,624)	($155,258)	($172,504)	($295,971)	$1,104,181
Cash on Hand	$1,883,539	$1,824,790	$1,766,041	$1,625,417	$1,470,159	$1,297,655	$1,001,684	$2,105,865

Fig. A.8. • A typical project master cash forecast for a product-oriented project. Note that the first year forecast is presented by month and that the next four years are presented by year. Also note that this project will require massive infusions of cash (to fund expansion and receivables). However, on an accrual basis, the project is highly *profitable* in every one of the five years. In general, although it is a simplified document and it leaves a lot out, the cash forecast is adequate for most project planning activities.

contain a description of the procedures that will be followed in maintaining the project budget throughout the duration of the project. For projects carried out within an institution with its own financial personnel, this should be a simple description of how the existing accounting systems will be employed on the project. For projects involving a new enterprise, the description should include a discussion of both who will do the various accounting functions, and how those functions will be done. For projects of any significant magnitude, auditors should be selected for the project and regular audits should be scheduled. For projects conducted within an institution, the audits can be carried out by independent auditors within the organization. For new enterprises, one of the "Big Six" accounting firms should be engaged for this purpose (actually, for years there were eight large accounting firms, but these have been reduced to six due to mergers between them—the number may yet shrink further). The reputations of these firms are unimpeachable and they bring with them an enormous amount of experience and expertise. Also, all of the Big Six firms have small-business divisions at most of their business offices which specialize in the needs of small enterprises and provide their services at (sometimes) a substantial discount. For a small company that looks like it may grow into a large

Sep-97	Oct-97	Nov-97	Dec-97	1997 TOTALS	1998	1999	2000	2001
$0	$0	$0	$0	$2,000,000	$8,000,000	$12,000,000	$15,000,000	$50,000,000
								(public offering)
1	1	1	2	8	63	150		
$500,000	$500,000	$500,000	$500,000	$500,000	$300,000	$250,000		
$500,000	$500,000	$500,000	$1,000,000	$4,000,000	$18,900,000	$37,500,000		
						320	310	150
						$100,000	$90,000	$90,000
						$32,000,000	$27,900,000	$13,500,000
							2380	5730
							$30,000	$20,000
							$71,400,000	$114,600,000
$500,000	$500,000	$500,000	$1,000,000	$4,000,000	$18,900,000	$69,500,000	$99,300,000	$128,100,000
$43,794	$49,794	$104,654	$94,654	$521,266	$2,221,867	$3,237,054	$5,347,568	$8,606,959
$48,183	$55,671	$55,671	$55,671	$539,724	$3,822,200	$6,115,520	$9,784,832	$15,655,731
$83,419	$75,319	$89,584	$92,342	$611,545	$4,631,700	$7,410,720	$11,857,152	$18,971,443
$151,740	$206,877	$526,277	$526,277	$1,470,049	$10,052,000	$48,963,704	$69,958,213	$85,735,797
$308,520	$120,968	$425,115	$225,000	$1,591,071	$5,278,100	$8,444,960	$13,511,936	$18,619,098
$635,656	$508,619	$1,201,301	$993,944	$4,733,655	$26,005,867	$74,171,958	$110,459,701	$147,589,028
($135,656)	($8,619)	($701,301)	$6,056	($733,655)	($7,105,867)	($4,671,958)	($11,159,701)	($19,489,028)
$1,970,209	$1,961,590	$1,260,289	$1,266,345	$1,266,345	$2,160,478	$9,488,520	$13,328,820	$43,839,791

company, accounting services are sometimes provided on a "loss-leader" basis, which can save a small company quite a bit of cash in the beginning. One general rule holds for all professional services: always go with the best practitioners (the best cost about the same as the worst).

Every large project should be audited by independent accountants on a yearly basis. The result of this audit should be a certified audit statement signed by the auditors. Summary audits and other types of audits short of a full-fledged audit are essentially useless and are a waste of money. Complete audits by independent internal auditors or by a Big Six accounting firm provide the project with an unassailable statement of the financial activities of the project over the previous year. This can save many headaches and allow project personnel to continue to focus on their responsibilities.

A.1.11 Financing and Ownership

Business plans for small projects, where the resources to be expended are entirely under the control of the organizers of the project, and where the ownership of the results is clearly defined, do not need this section (except perhaps to clearly document these arrangements). However, most projects do require resources from sponsors outside the group of project organizers, and will have ownership that is split many ways. In these instances, it is important to spell out where these resources will come from and how the ownership of the results of the project will be allocated. That is the purpose of this section of the business plan.

Financing for a project can come from a large variety of sources: capital funds of a company, research and development funds set aside from profit, a government contract (or grant), private investors, a university research endowment, a venture capital fund, etc. In the financing and ownership section of the business plan, the proposed source(s) of funding for the project should be identified. The amount of funding expected from each source and the timing of the resource infusions should both be spelled out. Almost all projects of any magnitude are funded incrementally. This allows the sponsoring institutions to monitor project progress and 'cut their losses' if the project is, for some reason, unsuccessful.

When submitting a business plan for consideration by funding sources, it is essential that the sources chosen be compatible with the planned project. Essentially every funding source has a limited range of project types that it funds. Here is another place where expert advice can be of great value. Finally, it is important to realize that the business plan format presented here, while essentially universal, may have to be rearranged or modified somewhat to be consistent with the format used by some funding sources.

The subject of ownership can be tricky. Most projects carried out within an existing institution have the characteristic that the ownership of the output of the project is usually not in question—all rights are transferred to that institution. However, for independent projects that produce tangible or intellectual property and/or lead to the founding of a company, ownership can be an important issue. It is essential in such instances that the ownership allocation be carefully planned *before* the project is started. These agreed-upon ownership arrangements should be spelled out clearly and unequivocally in the business plan to the satisfaction of all parties.

The amount of ownership of the output of a project by an individual or institution is usually roughly proportional to the contribution they made to the success of the project, with some exceptions. One typical exception is the founders or originators of the project. They tend to get somewhat more than they might otherwise, simply because they were the ones who took the early initiative and risks and got the whole thing going. Institutions and/or individuals who provide funding for a project also tend to get more than might seem appropriate, but this is because they are risking tangible liquid assets that could just as well have been invested in a much safer place.

One of the difficulties in spelling out ownership in a business plan is that the actual contribution of each of the named parties to the success of the project cannot be assessed until the project is already well underway. One practical solution to this problem is the concept of *vesting*. In vesting, each participant in the project is guaranteed a particular amount of ownership at the outset, but they do not get this ownership until they have earned it by actually participating in the project. For projects of finite duration, vesting should take place in accordance with a linear law (with ownership starting at zero on the day the project starts, and ending up with the full agreed-upon amount on the last day of the project). Ownership increments usually occur every quarter or every year on this linear scale. If the project is a new company, a four-year vesting schedule is traditional. Vesting should apply to all participants, even founders. Nothing is more annoying than having a non-vesting founder who quits the project or company (or gets fired) and simply sits back and waits for everyone else to do the work and to receive his/her payoff. Project participants who quit or are fired and leave with fractional ownership are typically constrained from selling that ownership to anyone else (until the current participants are allowed to sell theirs as well—as, for example, when a company's stock becomes publicly traded).

For projects to be funded by, and carried out within, an existing institution, the procedures for submitting project plans are usually well established. The chances of project success can be increased greatly by getting and following advice from individuals who have successfully completed similar projects.

For research and development projects to be funded by government agencies, foundations, or universities, there are essentially only two rules that must be followed. First, make sure that the project is appropriate in its subject matter, scope, and funding level for the organization(s) from which funding is sought. For example, the National Science Foundation would typically not support development of a neurocomputing-based hay baler. Nor would the Department of Agriculture support development of a neurocomputer pattern recognition system for particle accelerator bubble chamber photographs. Assuming that the subject matter is correct, the scope of the project is within the acceptable limits (the project doesn't attempt to do too much or too little, nor venture into areas of activity that are inappropriate), and the funding amount requested is within the acceptable range, then the only remaining question is the attractiveness of the business plan to your peers. If the current "in-crowd" of your field will judge the plan to be worthy of support, then it will probably be supported. If they don't find it worthy of support, then it probably won't be. It's that simple. A certain amount of the worthiness factor depends on who you are, where you are, who you work with, and who you know. A Nobel Prize winner can turn in virtually any grant request and have it funded. An obscure individual at an obscure institution with no credentials and no standing in the community must produce a spectacularly good proposal to get funding. But if the plan is good enough, it will almost certainly be funded. The existing system, while not completely fair, is consistent.

For new companies,[12] there are several sources of funding: corporate investment, private investment, venture investment, government grants, etc. These

---

[12] For anyone thinking about starting a company, I strongly recommend the book *Entrepreneuring* [28] by Steven Brandt. This concise, well written book presents a wealth of practical information on successfully starting and running a business.

sources have significantly different characteristics and the choice of source can have a large influence on the probability of success. The first fact that must be faced is that, unlike internal projects and sponsored research projects (which are usually successful), the vast majority of start-up companies fail. Although the failure of a small company can be caused by many factors, the most common root cause of company failure is inadequate management. Similarly, the success of start-up companies that prosper can usually be attributed to the actions of a good management team. Bluntly put, the success of a start-up company has very little to do with technology (although the technology may provide the reason for starting the company). Thus, anyone considering starting a new company should spend a great deal of time devising a plan for attracting and retaining a good management team.

There are basically two approaches for financing a new company: the bootstrap approach and the venture capital approach. The bootstrap approach involves starting the company on a shoestring and working to achieve self-financed growth through the profits from sales. Bootstrap companies can be very successful (for example, a company that later became IBM was started by Herman Hollerith as a part-time activity while he was an employee of the United States Census Bureau). However, such companies often suffer from the limitation that they quickly develop a culture of "going it alone" that makes it difficult for them to bring in substantive management talent and to attract the large amounts of capital required for growth and expansion. Thus, most bootstrap companies that succeed (the percentage that succeed is, of course, very low) tend to have their sales revenues level off at very modest levels (although some, like IBM, later become large public companies).

The venture capital approach involves giving up much of the ownership of the company in return for the capital to fund start up, product development and growth. Institutional venture capital investors essentially all operate in accordance with a standard, unvarying formula. The formula involves a sequence of events that start with the evaluation of the business plan and end with the company either selling its stock on the open market or being acquired by another company. The goal of venture capitalists is to make money over a five-year to seven-year cycle.

Venture capital firms set up large pools of money called *funds* (funds are typically 10 million to 100 million dollars in size) that are made up of investments by private individuals, large corporations, trust funds, pension funds, governments, etc. The venture capitalists then invest the money in the fund in small companies over a three to five year period. At the end of a period of approximately five to ten years, the fund is terminated and the proceeds are distributed to the original investors (with a percentage being retained by the venture capitalists as their fee). Thus, the goal of each investment is to achieve *liquidity* at the end of a period of four to seven years by having the company in which the fund invested begin selling its stock on the open market or by having another company buy its stock for cash. Any companies that have not gone public or been acquired by the time the fund ends simply have their stock distributed to the investors in the fund. Some well-run venture funds have been able to consistently achieve average returns of 40% per year.

The first step in obtaining venture funding is to write a first-class business plan that convincingly demonstrates the potential for the company to grow to fairly high levels of yearly revenue within the first five years of operation (most venture funds are not interested in companies unless they have the potential to reach annual revenues of 50 million dollars or more within five years). The next step is to submit this business plan to several reputable venture firms for analysis and review. The first response will likely be a number of criticisms of the plan that can then be used to refine the plan further. Only rarely will a venture fund invest in a company alone. Thus, all of the venture firms that like the plan should be put in contact with one another so that they can form a funding "syndicate". The average reputable venture firm receives hundreds of business plans every year. Of these, only a few are actually funded. The reason venture funding is so avidly sought is its impact on the overall probability of success. For non-venture funded companies, approximately 90% are out of business within two years after start up. Among venture-funded companies, approximately 50% go on to become permanently successful companies. However, fewer than 10% of the venture funded companies actually reach the 50 million dollar level (at which the venture companies can get a major payback). In other words, the venture capital business is a numbers game: only a small fraction of the companies funded by the firm actually make it big—but these more than make up for the investments lost in the companies that failed or leveled off at too small a revenue level.

In selecting venture capital firms, it is essential that only the most reputable firms be considered (ask for the names of companies they have funded and check them out). Also, only the individual venture capitalists who have the best reputations (again, check them out) should be dealt with. The importance of checking out the candidate venture firms, and the individual venture capitalists at those firms, cannot be overstated.

Besides capital, good venture capital firms bring many other things to a company. They often are of great assistance in attracting a good management team, they can introduce the company to larger companies that might be interested in joint R&D efforts or volume purchases of the product, and they can participate as members of the new company's Board of Directors; giving ongoing sage advice and providing access (via "networking") to expertise in a variety of areas. They can also be useful in helping select an appropriate Big Six accounting firm and law firm for the company. Thus, for those companies that have the potential to grow to medium or large size, venture capital is often the golden road to success.

Obtaining venture funding can take a long time. A year or more elapsed time between the completion of the first business plan and the actual deposit of the first check in the bank is not unusual. To allow the founders time to pursue venture capital and refine their business plan, interim financing (to allow the company to get started) in the form of *seed capital* is often a good approach. A number of specialized venture capital firms concentrate their activities in this area, with some even running "hothouses" in which the founders of the company can be given an office, secretarial support, telephones, and personal computer resources[13] with which to pursue the venture funding of their business. For anyone interested in considering starting a venture-funded company, the easiest approach is to simply contact the nearest office of any of the Big Six accounting firms and ask to speak with the partner who specializes in start-up businesses. This person will typically have a wealth of knowledge of the venture capital community and will be able to steer you to appropriate resources.

In the end, every for-profit project involves an investment by one or more parties. Therefore, as part of the business planning process it is always a good idea to estimate the return that each of these investments will bring (i.e., the actual return to the investing party—not the overall business profitability analysis contained in the business plan). Although these calculations are typically not presented in the business plan, they are useful in determining how the investment looks from the standpoint of the capital sources. If these returns are too low it may be difficult to find investors. In this case, the financing and ownership portion of the business plan may have to be restructured.

In conclusion, writing a business plan is a lot of work. It is almost a simulation of actually carrying out the project. That is why it is so valuable and essential: it is a way to find out whether the project really makes sense as it is currently planned. The fact is that most business plans do not make sense when they are first written. The writers may find, for example, that the entire project is out of sync with their personal goals. Or, perhaps the project is attempting to do something that is virtually impossible. By iteratively modifying and analyzing the business plan, either the bugs can be worked out, or the plan can be abandoned. If the plan is ultimately discarded, everyone has saved an enormous amount of time and effort (and in some cases, a good chunk of the lives of the participants). If the plan can be worked up into one that makes good sense, then the participants have gone a long way towards insuring the success of the project. A good business plan allows the project to get off and running and get up to speed with few problems. By the time the problems come along, the necessary management skills will either be on-board or accessible, and the problems can usually be successfully worked.

A.2 Writing a Proposal

Virtually all major human endeavors involve the efforts of multiple groups. As a result, a means for selecting those groups and coordinating their activities must be utilized. Among nations, the primary vehicles for achieving these aims are

---

[13] The use of a user–friendly personal computer with good word processing, graphics, and spreadsheet software for entering a business plan is almost mandatory for all but the smallest projects. A laser printer and a copy machine are also indispensable.

negotiations and treaties. In technology, the primary vehicles are the RFP/RFQ, the proposal, and the contract. This section of the appendix discusses proposal structure and proposal writing, following a brief overview of RFPs and RFQs.

A.2.1 RFPs and RFQs

Requests for Proposals and Requests for Quotations are documents that clearly specify a task to be accomplished and solicit proposals from qualified bidders to carry out that task. Except in rare instances, an RFP or RFQ will be distributed to several qualified groups. This introduces the all-important aspect of competition into the process. Without competition, there is no particular incentive for the bidder to prepare an attractive, high-value proposal. Nonetheless, there are situations where there will be only one bidder. Typically, this occurs because some element of the work to be performed can only be carried out by that group, or where there is only one source for a required piece of equipment. Such situations are called *sole-source* procurements.

An RFP describes a general task to be accomplished, or an item to be developed, in terms of a functional description of that task and/or item. By only providing a functional description, the bidders are given substantial latitude in formulating a specific set of plans and designs for meeting the RFP's requirements. In an RFQ, the exact work to be performed and/or the exact hardware to be procured and assembled is specified precisely. With an RFQ, all the sponsoring organization wants is a cost quotation from bidders telling them what it will cost to provide the specified services and/or equipment.

A.2.2 Proposal Organization

Proposals written in response to an RFP typically consist of three volumes: the *Technical Volume*, the *Management Volume*, and the *Cost Volume* (for small proposals, the first two of these are sometimes consolidated). RFQs usually only require Management and Cost Volumes. The outline of a typical proposal is given below (note: sometimes the Executive Summary sections of the Technical and Management Volumes are merged into a separate Executive Summary Volume):

TECHNICAL VOLUME

1.0 Executive Summary
    1.1 The End User Problem
    1.2 The Equivalent Technical Problem
    1.3 Our Technical Approach
    1.4 How We are Going to Conduct this Project
    1.5 Features and Benefits of Our Project Plan
    1.6 Why Our Approach is Superior
2.0 The End User Problem
    2.1 Succinct Description of the End User Problem
    2.2 Significance and Impact of the End User Problem

5.2 Relevant University Relationships
5.3 Relevant Industrial Relationships
5.4 Relevant Governmental Relationships
6.0 Facilities
   6.1 Physical Plant
   6.2 Proximity to Relevant Infrastructure
   6.3 Cultural, Philosophic, and Work Practice Advantages
7.0 Equipment
   7.1 Relevant General-Purpose Equipment
   7.2 Relevant Specialized Equipment
   7.3 Outside Equipment to Which We Have Access
8.0 Capabilities
   8.1 Review of Our Relevant Capabilities
   8.2 Benefits to the Project from Relevant Capabilities
9.0 Experience
   9.1 Relevant Experience
   9.2 References
Appendix: Resumes of Key Personnel and Outside Participants and Advisors
COST VOLUME

1.0 Executive Summary
   1.1 Benefits and Features of Our Cost Plan
   1.2 Sources of Extra Value in Our Project Plan
2.0 Project Statement of Work
   2.1 Listing of Formal Statement of Work
   2.2 Notes and Comments on the Statement of Work
3.0 Project Schedule
   3.1 Graphical Formal Project Schedule
   3.1 Notes and Comments on the Schedule
4.0 Project Deliverables/Receivables
   4.1 Formal Deliverables List
   4.2 Formal Receivables List
   4.3 Notes and Comments on the Deliverables/Receivables Lists
5.0 Project Budget
   5.1 Labor Categories and Hourly Rates
   5.2 Formal Budget Spreadsheet
   5.3 Notes and Comments on the Budget
6.0 Project Accounting
   6.1 Our Tracking System for Labor Hours, Materials Costs, and Other Expenses
   6.2 Our Billing Generation System
   6.3 Our Audit and Compliance Monitoring Systems
7.0 Payment Arrangements
   7.1 Our Planned Billing Procedure
   7.2 How and When We Expect You to Pay Us
8.0 Representations and Certifications

The Cost Volume of the proposal is usually not supplied to the technical evaluators, since their role is usually restricted solely to technical evaluation. Most of the section titles used in the outline shown are somewhat different than those used in an actual proposal. They are designed to emphasize the tone in which the sections should be written. In particular, the terms "we" and "our" should be used whenever appropriate (but not to excess, as in this outline). Dry, impersonal prose detracts significantly from a proposal, since most readers interpret it as an indication of embarrassment or as an attempt on the part of the writer to express personal disagreement with the contents of the proposal.

A.2.3 Proposal Writing

The previous subsection of this appendix discussed proposal organization. It briefly described what should be in a proposal. In this subsection we examine the process by which a proposal is actually written.

PREPARING TO WRITE THE PROPOSAL   Proposal writing is both an art and a technology. Most organizations which prepare large numbers of proposals every year have developed an elaborate, refined, and effective methodology for proposal writing. While this subsection cannot hope to present such a comprehensive methodology, at least the basic ingredients can be discussed.

The first consideration in proposal writing is the milieu. The proposal writing team should be provided with an environment that allows for concentrated, uninterrupted work on the proposal. The environment should also provide a means for tacking the proposal up on walls (corkboard walls and push pins with plastic handles are best, but ordinary walls and non-marring tape will do). Facilities (and personnel support) for word processing, draft and final printing, artwork production, and copying are also essential.

The most important ingredient in preparing a good proposal is to pick a good proposal team. Ideally, the proposal writing team will be the same people who later go on to actually perform the work of the resulting project. Unfortunately, the skills involved in project conception and proposal writing are quite different from those involved in actually carrying out a project. Thus, it will be rare that the project personnel also have outstanding project conception and proposal writing skills. For this reason, the best approach is to have experienced and talented project conceptual thinkers and proposal writers in charge of the proposal; but to also have the project performance personnel heavily involved as advisors, quality control inspectors, and "worker bees". Their involvement is crucial since they will ensure that what is proposed can actually be done. This also ensures continuity between the proposal and the actual project. Without project personnel involvement it is likely that the proposal will be unrealistic and that the proposed project will be unperformable. At an absolute minimum, every proposal should be subjected to a 'sanity check' by an experienced project manager—who has veto power — before it is submitted.

The best people to pick for a proposal team are those associated with past proposals that went on to be successful projects (notice that this is different from the most common criterion of a track record of winning proposals). Because all organizations have turnover, it is wise to include a small number of people who have never before worked on a proposal. This will ensure a continued supply of proposal writers. However, such novices are typically not very effective. In fact, they often cause considerable rework effort. Thus, the number of such people included on the proposal team must be kept to the absolute minimum necessary.

Every proposal should have an overall Proposal Manager who is personally accountable both for winning the procurement competition *and* for proposing a project that can actually be successfully performed as proposed (a much more difficult goal). Working for the Proposal Manager are the Volume Captains (one Captain for each volume of the proposal). The Captains are individually totally in charge of their volume. However, their primary job is coordinating between one another to ensure total consistency of material and presentation style between volumes.

THE ROLES OF THE VOLUME CAPTAINS   The primary job of the Technical Volume Captain is to clearly and precisely define the end user problem, translate this into the associated technical problem, and then ensure the early development of an innovative, effective, and practical technical approach for solving this technical problem[14]. Following this, the first drafts of the statement of work, schedule, deliverables, receivables, and budget are produced. These are subsequently put through many cycles of revision and refinement during the writing cycle. The Cost Volume Captain's team should take over the task of maintaining and inserting updates into the statement of work, schedule, deliverables, receivables, and budget immediately after the first drafts are produced by the Technical Volume team. The Technical Volume team also produces the initial drafts of the project organization chart and project management plan.

The most difficult challenges in preparing the Technical Volume are devising the technical approach and developing the project plan.[15] Because the rest of the proposal is built around these two items, they must be developed early in the proposal cycle and must be right. If the approach or project plan are later shown to have fundamental flaws this can be disastrous. The ability to conceive

---

[14] Top-notch Technical Volume Captains often create the overall project concept and then work with the sponsor to structure the RFP. While this does not (necessarily) "wire" the outcome, it usually introduces a high barrier that any competitor will have to get over to win.

[15] Oddly, definition of the end user problem and translation of this into the technical problem are also usually difficult.

a winning technical approach and develop a good project plan is very rare, particularly for larger projects. But at least one such individual or (for really large projects) a team of them must be enlisted if the proposal effort is to be a success.

The Management Volume Captain is primarily responsible for pulling together the diverse material that makes up the Management Volume. Many organizations maintain full and current resumes on all key technical personnel as well as periodically updated descriptions of past experience, outside resources, facilities, and equipment. Creation of the Management Volume is made much easier if such preexisting material is available. Regardless of whether they are already available or are generated from scratch, all of these materials need to be checked extensively for accuracy, currency, and internal consistency. They should not be treated merely as "boilerplate" to be used as-is; since this approach is usually quite obvious and detracts significantly from the appeal of the proposal.

The Cost Volume Captain's time is primarily spent modifying and checking the the formal statement of work, formal schedule, deliverables list, receivables list, and budget in response to Technical and Management Volume changes. One of the key factors to success in proposal writing is the ability to make these changes rapidly with little effort. Here again, computerized spreadsheets and other integrated planning tools are of great value.

The next section discusses the essential subjects of project planning and project management for development projects. As with business plans and proposals, almost every neurocomputing project involves these elements.

A.3 Planning and Managing Development

Once the decision to proceed with a project has been made, the development plan must be refined and executed. The technical members of the project team are typically responsible for carrying out these activities. The purpose of this section is to discuss a practical methodology for creating a detailed development plan and then managing the project to that plan. The methodology presented here (which extensively exploits the capabilities of modern personal computers) is simpler than most taught in university engineering economics and project management courses. But, experience has shown that maximum simplicity is essential if a methodology is to actually be used on a day-by-day basis in the real world.

A.3.1 The Development Planning Process
A plan for a development project consists of four documents:

- Statement of Work
- Schedule
- Milestone Definitions

⋮

Task 2—Software Development and Test. This task shall develop the software for the prototype system. The design of this software shall meet the requirements of the system specification produced in Task 1 and incorporate the relevant elements of the system design produced in Task 1. The software shall be thoroughly and iteratively tested and improved and be ready for integration with the hardware portion of the system no later than 1 October 1997.

- Subtask 2.1—Rapid Prototype. A rapid prototype of the final software shall be constructed. This prototype shall be consistent with the system specification and draft design document of Task 1 and shall include a simulated operational system environment. The completed rapid prototype shall demonstrate the capabilities that can be expected of the final software configuration.

- Subtask 2.2—Software Development. The system software shall be designed and developed and then tested at the module level. This software shall meet the requirements of the system specification produced in Task 1 and shall be consistent with the system design produced in Task 1. The software development process of this task is expected to draw heavily from the results of Subtask 2.1.

- Subtask 2.3—Iterative Test and Modification. The software produced in Subtask 2.2 shall be iteratively tested and modified to eliminate faults and design deficiencies

⋮

Fig. A.9. • A portion of a two-level WBS.

- Staffing Plan and Budget

The creation of these documents is discussed in this subsection. Their use in project management is discussed in the next subsection.

STATEMENT OF WORK   The statement of work (also known as a *Work Breakdown Structure*—WBS) is a hierarchical description of all of the work that is to be done on the project. The high-level work elements are the tasks from the business plan or proposal statement of work. These are brought over intact. The original high-level statement of work should not be modified without extensive discussion with all project participants and sponsors. Any change at this level represents a major deviation from the agreed-upon plan and must be ratified by all participating parties.[16]

The first step in creating the detailed WBS is to take each of the major tasks of the project and decide what subtasks need to be carried out in order

---

[16] Changing the top-level plan is often necessary if the plan extends beyond 12 to 18 months in duration, since conditions change and new facts become known.

to complete each major task. This creates the second level of the WBS. Each of the subtasks are then analyzed to determine the individual work elements that are required to complete them—thus creating the subsubtasks, and so on. Each task, subtask, and subsubtask, etc., is accompanied by a text description (typically a short paragraph using the word *shall*—to emphasize the contractual nature of the document) that spells out in precise detail what the task includes, indicating any particular agreed-upon specifications or requirements that must be met.

Small projects lasting only a few weeks can usually be conducted from a one-level WBS. With experience, such a structure can be put together in an hour or so. Larger, more ambitious, projects may require a WBS with four or more levels. Most projects end up using a two-level WBS. A portion of a typical development project WBS is shown in Figure A.9.

SCHEDULE   Just as the WBS is based on the statement of work in the business plan or proposal, the schedule is merely an extension of the schedule portion of the development plan section of the business plan or proposal. Figure A.10 shows a portion of a typical development schedule. As with the WBS, any deviation of the highest-level task schedules or milestones from those stated in the business plan should be discussed with all key project participants and ratified. Naturally, the high-level schedule is developed iteratively from the lower level schedules for each of the subtasks, subsubtasks, etc.

MILESTONE DEFINITIONS   Binary milestones are then developed for each of the lowest level elements of the WBS. Each milestone is described in detail in an appendix that accompanies the schedule (see Figure A.11 for some examples of milestone descriptions). Remember, milestones must be yes-or-no (i.e., binary) and must be objectively measurable by outside personnel not connected with the project. Each lowest-level element of the WBS (i.e., each element that has nothing beneath it in the hierarchy) must have a binary milestone developed for it at intervals of no greater than two technologist weeks of effort. The process of developing these milestones greatly assists project personnel in focusing on the actual work that will be carried out in each WBS element. This tightens up the planning process and makes it more realistic.

STAFFING PLAN AND BUDGET   Given the WBS, schedule, and milestone descriptions, the next step is to create the combination staffing plan and budget. Typically, a single spreadsheet, such as the one shown in Figure A.12, is used to encapsulate both of these into one document (this facilitates the many iterations that are typically required). The staffing plan spells out in detail who is going to work on each element of the WBS and when. The traditional approach is to not list people by name, but by *labor category*. Typical labor categories are: Support, Technician, Engineer, Senior Engineer, Principal Engineer, etc. By using labor categories the aggregate work of multiple people in the same labor category can be agglomerated in the staffing plan. Another advantage to using labor categories, particularly on larger projects, or within larger organizations,

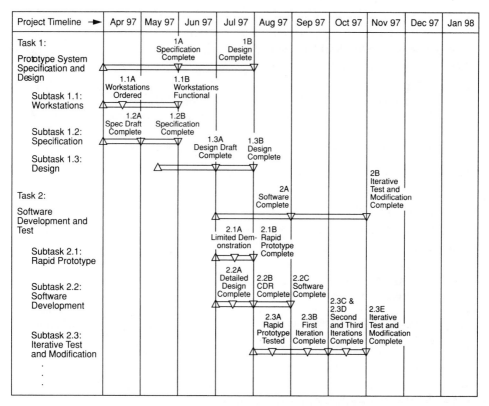

Fig. A.10. • A portion of a typical development schedule. Note that each of the two tasks shown consist of three subtasks. Task 2 of this project is described in the WBS of Figure A.9. Figure A.11 presents a description of the milestones of Subtask 2.2.

is that the budget portion can list the average hourly salary of workers in each category without revealing the salaries of individual participants (salary data is very sensitive). Without this provision, the staffing plan/budget could only be seen by people who would have a need to know salary information—which is typically a very small group of managers and administrative people.

In the staffing plan, each lowest-level element of the WBS is listed, followed by the labor categories that will directly work on that element. Each category is allotted one horizontal row of the sheet (see Figure A.12). The vertical columns of the sheets are months (weeks for small projects), beginning with the first month of the project at the left and going to the last month of the project at the right. The number of hours that people in each labor category will work on each of the WBS elements is listed for each month of the project. Note that only people directly working on the project are listed. People who carry out administrative, sales, marketing, and management duties are paid for out of *overhead* and *general and administrative* monies. These monies are added later

⋮

Subtask 2.2—Software Development

- Milestone 2.2A—Detailed Software Design

   This milestone is complete when the detailed software design document, based upon the system specification produced in Subtask 1.2 and the draft system design document produced in Subtask 1.3 is finished.

- Milestone 2.2B—Software CDR

   The detailed software design document produced earlier in this Subtask (see Milestone 2.2A) shall be iteratively improved and (in close consultation with the people working on Subtask 1.3) made consistent with the final system design document being produced contemporaneously in Subtask 1.3. This milestone is complete when the final detailed software design document has successfully passed a Critical Design Review (CDR) conducted by the Project Manager.

- Milestone 2.2C—Software Complete

   The modules of the final software design produced earlier in this subtask shall be completely coded. Each module will pass a functional test (produced by the module developer) that is sufficient to show that the module meets the requirements of, and is consistent with, the system specification, system design, and detailed software design. This milestone is complete when the modules, the test routines, and the functional testing results have passed a final design review conducted by the Project Manager.

⋮

Fig. A.11. • A portion of a typical milestone definition document.

in the budget as burdens applied to labor and cost (as will be shown). The main point is that these personnel do not show up in the staffing plan.

To make planning easy it is useful to list the materials costs, equipment rental costs (purchased equipment is not charged against the project unless it will be used only for that project and discarded at the end of the project—is is charged to operations), travel costs, and other direct costs associated with each WBS element (other direct costs include incidentals such as copying, photography, videotaping, services, etc.). In formulating both the staffing plan and estimating these costs it is helpful to be able to view the schedule and milestones. The easiest way to do this is to simply add these above each WBS element, as shown in Figure A.12. Note that in Figure A.12 there are two rows for each entry. One of these rows is for entering the *planned* resource expenditures (labor hours, materials costs, travel costs, and other direct costs). The other is for entering the *actual* expenditures as the project proceeds. For example, in the budget presented in Figure A.12 the actual hours worked and the actual direct costs have been filled in up through September of 1997. Using this data, charts can be built that show the variance between the planned costs and the actual costs. These are used in project management (see the next subsection for details on how these are used).

After the labor hours and costs have been determined for each lowest-level WBS element they are then accumulated for the higher level elements; up to the task level. For very large projects (say, 10 technologist years or greater) the budget is then calculated at the task levels and later accumulated. However, for all but these very large projects it is usually adequate to simply accumulate all of the task labor and cost totals at the bottom of the spreadsheet and figure the budget for the project as a whole (as in Figure A.13).

To calculate the budget (which is usually done for each month and then accumulated to get a project total—see Figure A.13) the first step is to add two new sets of rows (under the project-total labor hours by category, but before the materials, equipment, travel, and other direct costs) listing the labor hours and labor costs in each labor category. These are obtained by multiplying the total labor hours in each category in each month by the established hourly labor rate for that category (listed in column B of Figure A.13). These costs are then summed to get the total labor cost for that month. Again, as in the staffing plan, two rows—planned and actual—are provided for each item.

Following the calculation of labor costs a row for stating the overhead cost is added. Overhead is figured by simply multiplying the total labor cost by the *overhead rate.* The overhead rate is calculated by taking all of the indirect expenses that scale with labor hours (facilities expenses, employee fringe benefits, the employer–paid portion of social security taxes, gas and electricity costs, generally available computers, software, and office equipment costs, the cost of secretaries and other support personnel, test equipment costs, office furnishings, employee benefits, accounting/sales/marketing/support/operations labor costs, advertising expenses, supplies, etc.) and dividing the sum of them by the corresponding cost of direct labor expended on projects. Overhead rates in the range of 80% to 200% are common. The use of an overhead rate makes project budgeting much easier by providing a simple mechanism for taking a wide variety of indirect costs (the ones that scale with the direct labor expended by the organization) into account. Underneath the calculation of overhead, the direct costs (materials, rented equipment, travel, and other) and the monthly costs of any subcontracts are listed. The sum of these costs (total labor, overhead, materials, rental equipment, travel, other direct, and subcontract costs) is the total *cost* of the project.

After the cost has been determined, the next step is to add the *General and Administrative* (G&A) burden. This burden is obtained by multiplying the cost by the G&A rate. The G&A rate is determined by adding the expenses of the organization (over a fixed period of time — usually the last fiscal year) for items other than those counted in overhead, such as management labor cost, accounting firm audit costs, legal fees, etc. (i.e., those costs that do not scale linearly with direct labor) and divide this sum by the total costs of the projects of the organization over the same period of time. G&A rates are almost always in the range of 10% to 40%, with the vast majority close to 20%.

Project Timeline --->	Apr-97	May-97	Jun-97	Jul-97	Aug-97	Sep-97	Oct-97	Nov-97	Dec-97	Jan-98	TOTALS
Project Element V											
	Start	1A Prototype Specification Completed		1B Prototype Design Completed							
Task 1: Prototype System Specification and Design											
Principal Engineer -- Actual	145	170	180	82							577
Principal Engineer -- Planned	170	170	170	80							590
Senior Engineer -- Actual	518	412	772	489							2191
Senior Engineer -- Planned	510	510	510	510							2040
Engineer -- Actual	121	520	544	204							1389
Engineer -- Planned	510	510	510	300							1830
Technician -- Actual	62	3	45	12							122
Technician -- Planned	20	20	20	20							80
Material -- Actual	$345	$18,735	$4,289	$3,174							$26,543
Material -- Planned	$200	$200	$3,600	$3,600							$7,600
Rental Equipment -- Actual	$4,000	$3,308	$4,023	$1,892							$13,223
Rental Equipment -- Planned	$4,000	$4,000	$4,000	$4,000							$16,000
Travel -- Actual	$1,448	$1,634	$6,290	$612							$9,984
Travel -- Planned	$1,500	$1,500	$6,000	$1,000							$10,000
Other -- Actual	$2,508	$122	$715	$280							$3,625
Other -- Planned	$2,500	$300	$300	$100							$3,200
				Start	2A Prototype Software Completed		2B Iterative Test & Modif. Completed				
Task 2: Software Development and Test											
Principal Engineer -- Actual				78	54	86					218
Principal Engineer -- Planned				90	80	80	50				300
Senior Engineer -- Actual				288	368	331					987
Senior Engineer -- Planned				340	340	340	340				1360
Engineer -- Actual				145	267	419					831
Engineer -- Planned				170	340	340	170				1020
Technician -- Actual				33	17	22					72
Technician -- Planned				20	20	20	20				80
Material -- Actual				$231	$182	$0					$413
Material -- Planned				$100	$300	$300	$300				$1,000
Rental Equipment -- Actual				$0	$0	$0					$0
Rental Equipment -- Planned				$0	$0	$0	$0				$0
Travel -- Actual				$329	$112	$0					$441
Travel -- Planned				$200	$200	$200	$200				$800
Other -- Actual				$170	$55	$129					$354
Other -- Planned				$150	$400	$400	$500				$1,450

Fig. A.12. • Two task allocation budget examples from a combination staffing plan and budget.

Project Timeline --->	Rate	Apr-97	May-97	Jun-97	Jul-97	Aug-97	Sep-97	Oct-97	Nov-97	Dec-97	Jan-98	TOTALS
TOTALS:												
Labor Hours:												
Total Principal Engineer Labor Hours -- Actual		145	170	180	160	354	286	0	0	0	0	1295
Total Principal Engineer Labor Hours -- Planned		170	170	170	170	170	170	170	170	170	170	1700
Total Senior Engineer Labor Hours -- Actual		518	412	772	993	1115	699	0	0	0	0	4509
Total Senior Engineer Labor Hours -- Planned		510	510	510	1020	1020	1020	1020	1020	780	510	7920
Total Engineer Labor Hours -- Actual		121	520	544	701	687	688	0	0	0	0	3261
Total Engineer Labor Hours -- Planned		510	510	510	680	680	680	680	850	620	510	6230
Total Technician Labor Hours -- Actual		62	3	45	145	170	166	0	0	0	0	591
Total Technician Labor Hours -- Planned		20	20	20	170	170	170	170	170	170	80	1160
Total Labor Hours -- Actual		846	1105	1541	1999	2326	1839	0	0	0	0	9656
Total Labor Hours -- Planned		1210	1210	1210	2040	2040	2040	2040	2210	1740	1270	17010
Labor Cost:	Rate											
Principal Engineer Hourly Labor Cost -- Actual	$35.87	$5,201	$6,098	$6,457	$5,739	$12,698	$10,259	$0	$0	$0	$0	$46,452
Principal Engineer Hourly Labor Cost -- Planned	$35.87	$6,098	$6,098	$6,098	$6,098	$6,098	$6,098	$6,098	$6,098	$6,098	$6,098	$60,979
Senior Engineer Hourly Labor Cost -- Actual	$29.12	$15,084	$11,997	$22,481	$28,916	$32,469	$20,355	$0	$0	$0	$0	$131,302
Senior Engineer Hourly Labor Cost -- Planned	$29.12	$14,851	$14,851	$14,851	$29,702	$29,702	$29,702	$29,702	$29,702	$22,714	$14,851	$230,630
Engineer Hourly Labor Cost -- Actual	$21.56	$2,609	$11,211	$11,729	$15,114	$14,812	$14,833	$0	$0	$0	$0	$70,307
Engineer Hourly Labor Cost -- Planned	$21.56	$10,996	$10,996	$10,996	$14,661	$14,661	$14,661	$14,661	$18,326	$13,367	$10,996	$134,319
Technician Hourly Labor Cost -- Actual	$26.81	$1,662	$80	$1,206	$3,887	$4,558	$4,450	$0	$0	$0	$0	$15,845
Technician Hourly Labor Cost -- Planned	$26.81	$536	$536	$536	$4,558	$4,558	$4,558	$4,558	$4,558	$4,558	$2,145	$31,100
Total Labor Cost -- Actual		$24,556	$29,387	$41,872	$53,656	$64,536	$49,897	$0	$0	$0	$0	$263,906
Total Labor Cost -- Planned		$32,481	$32,481	$32,481	$55,019	$55,019	$55,019	$55,019	$58,684	$46,736	$34,090	$457,028
Overhead on Labor Cost -- Actual	169%	$41,500	$49,664	$70,764	$90,679	$109,066	$84,327	$0	$0	$0	$0	$446,000
Overhead on Labor Cost -- Planned	169%	$54,893	$54,893	$54,893	$92,982	$92,982	$92,982	$92,982	$99,176	$78,985	$57,611	$772,377
Total Materials Cost -- Actual		$345	$18,735	$4,289	$9,367	$7,534	$18,973	$0	$0	$0	$0	$59,243
Total Materials Cost -- Planned		$200	$200	$3,600	$7,700	$6,800	$16,900	$1,300	$14,000	$200	$200	$51,100
Total Rental Equipment Cost -- Actual		$4,000	$3,308	$4,023	$3,729	$6,864	$4,236	$0	$0	$0	$0	$26,160
Total Rental Equipment Cost -- Planned		$4,000	$4,000	$4,000	$7,500	$7,500	$7,500	$7,500	$6,000	$6,000	$1,500	$55,500
Total Travel Cost -- Actual		$1,448	$1,634	$6,290	$1,815	$4,504	$891	$0	$0	$0	$0	$16,582
Total Travel Cost -- Planned		$1,500	$1,500	$6,000	$1,500	$1,500	$1,500	$9,000	$4,500	$4,500	$1,500	$33,000
Total Other Costs -- Actual		$2,508	$122	$715	$450	$563	$1,294	$0	$0	$0	$0	$5,652
Total Other Costs -- Planned		$2,500	$300	$300	$300	$2,500	$2,500	$2,500	$6,400	$8,500	$1,200	$27,000
Subcontract Costs -- Actual		$0	$0	$0	$0	$0	$0	$0	$0	$0	$0	$0
Subcontract Costs -- Planned		$0	$0	$0	$0	$0	$0	$0	$0	$0	$0	$0
Total Cost -- Actual		$74,357	$102,850	$127,954	$159,697	$193,067	$159,618	$0	$0	$0	$0	$817,543
Total Cost -- Planned		$95,574	$93,374	$101,274	$165,001	$166,301	$176,401	$168,301	$188,760	$144,921	$96,101	$1,396,005
G&A on Costs -- Actual	19%	$14,128	$19,541	$24,311	$30,342	$36,683	$30,327	$0	$0	$0	$0	$155,333
G&A on Costs -- Planned	19%	$18,159	$17,741	$19,242	$31,350	$31,597	$33,516	$31,977	$35,864	$27,535	$18,259	$265,241
Profit on Cost and G&A -- Actual	11%	$9,733	$13,463	$16,749	$20,904	$25,273	$20,894	$0	$0	$0	$0	$107,016
Profit on Cost and G&A -- Planned	11%	$12,511	$12,223	$13,257	$21,599	$21,769	$23,091	$22,031	$24,709	$18,970	$12,580	$182,737
Total Price -- Actual		$98,219	$135,854	$169,014	$210,943	$255,023	$210,840	$0	$0	$0	$0	$1,079,893
Total Price -- Planned		$126,243	$123,337	$133,772	$217,949	$219,666	$233,008	$222,308	$249,333	$191,426	$126,939	$1,843,983
Cumulative Price -- Actual		$98,219	$234,073	$403,087	$614,030	$869,053	$1,079,893	$1,079,893	$1,079,893	$1,079,893	$1,079,893	$1,079,893
Cumulative Price -- Planned		$126,243	$249,580	$383,353	$601,302	$820,968	$1,053,976	$1,276,284	$1,525,617	$1,717,043	$1,843,983	$1,843,983

Fig. A.13. • The budget total portion of a combination staffing plan and budget. This is the bottom of the spreadsheet that Figure A.12 is the top of.

Next, the *profit* or *fee* that is to be charged is calculated. Naturally, if a development effort is carried out within the sponsoring institution then the profit will usually be zero. For projects that earn a profit the traditional range is 5% to 30% profit, with 10% being very commonly encountered. Although it is not unusual for the gross profit from sale of a product to exceed 25%, this level of profit on development projects is usually considered outrageous. In fact, for development projects funded by the U.S. Government profit is limited by law to a maximum of 10% of the total amount (this level of profit, measured as a fraction of the price, can be figured by multiplying the sum of cost and G&A by 11.11%).

The sum of cost, G&A burden, and profit is called the *price*. The price is what the customer or sponsor must pay for the effort. Note that along the bottom of the budget there are two additional rows. These are for planned and actual cumulative price by month. The final entry in these rows (which accumulates all of the months of the project) gives the planned and actual total price of the project.

A.3.2 Project Management

Detailed development plans are usually produced twice—once when the project is being defined and again when it is executed. The initial plan is used to write the business plan or proposal. This plan (which is usually developed by means of the kind of detailed "bottoms up" planning effort described in the last subsection) leads to a definition of the overall high-level tasks that will be carried out and a definition of the schedule, milestones, and budget. However, unless the project is very short and the delay in starting the project is minimal, the initial project plan will be unusable because of changes in conditions.

The solution to this problem is to replan the project once it gets underway. The first step in this replanning process is to break the project up into disjoint time *phases* lasting a few months each (the development project described in the figures of this section is scheduled to last 10 months). Each phase is then replanned in detail shortly before it begins. In this way, the development plan that is actually executed is correctly formulated.

Once the development plan for a particular phase of the project has been formulated (which, like the initial plan, usually requires several iterations), it is then "frozen." Following this freeze, the only way the plan for that phase can be changed is through another re-planning process. However, replanning of a frozen plan is invoked only under the most dire circumstances, such as the death of a key project leader, the burning down of the project facility, etc. Except in such circumstances, the changes to the plan are made by *reforecasting*—a process in which the original plan stays in place but deviations from it are noted on top of it. For example, if a milestone slips a month then the original milestone symbol on the schedule is retained, but a slash is put through it to indicate that it has been changed. A new milestone symbol bearing the same milestone number is then added at the new location. Similarly, changes in WBS element starting and ending times are indicated by putting slashes through now unused lines and adding new dashed lines where needed. Changes to labor and other resource requirements are made by creating new rows showing the reforecast numbers. The original plan numbers are left intact. Whether a plan has been reforecast or not, once it is set the management process is designed to guide the project through the execution of the current plan.

The process of managing the development activity primarily revolves around *project reviews*. For most small projects, project reviews should be held weekly and should involve all project personnel. For larger projects, each currently active task team should have its own weekly project review, and the overall project should have monthly reviews (which are usually attended only by the task leaders and the project manager(s)).

Every project review, which is run by the project or task manager, is operated in accordance with essentially the same fixed format: schedule review, milestone review, and budget review. Project reviews are typically conducted with the use of both a "hand-out" package (a copy of which is given to each of the participants), and a set of overhead projection viewcells (transparencies) made from the material in the package (these are used by the project leader to make the presentation to the group).

The package contains copies of the project WBS, milestone descriptions document, schedule, and combined staffing plan and budget. The schedules have the progress that has been made in each WBS element indicated by filling in and darkening the appropriate open triangles and open lines. Filling in a triangle indicates that the corresponding milestone has been completed (the verification of this completion takes place in the next section of the review). Once a triangle has been filled in, the parallel lines containing that triangle are also filled in up to that point (by only allowing the parallel lines to be filled in when milestones are positively completed this prevents the problem of subjective progress measurement—such as the famous '99% complete software module'). Filling in the parallel lines of a task, subtask, etc. indicates how far along that task has progressed. Comparing how much of the task lines have been filled in with the actual calendar date indicates whether that particular WBS element is ahead or behind schedule. This is illustrated in Figure A.14. As shown in the figure, at the early October 1997 progress review, Task 1 has been completed (and thus all of its schedule bars are filled in), but Task 2 is still in progress.

Subtask 2.2 has been completed on time (there are no slipped milestones— which would be indicated by slashes through the original milestone triangles and the appearance of newly placed triangles). However, Subtask 2.3 has only been completed up through Milestone 2.3B. Due to a major software design flaw (which was not noticed until late September), the planned completion dates of Milestones 2.3C, 2.3D, and 2.3E have all slipped one month.

Even though it turns out that Task 2.3 is now about one-half completed, the Subtask 2.3 schedule line is not filled in past Milestone 2.3B (which was completed on time). As mentioned above, schedule lines are only filled in up to the last completed milestone. This prevents "fudging," and keeps the project review process objective and honest.

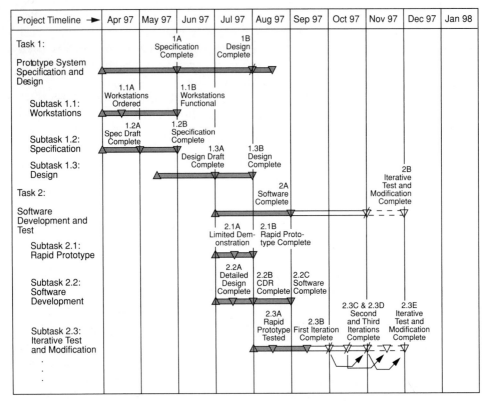

Fig. A.14. • Example of a partially completed project schedule. It is now early October 1997 and there has been some slippage in Subtask 2.3 due to a major software design flaw that was only recently discovered.

The *schedule and milestone review* portion of the project review is a discussion of which milestones have been met. The progress made on each milestone passing project element is carefully checked to make sure that all of the milestone completion criteria have been met. To borrow President Ronald Reagan's phrase, project managers should "trust but verify".

Following the schedule and milestone review, the next part of the project review is the *staffing plan and budget status review*. This is best carried out by preparing a viewcell that lists any significant recent deviations from the staffing plan and a graph that shows the (superimposed) planned and actual cumulative cost expenditures of the project to date. An example of such a spending chart is shown in Figure A.15.

Following the review of the schedule, milestones, staffing plan, and budget, the final step is to review *action items* from the previous meeting and set action items to be completed before the next meeting (action items from previous meetings are sometimes reviewed as the first activity of a project review meeting—rather than doing this at the end). The typical result of the action

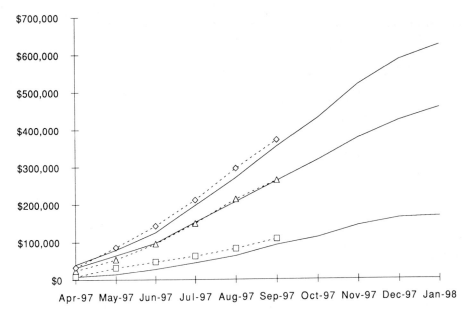

Fig. A.15. • Cumulative expenditure chart for an early October 1997 project review. The three lines (bottom, middle, and top) extending across the entire schedule represent, respectively, the planned cumulative non-labor, labor, and total costs of the project. The three additional dotted lines represent the records of actual cumulative (non-labor, square ticks; labor, triangular ticks, and total, diamond ticks) cost expenditures in each of the months of the project. Note that the labor cost is running close to plan but that the non-labor costs have overrun. This overrun was caused by an unanticipated materials expense in Task 1 in May (see Figures A.12 and A.13).

item portion of a project review is the identification of problems with the project and the development of plans for solving those problems. The action items are the brief written descriptions of those plans. At the end of the review copies of the action items (including the date by which the action must be accomplished) should be given to the relevant project participants. These action items are recorded in the *minutes* of the project review maintained by the project leader.

At each project review, the pending action items developed at previous reviews are discussed to verify that the required actions have been taken and that the action did indeed solve the problem that led to the formulation of the action item. If the action could not be completed or if it was completed but failed to solve the problem, then further action items are generated to continue the attack on the problem. When all of the participants know what they are doing, it takes the relevant project manager approximately an hour to pull together the necessary information and prepare the charts for the review. The review itself usually takes only 15 to 30 minutes, although it can take longer if major problems are identified, and intricate work-arounds and solutions need to be developed. Project reviews take relatively little time and for well-run projects often seem like a waste of time. However, they are the primary technique for keeping a project running correctly.

Being a project leader involves many responsibilities, but perhaps the most important of these is setting and enforcing standards of performance, honesty, and forthrightness; and creating a non-hostile environment in which problems and failures can be comfortably and openly discussed. Beyond leadership, the next most important element of project management is deep involvement ("management by walking around" is a good project management technique).

Bibliography

[1] Aarts, E., and Korst, J., **Simulated Annealing and Boltzmann Machines**, Wiley, New York, 1989.

[2] Ackley, D. H., "Stochastic iterated genetic hillclimbing," Doctoral Dissertation, Carnegie Mellon Computer Sci. Dept., 1987. Published as *Carnegie Mellon Technical Paper*, **CMU-CS-87-107**, Carnegie Mellon University, Pittsburgh PA, March 1987.

[3] Ajmera, R. C., Kohli, C. K., and Newcomb, R. W., "Retinal-type neuristor sections," *Proc. Southeastcon Conf.*, 267–268, IEEE Press, New York, April 1980.

[4] Albert, A., **Regression and the Moore–Penrose Pseudoinverse**, Academic Press, New York, 1972.

[5] Albus, J. S., **Brains, Behavior, and Robotics**, Byte Books, Peterborough NH, 1981.

[6] Almeda, L., "Backpropagation in Perceptrons with Feedback," in Eckmiller, R. and von der Malsberg, C. [Eds.], **Neural Computers**, NATO ASI Series, F (41), 199–208, Springer–Verlag, Berlin, 1988.

[7] Aluffi-Pentini, F., Parisi, V., and Zirilli, F., "Global Optimization and Stochastic Differential Equations," *Journal of Optimization Theory and Applications*, **47**, 1-16, September 1985.

[8] Amari, S., "Learning patterns and pattern sequences by self-organizing nets of threshold elements," *IEEE Trans. Computers*, **C-21** (11), 1197–1206, November 1972.

[9] Amari, S., "A theory of adaptive pattern classifiers," *IEEE Trans. Electronic Computers*, **EC-16** (3), 299–307, 1967.

[10] Amari, S., "Geometrical theory on manifolds of linear systems," Dept.

Mathematical Engineering and Instrumentation Physics Technical Reports, University of Tokyo, METR 86-1, March 1966.

[11] Anderson, J. A., and Rosenfeld, E. [Eds.], **Neurocomputing: Foundations of Research**, MIT Press, Cambridge MA, 1988.

[12] Anderson, J. A., "Cognitive capabilities of a parallel system," in Bienenstock, E., et al [Eds.], **Disordered Systems and Biological Organization**, NATO ASI Series, **F20**, Springer–Verlag, New York, 1986.

[13] Anderson, J. A., Golden, R. M., and Murphy, G. L., "Concepts in distributed systems," *SPIE Proc.*, **634**, 260–276, Bellingham WA, 1986.

[14] Anderson, J. A., Silverstein, J. W., Ritz, S. A., and Jones, R. S., "Distinctive features, categorical perception, and probability learning: Some applications of a neural model," *Psychol. Rev.*, **84** (5), 413–451, 1977.

[15] Anderson, J. A., "A simple neural network generating an interactive memory," *Math. Biosci.*, **14**, 197–220, 1972.

[16] Anderson, J. A., "A memory storage model utilizing spatial correlation functions," *Kybernetik*, **5**, 113–119, 1968.

[17] Ash, T., "Dynamic node creation in backpropagation networks," ICS Report 8901, Cognitive Sci. Dept., University of California, San Diego, February 1989.

[18] Baldi, P., and Hornik, K. "Neural networks and principal component analysis: Learning from examples without local minima," *Neural Networks*, **2**, 53–58, 1989.

[19] Banks, S. P., **Mathematical Theories of Nonlinear Systems**, Prentice–Hall, New York, 1988.

[20] Barron, R. L., Gilstrap, L. O., and Shrier, S., "Polynomial and neural networks: Analogies and engineering applications," *Proc. of the Int. Conf. on Neural Networks*, **II**, 431–493, IEEE Press, New York, June 1987.

[21] Barron, R. L., "Learning networks improve computer-aided prediction and control," *Computer Design*, 65–70, August 1975.

[22] Barto, A., Sutton, R., and Anderson, C. "Neuron-like adaptive elements that can solve difficult learning control problems," *IEEE Trans. Systems, Man & Cyber.*, **SMC-13** (5), 834–846, 1983.

[23] Bashe, C. J., Johnson, L. R., Palmer, J. H., and Pugh, E. W., **IBM's Early Computers**, MIT Press, Cambridge MA, 1986.

[24] Becker, S., and le Cun, Y., "Improving the convergence of backpropagation learning with second order methods," Technical Report CRG-TR-88-5, Connectionist Res. Group, University of Toronto, Canada, September 1988.

[25] Blanchard, K., **The One-Minute Manager**, Morrell Publishing, New York, 1986.

[26] Boender, C. G. E., Rinnooy Kan, A. H. G., and Timmer, G. T., "A Stochastic Method for Global Optimization," *Mathematical Programming*, **22**, 125-140, 1982.

[27] Brady, D., Gi, X-G, and Psaltis, D., "Photorefractive crystals in optical neural computers," *Proc. of the SPIE Conf. on Neural Network Models for*

Optical Computing, SPIE Proc., **882**, 132–136, Bellingham WA, 1988.

[28] Brandt, S. C., **Entrepreneuring**, Addison-Wesley, Reading, MA, 1982.

[29] Bryson, A. E., and Ho, Y-C, **Applied Optimal Control**, [Revised Printing of the 1969 Edition], Hemisphere Publishing, New York, 1975.

[30] Buhmann, J., Lange, J., and v.d.Malsburg, C., "Distortion invariant object recognition by matching hierarchically labeled graphs," *Proc. of the Int. Joint Conf. on Neural Networks*, I, 155–159, IEEE Press, New York, June 1989.

[31] Carpenter, G. A., and Grossberg, S., "A massively parallel architecture for a self-organizing neural pattern recognition machine," *Computer Vision, Graphics and Image Processing*, **37**, 54–115, 1987.

[32] Carpenter, G. A., and Grossberg, S., "ART 2: Self-organization of stable category recognition codes for analog input patterns," *Applied Optics*, **26** (23), 4919–4930, December 1987.

[33] Carpenter, G. A., and Grossberg, S., "Associative learning, adaptive pattern recognition, and cooperative-competitive decision making by neural networks," in Szu, H. [Ed.], **Optical and Hybrid Computing**, SPIE Institute Series, published as *SPIE Proc.*, **634**, 218–247, Bellingham WA, 1986.

[34] Carson, D. L., **Comparison of 2-D Fourier and Spatial Techniques for Removing Noise in Real-Time X-Ray Radiography**, DTIC 88 4 18 107, April 1988.

[35] Cater, J. P.,"Successfully using peak learning rates of 10 (and greater) in back-propagation networks with the heuristic learning algorithm," *Proc. of the Int Conf. on Neural Networks*, II, 645–651, IEEE Press, New York, June 1987.

[36] Cerny, V., "Thermodynamical approach to the travelling salesman problem: An efficient simulation algorithm," *J. Optimization Theory & Appl.*, **45**, 41–51, 1985.

[37] Cerny, V., "A thermodynamical approach to the travelling salesman problem: An efficient simulation algorithm," *Inst. Physics & Biophys.*, Comenius University, Bratislavia, Czechoslovakia, 1982.

[38] Churchland, P. S., **Neurophilosophy**, MIT Press, Cambridge MA, 1986.

[39] Cohen, M. A., Grossberg, S., "Absolute stability of global pattern formation and parallel memory storage by competitive neural networks," *IEEE Trans. Systems, Man & Cybern.*, 1983.

[40] Coolidge, J. L., **A History of Geometrical Methods**, Dover Publications, New York, 1963.

[41] Cottrell, G. W., Munro, P., and Zipser, D., "Image compression by back propagation: An example of extensional programming," ICS Report 8702, University of California at San Diego, February 1987.

[42] Crane, H. D., "Neuristor — A novel device and systems concept," *Proc. of the IRE*, **50**, 2048–2060, October 1962.

[43] Crofts, A., University of Illinois, Dept. of Biology, personal communication, 17 April 1990.

[44] Daugman, J. G., "Relaxation neural network for non-orthogonal image

transforms," *Proc. of the Int. Conf. on Neural Networks,* **1**, 547–560, IEEE Press, New York, July 1988.

[45] Daugman, J. G., "Complete discrete 2-D Gabor transforms by neural networks for image analysis and compression," *IEEE Trans. Acoustics, Speech & Signal Processing,* **36** (7), 1169–1179, 1988.

[46] Daugman, J. G., "Pattern and motion vision without laplacian zero crossings," *J. Optical Soc. Am. A,* **5** (7) 1142–1148, 1988.

[47] Daugman, J. G., and Kammen, D. M., "Image statistics, gases, and visual neural primitives," *Proc. of the Int. Conf. on Neural Networks,* **IV**, 163–175, IEEE Press, New York, June 1987.

[48] Daugman, J. G., "Image analysis and compact coding by oriented 2D Gabor primitives," *SPIE Proc.,* **758**, Bellingham WA, April 1987.

[49] Daugman, J. G., "Uncertainty relation for resolution in space, spatial frequency, and orientation optimized by two-dimensional visual cortical filters," *J. Optical Soc. Am. A,* **2** (7), 1160–1169, 1985.

[50] Dertouzos, M. L., **Threshold Logic: A Synthesis Approach**, MIT Research Monograph No. 32, MIT Press, Cambridge MA, 1965.

[51] Desieno, D., "Adding a conscience to competitive learning," *Proc. Int. Conf. on Neural Networks,* **I**, 117–124, IEEE Press, New York, July 1988.

[52] Devijver, P. A., and Kittler, J., **Pattern Recognition: A Statistical Approach**, Prentice–Hall, Englewood Cliffs NJ, 1982.

[53] Diamond, M. C., **The Human Brain Coloring Book**, Barnes & Noble Books, New York, 1985.

[54] Dreyfus, H. L., and Dreyfus, S. E., "Making a mind verses modeling the brain: Aritificial intelligence back at a branchpoint," *Dædalus: Proc. Am. Acad. Sci.,* **117**, 15–43, Winter 1988.

[55] DTIC Technical Report No. RADC-TDR-64-123, **Neuristor Logic Technology**, Distributed by Information Processing Branch, Rome Air Development Center, Research and Technology Division, Air Force Systems Command, Griffiss Air Force Base, New York, June 1964.

[56] Duda, R. O., and Hart, P. E., **Pattern Classification and Scene Analysis**, Wiley, New York, 1973.

[57] Duncan, R., "A survey of parallel computer architectures," *IEEE Computer,* **23**, 5-16, February 1990.

[58] Dunford, N., and Schwartz, J. T., **Linear Operators**, Part I, Third Printing, Wiley, New York, 1966.

[59] Dunning, G. J., Marom, E., Owechko, Y., and Soffer, B. H., "Optical holographic associative memory using a phase conjugate resonator," *SPIE Proc.,* **625**, Bellingham WA, January 1986.

[60] Eberhardt, S., Duong, T., and Thakoor, A., "Design of parallel hardware neural network systems from custom analog VLSI 'building block' chips," *Proc. of Int. Joint Conf. on Neural Networks,* **II**, 183–190, IEEE Press, New York, June 1989.

[61] El-Leithy, N., Newcomb, R. W., and Zaghloul, M., "A basic MOS neural-type junction: A perspective on neural-type microsystems," *Proc. of the*

Int. Conf. on Neural Networks, III, 469–477, IEEE Press, New York, June 1987.

[62] Eriksson, L. J., and Allie, M. C., "Use of random noise for on-line transducer modeling in an adaptive active attenuation system," *J. Acoustic Soc. Am.*, **85**, 797–802, February 1989.

[63] Farhat, N.H., Psaltis, D., Prata, A., and Paek, E. "Optical implementation of the Hopfield model," *Applied Optics*, **24** (10), 1469–1475, 1985.

[64] Farlow, S. J. [Ed.], **Self-Organizing Methods in Modelling**, Marcel Dekker, New York, 1984.

[65] Finkler, S. A., **The Complete Guide to Finance & Accounting for Nonfinancial Managers**, Prentice–Hall, Englewood Cliffs NJ, 1983.

[66] Fisher, A. D., and Lee, J. N., "The current status of two-dimensional spatial light modulator technology," in Szu, H. H. [Ed.], **Optical and Hybrid Computing**, SPIE Institute Series, published as: *SPIE Proc.*, **634**, 352–371, SPIE, Bellingham WA, 1986.

[67] Fletcher, R., **Practical Methods of Optimization**, Second Edition, Wiley, New York, 1987.

[68] Fukushima, K., "A hierarchical neural network model for selective attention," in Eckmiller, R. and von der Malsberg, C. [Eds.], **Neural Computers**, 80–90, Springer–Verlag, Berlin, 1988.

[69] Fukushima, K., "Neocognitron: A hierarchical neural network capable of visual pattern recognition," *Neural Networks*, **1**, 119–130, 1988.

[70] Fukushima, K., and Miyake, S., "Neocognitron: A new algorithm for pattern recognition tolerant of deformations and shifts in position," *Pattern Recognition*, **15** (6), 455–469, 1984.

[71] Fukushima, K., Miyake, S., and Ito, T., "Neocognitron: A Neural network model for a mechanism of visual pattern recognition," *IEEE Trans. Systems, Man & Cyber.*, **SMC-13** (5), 826–834, 1983.

[72] Fukushima, K., and Miyake, S., "Neocognitron: A new algorithm for pattern recognition tolerant of deformations and shifts in position," *Pattern Recognition*, **15** (6), 455–469, 1982.

[73] Fukushima, K., "Cognitron: A self-organized multi-layered neural network model," *NHK Technical Monograph*, **30**, NHK Technical Research Laboratories, Tokyo, 1981.

[74] Fukushima, K., "Neocognitron: A self-organizing neural network model for a mechanism of pattern recognition unaffected by shift in position," *Biol. Cyber.*, **36** (4), 193–202, 1980.

[75] Fukushima, K., "Cognitron: A self-organizing multi-layered neural network," *Biol. Cyber.*, **20** (3/4), 121–136, 1975.

[76] Fukushima, K., "A feature extractor for curvilinear patterns: A design suggested by the mammalian visual system," *Kybernetik*, **7** (4), 153–160, 1970.

[77] Fukushima, K., "Visual feature extraction by a multilayered network of analog threshold elements," *IEEE Trans. Systems, Sci. & Cyber.*, **SSC-5** (4), 322–333, 1969.

[78] Gabor, D., "Associative holographic memories," *IBM J. Res. Develop.*, 156–159, March 1969.

[79] Gabor, D., "Theory of communication," *J. of IEE*, **93**, 429–457, 1946.

[80] Gallant, A. R., and White, H., "There exists a neural network that does not make avoidable mistakes," *Proc. of the Int. Conf. on Neural Networks*, **I**, 657–664, IEEE Press, New York, July 1988.

[81] Gallant, S. I., "Connectionist expert systems," *Communications of the ACM*, **31** (2), 152–169, 1988.

[82] Gallant, S. I., "Automated generation of connectionist expert systems for problems involving noise and redundancy," *AAAI Workshop on Uncertainty*, Am. Assoc. for AI, Menlo Park CA, 1987.

[83] Geman, S., and Hwang, C. R., "Diffusions for global optimization," *SIAM J. of Control and Optimization*, **24**, 1031–1043, 1986.

[84] Geman, S., and Geman, D., "Stochastic relaxation, Gibbs distributions, and the Baysian restoration of images," *IEEE Trans. Pattern Analysis and Machine Intel.*, **PAMI-6**, 721–741, 1984.

[85] Gill, P. E., Murray, W., and Wright, M. H., **Practical Optimization**, Academic Press, San Diego, 1981.

[86] Glover, D. E., "An optical Fourier / electronic neurocomputer automated inspection system," *Proc. of the Int. Conf. on Neural Networks*, **I**, 569–576, IEEE Press, New York, July 1988.

[87] Goldberg, S., **Introduction to Difference Equations**, Dover Publications, New York, 1958.

[88] Goodman, J., **Introduction to Fourier Optics**, McGraw–Hill, San Francisco, 1968.

[89] Gray, C. M., König, P., Engel, A. K., and Singer, W., "Oscillatory responses in cat visual cortex exhibit inter-columnar synchronization which reflects global stimulus properties," *Nature*, **338**, 334–337, 23 March 1989.

[90] Gray, R. M., "Vector quantization," *IEEE ASSP Magazine*, **1**, 4–29, April 1984

[91] Grossberg, S. [Ed.], **Neural Networks and Natural Intelligence**, MIT Press, Cambridge MA, 1988.

[92] Grossberg, S., **Studies of Mind and Brain: Neural principles of learning, perception, development, cognition, and motor control**, Reidel Press, Boston, 1982.

[93] Grossberg, S., "A theory of human memory: Self-organization and performance of sensory motor codes, maps and plans," in Rosen, R., and Snell, S. [Eds.], **Progress in Theor. Biol.**, **5**, 233–374, Academic Press, New York, 1978.

[94] Grossberg, S., "Adaptive pattern classification and universal recoding: I. Parallel development and coding of neural feature detectors," *Biol. Cyber.*, **23**, 121–134, 1976.

[95] Grossberg, S., "Contour enhancement, short term memory, and constancies in reverberating neural networks," *Studies in Appl. Math.*, **52**, 213–257, 1973.

[96] Grossberg, S., "Pattern learning by functional-differential neural networks with arbitrary path weights," in Schmitt, K. [Ed.], **Delay and Functional Differential Equations and their Applications**, 121–160, Academic Press, New York, 1972; reprinted in Grossberg, S., **Studies of Mind and Brain**, Reidel Press, Boston, 1982.

[97] Grossberg, S., "Embedding fields: Underlying philosophy, mathematics, and applications to psychology, physiology and anatomy," *J. Cyber.*, **1** (1), 28–50, 1971.

[98] Grossberg, S., "On the production and release of chemical transmitters and related topics in cellular control," *J. Theor. Biol.*, **22**, 325–364, 1969.

[99] Grossberg, S., "Embedding fields: A theory of learning with physiological implications," *J. Math. Psych.*, **6**, 209–239, 1969.

[100] Guyon, L., Poujaud, I., Personnaz, L., Dreyfus, G., Denker, J., and Le Cun, Y., "Comparing different neural network architectures for classifying handwritten digits," *Proc. of the Int. Joint Conf. on Neural Networks*, **II**, 127–132, IEEE Press, New York, June 1989.

[101] Haines, K., and Hecht-Nielsen, R., "A BAM with increased information storage capacity," *Proc. of the Int. Conf. on Neural Networks*, **I**, 181–190, IEEE Press, New York, July 1988.

[102] Hecht-Nielsen, R., "On the algebraic structure of feedforward network weight spaces," in Eckmiller, R. [Ed.], **Advanced Neural Computers**, Elsevier North Holland, Amsterdam, 1990.

[103] Hecht-Nielsen, R., "Annual report: Attentional neurocomputers deserve more attention," *Electronic Engineering Times*, T28 and T44, Manhassett, NY, 29 January 1990.

[104] Hecht-Nielsen, R., "Attentional focusing for spatiotemporal patterns," *Proc. of the Int. Joint Conf. on Neural Networks*, **II**, 40, Washington DC, INNS, New York, January 1990.

[105] Hecht-Nielsen, R., "Theory of the backpropagation neural network," *Proc. of the Int. Joint Conf. on Neural Networks*, **I**, 593–611, IEEE Press, New York, June 1989.

[106] Hecht-Nielsen, R., "Neurocomputing," *IEEE Spectrum*, 36–41, March 1988.

[107] Hecht-Nielsen, R., "The impact of neurocomputing on our future," Paper written for the Res. & Develop. Assoc. for Future Electron Devices, Tokyo, Japan, 1988.

[108] Hecht-Nielsen, R., "Applications of counterpropagation networks," *Neural Networks*, **1**, 131–139, 1988.

[109] Hecht-Nielsen, R., "Counterpropagation networks," *Proc. of the Int. Conf. on Neural Networks*, **II**, 19–32, IEEE Press, New York, June 1987.

[110] Hecht-Nielsen, R., "Counterpropagation networks," *Applied Optics*, **26**, 4979–4984, December 1987.

[111] Hecht-Nielsen, R., "Kolmogorov's mapping neural network existence theorem," *Proc. of the Int. Conf. on Neural Networks*, **III**, 11–13, IEEE Press, New York, 1987.

[112] Hecht-Nielsen, R., "Nearest matched filter classification of spatiotemporal patterns," *Applied Optics*, **26** (10), 1892–1899, 1987.

[113] Hecht-Nielsen, R., "Book review-Studies of mind and brain by S. Grossberg," *J. of Math. Psychol.*, **27** (3), 335–340, 1983.

[114] Hecht-Nielsen, R., "Neural Analog Processing," *Proc. SPIE*, **360**, 180–189, Bellingham WA, 1982.

[115] Hebb, D., **The Organization of Behavior**, Wiley, New York, 1949.

[116] Hestenes, D., **New Foundations for Classical Mechanics**, Reidel Press, Dordrecht, Holland, 1987.

[117] Hestenes, D., and Sobczyk, G., **Clifford Algebra to Geometric Calculus**, corrected printing, Reidel Press, Dordrecht, Holland, 1985.

[118] Hestenes, D., **Space-Time Algebra**, Gordon and Breach, New York, 1966.

[119] Hicks, N. J., **Notes on Differential Geometry**, van Nostrand, Princeton NJ, 1965.

[120] Hinton, G. F., Sejnowski, T. J., and Ackley, D. H., "Boltzmann machines: Constraint satisfaction networks that learn," *Carnegie Mellon University Technical Report # **CMU-CS-84-119**, Carnegie Mellon University, Pittsburgh PA, May 1984.

[121] Hirsch, M., "Dynamical systems review," a tutorial presented at the 1988 IEEE Int. Conf. on Neural Networks, videotape and notes available from: IEEE Press, New York, July 1988.

[122] Holler, M., Tam, S., Castro, H., and Benson, R., "An electrically trainable artificial neural network (ETANN) with 10240 'floating gate' synapses," *Proc. of the Int. Joint Conf. on Neural Networks*, **II**, 191–196, IEEE Press, New York, June 1989.

[123] Hopfield, J. J., "Neurons with graded response have collective computational properties like those of two-state neurons," *Proc. Natl. Acad. Sci.*, **81**, 3088–3092, 1984.

[124] Hopfield, J. J., "Neural networks and physical systems with emergent collective computational abilities," *Proc. Natl. Acad. Sci.*, **79**, 2554–2558, 1982.

[125] Hornik, K., Stinchcombe, M., and White, H., "Multilayer feedforward networks are universal approximators," Manuscript, Dept. of Economics, University of California at San Diego, June 1988.

[126] Horst, R., and, Tuy, H., "On the Convergence of Global Methods in Multiextremal Optimization," *Journal of Optimization Theory and Applications*, **54**, 253-271, August 1987.

[127] Hush, D. R., and Salas, J. M., "Improving the learning rate of backpropagation with the gradient reuse algorithm," *Proc. of the Int. Conf. on Neural Networks*, **I**, 441–446, IEEE Press, New York, July 1988.

[128] Irie, B., and Miyake, S.,"Capabilities of three-layered perceptrons," *Proc. of the Int. Conf. on Neural Networks*, **I**, 641–648, IEEE Press, New York,

July 1988.

[129] Ito, K., **Introduction to Probability Theory**, Cambridge University Press, Cambridge MA, 1978.

[130] Ivakhnenko, A. G., "Polynomial theory of complex systems," *IEEE Trans. Systems, Man & Cyber.*, **SMC-12**, 364–378, 1971.

[131] Ivakhnenko, A. G., "The group method of data handling — A rival of stochastic approximation," (in Russian) *Soviet Automatic Control*, **1**, 43–55, 1968.

[132] Jackel, L. D., Graf, H. P., Hubbard, W., Denker, J. S., Henderson, D., and Guyon, I., "An application of neural net chips: Handwritten digit recognition," *Proc. of the Int. Conf. on Neural Networks*, **II**, 107–115, IEEE Press, New York, July 1988.

[133] John, E. R., Prichep, L. S., and Chabot, R. J., "Quantitative electrophysiological maps of mental activity," *Springer Series in Brain Dynamics*, **2**, 316–330, 1989.

[134] Kaufman, L., and Rousseau, P. J., **Finding Groups in Data: Cluster Analysis with Computer Programs**, Wiley, New York, 1988.

[135] Kirkpatrick, S., Gelatt, C. D. Jr., and Vecchi, M. P., "Optimization by simulated annealing," *Science*, **220** (4598), 671–680, 1983.

[136] Klopf, A. H., "A neuronal model of classical conditioning," *Psychobiology*, **16** (2), 85–125, 1988.

[137] Klopf, A. H., and Gose, E., "An evolutionary pattern recognition network," *IEEE Trans. Systems, Sci. & Cyber.*, **SSC-5** (3), 247–250, 1969.

[138] Koch, C., "Seeing Chips: Analog VLSI Circuits for Computer Vision," *Neural Computation*, **1**, 184–200, Summer 1989.

[139] Köhle, M., and Schönbauer, F., "CONDELA — A language for neural networks," Proceedings of the nEuro88 Conf., Paris, France, June 1988.

[140] Kohonen, T., "An introduction to neural computing," *Neural Networks*, **1** (1), 3–16, 1988.

[141] Kohonen, T., **Self-Organization and Associative Memory**, Second Edition, Springer–Verlag, Berlin, 1988.

[142] Kohonen, T., "Self-learning inference rules by dynamically expanding context," *Proc. of the Int. Conf. on Neural Networks*, **II**, 3–9, IEEE Press, New York, 1987.

[143] Kohonen, T., **Self-Organization and Associative Memory**, Springer–Verlag, Berlin, 1984.

[144] Kohonen, T., "A simple paradigm for the self-organized formation of structured feature maps," in Amari, S., and Arbib, M. [Eds.], **Competition and Cooperation in Neural Nets**, (Lecture Notes in Biomathematics), **45**, Springer–Verlag, 1982.

[145] Kohonen, T., "Self-organized formation of topologically correct feature maps," *Biol. Cyber.*, **43**, 59–69, 1982.

[146] Kohonen, T., "Correlation matrix memories," *IEEE Trans. Computers*, **C-21** (4), 353–359, 1972.

[147] Kohonen, T., "Correlation matrix memories," Helsinki University of

Technology Report TKK-F-A130, 1970.

[148] Kolmogorov, A. N., "On the Representation of Continuous Functions of Many Variables by Superposition of Continuous Functions of One Variable and Addition" [in Russian], Dokl. Akad. Nauk USSR, **114**, 953–956, 1957.

[149] Korn, G. A., and Korn, T. M., **Mathematical Handbook for Scientists and Engineers**, Second Edition, McGraw–Hill, New York, 1968.

[150] Kosko, B., "Unsupervised learning in noise," *Proc. of the Int. Joint Conf. on Neural Networks*, I, 7–14, IEEE Press, New York, June 1989.

[151] Kosko, B., "Bidirectional associative memories," *IEEE Trans. Systems, Man & Cyber.*, **18** (1), 49–60, 1988.

[152] Kosko, B., "Fuzzy Cognitive Maps," *Int. J. Man-Machine Studies*, **24**, 65–75, 1986

[153] Kronland-Martinet, R., Morlet, J., and Grossmann, A., "Analysis of sound patterns through wavelet transforms," *Int. J. Pattern Recog. & AI*, **1** (2), 273–302, 1987.

[154] Kryukov, V. I., Borisyuk, G. N., Borisyuk, R. M., Kirillov, A. B., and Kovalenko, E. I., **The Metastable and Unstable States in the Brain** (in Russian), U.S.S.R. Academy of Sciences, Pushchino, 1986.

[155] Kuffler, S. W., Nicholls, J. G., and Martin, A. R., **From Neuron to Brain**, Second Edition, Sinauer Associates, Sunderland MA, 1984.

[156] Lapedes, A., and Farber, R., "How neural nets work," in Anderson, D. Z. [Ed.], **Neural Information Processing Systems** (Proc. of the IEEE NIPS Conf., Denver CO, 1987), 442–456, Am. Inst. of Physics, New York, 1988.

[157] Leake, B., and Anninos, P. A., "Effect of connectivity on the activity of neural net models," *J. Theor. Biol.*, **58**, 337–363, 1976.

[158] le Cun, Y., "A theoretical framework for back-propagation," Technical Report CRG-TR-88-6, Connectionist Research Group, University of Toronto, Canada, September 1988.

[159] le Cun, Y., "Modeles connexionnistes de l'apprentissage," Doctoral Dissertation, University of Pierre and Marie Curie, Paris, France, 1987.

[160] Linsker, R., "Self-Organization in a Perceptual Network," *IEEE Computer*, **21**, 105–117, March 1988.

[161] Little, W. A., "The existence of persistent states in the brain," *Math. Biosci.*, **19**, 101–120, 1974.

[162] Lookabaugh, T. D., and Gray, R. M., "High-resolution quantization theory and the vector quantizer advantage," *IEEE Trans. Inf. Th.*, **35**, 1020–1033, September 1989

[163] Lorentz, G. G., "The 13-th problem of Hilbert," *Proc. of Symposia in Pure Math.*, **28**, 419–430, Am. Math. Soc., 1976.

[164] Marcelja, S., "Mathematical description of the responses of simple cortical cells," *J. Opt. Soc. Am.*, **70** (II), 1297–1300, November 1980.

[165] McCulloch, W. S., and Pitts, W., "A logical calculus of the ideas immanent in nervous activity," *Bulletin of Math. Bio.*, **5**, 115-133, 1943.

[166] McEliece, R. J., Posner, E. C., Rodemich, E. R., and Venkatesh, S., "The capacity of the Hopfield associative memory," *IEEE Trans. Information Theory*, **IT-33** (4), 461–482, 1987.

[167] McEliece, R. J., **The Theory of Information and Coding: A Mathematical Framework for Communication**, part of *Encyclopedia of Mathematics and Its Applications Series*, 3, Addison–Wesley, Reading MA, 1977.

[168] McInerney, J. M., Haines, K. G., Biafore, S., and Hecht-Nielsen, R., "Can backpropagation error surfaces have non-global minima?," *Int. Joint Conf. on Neural Networks*, **II**, 627, IEEE Press, New York, 1989.

[169] Mead, C., **Analog VLSI and Neural Systems**, Addison-Wesley, Reading MA, 1989.

[170] Metropolis, N., Rosenbluth, A., Rosenbluth, M., Teller, A., and Teller, E., "Equation of state calculations by fast computing machines," *J. Chemical Physics*, **21** (6), 1087–1092, June 1953.

[171] Minsky, M., and Papert, S., **Perceptrons**, MIT Press, Cambridge MA, 1969.

[172] Minsky, M., "Neural nets and the brain — Model problem," Doctoral Dissertation, Princeton University, Princeton NJ, 1954.

[173] Moore, B., and Poggio, T., "Representation properties of multilayer feed-forward networks," Presented at the 1988 Annual Meeting of the Int. Neural Network Soc., Boston MA, September 1988. Note: an abstract of this section was published as a Supplement to Volume 1 of *Neural Networks*, 1988.

[174] Murakami, K., and Aibara, T., "An improvement on the Moore–Penrose generalized inverse associative memory," *IEEE Trans. Systems, Man & Cyber.*, **SMC-17** (4), 699–707, July/August 1987.

[175] Nakano, K., "Associatron — A model of associative memory," *IEEE Trans. Systems, Man & Cybern.*, **SMC-2** (3), 380–388, 1972.

[176] Nasser, A. L., **Analysis of Edge Detection Techniques for Radiographic Image Measurement**, DTIC 88 4 18 055, April 1988.

[177] Nguyen, D., and Widrow, B., "The truck backer-upper: An example of self-learning in neural networks," *Proc. of the Int. Joint Conf. on Neural Networks*, **II**, 357–363, IEEE Press, New York, June 1989.

[178] Nilsson, N., **Learning Machines**, McGraw–Hill, New York, 1965.

[179] Nilsson, N., **Learning Machines** (reprinted version of 1965 McGraw–Hill book with a new Introduction by Terrence J. Sejnowski and Halbert White), Morgan Kaufmann Publishers, San Mateo, California, 1990.

[180] North, D. O., "An analysis of the factors which determine signal / noise discrimination in pulsed-carrier systems," *RCA Technical Report PTR-6C*, June 1943; reprinted in *Proc. IEEE*, **51**, 1016–1027, July 1963.

[181] Olson, H. F., and May, E. G., "Electronic sound absorber," *J. Acoustic Soc. Am.*, **25**, 1130–1136, November 1953.

[182] O'Shaughnessy, D., **Speech Communication**, Addison–Wesley, Reading MA, 1987.

[183] Palm, G., "On associative memory," *Biological Cybernetics*, **36**, 19-31,

1980.

[184] Papert, S., "One AI or many?," *Dædalus: Proc. Am. Acad. Sci.*, **117**, 1–14, Winter 1988.

[185] Papoulis, A., **Signal Analysis**, McGraw–Hill, New York, 1977.

[186] Parker, D. B., "Optimal algorithms for adaptive networks: Second order back propagation, second order direct propagation, and second order Hebbian learning," *Proc. of the Int. Conf. on Neural Networks*, **II**, 593–600, IEEE Press, New York, June 1987.

[187] Parker, D. B., "A comparison of algorithms for neuron-like cells," in Denker, J. [Ed.], *Proc. Second Annual Conf. on Neural Networks for Computing*, **151**, 327–332, Am. Inst. of Physics, New York, 1986.

[188] Parker, D. B., "Learning-logic," Technical Report TR-47, Center for Computational Res. in Economics and Management Sci., MIT, April 1985.

[189] Pineda, F. J., "Recurrent backpropagation and the dynamical approach to adaptive neural computation," *Neural Computation*, **1**, 161–172, Summer 1989.

[190] Pollen, D. A., and Ronner, S. F., "Spatial computation performed by simple and complex cells in the visual cortex of the cat," *Vision Res.*, **22**, 101–118, 1982.

[191] *Proc. of the Int. Joint Conf. on Neural Networks*, IEEE Press, New York, June 1989.

[192] *Proc. of the Int. Conf. on Neural Networks*, IEEE Press, New York, July 1988.

[193] *Proc. of the Int. Conf. on Neural Networks*, IEEE Press, New York, June 1987.

[194] Quate, C., personal communication, 1985.

[195] Raibert, M. H., **Legged Robots That Balance**, MIT Press, Cambridge MA, 1986.

[196] Ricotti, L. P., Ragazzini, S., and Martinelli, G., "Learning of word stress in a sub-optimal second order back-propagation neural network," *Proc. of the Int. Conf. on Neural Networks*, **I**, 355–361, IEEE Press, New York, July 1988.

[197] Robbins, H., and Monro, S., "A stochastic approximation method," *Annals of Math. Stat.*, **22**, 400–407, 1951.

[198] Rosenblatt, F., **Principles of Neurodynamics**, Spartan Books, Washington DC, 1961.

[199] Rosenblatt, F., "The perceptron: A probabilistic model for information storage and organization in the brain," *Psychol. Rev.*, **65**, 386–408, 1958.

[200] Rousseeuw, P. J., and Leroy, A. M., **Robust Regression & Outlier Detection**, Wiley, New York, 1987.

[201] Ruelle, D., **Elements of Differentiable Dynamics and Bifurcation Theory**, Academic Press, San Diego, 1989.

[202] Rumelhart, D. E., "Parallel distributed processing," Plenary Lecture, *Int. Conf. on Neural Networks*, San Diego, July 1988.

[203] Rumelhart, D. E., and McClelland, J. L., **Parallel Distributed Processing: Explorations in the Microstructure of Cognition, I, & II**, MIT Press, Cambridge MA, 1986.

[204] Rumelhart, D. E., Hinton, G. E., and Williams, R. J., "Learning internal representations by error propagation," in Rumelhart, D. E., and McClelland, J. L. [Eds.], **Parallel Distributed Processing: Explorations in the Microstructure of Cognition, 1**, 318–362, MIT Press, Cambridge MA, 1986.

[205] Sage, J. P., Thompson, K., and Withers, R. S., "An artificial neural network integrated circuit based upon MNOS/CCD principles," in Denker, J. S. [Ed.], *Neural Networks For Computing*, AIP Conf. Proc., **151**, 381–385, Am. Inst. of Physics, New York, 1986.

[206] Sejnowski, T. J., and Rosenberg, C. R., "NETtalk: A parallel network that learns to read aloud," Johns Hopkins University EE & CS Technical Report JHU/EECS-86/01, January 1986.

[207] Shepanski, J. F., and Macy, S. A., "Teaching artificial neural systems to drive: Manual training techniques for autonomous systems," in Anderson, D. Z. [Ed.], *Proc. of the 1987 Neural Information Processing Systems Conf.*, 693–700, Am. Inst. of Physics, New York, 1988.

[208] Shepanski, J. F., "Fast learning in artificial neural systems: Multilayer perceptron training using optimal estimation," *Proc. of the Int. Conf. on Neural Networks*, **I**, 465–472, IEEE Press, New York, July 1988.

[209] Sheu, B., "Recent progress on VLSI neuro-computing at USC," Dept. of Electrical Engineering / Electrophysics, University of Southern California, October 1989.

[210] Shrier, S., Barron, R., and Gilstrap, L., "Polynomial and neural networks: Analogies and engineering applications," *Proc. of the Int. Conf. on Neural Networks*, **II**, 431–439, IEEE Press, New York, June 1987.

[211] Silva, F. M., and Almeda, L. B., "Accelerating Backpropagation," in Eckmiller, R. [Ed.], **Advanced Neural Computers**, Elsevier North Holland, Amsterdam, 1990.

[212] Special Issue devoted to articles on European approaches to silicon neural networks (contains 7 articles), *IEEE Micro*, **9** (6), December 1989.

[213] Sprecher, D. A., "On the structure of continuous functions of several variables," *Trans. Am. Math. Soc.*, **115**, 340–355, March 1965.

[214] Stark, L. M., Okajima, M., and Whipple, G. H., "Computer pattern recognition techniques," *Comm. of the ACM*, **5**, 527–532, October 1962.

[215] Strang, G., **Linear Algebra and Its Applications**, Academic Press, New York, 1976.

[216] Steinbuch, K., **Automat und Mensch**, Second Edition, Springer-Verlag, Heidelberg, 1963.

[217] Steinbuch, K., "Die lernmatrix," *Kybernetik (Biol. Cyber.)*, **1** (1), 36–45, 1961.

[218] Stroyan, K. D., and Luxemburg, W. A. J., **Introduction to the Theory of Infinitesmals**, Academic Press, New York, 1976.

[219] Stryker, M. P., "Is grandmother an oscillation?," *Nature*, **338**, 297–298, 23 March 1989.

[220] Tolat, V. V., and Widrow, B., "An adaptive 'broom balancer' with visual inputs," *Proc. of the Int. Conf. on Neural Networks*, **II**, 641–647, IEEE Press, New York, July 1988.

[221] Tsypkin, Y. Z., **Foundations of the Theory of Learning Systems**, Academic Press, New York, 1973.

[222] Tsypkin, Y. Z., **Adaptation and Learning in Automatic Systems**, Academic Press, New York, 1971.

[223] von der Malsburg, C., "Self-organization of orientation sensitive cells in the striate cortex," *Kybernetik*, **14**, 85–100, 1973.

[224] Von Neumann, J., "Probabilistic logics and the synthesis of reliable organisms from unreliable components," in Shannon, C. E., and McCarthy, J. [Eds.], **Automata Studies**, 43–98, Princeton University Press, Princeton NJ, 1956.

[225] Von Neumann, J., "The general and logical theory of automata," in Jeffress, L. A. [Ed.], **Cerebral Mechanisms in Behavior**, 1–41, Wiley, New York, 1951.

[226] Waibel, A., "Modular construction of time-delay neural networks for speech recognition," *Neural Computation*, **1**, 39–46, Spring 1989.

[227] Waibel, A., Hanazawa, T., Hinton, G., Shikano, K., and Lang, K., "Phoneme recognition: Neural networks vs. hidden Markov models," *Proc. ICASSP*, **S3.3**, 107–110, April 1988.

[228] Watrous, R. L., "Learning algorithms for connectionist networks: Applied gradient methods of nonlinear optimization," *Proc. of the Int. Conf. on Neural Networks*, **II**, 619–627, IEEE Press, New York, June 1987.

[229] Watson, G. S., **Statistics on Spheres**, Chapter 2, Wiley, New York, 1983.

[230] Wellstead, P. E., and Zanker, P. M., "Application of self-tuning to engine control," in Harris, C. J., and Billings, S. A. [Eds.], **Self-Tuning and Adaptive Control**, Peter Peregrinus Publishers, New York, 1981.

[231] Werbos, P. J., "Backpropagation: Past and future," *Proc. of the Int. Conf. on Neural Networks*, **I**, 343–353, IEEE Press, New York, July 1988.

[232] Werbos, P. J. "Learning how the world works: Specifications for predictive networks in robots and brains," *Proc. of the Conf. on Systems, Man, & Cyber.*, IEEE Press, New York, 1987.

[233] Werbos, P. J., "Beyond regression: New tools for prediction and analysis in the behavioral sciences," Doctoral Dissertation, Appl. Math., Harvard University, November 1974.

[234] White, H., "Learning in Artificial Neural Networks: A Statistical Perspective," *Neural Computation*, **1**, 425–464, Winter 1989.

[235] White, H., "Learning in artificial neural networks: A statistical perspective," manuscript, University of California at San Diego, August 1989.

[236] Widrow, B., and Stearns, S. D., **Adaptive Signal Processing**, Prentice-Hall, Englewood Cliffs NJ, 1985.

[237] Widrow, B., "Generalization and information storage in networks of

ADALINE neurons," in Yovitts, G. T. [Ed.], **Self-Organizing Systems**, Spartan Books, Washington DC, 1962.

[238] Widrow, B., and Hoff, M. E., "Adaptive switching circuits," *1960 IRE WESCON Convention Record*, 96–104, New York, 1960.

[239] Williams, R. J., and Zipser, D., "A learning algorithm for continually running fully recurrent neural networks," *Neural Computation*, **1**, 270–280, Summer 1989.

[240] Williams, R. J., "A class of gradient-estimating algorithms for reinforcement learning in neural networks," *Proc. of the Int. Conf. on Neural Networks*, **II**, 601–608, IEEE Press, New York, June 1987.

[241] Williams, R. J., "Feature discovery through error correction learning," ICS Report 8501, Inst. of Cognitive Science, University of California, San Diego, May 1985.

[242] Willshaw, D. J., and von der Malsburg, C., "How patterned neural connections can be set up by self-organization," *Proc. R. Soc. Lond. B*, **194**, 431–445, 1976.

[243] Willshaw, D. J., Buneman, O. P., and Longuet-Higgins, H. C., "Non-holographic associative memory," *Nature*, **222**, 960–962, 1969.

[244] Wu, K. K. M., Quinn, J. D., and Hedger, D. F., **Computer Aided Ammunition Radiography**, DTIC AD-A 160 759, July 1985.

[245] Zadeh, L. A. , "Fuzzy sets," *Information and Control*, **8**, 338–353, 1965.

[246] Zeevi, Y. Y., and Porat, M., "Computer image generation using elementary functions matched to human vision," in Earnshaw, R. A. [Ed.], **Theor. Foundations of Computer Graphics and CAD**, NATO ASI Series, **F40**, 1197–1241, Springer–Verlag, Berlin Heidelberg, 1988.

[247] Zipser, D., and Rabin, D. E., "P3: A parallel network simulating system," in Rumelhart, D. E., and McClelland, J. L. [Eds.], **Parallel Distributed Processing: Explorations in the Microstructure of Cognition**, I & II, MIT Press, Cambridge MA, 1986.

Index

422